# Post Mishnaic Judaism in Transition

Number 17

Post Mishnaic Judaism in Transition
Samuel on Berakhot and the Beginnings of Gemara

by Baruch M. Bokser

# Post Mishnaic Judaism in Transition

## Samuel on Berakhot
and the
Beginnings of Gemara

## by
## Baruch M. Bokser

*Scholars Press*

Distributed by
SCHOLARS PRESS
101 Salem Street
Chico, CA 95926


Post Mishnaic Judaism in Transition
Samuel on Berakhot and the Beginnings of Gemara

by
Baruch M. Bokser

Library of Congress Cataloging in Publication Data

Bokser, Baruch M
    Post Mishnaic Judaism in Transition.

    (Brown Judaic studies ; no. 17)
    Bibliography: p.
    Includes index.
    1. Samuel bar Abba, 179 (ca.)-257. 2. Mishnah. Berakot--
Commentaries. I. Title. II. Series.
BM502.3.S3B63          296.1'2307          80-19702

ISBN 0-89130-432-0
ISBN 0-89130-433-9 (pbk.)

Printed in the United States of America
1   2   3   4   5
Edwards Brothers, Inc.
Ann Arbor, Michigan 48106

For

Jacob Neusner

TABLE OF CONTENTS

# Table of Contents

LIST OF CHARTS

## PREFACE AND ACKNOWLEDGEMENTS

i

This volume is an extension and expansion of a project
begun in my Ph.D. dissertation, a revised version of which
appeared as *Samuel's Commentary on the Mishnah. Its Nature,
Forms, and Content. Part One. Mishnayot in the Order of Zera$^c$im*
(Leiden, 1975). Here we apply the methodology developed in that
volume to the additional sample of sources in tractate Berakhot.
We confirm the results presented in Volume One. First, Samuel
did undertake a sustained effort at commenting on Mishnah and,
secondly, it took the form of a Commentary, that is, the comments
were designed to be tightly tied to the text of Mishnah. As we
discuss in chapter one, the Introduction, we expand our inquiry
to evaluate the relative impact of Mishnah upon Samuel's teaching
and we demonstrate that Mishnah greatly affected the non-
"Commentary" traditions as well. In chapter three, we present
the full corpus of teachings and, in chapter four, we analyze the
spread of all the teachings and their relationship to Mishnah.

The expansion of our scope enables us to devote more
attention to the literary and historical implications of our
study. We do so in chapters five through ten, especially in chapters nine and ten. In turn, the study throughout is enhanced by
a more sophisticated understanding of the issues which one faces
in evaluating the characteristics and significance of Samuel's
teachings.

The nature of the talmudic sources creates the specific
problems with which we deal but it also provides us with the
means to pursue a solution. We trace the transformation of Samuel's teachings from an originally oral stage designed to circulate along with Mishnah to one which provided a framework for
additional teachings. In this new stage the teachings functioned
no longer just as a commentary to another text but became the
antecedent text and framework for other traditions. Eventually
this framework received a written form and made up the rubric for
the developing *Gemara*. Moreover, the *Gemara* itself has had its
own textual and literary history. But despite numerous changes
in their role and application, Samuel's teachings preserved some
of the traits of their original function. These consist of literary and formal elements and they provide the raw material for this
study and hence we focus upon their characteristics. The sharper

appreciation of these overall problems has greatly enriched the
analysis of the individual teachings as well as of the systematic
presentation of their traits in chapters four through nine.

In our synthetic portion of the study, the present volume
examines the "content" of Samuel's commentary and teachings to a
greater degree than Volume One. This analysis makes up a large
portion of chapter four and sections of chapters nine and ten.
The matter is relevant to an evaluation of Samuel's focus and how
his teachings deal with the main subjects of each chaper and section of Mishnah and how those comments not directly on Mishnah,
in effect, complement and expand that response to Mishnah. The
concern for the substance of Samuel's comments also relates to
our theory concerning the origins of *Gemara*. In chapter ten we
suggest that Mishnah's and Samuel's disparate purposes account
for Samuel's far-ranging response to Mishnah which led into the
formation of *Gemara*. Naturally, therefore, it became necessary
to have a more exact description of the substance of Samuel's
efforts.

ii

We have had to face many complex problems in the history
and literature of Judaism in addition to those directly tied to
the analysis of the sources. We have tailored our discussion to
suit the purposes of our exposition. In the analysis of the
texts we have comprehensively studied the history of a passage's
interpretation in post-talmudic and modern authorities. We also
have fully reviewed all the textual evidence in manuscripts and
medieval citations. In chapter two and its footnotes, we frequently draw upon this material. But in the systematic analysis
and discussion of the implications and conclusions, in chapters
four through ten, we cite secondary literature only as an aid in
our argument and to provide a perspective on our observations and
results. Indeed, in chapter ten, we indicate that much work
remains in carefully relating our conclusions to earlier scholarship. Hence while we may have consulted numerous works on a
problem, in these chapters we have not written a history of the
various literary and historical problems and we do not purport to
have cited every view on a matter. Generally, we have consistently presented a cross section of modern authors.

Our task in referring to earlier scholarship has considerably lightened since publication of Volume One of this project.
In the interim three works which comprehensively present and

comment upon most of the modern literature have appeared.  First,
Shamma Friedman, "A Critical Study of Yevamot X with a Methodological Introduction," in *Tests and Studies.  Analecta Judaica*, vol.
1, ed. H. Z. Dimitrovsky (New York, 1977), pp. 275-442, deftly
surveys the work of modern literary critics on the Babylonian
Talmud, in particular in terms of the differences between the
anonymous and attributed materials.  He also complements our
emphasis on the importance of form criticism.  Friedman points to
several important literary and formal elements of the amoraic
materials.

Secondly, David Goodblatt, "The Babylonian Talmud, in
*Aufstieg und Niedergang der Römischen Welt* II. 19, 2 (Berlin,
1979), pp. 257-336, provides a critical history of scholarship on
the b.  Goodblatt's presentation of the modern works is significantly enhanced by his own observations.  Thirdly, the present
writer's contribution to the same volume of *ANRW*, pp. 139-256,
systematizes and analyzes earlier scholarship on the y.  We have
called it "An Annotated Bibliographical Guide to the Study of the
Palestinian Talmud," because scholarship on the PT lags so far
behind that of the BT and the former has elicited far fewer
"Introductions" and "critical surveys."  As a "Guide" this monograph constitutes a basis for a true history of the issues which
can be written in the future.  These three works and several less
comprehensive ones have enabled us to cite numerous studies which
we directly made use of but without making our footnotes too cum-
bersome.  We refer to the original materials only where they are
appropriate to our argument or where they exemplify a trend in
scholarship.

iii

We follow our transliteration conventions laid down in
Volume One though we have tried where possible to simplify them
slightly.  In transcribing a text we generally try to represent
the name of work or person in the way in which it is cited or
spelled.  Since different texts and pericopae may spell the same
name differently, at times we end up with several different spell-
ings.  On the other hand, in our discussion, we refer to the person or item with a single system of spelling.  We generally have
transcribed the names according to the Hebrew or Aramaic except
where we have followed a conventional rendering.  Thus we use the
spelling "Samuel" and not "Shmuel" for the name of the person
whose teachings make up the subject of this study.  The section

of Transliterations and Transcriptions presents the system which
we follow.

In the translation of texts, we italicize the Aramaic
passages.

We have also employed a system of abbreviations. The list
of Abbreviations lays out this material. One entry deserves particular note. We employ a capital "M" to connote Mishnah as a
complete work. We write out "mishnah" with a small "m" to refer
to an individual passage in Mishnah, especially where we differentiate between it and the whole corpus.

We omit quotation marks before and after statements which
are attributed to an individual master and which are presented as
a text. When a citation appears within a cited text, however, we
include the quotation marks as we likewise do when we cite a passage in the midst of our discussion.

Finally, when we refer to sources we generally list them
in the sequence in which they appear in the literature. We deviate from this pattern to present references in the order of
importance and relevance.

iv

Many people in numerous ways have contributed to the completion of this work. I owe special thanks to my teacher, colleague, and friend, Professor Jacob Neusner, who as I mentioned
in Volume One, initially suggested the topic of this research and
who has remained quite supportive and helpful as my research has
led to new directions and problems. I am appreciative of his
challenge to tackle significant problems involved in projects such
as this and of his constant prodding and demanding that I live up
to my best abilities. He generously offered his reactions and
thoughts on numerous problems which I faced during the course of
my study.

I express thanks to the following individuals who read
portions of this work and who offered numerous improvements to
the text, Professor William S. Green, University of Rochester,
Professor Gary G. Porton, University of Illinois, Champaign-
Urbana, Professor Morton Smith, Columbia University, Professor
Tzvee Zahavy, University of Minnesota, and Professor David Goodblatt, University of Haifa. Frequently, they made me realize the
implications of my own thoughts.

Many individuals exemplified the highest standards of
academic collegiality and willingly gave of their time to discuss

specific issues and to offer bibliographical references.  These
include Guitty Azarpay, Arnold Band, Peter Brown, William M.
Brinner, Joel Gereboff, Robert Goldenberg, William C. Hickman,
Anne D. Kilmer, Reuven Kimelman, Leonard H. Lesko, Ivan Marcus,
Jacob Milgrom, Lawrence H. Schiffman, Martin Schwartz, Justin
Sweet, Shemaryahu Talmon, David Weiss Halivni, Jean Weininger,
and David Winston.

        I am indebted to Professor Tzvee Zahavy for providing me
with a pre-publication copy of his study of Mishnah and Tosefta
Barakhot, "A History of the Mishnaic Law of Blessings."  I am
likewise grateful to Professor David Gordis for sending me a copy
of his dissertation, "On Rav's and Samuel's Exegesis of Mishnah
and Baraita" (Ph.D. diss., Jewish Theological Seminary of America,
1980).  I received both after completion of the present work and
just prior to sending it to the printer.  Since both throw considerable light on diverse aspects of this project, in the footnotes
I have added references to their discussions.  But in the body of
the study I have not been able fully to draw upon their findings
and to respond to their specific arguments.  I was happy to discover that their results complement mine and that Gordis's investigation, which approaches Samuel's Mishnah teachings from a
different perspective, generally accords with my conclusions.

        I am appreciative of the British Museum, London, the
Bibliothèque Nationale, Paris, Columbia University Library, New
York, and Library of the Jewish Theological Seminary of America,
New York, which provided me with microfilms of several manuscripts
which I needed in my research.  The staffs of the Library of the
Jewish Theological Seminary of America as well as of the several
libraries of the University of California at Berkeley and of the
Graduate Theological Union, Berkeley, proved in untold ways to be
of assistance in providing books and various bibliographical
information.

        I am grateful to the University of California at Berkeley
which has provided an institutional atmosphere conducive to serious research and which has offered financial support for my work.
The latter includes yearly research grants to cover typing,
xeroxing, and other technical expenses, and a Career Development
Summer Research Grant, 1976, a Humanities Research Fellowship,
Winter, 1978, to complement a Sabbatical Leave, Spring, 1978, and
a Regents' Junior Faculty Summer Fellowship, 1979.  These fellow-
ships enabled me to devote long periods of full-time work to my
research.  I am likewise appreciative of the Max Richter

Foundation of Providence, Rhode Island, for a grant for the publication of this book.

I thank as well Ms. Helen Green, who has patiently typed and retyped numerous drafts of this work; Ms. Rosalyn Paul Moss, who has edited the text; and Ms. Miriam Petruck, who has edited the bibliography and abbreviations.

I remain indebted to my parents, Rabbi Ben Zion Bokser and Mrs. Kallia Halpern Bokser, for their constant encouragement, support, and interest in me and my academic research.

Finally, I must mention my friends in the Berkeley and Albany community. While many are counted among my colleagues, many others are not. They provided much personal support, understanding, and interest while I pursued my research and had to devote considerable efforts and time in that area. They greatly contributed to making my research an enjoyable and satisfying task.

# ABBREVIATIONS

## A. Talmudic Literature

Arak.  = $^C$Arakhin
A.Z.   = $^C$Avodah Zarah
b.     = Babylonian Talmud; ben. or bar.
B.B.   = Bava Batra
B.M.   = Bava Mesi$^C$a
B.Q.   = Bava Qamma
Bekr.  = Bekhorot
Ber.   = Berakhot
Bes.   = Besah
Bik.   = Bikurim
BT     = Babylonian Talmud
Dem.   = Dem$^\ni$ai
Ed.    = $^C$Eduyyot
Eruv.  = $^C$Eruvin
Git.   = Gittin
Hag.   = Hagigah
Hal.   = Hallah
Hor.   = Horayot
Hul.   = Hullin
Ker.   = Keritot
Ket.   = Ketubot
Kil.   = Kila$^C$im
M.     = Mishnah
M.Q.   = Mo$^C$ed Qatan
M.S.   = Ma$^C$aśer Sheni
Maas.  = Ma$^C$aśerot
Mak.   = Makot
Meg.   = Megillah
Maks.  = Makhshirin
Meil.  = Me$^C$ilah
Men.   = Menahot
Miqv.  = Miqvaot
Naz.   = Nazir
Ned.   = Nedarim
Nid.   = Niddah
Oh.    = Ohalot
Orl    = $^C$Orlah
Pes.   = Pesahim

| | | |
|---|---|---|
| PT | = | Palestinian Talmud |
| Qid. | = | Qiddushin |
| R.H. | = | Rosh Hashanah |
| Sanh. | = | Sanhedrin |
| Shab. | = | Shabbat |
| Sheq. | = | Sheqalim |
| Shev. | = | Shevi$^c$it |
| Shevu. | = | Shevuot |
| Sot. | = | Sotah |
| Suk. | = | Sukah |
| T. | = | Tosefta |
| Taan. | = | Ta$^c$anit |
| Tem. | = | Temurah |
| Ter. | = | Terumot |
| Tos. | = | Tosefta |
| T.Y. | = | Tevul Yom |
| Uqs. | = | Uqsin |
| y. | = | Palestinian Talmud |
| Y.T. | = | Tom Tov |
| Yad. | = | Yadayim |
| Yev. | = | Yevamot |
| Zer. | = | Zera$^c$im |
| Zev. | = | Zevahim |

## B.  Other

Entries include bibliographical information necessary to clarify a reference to a volume or edition.  Complete information appears in the Bibliography.

Abramson, *Inyanut* = Shraga Abramson, *Inyanut BaSifrut HaGaonim*.

Agamati = See *HaNer*.

*Aggadot HaTalmud = Haggadoth HaTalmud*, Constantinople, 1511.

Albeck = Chanoch Albeck, *Shisha Sidre Mishnah*, 6 vols.  Mishnah
　　　　ed. with commentary and supplementary notes.  Cited by
　　　　volume and page or ad loc.

_____, *Introduction = Introduction to the Talmud, Babli and
　　　　Yerushalmi*.

_____, *Studies = Studies in the Baraita and Tosefta*.

*Aruch* = Alexander Kohut, *Aruch Completum*, 8 vols., and *Sup. Vol.*,
　　　　ed. Samuel Krauss et al.

Abbreviations

Ashbili, in *Ginze Rishonim* = Abraham Ashbili [or al-Ishbili = of
Seville], "Shitah Lehar'a Alshibili," in *Ginze Rishonim.*
*Berakhot*, ed. Moshe Hershler. [Author of work may
actually be Yom Tov Ashbili.] Cited by page.

Azikri = See Sefer Haredim.

Bacher, *EM* = B. Z. Bacher, *Erkhē Midrash*, 2 vols.

Bacher, *Tradition* = Wilhelm Bacher, *Tradition und Tradenten in den
Schulen Palästinas und Babyloniens.*

Bertinoro = Obadiah ben Abraham of Bertinoro (b. ca. 1500), Commentary on the Mishnah, published in standard editions of
Mishnah.

*Beth Nathan* = Nathan Cornel, *Beth Nathan.*

BH = R. Joel Sirkes, "Bayit Hadash," commentary to Jacob b. Asher,
*Arba^c ah Turim* [= *TurSA*]. Cited by location in *TurSA*, ad
loc.

*BIA* = *Bar-Ilan Annual.*

Bokser = Baruch M. Bokser, *Samuel's Commentary on the Mishnah.
Part One: Mishnayot in the Order of Zera^c im.*

Brand, *Ceramics* = Yehoshua Brand, *Ceramics in Talmudic Literature.*

Cam MS = *The Mishnah on which the Palestinian Talmud Rests*, ed. W.
H. Lowe (Cambridge, 1883, Jerusalem, 1967).

Cato = Marcus Cato, *On Agriculture.*

*CBQ* = *Catholic Biblical Quarterly.*

Columella = L. J. Moderatus Columella, *On Agriculture.*

David b. Levi = R. David b. Levi of Narbonne, "Sefer HaMiktam" on
Berakhot. In *Ginze Rishonim. Berakhot.* Cited by page.

*DS* = Raphaelo Rabbinovicz, *Diqduqē Sofrim*, 12 vols. Cited by page
and line or footnote, if so marked, thus DS 10:4 = *Diqduqē
Sofrim* to tractate under discussion, p. 10, line or footnote 4. To tractate b. Gittin, ed. Mayer Feldblum, cited
by page. To tractate b. Ketubot, 2 vols., ed. Moshe
Hershler, cited by page and footnote, where relevant, or
ad loc.

*EI* = *Eretz Israel.*

*EJ* = *Encyclopedia Judaica*, 16 vols. Cited by s.v., and, where
appropriate, volume and page.

Elbogen = Ishag (Ismar) Elbogen, *HaTefillah BeYisrael. A Hebrew Revised and Expanded Edition.*

*Eliezer* = See Neusner.

Elijah of London = R. Elijah of London, Commentary on Mishnah Berakhot, in *The Writings of.*

*EM = Encyclopaedia Miqrait.*

Emunat Yosef = Haim Yosef Dinglas, "Emunat Yosef," Commentary on Yerushalmi and Sirillo's Commentary, published with ed. of Sirillo. See S.

Engel = Joseph Engel, *Giljonei HaSchass.* Notes to b. and y.

Feldman = Uriah Feldman, *Samhē HaMishna.*

Feliks = Yehuda Feliks, *Agriculture in Palestine in the Period of the Mishna and Talmud.*

_____, *Marot HaMishnah* = Judah Feliks, *Marot HaMishnah*, "Simhet HaMishnah." Cited by page.

_____, *Mixed Sowing = Mixed Sowing, Breeding and Grafting.*

_____, *Plant World = Plant World of the Bible.*

Flr MS = *Babylonian Talmud. Codex Florence*, 3 vols.

Forbes = R. J. Forbes, *Studies in Ancient Technology*, vols. 1-3.

Frankel, *Introduction* = Zechariah Frankel, *Introduction to the Palestinian Talmud.*

_____, *PT* = Zechariah Frankel, *Talmud Yerushalmi, Seder Zera^c im. I: Berakhot, Pe^ɔah.*

Fulda = R. Elijah b. Loeb of Fulda, Commentary on PT. Cited ad loc.

*GBA* = J. N. Epstein, *Grammar Babylonian Aramaic.*

Gershom = Commentary of R. Gershom to b., on side of the page in standard editions of Bavli.

Gilat = Yitzhak D. Gilat, *The Teachings of R. Eliezer ben Hyrcanos.*

Ginzberg, *Commentary* = Louis Ginzberg, *A Commentary on the Palestinian Talmud*, 4 vols. On y. Ber. chs. 1-5. Cited by volume and page.

Gn. Fr. Epstein = Geniza Fragments to Palestinian Talmud, ed. by J. N. Epstein, *Tarbiz*, 3 (1932), cited by page and line.

*GnK* = *Ginze Mishna*, ed. A. I. Katsh (Jerusalem, 1970).

Goldschmidt = Notes on H MS to b. B.Q., b. B.M., and b. B.B.,
        printed in Makor reprint of H MS.  See H MS.

Gordis = David Gordis, "On Rav's and Samuel's Exegesis of Mishnah
        and Baraita."

Goren = Shelomoh Goren, *HaYerushalmi HaMeforash*.  Commentary to y.
        Berakhot chapters one through six.

GRA = Elijah of Vilna, *Gaon* (1720-1797), Commentary on Palestinian
        Talmud, in back of modern standard editions of y. with
        commentaries.

GRA, *Hiddushe* = Elijah of Vilna, Gaon, *Sefer Hiddushe UBeure*
        *HaGRA <sup>c</sup>al Masekhet Berakhot.*

GRA, SE = Elijah of Vilna, Gaon, "Shenot Eliyahu."  Commentary on
        M. Zera<sup>c</sup>im in standard editions of Mishnah, Vilna reprint.

*GYF* = Louis Ginzberg, *Yerushalmi Fragments from the Geniza.*

H MS = *The Babylonian Talmud, Seder Nezikin: Codex Hambourg,*
        Facsimile of the Original MS and a Reprint of the Gold-
        schmidt Edition.

Ham MS 169 = *Babylonian Talmud, Tractate Hullin: Codex Hamburg*
        *169.*

HD = David Pardo, *Hasde David on Tosefta*, 6 vols.

*HaEshkol* = Abraham b. R. Isaac of Narabonne, *Sefer HaEshkol.*
        Editions by Albeck and Ehrenrich.

*HaNer* = R. Zekharya b. Yehudah Agamati, *Sefer HaNer to Tractate*
        *Berakhot.*  In sequence of *Gemara.*  Cited ad loc. or by
        page.

Heinemann, *Prayer* = Joseph Heinemann, *Prayer in the Period of the*
        *Tannaim and Amoraim.*

_____, *Tefillot HaQeva* = Joseph Heinemann, *Tefillot HaQeva*
        *VeHaHovah Shel Shabbat VeYom-Tov.*

*HG*, I, II, or III = *Halakhot Gedolot.*  In three recensions or
        editions.  Cited by edition and page.

Higger = Michael Higger, *Osar HaBaraitot*, 10 vols.  Cited by
        volume and page, and where appropriate paragraph number.

Hokhmat Shelomo = Solomon Luria, "Notes," in back of standard
        editions of Bavli.

*HUCA = Hebrew Union College Annual.*

*HY* = Saul Lieberman, *Hilkhoth HaYerushalmi of Rabbi Moses Ben Maimon.*

Hyman = Aaron Hyman, *Toldot Tannaim VeAmoraim.* Cited by page.

*IAL* = J. N. Epstein, *Introduction to Amoraitic Literature.*

Ibn Ezra = Abraham Ibn Ezra, Commentary to the Pentateuch. Cited by biblical verse, ad loc.

*IDBSup = Interpreter's Dictionary of the Bible, Supplementary Volume.*

*IEJ = Israel Exploration Journal.*

*ITL* = J. N. Epstein, *Introduction to Tannaitic Literature.*

*ITM* = J. N. Epstein, *Introduction to the Text of the Mishnah.*

*JAOS = Journal of the American Oriental Society.*

Jastrow = Marcus Jastrow, *Dictionary of Talmud Babli.*

*JBL = Journal of Biblical Literature.*

*JE = Jewish Encyclopedia,* 12 vols.

*JJLG = Jahrbuch der Juedische-Literarischen Gesellschaft.*

*JJS = Journal of Jewish Studies.*

*JQR = Jewish Quarterly Review.*

*JSJ = Journal for the Study of Judaism in the Persian, Hellenistic, and Roman Period.*

Kesef Mishneh = Yosef Qaro, on Maimonides, *Mishneh Torah,* in standard editions and in Reprint Constantinople, 1509 edition.

K MS = *Mischnacodex Kaufmann A 50.*

Krauss, *LW* = Samuel Krauss, *Lehnwörter. 2:Wörterbuch.*

_____, *QT* or *Qad. Hat.* = *Qadmoniot HaTalmud.* 2 vols. in 4 parts.

_____, *Tal. Arch. Talmudische Archaeologie.* 3 vols.

Levy = Levy, *Wörterbuch.* 4 vols.

Lieberman, "Brief Commentary," = Saul Lieberman, *The Tosefta* and a Brief Commentary, 1- .

_____, *Caesarea = The Talmud of Caesarea.*

_____, *GJP = Greek in Jewish Palestine.*

_____, *HJP = Hellenism in Jewish Palestine.*

_____, *HY = Hilkhoth HaYerushalmi of Rabbi Moses Ben Maimon.*

_____, *OY = On the Yerushalmi.*

_____, *SZ* or *Siphre Zutta = Siphre Zutta.*

_____, *TK = Tosefta Ki-Fshutah* 1- .

_____, *TR = Tosefeth Rishonim.*

_____, *YK = HaYerushalmi Kiphsuto.*

L MS = *Palestinian Talmud: Leiden MS Cod. Scal 3.*

Loew or Löw = I. Low, *Die Flora der Juden.*

Luncz = A. M. Luncz, *Talmud Hierosolymitanum.* Edition and commentary to y. Berakhot through Shevi[c]it.

Maharsha = Shmuel Eliezer Halevi Eidels, "Novellae," in back of standard editions of Bavli.

*Makhon-Mishnah = Mishnah Zera[c]im,* 1. [= Makhon HaTalmud edition.]

Mareh Hapanim = Moses Margaliot, Commentary on y. In standard edition with commentaries.

Margalioth = Mordechai Margalioth, *Encyclopedia of Talmudic and Geonic Literature.*

Meir Netiv = Meir HaLevi Lehmann, "Meir Netiv." Notes on Sirillo to y. Berakhot. Cited by the number of the note, ad loc.

Meiri = Menahem HaMeiri of Perpignan (d. 1306), *Bet HaBehirah.* Commentary on Individual Tractates of Talmud, and on certain Mishnayot, separately published.

Mel. S. = Solomon Haedani, *Melekhet Shelomo.* In standard editions of Mishnah.

*Midrash HaGadol* = R. David b. R. Amram Adeni [of Eden], *Midrash HaGgadol* on the Pentateuch, in 5 vols., Genesis to Deuteronomy, cited by volume and verse, ad loc. and page, or page and line.

Mis. Ris. = Ephraim of Premishla, "Mishnah Rishonah," Commentary on Mishnah published in standard editions of Mishnah.

*MGWJ = Monatschrift für die Geschichte und Wissenschaft des Judentums.*

M MS = *Babylonian Talmud: Codex Munich 95.*

Mordekhai = Mordekhai b. R. Hillel Ashkenazi, Commentary on Bavli,
in back of standard editions of Babylonian Talmud.

*MT* = *Mishneh Torah* of Maimonides.

Nemuqe Yosef = R. Yosef b. R. Habiba.  On Hilkhot HaRif.  In back
of standard editions of Bavli.

Neusner, *Eliezer* = Jacob Neusner, *Eliezer Ben Hyrcanus*.  2 vols.

_____, *History* = *History of the Jews of Babylonia*.  5 vols.

_____, *Purities* = *History of the Mishnaic Law of Purities*.  22
vols.

_____, *Pharisees* = *The Rabbinic Traditions About the Pharisees
Before 70*.  3 vols.

*Nir* = Meir Marim of Kobrin (d. 1873), *Sefer Nir*, on Y. *Zera^cim*.

N MS or Naples ed. = *Naples p.e. of Mishnah*, 1492.

*NY* = Yehoshua Isaac Shapiro of Slonim (1801-1873), *Noam Yerushami*.
2 vols.

OH = "Orah Hayyim," one of the four divisions of the *Shulhan
Arukh* and of the *Arba^cah Turim*.

*OhG* = B. M. Levin, *Ozar HaGaonim*.  13 vols.  Citations by reference to section, "Responsa," "Commentaries," or RH, and
page, and, where appropriate, number of item.

*OZ* = Isaac b. Moshe (d. 1260), *Or Zarua*.

*PAAJR* = *Proceedings of the American Academy of Jewish Research*.

Paris MS = *Mishna Codex Paris: Paris 328-329*.

Payne Smith = R. Payne Smith, *A Compendious Syriac Dictionary*.
Edited by J. Payne Smith.

Pliny = Pliny, *Natural History*.

PM = Moses Margaliot (d. 1780), "Pene Moshe."  Commentary on y.
In standard editions of y. with commentaries.

P MS = *Mishna Codex Parma* (De Rossi 138).

Qorban Haedah = David Fraenkel of Berlin (1704-1762).  Commentary
on y.  In standard editions of y. with commentaries.

Rabiah = R. Eliezer b. R. Joel HaLevi.  *Sefer Rabiah*.  4 vols.
Cited by volume and page.

Rambam = Maimonides' Commentary on Mishnah.

# Abbreviations

Ramban = Nahmanides, *Novellae* on Babylonian Talmud. Separately
  published, in several editions and new critical edition,
  *Complete Novellae*.

Rashba = R. Solomon b. Adret, *Novellae on Bavli*. Separately
  published.

Rashbas = Simeon bar Semah, *Perush HaRashbas* <sup>c</sup>*al Berakhot*.

Rashi = Solomon b. Isaac (1040-1105), Commentary on Bavli or Commentary to Bible.

Ratner = B. Ratner, *Ahawath Zion We-Jeruscholaim*. 10 vols. Cited
  by ad loc. or page.

*REJ* = *Revue des Etudes Juives*.

RH = Rabbenu Hananel (ca. 990-1055). Commentary on b., published
  on the side of the page in the standard editions of b. or
  in *OhG*.

Riaz = R. Isaiah the Younger of Terrani, "The Rulings of" =
  Piskei Hariaz. Published with The Rulings of Isaiah the
  Elder of Terrani, in *Piskei Harid and Piskei Hariaz*. In
  sequence of BT. Cited by page.

Ribban = R. Judah b. Benjaim, "Perushe." In *Ginze Rishonim.
  Berakhot*. Cited by page.

Rid = Isaiah the Elder of Terrani, *Piskei Harid*.

Ridbaz = Aryeh Loeb of Bielsk (1820-1886). Commentary on Palestinian Talmud.

Ridbaz on *MT* = Commentary on Maimonides' *MT*, in standard editions
  of *MT*.

Rif = Isaac Alfasi (d. 1103), "Halakhot Rabbati" [= "Hilkhot
  HaRif"].

Ritba = R. Yom-Tov b. Abraham Ashbili (d. 1340), *Novellae* on
  Bavli.

Rosh = Asher ben Yehiel, "Piskei haRosh" [= "Hilkhot HaRosh"].
  Reference to tractate under discussion, ad loc.

R. Yonah [on Rif] = R. Jonah b. Abraham Gerondi, "Perush" on
  "Hilkhot HaRif."

S or Sirillo = Solomon Sirillo (ca. 1530). Commentary to
  Yerushalmi.

*SA* = R. Joseph Cairo, *Shulhan Arukh*.

Saadja, *Siddur* = R. Saadja Gaon, *Siddur*.

*Samuel's Commentary* = Baruch M. Bokser, *Samuel's Commentary on the Mishnah.  Part One: Mishnayot in the Order of Zera^cim*.

*Śedah Yehoshua* = Yehoshua Benvenisti.  *Śedeh Yehoshua*.  Commentary to y.

*Sefer HaItur* = Isaac b. Abba Maari, *Sefer HaItur*.

Sefer Haredim = Eleazar Azikri, "Sefer Haredim."  Commentary to PT, in Vilna editions.  Cited ad loc.

*Semag* = Moses of Quizi.  *Sefer Miṣvot Gadol*.

Sens = Samson b. Abraham of Sens, ca. 1150-1230, Commentary on Mishnah Zera^cim in standard editions of Babylonian Talmud.  Also, Commentary to Sifra.

*Sheiltot* = R. Ahai Gaon, *Sheiltot*.  Editions of Mirsky and Berlin.

Shire Qorban = David Fraenkel, "Shire Qorban."  Commentary on y.  In standard editions with commentaries.

Shitah Mequbeset = Bazalel Ashkenazi, Shitah Mequbeset, 4 vols.  On Berakhot in *Berakhah Meshuleshet* [incorrect attribution, however; probably of Yom Tov--or Abraham--Ashbili].

Shulsinger, *YE* = Eliahu Shulsinger, *Yad Eliahu*.  Volume One.  Notes to y. and b., in sequence of *Gemara*.

*ST* = David Weiss Halivni, *Sources and Traditions*.  2 vols.

*STEI* = Z. W. Rabinovitz, *Sha^care Torath Eretz Israel*.

Sussmann = Jacob Sussman, "Babylonian Sugyot to the Order Zera^cim and Tehorot."

*SRAG* = R. Amram b. Sheshna Gaon, *Seder*.

*Thes. Mis.* = C. Y. Kosovsky, *Thesaurus Mishnae*.

*Thes. Nom.* = B. Kosowsky, *Thesaurus Nominus*.

*Thes. Tal.* = C. Y. Kosovsky, *Thesaurus Talmudus*.

*Thes. Tos.* = C. Y. Kosovsky, *Thesaurus Tosephthae*.

*TK* = See Lieberman, *TK*.

Tosf. = Tosafot.  Abbreviation alone = on page of standard edition of Babylonian Talmud.

Tosf. Anshe Shem = "Tosefot Anshē Shem."  Commentary on M.  In standard editions of Mishnah.

Tosf. Hakhme Anglia = (on Qid.).

# Abbreviations

Tosf. HaRosh = Asher ben Yehiel, Tosefot to Berakhot.  In *Berakhah Meshuleshet.*

Tosf. R. Judah = R. Judah ben Isaac Sir Leon, *Tosefot.*  2 vols.  Cited by volume and page.

Tosf. Rid. = Isaiah the Elder, *Tosefot HaRid*, and Rulings, *Pisqe HaRid*, on specified tractates, separately published.

Tosf. Y. T. = R. Yom Tov Lippman Heller, "Tosefot Yom Tov."  In standard editions of Mishnah.

Tosf. Yeshenim = In Vilna edition of Bavli.

*TR* = See Lieberman, *TR.*

*TurSA* = R. Jacob B. Asher, *Arba^cah Turim* [= *Tur Shulhan Arukh*].

Unk. or Unknown ed. = *Mishna Sedarim Zeraim, Moed, Nashim:* Unknown Edition.

V MS = Vatican MS to the Palestinian Talmud.

Varro = Varro, *On Agriculture.*

Vatican BT MS = *MSS of the Babylonian Talmud in the Collection of the Vatican Library.*  Series A.  Vols. 1-3; Series B.  Vols. 4-6.  (Jerusalem: Makor Publs.)  Cited by volume and page in Makor edition.

Ven. p.e. = Venice first edition of Babylonian Talmud or of Palestinian Talmud.

Vilna ed. = Vilna edition or reprint of Mishnah, Babylonian Talmud, or Palestinian Talmud.

Volume One = Baruch M. Bokser, *Samuel's Commentary on the Mishnah.  Part One: Mishnayot in the Order of Zera^cim.*

A. Weiss, *Development* = Abraham Weiss, *The Talmud in its Development.*

_____, *Leqorot* = Abraham Weiss, *Leqorot Hithavut HaBavli.*

_____, *Literary Unit* = Abraham Weiss, *The Babylonian Talmud as a Literary Unit.*

_____, *Notes* = *Notes to Talmudic Pericopae* [= Collection of reprinted articles].

_____, *On the Mishnah* = *On the Mishnah* [= Collection of reprinted articles].

_____, *Studies* (1962) = Abraham Weiss, *Studies in the Literature of the Amoraim.*  New York, 1962.

_____, *Studies* (1975) = Abraham Weiss. *Studies in the Talmud*.
    Jerusalem, 1975.

White, *Roman Farming* = K. D. White, *Roman Farming*.

*Yalqut HaMakhiri* = R. Machir ben Abba Mari, *Jalkut Machiri*. To
    Psalms and Isaiah. Cited by verse and page.

*Yalqut Shimoni* = Shimeon HaDarshon, *Yalqut Shimoni*.

Yellin = Aryeh Loen Yellin, "Yefeh Enayim," notes to Babylonian
    Talmud with cross-references to PT and notes thereon.
    Cited by page of BT, ad loc.

*YK* = See Lieberman, *YK*.

Zahavy = Tzvee Zahavy, "A History of the Mishnaic Law of Bless-
    ings."

program for a Judaism freed from central cultic institution, and
to demonstrate the efficacy and significance of extra-Temple
institutions and practices.  The early rabbis drew upon and shaped
the teachings of different circles to present a comprehensive
statement on all facets of life.  Third-century and later masters
had to present this body of teachings to Jews for whom the
Temple's loss was a fact.  Therefore, they found it necessary to
concretely apply Mishnah's teachings and develop their full ramifications.  They had to facilitate a more intricate knowledge of
the Written Torah especially in terms of the new rabbinic perspective of its institutions and ideas.  Concurrent with this we find
changes in people's attitudes to the location of and access to the
divine in this world.  Jews and non-Jews become more willing to
see their religious leaders as special people with certain qualities who personally could do something for the religious followers.  Hence the people's religious needs changed along with their
perception as to the nature of a religious leader.[3]

        Accordingly, when we study Samuel's teachings on Mishnah
we analyze the ways in which this central work of Early Rabbinic
Judaism is related to the lives of Jews living in a new context.
Thus we should expect that Samuel's exposition of Mishnah will not
constitute merely a simple rendering of the text to enable people
to comprehend the meaning of its words--though this is included
within the larger effort.  Samuel's response to Mishnah is more
than a "scribal" activity and is designed to enable people to
apply Mishnah to their own lives in their own situation.

        Samuel's teachings on Berakhot, which makes up the present
sample of Samuel's heritage, provides a fine example of this
process.  We deal with teachings which develop the texts and
formulae of blessings and liturgy and lay out the concrete ways
in which the prayers may be said.  The transformation of the
service of God from primarily a cultic activity in a central
Temple to that of a service of the heart, in prayer, lies at the
core of M. Berakhot.[4]  Third-century Jews, as mentioned, accepted
the alternatives to the cult as a given.  Consequently, rabbis
faced the task of making Mishnah's rules practical, correlating
its numerous specific cases so as to develop and extend Mishnah's
principles and in the process adapt them to third-century Jewish
life.  And they did this to one of the most central areas of religious expression and experience.  Samuel's teachings, for example,
confront the vexing problem of legislating proper intent.  Mishnah
requires intent in prayer and provides some limited examples of

# CHAPTER ONE

## INTRODUCTION

i

The study of the teachings of Samuel, a Babylonian rabbi
from third-century Iran, poses many problems. Samuel, like many
other religious figures from antiquity, is known to us not through
a literature which he personally composed and edited but from one
which others compiled. In particular, the teachings of such
individuals, whether originally formulated in written or oral
form, frequently are those which disciples transmitted in the
master's name. Since issues and concerns important to the disciples often color the master's image, our picture of the master is
refracted through the perception of later circles and their use of
his teachings. Moreover, the extant version of the teachings
often are found in a written work which has had its own literary
and textual history.[1] Therefore in dealing with the teachings of
such figures we confront two basic problems. First, what is the
nature of the literature in which we find the teachings, and how
are the teachings integrated into their present context? Second,
how does the picture that emerges from that literature relate to
earlier stages of the teachings, especially their earliest stage?

While these problems are thus not unique to third-century
rabbinic figures, they take on added complexities due to the
specific nature of the rabbinic sources. They especially apply
to the teachings of Samuel due to his transitional role in Judaism. Samuel lived in the first post-mishnaic generation. Mishnah
was produced in Palestine, ca. 200 C.E., and Samuel devoted a
considerable portion of his efforts to presenting and mediating
that work to third-century Iranian Jewry. In so doing, Samuel
played a key role in the rabbinic movement's expansion in Babylonia.[2]

The differences between the period preceding Samuel, first-
and second-century Judaism, and that which followed, third century
to sixth, are not differences just in the nature of our sources
for those periods. Mishnah and Tosefta constitute the primary
sources of the former. The Midrashim and especially the Babylonian and Palestinian Talmuds constitute the main sources for the
latter. Each set of sources derives from a different cultural,
intellectual, and religious context. In the first, Early Rabbinic
Judaism sought to overcome the loss of the Temple, to organize its

1

# TRANSLITERATIONS AND TRANSCRIPTIONS

To transliterate, I reproduce the consonants of the Semitic words by using capital letters of the Roman alphabet.  The following symbols are used:

| | | | | |
|---|---|---|---|---|
| א | = ʾ | ם מ | = | M |
| ב | = B | ן נ | = | N |
| ג | = G | ס | = | S |
| ד | = D | ע | = | ʿ |
| ה | = H | ף פ | = | P |
| ו | = W | ץ צ | = | Ṣ |
| ז | = Z | ק | = | Q |
| ח | = Ḥ | ר | = | R |
| ט | = Ṭ | שׁ | = | Š |
| י | = Y | שׂ | = | Ś |
| ך כ | = K | ת | = | T |
| ל | = L | | | |

I employ also a second system, transcription.  Here I attempt to reproduce the vowel structure as well as consonants. I use most of the same symbols as in the transliteration symbol, except that they appear as lower case letters in italics.  There are several different and additional symbols.  In transcription I use *v* for W and *sh* for Š, and *v*, *kh*, and *f* for spirant B, K, and P, respectively.  I generally do not represent the different types of *sheva*.  Furthermore, I am not consistent in the indication of *alef* at the beginning of words.  As to the exceptions in rendering names, see the Preface, pp. xv-xvi.

its application.  But Samuel and other third-century masters are
sensitive to the human difficulty in always maintaining the proper
and preferred personal involvement.  Through a series of teachings
he provides a basis by which a person may securely know what is
required, how to achieve the intent, what to do when one is not
sure if one has maintained it, and various other aspects of what
it entails.[5]

The study of Samuel's comments on Mishnah also deals with
a literary problem.  Samuel's teachings with those of several
other early Amoraim, chiefly Rav, somehow became the central
rubric around which *Gemara* was structured.  The work which eventually emerged has shaped the mentality and lives of Jews for
centuries and makes up one of the great sources of religious
history.  What were the stages that produced this text?  We are
better able to answer this question today than scholars were
fifty years ago.  Today modern talmudic research has proven that
the Talmud is made up of many different, and often inconsistent,
sources and traditions and is the result of an ongoing process of
teaching, interpretation, and application, of revision and expansion of earlier teachings, as well as of a post-amoraic literary
arrangment, filling in of anonymous introductory and bridging
language, and recasting often on the basis of later concerns.
These later anonymous authorities structured the individual
teachings to relate to each other, to form arguments and debates,
and to make up or reflect wider conceptual units.  While they
added this anonymous literary enrichment and glossed a tradition
to expand it, or rephrased it to emphasize a particular point, or
transferred a teaching to other relevant locations throughout the
*Gemara*, but where they may not actually exactly fit, nevertheless
they did not actually change teachings in a wholesale fashion.
In particular they did not fully harmonize and level differences
between teachings and pericopae.  Hence the sensitive reader can
discern traits of disparate sources and often distinguish between
the component parts and separate earlier from later elements.[6]
Consequently, our study addresses the question of the form of
Samuel's teachings in their pre-literary stage and of the processes through which they later became the rubrics of the literary
work Talmud.

Accordingly, our study of Samuel's teachings is one
instance of a general problem facing the historian of numerous
cultures and literatures.  What are the stages in the history of
a master's teachings?  In Samuel's case, the problem involves

central issues in the history of Judaism, in particular the
expansion of rabbinic Judaism and the beginnings of *Gemara*.  Hence
our project throws light on the transition of Early Rabbinic Judaism into a larger social movement and on the transmission and
shaping of logia and the transformation of an oral account into a
written composition.  Since Jews and Judaism constitutes one
element of late antique society and culture, the study likewise
contributes to our understanding of the changing intellectual and
religious currents of the second and third centuries.


ii

In Volume One we initiated this study.  We drew upon and
adapted the methods of modern talmudic textual, literary, and
historical criticism as well as those of form criticism and applied
them to amoraic sources.  We chose the sample of Samuel's teachings
on M. Zera$^c$im, less Berakhot,[7] and focused on a single and limited
question.  Do the traditions represent the remains of a comprehensive response to Mishnah which we could call a "Commentary"?  We
answered in the affirmative and in the analysis of individual
pericopae we demonstrated how Samuel's teachings were transmitted
and used and we traced their later history.  We found that close
attention to the way in which small units of teachings are formulated and employed enable us to transcend the later contexts in
which they presently appear.  The forms and phrasings to some
degree preserved the earlier traits of the traditions.
Here we present the results of the continuation and extension of this project.  Once we proved the effectiveness of our
methods we sought to confirm our results based upon an additional
sample of sources and to build upon those conclusions.  Hence we
expanded our focus.  Taking as a fact that Samuel did compose a
Commentary to Mishnah, we asked what do we make of the non-Mishnah
commentary teachings?  How did they originate?  Did Mishnah in
some way also affect them?  What is the relationship between these
two types of teachings?
In chapter two, "Analysis of Traditions," we carefully
study Samuel's comments which directly deal with Mishnah.  As in
Volume One, we present each source, cite relevant textual variants,
and analyze the component parts of its wider context to isolate
the role of Samuel's teaching within it.  Thus we are able to
examine how other masters may have employed Samuel's comment and
the degree to which it may have been adapted to fit transmissional
and redactional needs.  Likewise we deal with a passage's analogues

whether parallel or different, whether similar or divergent, and
then compare the several versions of Samuel's teachings.  Once we
trace the use of Samuel's teaching in each location we can more
effectively answer the following questions.[8]

1.  Are the forms of the comments and the introductory formu-
    lae consistently used for the same purpose?

2.  Who attests to Samuel's comments?  That is, who adds
    something or refers to the tradition of Samuel?  Which
    circles, in which generation, knew the materials?

3.  What is the role of the tradents in the transmission of
    the traditions, especially where different versions
    exist?

4.  What types of comments do we find?  Are they what we would
    expect to find in a commentary on a text like Mishnah?

5.  Are the comments designed to circulate along with Mishnah
    or independently of it?  What was the Mishnah of Samuel?
    What is the relative number of comments?  Do they consti-
    tute a sustained effort on significant portions of Mishnah?

In chapter three, "The Full Corpus," we present all of
Samuel's teachings in b. and y. Berakhot and on M. Berakhot, even
if found in another tractate.  To enable the reader to have a
sense of the whole corpus and of the overall and individual relationship of the traditions to Mishnah, we cite each Mishnah passage and then at their appropriate places the non-Mishnah Commentary traditions along with the Mishnah-Commentary ones.  We
classify each tradition by the way in which it relates to Mishnah.
The main categories include "Mishnah Commentary," "Related and
Complements Mishnah," "Related and Supplements Mishnah," "Unrelated to Mishnah," and "Unrelated Extensions."  We place notational abbreviations to denote these categories on the margin to
the right of each text.  In the footnotes we comment on the essential textual problems and on how the teachings, especially the
non-Mishnah Commentary ones, fit in their contexts, and how, if at
all, they relate to Mishnah.

The results of our analyses in chapters two and three, as
for the materials studied in Volume One, contribute to a better
understanding of each pericope and its parts, a more accurate
understanding of the fundamental meaning of Samuel's teachings, a
possible indication of the sources and traditions that Samuel may
have used, and an appreciation of the role of the work of Samuel's
tradents, students, and later authorities who may have worked over
Samuel's teachings.  We have thrown considerable light, in particular, on the role of the travelers who transmitted Samuel's

traditions to Palestine and on the different treatments of
Samuel's teachings in b. and y.

Chapters four to ten likewise throw light on the above
matters though each is devoted to a specific question.  In chapter
four, "The *Prima Facie* Case for a Mishnah Commentary," we analyze
the spread of Samuel's teachings and demonstrate that they represent a comprehensive response to Mishnah.  We compare this with
the spread of the non-Mishnah Commentary teachings and find that
Mishnah has greatly shaped many of them as well.  We then indicate
the ways in which these traditions extend or complement the Mishnah Commentary teachings.  In chapter five, "The Types of Comments," we catalogue the types of comments by the kinds of information which they elicit from or add to Mishnah.  We find that
they provide the spectrum of information that we would expect in
a commentary on a work like Mishnah.  In chapter six, "The Literary Phrasing of the Traditions," we similarly catalogue the ways
in which the traditions are formulated.  We find that they employ
in a disciplined fashion a series of precise usages and patterns
which we would expect to find in a commentary designed to be
tightly knit to Mishnah.  A significant portion of these depend
upon Mishnah in formulation and most rely upon it for comprehension.  In chapter seven, "The Modes of Presentation: The Dispute
Form," we examine the manner in which the traditions are presented
whether alone or in juxtaposition and ostensibly in dispute with
the opinion of another master.  We confirm our results from
Volume One that the dispute form is not the usual and standard
way in which traditions are presented and is not fundamental to
the traditions where they do appear.  Initially teachings constituted single comments directly on Mishnah.  As part of our
discussion we suggest how the dispute form originated and throw
light upon the roles played by the master's disciples and by the
travelers.

In chapter eight, "Tradents and Attributive Formulae," we
turn to the chain of masters which precedes the substance of the
tradition and evaluate the significance of the presence or absence
of a tradent before Samuel's name.  We find that those teachings
which probably made up the essential portions of a Mishnah Commentary had an integrity of their own and generally appear without a
tradent.  Samuel's name and the comment itself formed some type of
a unit or structure with the referent and it was inappropriate to
interpolate the name of an additional master.  On the other hand,
the formulae which include a tradent's name introduce traditions

for which that reference was significant.  The mention of his
name either adds his weight to the tradition's authority, as in
Decisions, or reflects a specific context in which the teaching
was cited.  We also delineate the history of the representation
of Samuel's teachings and indicate which portions elicited the
interest of which generations of masters.  Since we rely in part
upon the types and formulations of the teachings to conclude that
a portion of the teachings circulated in an early period, we
investigate these phenomena in the non-Mishnah commentary items.
We find that our results are not vitiated by the presence of
similar traits among these materials.

　　　In chapter nine, "Correlations and Conclusions: The Nature
of Samuel's Commentary," we correlate all the data from chapters
four through eight in terms of the individual tradents and indicate how the results prove our case.  Since chapters four through
nine focus on individual problems and the systematic presentation
and analysis of data in terms of certain questions specified at
the onset of each chapter, we review our argument as a whole.  We
demonstrate how the building blocks fit together.

　　　Once we clearly see the wider picture, we provide a composite picture of the Mishnah commentary and its characteristics.
With this information we are better able to evaluate the distinctive elements of Samuel's response to Mishnah.  To do so we review
the nature of commentaries in general and in Judaism in particular.
We trace the characteristics of this genre of interpretation and
its literary and formal traits which may have constituted a model
for Samuel.  We find that Samuel's efforts are not the result of
a linear development of earlier intellectual activity.  While his
response to Mishnah exhibits characteristics similar to those in
other commentaries, we lack an extant instance of such a genre in
Judaism until the Hellenistic period.  From that period we have
the Qumran *pesharim* and Philo's allegorical interpretations of the
Bible.  But Samuel's teaching differs from both in significant
ways.  Likewise we find interesting analogues to Samuel's work in
the responses to tannaitic teachings within Mishnah itself, one
layer glossing another, an ostensibly earlier, layer, or in
Tosefta, which glosses, complements, and supplements Mishnah, and
in the responses of Midreshe Halakhah to the Bible.  Nevertheless,
these analogues and Samuel's teaching differ in the scope of their
effort and in the degree to which they develop the antecedent
text.  We argue that these differences derive from the disparate
purposes of each activity.  The nature of Samuel's efforts is

shaped by his goals.  He uses Mishnah as a point of departure to
teach the rabbinic interpretation of Judaism to Babylonian Jewry.
He did not engage in a simple literary and intellectual exercise.
To provide a wider perspective on this conclusion we briefly indicate how Samuel's effort reflects the notion of Oral Torah and the
image of a rabbi which Samuel and other masters projected.

In chapter ten, "Third-Century Judaism and the Beginnings
of *Gemara*," we take up the historical and literary implications
of our study.  We extensively treat three matters.  First, we
relate our study to our understanding of the social and religious
situation of third-century Judaism and the role of the rabbis.
We further place the notion of an oral commentary on a holy work,
Mishnah, within its context.  We note a striking parallel to
Samuel's commentary in the Middle Persian commentary, *Zand*, to
the Middle Persian translations of the Avesta.  The *Zand* represents a late literary reworking of originally individual oral
glosses and comments to the Avesta which were combined and
redacted into a larger composition.

Second, we discuss the nature of the creative transmission
of Samuel's teachings.  The rabbis were not antiquarians and they
designed their teachings for a purpose.  Hence the shaping of
teachings and the characteristics of each stage of a tradition
have implications on the ways in which practical and didactic
concerns of transmitters and redactors affect teachings.[9]  The
history of the traditions by and about Samuel also enables us to
focus on the ways in which later authorities in Babylonia and
Palestine perceived Samuel and other early masters.

Third, our study throws light on a stage of the formation
of *Gemara* which scholars generally pass over and to which they
often do not at all allude.  Even those who appreciate the fact
that the *Gemara* is not a record of debates between Amoraim generally say very little concerning the transformation of discrete
teachings of individual masters into the rubric of *Gemara* and how
they became the structure for organizing and presenting other
teachings.  Our theory, as mentioned, proposes that the originally
oral commentary to Mishnah circulated tied to or in conjunction
with Mishnah and the study of Mishnah with this Commentary provided the framework and point of departure for subsequent teaching.  We are still not clear as to when this arrangement of
teachings received the written form which eventually went through
the process of anonymous expansion and enrichment.

We conclude with an observation which we made in Volume One.[9] The sample of sources which we investigate affects our results and we cannot draw definite conclusions until we have fully analyzed the complete data. But research must begin somewhere and we need tentative theories to guide the ongoing study. The results of Volume One justified our efforts and we find further justification in what we now present as Volume Two. We also confirm our observation that a particular sample may involve special problems. The sources in Volume One and Volume Two exhibit one main variation. In the latter we more frequently find that later masters slightly adapted or worked over Samuel's teachings. This reflects the fact that M. Berakhot sustained greater and more extensive interest among the Amoraim especially the Babylonian ones than did the other tractates of M. Zera[c]im. M. Berakhot lays out the basic structures of liturgy and blessings, both central religious concerns. With this awareness of the impact of the sample, we suggest how other samples of Samuel's teachings might provide implications on several specific literary and historical problems.

Thus the nature of our sources is responsible for the problems which we face. But it also provides us with the keys with which to pursue a solution. We seek to understand the nature of Samuel's teachings in their pre-literary and fundamental state and how in turn they took on a new role within *Gemara*. But while the teachings assumed traits for their new function they continued to retain certain traits from their earlier role. It is these traits that we focus upon, in particular their formal aspects. In the process this effort has thrown considerable light on the simple meaning of a passage and on wider historical and literary issues.

[1]See chaper nine, n. 62 and text thereto, and chapter ten, nn. 34-35, 49-51, and texts thereto; William S. Green, "What's in a Name?--The Problematic of Rabbinic 'Biography,'" in *Approaches to Ancient Judaism: Theory and Practice*, ed. William S. Green (Missoula, 1978), pp. 77-96, esp. 80-81; and Neusner, *Purities*, vol. 21. Cp. Mary Boyce's formulation of the problem in the study of Zoroaster, in *A History of Zoroastrianism* (Leiden, 1975), pp. xii-xiii.

[2]See chapter ten, nn. 1-21 and text thereto.

[3]See chapter ten, n. 33; Morton Smith, *Tannaitic Parallels to the Gospels* (Philadelphia, 1951, 1968), p. 81; W. S. Green, "Palestinian Holy Men: Charismatic Leadership and Rabbinic Tradition," in *ANRW*. II.19.2: 619-647; and Baruch M. Bokser, "Reflections from Jewish Sources on the Religious Crisis of the Third Century. A Response to Peter Brown," in Peter Brown, *A Social Context to the Religious Crisis of the Third Century A.D.*, Center for Hermeneut-ical Studies in Hellenistic and Modern Culture. *Protocol of the Fourteenth Colloquy*: February 9, 1975, ed. Wilhelm Wuellner (Berkeley, 1975), pp. 19-24. In the response to Brown, we discuss this problem and cite literature on dif-ferent indicators of change including, e.g., the rise of a martyrdom ideology and the new image of a master of Torah who exhibits holy man traits. See, for example, Saul Lieberman, "Martyrs of Caesarea," in *Annuaire de l'Institut de Philologie et d'Histoire Orientales et Slaves* 7 (1939-1944), pp. 395-445, and Moshe David Herr, "Persecutions and Martyrdom in Hadrian's Days," in *Scripta Hierosolymitana* 23 (1972): 85-125. While we evaluated both the similarities and differences between the second and third centuries, perhaps in retrospect we should have further emphasized the differences. See Baruch M. Bokser, "Responding to Catastrophe: From Continuity to Discontinuity" (forthcoming).

[4]See chapter four; and chapter ten, nn. 62-66 and text thereto.

[5]See chapter four. On the notion of "intent," see, e.g., traditions #13-14 = 18-19, 20, 21, 23, 36, 37, 38, 57. #21 is analyzed in chapter two, and the rest are presented in chapter three. See also Baruch M. Bokser, "Proper Intent in Early Rabbinic Judaism. A Response to H. D. Betz," in H. D. Betz, *Paul's Concept of Freedom in the Context of Hellenistic Discussions About the Possibilities of Human Freedom*, Center for Hermeneutical Studies in Hellen-istic and Modern Culture, *Protocol of the Twenty-Sixth Colloquy*: January 9, 1977, ed. Wilhelm Wuellner (Berkeley, 1977), pp. 35-37, where we cite litera-ture on this problem, to which add Zahavy.

[6]See chapter ten, nn. 43, 45-57, and texts thereto, and Shamma Friedman, "A Critical Study of Yevamot X with a Methodological Introduction," in *Texts and Studies. Analecta Judaica*, vol. 1, ed. H. Z. Dimitrovsky (New York, 1977), pp. 275-442.

Gordis likewise found that the traditions may have been recast and placed into new contexts and he offers criteria to evaluate the primary or secondary nature of the context of a tradition. But for some reason, Introduc-tion, n. 28, he believes that we hold that the present locations and functions are primary. But this is not so. We extensively cite the larger contexts in which the traditions appear to demonstrate how transmissional and redactional considerations may have changed the traditions, in the course of which the comments may even be applied to different referents. See Volume One, passim, e.g., pp. 34-38, 157-162; and throughout the present volume, e.g., chapter two, analysis of traditions #8, 11, 15=16, 54-56, 101 (and our longer study thereon, in "Minor for Zimmun"), 115-116, 117-119, 134, esp. 136-137; and chapter three, #39 (and n. 43), 40-41 (and n. 50), 42-43 (and nn. 51-52), 63 (and n. 73), and esp. 90-91 (and n. 86). Note our analysis of 81=82=84; 83; and 72=85 and our argument concerning the formation of the third version (72=85).

Due to the realization that logia have been reused and recast, we have stressed the impact of the tradents upon the traditions, especially the way in which the travelers have adapted the comments in Palestine. Our task has been to isolate factors that may indicate which traits may derive from the fundamental stage of the traditions and what may have been the fundamental function of the teachings. For example, we found that the presence of identical or closely analogous traditions in structurally similar places in both *Gemarot*, e.g., 58 and 59, 102, and 103, may indicate that that comment has maintained its early function. See our discussions in chapters eight through ten.

[7] Berakhot may not have originally been integral to the Order of Zera[c]im. See Sussmann, *Babylonian Sugyot*, pp. 71-72, and n. 120; Volume One, p. 4; and below chapter ten, nn. 71-72 and text thereto.

[8] We reproduce these questions from Volume One, p. 5.

[9] See Green, "What's in a Name?"[3]

PART ONE

# CHAPTER TWO

ANALYSIS OF TRADITIONS

In chapter two we present and analyze Samuel's comments
which directly deal with Mishnah and evaluate whether or not they
may have originally belonged to a Commentary.  Accordingly, we
focus on a tradition's formulation, form, and function.  Since a
tradition's history may have obfuscated its original purpose, we
must also examine its transmission and its role within its present context.

At the onset of the citation of each set of traditions
appear numbers (1-140).  These numbers denote the number and place
of the comment within the full sequence of the 143 Samuel traditions on Mishnah Berakhot or in the *Gemara* to Mishnah Berakhot.
In chapter three we present the whole corpus, the Mishnah comments
along with the other traditions.  Using this single numbering
system facilitates our discussion and easy cross-reference.

*1.  Berakhot Chapter One*

1.

### M. Ber. 1:1

1.  From what time do they recite the *Shema*[c] in the
evening?

From the time that the priests start[1] (NKNSYM) to eat
their heave-offering;

2.  [and they read the *Shema*[c]] until the end of the
first watch [= 1/3 of the night]--the words of R. Eliezer.

And Sages say, Until midnight (HSWT).

Rabban Gamaliel says, Until the first light from the
East appears [lit., "until the pillar of morning, [c]MWD HSHR,
rises," which precedes sunrise[2]].

(M. Ber. 1:1)

A.  R. Gamaliel says, etc. [= citation of M.]

B.  Said R. Judah said Samuel, "The *halakhah* follows
(HLKH K-) R. Gamaliel.

(b. Ber. 8b)

Mishnah deals with one aspect of the evening recitation
of the *Shema*[c], a prayer which consists of several biblical

passages and which opens with the declaration, "Hear O Israel, the
Lord is our God, the Lord is One" (Deut. 6:4). Mishnah takes for
granted that the prayer exists and that it is to be recited twice
daily.[3] Clause 1 deals with the earliest hour in which the *Shema*[c]
may be recited, and 2, the latest hour. Mishnah records three
opinions on the latter matter. Samuel's tradition constitutes a
ruling as to the authoritative position.

A is a citation from Mishnah. B presents Samuel's comment. The attributive formula is "Said R. Judah said Samuel."
The tradition employs the structure of HLKH K-.

Samuel supports Gamaliel's position and provides the
individual with the greatest latitude.[4]

7.

### M. Ber. 1:2

From what time does one recite the *Shema*[c] in the
morning?

From the time that one can distinguish between blue
and white.

R. Eliezer says, Between blue and green,
until the sun shines (HNS HHMH).

R. Joshua says, Until the third hour of the day, for
such is the custom of kings to rise at the third hour [and
therefore, it is within the period of "getting up" specified
in Deut. 11:19].

One who recites the *Shema*[c] from then on, has not lost
[anything]. [It is] like a person who reads the Torah.

(M. Ber. 1:2)

R. Joshua says, Until the third hour of the day.
[= M. lemma.]

Said R. Judah said Samuel, The *halakhah* follows
(HLKH K-) R. Joshua.

(b. Ber. 10b)

M. Ber. 1:2 records disputes as to the proper hour for
the morning *Shema*[c]. Samuel decides in favor of R. Joshua, the
most lenient opinion. As with the law in M. Ber. 1:1, Samuel's
ruling allows the latest possible hour and gives the individual
the greatest latitude.

Judah is the tradent and the tradition follows the HLKH
K- form.[5]

8.   [Below: 11, 15, 19]

### M. Ber. 1:4A

[As to] the morning [Shema[c]] one blesses two [bless-ings] before it and one after it;

And[6] [as to] the evening [Shema[c]] one blesses two before it and two after it, one long [in length] and one short [in length].[7]

(M. Ber. 1:4A)

A.   What blessing does one say [prior to the morning Shema[c][8]]?

B.   . . . [= Gemara cites and then analyzes a tradi-tion which identifies the first blessing.]

C.   What is the other one [i.e., the second of the two blessings immediately before the Shema[c]]?

D.   Said R. Judah said Samuel, "With great love" (ƆHBH RBH).   [= A prayer which opens with the clause, "With great love (God has loved us)."]

E.   And thus R. Eleazar taught R. Padat, his son, "With great love" (WKN ƆWRY LYH . . . .).

[Two early versions exist for F and G:]

| | |
|---|---|
| F.   And Rabbis say, "With eternal love" (ƆHBT [c]WLM).   [ = A prayer opening with this clause.] | F'.   It was taught likewise, They do not say, "With eternal love," rather, "With great love." |
| G.   It was taught likewise[9] (WTNYƆ NMY HKY): They do not say, "With great love," rather, "With eternal love." | G'.   And rabbis say, "With eternal love." |
| [F and G = many MSS and citations.[10]] | [F' and G' = Ven. p.e. and certain citations.] |

H.   And thus it says, "With an eternal love I have loved you" (Jer. 31:2).

(b. Ber. 11a-b)

i

Mishnah prescribes blessings to precede and to follow the recitation of the Shema[c].   Gemara contains traditions that define the appropriate blessings, A - H, and additional related laws and sources.   We examine Samuel's identification of the prayer and then relate the pericope to an alternative context for the tradition on M. Tamid 5:1.

Samuel's tradition is transmitted by Judah and employs the attributive formula, "Said R. Judah said Samuel." The content of the tradition is made up of two words, the opening of the appropriate blessing. The comment is thus not formulated as an autonomous statement but as a gloss, which for comprehension, depends upon its referent or context. While Samuel's tradition ("With great love") accords with the teaching of Eleazar, E, a second-generation Babylonian who emigrated to Palestine, and with one version of the *baraita*, F', it differs from that of the "rabbis," in F or G', and from the other version of the *baraita*, G.[11] The latter text opens with the words, "With eternal love."

Judging on the basis of their later preserved texts, both prayers deal with the Torah as a token of God's love for Israel and Israel's responsibility to study it, though the "With great love" prayer is longer and more complex. It stresses the notion of Israel's election and adds the themes of God's unity and of His kingship and kingdom. The latter entails an appeal for an ingathering of the exiles, which may have messianic overtones. But we cannot positively know if the two prayers originally substantively differed. All the talmudic references to these prayers include only the opening words. While separate texts have crystallized in the course of the liturgy's history, we cannot automatically rely on the later preserved texts of the two versions. For example, certain versions of the "With eternal love" text are in substance partially similar to that of the "With great love." One fragment of a prayer opens with the phrase "With eternal love" and includes the theme of God's unity and a request from God that He enable a person to understand, teach, and follow the Torah, language reminiscent of the "With great love" prayer.[12]

## ii

Samuel thus identifies an item in Mishnah, a concern appropriate to a Mishnah commentary, and from the perspective of the history of the tradition, he appears as interested in the proper text of the prayer. Nevertheless, it is not clear if Samuel's comment originated as a commentary on Mishnah, and if so, on M. Ber. 1:4.

Bavli Ber. 11b provides a second context for Samuel's tradition. In the part of the *sugya* which follows A - H, also on

M. Ber. 1:4, b. cites M. Tamid 5:1 and then Samuel's tradition.
The Mishnah deals with liturgical procedures in the Temple.

> I.   There we learned (TNN HTM),
> The appointed one said to them [i.e., to the priests,
> in the morning], "Say a blessing" (BRKW BRKH ᵓHT).
> And they said the blessing and read the Ten Command-
> ments, *Shema*ᶜ, . . .
> J.   Which blessing?  [Lit., "what is a 'blessing'?"]
> K.   Like that of (KY Hᵓ D-) R.   Abba[13] and R. Yosi
> bar Abba[14] who chanced to be in a certain place; they [assum-
> edly people of that place] asked of them, "Which blessing?"
> They did not know.
> They came, they asked R. Mathah.[15]   He did not know.
> They came, they asked R. Judah.[15]   He said to them,
> Thus said Samuel, "With great love."
>
> (b. Ber. 11b)

Y. Ber. 1:8, 3c, on M. Ber. 1:4, likewise cites M. Tamid.
To its question of, "What blessing did they say," y. presents a
different version of Samuel's comment.

> R.  Matnah  said  in  the  name  of  Samuel, This is (ZW)
> the blessing over the Torah.
>
> (y. Ber. 1:8, 3c)

The y. version apparently provides the conceptual name for the
blessing.  This formulation underlines the function of Samuel's
tradition as applied to M. Tamid.  In both b. and y. the tradition serves to establish which prayer precedes the *Shema*ᶜ and not
which version of which prayer is recited.[16]

If I - K preserves a reliable account, the several individuals mentioned in K, all from the second to third amoraic
generations, did not know Samuel's tradition or its application
to M. Tamid 5:1.[17]   For them, in contrast to Judah, the comment
did not belong to their corpus of materials that circulated along
with Mishnah.  If so, considering Matnah's role in b. and y., y.
represents a later stage of the tradition.  Someone who learned
the comment applied it to M. Tamid.

### iii

The alternative uses of Samuel's tradition reflect its
particular function and formulation.  In both instances it serves
as a definition of a prayer which precedes the *Shema*ᶜ, which is
formulated as a gloss, and which, accordingly, could be easily

applied to different texts.  But we remain unsure as to the
original context of the teaching.

Three possibilities could explain the two locations.
Samuel's teaching might have originated on M. Ber., and I - K
then provide a confirmation of the attribution of "With great
love" formula to Samuel.[18]  Secondly, it might have originated on
M. Tamid and then I - K constitute the text from which *Gemara* or
its source spun out Samuel's tradition on M. Ber. 1:4.  Thirdly,
at the earliest stage of the tradition, Samuel's tradition might
have been associated with both M. Ber. and Tamid and served, if
not originated, as glosses to both.

We note, b. and y. contain additional teachings on both
M. Tamid and M. Ber.  On b. Ber. 12a Judah transmits a comment
by Samuel on M. Tamid 5:1's mention of the Ten Commandments.[19]
On b. 11b we find the following:

> Said R. Judah said Samuel, If one awoke early to
> study--before one recited the *Shema$^c$*, one is required to say
> a blessing [over study]; after one recited the *Shema$^c$*, one is
> not required to say a blessing.[20]

This tradition attests that the *Shema$^c$* complex, i.e., the blessing preceding the *Shema$^c$*, functions as a blessing over the study
of Torah.  This tradition including the attribution to Samuel
appears likewise in y. Ber. 1:8, 3c.[21]  The comment thus appropriately fits within the *Gemara* on M. Ber. 1:4.

We conclude that as K indicates, Samuel's tradition did
not widely circulate as part of a commentary on M. Tamid among
second-to-third-generation Babylonian masters.  Judah specifically
had to point out the teaching, or, perhaps relate it to M. Tamid
5:1.  Alternatively, K indicates how someone could cite a tradition with the attribution of R. Judah said Samuel, and how that
tradition could be used as an identification of M. Ber. 1:4.
PT's version of K further indicates how the same tradition could
circulate along with M. Tamid.

Samuel's teaching thus focused on the prayer that precedes
the *Shema$^c$*.  His remarks reflect a concern to identify a general
reference to such a blessing, an interest relevant to a commentary.
But we remain unsure whether it originated in the context of M.
Ber. 1:4, M. Tamid 5:1, or both.  Evidence suggests that Samuel
focused upon both texts.

2.  *Berakhot Chapter Two*

21.

### M. Ber. 2:1A

[If] one reads the Torah and the time of the recitation [of *Shema*[c]] came--if he directed his heart, he fulfilled
[his obligation to say *Shema*[c]], and if not, he did not fulfill
[his obligation].

(M. Ber. 2:1A)

A.  R. Huna, R. Idi, R. Joseph, R. Judah in the name
of Samuel,[22] [One] has to (SRYK L-) to take upon oneself the
Kingdom of Heaven--standing.

B.  What, if he was sitting, he stands?
No, if he was walking, he stands.[23]

(y. Ber. 2:1, 4a)

Samuel's comment is an independent and autonomously formulated teaching.  With the adverbal phrase SRYK L- "[One] has to,"
it in effect glosses M. Ber. 2:1, by adding supplementary material.[24]  M. Ber. 2:1 deals with the integrity of the recitation of
the *Shema*[c].  Its first part focuses on reciting the *Shema*[c] while
reading it in the Bible, and the second, not cited above, with
permissible and prohibited interruptions during the recitation.

It is not unnatural for M. Ber 2:1 to elicit developments
of its principle.  T. Ber. 2:2, for example, includes a general-
ized rule on proper intention during the recitation.  Samuel's
comment offers the additional requirement of standing and may
reflect the notion, known elsewhere, to employ this posture to
give testimony.[25]  This accords with the reference to accept "the
(yoke) of the Kingdom of Heaven, which refers to the first verse
of the *Shema*[c], Deut. 6:4.[26]  The SRYK L- wording provides a
standard way to make such additions.

B interprets that Samuel's tradition excludes reciting
*Shema*[c] when walking.  It does not prescribe rising when one is
seated, a position which Mishnah had associated with Shammai.  We
do not know whether B accurately interprets Samuel or whether it
imposes a Palestinian or secondary concern on his comment.[27]

Samuel's comment thus develops Mishnah's problematic.

3.  *Berakhot Chapter Three*

44, 45-46.

## M. Ber. 3:5

1.  [If] one is engaged in the *Tefillah* and remembers
that he had had a nocturnal emission, he should not terminate
[his prayer] but rather shorten [it].

2.  [If] one goes down to immerse oneself--
if he can come up, cover himself, and recite [the
*Shema*<sup>c</sup>] before the sun rises, he should come up, cover himself
and recite [it],

and if not, he should cover himself with water and
recite [it],

but he should not cover himself with foul water or
soaking water [for flax], until he pours therein [fresh]
water.

3.  And how far should one distance oneself from them
[= the "foul water" and "soaking water," mentioned above, or
alternatively, from "urine"[28]] and from excrement?  Four cubits.
                         (M. Ber. 3:5)

A.  And in the case of certainty [that urine is
present] how long [is it prohibited] (<sup>c</sup>D KMH)?

B.  Said R. Judah said Samuel, So long as they
moisten [the ground].

C.  Thus said Rabbah bar Bar Hanah,[29] So long as they
moisten.

D.  Geniva in the name of Rav said, So long as their
mark is discernible.

E.  And R. Joseph, May his master forgive Geniva.  For
as to excrement said R. Judah said Rav, that as soon as its
top has dried it is permitted.  Is there any question as to
urine?

F.  Said Abaye to him, Why do you rely upon this
[report of Rav]?  Rely rather on this which said Rabbah bar R.
Hunah said Rav,[30] Excrement even as a potsherd is forbidden.
                         (b. Ber. 25a)

G.  R. Abba in the name of Rav, Excrement [prohibits]
until it dries up like a bone, urine (MYM) as long it moistens.

Geniva said, Urine--as long as its mark is discernible.

H.  Samuel said,[31] Until its top has dried.

     I.   Simeon b. Ba in the name of R. Yohanan, Until its
top has dried.

     J.   R. Yermiah, R. Ze$^c$ira in the name of Rav, Excre-
ment, even like a bone is forbidden.

     K.   Samuel said, Until its top has dried.

     L.   Simeon b. Ba said in the name of R. Yohanan,
Until its top has dried.

     M.   Said R. Hezkiah,[32] R. Abba is more stringent as
to urine than as to excrement.

     N.   Said R. Mana, From this [statement] of Geniva.

     O.   He said to him, Even if it has become like a
bone, it is forbidden because its essence lasts; urine
[however]--its essence does not last.[33]

            (y. Ber. 3:5, 6d)

                i

     Mishnah requires purity and cleanliness during prayer.
Lev. 15:16-18, Num. 5:1-5, especially Deut. 23:10-15, and other
biblical passages applied this rule to the locus of God's presence
in the Temple or in the camp.[34]  As rabbinic prayer could be
recited in any locale, the requirement would be extended to the
whole world.  M.'s last clause, however, states that unclean things
disqualify the surrounding area only up to a fixed distance.
Samuel and other Amoraim discuss how long that prohibition lasts.

     BT and PT present complementary traditions attributed to
Samuel and divergent versions attributed to Rav.  We concentrate
on Samuel's comment.

     In b., Samuel rules that the place remains forbidden as
long as the item "moistens," a process characteristic of a liquid.
This criterion fits the introductory question and context which
refers to "urine."  In y., Samuel (and Yohanan), in both versions
of the *sugya*,[35] similarly employs the criterion of "moisture."
Here, however, the criterion defines the end of the prohibited
stage and is accordingly formulated in terms of the lack of the
desired element, viz., "until its top becomes dry."  The language
of "its top," fits excrement.  Samuel thus applies a similar principle to both urine and excrement, and provides for the briefest
criteria.

     Samuel's comment probably originated as a gloss on Mishnah.
Bavli's introductory question, A, is required only due to the
immediately preceding pericope's focus on doubtful presence of

urine and excrement.  This accords with the tradition's actual
formulation as a gloss both in b. and in its analogue in y.[36]

ii

The appropriateness of Samuel's comment on Mishnah is
reflected in T. Ber. 2:16, 19, pp. 9-10, ls. 50-58, 61-64.
Tosefta deals with the type of excrement and urine which render
them potent to disqualify a place from prayer.  Note the formulation of T. Ber. 2:19.

1.  A person should not urinate in the place where he
prays the *Tefillah* unless he distances himself four cubits.
2.  The one who urinates should not pray the *Tefillah*
in that same place unless he distances himself four cubits.
3.  If they have dried up [e.g., on a rock] or been
absorbed [e.g., in the ground], lo this one is permitted.
(T. Ber. 2:19, p. 10, ls. 61-64)

Clauses 1-2 of Tosefta employ the same pattern as Mishnah and
apply its rule to *Tefillah*.  Clause 3 appends a criterion as to
the durability of the prohibited item.  This is exactly what the
Amoraim, including Samuel, had done to Mishnah.  Lieberman
suggests that clause 3 was understood to refer not to 2, the
preceding clause, but to Mishnah Ber. 3:5, end, "And how far
. . ."[37]  If so, Samuel and the other Amoraim have an exact
precedent in their commenting on Mishnah, though they differ in
their specific criterion.  Samuel's position, in contrast to some
versions of Rav, would then seem to differ from Tosefta's.

*4.   Berakhot Chapter Four*

51.

M. Ber. 4:1

1.  The morning *Tefillah* [is said] until noon,
R. Judah says, . . .
2.  The afternoon *Tefillah* . . . R. Judah says, . . .
3.  The evening *Tefillah* has no fixity [= has no
fixed time].
4.  And that of the extra service . . .
(M. Ber. 4:1)

A.  For [deleted in certain readings[38]] said R. Judah
said Samuel, The evening *Tefillah*--

R. Gamaliel says [It is] compulsory.

R. Joshua says [It is] optional.

B.  And the *halakhah*[39] follows the words of the one
who says, "Compulsory."[40]

C.  Rav[40] said, The *halakhah* follows the words of the
one who says, "Optional."

(b. Ber. 27b)

Samuel supplements Mishnah's mention of the evening
*Tefillah*.  He supplies information as to a tannaitic dispute on
the obligation to say it and then offers a decision as to the law.
The basis of this *Tefillah* differed from that of the other services
and accordingly it lacked a fixed time in which to be said.[41]

Samuel's comment apparently consists of both A and B.  In
A, he formulates the opposing views into a dispute form.  PT Ber.
4:1, 7c may contain an analogue, if not a parallel, to Samuel's
formulation:

A'.  Said R. Jacob bar Aha, It was taught there
[= Babylonia[42]].

B'.  [As to] the evening *Tefillah*, what is the law?
(MHW‎ᵓ)?

C'.  Rabban Gamaliel says, Obligatory.

R. Joshua says, Optional.

A'-C' is identical to A except for the interpolated
question in B', MHW‎ᵓ.  This word clearly is an addition to introduce the dispute.

As Jacob bar Aha elsewhere cites Samuel's traditions,
even a *baraita* of Samuel, and b. Ber. 27b apparently attributes
this teaching to Samuel, Epstein argues that likewise here Jacob
b. Aha cites the teaching from a *baraita* of Samuel.[43]  For our
purposes, y., at the minimum, indicates that the formulation of
the dispute is assumed to be Babylonian (amoraic) and supports
the possibility that A makes up part of Samuel's teaching.
Moreover, A, in substance, might then fit into the category of
Samuel's teachings which are formulated as a *baraita* and which
supplement Mishnah.[44]

The presence of the tradent Judah may correlate with a
second observation.  Elsewhere where Samuel decides between
opposing views, his tradition is generally cited by a tradent,
chiefly Judah.[45]  Accordingly, perhaps Judah cites the formulation of the Gamaliel-Joshua dispute, for which he drew upon a

Samuel *baraita* that supplements Mishnah, and then he cites
Samuel's decision as to the law.[46]

54, 55, 56 [and 56a].

## M. Ber. 4:3

1.   Rabban Gamaliel says, Every day a person prays
eighteen [prayers].

2.   R. Joshua says, The substance of ($M^CYN$) eighteen.

(M. Ber. 4:3A)

A.   R. Joshua says, The substance of eighteen.   [=
Citation of M.[47]]

B.   What is [the meaning of the phrase] "the substance of eighteen."

C.   Rav says, The substance of each blessing[48] ($M^CYN$
KL BRKH WBRKH).

D.   And Samuel said, Give us discernment, Lord our
God, to know Thy ways;

and circumscribe our hearts to fear Thee;

so that we be forgiven;[49]

and be redeemed;

and keep us far from agony;

and fatten us in the pastures of Your land;

and the [alt., "our"] dispersed from the four
[corners of the earth] gather;

and those who go astray by [alt. "in" or "from"]
Your knowledge judge;[50]

and against the wicked raise Your hand;

and let the righteous rejoice,

in the building of Your city and establishment of
Your Temple,

and in the growth of the horn of David, Your servant;

and in the preparation of a light for the son of
Yishai, Your annointed one [= messiah].

Before we call, may You answer.

Praised are You, Lord, who hearest prayer.

E.   Abaye cursed (LYYT ᵓBYY) anyone who prayed, "Give
us discernment" (HBYNNW).[51]

F.   Said R. Nahman said Samuel,

Throughout the year a person prays, "Give us discernment," except on the outgoing of Sabbath and festivals[52]
because [he] has to say *havdalah* in [the prayer which opens
with the phrase] "Who graciously gives knowledge."   [= The

fourth blessing of the *Tefillah*, which, when abridged, cannot take the addition.]

G.  Attacked Rava bar Ishmael,[53] . . . [= a question on F].

H.  . . . [A response to G.]

I.  Attacked Mar Zutra, . . . [= a further question].

J.  It is difficult (QŠYᵓ).

K.  Said R. Bibi b. Abaye.

Throughout the year a person prays "Give us discernment" except for the rainy season because he has to say [a] request [for rain] in the "benediction of the years" [= one of the abridged blessings].

L.  Attacked Mar Zutra . . . [= Question followed by an anonymous answer and a second question and answer.]

M.  Attacked Rav Ashi. . . . [A question followed by an anonymous answer.]

(b. Ber. 29a)

A'.  HYL[KH]  R. Joshua says, The substance of (MᶜYN) eighteen.[54]  [= Lemma of M.]

B'.  What is, "(Seven) the substance of (ŠBᶜ MᶜYN) eighteen"?  [The reference to "seven" either reflects a reading or interpretation of M., or else is the result of a contamination from E' or F'.[55]  See below.]

C'.  Rav said, The end of each blessing (SWP KL BRKH WBRKH).

D'.  And Samuel said, The beginning (RᶜŠ) of each blessing.

E'1.  There are teachers who teach (ᵓYT TNYY TNY), "Seven the substance of eighteen."

2.  And there are teachers who teach, "Eighteen the substance of eighteen."

3.  The one who says, "Seven the substance of eighteen" supports Samuel.

4.  The one who says, "Eighteen the substance of eighteen" supports Rav.

F'.  R. Zeᶜira sent to R. Nahum[56] via (GBY) R. Yanai b. R. Ishamel,

What is, "Seven the substance of (ŠBᶜ MᶜYN) eighteen" of Samuel?[57]

G'.  He said to him, Give us discernment (HBYNYNW);

Desire our repentance;

Forgive us;

Redeem us,

Heal our sickness;

Bless our years.

(H'.  Said R. Hagai, If it was [the time of[58]] the rains, they say, "In rains of blessing."[59]

If it was [the period of] dews,[60] they say, "In dews of blessing.")

I'.  For, the dispersed You [hopefully will] gather,[61]

And those who go astray against You [alt. "for You to"], judge;[62]

And upon (W<sup>C</sup>L) the wicked place Your hand;[63]

And let all those who rely upon You rejoice,

In the building of Your city and in the renewal of Your holy-house;[64]

For before we call, may you answer, As it is said, "And it shall be, before they call I will answer; while they are yet speaking, I will hear" (Is. 65:24).

J'.  And he says, Praised Lord, For You hear the voice of my supplication.

K'.  Praised be Thou Lord, who hears prayer.

L'.  And he says the first three blessings and the last three.  [The readings and suggested readings for J'-L' vary.[65]]

(y. Ber. 4:3; 8a = y. Taan 2:2; 65c)


i

M. Ber. 4:3a focuses upon the individual's obligation to pray the *Tefillah* and assumes that the matter was still not formalized, though there was an agreed upon structure of prayers containing eighteen blessings and defined themes.  The eighteen-- and later, in Babylonia, nineteen--consisted of three opening and three closing blessings and twelve--or thirteen--middle items, which were later referred to as petitionary prayers.[66]  The first of the inner passages asks for "understanding" and the last one appeals to God "to receive" an individual's prayer.

Samuel's traditions in b. and y. relate to Joshua's cryptic M<sup>C</sup>YN, "The substance of eighteen."  As the traditions appear in two different formulations, our analysis focuses upon the relationship between the two.

A is a citation of Mishnah.  B introduces[67] the traditions of Rav and Samuel, which, however, do not make up a balanced dispute form.  While both lack a tradent, Rav's opinion responds

to the question and clarifies Joshua's language, but Samuel's
neither formally responds to the question nor does it employ
Joshua's language.  The substance of the latter, the full text of
a prayer,[68] opens with the word *havinenu*, "Give us discernment,"
the term by which the prayer is often called.  It contains thirteen clauses which represent the inner part of the *Tefillah*.
They, along with the opening and closing sets of three blessings,
constitute the nineteen units.  As stated, this total follows the
Babylonian practice which mentions the Davidic hope as an independent prayer.[69]  Samuel's abridgement constitutes a reinterpretation of the original prayer and focuses on "the messianic and
eschatological aspects of Eighteen Benedictions, to the neglect
of themes which are more central in the original."[70]

     E-M attests Samuel's connection with the *havinenu* prayer.
Abaye, a fourth-generation Babylonian Amora, reportedly reacted
to Samuel's tradition.  In F, the second Samuel tradition concerning *havinenu*, a third-generation master assumes Samuel's interest
in this prayer.  Furthermore, another third-generation master, G,
and a sixth-generation one, I, discussed that tradition.  But as
indicated by the repetition of phrasing in K-M, these reports may
be shaped by the *sugya*'s redaction.  The pattern of K, a tradition attributed to a fifth-generation master, is identical to F.
Either F provided a model for K or else both received their present formulation at the same time.  Moreover, I and L, Mar Zutra's
questions on F and K, are likewise similarly formulated, "Let
them include in it. . . ."  The pericope is thus redacted together
and is not made up of merely an accretion of layers, each of which
is unrelated to the other.[71]  As we shall see, the y. pericope
throws further light on this matter.

     Traditional commentators[72] have tried to relate E, F, and
K to each other.  While that is not our task, we may notice that
three items limit the use of *havinenu*.  Abaye, in E, in accord
with the depiction of him elsewhere, reportedly "cursed" anyone
who followed Samuel's tradition.[73]  Secondly, certain circles
considered it necessary to associate one such limitation, F, with
Samuel's name.  Perhaps the differences in attitudes reflect the
fact that the need for *havinenu* was greater in Samuel's day, at
the beginning of amoraic rabbinic activity in Babylonia, than
later.  For as a result of the growth of the rabbinic movement,
more individuals, whether disciples or other adherents, were more
familiar with the fuller liturgical texts.  It may also reflect a
general greater degree of freedom in liturgical matters whereby

prayers could be abridged.  This freedom decreased with the
increased efforts at standardization.[74]  Of note, the y. pericope
lacks such limitations.  Indeed one comment there, I', is inconsistent with one of the b. limitations.  Thus the limitations
should not necessarily determine our interpretation of Samuel's
comment.[75]

ii

In y.'s *sugya*, Samuel's and Rav's traditions follow a
lemma of Mishnah[76] and refer to its second line.  B' introduces
the comments.  The mention of "Seven" in the introductory question,
is problematic.  It is either a contamination from below or else a
reflection of the reading of Mishnah which is made explicit in the
*baraita*, E', and which accords with Samuel.[77]

C' and D', two explanatory traditions, appear without a
tradent.  Neither one, in contrast to C of b., employs Joshua's
language.  But this time, they make up a balanced dispute form,
and their wording directly contrast, "end" versus "beginning."
Below we shall analyze the significance of this formulation.

E' presents two *baraitot* which give support to Rav and
Samuel.  Both are clearly formulated as a gloss so as to comment
upon, enter, or replace a clause in a text like Mishnah.  In F',
Zeiri, a third-generation Babylonian emigré to Palestine, is
represented as if he inquired from a Palestinian as to the meaning of Samuel's comment and thus attests the attribution to
Samuel.  His question, though, refers to Samuel's tradition in
terms of the language in E' and not D' and thereby attests to a
certain interpretation of Samuel's comment.  G' and I', the text
of a prayer, constitute the response.  H' is an interpolation
which indicates that a text of *havinenu* circulated in the time of
Hagai, a third-fourth-generation Palestinian Amora.[78]

The wording of y.'s version of *havinenu* somewhat differs
from b.'s.  It lacks a reference to the Davidic hope, the "thirteenth" clause, for in Palestine this sentiment was incorporated
into an existing prayer.[79]  Evidently, then, we have a Palestinian
analogue to Samuel's abridgement.[80]  At the end, the prayer
includes a biblical verse, not found in b.'s version.  It also
mentions the ending formulation of the blessing, which normally
constitutes the fifteenth of the eighteen blessings.  It sets
forth a requirement which commentators of b. Ber. 29a generally
assume to be Samuel's meaning, an assumption explicity spelled out
in an anonymous pericope, in b. Ber. 30a.

iii

C and D and C' and D' substantively accord with each
other.  BT and PT therefore both attest that Samuel deals with
Joshua's comment in Mishnah and that he is associated with the
*havinenu* prayer.  Recent scholarship argues that Samuel did not
invent this prayer; rather, he provided the text for Babylonians.[81]  Even if we assume this, what version of his tradition is
"prior" and which, if either, initially functioned as a Mishnah
commentary?  The formulation of Samuel's comments may provide an
answer.  As noted above, in y., Samuel's comment is in a balanced
dispute form with Rav's.  But the language appropriately fits
only Rav's position and not Samuel's.  According to Rav, a person
abbreviates the *Tefillah* by saying something of each of the benedictions and something of the end, "the seal," of each.[82]  But
Samuel's precís is a digest and is not made up of the "beginning"
of each blessing.  Accordingly, the word the "beginning," literally the "head," serves to contrast with Rav's term, the "end,"
and refers to the topic of each prayer.[83]  Samuel's tradent or a
later authority who worked over the tradition, therefore, shaped
his language to respond to Rav's.  This accords with our argument
that the presentation as a dispute is not the most fundamental
form of the tradition.[84]

We note, as elsewhere where Zeira follows a comment of
Samuel, it is possible that he cited it and shaped it in the
course of transmission and application.[85]  He may have thus
presented Samuel's tradition along with Rav's together in a dispute form, and the need of that dispute form required that both
traditions appear in a certain formulation.  We should, therefore, not assume that because D' and not D is formulated as a
Mishnah comment, it precedes D in the history of the tradition.
Indeed if C' provides an indication, both C' and D' may be
reformulations.  Thus while C' is formulated as a Mishnah comment,
bavli's version, C, is a gloss and thereby so constitutes an
equally acceptable if not more fundamental formulation of a
Mishnah explanation.

The *havinenu* prayer, D, is simply a text of a prayer, and
not a formal comment on Mishnah.  Clearly, however, as indicated
by the introductory questions (B and B'), D just as D', is used
as a comment on Mishnah.[86]  The *havinenu* prayer accordingly may
assume and have developed a simple interpretation of Mishnah and
thereby constitute a "second level" Mishnah comment.  Alternatively, it may have originated not in response to Mishnah but in

another context and, due to its assumed relevance, have been
cited in conjunction with Mishnah.  The former more likely
describes the history of the tradition.  F', in fact, provides us
with an example of what might have actually happened.  It specifically identifies the *havinenu* prayer with Samuel's interpretation of Mishnah.

        To conclude, in tracing the history of Samuel's teachings,
we must distinguish between logically necessary stages in the
explanation of Mishnah and the relative priority of extant formulations of teachings.  As indicated by Nahman's comment, F, and
by the y. *sugya*, third-generation masters associated Samuel with
the *havinenu*.  Therefore, b.'s formulation of Samuel's tradition
need not be a late reformulation of his thought.  Rather, Babylonians preserved and transmitted the upshot of his opinion--the
*havinenu* prayer--and not a comment which logically was more
fundamental, which explained Mishnah, and which in thought must
have preceded the *havinenu*.  Our analysis thus demonstrates that
Samuel's traditions which respond to Mishnah may take different
forms and be transmitted in different fashions.[87]

58, 59.

## M. Ber. 4:7

        1.  R. Eleazer b. Azariah says,
        There is *Tefillah* of *Musafim* [= the additional
*Tefillah*] only where there is [alt. = "in"] (B-) a *hever* $^c$*ir*
(HBR $^c$YR) [a term variously vocalized and rendered = "town
congregation," or "assembly," "community," "communal city,"
"community leader."][88]
        2.  And Sages say, Whether there is a *hever* $^c$*ir* or
whether there is no *hever* $^c$*ir*.
        3.  R. Judah says in his name [i.e., of R. Eleazer b.
Azariah],
        Wherever there is a *hever* $^c$*ir* an individual is exempt
from *Tefillah* of *Musafim*.
                        (M. Ber. 4:7)

        A.  Said R. Huna bar Hinena said R. Hiyya bar Rav,[89]
        The *halakhah* follows R. Judah who said in the name of
R. Eleazar b. Azariah.
        B.1.  Said to him R. Hiyya bar Abin,
        You are right.

B.2.   For said Samuel (D'MR ŠMW'L), During my days I
individually in Nehardea[90] never prayed the *Tefillah* of
*Musafim* except on the day in which the king's [a word deleted
in certain texts[91]] force[92] (PWLMWS) came to the city and the
rabbis became terrified and did not pray,

and I individually prayed (BYHYD).

(B.3.   and I was an individual not in the context of
a *hever* *c*ir.)[93]

(b. Ber. 30a-b)

A'.   R. Bibi BŠM R. Hanina[94] said,

The *halakhah* follows R. Judah who said in the name of
R. Eleazar b. Azariah.

B'.1.   The matter [alt., "word"] of Samuel said thus
[i.e., accords with A].

B'.2.   For said Samuel (DŠMW'L 'MR),

I never prayed that of *Musaf* except once when (D-)
the son of the exilarch died and the community did not pray
[it] and I prayed it.

C'.   The matters [alt. "words"] of the rabbis dispute
[A'],  . . .[95]

D'.   The matter [alt. "word"] of R. Yohanan said thus
[i.e., accords with C'], . . .

E'.   One hears three things from this:

. . . and one hears that they dispute R. Judah who
said in the name of R. Eleazar b. Azariah; . . .[96]

(y. Ber. 4:7 [6], 8c)

i

M. Ber. 4:7 provides the context for three traditions of
Samuel.  In the first two Samuel reports different but related
incidents which at an early time were considered relevant to
Mishnah's law.

M. Ber. Ch. 4 deals with the regularization of the
*Tefillah* service which became central in the rabbinic, post-70,
emphasis on prayer as the essential, and not just supplementary,
means of divine worship.  M. Ber. 4:7 focuses on the special case
of *Musaf*, the "additional" *Tefillah* reserved for Saturdays, New
Moons, and holidays.  It has an anomalous place within the twofold dimension of rabbinic prayer.  One type is said by the group,
led by a representative, and the other, by an individual.  The
latter may offer these noncommunal prayers, though, when with a
group and privately.  Since *Musaf* retains the sense of its

communal origin,[97] it was not automatically clear if the individual has a responsibility to say it.


ii

Samuel's traditions appear within *sugyot* which evaluate
Mishnah's authoritative position.  In the BT *sugya*, Samuel's
comment, B, is one of seven items, each of which has halakhic
implications.  The pericope opens with a decision attributed to
Hiyya bar Rav, a second-generation Babylonian master, and transmitted by R. Huna bar Hinena, a third-to-fourth-generation Babylonian Amora.  His colleague, Hiyya bar Abin, concurs and cites
Samuel's comment.  Samuel is thus redactionally represented to
accord with Judah's tradition in the name of Eleazar b. Azariah.
Where there is a *hever* $^c$*ir* the individual is exempt from *Musaf*.

The printed editions of *Gemara* contain an apparent gloss
on Samuel's comment, B.3.  It is generated by an anonymous pericope which immediately precedes A and which opens the *Gemara* on
the Mishnah.  That pericope distinguishes between clauses 3 and 1
of Mishnah.  According to Judah, and not Eleazar (clause 1), an
individual outside the *hever* $^c$*ir*'s presence says *Musaf*.[98]  But
this does not necessarily represent Samuel's position.  The substance of his comment B.1-2 explicitly mentions only praying
*Musaf* alone and makes clear that this is an unusual procedure.

While pericope A-B supports Judah, the remaining five
parts of the *sugya* oppose that decision.[99]  The latter consist of
opinions and practices of Palestinians and comments thereon by
Babylonian emigrés.  Following Abraham Goldberg's observation
elsewhere, the *sugya* apparently thus reports on or projects
Babylonian emigrés' attempts in Palestine to relate Samuel's
position to Palestinian views.  While certain points of the *sugya*
present difficulties, it clearly represents the Palestinians as
rejecting the Babylonian custom and apparently supporting sages'
position (clause 2).[100]


iii

In PT, Samuel's report forms the second part of a four-
part *sugya* which directly comments on the Mishnah.  A'-B' are
structurally equal to A-B of BT.  The first clause, while here
attributed to a different Amora, likewise rules that the *halakhah*
follows Judah.  An anonymous comment from the *sugya*'s editor
mentions that Samuel holds likewise, as evidenced in his report.

The anonymous authority cites additional traditions, C' and D',
which are understood to agree with sages (clause 2).[101]

The two versions of Samuel's report, B.2 and B'.2, mention
different contexts.  PT refers to the death of the exilarch and
b. to an army incursion.  At this point we cannot know why each
*Gemara* has a different incident.  It may, however, reflect an
observation which we discussed elsewhere.[102]  Such variations may
accord with varying views each *Gemara* has of the overall issues.
First, B' is introduced and formulated to fit its context and
explicit to differ with D'; B has thus been shaped on the basis
of redactional considerations.  Secondly, PT, in contrast to BT,
does not apparently distinguish between Judah and Eleazar b.
Azariah.[103]  According to Judah, when the *hever* $^c$*ir* prays *Musaf*,
the individual does not.  In BT, on the other hand, as mentioned,
the (late) gloss in B.3 accords with b.'s anonymous distinction
between Judah and Eleazar.  Moreover, the formulation of the rest
of the report, "I individually in Nehardea . . . ,"[104] further
reflects the view that Mishnah's rule applies only in the context
of the *hever* $^c$*ir*, and that elsewhere an individual prays *Musaf*.

Alternatively, the differences between the b. and y. versions may be tied to rabbinic-exilarchic politics.  Bavli circles
may have preferred not to indicate that rabbis respected the
exilarch and therefore reworked or transmitted the incident in
the way in which they did.  This suggestion may receive support
from the observation that elsewhere b. does not mention the son
of an anonymous exilarch.  But since references to inroads
(PWLMWS) into Iranian cities do appear elsewhere in b., that
context would be a viable one.[105]


                                iv

Samuel in both the b. and y. versions emerges as in
agreement with Judah in the name of R. Eleazar b. Azariah.  The
tradition is cited by someone else, formulated as a report of
Samuel's statement, and forms part of structurally parallel
*sugyot*.  Variations in the report may reflect the later Babylonian
and Palestinian conceptions and use of the materials.  In b., the
opposing view is tacitly presented and supported by including a
*sugya* of Babylonian emigrés in Palestine and the comments of
Yohanan.  In y., while the differing view is likewise attributed
to Palestinians, its opposite position is explicitly stated.

The structural parallels indicate that some type of early
pericope formed around the Mishnah.  It consisted of a ruling in

favor of R. Judah, and then Samuel's report.  Alternatively,
Samuel's report circulated and someone later appended it to an
explicit decision.  Either way, the pericope was reported in
Palestine and became subject to further discussion.[106]  In the
process, Palestinian circles rejected Samuel's position.[107]  Babylonian circles, furthermore, became aware of the Palestinian
scrutiny.  The report of Samuel's comment thus in an early period
became associated with Mishnah.  But it is not formulated so as
to circulate along with Mishnah as part of a "commentary," and
therefore someone has to cite it.[108]

60.

### [M. Ber. 4:7]

A. Rav said,

[One] has to (SRYK L-) innovate something in it (LHDŠ
BH DBR) [in *Tefillah* of *Musaf*].

B.  Samuel said,

[One] does not[109] have to innovate something in it.

C.  R. Ze[c]ira asked R. Yose [V MS = "Yosa"],

What is [the meaning of] "to innovate something in
it"?[110]

D.  He said to him,

Even if he said, "And [so that] we will prepare before
you our obligations of [or 'with,' B-[111]] daily offerings
(BTMYDY YWM] and of [or 'with'] the sacrifice of *Musaf*"--
he has fulfilled his requirement (YS[ɔ]).

(y. Ber. 4:6 [7], 8c)

The third tradition concerning M. Ber. 4:7 and attributed
to Samuel forms a dispute with Rav as to the text of *Musaf*.  The
comments reflect the early stage of this *Tefillah* in which it was
identical to that of the morning, the *Shaharit*.[112]

The two traditions appear in a dispute form and use identical language except for B's added negative, [ɔ]YN, "not."  The
comments employ the gloss-like verbal phrase, ṢRYK L-, "[One]
has to," and the inexplicit word "in it," BH, and therefore
cannot circulate by themselves but require a context for comprehension.  They undoubtedly refer back to the additional *Musaf*
*Tefillah*, as indicated by Yose's mention of "sacrifices of
*Musaf*,"[113] and by the general context, which focuses on *Musaf*.[114]

Zeira attests the formulation of A.  Following our observation elsewhere, where Zeira's comments in y. are placed after a

tradition of Samuel, Zeira may have transmitted A and B to Palestine and even formulated the two traditions as a dispute.[115]

The comment, like the previous one which supported Judah's
position in M. Ber. 4:7, indicates that Samuel is concerned with
*Musaf*.[116]  Moreover, his view here may relate to that previous
tradition.  As private individuals need not say *Musaf*, naturally
one does not have to innovate anything in the text.  But the
opposite position which requires *Musaf*, logically may also obli-
gate an individual to distinguish or set aside that *Tefillah* from
that of the morning.[117]

As Samuel's and Rav's traditions appear in dispute form
we remain uncertain as to whose formulation is fundamental.
First, it may not be original to Samuel; rather, as elsewhere,
the transmitter or editor when he presented the dispute may have
employed Rav's language or may have imposed the language upon
both Rav and Samuel.  Alternatively, Rav and Samuel may have
fortuitously used this language, in which case it would be fundamental to both masters.  For sure, Rav requires an additional
action and only once such a view circulates does it become necessary to stress the opposite position.  Moreover, the opening
formulation fits a pattern in which both opinions in a dispute
appear.  Already in Mishnah and Tosefta we find, "X says, [One]
has to (SRYK L-) . . ., and Y says, [One] does not have to
(ᵓYN SRYK L-) . . ."  We also find just the first portion alone,
or just the second one, but appended to a different formulation
of a preceding opposite opinion.[118]  Thus, the second opinion is
presently formulated to circulate along with the first one.
Nevertheless, we do not deal with a foreign notion imposed upon
Samuel.  Samuel's position remains consistent with his other
views.  He and Rav, in fact, are discussing the applicability of
a principle known in their day.

First, the phrase LHDŠ BH DBR, "to innovate something in
it," appears in b. Ber. 21a-b in a teaching of Samuel, the third
in a series of traditions which Judah transmits in Samuel's name.
An individual who has already prayed the *Tefillah* before entering
a synagogue, may participate and repeat the *Tefillah* with others
only if he can innovate something.  That tradition is not inconsistent with the principle that *Musaf* does not require innovation.
Indeed, as innovation does not apply to the standard, here the
first, recitation of the *Tefillah*, it can be operative in the
special case of repeating the *Tefillah* with a group.[119]

Secondly, the principle to innovate and therefore to vary
something and the formulation HDŠ [BH DBR] exists in tannaitic
literature.[120]  It thus constitutes a formulaic principle which
Samuel or Rav or both may have known.

Samuel's tradition directly comments on Mishnah, though
it is presented as part of a dispute.  While the view attributed
to Samuel is not anachronous or inappropriate to Samuel, we remain
uncertain whether or not the language is fundamental to him.

*5.  Berakhot Chapter Five*

65, 66.

### M. Ber. 5:2

1.   They mention the "Powers of Rain" in [the bless-
ing] "Resurrection of the Dead,"
2.   and ask for rain in the "Blessing of the Years,"
3.   And *havdalah* [they say][121] in "Favors [a person
with] knowledge."

R. <sup>C</sup>Aqivah says, He says it (W<sup>Ɔ</sup>MRH) as a fourth
blessing by itself.  [He interpolates *havdalah* before the
regular blessing of "Favors (a person with) knowledge," which
thus becomes the fifth blessing.]

R. Eliezer says, "In Thanksgiving." [= The next-to-
last blessing in the *Tefillah*.]

(M. Ber. 5:2)

A.   And *havdalah* in "Favors [a person with] Knowledge."  [= M. lemma.]

B.   Simeon B. Va [= "Ba," which is the reading in V
MS] asked R. Yohanan,

A matter which is a present custom,[122] sages are in
dispute[123] over it?

C.   Said [Yohanan] to him [to Simeon],

Because its essence [= the essential ceremony] is over
a cup (BKWS), they forgot [its place] in the *Tefillah*.[124]

D.   That indicates (MLTYH <sup>Ɔ</sup>MRH) that its essence is
over a cup.

E.   R. Yaaqov bar Idi BŠM R. Yishaq the Great,

[If] he said it over a cup, he says it in the *Tefillah*
[add or correct to: "If he said it in the *Tefillah*, he says it
over a cup"] so as to involve (LZKWT) the children.  [= A
clause variously rendered.  In light of line F, the purpose

clause, E indicates that one says *havdalah* over a cup not for
its own sake to fulfill the requirement of *havdalah* but for a
separate, secondary purpose.][125]

F.   That indicates that its essence is in the *Tefillah*.

G.   R. Ze<sup>c</sup>ira, R. Judah BŠM Samuel,

[If] he said[126] it over a cup, he says it in the
*Tefillah*.

[If] he said it in the *Tefillah*,[127] he says it over a
cup.

H.   That indicates that its essence is in both.

                    (y. Ber. 5:2, 9b)


I.   And did not say (WH<sup>ɔ</sup>MR) R. Judah said Samuel,

And the one who says *havdalah* (WHMBDYL) in *Tefillah*
must say *havdalah* over a cup?

                    (b. Shab. 150b)


                              i

     PT and BT each contain two comments attributed to Samuel
which concern M. Ber. 5:2's reference to *havdalah*, the formal
separation verbally proclaimed to distinguish between one period
of holiness, e.g., the Sabbath, from a second, less holy, one,
e.g., a regular weekday.  We first examine the set of comments
which focus on the proper context for *havdalah* and which are
presented above.  We then cite and analyze the second set which
deals with Mishnah's dispute as to the exact place of *havdalah*
in *Tefillah*.  While all the traditions may not formally comment
on Mishnah, some, if not all, have been generated by Mishnah and
may thus constitute part of a commentary.


                             ii

     The authorities behind the y. *sugya*, A-H, cite G as one
of three texts to determine the essential context for *havdalah*.[128]
After each text the redactor makes explicit the implications, D,
F, and H.

     As the origin and history of the *havdalah* undoubtedly
caused the uncertainty as to the context, we briefly review the
developments.  The *havdalah* over a cup and in the *Tefillah* are
both mentioned in tannaitic sources.[129]  *Havdalah* probably originated at the Saturday late-afternoon meal as a home ceremony over
a cup of wine.  The sequence of this *havdalah* is disputed by the
Houses of Hillel and Shammai and it may thus well predate 70 and

the standardization and formalization of prayers.  Moreover,
people apparently even without the meal recited *havdalah*.  As the
evening service originally was not obligatory, *havdalah* had to be
said in a separate context.  Once the evening service, however,
became common or commonly accepted, *havdalah* was included in it.
Only then did the relationship between the two contexts become a
problem.  The two locations, moreover, may form part of a wider
phenomenon.  The evening meal in Pharisaic and other circles may
have constituted a table fellowship, whereas in other groups it
was a ritual meal.  Perhaps the transformation in contexts,
accordingly, relates to the transition from Pharisaic and other
"meal"-oriented pieties to that of the emerging and expanding
rabbinic movement.  Indeed the recitation of *havdalah* in *Tefillah*
undoubtedly reflects not only the growing standardization of the
liturgy but also the heightened importance of prayer and its
function in early rabbinic Judaism.[130]

    Initially, one context of *havdalah* probably sufficed, a
point reflected in T. Ber. 3:9.  That text accords with Mishnah's
anonymous position of "Favors Knowledge," and indicates that if
one forgot *havdalah* in one place one could, and should, say it in
the other.[131]

    E presents one view as to the proper context.  Abraham
Goldberg aptly points out that Yishaq the Great was the reciter
of R. Judah the Patriarch and may thus represent some type of
early Palestinian position.[132]  As we shall see, Samuel's opposite
position may reflect a differing Babylonian approach.

    Samuel's tradition, G, like E, does not specify the
subject, which, however, is clear.  Both G and E, in contrast to
B, employ Mishnah's language, "say it," and thus refer back to
Mishnah.[133]  The b. version of the tradition, I, provides an
example of what an autonomous formulation might have looked like.

    The b. version is secondary to its context.  While Judah,
like in y., transmits the tradition, the anonymous author of the
pericope cites it to bolster a question against M. Shab. 23:3.[134]
But the tradition serves to attest Samuel's position.  Elsewhere
we also find other Samuel traditions which primarily do not
address the issue of *havdalah* per se, but which reflect or mention
Samuel's view and confirm his opinion.[135]


                                iii

    The attributive formula of the y. tradition is R. Zeira
R. Judah, BŠM Samuel.  Zeira probably brought the tradition to

Palestine.  As the name of the tradent is not always included
when Zeira cites a tradition, perhaps it was appropriate here
because it ultimately represents a decision as to the proper context.  Elsewhere we found that adjudications are generally transmitted by tradents.[136]

Building upon one of Goldberg's suggestions, we may
appreciate the role of Zeira, and relate G to B-C, and both to a
b. analogue to the whole *sugya*, b. Ber. 33a-b.  Goldberg specifically analyzes aspects of this *sugya* and several other passages
and suggests that Babylonian emigrés to Palestine tried, in Palestine, to give currency to Babylonian traditions.  Thus in G, Zeira
cites Samuel, and in B, Simeon b. (Ab)ba, another emigré, through
his pointed question, has Yohanan mention the context over a
cup.[137]  Moreover, the importance of Samuel's position may be
reflected in the fact that *Gemara* elsewhere contains instances of
the tradition formulated identical to I though not attributed to
Samuel.  An anonymous authority in b. Pes. 105b deduces the tradition as one of eight items inferred from a *baraita* cited there.
In b. Pes. 107a, the tradition appears as one of a threefold
deduction made from a report of the actions of certain Amoraim.
Finally, the b. analogue on b. Ber. 33a contains several instances
of this identical tradition, again not attributed to Samuel.  The
b. Ber. 33a analogue to A-H is particularly relevant and we
accordingly focus on it.

The analogous b. *sugya* presents a slightly different
version of Simeon b. Ba's question and several traditions which
explicitly require *havdalah* both over a cup and in the *Tefillah*.
As mentioned, b. uses a formulation identical to I.  Yohanan,
among others, is thus represented as mentioning *havdalah* over a
cup.[138]  A second Babylonian, Hiyya b. Abba, a third-generation
Babylonian emigré to Palestine,[139] either transmits it in the
name of Yohanan or, apparently, appends it to his (Yohanan's)
tradition.  Further, Benjamin b. Yefet in the name of R. Asi,[140]
a third-generation Babylonian emigré, transmits a conversation
in which Yohanan confirms the importance of *havdalah* over a cup.
In addition, Rabbah apparently through an emendation, reads it
into a *baraita*.[141]  The extent of the emphasis is reflected in
the next question which b. logically poses.  If one says *havdalah*
over a cup, is it necessary also in the *Tefillah*?  R. Nahman b.
Yishaq answers affirmatively.  Rav likewise presents Ravina with
a decision that it is necessary in both.[142]  BT's *sugya* thus

contains elements and a conclusion similar to y.'s, though, as
indicated, it does not mention Samuel's name.

Samuel's tradition, in y., comments on Mishnah.  It represents a view which Palestinian circles evidently somewhat originally opposed, a view which Yohanan rejected, but which later
circles partially recognized.  Babylonian circles responsible for
b. Ber. 33a-b surely see it in those terms whereby Yohanan himself
adapts this position.  In addition, Samuel's comment accords with
the possibly "earlier" practice of *havdalah* over a cup.  He
thereby affirms the importance of various forms of religious
ceremonies in addition to those of *Tefillah*.[143]

## 67, 68 [and 55].

### [M. Ber. 5:2]

A.  R. Eliezer says, In [the prayer] "Thanksgiving."
[= lemma of M.]

B.  R. Yohanan in the name (BŠM) of Rabbi, "They
incline (MTYN) following R. Eliezer[144] on a holiday that
occurs at the outgoing of a Sabbath[145] [when the regular
*Tefillah* with the prayer, "Favor a person with Knowledge" is
not said and thus cannot be the place for *havdalah*.]

C.  R. Yishaq the Great BŠM Rabbi, The *halakhah*
follows R. Eliezer on a holiday that occurs at the outgoing
of a Sabbath.[145]

D.  R. Yishaq bar Nahman BŠM R. Hunaniah[145] b.
Gamaliel [says], The *halakhah* follows R. Eliezer in all cases
(L^CWLM).

E.  R. Abbahu BŠM R. Eleazar [says], The *halakhah*
follows R. Eliezer in all cases.

F.  Said R. Yaaqov b. Aha . . . [= Comment on above:
Eleazar in E--like Yishaq in D--transmits in the name of R.
Hanina b. Gamaliel, and D and E therefore represent only one
tradition.][147]

G.  The words of the sages (DBRY HKMYM) [= the following item is the *halakhah*:][148]

H.  R. Yaaqov b. Aha BŠM Samuel, [He] says it ["as,"
or "in," which Sirillo makes explicit with a prefix, B-] the
Fourth blessing.[149]

### (y. Ber. 5:2, 9b)

[As to the position of R. Eliezer on the outgoing of
the Sabbath which coincides with a holiday:]

A'.  It was said ($^{\text{3}}$TMR),[150] R. Yishaq bar Avudimi
[= R. Yishaq the Great][151] in the name of Rabbenu [= Rabbi
Judah the Patriarch][152] said, *Halakhah.*

And some say, "They incline (MTYN) [to his position].

B'.  R. Yohanan said . . . [= Citation of Yohanan's
position and a dispute between several masters as to what
Yohanan had supposedly said, viz., the degree to which he
supported R. Eliezer's position.][153]

C'.  Said R. Joseph, I [MSS, "We"] know neither this
nor that.[154]  Rav and Samuel already arranged for us [155] a
pearl in Babylonia,

C'.2.  "And You informed us, O Lord, our God, Your
righteous judgments,

"and taught us to do your desired statutes,

[Rid adds, "And in love gave us, O Lord our God,
equitable judgments and true instructions, good laws and
commandments, which if a person does them he might live by
them,]

"and You caused us to inherit occasions of gladness
[Rid adds, "and holy festivals,"] and celebrations of free
will offerings,

"and You transmitted to us the holiness of the
Sabbath and the glory of the festive days, and the celebration of the festival,

"[Rid adds, "And"] You divided between the holiness
of the Sabbath and that of holiday,

"and You sanctified the seventh day above the six
days of creation [missing in Rid],

"You separated [missing in Rid] and sanctified Your
people Israel with Your holiness,

C'.3.  "and You have given us etc."[156]  [= The next,
regular festival prayer.]

(b. Ber. 33b)


i

In y., the tradition attributed to Samuel adjudicates
between the several views in Mishnah.  The comment appears within
a *sugya* that initially focuses on a special case of *havdalah.*  On
a Saturday night on which a holiday occurs one does not say the
regular *Tefillah* and thus one cannot interpolate *havdalah* or
anything else into the now nonpresent "He Who Favors a person
with Knowledge."  In such a case should one follow Eliezer, Aqiva,

or some other procedure?  The identical problem is central also
to the b. *sugya* which presents a related tradition of Samuel.
PT's and especially BT's pericopae strikingly indicate the ways
in which Babylonian emigrés handled Yohanan's tradition and thus
represent the Babylonians as trying to make a place for Samuel's
comment.

ii

Samuel's comment, H, provides a *halakhic* ruling which
rejects both D and E, and, if we follow the impression imparted
from the pericope's arrangement, B and C.  These four traditions
present decisions in one form or another in favor of R. Eliezer.
B and C deal with a special case, which is specified perhaps to
contrast with the phrase "in all cases" in D and E.  B presents
this as an "inclination" of R. Eliezer, i.e., less than a full
ruling, and C does so as an explicit *halakhah*, i.e., the regular
normative position.  D is attributed to a second-third-generation
Palestinian Amora in the name of a fourth-generation Tanna; and
E, to a third-generation master in the name of a second-generation
Babylonian emigré to Palestine.  Yaaqov B. Aha, a third-fourth-
generation Palestinian Amora, who transmits Samuel's tradition,
comments on D and E.[157]

H, in formulation, is not restricted to any special case,
though, redactionally, it is used for a particular purpose.  H
employs the language of Mishnah, "say it," WƆMRH, and lacks
either of the clarifications found in B-E.  On the other hand,
the *sugya* has the redactional clause G, which indicates that what
follows, and not what precedes, is the correct decision.  Moreover, R. Yaaqov b. Aha, Samuel's tradent, appears also in F.  We
are thus given the impression that H, like the previous decisions,
refers to the specified special case and rejects Eliezer.  Our
understanding of Samuel's tradition is accordingly shaped by its
use.

If H rejects Eliezer, whom does it support?  There are two
possibilities.  First, H may accord with Aqiva.  It thus employs
the same term as in Aqiva's tradition.  It lacks, however, his
final phrase, "by itself," and it does not, following the usual
pattern of a decision, state the name of the Tanna whom it supports.

Alternatively, H may refer to the anonymous first opinion
in Mishnah.  If it does the lack of Aqiva's final phrase, "by
itself," and the mention of his name makes sense.  Moreover, the

present formulation is not problematic.  As the first opinion is
anonymous, H could not name the authority.  Nor could it simply
refer to the authority with the attribution "rabbis" or "sages,"
or mention "He who Favors with Knowledge"; for, while H accepts
the principle of that anonymous authority, it does not literally
follow its view.

        The only problem with the latter interpretation is the
lack of a B- before the word "blessing."  While Sirillo's text
includes it, this is a unique reading and therefore may be an
emendation.[158]  Nevertheless, we may be able to render the clause
in the same way even when it lacks the B-; at times a prefix B-,
especially before a word starting with a B-, is deleted.[159]  PM,
Sefer Haredim, Epstein, and Ginzberg, favor the first possibility.
If they are correct, y.'s tradition apparently somewhat differs
from b.'s presentation of the materials, in which, as we shall
see, Samuel's "pearl" either follows or provides a structural
analogue to the anonymous first opinion in Mishnah or else it
constitutes a special compromise between the several opinions.
Sirillo and Yellin follow the second alternative, to which I also
incline.  If the latter is correct, y. fits b.[160]

        Yohanan's view in y. is thus subject to discussion.  Some
authorities consider Eliezer authoritative.  Samuel differs from
various Palestinian views mentioned in the pericope.  As we shall
now see, y. exhibits certain similarities with its b. analogue.


                                iii

        In b., A' and B' provide several decisions in favor of
Eliezer.  As Goldberg points out, the effect of B', the Babylonian emigrés' revision of that decision, is to state that
*Yohanan's position is only tolerated and not favored.  This
redactionally leads up to a statement of the preferred position
which C' supplies.*

        C' attributes "You have informed us," to Samuel and Rav.
At this point we are unable to know what the double attribution
means.  Did both come together to formulate the text?  Did one
compose it and the second accept that formulation?  But the
attribution to Samuel conforms to the fact that other traditions
concerning *havdalah* are attributed to Samuel.  The attribution
thus is not an arbitrary mistake.[161]

        C' supports which position in Mishnah?  First, it clearly
rejects R. Eliezer, and thereby accords with y.  Secondly, it
probably does not follow Aqiva; for he already requires an

individual to make a separate blessing for *havdalah*.  Accordingly,
one does not need a special prayer.  A person could simply revise
the existing prayer and mention the separation between the holiness of the Sabbath and that of the holiday.  Would, then, such a
modification be considered a "pearl"?[162]  This argument receives
support from the fact that Samuel does not follow Aqiva as to the
regular saying of *havdalah*.

> Said R. Nahman said Samuel, Throughout the year a
> person prays "Give us discernment," [= an abridged *Tefillah*],
> except on the outgoings of the Sabbath and holidays, because
> he has to say *havdalah* in "[He who] favors [a person] with
> knowledge."
>
> (b. Ber. 29a)

Thirdly, there remains the possibility that C' makes up a
structural analogue to the anonymous position in Mishnah, viz.,
that one interpolates *havdalah* into the fourth blessing.[163]  Note
the last clause, C'.3, resumes the next part of the festival
prayer.  While several authorities support this interpretation,
E. Wider considers C' a special, independent formulation which
does not totally agree with any of the Tannaim.[164]  The difference, however, is basically semantic.  If C' is a structural
analogue to the position of the anonymous authority, it is not
identical to that position.  Therefore, if one wishes one might
be justified to call it a "compromise."  But one must not forget
that in light of the b. and y. pericopae, which contain the ruling
in favor of R. Eliezer, the thrust of C' clearly serves to reject
Eliezer.  BT's tradition, as that of y., thus constitutes a rejection.  The position which it supports, however, cannot be totally
identified with one of the remaining views.

The import of the tradition further emerges in light of
several *geniza* fragments.  They indicate that in later times,
some Palestinians followed Eliezer.[165]  This may make us appreciate the nature of *Gemara*'s "representation" of Samuel and his
"rejection" of Eliezer.  We see the role of Samuel's traditions
through the perceptions and use of later generations.  BT may
project how Babylonian emigrés transmitted Yohanan's ruling to
give currency to Samuel.  Likewise, y. may indicate that Samuel
held an authoritative position.  But we cannot automatically
assume that that image of Samuel accords with the actual practices of people over many generations.

iv

When one compares b. and y., one wonders why PT does not
mention the blessing "You have informed us." We remain uncertain
whether or not Palestinian circles knew this text. Yet what y.
does have, viz., H, accords with the principle behind the "pearl"
and that apparently is what in Palestine was transmitted or cited
in this context. Indeed, when one considers how the formulation
in H varies from B-E, it is difficult to assume that the redactor
of the pericope altered the formulation of the text of a prayer
into its wording in H.

The last point also throws light on the logical relationship between the b. and y. formulations of the tradition. H makes
up an appropriate adjudication of Mishnah and the position which
one must first hold before one can compose b.'s "pearl." The
formulation in y. thus logically precedes the liturgical text in
b. Earlier we dealt with an analogous situation in the case of
the abridged *Tefillah*, the *havinenu*. PT's tradition contained
the comment which provided the logic behind b.'s liturgical text
of *havinenu*. But in our instance, y.'s use of Mishnah's language
"say it" and the apparent preservation of the tradition's formulation *despite* the context, would seem to preclude the possibility
that within y.'s context, the y. version of Samuel's tradition
has been generated by another text.

Samuel's interest in liturgical matters is thus further
attested. A b. tradition (*Tefillah* and cup) is formulated as an
autonomous tradition, while its y. analogue constitutes a comment
on Mishnah. Samuel, in effect, legitimizes or reestablishes as
necessary the *havdalah* on a cup. He, moroever, is assumed to
(co)author a special prayer, "You informed us." In y. the
latter's basis is formulated as a gloss on Mishnah, though that
tradition is used as a decision against R. Eliezer's view in
Mishnah. In addition, BT projects Samuel in Palestine as a
representative of the Babylonian tradition as well as an authority
in support of a tannaitic opinion. Similarly, y. in both
instances presents Samuel's comments integrated into its context,
placed at the end of each *sugya*, and thus as a significant
authority.

*6.  Berakhot Chapter Six*

70.

## M. Ber. 6:1

1. How do (KYSD) they say blessings over fruit?

2a. Over fruit of the tree one says (ᵓWMR), "Who createst the fruit of the tree";

2b. except for wine,

for over the wine one says, "Who createst the fruit of the vine."

3a. And over fruit of the earth one says, "Who createst the fruit of the earth";

3b. except for bread,

for over bread one says, "Who bringest forth bread from the earth."

4. And over vegetables (HYRQWT) one says, "Who createst the fruit of the earth."

R. Judah says, "Who createst various types of grasses."

(M. Ber. 6:1)

M. Ber. 6:1 is the subject of nine separate b. and y. traditions attributed to Samuel. Taking into accout different versions and the several instances of a single tradition, they make up twenty items. The first, immediately below, deals with the conceptual basis of the Mishnah. After the analysis of that pericope, there follows the remaining texts along with their analyses.

A. It was taught (TNW RBNN), A person is forbidden to benefit from this world without a blessing,

and whoever benefits from this world[166] without a blessing performs a sacrilege [or "trespass"] (MᶜL).

B. What is his remedy?[167] Let him go to a sage . . . [= b. asks what a person should then do and as part of the final answer presents a tradition attributed to Rava.]

C. Said R. Judah said Samuel,

Whoever benefits (KL HNHNH) from this world[168] without a blessing is as if he benefits from items dedicated to Heaven.

as it is said, "The earth is the Lord's and all that it holds" (Ps. 24:1).

D.   R. Levi . . . [= derivation of the necessity for a
blessing by comparing Ps. 24:1 with Ps. 115:16.]

E.   Said R. Hanina bar Papa,

Whoever benefits from this world without a blessing
is as if he steals from the Holy One, blessed be He, and the
Congregation of Israel,

as it is said, "He who robs his father or his mother
and says, 'That is no transgression,' he is the companion of
a man who destroys" (Prov. 28:24).

F.   "His father refers to the Holy One blessed be
He, . . .

"His mother" refers to the Congregation of Israel . . .

. . . [= referent of the "companion of a man who
destroys."][169]

(b. Ber. 35a-b)

M. Ber. 6:1, like the rest of the chapter, deals with
blessings said over foods.  Rabbis regularize and standardize
what previously may have been a personal act of piety and prescribe that every individual should say a blessing over all kinds
of food.  Samuel's tradition provides a proof test and a metaphoric basis for the principle behind Mishnah.  The lack of a
blessing before eating constitutes a sacrilege of divine prop-
erty.  As we will see, this notion had apparently circulated
without a verse and various traditions ascribed to it different
bases.

To focus on the distinctive meaning of Samuel's comment
we examine the rest of the larger *sugya* and other reasons offered
for the blessings as well as several additional texts.[170]

Judah transmits Samuel's comment which is formulated as
an autonomous statement.  The tradition focuses on one of the two
dimensions of the general notion of blessings before eating.  Some
sources prescribe that one should say a blessing and explain why
(= "prescription").  Other traditions, including Samuel's comment,
state the consequences of violating that prescription (= "result").[171]  Ps. 24:1 is used to support both propositions.  Certain texts, as A in BT, contain both dimensions, the "prescription" and the "result."  Thus we find in T. Ber. 4:1, p. 18, ls.
1-2, these notions along with Ps. 24:1:

1a.  A person should not taste anything (L$^\supset$ YT$^c$WM)
until he says a blessing.

1b.   For it is said, "The earth is the Lord's and all that it holds" [Erfurt MS adds: "the world and all its inhabitants].

2a.   One who benefits (HNHNH) from this world without a blessing [Erfurt MS adds: "Lo, he"] performs a sacrilege ($M^CL$).

2b.   Until all the commandments [Lieberman: the last of which is the blessing][172] permit him.

(T. Ber. 4:1, p. 18, ls. 1-2)

Clause 1 presents the first principle and uses the verb "to taste," $T^CM$. Clause 2 presents the effect, as expressed in the concept of "sacrilege," or "trespass," $M^CL$, and uses the verb "to benefit," HNHNH. The last clause, 2b, which balances 1b, apparently repeats the first principle. Considering the presence of different verbs, "benefit" and "taste," 1 and 2 probably originally represented separate sources.

PT opens the *Gemara* on Ber. 6:1, p. 9d, with a midrashic exegesis which deduces the second principle:

3.   It is written, "The earth is the Lord's and all that it holds, the world and its inhabitants."

4.   Whoever at all benefits (HNHNH KLWM) from this world performs a sacrilege ($M^CL$),

5.   until the [or "all the"][173] commandments permit him.

As clauses 4 and 5 are presented as deductions based upon Ps. 24:1, we notice that the verse can lay the basis for both the "prescription" and the "result."[174]

A of BT mentions "trespass" and while it does not refer to "all the commandments," as found in 2b and 5, it does speak of "blessings" prior to the eating. A thus includes both principles. Moreover, it uses the same verb, "to benefit," HNHNH, in both clauses and thereby presents them as a single source.[175]

D provides a somewhat different use of Ps. 24:1 but also asserts that a blessing frees an object from God's possession. But Levi drops all allusions to cultic notions.[176] A different source uses Lev. 19:24 as a proof text. It appears in Sifra *Qedoshim*, #5 (3), 9, p. 90b, in y. Ber. 6:1, 10a, with an introductory TNY RBY HYYᵓ, and in b. Ber. 35a with TNW RBNN.[177] The verse concerns fourth-year produce. "Three years it [= the fruit of a new tree] shall be forbidden ($^CRL$) for you, not to be eaten. In the fourth year all its fruit shall be set aside for jubilation

before the Lord."  The biblical passage reflects the notion that
these items belong to the Lord.  The tradition is attributed to
Aqiva, is formulated with the verb "to taste," $T^CM$, and specifies
only the prescriptive principle, "one should not taste. . . ."

PT also presents a derivation based upon Ps. 16:2[178] and
an analogy based upon Deut. 22:9, viz., a blessing is necessary
to redeem the plentitude of the world which is like a vineyard.
In addition, at the end of the pericope that precedes A, b.
asserts that simple logic mandates a blessing.  Earlier nonrab-
binic literature, moreover, knows of the concept that a blessing
constitutes a thanksgiving sacrifice to God.  The Bible itself,
e.g., Deut. 26:15, makes explicit the underlying principle that
God provides food and a person must acknowledge it.[179]

The necessity to provide different metaphors, proof
texts, and bases probably indicates that the comments address the
wider Jewry and not just the disciples of the rabbis.[180]

Now that we have reviewed the diverse justifications for
the blessing requirement, we can ask what is distinctive to
Samuel's teaching.  Samuel defines the term $M^CL$ and in the process replaces this technical term with the phrase, "as if he
benefits from items dedicated to Heaven."  He thus adapts an
earlier teaching, one version of which we find in A and another
in Tosefta, line 2a.[181]

Consequently, the question becomes, why does Samuel
replace the term $M^CL$ and what is the significance of that
change?[182]

$M^CL$ in the Bible generally has two usages.  It refers to
a trespass against an item dedicated to the Temple and other such
sancta, and, secondly, a violation of the oath to God.  Lev. 5:15
provides an example of the former usage: "When a person commits a
trespass ($TM^CL\ M^CL$), being unwittingly remiss about any of the
Lord's sacred things . . ."  This makes up the standard usage in
Middle Hebrew, where it serves as a technical term, as, for
example, throughout the tractate $Me^Cilah$.[183]  The second usage
covers a wider area and includes  metaphoric instances of unfaith-
ful acts towards God.  These actions constitute violations of an
oath and the Covenant.  Both types of trespass affect the status
of the violator and the violator's community and may provoke
God's reaction, even to the extent of exiling the people.  See,
e.g., Num. 31:16, Ezek. 17:20, 2 Chron. 28:19f., and Dan. 9:7,
and 1 Chron. 9:1.[184]

The *baraita*'s application of the word "trespass," $M^C L$,
thus remains within its common (biblical) usage.  It further
employs the rabbinic notion which makes "benefit" a prerequisite
of the sacrilege.  Rabbinic sources thus pair benefit, $HN^{\supset}H$, with
trespass, $M^C L$, as in, "One who benefits does a trespass."[185]
This usage of HNHNH is particularly appropriate to the present
context of eating food.

The use of the term $M^C L$ undoubtedly fulfills a twofold
need.  First, the very act of saying a blessing permits one to
partake of God's bounty and fulfill one's obligations toward
Temple rituals and requirements.  This notion addresses those
Israelites who wonder if their inability to fulfill all the
various agricultural laws which are specified in the Bible and
tied to the Temple and Jerusalem, prevents them from legitimately
making use of agricultural products.  It thus offers reassurance
that with the blessings they fulfill their responsibility.
Secondly, it forms part of an extension of cultic notions to
extra-Temple institutions to legitimate them and to provide them
with greater meaning.  The earlier concern to avoid $M^C L$ and the
motivation to express one's piety through giving *terumot* and
*ma^C aserot* and the other agricultural dues are not lost, but
channeled into saying a blessing before eating.  Hence, the originally Temple-centered means of religious expression can continue
in a new way.[186]

Samuel's teaching reflects a stage of consciousness somewhat more removed from the Temple than that assumed in the
*baraita*.  He replaces the technical term $M^C L$ with the clause "as
if he benefits from items dedicated to Heaven."  The words
"dedicated" (QDŠ) and "Heaven" (ŠMYM) make up a phrase in cultic
and non-cultic contexts though the present pattern is used only
for items that belong to the Temple, especially sacrifices.  But
this is not the standard formulation to denote such objects and
very few instances are found in the sources.  Moreover, "Heaven"
as an appellation for God serves to emphasize God's role throughout the world--even in Babylonia.[187]  Hence, Samuel's less technical language provides a reason understandable to anyone, even
to someone for whom cultic notions would have been too distant
from his or her experience, as in third-century Babylonia.

While Samuel draws upon the idea behind the concept of
$M^C L$, he implicitly extends its applicability.  Therefore, both
his use of NHNH and his citation of Ps. 24:1 are appropriate.
This verse reflects the biblical strand which emphasizes the

divine role and presence throughout the world.  The whole world
is the divine domain and all creation is in the state of dedication
to God., i.e., belongs to God.[188]  We thus find that Samuel adapts
a cultic notion but drops all explicit associations with Temple
institutions.

Hanina bar Papa, a third-generation Palestinian Amora,[189]
totally breaks the association with the Temple imagery and ideas.
His comment, E, employs a formulation identical to Samuel's
tradition but substitutes both the metaphor, "steals from God and
the Congregation of Israel," and the proof text.  Hanina uncon-
ventionally uses the word "benefit," NHNH, as part of his comparison with stealing.  While a few rabbis hold that a person does
not perform a "theft" unless one derives benefit from the stolen
objects, this is not the general notion.  This contrasts with
Samuel's application of the word NHNH which integrally fits his
definition of $M^CL$.  Accordingly, Hanina employs the word "benefit"
only because his comment is patterned ultimately after the *baraita*
which employs the word $M^CL$ and more directly after Samuel's teaching which also includes the language, "as if he (derives benefit
from)."

Hence, Hanina totally replaces the notion of Temple with
that of "community" as his source of imagery.  His use of Prov.
28:24 reflects this non-cultic and extra-Temple perspective.
While he may provide a more "humanistic" and national rationale,
he loses the power of the original metaphor.  Apparently, however,
for him and his projected audience the old source of meaning was
not sufficiently viable.[190]

Samuel's focus on the nature of blessings over food deals
with the conceptual notion behind M. Ber. 6:1 and thus with an
item central to any commentary on Mishnah.  His distinctive contribution apparently lies in his formulation, or reinterpretation,
of the meaning of $M^CL$ and its association with one of the classic
verses on the subject.  His thought represents one stage in the
emotional and intellectual distancing from the Temple and in the
use of cultic notions as a basis for imparting meaning in extra-
Temple institutions and practices.[191]

71, 72, 73, 74, 75.

[M. Ber. 6:1]

The second to ninth traditions, items 2-20, focus on
specific types of foods and their appropriate blessings.  In their
present formulation and use they do not formally comment on

Mishnah.  Initially, however, they were generated by consideration of Mishnah, its principles, and themes.  Moreover, even now
they serve to clarify Mishnah's principles.  To the degree that
they extend the rule in Mishnah they constitute even primary
aspects of a Mishnah commentary.  Furthermore, as they focus on
special and additional cases, something which Tosefta on M. Ber. 6
does, they make up supplements to Mishnah.  We separately analyze
each group of comments, and the relationship between their several
versions, and at the end take stock of them all.

    [Three different traditions follow: C, G, and J-K; E;
and O.]

    A.  Except for wine etc. [= 2b of Mishnah.]

    B.  *What is the reason*[192] *concerning wine?  If one
says, because it is changed for the better* (D$^{\jmath}$ŠTNY L$^{C}$LWY )
[i.e., improved] *it is also changed* ($^{\jmath}$ŠTNY) *as to the blessing, but behold, olive*[193] *oil which is changed for the better,
does not change as to the blessing.*

    C.  *For said* R. Judah said Samuel, and thus said R.
Yishaq said R. Yohanan, Olive oil, over it they say (MBRKYN)
the blessing, "Who createst the fruit of the tree."

    D. . . . [= Answer and further discusion.  As part of
a question, the *sugya* cites a pericope from b. Eruv. 30a which
contains a second tradition of Samuel:]

    E.  *Let us say that constitutes a refutation of Rav
and Samuel who both*[194] *say that,* They say the blessing, "Who
createst various kinds of foods" only over the five kinds
[of grain distinctive to the land of Israel].

    F.   . . . [Further discussion.]  GWP$^{\jmath}$ [= "Essence."
The above-cited text:]

    G.  Said R. Judah said Samuel, and thus said R. Yishaq
said R. Yohanan, Olive oil--over it they say the blessing,
"Who createst the fruit of the tree."

    H.  How is this?  . . . [= An anonymous discussion
whether the oil is consumed as a drink by itself, or with
bread, or as part of a *gorion* mix, or as a huge amount with
the *angarion* for a sore throat.][195]

    (b. Ber. 35b-36a)

    I.  *Wheat flour* [requires the blessing of]--
R. Judah said, "Who createst the fruit of the earth."
And R. Nahman said, "By whose word all things come
into existence."[196]

J.  *Said Rava to R. Nahman, Do not dispute R. Judah,*
*for Samuel and R. Yohanan*[197] *hold like him,*

K.  *For said* R. Judah said Samuel, and thus said R.
Yishaq said R. Yohanan, Olive oil--over it they say the
blessing, "Who createst the fruit of the tree."

L.  *Thus* (ᵓLMᵓ), *even though it changes* (Dᵓ ŠTNY) *it*
*remains in its same status, likewise here* [i.e., wheat flour],
*even though it is changed, it remains in its same status.*

M.  [He said to him,][198] Are they comparable?  There
it cannot be further improved; here [the flour] can be further
improved as bread.

N.  And if it [= something] can be further improved,
over it they do not say *the blessing,* "Who createst the fruit
of the earth," *but* "[By whose word] all [exists]?"

O.  And did not say (WHᵓMR) R. Zera said R. Mattena
said Samuel, *Over raw bottle-gourd* [199] *and barley flour--over*
*them we say the blessing,* "By whose word all things come into
existence."

P.  Is not it (MᵓY LᵓW) [that this applies only to the
specified type of flour, and that over the flour] of wheat--
[they say the blessing] "Who createst the fruit of the earth"?

Q.  No.  [Flour] of wheat also [requires] "By whose
word all things come into existence."

R.  . . . [= A question on the logic of I and an
answer.]

(b. Ber. 36a)

A-E, F-H, and I-R make up three successive and separate
pericopae.  A-E, an anonymous pericope,[200] focuses on the qualities of wine which, as clause 2b of Mishnah rules, require it to
have a distinctive blessing.  The *sugya* cites from elsewhere two
traditions of Samuel.  The first one, C, serves to bolster a
question on the first suggested quality.  The second comment forms
part of a pericope from b. Eruv. 30a which along with M. Eruv. 3:1
is cited to challenge the second proposed explanation.[201]  We
treat the latter tradition with its analogues, below.

F-H presents for separate analysis the tradition to which
C had earlier referred.  The opening term, in F, GWPᵓ, regularly
introduces such pericopae which generally derive from a late
amoraic--or saboraic--period.[202]  B and G are identically formulated except for B's relative prefix, "For," used to cite the
reference.

I-R is built around a dispute between Judah and Naḥman.
In it, Rava, J-K, comments on the dispute, I, and tells Naḥman of
the olive oil tradition, earlier presented in C and G.  L spells
out the force of the reference and M analyzes it.  A challenge to
the latter provides a transition to the third tradition which
deals with a gourd and flour.  An anonymous authority,[203] O, cites
that tradition to support a question, N-P, against the logic of M.
Q responds that O is an inappropriate proof text.

According to its attributive formula, the tradition in O
originally was cited by R. Zeira, a third-generation master, in
the name of R. Mattena, a second-generation master, student of
Samuel.[204]  People normally did not eat plain barley flour, and
infrequently the bottle-gourd, especially when raw.  The edible
part contained a hard covering which required cooking.  People,
on the other hand, used the hard shell as a bottle.[205]  The particular states of these two items apparently account for their
special treatment.

A-R thus presents us with three Samuel traditions.  One,
the olive oil tradition, appears in three identical formulations,
C, F, and K.  Only in the third instances, K, does *Gemara* identify
the individual who cites the tradition.  Moreover, it forms part
of a discussion between named masters.[206]  On the other hand, C
and F make up part of anonymous and probably late pericopae, or
in the case of C, perhaps at most, a late addition to an earlier
pericope.  That is, the earlier material consisting of comments
of Rava and R. Naḥman b. Yishaq is structured to follow the anonymous material and to end the *sugya* which precedes the GWPᵓ in
F.[207]  Accordingly, I-K most probably constitutes the original
context of the tradition.  K subsequently served as a source in
the discussion in C.  F-G with its GWPᵓ introductory term cites
the tradtion so as to clarify it.  G either responds to the citation in C, or originates as a response to K but was placed after
A-C, which had been set first in the *sugya*.[208]

The olive oil tradition may make up an integral part of a
Mishnah commentary, though it is formulated as an autonomous
statement and deals with an item analogous to, but different from,
"wine" of Mishnah.  First, Tosefta in its section paralleling M.
Berakhot Ch. 6, likewise includes  special cases of other juices
from fruit, though not wine,[209] and these, as well, are autonomously formulated.  Secondly, the particular concern for olive
oil is natural considering the fact that sources regularly couple
or associate together grape vines and olive trees or wine and

olive oil.[210]  Samuel's interest in olive oil would, therefore,
not be out of place in a Mishnah commentary.  Moreover, even his
formulation which differs from Mishnah's "Over . . . one says
(ᵓWMR) . . . ," does not prove that his comment was formulated
outside the context of Mishnah.  For in the above-mentioned
pericope from T. Ber 4, as well as in the surrounding passages,
we find "Samuel's" formulation.  For example, "Raw [= undiluted]
wine, over it they say the blessing (MBRKYN ᶜLYW), [Who] createst
fruit of the tree . . ."[211]  Samuel's pattern is thus merely an
alternative one which can be used alongside of Mishnah.[212]
Samuel's comment, though, does not constitute a simple gloss,
but rather a supplement to Mishnah.  Accordingly, we appropriately
find a tradent, Judah, who stands behind the tradition.  Evidently,
the tradition did not circulate along with the text of Mishnah
but had to be cited.

The second tradition, E, has numerous parallels and
appears in three different formulations (E, HH; Y, Z, EE; and
AA).  Below we examine these materials.

The third tradition, O, concerning barley flour and a
bottle gourd, lacks any parallels.  Like the olive oil tradition
it is formulated as an autonomous teaching and not as a gloss to
Mishnah.  But as with that tradition, O deals with the issues of
Mishnah.  As olive oil's blessing differs from that of wine, the
items in O do not follow their analogues in Mishnah.  Above we
suggested that the fact that they are not normally eaten might
make up their special quality.  Below we shall consider other
traditions which further relate to this problem.  In any event,
O can serve as a supplement to Mishnah.  It represents a special
case of Mishnah's rules concerning fruit of the earth and the use
of the blessing, "Who createst the fruit of the earth" (clause 3a
of Mishnah), as well as the application of the blessing, "By
whose word all things come into existence" (mentioned in M. Ber.
6:3).  As indicated above, Tosefta to M. Ber. Ch. 6 contains
supplementary traditions which delineate proper blessings for
diverse items.[213]  O thus reflects concerns appropriate to a
Mishnah commentary.  But as a supplement, it fittingly is presented not as a gloss but as a citation by a master.  The pericope's editor, as others who employ other Samuel traditions, has
used this tradition to form the *sugya*.  But even without the
developed *suga*, the tradition constitutes material germane to
M. Ber. 6:1.

76=79, 77=80, 78.

[M. Ber. 6:1]

[S and U make up the fifth and sixth traditions of
Samuel relevant to M. Ber. 6:1:]
S. Palm-heart (QWR‍ᵓ) [= the soft inner part of the
top of the palm,[214] requires the blessing of:]--
R. Judah said, "Who createst the fruit of the earth."
Samuel said, "By whose word all things come into
existence."
T. R. Judah says, "Who createst the fruit of the
earth"--*it is a food* [alt. "*fruit*"].[215]
And Samuel said, "By whose word all things come into
existence"--since it eventually hardens [some texts add "*and
it is not a food*"].[216]
U. Said Samuel to R. Judah, *Shinena* [= "sharpy" or
"toothy"--a nickname],[217] *Your opinion makes sense. For
behold*, a radish[218] which (Š-) eventually hardens *and over it
we say the blessing*, "Who createst the fruit of the earth."
V.1. And it is not so. . . . [= Rejection of U, for
as the two items are planted for different purposes, U's
logic is erroneous.]
V.2-3. . . . [= Challenge to V.1 which the anonymous
pericope's editor rebuts by presenting a comment by R. Nahman
b. Yishaq. The latter tradition in effect supports Samuel's
position in S.][219]
V.4. And even though Samuel *praised* R. Judah, *the
halakhah follows* Samuel.
(b. Ber. 36a ≈ b. Eruv. 28b, less V. 2-3
[which is presented below as S' and U'])

[W.2 provides a different version of the tradition in
S:]
W.1. Palm-heart (QWR‍ᵓ)--
W.2. R. Yaaqov bar Aha in the name of (BŠM) Samuel,
Over it one says, "Who createst the fruit of the tree" [= V
and L MSS and Venice p.e.; "Who createst the fruit of the
earth" = S].
X. Taught [TNY = V and S MSS; TN‍ᵓ = L MS ] R. Halafta
b. Saul [Vat MS adds: "One says over it"], "By whose word all
things come into existence."
Y. Taught (TNY) R. Hoshia,[220] "Who createst various
kinds of grasses."

Z.  The teaching (MTNYTᵓ) of R. Hoshia disputes him
[= contradicts his teaching in Y]:

And these are the kinds of grasses: the artichoke,
*anchusa hybrida* (HLMH), *demua*$^c$ (DMW$^c$), and the thorn (ᵓTD).[221]
[As the palm-heart is not included, presumably it is not considered a "grass."]

(y. Ber. 6:1, 10b)


PALM-HEART

|          | b.                     | y.                            |
|----------|------------------------|-------------------------------|
| Judah    | Fruit of the earth     |                               |
| Samuel   | All exists; retraction | Fruit of the tree             |
|          |                        | (Sirillo: fruit of the earth.)|
| Ḥalafta  |                        | All exists                    |
| b. Saul  |                        |                               |
| Hoshia   |                        | Kinds of grasses              |


i

The fifth and sixth traditions, S and U, substantively
provide additional supplements to Mishnah.  The fifth tradition,
S, makes up a balanced dispute with an opinion attributed to R.
Judah.  T, the product of an anonymous authority, spells out the
reason for Samuel's and Judah's positions, and does so probably
on the basis of Samuel's comment in U.  V.1 and 4, two anonymous
clauses, reject Samuel's retraction in U.

Samuel's opinion in S appears consistent with his opinion
above in O, that a raw bottle-gourd and barley flour require the
blessing, "By whose word all things come into existence."  That
ruling apparently assumes that the latter blessing is said when a
person eats a food not in its normal, final, and edible state.
This would apply to a palm-heart even though it is edible, as
people do not normally eat that part of the palm tree.[222]  According to U, some other factor undermines the application of the
above principle.

The sixth item, U, presents a quotation of what Samuel
said to Judah and, in the process, a tradition concerning a
radish.  We note U's implications as to the history of S and then
focus on its own characteristics.

U provides attestation to the fact that Samuel and Judah had expressed opposing opinions on a matter of the proper blessing.  In the context of that dialogue or discussion, Samuel expressed his remarks in U.  But the language and sentiment of U is inappropriate after a formalized dispute.  Accordingly, Samuel's and Judah's opinions must not have been initially expressed in such a form.  The dispute formulation, as we have suggested elsewhere,[223] must therefore represent a secondary stage of the tradition.  But this "secondary stage" becomes suitable once the views are to circulate in opposition to each other.  It fulfills the needs of the later history of the tradition, in particular V, which avers that one should follow Samuel and not Judah.  We further comment on Samuel's tradition, below, where the y. analogue supports our contention that the dispute form is secondary.

U, in contrast to the Tosefta *baraitot* and several of the other Samuel-traditions relevant to M. Ber. 6:1, is not formulated as a simple supplement to Mishnah.  The dialogue portion and part of the tradition itself employ Aramaic, which we have represented by italics, while the rest use Hebrew.  The tradition is in two parts.  We have, in Hebrew, the reason ("Which eventually hardens") into which is interpolated the pattern which delineates the blessing (lit. "a radish . . . we bless over it etc.").  A conjunctive "and," W-, prefixed to "we bless," serves to join the two portions.  Moreover, the verb and pronominal phrase, "we say the blessing over it," MBRKYNN [C]LYH, appear in Aramaic.

If U represents the way in which Samuel might have actually expressed his comment, we note that while the tradition's formulation is influenced by the mishnaic-toseftan pattern used to set out a blessing, it significantly differs from it.  That pattern would have been appropriate to define a radish's blessing, but the tradition does more than that.  It also addresses a discussion as to the blessing on another food.  We must, accordingly, distinguish between the thought process involved in the tradition's formation and its actual presentation.  The notion behind U undoubtedly was *generated* by consideration of M. Ber. 6:1 or some other analogous text which deals with blessings over foods. But Samuel's activity evidently was not defined just by the desire to explain Mishnah.  Therefore, to fit his particular purpose he shapes the comment's formulation.  At an early stage of the tradition, if not within Samuel himself, the concern and

form of a commentary-supplement on Mishnah has thus been transformed into something quite different.

## ii

In b. Eruv. 28b we find an earlier or abbreviated version
of the pericope S-V.  The larger *sugya* is structured around two
attempts to differentiate between two tannaitic views concerning
the palm-heart.[224]  The pericope parallel to b. Ber. 36a supports
the second attempt.  The two tannaitic opinions are thus assumed
to represent opposing positions as to the proper blessing.[225]
The pericope opens with:

> 1.   Rather said Rava,[226] they differ as to [the]
> blessing.
> 2.   For (D-)[227] it was said,
> 3.   [= S'-U'] A palm-heart--R. Judah said, . . .
> [= Equivalent to S-U.]

As 3 leads into a parallel to S-U, we can designate this material
as S'-U'.  Except for the lack of an analogue to V.2-3 and minor
variations,[228] the b. Eruv. passage is identical to that of b. Ber.
36a.  Eruv. draws upon b. Ber. and either deletes V.2-3 or else
lacks the clause in its text of b. Ber.[229]  In any event, the
absence of the clause indicates that V.4 can stand alone without
V.2-3 and, as we suggested above, is to be assigned to an anonymous authority and not Nahman b. Yishaq (who is mentioned in
V.3).[230]

While the pericope in b. Eruv. may have been cited by Rava,
most likely it was presented by someone else to support Rava's
position.  The first attempted differentiation lacks a supporting
text and, accordingly, one is not integrally needed.  A later
hand, undoubtedly, thought it appropriate to add the reference in
the second case, especially since it emerged or was represented
as the accepted explanation.[231]  As a result, the referent appropriately serves its function but Rava attests only the theme of S
and not any specific opinion or formulation.  From the point of
view of the one who supplied the b. Ber. parallel, though, that
passage, and S in particular, constituted the classic statement
concerning a palm-heart's blessing.

## iii

The y. analogue differs from b.  It adds a third opinion
on the matter, Y, reverses Samuel's position with his ostensible

disputant, W-X, and further varies the text that Samuel prescribes.
In y., Samuel requires the blessing, "Who createst the fruit of
the tree." According to S in b., Samuel requires "By whose word
all things come into existence," which, in y., constitutes the
opinion of R. Tahlifa [= Halafta] b. Saul, a first-generation
Palestinian Amora.[232]   Given U's retraction, Samuel ostensibly
requires the blessing "Who createst the fruit of the earth." This
is Sirillo's reading for Samuel in W. But in the face of the
other texts and Sirillo's known tendency to emend y. on the basis
of the BT, this reading undoubtedly is a "correction."[233]

X-Y appear as separate and independent teachings though
they have been presented together. They differ in their attributive formulae. Samuel's opinion alone is transmitted by a tradent,
Yaaqov bar Aha, a third-generation Palestinian Amora,[234] and his
comment is formulated as a statement. Halafta's and Hoshia's
teachings are formulated as *baraitot*, and following that pattern,
lack the name of a tradent.[235]  On the other hand, all three opinions require the presence of W.1, or some other statement of the
subject. The three are thus redacted together as the apodosis
after the protasis in W.1. In addition, only Samuel's comment
employs the verbal subject, "one says over it." V MS's inclusion
of this phrase in X, though, indicates that that comment may have
been balanced with Samuel's. If so, W-X would make up an early
stage of the dispute, to which Hoshia's opinion, Y, was added.
Alternatively, if the V MS's addition is secondary, the original
dispute form may have included only Halafta and Hoshia, X-Y, and
someone later interpolated Samuel's tradition. This would accord
with our observation, noted elsewhere, as to the place of Samuel
traditions in the y. pericope. Lieberman's observation that the
terminology opening Z and the structure in which it appears would
support a reading ƆMR and not TNY in Y has implications as to the
makeup of the primary dispute. Presumably the presence of TNY
might be the result of X's usage; the word TNY may have been generated by the desire to have similar terms open X and Y.[236]
Considering the above analysis, we can correlate the reading of
TNY and ƆMR with each alternative as to what makes up the original
dispute. The presence of the dispute thus emerges as the work of
the redactor, his source, or possibly even the transmitter, Yaaqov
b. Aha.

What is the significance of the variation in the blessing
attributed to Samuel? While Yaaqov b. Aha may simply present an
alternative version, a careful review of the pericopae may suggest

a slightly different solution.  BT does not explicitly state that
Samuel requires the blessing, "Who createst the fruit of the earth."
Samuel refers to radishes but does not explicitly state that its
blessing applies also to the palm-heart.  At most he says, "Your
opinion makes sense" (literally, "According to you it makes
sense").  U can therefore be construed to constitute only a retraction from Samuel's original position and thus the exemption of a
palm-heart from the general rule that a food not eaten in its
final and normal edible state requires the blessing, "By whose word
all things come into existence."  U would then leave open what
blessing Samuel requires and it could be "Who createst the fruit
of the tree."  Accordingly, W.2 need not contradict S and U.[237]
While Samuel might have intended one thing, Yaaqov b. Aha or his
source might have understood things differently and misrepresented
Samuel.

While we remain unsure as to the exact reason for the
variation between the two analogues, any rendering of y. supports
b.'s report that Samuel retracted from requiring the blessing,
"By whose word all things come into existence."  Moreover, his
position evidently circulated in Palestine in the third generation.  Finally, y. confirms the earlier suggestion that the dispute form in S represents a secondary stage of the tradition.
Clearly it was not known in the Palestinian circles responsible
for the y. pericope.[238]

iv

Whether S, or the view projected and assumed by U, or W
represents Samuel's true opinion as to the palm-heart's blessing,
we deal with a tradition which supplements Mishnah, in particular
clause 2 or 3.  If we classify the palm-heart as a fruit it would
be clause 2.  But as the palm-heart is not exactly a fruit in a
way analogous to other fruits, one could consider it part of the
tree itself.[239]  If so, Samuel's comment would relate to clause 3.
In none of the three instances, however, do we have the form of a
Mishnah supplement.  Nevertheless, since in substance the tradition responds to Mishnah, we can reconstruct such a formulation.
One such reading consists of: "A palm-heart--over it they say the
blessing, 'Who/By . . .'"

Undoubtedly the existence of a dispute demands that a name
be mentioned and thus an attribution separates the apodosis and
protasis.  Mishnah 6:1 and T. Ber. 4:4, p. 19, 1. 11, in fact,

provide examples of the way in which a differing opinion is
expressed.

> And over vegetables one says, "Who createst fruit of
> the earth."
>
> R. Judah says, "Who createst types of trees."
>
> (M. Ber. 6:1, clause 4)

Judah's tradition and S employ an identical pattern for an opinion
which disputes a preceding position.

The formulation of W is even closer to known paradigms.
W opens with the subject, the pattern which we earlier saw in T.
Ber. 4:2-3.[240]  Secondly, it continues with the verbal clause
followed by the prepositional phrase, and ends with the blessing
"one says over it, 'Who . . .'"  Thirdly, it employs the verb,
"one says" ($\supset$MR) found in Mishnah and not the verb "They say the
blessing" (MBRKYN), the word used in several toseftan *baraitot* and
Samuel-traditions in b.  This pattern combines the choice of verb
of Mishnah with the sequence of the toseftan, Samuel supplement
pattern:

| Mishnah: | And over | subject | one *says* "Who . . ." |
|---|---|---|---|
| Tos. supl. form: | Subject | *They say blessing* over it | "Who . . ." |
| W.1-2: | Subject | one *says* over it | "Who . . ." |

Naturally, here, as well, the attribution interrupts after the
protasis.

Neither S or W is thus presented as part of a Mishnah
commentary.  Nevertheless, the thought involved in each may have
been generated by Mishnah and its principles.  Tosefta, as indicated, includes examples of various supplements.  Just because
different views existed as to the proper blessing, that does not
preclude the fact that the comments deal with the substance of
Mishnah.  Their formulation--just like in Tosefta--however, is
affected by their use.  At the most fundamental level of the
tradition, accordingly, Samuel is motivated by a desire to set
forth the proper blessings for additional and special cases of
food.  But the needs of the particular use and the later history
of Samuel's comments have shaped the formulation of both S and W.
At the same time, the early nature of Samuel's comments has not
been totally obliterated.  Despite U's "retraction," Samuel
emerges, be it in the secondary formulation of a dispute form, as
one maintaining a distinct position.  Likewise, W, X, Y have not
been redacted into a three-way balanced dispute form.  To

conclude, while we remain unsure as to the exact blessing Samuel
prescribed, we can know the type of activity he undertook, appreciate his attempt, and trace the contours of the later history of
his teaching.

81=82, 83, 84, 85 [and 72].

[M. Ber. 6:1]

[The following pericopae, AA-GG, HH-II, JJ-OO, and E,
above, contain three different versions of a tradition which
deals with food containing grain (E, LL; CC, DD, II; and EE).
As E appeared earlier we have labeled this the "third tradition."]

AA.  Cooked *habis* [a pounded mixture of flour with
honey or oil cooked in a pot] and likewise (WKN) pounded grain
(DYYS⊃)[241] [require the blessing]--

R. Judah said, "By whose word all things come into
existence" (ŠHKL . . . .).

R. Kahana said, "Who createst various kinds of foods"
(MZWNWT).

BB.  As to *plain* pounded grain *no one argues*--that
[it requires] "Who createst [various] kinds of foods."[242]
*But they argue as to* pounded grain *that is like* cooked
*habis*:[243]

R. Judah says, "All" (ŠHKL)--He holds that the honey
is the basic ingredient.

R. Kahana said, "Who createst various kinds of foods."
--*He holds that the flour is the basic* [ingredient].

CC.  Said R. Joseph, Seize that of R. Kahana [i.e.,
his opinion],

*for Rav and Samuel both say* (DRB WŠMW⊃L D⊃MRY
TRWWYHW), Whatever contains anything (KL ŠYŠ BW) of the five
kinds [of grain]--over it they say the blessing, "Who createst
various kinds of food.[244]

DD.  GWP⊃ *Rav and Samuel both say* (RB WŠMW⊃L D⊃MRY
TRWWYHW), Whatever contains anything (KL ŠYŠ BW) of the five
kinds--over it they say the blessing, "Who createst various
kinds of foods."

EE.  And it was said also (W⊃TMR NMY), *Rav and Samuel
both say* (RB WŠMW⊃L D⊃MRY TRWWYHW), Whatever (KL SHW⊃) of the
five kinds--over it they say the blessing, "Who createst various kinds of foods."[245]

FF.  And it is *necessary* [to have both traditions, DD
and EE] . . .  [An anonymous pericope asserts that each tradition teaches something not otherwise known.  In the course of
the argument, b. mentions rice and sorghum, which become subject to analysis.[246]  The KL ŠHWᵓ formulation, EE, indicates
that the blessing, "Who createst various kinds of foods,"
applies only to the five grains and, thereby, excludes rice
and sorghum even when in a separate and distinguishable state.
The KL ŠYŠ BW formulation indicates that the blessing applies
to these grains even when they are not distinguishable, but
mixed in with other food.]

GG.   . . . *And it is a refutation of Rav and Samuel, a
refutation* (WTYWBTᵓ DRB WŠMWᵓL TYWBTᵓ).  [EE is rejected and
rice has the same blessing as the five grains.][247]

(b. Ber. 36b-37a)


HH.   Said Rava, "*Rihatā* [a mixture similar to *habis*][248]
*Of the field workers, in which they have packed
flour*[249]*--Over it one says the blessing,* "Who createst various
kinds of foods."  *Why? Because flour is the basic* [ingredi-
ent].

*Of the city, in which they have not packed flour--over
it one says the blessing,* "By whose word all things come into
existence."  "*Why? The honey is the basic* [ingredient]."

II.  *And it is not so* (WLᵓ HYᵓ).[250]  *Both require,*
"Who createst various kinds of foods," *for Rav and Samuel
both say* (DRB WŠMWᵓL DᵓMRY TRWWYHW), Whatever contains anything of the five kinds--over it they say the blessing, "Who
createst various kinds of foods."[251]

(b. Ber. 37b)


JJ.  "One who disavows food (HNWDR MN HMZWN) is permitted water and salt." [= M. Eruv. 3:1.]

KK.  "Water and salt"[252] *are not called* food (MZWN)
[and therefore permitted in JJ], *but by implication everything*
[else] *is called* food [and thus forbidden].

LL.  *Let us say that it constitutes a refutation*
(TYWBTᵓ) *of Rav and Samuel who both say* (DRB WŠMWᵓL DᵓMRY
TRWWYHW),[253] *They say the blessing,* "Who createst various kinds
of foods" *only over the five kinds* (ᵓYN MBRKYN . . . ᵓL ᶜL
. . . BLBD).  [This seemingly implies that only the five kinds
are called "food."]

MM.  *And did we not already refute it?*   [See E and
GG.]

NN.  *Let it be a refutation also from here.*[254]

OO.1.  Said R. Huna [it, KK, is not a refutation,
because the Mishnah deals] with a case in which (B-) one says,
"All that supports me" (KL HZN <sup>C</sup>LY) [and not someone 'disavow-
ing food.'"  Thus:]

OO.2.  *Water and salt do not support, but--by implication everything* [else] *supports* (ZYYNY).  [Accordingly there
is no refutation of the tradition of Rav and Samuel.]

(b. <sup>C</sup>Erub. 30a)


i


*Gemara* contains three related traditions concerning the
"five species" of grain, wheat, barley, emmer, *shibolet shual*,
and einkorn.  Elsewhere Mishnah speaks of these special five species which are subject to the laws concerning the agricultural
produce of the land of Israel.[255]  Samuel's traditions prescribe
for these grains a blessing not mentioned in Mishnah.  The comments, accordingly, either dispute Mishnah or supplement it with
an exception.  In addition, the three items may make up three
versions of a single tradition.

So as to clarify the relationship between the three
versions, we examine each formulation and the redactional considerations that may have affected their wording.  We already encoun-
tered one version of the tradition in E.  It forms part of a pericope cited from b. Eruv. 30:

E.  *Let us say that it constitutes a refutation of
Rav and Samuel who both say* that, They say the blessing, "Who
createst various kinds of foods" only over the five kinds.

(b. Ber. 35b = citation of LL from b. Eruv. 30a)

In the Eruv. 30a *sugya*, JJ-OO, Samuel's tradition appears at LL.
Before we examine the latter *sugya* and the parallel versions of
Samuel's tradition in E and LL, we focus on the other two versions.  This is appropriate since the Eruv. *sugya* may allude to
the other versions and its *sugya* at b. Ber. 36b-37a.


ii


The version in CC, DD, and II, though not identical with
the version in EE, shares a pattern with the latter which differs
from that of E and LL.  We find the sequence of: the type of food;

verb, MBRKYN <sup>C</sup>LYW; and the specified blessing.  This pattern is
used elsewhere by Samuel in traditions concerning the blessings
over olive-oil in C, G, and K, and over a bottle-gourd and barley
flour, in O.

The first of the two similarly structured versions appears
in pericope AA-CC.  Joseph in CC attests a dispute between Kahana
and a second master, presumably Judah, and cites the tradition.
It employs the standard double attributive formula.  As usual in
such cases one cannot know whether the formulation is to be
attributed to Rav or Samuel, or somehow to both.  DD-GG cites the
tradition mentioned in CC and to it adds a related tradition, EE.
Both CC and EE share the same attributive formula.

FF-GG notes the similarity between the traditions but
argues that the different formulations serve to emphasize different points.  The focus on the formulation is important and below
we shall return to it.  GG ends the pericope with a refutation.
Medieval commentators differ whether the conclusion rejects the
tradition as a whole or only the implication *Gemara* had suggested,
viz., that rice and possibly sorghum prepared by themselves, do
not require the blessing, "Who createst various kinds of food."
But GG employs the standard formulation for the refutation of a
tradition and speaks in general of "[that] of [= the tradition of]
Rav and Samuel."  Moreover, as we shall see, the pericope in b.
Eruv. 30a, MM, assumes that the refutation is against the thrust
of the tradition.

The formulation in CC appears also in HH-II.  Rava or an
anonymous authority, depending upon the correct reading, cites the
tradition.  If the attribution to Joseph in CC is correct, it is
reasonable to assume that Rava may have known the tradition.
Alternatively, the two pericopae initially developed independently
and a later individual who knew the tradition of Rav and Samuel
cited it here, where he thought it appropriate.[256]  As medieval
commentators already noticed, although GG presents a refutation,
CC and II use one form of the tradition.  The commentaries' analyses are tied to their understanding of the refutation.  We may
assume, however, that DD-GG, in particular FF-GG, derives from a
separate or later source from that of the other citations of the
tradition, a phenomenon present elsewhere in BT, and therefore
the "contradiction" is not problematic.[257]

### iii

In b. Eruv. 30a, an anonymous authority examines M. Eruv.
1:1 and cites a tradition of Samuel, LL.  The formulation of

Samuel's tradition fits the pericope's redactional purposes.   The
*sugya* focuses on the definition of "food," MZWN.   Rav and Samuel's
tradition appropriately responds to this issue by emphasizing that
the blessing which employs the word "food," MZWN, applies only to
the five kinds of grain.   The possibility that the tradition has
been adapted accords with the arrangement of the materials within
the pericope itself.

First, KK-LL are anonymous and exhibit characteristics of
late, saboraic, material.   Secondly, Huna, in OO, employs the B-
form, which is used to comment directly on a text.   Accordingly,
OO probably originated directly on Mishnah and the pericope's
editor placed the anonymous material before Huna's tradition so
as to introduce it.[258]   Furthermore, MM-NN provide an explicit
hint as to the effect of the redactional purpose.   MM mentions a
previous refutation of the tradition which should be identified
with GG, a rejection of the KL ŠHWᵓ version of the tradition, in
EE.   As the latter is part of a late *sugya*, MM must represent
even later material and it, along with NN, probably consist of
interpolations to take GG into account.

The author of MM-NN thus evidently assumed that the versions of Samuel's traditions in LL and EE did not substantively
differ.   We, therefore, should not consider the formulation in LL,
ᵓYN . . . ᵓLᵓ . . . BLBD, "there is only," as an independent
tradition.   Rather the formulation has been adapted to serve the
purpose for which it has been cited.   Whoever shaped the tradition
did so because the other two formulations of the tradition do not
emphasize the point of b. Eruv. 30a, to limit the word "food,"
MZWN, to the five species.   Those two formulations, as indicated
above, fit a pattern used elsewhere in the chapter to specify the
appropriate blessings for different foods.[259]

iv

The formulation in LL also appears in b. Ber. 35b, where
it does not, however, make up an independent instance of this
version of the tradition.   Rather the tradition forms part of a
*sugya* which cites b. Eruv. 30a.   Earlier we presented and briefly
analyzed that pericope, E.   One aspect of the pericope's citation
may itself indicate that it totally relies upon the b. Eruv. 30a
*sugya*.   In its citation of b. Eruv. 30a, it lacks an equivalent
to MM-NN.   It presents a citation of M. Eruv. 3:1, i.e., an
equivalent to JJ; an editor's bridging language, WHWYNN BH, "and
[there] we asked/analyzed it," which is standard language to

introduce a pericope on a text from elsewhere; equivalents to KK
and LL; and then immediately an equivalent to 00.1, to which is
prefixed a conjunctive W-, "and."  The b. Ber. 35b *sugya* spells
out the implication of the cited pericope to make explicit why it
cites b. Eruv. 30a and how that text may serve as a question.
Accordingly, the lack of MM-NN may mean that at the time of the
citation of the Eruv. 30a pericope, these two clauses had not yet
become integral to the text.  This accords with our earlier suggestion that MM-NN consists of very late additions to b. Eruv.
30a, interpolated to take into account the refutation in GG.[260]

v

The other two formulations employ patterns used to delineate blessings.  They exhibit certain variations which are not
insignificant.  Joseph, in CC, and the authority in II, cite one
tradition for its principle that the blessing applies even when
the food contains ingredients other than the specified species.
This usage accords with the nature of the KL ŠYŠ BW pattern which
elsewhere serves to indicate that an object or institution exhibits a specific characteristic or feature.  See, for example, M.
Ter. 8:6; M. Meg. 4:2; M. Bek. 8:9, and M. Ohl. 15:9.  On the
other hand, a pattern so formulated to focus on the amount of an
object, e.g., KL ŠHWᵓ, in EE, would not have so explicitly made
the point in CC and II.  For such a formulation might convey the
notion that any small *but undiluted* amount of the object suffices.

The KL ŠYŠ BW formulation thus fits redactional needs.  It
is the only one of the three versions cited by a tradent, and,
consequently, that tradent may have applied the tradition to his
context.  Even if this were the case, and Joseph revises the
tradition, we should not automatically assume that he introduced
a novel concept; for M. Hal. 3:7 may provide a partial precedent
for this notion.  It deals with dough consisting of one of the
five species as well as an additional kind of dough.  The Mishnah
rules that when the taste of the former, dough irrespective of
the amount, is present, the law as to *Halah* and Passover applies
due to the five species-ingredients.[261]

On the other hand, the KL ŠHWᵓ formulation is cited as
"an additional tradition," ᵓTMR NMY, and not to fulfill specific
redactional purposes within the *sugya*.  The wording consists of a
very common tannaitic and amoraic pattern.  It is one used more
frequently than the KL ŠYŠ BW pattern and is employed to define
the status of objects, including the appropriate blessings for

various foods.  It is often preceded by an introductory formula of
"This is the rule," ZH HKLL.  Several instances are particularly
relevant to the present case.[262]

      The first appears in the b. Ber. 37a *sugya* which follows
DD-GG and which analyzes the *baraita* used in the refutation in FF.
BT cites another *baraita*, in which Gamaliel and sages differ as to
the blessing after eating:

> This is the rule, For whatever of the seven kinds (ZH
> HKLL KL ŠHWᴐ MŠBᶜT HMYNYM)--
> R. Gamaliel says, . . .

This text in a slightly different wording appears in y. Ber. 6:1,
p. 10b, and T. Ber. 4:15, p. 21, 1. 52:[263]

> This is the rule, For whatever from a kind [of the]
> seven . . . (ZH HKLL KL ŠHWᴐ MMYN ŠBᶜH . . .)

      The b. version of this common KL ŠHWᴐ pattern thus makes
up an exact parallel to the wording of Samuel's tradition:

> For whatever of the seven kinds . . .
> For whatever of the five kinds . . .

      We also find a tradition which in part is identical to EE:

> Said R. Jacob bar Idi said R. Hanina, For whatever of
> the five kinds (KL ŠHWᴐ MHMŠT HMYNYN)--at the beginning one
> says the blessing, "Who createst various kinds of foods," and
> at the end, "One Blessing which is like three."[264]
> (b. Ber. 44a)

> R. Yaaqov bar Idi in the name of R. Hanina, For what-
> ever that is like (KL ŠHWᴐ Kᶜyn) flour and like *halitah*
> [flour dumplings in boiling water], and made from the five
> kinds--over it one says (ᴐWMR ᶜLYW), "Who createst various
> kinds of foods," and after it one says the blessing, "One
> blessing that is like three."[265]
> (y. Ber. 6:1, p. 10b)

While both versions of this tradition open with the phrase KL ŠHWᴐ,
the b. one, as in EE, immediately mentions the five species.

      The question thus emerges, could the tradition with the
KL ŠHWᴐ formulation also include what the alternative KL ŠYŠ BW
formulation is assumed to teach?  Above we indicated that the
former need not imply the latter.  Nevertheless, it is not insignificant that the passage from T. Ber. 4:15 cited above ("For
whatever from a kind of the seven") might imply a mixture as

well.  For it follows a series of examples preceded by the following general principle:

>    They say the blessing over the grain which is pre-
>    ferred (HMWBHR) [= the better one, when there are more than
>    one type].
>
>    How so? . . .

This principle assumes that a mixture does not alter the status
of the five-species grain.  Accordingly, if our understanding of
T. Ber. 4:15 is to be shaped by its overall context, we would
conclude that the opening formula of KL ŠHW⊃ has a usage more
inclusive than b. assumes.


                                  vi

        We thus have three formulations of a Rav and Samuel tradi-
tion which deals with the five species.  The formulation in b.
Eruv. 30a, ⊃YN . . . ⊃L⊃ . . . BLBD fits redactional needs and,
given the nature of its *sugya*, may be saboraic.  The second
version, KL ŠYŠ BW, likewise fits redactional purposes though it
employs a less frequently used formulation and appears with an
early master as a tradent.  On the other hand, the third version,
formulated with the common pattern of KL ŠHW⊃, lacks a tradent
and appears in a *sugya* apparently later than the core of b. Eruv.
30a, that is, the portion of the pericope cited in b. Ber. 35b,
and perhaps later than the citations by Joseph in CC, and the
authority in II.[266]
        To conclude, first, what do we make of the existence of
three different versions of the tradition?  We remain uncertain
whether the tradition at its earliest stage served to delineate
the blessing for the five grains as such or to deal with a special case of the five species.  Since all three versions--even
the first--refer to the five species and include the standard
double attribution formula, theoretically one might speculate
that the three derive from a single tradition such as, "Five
kinds, over it they say the blessing . . ."  This single formulation would then have generated the extant three traditions.  The
pattern for this reconstructed tradition is used in traditions
attributed to Samuel and others.  The subjects usually are not
formulated so as to address the issue of the amount of the
item.[267]  Moreover, we can understand why each of the three
traditions was generated.  The first is to emphasize the number
of five species.  MM assumes that it does not substantively differ

from one of the other two versions.  The second serves to assert
the significance of the mere presence of some amount, irrespective
of its strength or dilution.  We noted, however, that this notion
is not without precedent.[268]  The third version employs a standard
pattern into which BT reshapes traditions.

As we saw with other Samuel traditions, the extant versions and formulations are often affected by their later history.
In this case, Samuel's tradition served as a precedent for third-
generation masters and it may have been shaped accordingly.

Secondly, how do the comments including a reconstructed
Uhr form relate to Mishnah?  The tradition assumes that an item
of the five species is not bread and yet does not fall within the
category of "fruit of the earth" and its blessing.  The concern
for this problem appears in Tosefta in a passage cited in b. Ber.
36a.[269]  It specifies that where the grains are treated they fall
into different categories:

> One who chews grain, over them one says the blessing
> (MBRK [C]LYHM), "Who createst various kinds of seeds."
> [If] one baked them [or][270] cooked them--
> if the pieces are extant, over them one says the
> blessing, "Who brings forth bread from the earth" . . .
> [if] the pieces are not extant, over them one says
> the blessing, "Who createst various kinds of food" . . .

Tosefta thus indicates that the subject of Samuel's tradition is
not inappropriate to a supplement on Mishnah.  Above we saw various examples of such supplements.  The olive oil tradition in particular parallels the focus of Mishnah Ber. 6:1 on the special
case of wine and bread.  The present tradition may similarly deal
with a special case--that of grain.  But as in the traditions
concerning palm-heart and radish, in S, U, and W, we do not have
a supplement, and, surely, not a gloss formulation.  But as in
those other items, the notion behind the traditions is generated
by consideration of Mishnah, its principles, and issues.  Moreover, as autonomous statements are used in Tosefta for traditions
which supplement Mishnah, the type of comment may have facilitated
the reuse of the tradition.[271]  Such autonomous formulations do
not directly circulate along with the text of Mishnah which they
supplement and therefore can easily become applied to new contexts.  We, accordingly, have an additional instance in which our
evaluation of the emergence and fundamental nature of Samuel's
tradition is skewed by its use and later history.

86.

## [M. Ber. 6:1]

[PP presents the seventh tradition:]

PP. *Shatita* [= grain, especially barley, porridge][272]--

Rav said, "By whose word all things come into existence."

Samuel said,"Who createst various kinds of foods."

QQ.1. Said R. Hisda, And they do not differ. This speaks of (B-) the thick [= heavy type] (H⊃ B^C BH), and this [the other] speaks of (B-) the thin [= light type] H⊃ BRKH).

QQ.2. The thick, which is made for eating.[273] The thin, which is made for medicine.[273]

RR. R. Joseph [M MS = "Rava"][274] retorted . . . [= Question on QQ.1]

SS. Said Abaye to him, . . . [= Answer to RR, which thus supports Hisda.]

(b. Ber. 38a)

The seventh tradition on M. Ber. 6:1 focuses on another exception to Mishnah's ruling on "fruit of the earth." While it is not a simple gloss to Mishnah, it serves to elucidate the text.[275]

The tradition, part of *sugya* PP-SS, is presented with Rav's comment in a standard dispute form, PP. Hisda, QQ, attests the existence of that dispute form, yet he claims it has been imposed on two traditions that do not actually differ. He maintains the form is employed to transmit materials which deal with the same issue. Joseph further attests the dispute as well as QQ.2, unless his comment in itself generated QQ.2.[276]

The different rulings in PP could reflect different customs and attitudes in the use of barley as food. In antiquity the use of barley as food was widespread but later it decreased, except as poor persons' food and animal feed. As a porridge, however, it remained a favorite. *Shatita* was one such porridge. It apparently was made of roasted young grains of barley and millet, and then mixed and cooked with water, and sometimes honey.[277] The two masters may thus differ on whether or not the *shatita* constituted a normal or natural use of the barley. If it did not, then assumably the blessing, "By whose word all things come into existnce," would apply.

According to Hisda, Rav and Samuel refer to different
types of barley food and, by implication, do not differ whether
one or the other type constitutes the standard item.  We cannot
know whether or not this is the plain sense.  Joseph, for one,
assumes a dispute may exist.[278]  Moreover, Hisda may only be
following his tendency to minimize disputes and assert that each
of two contradictory views applies to different cases.  Furthermore y. Ber. 6:1, p. 10a-b, cites an analogue to Rav's opinion,
which makes up one in a series of autonomous traditions attributed
to Huna, but none to Samuel's position.  As y. does not clarify
the reference to the *shatita*, the statement would appear to be
inclusive of all types.[279]

On the other hand, Hisda's comment accords with our observation elsewhere.  A dispute form may indeed be imposed onto two
traditions which are not inconsistent.[280]  In addition, we know
that in antiquity people prepared and used barley in heavy and
light consistency for nourishment and medicine.[281]

The relevance of the tradition to Mishnah may be reflected
in a *baraita* in Tosefta Ber. 4:6, one version of which appears in
b. 37a, and y. Ber. 6:1, p. 10b, and cited above, at n. 269.  It
focuses on different ways in which grain may be treated.  Thus
commentary on Mishnah includes specification of appropriate blessings for different stages of the food.  We cannot know whether
Samuel--and Rav--directly focused on this issue and used the case
of *shatita* as a concrete example or whether they chose a specially
difficult or ambiguous item, which has qualities of a baked and
of a cooked and, perhaps, of a liquid substance.  If the latter,
the item generated or provided the opportunity or occasion for
the comment.  Earlier we examined other Samuel traditions which
deal with such problematic items, as olive oil, in C, G, and J,
and cooked *habis*, in AA.  Even the latter items, as we earlier
noted, may integrally belong to Mishnah's agendum, as demonstrated
by the interest of M. Ber. 6:1 in wine and bread and Tosefta's
concern for special cases.  Accordingly, Mishnah may have set the
groundwork for Samuel's tradition on *shatita*.

Finally, as in other Samuel traditions on blessings,
despite the extant formulation of the tradition, it may have
initially, if only in thought, supplemented Mishnah.  Already
third-generation circles knew the present form of the tradition,
but they also aver that we must transcend it and its implication
that a dispute exists.  Indeed, only then can we hope accurately
to understand the tradition's meaning and to uncover its earlier
and most fundamental function.

87, 88, 89.

[M. Ber. 6:1]

[TT-YY presents the eighth tradition. ZZ-BBB, a y. pericope, presents a different version of this tradition, ZZ, along with a ninth and separate tradition, BBB, which further bears on the subject.]

TT.    Taught (DRŠ) R. Nahman in the name of our Rabbi--and who is he Samuel?--Steamed foods (ŠLQWT), over them they say the blessing (MBRKYN), "Who createst the fruit of the earth."

And our friends who come from the land of Israel to Babylonia--and who are they? Ulla in the name of R. Yohanan--said, Steamed foods (ŠLQWT), over them they say the blessing, "By whose word all things come into existence."

UU.    And I [Nahman] say, "They were taught in a dispute."[282]

As it was taught (DTNYᵓ) . . .

VV.    And it is not so [it is not a dispute] . . .[283]

WW.    Said R. Hiyya bar Abba said R. Yohanan, Steamed foods (ŠLQWT)--over them they say the blessing, "Who createst the fruit of the earth."

XX.    And R. Benjamin bar Yefet said R. Yohanan,[284] Steamed foods (ŠLWQT)--over them they say the blessing, "By whose word all things come into existence."[285]

YY.    Said R. Nahman bar Yishaq, Ulla fixed his mistake [corruption of the tradition] (LŠBŠTYH) on the basis of R. Benjamin bar Yefet.[286]

(b. Ber. 38b)

ZZ.    R. Abba said: *Rav and Samuel both say* (RB WŠMWᵓL TRWYHWN ᵓMRYN), Steamed vegetables (YRQ ŠLWQ)--over it one says (ᵓWMR), "By whose word all things come into existence."

AAA.    R. Zeᶜira in the name of Samuel, Turnip heads that have been steamed, (ŠŠLQN):

If they are in their original [natural] state (ᵓM BᶜYYNW HN)--over them one says (ᵓWMR), "Who createst the fruit of the earth";

That have been ground (ŠHQN)--over them one says (ᵓWMR), "By whose word all things come into existence."

BBB.    Said R. Yose, And the Mishnah says likewise (WMTNYTᵓ ᵓMRH KN): "[One says the blessing, 'Who createst the fruit of the earth' on the fruit of the land] except for

bread, for over bread one says, 'Who bringest forth bread from
the earth.'"  And is not bread ground (ŠHWQH) [i.e., made of
ground items]?[287]  It only says "except for bread."  Thus
(H<sup>ɔ</sup>) other things, though ground,[288] are in their natural
state (B<sup>C</sup>YNN HN) [and require the blessing, "Who createst the
fruit of the earth."]

(y. Ber. 6:1; p. 10a)

i

     The final item in Mishnah, clause 4, vegetables, YRQWT,
is the subject of three comments attributed to Samuel, TT, ZZ,
and AAA.  As in the earlier traditions these focus on the effect
of the food's preparation on the choice of the blessing.  The
traditions likewise are formulated not as comments to Mishnah, but
as autonomous statements, within their own pericopae, and are
contrasted with similarly phrased traditions attributed to other
masters.  We include the comments within the present study for
they serve to focus on Mishnah.  Mishnah mentions fruit of the
earth and its blessing, 3a, an exception which happens to be
cooked, that is, baked, 3b, and then the vegetables, 4.  Judah
who requires specialized blessings requires a distinctive blessing.  The overall issue is whether the vegetables when cooked
maintain the specified blessing.  Some of the earlier Samuel-
traditions and their thematic analogues in Tosefta took into
account the cooking of the food.  But vegetables deserve special
attention, as they have their own peculiar types of preparations.
These include ŠLQ, steaming or steeping food in hot or boiling
water,[288] and pickling or setting the food in vinegar or salt.

ii

     Samuel's comment appears in an exposition (DRŠ) attributed
to Nahman.  The direct attribution to Samuel, however, is a gloss
to the standard phrase, "Our Rabbi," which in this case does fit
Samuel, Nahman's teacher.[289]  Nahman contrasts that tradition with
an opinion Ulla transmits in Yohanan's name.  The expounder adds
that the two opinions make up a dispute and thus each one refers
to all cases.  BT then includes two versions of Yohanan's opinion
and Nahman b. Yishaq's comment that Ulla relied on the wrong
version.  Yohanan would accordingly agree with Samuel.[290]  BT
further discusses the nature of Yohanan's position.
     TT-YY follows a pattern apparently worked over or at least
known in Nahman b. Yishaq's circle.[291]  This is indicated by an

exposition which immediately precedes that of Nahman and which
employs the identical structure.  As that text also throws additional light on Yohanan's position and the analogue in PT, we
cite it.

> A'.  Taught (DRŠ) R. Hisda in the name of our Rabbi--
> and who is he?  Rav--Steamed foods (ŠLQWT), over them they
> say the blessing, "Who createst the fruit of the earth."
>
> And our rabbis who came from the land of Israel to
> Babylonia--and who are they?[292]  Ulla in the name of R.
> Yohanan--said, Steamed foods (ŠLQWT), over them they say the
> blessing, "By whose word all things come into existence."
>
> B'.  I [R. Hisda] say,[293] "Whatever initially [i.e.,
> when raw, requires], "By whose word all things come into exis-
> tence," when steamed (ŠLQN) [require], "Who createst the fruit
> of the earth."  And whatever initially [i.e., in its raw
> state, requires], "Who createst the fruit of the earth," when
> steamed (ŠLQN) [require], "By whose word all things come into
> existence."  [Where "fruit of the earth" is eaten mainly in a
> raw state--then that state requires the blessing, "Who createst
> the fruit of the earth."  When it is eaten mainly steamed,
> then that blessing applies only to that state.]
>
> C'.  [= A question concerning B'].
>
> D'.  Said R. Nahman bar Yishaq . . . [= an answer to
> C'.]

>                    (b. Ber. 38b)

In A', Rav is in the place of Samuel and in B', the
expounder harmonizes the two positions.  The passage thereby
claims that Yohanan and Rav refer to not all but only certain--
and different--cases.  According to the implied principle, the
blessing applies to the food when it is in its regular edible
state.

Samuel's comment is thus not a direct citation but part
of an exposition and appears in a pericope with a patterned
phrasing.[294]  We, accordingly, cannot know if the present formulation represents the tradition's most fundamental stage.


                              iii

PT presents two versions of Samuel's comment.  They and
the pericope in which they appear make up part of a larger *sugya*.
The latter is the y. analogue to b.'s *sugya* which contains A'-D'
and TT-YY.  The two *sugyot* exhibit extensive parallels and some

variations, especially in sequence.  We find even a b. analogue
to AAA, which we cite below.  PT in particular focuses on the
different versions of Yohanan's tradition.  A. Weiss and A. Goldberg have analyzed the texts.[295]  Relevant to our study is the
observation that b. and y. exhibit close similarities, undoubedly
draw on common materials, and attribute to Zeira a central role.
Goldberg argues that in Palestinian circles Zeira tried to represent Yohanan's position as being close to Samuel's and that this
effort along with conceptual differences between the two *Gemarot*
account for many of the variations on Samuel's comment.[296]  Zeira
in the process, apparently, adapted Samuel's tradition, thereby
obscuring the fundamental form of his tradition.

      Abba attributes to Samuel and Rav the position that Ben-
jamin bar Yefet in XX and an uncited tradition in the analogue in
PT had attributed to Yohanan.[297]  The two b. expositions, TT-UU
and A'-B', attest that Rav and Samuel had opinions on this matter,
though assign them the blessing, "Who createst fruit of the earth."
On the other hand, ZZ, in contrast to B', is similar to TT in that
it does not qualify or limit the principle.  But if one applies YY
to the first exposition, one could argue that Rav, as well, actually offered a general rule.[298]  Goldberg suggests that Abba
palestinizes the Babylonian tradition.  Below we hesitantly offer
a different interpretation.

      Commentators differ as to the relation of Zeira's version
of Samuel, in AAA, to that of Abba's in ZZ.  While PM and Fulda,
e.g., hold that AAA disputes ZZ, Azikri is able to distinguish
between their cases and harmonize them: ZZ speaks of vegetables
that are regularly eaten raw, while AAA deals with an item not
regularly eaten in that state.  But that principle is not mentioned in the text and imposes a criterion that Hisda had offered,
in B', and which is found elsewhere in PT.  Moreover, it contradicts ancient eating habits, as people ate raw turnip heads.[299]
Goldberg, following his argument that Zeira had a purpose in citing what he did and in using the formulations which he employed,
aptly suggests that AAA is more of a revision or clarification of
ZZ than an outright dispute.  That is, Abba is correct with regard
to Samuel's position, but only when the vegetable has been ground
and not in its natural state.[300]  Whether or not Goldberg is
correct as to Zeira's intent, he does sense the impression one
receives from the placement of the traditions.  We should also
note that since ZZ and AAA are not placed in a dispute form, they
were not initially presented as two opposite opinions.

iv

We now turn to b.'s analogue to AAA:

C'. Said R. Zera, When we were at R. Huna's we used
to say [or: "he said," ],[301] Turnip tops[302] (GRGLYDY DLPTᵓ):
When cut up into large pieces--[over them one says the bless-
ing] "Who createst the fruit of the earth." When cut up into
small pieces--[over them one says the blessing] "By whose
word all things come into existence."

D'. And when we came before R. Judah, he said to us,
The former and the latter [over them one says the blessing],
"Who createst the fruit of the earth." And they cut them up
a lot [i.e., into small pieces] in order to sweeten their
taste.[303]

(b. Ber. 39a)

A. Weiss suggests this passage presents an early formulation of the material which generated AAA. Zeira had concluded
that Judah's comment represented Samuel's opinion, for Judah was
an important student of that master.[304] While the texts are not
exactly identical and only AAA explicitly mentions the principle
of "natural state" versus "ground up,"[305] A. Weiss's suggestion,
at least in part, is reasonable. Zeira adapted[306] C'-D'. But the
tradition which he transmitted may have been shaped by transmi-
tional and redactional needs of PT. This might account for the
fact that C'-D' does not use the example of "turnips" in the
formulation of its tradition.


v

BBB in PT is a problematic clause. We briefly review the
alternatives, for the matter underlies Samuel's relationship to
Mishnah and the nature of PT's *sugya*

Commentators differ on the point of BBB. Does it support
or contradict AAA?[307] Several, including Azikri, Frankel, and
Luncz, understand BB as a question against AAA and a rejection of
its criterion of a recognizable and natural state.[308] But this
does not fit the language of BBB. First, a y. pericope that
immediately precedes ZZ contains a tradition with a formulation
quite close to BBB. A master cites a tradition as to olive oil;
to support that opinion a different master presents before R.
Zeira[309] the mishnaic clause, "except for wine . . .," i.e., the
first exception in the Mishnah. BBB differs only in the mention
of Mishnah's second exception, "bread," and its attendant

blessing, "Who bringest forth bread from the earth." We, accordingly, have two texts. One is patterned after the other, or both are patterned after a third text, or both are shaped by a later and common transmissional or redactional process. Consequently, whatever be the history of the two texts, we cannot assume that the formula that opens BBB, "And the Mishnah says likewise," is a question. Such a rendering would break the pattern as evidenced in the first text. Secondly, this formula elsewhere is usually used to support, and not question, a preceding passage. This problem may have motivated the GRA to include the word L$^{\circ}$, "not" in the opening formula of BBB, viz., "And the Mishnah does not say likewise" [thus, as you presented].[310] A single formula is then not used in opposite ways.

On the other hand, to take BBB as a support following its usual language, involves the emendation of ŠHWQH to ŠLWQH; that, however, is unacceptable, as it requires a forced rendering and is further out of phase with the identical clause in the preceding --and structurally parallel--text.[311] We thus cannot easily explain the enigmatic clause BBB. Nevertheless, through our focus on the tradition we have carefully evaluated the relationship of Samuel's tradition to Mishnah.

There is, however, an additional possible solution to this crux. The root of the problem, to recapitulate, lies in the fact that BBB is identical to a clause in a preceding pericope and that the language which opens BBB normally serves to support a preceding text. But the pericope lacks an appropriate preceding text. We propose, therefore, that such a text did at one time exist, and it either has been corrupted into the present formulation of ZZ or is no longer extant in the *sugya*. ZZ, like TT in b., presents a general principle which does not limit its rule to "steaming," and thus accords with BBB. On the other hand, as emphasized above, the blessing specified in ZZ does not fit BBB nor b.'s version of Rav's and Samuel's opinions. The latter require, "Who createst fruit of the earth." If, however, ZZ originally prescribed the blessing, "Who createst fruit of the earth," the problems would be solved. Implicit in our logic is that this reconstructed ZZ would, if only in part, accord with AAA, for one could construe BBB as a qualification of AAA. Moreover, our suggestion solves the difficulty in the opening formula of BBB. A y. clause frequently refers to a penultima passage, from which it was separated by an interpolated clause.[312] In our case we could understand how someone interpolated an additional

opinion of Samuel between one opinion and the supporting text.
Moreover, if an emended ZZ and BBB constituted the early layout
of the pericope, it would make up a perfect structural parallel
with the preceding pericope.  The latter contains only the opinion
and then the support, i.e., two traditions.

        Our reconstruction assumes that a scribe altered the
blessing text in ZZ.  Our suggestion, however, remains only a
possibility.  Nevertheless it does indicate that we can--and
should--construe BBB to read it smoothly.  It also enables us to
appreciate the degree to which the present specified blessing in
ZZ does not conform to the other versions of Samuel's tradition.

        A variation of our suggestion consists of the possibility
that BBB originally referred to a now-no-longer-extant tradition
which had been formulated as ZZ but with the blessing, "Who
createst fruit of the earth."  This would, accordingly, conform
to Nahman's alignment with and citation of Samuel in TT.[313]

                              vi

        Samuel thus focuses on an extended development of the
final clause of M. Ber. 6:1.[314]  In his "extreme" formulation,
Samuel claimed that vegetables, whether or not steamed, require
the same blessing.  His view circulated among Babylonian emigrés
to Palestine and native Babylonians, such as Nahman.  Zeira may
have employed a precedent, C'-D', and, if we follow Goldberg,
somewhat modified that tradition in order to gain its acceptance
in Palestine, and at the same time supported a homogeneous version
of Yohanan's opinion.[315]

        In addition, ZZ, unless its blessing text has been cor-
rupted, provides an example of how someone might revise Samuel's
tradition and produce a version inconsistent with Zeira's in AAA.
As we suggested earlier, the existence of these variations and
adaptions may accord with the tradition's formulation and function.  In each of the three versions of the tradition, we can
discern the rubric used to specify blessings and to supplement
Mishnah, instances of which appear in Tosefta.  It constitutes an
autonomously formulated declarative sentence.  The tradition,
accordingly, originated as a supplement to Mishnah, and, employed
an autonomous formulation.  Since traditions in such formulations
by definition do not depend upon, and do not circulate along with
the text of Mishnah, they may not make up an inviolable text, but
may be reworded and used.  Moreover, as we earlier saw, the substance of the tradition in its earliest stage is generated by

consideration of the concerns and principles of Mishnah.  But as
in those earlier examples, the tradition is presented in its own
terms and is the subject of later amoraic (and at times, saboraic)
activity.

### Summary of Traditions on Mishnah Ber. 6:1

M. Ber. 6:1 is the subject of twenty separate comments
attributed to Samuel.  When one considers that three appear in
two duplicate *sugyot*, and that some of the others make up different versions or instances of the same tradition, we end up with
nine different traditions.

None of the items are formulated as glosses to circulate
along with Mishnah.  Yet each one, as evidenced by Tosefta's functional and thematic analogues,[316] properly belongs to a commentary
on Mishnah.  The first one provides a conceptual basis for Mishnah's law and the others supplement it with additional or special
cases.  These latter nineteen items originally employed a pattern
to specify an item's blessing.  Some, however, have been somewhat
recast, used, and placed into dispute forms and thus, in turn,
have become subject to subsequent transmissional and redactional
activity.

1.  B provides a conceptual, metaphoric basis and biblical
    proof-text for Mishnah's overall requirement that a person
    say a blessing over food.  With a blessing one avoids
    sacrilege.

2.  C, G, and J-K, identical comments, specify the blessing
    for olive oil.  They relate to Mishnah clause 2b's mention
    of wine as both wine and olive oil are made up of juice of
    a fruit.  PT's analogue is not attributed to Samuel.

3.  CC, DD, II; EE; and LL, E (which along with its pericope
    is drawn from LL's pericope, in b. Eruv. 30a), make up
    three different versions of a tradition specifying the
    blessing for the five kinds of grain characteristic of the
    land of Israel.  They deal with "fruit of the earth,"
    Mishnah clause 3, and require a blessing mentioned not in
    Mishnah but in Tosefta, "Who createst various kinds of
    foods."  While they may all derive from a now-not-extant
    formulation, each of the present formulations emphasizes
    something different.  EE employs a common formulation
    which focuses on whatever amount of the item, KL ŠHWᵓ.
    CC, DD, and II emphasize the presence of the item,

irrespective of the admixture of something else.  E and
LL, probably presented in a rather late reformulation to
fit redactional needs, focus on the number of the items
within this category.  Only this formulation lacks the
rubric to delineate a blessing.

4.  O specifies the blessing for a raw bottle-gourd and
    barley flour.  While, in part, it might relate to the pre-
    vious tradition, it can properly function as a supplement
    to Mishnah clause 3 and addresses the problem of eating
    food not generally considered edible for human consumption.

5-6.  S, W; U; and S' and U', in a duplicate *sugya*, in b.
      Eruv. 28b, deal with concrete cases of "fruit of the
      earth," the item in Mishnah clause 3.  S and its y. ver-
      sion W focus on a palm-heart, which while edible was not
      usually eaten due to the picking's negative impact upon
      the tree.  U provides a "retraction" and a separate tradi-
      tion on radish.  The latter's blessing accords with W
      but not S.

7.  PP specifies the blessing for (barley) porridge, and thus
    likewise deals with fruit of the earth but introduces the
    concern for the manner in which the food has been pre-
    pared.  Mishnah clause 3b, as well as Tosefta, provides
    precedents for the focus on the food's preparation and
    the latter's impact on the blessing.

8-9.  TT, AAA; ZZ focus on the blessings for steamed vege-
      tables and, in AAA, on the particular example of turnip
      heads.  These traditions thus deal with Mishnah clause 4,
      vegetables, and, like the previous item, address the
      issue of the produce's preparation.  TT may perhaps be
      construed to accord with its y. version in AAA but not the
      blessing in the present text of ZZ.  We hesitantly sug-
      gested that ZZ should be emended

As the traditions in items 2-9 deal with special cases,
they may, through concrete examples, actually deal with the identification of the principles which determine what constitutes the
proper blessing.  One such "emerging" principle focuses on whether
or not the food is in the state in which it is normally or primarily eaten.  If it is, one then employs the blessing which Mishnah
specifies for that item.  But the traditions do not enable one to
draw clear-cut identifications of the implicit principles and we

can accordingly understand why they have become subject to discussions and diverse conclusions.

Finally, these items exemplify both sides of the history
of Samuel's comments on Mishnah.  At their most fundamental stage,
they may have supplemented Mishnah.  Later, when they played an
essential role in the formation and growth of *Gemara*, they
provided the structure around which other comments were organized.
Moreover, while we can trace how they have been shaped in the
course of their later use and application, we can also discern
how the teachings originally related to Mishnah.[317]

### 7.  Berakhot Chapter Seven

### 99, 105 [and 96].

#### M. Ber. 7:1-2, 4

1.   Three who ate together are obligated to summon
[Grace = to have one person invite the others to say Grace
together].[318]

2.   [if] one ate . . .

(M. Ber. 7:1)

3.   Women, or slaves, or minors--they do not summon
Grace over them.  [= They are not counted to make up the
quorum of three.]

4.   From what amount [of food] do they summon Grace?
The size of an olive.  R. Judah says, The size of an egg.

(M. Ber. 7:2)

5.   Three who ate together are not permitted to
separate.

(M. Ber. 7:4A)

[The above *mishnayot* elicit several traditions
attributed to Samuel.  We first present related y. and b.
versions of a tradition which deals with M. Ber. 7:1 and 4.]

A.   Here [= M. Ber. 7:4] it says, "They are not
permitted to separate."  Here [= M. Ber. 7:1] it says, "They
are required to summon [Grace]?"

B.   Samuel said, Here [, M. Ber. 7:4,[319] speaks of a
case in which] (B-) it is in the beginning (BTHYLH).  And
here [, M. Ber. 7:1,[319] speaks of a case in which] (B-) it is
in the end (BSWP).

C.   What is "in the beginning" and what is "in the
end"?

D.1.  Two Amoraim [differ on the matter].

D.2.  One said, [If] they gave thought to eat--that is
"in the beginning."  [If] they ate an olive's amount--that is
"in the end."

D.3.  The other [Amora] said, [If] they ate an olive's
amount--that is "in the beginning."

[If] they finished eating--that is "in the end."
                    (y. Ber. 7:1, 11a)

E.  What does [M. Ber. 7:4] teach us?[320]

We have learned [it already] one time: "Three who ate
together are required to summon [Grace]" (M. Ber. 7:1).

F.  This [= M. Ber. 7:4] teaches us in accordance
with that which R. Abba[321] said Samuel.

Three who sat to eat together and still have not
eaten, are not permitted to separate.[322]

G.1.  *An alternative version* (L"ᵓ = LYŠNᵓ ᵓHRYNᵓ):

G.2.  Said R. Abba [321] said Samuel, Thus it [= M. Ber.
7:4] is taught, Three who sat to eat together, even though
each one eats by himself [alternatively some texts have: "each
one eats from his own plate"][323]--are not permitted to separate.

H.  Alternatively [M. Ber. 7:4 teaches] in accordance
with R. Huna, for R. Huna said, Three[324] who came from three
groups are not permitted to separate.

I.  Said R. Hisda, And it is when (WHᵓW Š-) they come
from three groups of three men.[325]

J.  Said Rava, And we do not say but . . . [= further
defines the comment in I].
                    (b. Ber. 50a-b)


                                i

M. Ber. 7:1-2 and 4 are subject to several Samuel traditions.  M. Ber. 7:1-2 rules that three individuals who eat together
must preface their Grace After Meals with an "invitation" to say
the Grace, and then lists those counted and excluded from the
quorum to make up the three.  In a series of refrains between one
individual and the other participants, the former leads the latter
in thanking God for the meal.[326]  M. Ber. 7:3 provides the opening
formula of the Summons.  With three individuals it opens with the
phrase, "Let us praise . . ."

ii

The first Samuel tradition we examine correlates M. Ber.
7:1's requirement of three individuals with a different formulation of the point in M. Ber. 7:4. The two texts seemingly make
up redundant *mishnayot*.[327] The tradition appears in y. Ber. 7:1,
11a. A different version may be represented by an analogous tradition, in b. Ber. 50a. After we separately examine each one we
compare the two.

Samuel's comment in B consists of two balanced parts, each
of which is formulated as a gloss which uses the B- form:

> K$^{\circ}$N BTHYLH
>
> K$^{\circ}$N BSWP

The presence of the demonstratives, "here . . . here
. . . ," indicates that the tradition is used to correlate two
texts but it does not explicitly identify them. A's introductory
question, however, makes the referents clear, as it cites two
passages. We note, though, in A, the citation of M. Ber. 7:4
precedes that of M. Ber. 7:1. This suggests that the *sugya* may
have originated in the *Gemara* on M. Ber. 7:4, which as we shall
see is the location of the b. analogue. If so, the pericope makes
up one of the numerous instances of a y. *sugya* which takes form
in one context, is transferred to a second one, and is later
deleted in the first location.[328]

An anonymous *sugya* employs additional materials to explain
Samuel's comment. The two unnamed authorities cited in D attest
Samuel's comment and explain what constitutes the "beginning" and
the "end." While commentators differ in their explanation of y.,
we follow the sequence of references in A.[329] Paraphrasing D, we
read:

> 1. [= D.2.] Three who initially intend to eat
> together are forbidden to separate, M. Ber. 7:4. The initial
> intent thus suffices to form the group.
> Three, even without the initial intent, who eat the
> minimum amount of food requiring Grace (an olive's amount)[330]
> must summon Grace, M. Ber. 7:1.
> 2. Alternatively [D.3]: Three who eat the minimum
> amount requiring Grace (an olive's amount) must not separate,
> M. Ber. 7:4.
> Three who finish eating together, even though they
> did not start together, must summon Grace, M. Ber. 7:1.

Samuel's tradition, accordingly, integrally fits into its context.  It provides two glosses to explain two texts and thereby directly responds to the presence of a seemingly redundant text, the question of A.  But we are unable to know if this is the most fundamental stage of the tradition.  Its original formulation may have focused on only one of the texts.  As we shall see, the b. Ber. 50a analogue provides an example of the latter type of formulation.  If the tradition has been expanded, the redactor of y. Ber. 7:1 or his source may have had access to one comment on one text and then generated the second half.  Alternatively, he may have provided both parts with the present language.

Whatever the original formulation, those who transmitted Samuel's tradition believed his remarks explained the distinctive characteristics of two different *mishnayot*.  At that stage of the tradition, Samuel appears as a commentator on Mishnah whose vision encompasses the chapter as a whole and who identifies the contexts of Mishnah's cases.  Moreover, those early circles deemed it appropriate to transmit Samuel's comment in the form of short glosses introduced by the B-form.  After we analyze the b. version, we can more closely examine this image of Samuel.

### iii

The version of Samuel's tradition in b. Ber. 50a, F-G, like the alternative one attributed to Huna, H, focuses on M. Ber. 7:4.  The anonymous question, in E, introduces F-H as if they explained the distinctive characteristics of M. Ber. 7:4 in contrast to that of M. Ber. 7:1.[330]

Samuel's tradition in the printed editions appears in two versions, F, and G.2, separated by the phrase, G.1, "alternative reading," L"ᵓ.  These two versions may derive from post-talmudic circles.[331]  Each is separately attested in Gaonic times.  As already noted by R. Jonah Gerondi, of the thirteenth century,[332] the two readings reflect two different interpretations of a briefer formulation of Samuel's comment.  It probably consisted of the material common to both versions.[333]

Three who sat to eat--are not permitted to separate.

Some commentators explained this as:

Those who sat to eat and still have not eaten--are not . . .[334]

Other commentators understood it thus:

Three who sat to eat, even though each one eats by himself . . .

There further emerged an alternative reading for one
phrase of the second version:

Three . . . even though each one eats *from his own plate.*

The alternative reading accords with a principle and
phrasing in a *baraita* found in b. Ber. 42b (= T. Ber. 5:23 and y.
Ber. 7:5, 11c):

> Ten who were travelling on the way even though they
> all eat from one plate, each one says the blessing by himself.
> [If] they sat to eat, even though each one eats from
> his own plate ($^{3}{}_{"}{}^{C}$P ŠKL $^{3}$HD W$^{3}$HD $^{3}$WKL MKKRW), one says the
> blessing for all of them.[335]

The group, by sitting together, forms its identity as a cohesive
whole.

In our presentation and translation of b. Ber. 50a, we
noted the variants in the second version, G. If the first reading, "each one eats by himself," is more original, the latter,
"each one eats from his own plate," may have been generated by
the *baraita*'s formulation. This is so because the phrase "from
his plate," appears in BT and Tosefta in only these two texts.

According to both b. versions of Samuel's comment, the
three individuals' initial intent is decisive. According to F,
the three need not have yet eaten; their mere sitting together
signifies their intention.[336] We find this notion also in the
second version, G, though it receives a different emphasis. The
initial intent is not compromised by subsequent action.

The "original" version of Samuel's comment which we posit
to have first existed, and which R. Johan Gerondi already suggested, enabled both of the above explanations to emerge. The PT
version we earlier examined demonstrates that Samuel's tradition
was so formulated that it could undergo at least two interpretations. The more fundamental form of the tradition problably
included the gloss of one word, [Š]YŠBW and drew upon Mishnah's
use of the verb to eat, Š$^{C}$KLW, changing it to the infinitive
form, L$^{3}$KWL. Our hypothesis gains some credence by the fact that
this "early" form of Samuel's tradition more closely balances with
Huna's tradition in H.

Both Samuel and Huna explain M. Ber. 7:4 by glossing it,
and both employ the apodosis from M. Ber. 7:4, "are not permitted
to separate." Hisda's comment glosses Huna and uses the form for
a clarification, WHW$^{3}$ Š-.[337] As is clear by the presence of the
introductory phrase in F, "This teaches us in accordance with that

which," and a comparable clause in H, an anonymous authority cites
the traditions of Samuel and Huna.  He uses them to answer the
question in A and accordingly may have shaped them.  We have
already seen the types of changes through which Samuel's tradition
may have gone.  Such transformations might apply, as well, to
Huna's tradition.  In y. Ber. 7:1, we find a different use for
Huna's remarks and Hisda's clarification:

> R. Huna said, Three who ate, each by himself, and
> came together--summon [Grace together].
> R. Hisda said, That is (WHN Š-) when they came from
> these three groups.

While these two lines have posed problems to the commentators,
they clearly indicate that Huna's notion and, even his language,
could be employed in the context of M. Ber. 7:1 and Mishnah's
formulation of, "obligation to summon [Grace]."

We thus again see that Samuel's tradition is presented
from the perspective of its later history.  The pericope's
editor or his source drew upon traditions which he molded to fit
his understanding of the matter.  In so doing, the editor
attempted to clarify why the masters read in what they did and
assumably did not find the Mishnah self-explanatory.  As a result,
the traditions of Samuel and Huna emerge as explanations why the
act of gathering prevents the three people from separating.

If our analysis is correct, we understand Samuel's and b.
Ber. 50's perception of M. Ber. 7:4.  But what of M. Ber. 7:1 and
how was it understood?  The editor of the b. pericope who supplied
the question in E assumes that M. Ber. 7:1 is clear.  But neither
he nor other b. circles, in contrast to y. Ber. 7:1, attribute to
Samuel an explicit comment that addresses that Mishnah.  But we
do have some indication.  First, we can draw an implication from
F-G-H that M. Ber. 7:1 deals with three who eat together.
Secondly, we have a pericope at b. Ber. 47a which may reflect or
assume the latter context for M. Ber. 7:1:

> 1.  Rav and Samuel sat at a meal.
> 2.  R. Shimi bar Hiyya entered and started to eat
> quickly.
> 3.  Said to him Rav, What is your intention, to join
> us [so as to say Grace together with a "Summons"]?  We have
> already eaten.
> 4.  Said to him Samuel, If they bring me mushrooms and
> pidgeons to Abba [= Rav], would we not eat them?[338]
>                    (b. Ber. 47a)

The pericope assumes that to summon Grace the parties need not
have eaten or, from the onset, have intended to eat the whole meal
together.  This notion accords with not only our suggestion as to
b.'s understanding of Samuel's position on M. Ber. 7:1, but also
y.'s version of Samuel on M. 7:1.  Samuel's BSWP, "at the end,"
means at the least, that the three did not begin their meal
together.  It further fits both amoraic interpretations of Samuel,
explicitly so with the second one, D. 3, "they finished eating,"
and substantively so with the first, D. 2, "they ate an olive's
amount."[339]

The b. version of Samuel's comment thus glosses Mishnah
and paraphrases it.  The circle of Rava knows an alternative
explanation attributed to Huna and glossed by Hisda.  The anonymous editor of the pericope employs both traditions.  Subsequently,
the wording of Samuel's teaching yields two interpretations, each
of which contaminates the original text; eventually both are conflated in the printed editions of BT.

iv

We now compare the b. and y. versions.  The two differ,
though they have striking similarities.  First, each version in
time became subject to two interpretations.  This suggests that
the comment did not circulate as an autonomous and fully comprehensible comment but rather as some brief comment or gloss.  Such
a formulation is found in the y. version and can be reconstructed
out of the b.'s.

Secondly, the versions substantively accord with each
other.  According to b.'s "preserved" versions and the reconstructed one, the individual's sitting serves as an act to signify
intent and to define the situation so as to require the communal
Grace (M. Ber. 7:4).  As above partially indicated, this accords
with the y. version.  Specifically, taking M. Ber. 7:4 as the
referent of "in the beginning," we have: (1) the principle, "They
gave thought to eat" together, D.2, and, therefore, something
which precedes the eating and which matches b. version's concern
for the prior intent; (2) the criterion of "eating an olive's
amount," D.3, which is the opposite of "finishing eating" and,
therefore, something which comes prior to the meal's completion.
Indeed, b.'s requirement of the act of sitting together to signify
the intent finds an analogue in the *act* of "eating the olive's
amount," something missing in the first explanation's unconcret-
ized "gave thought together."

Thirdly, the location of the versions are identical.  BT
deals with M. Ber. 7:4 and, based upon the y.'s sequence of the
references in A, the y. pericope similarly originated in y. Ber.
7:4.  In fact, one would logically ask a question as to redundancy
only once one has seen both texts, i.e., at 7:4 and not 7:1.

On the other hand, we remain unsure as to the original
form of the tradition.  As we have seen, both versions attest the
use of glosses.  While the b. version employs the language of M.
Ber. 7:4 and paraphrases it with a gloss, the y. version is formulated as single, one-word glosses preceded by the demonstratives,
"here" and "here."  As in other instances, the later use of the
traditions contribute to the difficulty in isolating its fundamental form.  In this case both pericopae and their wider *sugyot* have
been shaped redactionally.[340]  But as in other cases, the original
gloss-like formulation of the tradition at its earliest stage may
have facilitated the later transformations.

Babylonian and Palestinian circles accordingly use Samuel's
tradition and believed that it explains the distinctive characteristics of M. Ber. 7:4 and 1.  Both versions, in different ways,
employ glosses, and one incorporates the language of Mishnah.
Finally, both versions become building blocks in the expanding
*Gemara*.

## 101a, 101b [and 102, 102].

### [M. Ber. 7:2]

[PT and Gen. R. present two recensions of a y. *sugya*
containing a tradition attributed to Samuel.  In PT the comment has been integrated into the *sugya*'s wider problematic
and adapted to a Palestinian issue.  In Gen. R.'s earlier
recension of the y. *sugya*, the tradition appears in an earlier
stage and comments directly on M. Ber. 7:2's exclusion of a
minor from "the three" required to say Grace communally.]

A.  It was taught (TNY), a minor (QTN) and (W-) the
scroll of the Torah--they consider him as an adjunct [to make
up the ten] (ᶜWŚYN ᵓWTW SNYP).

B.  Said R. Yudan, *Thus is the teaching* [in A]: A
child for the scroll of the Torah--they consider as an
adjunct.[341]

C.  "From when" do they start to consider him as an
adjunct (MᵓYMTY ᶜWŚYN ᵓWTW SNYP)?[342]

D.1.  R. Avina said, *R. Huna and R. Judah both of*
*them in the name of Samuel, dispute* [the matter].

D.2. *One said*, When he knows the character of the blessing (KDY ŠYHꓘ YWD$^C$ ṬYB BRKH).[343]

D.3. *And the other said*, When he knows to whom he says a blessing (ŠYHꓘ YWD$^C$ LMY MBRK).[344]

(y. Ber. 7:2, 11b)

A'. And until when is he considered a minor (W$^C$D ꓘYKN YHYH QṬN).[345]

B'1. Said R. Avina, *R. Huna and R. Judah, both of them in the name of Samuel, dispute* [the matter]:

B'2. *One said*--Until he knows how to say a blessing ($^C$D ŠHWꓘ YWD$^C$ LBRK).[346]

B'3. *And the other said*--Until he knows the character of the blessing ($^C$D ŠHWꓘ YWD$^C$ ṬB BRKH).[346]

(Gen. R. 91.4)


i

Women, slaves, and minors are required to say Grace After Meals (M. Ber. 3:3) but may not be counted to make up the number to summon Grace and thus say Grace communally. Samuel's comment, D and B', define the category of a minor. We review the tradition's present location in PT, A-D, and by internal analysis trace how it has been reworked, and then turn to Gen. R. for confirmation of our reconstruction.


ii

The *baraita*, A, lists items which can be counted as an adjunct (to ten). The meaning of the word "adjunct" is made clear by its use elsewhere in the *sugya*. The beginning of y. Ber. 7:2 focuses on the issue. A tradition attributed to Rabbi Judah the Patriarch as well as to R. Yehoshua ben Levi, a first-generation Palestinian Amora, states that we may count a minor as an adjunct to a group of men to make up *the ten*.[347]

In B, Yudan, a fourth-generation Palestinian Amora,[348] clarifies the *baraita* and apparently takes the *vav* as an explanatory *vav*, a usage found elsewhere.[349] We should, accordingly, render the *baraita* thus: "A minor, that is, for the Scroll. . . ." which means, following many commentators, that a child may count as one of the seven individuals called to the Torah Scroll when it is read on the Sabbath.[350]

C employs the same language as A-B, $^C$WŚYN ꓘWTW SNYP. This suggests that C deals with a quorum of ten, or following the

interpretation of Yudan's explanation, a quorum of seven.   The
question in C thus raises a matter relevant to the concerns of
A-B: when is a minor counted to make up a required quorum?

D contains Samuel's tradition.   Avina, a third-generation
Babylonian Amora who emigrated to Palestine, transmits it in the
name of two second-generation Babylonian Amoraim,   Huna [Huna =
Huna] and Judah.   Each of the latter two, students of Samuel, had
reported the master's tradition in a different version.   Avina,
however, apparently did not know which tradent had transmitted
which version.[351]   Both versions of Samuel's comment lack a referent, make up balanced glosses, and offer criteria which qualify
(and do not disqualify) a person.

According to the first view, D.2, a minor who knows the
character, i.e., practices and make-up, of the blessing may be
counted.[352]   The second master claims that the requirement is for
the minor to know the referent of the benediction, the One
Addressed.   The first, D.2, thus employs a technical ability or
knowledge as a criterion, while the second, D.3, uses an abstract--
or theological--one.

Assuming the criteria fit the matter being defined[353] the
tradition sets out when a person *may say* some type of blessing.
The tradition itself does not say which.   As Mishnah deals with
the exclusion of an individual from saying the blessing, Mishnah
cannot supply the subject.   Can A-B, the immediately preceding
pericope, clarify the subject?   Yudan's interpretation of the
*baraita*, B, cannot constitute the subject of D, for Yudan lived
after Samuel and the masters, who in D, transmit his tradition.[354]
On the other hand, if A represents a tannaitic *baraita*, Samuel
theoretically could directly refer to it.   As it ostensibly deals
with the Summons to Grace, Samuel, too, could deal with that
issue.   This would accord with the *sugya*'s wider problematic of
Grace and the Summons thereto.   But, as we shall see, while Samuel
does refer to the Summons, he does not treat it in in terms of
the issue as presented in A.[355]

To recapitulate, Samuel's comment refers to the Summons
for Grace.   In terms of the wording of D we are not informed
whether this refers to the version of the Summons for three
people or the expanded one for ten people.   For sure the question
in C wants us to understand the tradition in the latter terms and
takes Samuel as commenting on "adjunct for ten."   But the question
is secondary and postdates the tradition.   As we have already
seen, it accords with the problematic of the wider *sugya* and

accordingly fulfills redactional needs to apply Samuel's comment
to the issue of "adjunct to ten." In general, such anticipatory
questions are late and postdate the traditions which they introduce.[356] We now turn to concrete evidence to support our suggestion.

First, while C appears in most texts of y., at least two
medieval works in their citations of A-D lack C or an analogue to
it.[357] Whether or not these works represent an actual literary
tradition of *yerushalmi*, they do reflect the fact that to understand Samuel's comment one need not rely on C. Secondly, this
observation does not demand an extraordinary reading of the pericope. It is assumed, for example, in Maimonides' and Sirillo's
commentaries to M. Ber. 7:2 which employ the two versions of
Samuel's comments in D and set them out as definitions of Mishnah's mention of a "minor."[358] Thirdly, a different recension of
the *sugya* in Genesis Rabba provides a text free from the above
difficulties and in which Samuel explains Mishnah.

### iii

The *sugya* in Gen. R. 91.4, Theodore and Albeck ed. 3:1111-
1118, parallels y. Ber. 7:2. The two versions exhibit several
differences in wording, in formulation, especially in clauses
which bridge or spell out implications of the traditions, and in
the sequence of the materials. Elsewhere, we extensively compared
these two versions and related them to the common differences
between PT and Gen. R. analogues. Scholars argue that each text
represents a different recension of y. and that Gen. R., at least
for the *halakhic* portions, used a recension of y. earlier than
that of the PT itself. Indeed, here Gen. R. presents Samuel's
comment in a state which has not been redactionally and completely
incorporated into its y. context.[359]

The sequence in the Gen. R. *sugya* justifies our focus on
Samuel's tradition and the introductory question alone and not in
terms of what in PT precedes, i.e., the *baraita* and its interpretation, A-B or equivalents thereto. Gen. R. does not juxtapose its
analogues of A-B and C-D. Moreover, it has a different location
for the following "story" whose point is that a minor can*not*
serve as an adjunct to make up the required three:

> Said R. Nisa, Several times I ate with R. Tahlifah my
> father and with Inaini bar Sis, my uncle, and they did not
> count me towards a *zimmun* until I grew two hairs [= signs of
> majority].[360]

While in PT the story closes the *sugya*, in Gen. R. the anecdote changes place with Samuel's tradition and introductory question.

The following chart lays out the different sequences in y., in PT and Gen. R.:

|        | PT |        | Gen. R. |
|--------|----|--------|---------|
| 1. | Yehoshua b. Levi and Rabbi: minor as adjunct to 10. | 1'. | same [= #1]. |
| 2-3. | Question and answer on #1. | 2'-3'. | same [= #2-3]. |
| 4. | Tradition re 9 as 10. | | |
| 5-6. | Question and answer on #4: 9 "with a minor."[361] | | |
| 7. | If minor for 10, why not for 3? | | |
| 8. | Answer. | | |
| 9. | Minor and Torah Scroll [= A]. | 4'. | same [= #9]. |
| 10. | Explanation of #9 [= B]. | 5'. | same [= #10]. |
| | | 6'. | as #4. |
| | | 7'-8'. | as #5-6. |
| | | 9'. | as #7 [with variation and addition][362] |
| | | 10'. | Story [= #13]. |
| 11. | Introductory question [= C]. | 11'. | Introductory question [as #11, but differs]. |
| 12. | Samuel's tradition [= D]. | 12'. | same [= #12 with different preposition]. |
| 13. | Story: Person with two hairs and no young minors. | | |

The sequence thus proves that Samuel's comment, 12', is not integrally connected to the *baraita* and its explanation, 4'-5'. Moreover, the reversed locations between Samuel's tradition and explanation and the story is significant in terms of y.'s literary style. A concluding story generally reflects the concluding and overall point of the *sugya*.[363] Accordingly, Samuel's tradition in PT is structurally integrated into the *sugya*. This accords with the changes between C and A', in the question which introduces Samuel's tradition and between D and B', in the prepositions which open the traditions. The language in PT, "when he knows . . . ," sets forth qualifying criteria, as when a minor may

be counted for the Invitation. But that in Gen. R., "Until he
. . . ," presents the disqualifying factors, as when a minor is
excluded from the Summons, the issue of M. Ber. 7:2.

We find additional differences as well. While one of each
pair employs the verb, "to know," follows with an object, and
offers the same criterion, the "character of the blessing," in PT
this version comes first, and in Gen. R. second. The other tradition in each pair employs the verb "to know" and then the prefix
L-, "to," before the object. In one case we find, "to know to
whom he says a blessing," and in the other," to know to bless."
Evidently there has been some confusion in the transmission.[364]
If the Gen. R. version represents the fundamental formulation of
the traditions, the differences between their criteria are insignificant. One refers to a child's physical ability or knowledge
to bless, while the second to the character of the blessing. In
the PT, on the other hand, the differences are sharp and, accordingly, that version probably is closer to the original.[365]

If we assume that the type of criteria formulated fit the
context in which they are used,[366] Samuel's tradition in Gen. R.
sets out until when someone remains in his or her present status
and *unable* to say a certain blessing. This is inappropriate to the
status of an adult, for then the person has become part of the
group that is liable and able to say the blessing. But it does
accord with M. Ber. 7:2's reference to a "minor." Thus in Gen.
R., Samuel's comment explains M. Ber. 7:2.

iv

We also have additional evidence to exclude an "adult" as
Samuel's referent, to prefer Gen. R.'s formulation, and to accept
our analysis of y. PT's version of Samuel's comment and especially the introductory question assume that Samuel refers to an
"adjunct of ten." But in the context of Summons to Grace this
term appears in traditions attributed to only Palestinians. In
PT we find it in a *baraita* that lacks a b. parallel, in traditions
attributed to Palestinians, and in anonymous parts of y. *Gemara*.
One of the y. traditions does appear in BT, significantly attributed to the first-generation Palestinian Amora, Yehoshua ben
Levi.[367] On the basis of usage, it is thus highly unlikely that
Samuel focuses on the issue of "adjunct to ten."

Given the above observations, a referent appropriate to
Samuel's comment could be a "minor," QTN, who is excluded from
participating in the blessing, which is exactly what we find in

M. Ber. 7:2.  Samuel thus refers to Mishnah and its mention of
minors who are excluded from the Summons.[368]

If Gen. R.'s formulation of Samuel's comment preserves the
literary form of his comment, the tradition had circulated as a
gloss to Mishnah.  Indeed the use of the formulation as a gloss
without an explicit reference and not as an autonomous statement
can account for the history of the tradition.  Someone could have
easily reapplied the gloss to another text without violating the
substance of the comment.  He had to change only the preposition,
from "until" to "when."

Our analysis has offered both negative and positive proof
to support the notion that Samuel glossed M. Ber. 7:2.  We now
turn to several supplementary observations which confirm Samuel's
interest in the Summons for Grace and which indicate that it was
appropriate for someone to define the term "minor" in M. Ber. 7:2.

v

First, b. Ber. 48a, in its analogous *sugya* to y. Ber. 7:2,
cites a tradition which is attributed to Nahman and which is very
close to one of the versions of Samuel's comment:

> And the halakhah does not follow all these [above]
> traditions.  Rather it follows what R. Nahman said, A minor
> who knows to whom they bless, They summon Grace with him
> (WLYT HLKT⁾ KKL HNY SM^CTT⁾ ⁾L⁾ KY H⁾ D⁾MR RB NHMN, QTN HYWD^C
> LMY MBRKYN MZMNYN ^CLYW).

(b. Ber. 48a)

Nahman's comment delineates the status which qualifies
one to participate in the Summons.  This accords with the perspective of PT's version of Samuel's comment--vis-à-vis that of Gen.
R.  Its criterion is identical with that of D.3, the second
version of Samuel's tradition but, in contrast to the latter, it
is formulated as an autonomous statement.  It makes use of the
language of M. Ber. 7:2, into which is glossed the phrase, "Who
knows to whom they bless," HYWD^C LMY MBRKYN.  The negative is
removed from Mishnah's formulation, "They (do not) summon the
Grace with him."  The context clearly is defined by Mishnah and
thus agrees with Gen. R.'s recension, "Summons for three," and
not PT's--worked over--"adjunct for ten."  To judge from the
language of the comment itself, Nahman precludes other criteria
and avers that his is sufficient.[369]

Nahman, a second-third-generation Amora, had access to
Samuel traditions,[370] and it is possible that he draws upon

Samuel's teachings.  While we remain unsure as to this possibility,
Nahman's tradition does attest to the beliefs of those responsible
for the *sugya*.  They associate an early Babylonian with a version
of the tradition which y. attributes to Samuel.[371]

The placing of Samuel's comment in the context of "Summons
for three," or "adjunct to ten," may reflect differing Babylonian
and Palestinian notions.  If so, it is not insignificant that the
autonomous authority who worked over--or, following Albeck,
revised--b. 47b-48a cites Nahman's comment as if it should be
authoritative.[372]


vi

Secondly, in addition to the preceding confirmation of
the second version of Samuel's comment, D.3, we also find attestation of the first one, D.2, as well as of Samuel's concern for the
proper formulation of the "Summoning" formula.  This information
is provided by a tradition of Samuel in b. Ber. 49b-50a and y.
Ber. 7:3.  The tradition relates to M. Ber. 7:3.

Mishnah Ber. 7:3 lists the different formulae for different occasions of the Summons for Grace:

> How do they summon [Grace]?
>
> In the case of three [people]--he [the summoner] says,
> "Let us bless."
>
> In the case of three and he [= in addition to the
> summoner]--he says, "Bless."
>
> (M. Ber. 7:3A)

> Said Samuel, Let a person never exclude himself from
> the group (L$^C$WLM $^⊃$L YWSY$^⊃$ $^⊃$DM $^⊃$T $^C$SMW MN HKLL).
>
> (b. Ber. 49b-50a)

> Samuel said, I do not exclude myself from the group.
> (y. Ber. 7:3, 11c)

In their discussions of the formulae in M. Ber. 7:3A, b.
and y. cite Samuel's comment.  Both Babylonian and Palestinian
circles believed Samuel to be punctilious as to the appropriate
formula by which to summon Grace.  Given this concern it is understandable that he might employ the criterion of "one's knowledge
of the character of the blessing" so as to evaluate a person's
fitness to summon Grace.[373]

Both versions of Samuel's comment thus receive support.
Nahman's tradition demonstrates an early Babylonian interest in a
definition of a "minor," mentioned in M. Ber. 7:2.  It is

formulated in terms of the second version of Samuel's comment,
D.3, and defines the end of the disqualified stage.  A second
independent tradition of Samuel, in b. Ber. 49b-50 and y. Ber.
7:3, 11c, attests that the alternative version, D.2, fits within
Samuel's concerns.


vii

        The third item which confirms our suggestion as to the
original form of Samuel's comment--as a gloss on Mishnah--lies in
the history of the mishnaic category "minor."  Often a reference
to a minor (QTN or TYNWQ) is subject to a comment, definition,
and limitation, both within Mishnah itself and Tosefta and within
*Gemara*.  We find instances where one clause of Mishnah excludes a
minor from liability or permission to perform some activity.[374]
But another passage in that same Mishnah or one adjoining it, or
in Tosefta limits Mishnah's rule and defines what type of minor
is so excluded.  Likewise a ruling excluding a minor often includes
a clause modifying or defining the type of minor.  There is thus
no single standard as to who constitutes a "minor."  Moreover, the
language of the definitions are generally formulated in terms of
their application and context, viz., whether or not a minor knows
or is able to do something.  Thus M. Suk 3:15 incorporates the
definition into the reference:

        And every minor (QTN) who knows how to shake [the
*lulav*] is liable as to *lulav* (WKL QTN ŠYŠ BW D^CT LN^CNY^C HYYB
BLWLB).[375]
                        (M. Suk. 3:15)

     M. Suk 2:8 presents a general rule and then limits it:

        Women, and slaves, and minors (WQTNYM) are exempt
from the [requirement to have a] *sukkah.*
        And every minor (QTN) who does not need his mother
[= but moves about without her] is liable as to the *sukkah.*[376]
                        (M. Suk. 2:8)

        Samuel's definition of M. Ber. 7:2 thus prima facie is not
unusual.  It is natural to find a definition of Mishnah's rule and
it should not be exceptional in the context of blessings to find
it formulated in terms of the blessing and the youth's knowledge
thereof.  This suggestion finds confirmation in T. Ber. 5:18, p.
28, ls. 36-38, which deals with M. Ber. 7:2's mention of a minor.

        1.  A minor who is able to eat an olive's amount--
        they summon Grace with him;

who cannot eat an olive's amount [= the minimum amount
necessary to become liable to say Grace]--they do not summon
Grace with him.

    2.  (And) they are not exacting as to a minor.

    3.  Whether he says, "Let us bless," whether he says,
"Bless"--they do not seize him on that.

    4.  The fault-finders (HNQDQYN) seize him on that [if
he says, "Let us bless"].[377]

           (T. Ber. 5:18, p. 28, ls. 36-38)

Clause 1 defines the type of minor excluded and included.
Tosefta thus follows the perspective of M. Ber. 7:2, which lists
disqualifications, as well as its opposite, those counted.  While
it is not formulated as a simple gloss, Tosefta does consist of
what might have circulated as a 'composite gloss'.  That is, it
employs the language of Mishnah with a gloss interpolated into it.

    Clause 2 deals with examining a minor, probably as to the
presence of two hairs.[378]  If so, its principle accords with that
of clause 1.  When a person exhibits the qualifications in clause
1 but not clause 2, the individual may be counted.  While Samuel
and Tosefta may offer different concrete criteria, they share the
notion that a child who has reached a certain stage, even before
physical maturity, may be counted.[379]  Moreover, Tosefta attests
that Mishnah's reference to a "minor" became subject to explanation already before Samuel's day.[380]


                viii

    We have thus traced the history of Samuel's comment.  We
focused upon its wording and its place within its context in y.
The Gen. R. parallel to y. Ber. 7:2 supports our internal analysis
and represents an early recension of y. and of Samuel's comment.
Already in this "earlier" recension a question to introduce
Samuel's tradition appears.  In the later recension, as found in
y. Ber. 7:2, the editor of the *sugya* used the tradition to focus
on an issue which slightly differs and which fits into the wider
topic of *snif*, "adjunct"--all this despite difficulties in chronology and usage.  BT Ber. 48a attests that the substance of
Samuel's comment circulated as part of an early Babylonian tradition relating to M. Ber. 7:2.  PT Ber. 7:3 and b. Ber. 49b-50a
indicate that Samuel, indeed, was concerned with the proper formulation of the Summons and thus it is appropriate for him to have
used a blessing formula to determine whether or not to include a
minor.  The usage of "minor" in Mishnah and the need in Mishnah

and Tosefta to define that category in language appropriate to
the case at hand demonstrates that such a definition of M. Ber.
7:2 would be appropriate.  T. Ber. 5:18 finally proves that the
word "minor" in M. Ber. 7:2 in fact did elicit a definition.

Samuel's comment thus forms part of a concern integral to
Mishnah-commentary.  For sure, a definition which specifies the
type of "minor" limits Mishnah, but such limitations are found
elsewhere as well.  Samuel's comment may have originated as a
gloss to Mishnah.  This would explain how once it no longer circulated as a gloss onto Mishnah, it might require a question to
introduce it, how it could also be applied to new contexts, and
how the change of a preposition might yield a change in emphasis.

102, 103.

## M. Ber. 7:3

1.  How do they summon [= say the Invitation to
Grace]?

2.  In the case of three [people]--he [the summoner][381]
says, "Let us bless."

In the case of three and he [= in addition to the
summoner]--he says, "Bless."

3.  . . . [= gradations of the formula]

4.  R. Yose the Galilean says, According to the size
of the congregation (HKHL) they bless, for it is said, "With
the congregation bless God, the Lord, O you fountain of
Israel" (Ps. 68:27).

5.  Said R. Aqivah, What do we find in the house of
assembly?  Whether many or whether few, [the person] says,
"Bless the Lord."

6.  R. Ishmael says, "Bless the Lord, who is blessed."
(M. Ber. 7:3)

Said Samuel, Let a person never exclude himself from
the group (L<sup>C</sup>WLM ꜣL YWSY ꜣDM ꜣT <sup>C</sup>SMW MN HKLL).
(b. Ber. 49b)

Samuel said, I do not exclude myself from the group
(ꜣNY ꜣYNY MWSYꜣ <sup>C</sup>SMY MN HKLL).[382]
(y. Ber. 7:3, 11c)

i

M. Ber. 7:3 focuses on the appropriate formula for the
Invitation to Grace.  BT and PT both associate a tradition of
Samuel with this issue.

Mishnah 1-3 lists a series of graded patterns, first, for
3, then 10, 100, 1,000, and 10,000 individuals, and secondly, for
the number plus one, that is, in addition to the summoner.  This
anonymous position accords with the principle which Mishnah,
clause 4, attributes to Yose the Galilean.  Mishnah's editor
adapts to the issue of the Summons to Grace a separate dispute
between Aqiva and Ishmael, 5-6.  The latter differed as to the
blessing said at the reading of the Torah.  Aqiva holds that the
formulae remain constant.  As a result, Aqiva appears to dispute
Yose, 4, and the anonymous first opinion, 1-3.  We cite 5-6, for
Samuel's tradition, as we shall see, in effect agrees with
Ishmael's principle.[383]

ii

The two *Gemarot* discuss the different patterns of the
Summons.  BT on Mishnah 7:3 opens with Samuel's tradition and
then analyzes it.[384]  PT precedes it with other traditions on the
subject.

In both versions Samuel rules that one should not exclude
oneself from the group.  In our context this notion means that an
individual should not act as an observer who calls others to act
but rather should be personally involved.[385]  In b. this is presented as a general principle for anybody, while in y. it appears
as a principle which Samuel himself follows.[386]  Nevertheless,
the two texts employ a similar phraseology.

In addition, both versions are formulated as autonomous
statements and could circulate as independent teachings.  But
neither specifies the rule's application and thus depends upon a
context for clarification.  The fact that both b. and y. place
Samuel's tradition in the *Gemara* on M. Ber. 7:3, however, indicates that it was natural to associate the teaching with this
text and that the connection must have occurred at a relatively
early period.  A third-fourth-generation master furthermore so
attests the tradition.  R. Avun, a traveler between Babylonia and
Palestine, in the pericope which follows Samuel's tradition,
responds to a question against that tradition and employs language
identical to it, viz., "exclude himself from the group":[387]

They responded, Lo the blessings over the Torah?  [In
such cases a person says, "Bless," and does he not exclude
himself?][388]

Said R. Avun [or "Abin"], Since he says, "[Bless the
Lord] who is blessed," even he does not exclude himself from
the group.

As Avun's comment indicates, Samuel's tradition accords
with the view that the person who recites the Torah blessing says,
"Who is blessed."  In Mishnah this is associated with R. Ishmael.
Samuel, accordingly, agrees with his position and not Aqiva's.[389]

Samuel, therefore, emerges as a teacher of a general
principle which has direct implications as to the law of Mishnah.
In effect he decides between opinions set forth in Mishnah and,
thereby, fulfills a function central to commentary on a legal
work.  In this case, however, the adjudication does not employ the
decision pattern of HLKH K-, "The *halakhah* follows . . . ," but is
formulated as an abstracted principle and as an independent
teaching.  Perhaps, though, this wording is used because Samuel's
opinion does not actually coincide with one of the views in
Mishnah.  It accords with both patterns, "Let us bless," and
"Bless . . . who is blessed."  One can, therefore, adapt several
tannaitic views to Samuel's position.

### 8.  *Berakhot Chapter Eight*

115a, 115b, 116.

#### M. Ber. 8:5

1.  The House of Shammai say, [The order of the Benedictions at the outgoing of the Sabbath is] lamp, and food,
and spices, and *havdalah.*

And the House of Hillel say, Lamp, and spices, and
food, and *havdalah.*

2.  The House of Shammai say, [The Benediction over
the lamp is, "Blessed art Thou] who did create the light of
fire."

And the House of Hillel say, "[. . .] who createst
the lights of fire."

(M. Ber. 8:5)

[A tradition attributed to Samuel focuses on the reason
for saying a blessing over fire at the outgoing of the Sabbath,
one of the elements of *havdalah* mentioned in M. Ber. 8:5.  We cite

and analyze first two y. recensions of Samuel's comment, one in
PT Ber. 8:5, and the second, a slightly less worked-over version,
in Gen. R. #82 and Pesiqta Rabbati, #23, and then we turn to the
version in b. Pes. 53b.][390]

      A.   Samuel said, Therefore (LPYKK) we say a blessing
over the fire[391] ($^C$L H$^{\circ}$Š) on the outgoing of the Sabbath
since it (ŠHY$^{\circ}$) is the beginning of its creation.

      B.   R. Huna in the name of [SRAG adds Rav][392] Rabbi
Abbahu in the name of R. Yohanan, Even ($^{\circ}$P) at the outgoing of
Yom Kippur one says the blessing over it, since the fire
rested that whole day.[393]

                   (y. Ber. 8:5, 12b)


                         i


      Samuel connects the time at which one says the blessing
over fire with the etiology of fire. At the outgoing of the
Sabbath Adam first needed and used fire. Earlier in the day,
thoroughout the Sabbath he had experienced natural light, provided
by God. But Saturday night he faced darkness. Yohanan in B claims
the blessing should also be said on the outgoing of the Day of
Atonement because fire then was not used. He evidently refers to
the practice of some localities not to leave the lights on in the
house on Yom Kippur, as mentioned in M. Pes. 4:4. The use of the
word "even" in Yohanan's remarks serves to imply that what he
includes, the first view has excluded.[394] Thus A-B make up a
dispute.

      Samuel's and Yohanan's comments form part of a wider *sugya*
which deals with the origin of fire. In PT, Samuel's comment is
cited as an *independent* statement that *glosses* the previous
material.[395] Two possibilities could account for this anomalous
situation. The pericope's editor joins A with the preceding
pericope by including the word, "therefore," LPYKK, as if the
previous material constitutes the reason for Samuel's rule--
despite the fact that Samuel's tradition itself contains a sufficient reason, "since it is the beginning of its creation."
Alternatively, the "therefore" is fundamental to the tradition,
and the reason included in A, "since it was the beginning of its
creation," is redundant and secondary. But the latter possibility
is precluded by chronological considerations. The relevant
preceding material is attributed to a R. Levi, a second-third-
generation Palestinian Amora.[396] Samuel could not have glossed

his comment.  Samuel's and Yohanan's comments thus are separate
from what precedes and the word "therefore" represents an editorial and transitional term to integrate the former with the latter.[397]

ii

The internal analysis of the *sugya* is confirmed by an
examination of Palestinian Midrashim which cite  the whole *sugya*
but lack  the bridging word, "therefore," LPYKK.[398]  We cite from
Pesiqta Rabbati and Gen. R. only Samuel's tradition:

> This follows Samuel, for Samuel says (ᵓTYᵓKŠMWᵓL
> DᵓMR ŠMWᵓL), Why do they say the blessing over the lamp at the
> outgoing of the Sabbath?  Because it is the beginning of its
> creation.

(Gen. R. #11, p. 89 = Pesiqta Rabbati,<br>#23, Friedman ed., p. 118b)[399]

The introductory language used in these Midrashim, "This
follows . . ."[400] is the normal y. formulation to cite a view or
statement to which a previous one is analogous.  None of the MSS
or medieval citations of PT, however, has this reading.  Nevertheless, this reading probably is primary.  This observation accords
with the theory which accounts for the differences between Gen. R.
and PT parallels.  The former used a recension of y. earlier than
the one presented in the PT.[401]  The "therefore" in A, accordingly,
is not original to Samuel's remarks.  On the other hand, the version in the Midrashim includes a question in its version, "Why
. . ."  We are unable to determine whether or not this is integral
to the tradition.  But the comment itself responds to the fact that
a blessing for fire is said Saturday night and in the context of
M. Ber. 8:5 it functions as an explanation of something assumed in
Mishnah.  Such explanations constitute an element intrinsic to a
commentary on a text and we can therefore understand why it appears
in the *Gemara* on M. Ber. 8:5.

iii

We now turn to the parallel in b. Pes. 53b-54a.

> A.  Said R. Judah said Samuel, They do not say the
> blessing over the fire (HᵓWR) except at the outgoing of the
> Sabbath, since (HWᵓYL W-) it is the beginning of its creation.
> B.  Said to him a certain elder and some say Rabba bar
> bar Hana [said the following], Right (YŠR), and similarly R.
> Yohanan said, Right.[402]

C.   Ulla was riding on an ass.   R. Abba was walking
on his right, and Rabba bar bar Hana on his left.

D.   Said R. Abba to Ulla, Is it true that you said in
the name of R. Yohanan, They do not say the blessing over the
fire except at the outgoing of the Sabbath, since it is the
beginning of its creation?

E.   He[403] looked askance at Rabba bar bar Hana.

F.   He said to him, I did not speak in reference to
that but in reference to the following:[404] For it was taught
(DTNY) before R. Yohanan, R. Simeon b. Eleazar says, Yom
Kippur that occurs on the Sabbath, even where they said not to
light candles, they light [candles] out of respect of the
Sabbath.

R. Yohanan[405] said after him, And the Sages forbid.

G.   He said to him, Verily.

. . .

H.   And they hold[406] according to this which said
(KY HᵓDᶜMR) R. Benjamin bar Yefet said R. Yohanan, They say
the blessing over the fire whether at the outgoing of the
Sabbath or whether at the outgoing of Yom Kippur.

And thus the people practice.

(b. Pes. 53b-54a)

The pericope presents us with a tradition of Samuel with
the attributive formula of "said R. Judah said Samuel."  Judah
transmits an explicit statement that the blessing over the fire is
said only Saturday night.  On the other hand, we find different
and contradictory opinions attributed to Yohanan.  According to B
and D, Yohanan agrees with Samuel.[407]  According to F, however,
Yohanan did not comment at all about a blessing over the fire.
Finally, according to H, he requires the blessing over the fire
at the conclusion of the Sabbath and of Yom Kippur.  The pericope
indicates that Samuel's view circulated autonomously and apart
from Yohanan's; indeed, Yohanan's opinion was known to various
degrees, and in different forms, and not by all circles.[408]

BT's pericope attests to the tradition of Samuel which PT
had cited.  BT and PT both include the same "reason": "since it
is the beginning of its creation."  BT thereby supports our contention that Samuel did not originally, as reported in y. Ber. 8:5,
12b, say his remarks as a gloss of someone else's statement.  In
addition, the exclusive nature of the tradition of Samuel in PT,
only implied by Yohanan's opening word "even," is confirmed here
by the wording of Samuel's own remark.  Nevertheless, one must

inquire which version may more accurately preserve Samuel's own
words.  PT's version, without the "therefore,"[409] is a simple
statement.  It explains why the blessing for fire is said Saturday
night.  The reason fits in well.  It is not presented in a dispute
form.  BT's version, transmitted by Judah, has the added words of
emphasis "one does not . . . except," ꝉYN . . . ꝉLꝉ . . . This
formulation argues that one says the blessing that night and not
another night.  The emphasis comes to exclude Yom Kippur.  But
Samuel's saying, if originally presented independently of other
amoraic views on the subject, probably originated as a discrete
statement with no intention to dispute an alternative position.
In addition, the clause, "since it is the beginning of its creation," is more of an explanation for the recitation of the blessing Saturday night than a reason for excluding it another night.
Just because the beginning of the creation of fire was on a Saturday night does not logically preclude that another night might
have a different reason for the same blessing.[410]  Accordingly,
the plain sense of the clause supports the authenticity of y.'s
version of Samuel's tradition (without the added "therefore").
Hence, we must attribute the added words of emphasis in b.'s version either to Judah or to the pericope's arranger.  As the tradition serves a purpose within b.'s context it undoubtedly was shaped
by redactional considerations.  Indeed, it appears in b. Pes. 53b-
54a due to the presence of Yohanan's traditions.  The latter's
ruling appropriately belongs there as part of a *Gemara* on M. Pes.
4:4, which focuses on lights in houses on Yom Kippur.

Thus both b. and y. attest to Samuel's comment concerning
the blessing for fire which is said Saturday night.  As M. Ber.
8:5 contains the only mishnaic reference to God's creation of
light and deals with light as part of *havdalah* Saturday night,
that Mishnah provides a fitting location for Samuel's comment.
Furthermore, the tradition provides information relevant to a
commentary on M. Ber. 8:5.

## 117 [and 118, 119], 120.

### M. Ber. 8:6B

They do not say the blessing over the lamp until they
enjoy (SYꝉWTW) its light.

(M. Ber. 8:6B)

[PT on M. Ber. 8:6B contains two traditions attributed
to Samuel.  One focuses on the reading of a word with a

possibly weakened guttural (B), and the other on the criterion
of the law (L). The former makes up the basic element of the
first part of a tripartite *sugya*. The *sugya* derives exegetical
implications from three such grammatical phenomena in Mishnah.][411]

A.   They do not say the blessing over the lamp until
they enjoy its light.  [= M. Ber. 8:6B.]

B.   Rav said, *yeoto* ($Y^{\supset}WTW$).  [= With an *alef*,]

And Samuel said, *yeoto* ($Y^{C}WTW$).  [= With an *ayin*,]

C.   The one who said, *yeoto* ($Y^{\supset}WTW$)--[may find support
in the verse:] "Only on this [condition] will we agree ($N^{\supset}WT$)
with you" (Gen. 34:15).  [Literally, "will it be fitting" or
"good for us." This rendering derives *yeoto* from a verb meaning "yielding enjoyment/satisfaction."]

The one who said, *yeoto* ($Y^{C}WTW$)--[may find support in
the verse:] "To know to help ($^{C}WT$) with a word the one who is
weary" (Is. 50:4).  [This rendering derives *yeoto* from a verb
meaning "to employ/use."][412]

D.   There we learnt, How do they extend the [Sabbath]
limits of cities? [= M. Eruv. 5:1.]

E.   Rav said, *Me$^{\supset}$abrin* ($M^{\supset}BRYN$).  [= With an *alef*.]

And Samuel said, *Me$^{C}$abrin* ($M^{C}BRYN$).  [= With an *ayin*.]

F.   The one who said, *Me$^{\supset}$abrin* ($M^{\supset}BRYN$)--[that is as
if] they add a limb ($^{\supset}BR$) to it.  [= This rendering takes
*me$^{\supset}$abrin* as "add."]

The one who said, *Me$^{C}$abrin* ($M^{C}BRYN$)--[that is] as a
woman who is pregnant ($^{C}WBRH$).  [= This rendering takes
*me$^{C}$abrin* as "increase."][413]

G.   There we learnt, Before the festivals ($^{C}DYHN$) of
the nations.  [= M. A.Z. 1:1.]

H.   Rav said,[414] *$^{\supset}$edehen* ($^{\supset}YDYHN$).  [- With an *alef*.
Many texts, however, have *$^{C}$edehen*, with an *ayin*.][415]

And Samuel said,[414] *$^{C}$edehen* ($^{C}YDYHN$).  [= With an *ayin*.
Many texts, however, have *$^{\supset}$edehen*, with an *alef*.][415]

I.   The One who said, *$^{\supset}$edehen*--[may find support in
the verse:] "For near is the day of their calamity ($^{\supset}YDM$)"
(Deut. 32:35).  [The word *$^{\supset}$ed*, meaning "festival," is pejora-
tively distorted and has the popular usage as "calamity."][416]

And the one who says *$^{C}$edehen*--[may find support in the
verse:] "Their testimonies neither see nor know, that they may
be put to shame" (Is. 44:9).  [Following a literary usage,
*$^{C}$edehen* is taken as "their witnesses."]

J.1.  How[417] does Samuel deal with the reason [= verse]
of Rav, "And their testimonies (W$^C$YDYHN) . . ." [Is. 44:9]?
[J.1. goes along with the variant reading in H that Rav said
$^c$edehen, with an ayin, and Samuel $^ɔ$edehen, with an alef.  But
this clause may constitute a secondary addition to the pericope.][418]

J.2.  --That they [= their idols] are destined to
embarrass those who serve them on the day of judgment.  [The
idols will give testimony ($^C$DWT) against them.  The citation
of Is. 44:9 fits the usage and perspective of $^c$edehen in M.
A.Z. 1:2 which lists different types of pagan festivals, viz.
these holidays in the future will bear witness against the
nations.][419]

K.  They do not say the blessing over the lamp until
they enjoy its light.  [= M. Ber. 8:6B.][420]

L.1.  R. Judah in the name of (BŠM) Samuel, Sufficient
that women spin by its light.

L.2.  Said R. Yohanan,[421] Sufficient that his eyes see
what is in the cup and what is in the plate.[422]

L.3.  Said R. Hanina [alt. = "Hinana"],[423] Sufficient
that one be able to distinguish between one coin and another
coin.

M.  Teaches (TNY) R. Hoshiah, Even [in a] triclinium
[= a large room][424] ten by ten [cubits].  That is, one need
not stand adjacent to the illumination.]

N.  R. Ze$^C$ira . . .[425]

(y. Ber. 8:6, 12c [A-J = y. Eruv. 5:1,
22b.  A-I = y. A.Z. 1:2, 39c])


i

M. Ber. 8:6B defines when one may say the blessing over
the lamp, that is the fire, in havdalah.  Samual responds to two
aspects of the definition.  He focuses on a textual problem in
the word "enjoy" (Y$^ɔ$WTW) and on the indefiniteness of the criterion.[426]  We first analyze the former comment (B) and its context
(A-J) and then turn to the latter one.


ii

A-J presents three separate disputes between Rav and
Samuel as to the proper spelling of a word in three different
mishnayot.  Due to the weakening of the gutturals alef and ayin,
their pronunciation was not distinguished.[427]  As indicated by the

presence of pericopae in y. Ber. and b. and y. Eruv. and A.Z.,
Amoraim at a relatively early period associated these linguistic
observations with different interpretations of Mishnah.  The
Amoraim suggested the variations in spelling reflected different
verbal roots and therefore different meanings in the words.  B
thus does not necessarily presume different understandings of
Mishnah while C does.[428]

The set of three pericopae appear in y. in each of the
three locations and, as indicated, have analogues in b.  In each
y. *sugya* the portion relevant to the location appropriately opens
the *sugya*.  The three units have thus been integrated into a single
*sugya*.  They consist of a citation of Mishnah (A, D, G), the
opinions of Rav and Samuel (B, E, H), and later supportive or
clarifying comments on the opinions (C, F, I), which in two cases
present parallel biblical usage (C, I).  The third pericope--in
y. Ber. and in some texts of y. Eruv--includes a response to one
of the proof texts and thereby support for the other position (J).
As the question and answer in J break the pattern of A-J and does
not appear in all locations, not even in its assumably primary
context in y. A.Z., it probably postdates the *sugya*'s basic
rubric.  Accordingly, J.2 could even convey the meaning of the
verse in the second opinion in I.[429]

Other than for J, the three pericopae employ similar
patterned phrasing.  From the point of view of this formulation,
the *sugya* may have originated as a whole in one place, and a later
hand transferred it to the several locations and placed the
appropriate part first.[430]  But the masters must have observed
the problematic nature of each word with the *alef* or *ayin* and
discretely responded with remarks on each Mishnah.  Each such
response would form part of a commentary to each text.  On the
other hand, in addressing problems like these a master theoretically could respond to the linguistic-textual problem in terms of
the phenomenon as a whole, and formulate his remarks in the context
of one instance and word them in terms of them all.  But in that
case the comments would be presented as a unit and not in three
parts, as we find them in y. Ber. 8:6.  In any event, however a
master formulated his thought, his observation would belong to a
commentary on each text.  Moreover, as Lieberman has pointed
out,[431] the two different interpretations of *edehen*, based upon
the use of an *alef* or an *ayin*, probably arose in different
contexts.  M. A.Z. 1:1 proscribes certain types of transactions
with gentiles three days before their festivals, and M. A.Z. 1:2

lists pagan holidays.  The notion that the festival constitutes
a calamity fits the former context while that of a witness against
the worhipers fits the latter.  Each of the festivals in 1:2 can
provide testimony.  This observation suggests that those who drew
implications from the orthographic variations separately focused
upon each instance of the item in Mishnah.  If so, we have an
example in which an initial commentary and interpretation of that
commentary grew into the larger whole of *Gemara*.


iii


       Samuel's second tradition makes up one of three opinions
along with a *baraita* which define the minimum use of the lamp so
as to enable one to say the benediction over it.  While Judah is
the tradent, in B, Zeira may have played a role in the transmission of the tradition to Palestine.  He has a conspicuous place
within the larger context.  The first pericope on M. Ber. 8:6B,
not presented above, is attributed to Zeira and by implication
rules that one must use the light before one may say the blessing
over it.  In N, a narrative, Zeira appears in the final pericope
on this clause of Mishnah.  He draws the light close, an action
that students challenge through the citation of a *baraita* which is
attributed to Hoshiah and which is identical to the one in line
M.[432]
       The three traditions, L. 1-3, employ a similar pattern.
Each assumes a subject and glosses it with a definition formulated
in terms of an amount of activity.  As each one deals with the
ability to see or distinguish something, the subject must involve
illumination.  The three, therefore, appropriately appear as comments on M. Ber. 8:6B.  In contrast, while Hoshiah's *baraita* in M
also glosses a text, it opens with the word "Even."  This formulation serves to extend the rule of antecedent text.[433]  The forms
of the comments accord with the nature of the definitions.  The
three activities in L. 1-3 progressively require an increasing
amount of light.  Distinguishing the contents of plates requires
more illumination than spinning, but both of these need less light
than distinguishing between coins which may differ only in their
stamp.  M, on the other hand, requires that one see the light
within the room even if it is a large room ten by ten cubits.[434]
M thus implicitly rejects the principle of amount of light which
might suffice for a given activity.[435]

iv

Samuel thus tried to set the correct orthography of
Mishnah as well as to define its general principle.  In the former
instance another Babylonian, Rav, likewise believed it necessary
to comment, and in the latter he is joined by Palestinians and
Babylonians.[436]  T. Ber. 5:31 contains a *baraita* which rules that
one must see and use the light.  That text indicates that the rule
in M. Ber. 8:6B naturally elicits comments.  In L Samuel does so
and concretizes Mishnah's rule.[437]

121.

## M. Ber. 8:7

A'.  [As to] whoever ate and forgot to say the blessing [of Grace After Meals]--

The House of Shammai say, He should return to his
place and say the blessing [of Grace].

And the House of Hillel say, He should say the blessing [of Grace] in the place where he remembers.

B'.1.  And until when ($^C$D MTY) [after eating] does he
say the blessing [of Grace]?

B'.2.  Until the food in his bowels is digested.
(M. Ber. 8:7)

A.  Until when does he say the blessing [of Grace]?

Until the food in his stomach is digested.  [= M. Ber.
8:7.]

B.  R. Hiyya[438] in the name of (BŠM) Samuel, As long
as (KL ZMN Š-) he is thirsty from that meal.[439]

R. Yohanan said, Until[440] ($^C$D Š-) he becomes hungry.
(y. Ber. 8:7, 12c)

PT 8:7, like b. Ber. 53b, contains traditions which focus
on Mishnah's definition of the duration of one's liability to say
Grace (B' of Mishnah).  The two traditions in B of y. provide
glosses which, for comprehension, require either an introductory
question or text.  B'.1 of Mishnah, "Until when does he say the
blessing [for Grace]?", constitutes such a question.

The comments attributed to Samuel and Yohanan do not make
up a balanced dispute form.  In such a form, Yohanan's tradition
would have employed the formulation, "*As long as* he is *not*
hungry."[441]  The latter is not just a theoretical possibility, for
such a wording is attested by b.'s version of Yohanan's teaching
which reads:

> What is the measure of digestion?
> Said R. Yoḥanan, As long as he is not hungry.[442]
>                     (b. Ber. 53b)

Accordingly, Samuel's comment does not form an integral unit with
Yoḥanan's but may circulate alone without it.

Samuel's and Yoḥanan's criteria in effect replace those of
Mishnah. While one might, therefore, suggest that they dispute
Mishnah,[443] they actually concretize its standard and thus make up
a common type of gloss to a definition in Mishnah. People normally
do not know when their food is digested. On the other hand, they
readily know when they lose their thirst or become hungry again.[444]
Nevertheless, the two concrete measures may differ. Commentators
suggest that Yoḥanan prescribes a longer time than Samuel.[445] If
true, that is still not inconsistent with the fact that both masters interpret and define the same norm in Mishnah. Samuel thus
glosses Mishnah with a concrete definition. In the process of
refining Mishnah's definition, from a practical point of view he
replaces it. For, considering the place of the introductory question in Mishnah, clause B'.1, Samuel's comment could circulate as
part of Mishnah and as an answer to that question.

122.

## M. Ber. 8:8B

They respond "Amen" after an Israelite who says a
blessing.

And they do not respond "Amen" after a Samaritan who
says a blessing--until one hears the whole blessing.
                    (M. Ber. 8:8B)[446]

A. *Samuel asked Rav*, "Should a person respond "Amen"
after school children?

| B. [Venice, M and Flr MSS:[447]] | B'. [P MS and citations:[448]] |
|---|---|
| He [= Rav] said to Him, After every one they respond "Amen," except [after] school children,[449] as they [= the blessings] are said [literally "done"] for study. | He said to him, They do not respond ["Amen"]. It was taught likewise, After every one they respond "Amen" except [after] school children as they [= the blessings] are said for study.[450] |

C'. And in these situations, . . .
                    (b. Ber. 53b)

M. Ber. 8:8 rules as to one's responsibility to say "Amen" so as to affirm another person's blessing.  One must hear the full blessing of the Samaritan to insure that he has not changed the liturgical text or pattern of the blessing.[451]  Samuel's comment forms part of a narrative which focuses on the extent of Mishnah's general rule.

A represents Samuel as a questioner of Rav.  We have two versions of the response, in B.  One version provides Rav with an answer formulated as an autonomous tradition which for comprehension does not need Samuel's question.  The second version presents Rav's answer in the form of a reply.  It constitutes an incomplete sentence.  A complete statement, on the other hand, appears as an autonomous tradition and is formulated as a *baraita*.  It is difficult to know which version is original, though it is more logical to assume that the first one generated the second rather than vice versa.  The latter one may represent a reformulation of the teaching as a general principle for *halakhic* purposes.[452]

The pericope indicates that Samuel focused upon the principle behind M. Ber. 8:8B and inquired into the extent of its rule. His interest constitutes a concern which we would expect to find in a commentary.[453]

### 9.  *Berakhot Chapter Nine*

125.

#### M. Ber. 9:1

Whoever sees a place where miracles were wrought for Israel--says, "Blessed who wrought miracles for our ancestors in this place."

(M. Ber. 9:1A)

Rav said, [A person] has to say "Thou" ('TH).
And Samuel said, [A person"

| [L MS:] does not have to say "Thou."[454] | [V and S MSS and many citations:] has to say "Our God."[455] |

(y. Ber. 9:1, 12d)

i

M. Berakhot chapter nine focuses on private prayers.  M. 9:1 deals with the response to the site of a divine miracle.  The experience should lead one to thank and praise God.  Mishnah provides a text of the blessing.  It opens with the word "Blessed"

and then mentions the subject.  The benediction lacks a full
liturgical opening formula.  Rabbis applied such formulae, e.g.,
"Blessed art Thou, king of the universe, who . . ." to public
mandatory prayers.  Later masters discussed if, and to what degree,
such norms should apply to voluntary and private mandatory prayers,
especially those which involve praise and thanks.[456]  Passages
like M. Ber. 9:1 provided insufficient guidelines, as the style of
Mishnah and Tosefta to provide only part of the liturgical text
left room for later divergent interpretations.[457]  Samuel's
comment in y. Ber. 9:1 consitutes an instance of this concern for
the proper liturgical pattern.[458]

Rav requires in the benediction the use of the word "Thou,"
while Samuel does not.  The first version expresses this through
the negation of Rav's comment, and the second version through a
statement of an alternative requirement.  By implication, if one
has to say, "our God . . . ," one does not have to say "Thou."[459]

ii

We can understand the import of the dispute once we appreciate the history of the liturgy as well as the forms and referent
of the comments.

The two opinions follow an identical pattern except for
the negative in the first version of Samuel's comment.  They do
not actually make up a dispute form.  A statement of the disputed
issue does not precede the traditions nor is it incorporated into
the first opinion.  Moreover, the comments do not make their
referent explicit; it must be learned from the wider context and
the assumed possible applications of the words "Thou" and "Our
God."  Each item thus shares affinities with a gloss and could
independently be tacked onto an earlier text, e.g., Mishnah.
While the traditions might refer to the opening formula of all
blessings, their presence in this *Gemara* on M. Ber. 9:1 is especially appropriate.  They focus on a question integral to that
Mishnah,[460] for as pointed out above, M. Ber. 9:1 lacks a full
text of the blessing; it is unclear whether or not this merely
follows the common Mishnah practice.  Indeed medieval legal authorities debated this very issue in the context of M. Ber. 9:1.[461]
But the appropriateness of the issue disputed emerges also in
light of the history of the blessing formulae.

The common biblical benediction pattern which refers in
the third person to God appears in the context of a response to a
divine manifestation or wondrous act.  For example, "'Blessed be

the Lord," Jethro said, 'who delivered you from the Egyptians and
from Pharoah, and who delivered the people from under the hand of
the Egyptians . . .'" (Ex. 18:10).[462]

Scholars have noted the two biblical instances of the
"Thou" formula, its use in the DSS, and its role as a pattern to
close rabbinic benedictions.  They discuss how the "Thou" pattern
in the rabbinic opening formula became combined with a specific
praise of God formulated in the third person, and they evaluate
the relationship of the closing formula to that of the opening
formula.[463]  Heinemann has decisively demonstrated that *the
"combined" opening pattern*, with the "Thou" pattern in the second
person and then the reference to God in the third person, *regularly
appears only in public mandatory blessings.*[464]  *Accordingly, if
the pattern without the "Thou," in its biblical precedent, appears
as a response to divine wondrous acts, one can understand why
masters might conclude that this pattern suffices for contemporary
expressions of this experience.*  Samuel apparently followed this
biblical precedent and, according to both versions, did not require
the "Thou."  As a result, non-normative patterns which rabbis could
not exclude from popular usage, remained not only current, but
acceptable, to rabbinic circles.  On the other hand, the position
attributed to Rav evidently claimed that the general pattern with
the "Thou," chosen as the standard, should apply also here.[465]

We remain unsure if the dispute originated in the context
of M. Ber. 9:1 or if it deals with opening formulae in general.
In terms of its surrounding pericopae, the latter would seem to be
the case.  The preceding tradition speaks of "all blessings," and
the following one narrates an incident of community prayer.[466]
Yet, as argued above, the assignment of the dispute to the *Gemara*
on M. Ber. 9:1 remains especially appropriate.  Accordingly, we
may deal with the application of a general tradition to this
specific case, and, if so, the text provides an example of one way
in which *Gemara* developed.  What one generation or circle may have
considered subject to dispute--here prayer formula in general--
another did not.  Consequently, the latter applies the dispute to
a more refined issue--seeing the site of a miracle.[467]

126, 127a, b (,c), 128a (,b), 129.

## M. Ber. 9:2

1.  Over [= upon seeing] *ziqim* [literally, "sparks" =
a coment or meteor], and over earthquakes, and over lightning,
and over *reamim* [= thunder], and over tempests--He says,
"Blessed [. . .] whose strength fills the world."

2.  Over mountains, and over hills, and over seas, and
over rivers, and over deserts--He says, "Blessed [. . .] Maker
of creation."

R. Judah said, Whoever sees the Great Sea says,
"Blessed [. . .] who makes the Great Sea"--when he sees it at
intervals.

3.  Over rain and over good tidings--He says, "Blessed
[. . .] who is good and does good."

And over bad tidings--He says, "Blessed [. . .] the
true judge."[468]

(M. Ber. 9:2)

[Samuel's comments deal with *"ziqim," "reamim,"* and
"rain," and we separately present and analyze the traditions
on each one.]

A.  What is *Ziqin?*

B.  Said Samuel,[469] *kokhba deshevit*[470] [or *deshavet*]
(KWKB$^{\circ}$ DŠBYT) [= "shooting star," i.e., "meteor" or "comet"].

C.1.  And said Samuel,

C.2.  I am as familiar with the paths of the firmament[471] as with the paths of Nehardea--

C.3.  Except for *kokhba deshevit*, which I do not know
what it is,

C.4.  though I have learnt that it does not pass
through the constellation of Orion (KSL$^{\circ}$).[472]

and if it passes through Orion, it destroys the world.

D.  And lo, we see that it passes through [Orion]?

E.  Its brightness passes through and it appears as
if it itself passes through.[473]

(b. Ber. 58b)

F.  Over *ziqim.*[474]

G.  Samuel said, If this[475] *ziqa*[476] passes through
Orion, it will destroy the world.

H.  They challenged Samuel, And we saw it pass through.

I.  He said to them, It is not possible.[477]  It either
[passed] above it or below it.

J.1.  Samuel said, I am as familiar with the alleys
of the heavens[478] as with the alleys of Nehardea my city--[479]

J.2.  Except for this[475] *ziqa*, which I do not know what
it is.[480]

(y. Ber. 9:2, 13c)

i

Mishnah prescribes a specific blessing for the sighting
of one of the occasional, natural occurrences of divine power in
the world.  Even these "normal" experiences involve an experience
of the divine.  The blessing makes one especially conscious of
that fact and enables a person to generalize that experience so
as to offer praise to God.[481]

In the b. and y. *Gemarot* on M. Ber. 9:2A several analogous
traditions attributed to Samuel focus on the item *ziqim*.  B of b.
renders the word *ziqim* with the brief definition of *kokhba
deshevita*.  While post-talmudic commentaries are divided in their
explanation of the latter term, Samuel apparently refers to a
shooting star, i.e., a meteor, or a comet.[482]  In C, Samuel makes
a general claim as to his astronomical knowledge.  That statement
appears here due to its second half, C.3-4, which refers to *kokhba
deshevita*.

Samuel's lack of familiarity with the characteristics of a
meteor or a comet, C.3, is understandable.  Meteors are items
which do not maintain an orbit but rather vaporize within the
earth's atmosphere, though at times not completely; it is these
remnants which then strike the earth as meteorites.  Comets have
very elongated orbits.  The elliptical ones lack periodic orbits
or have orbits with periods so long that we lack records of their
reappearance.[483]  Nevertheless, despite his ignorance as to the
nature of *kokhba deshevita*, according to C.4 Samuel had learned
that a path through Orion would yield disaster.[484]

PT's analogue is also on M. Ber. 9:2A and though it lacks
an actual definition of *ziqim*, it serves as a commentary to
Mishnah's referent to *ziqim*.[485]  Likewise, the content of the
*sugya* closely matches BT, though it follows a different sequence.

PT's *sugya* is in two parts.  First comes Samuel's comment
on the impending danger if *ziqa* does pass through Orion.  The
tradition employs not BT's phrase, *kokhba deshevita*, but the word
*ziqa*, common in various Aramaic dialects as a shooting star.
Here it serves as an equivalent of Mishnah's Hebrew word *ziqim*.
This is understandable as PT did not introduce the term *kokhba
deshevita* as a definition of *ziqim*.  Samuel, as in BT, follows
with a response to a challenge (H, I).  The b. and y. versions of
his response substantively agree.  The challengers' misconception
is visual.  In the second part of the *sugya*, J, Samuel makes a
general observation as to his astronomical knowledge, which is
limited concerning *ziqa*.

BT, on the other hand, consists of three parts, a definition of *ziqim*, B; Samuel's claim as to his astronomical knowledge
except for *kokhba deshevita* (comet), C.1-3; and, as a continuation
of the second item, Samuel's comment as to the danger of a comet's
path through Orion, C.4.  This claim is challenged and defended,
D-E.  Given PT's lack of the definition, we can understand why it
opens with the observation on *ziqa* in Orion.  *Gemara* had to open
with a comment directly on Mishnah's *ziqim* and not with a general
observation.  We do not know, however, why BT and not PT presented
Samuel's definition.

ii

Samuel thus defines a term in M.  BT presents a direct
definition of the term *ziqim*, while PT offers an astronomical
observation on the danger of that item, *ziqim*, and thereby, by
implication, identifies *ziqim*.  Samuel's comment was remembered
and transmitted along with additional remarks which defend his
astronomical traditions.  Considering the similarity between the
comments on the comet in Orion and between the questions and
answers, the pericope must have taken shape at a relatively early
date.[486]  This indicates the degree to which those early generations who transmitted the materials perceived the extent and
exactness of Samuel's astronomical knowledge.  The early material,
however, was adapted.  PT, which lacked the formal definition of
*ziqim*, reshaped the danger-comment so that the pericope would open
with a Mishnah-related item.  Furthermore, the reason both b. and
y. included a statement of Samuel's astronomical knowledge was not
for the information the comment originally intended to convey, but
rather for its aid in understanding the Mishnah and its themes.[487]

We may gain an additional insight into an early stage of
the tradition as a result of the analysis of J. N. Epstein.[488]  He
argues that Mishnah originally lacked the term *ruhot*, which we
have translated as "tempests," and that the word *ziqim* means
"winds."  The latter usage is known in Aramaic and other Semitic
languages and in rabbinic literature elsewhere.[489]  Epstein demonstrates that though the word *ruhot* is not integral to the Mishnah,
once it entered the text it prevented commentators from identifying
*ziqim* with "winds."[490]  If Epstein is correct, the thrust of
Samuel's comment lies in defining *ziqim* as an astronomical phenomenon.  Moreover, Samuel may have understood the term in this way
due to not only the usage elsewhere but also a personal predilection, shaped by his astronomical interests.

132.

<u>132.</u>

### [M. Ber. 9:2]

A.   And over *reamim* [usually rendered as "thunder].
[= M. Ber. 9:2.]

B.   What is *reamim*?

C.   Said Samuel, *Clouds joining in a circle* [i.e.,
*reamim* = a "whirlwind"; alternative, the noise of thunder
caused by clouds joining].

as it is said, "The sound of Thy *reamim* in the whirlwind, the lightning illuminating the world, the earth trembled
and shook" (Ps. 77:19).[491]

D.   Rav [alternatively "Rabbis'][492] said, *Clouds that
throw water into one another,*[492]

as it is said, "When he makes his voice heard, there
is a rumbling of water in the skies" (Jer. 10:13).

E.   R. Aha bar Yaaqov said, *A powerful lightning that
flashes in the clouds and breaks hailstones.*[493]

F.   R. Ashi said, *Clouds become puffed up and a wind
comes and blows across them and it* [= the noise] *appears like
a wind* [which blows] *across a jar.*[494]

G.   *And it makes sense according to R. Aha bar Yaaqov,
for the lightning flashes, the clouds rumble, and rain
comes.*[495]

### (b. Ber. 59a)

Mishnah 9:2 includes *reamim* as one of the items which
elicit a blessing.  An anonymous question introduces a series of
definitions of this term.  As elsewhere, the question probably
postdates the traditions.

While the word *reamim* is generally rendered as "thunder,"
we can understand why someone might define it as some other type
of heavenly noise.  First, a similar root means "rumbling."
Secondly, there are biblical instances of *reamim* which do not
precede or appear in the context of rain.[496]  For sure, though,
elsewhere in tannaitic literature, e.g., T. Shab. 6:19, p. 25,
l. 42, *reamim* is coupled with lightning and the context definitely
proves that the former word means thunder.[497]  In M. Ber. 9:2, the
latter two items are joined with other divine manifestations.

The comments of Samuel and Rav (or "rabbis"), C-D, employ
a similar structure.  Both open with the word "clouds," and both
are followed with a verse which associates "clouds" and "noise"
with some kind of natural phenomena.  They thus are formulated as

a gloss along with a biblical proof text.  E-F presents additional
explanations.  G supports E as it receives confirmation from the
common observation of nature.[496]

Mishnah provides the context for these amoraic comments on
*reamim*.  Samuel and the others use their familiarity with natural
science to focus on the item in Mishnah.  Alternatively, the
editor of the pericope or of one or more of the explanations,
applied the traditions, formulated originally in another context,
to M. Ber. 9:2's mention of *reamim*.  The type of comment, though,
properly fits into a Mishnah commentary.  If Samuel defines *reamim*
as the whirlwind, he offers a standard definition of a word.  If he
explains the cause of the noise of thunder, he offers a regular,
though less usual, explanation of a phenomenon mentioned in Mishnah.  While such natural scientific information is not always
elicited by Mishnah, it is not foreign to a Mishnah commentary.
In addition, Jewish and non-Jewish late antique sources indicate
that people discussed the nature of *reamim* or thunder.  Gen. R.
12.1, Theodore and Albeck, ed., p. 97, contains a tradition which
is attributed to Huna and which in effect claims that people did
not fathom the course of *reamim*.[499]  Pliny devotes space in his
*Natural History* to a discussion of the types and nature of thunder
as well as of winds.[500]  Accordingly, it is appropriate to find a
discussion on *reamim* and given Samuel's interest in natural science
we should not be surprised to find his thought on the matter
formulated as a gloss or tradition directly on M. Ber. 9:2.
Moreover, since the meaning of *reamim* was subject to doubt, we
can understand why a master would cite a biblical verse to support
an interpretation.  The verse thus provides evidence for the
usage.

134.

### [M. Ber. 9:2]

[Over rain and good tidings--He says, "Blessed [is
He] who is good and does good (HTWB WHMTYB)."]
(M. Ber. 9:2C)

A.  And how much rain must fall so that a person will
have to bless [the benediction over rain].
B.  R. Hiyya in the name of R. Yohanan,
In the beginning (KTHYLH) [= Before any rain][501]--
sufficient for fructification (KDY RBY^CH);
and afterwards (BSWP)--sufficient to rinse off the
shutters [on a roof].[502]

C.   R. Yannai bar Ishmael in the name of R. Simeon b. Laqish,[503]

in the beginning--sufficient for fructification;

and afterwards--sufficient to soak [alternatively, "to dissolve"] the stopper.[504]

D.   And does a stopper become soaked [alternatively, "dissolved"]?   Rather [it means] we consider it as if it [the mud] would be able to form a stopper [alternatively, "would dissolve"].[505]

E.   R. Yose in the name of R. Judah, And R. Yonah and R. Judah in the name of Samuel,

in the beginning--sufficient for fructification;

and afterwards--even any amount (ᵓPYLW KL ŠHWᵓ).

(y. Ber. 9:3, 13d-14a = y. Taan. 1:3,
64a-b = Gen. R. 13.13, pp. 122-123,
in sequence of A, E, B, C, D)

Mishnah includes rain in its list of phenomena which elicit praise of God, as rain is a universal bounty and a basic necessity.   The land of Israel, in particular, relied upon rain for its water resources, and droughts had the potential to cripple the country.[506]

Samuel's comment defines when one should say the blessing. His comment appears in y. as the third of three explanations, and in Genesis Rabba, as the first of the three.   The pericope opens with an introductory question, A.   B, C (clarified in D), and E provide the three answers and presumably indicate what represents the "good" which God brings.   Each of the three employs a similar two-part structure, "in the beginning . . . afterwards . . . (KTHYLH . . . BSWP . . .)."

While commentators differ as to the exact meaning of these time periods, the first refers apparently to a stage prior to any rain or to the period of the first rain, and the second to the time after the rainfall.[507]   All three opinions agree as to the first criterion.   People initially bless God for rain when it suffices to satiate the ground.   The masters' common use of the phrase, "sufficient for fructification," KDY RBYᶜH, reflects an assumed definition of this term.   Such a definition is supplied in a *baraita* found in T. Taan. 1:4 and in a slightly variant version elsewhere in the *sugya* in y. and Gen. R.[508]   The *baraita* offers several definitions of the criterion.

The three opinions differ, however, as to the "afterwards," BSWP, situation.   Yohanan and Simeon b. Laqish, in B and C (and D), require a substantive amount of rain,[509] while Samuel, in E, requires a minimal amount.   This may reflect the latter's

geographical location in Babylonia.  There the Tigris and
Euphrates provided the source for water.  Once rain appeared early
in the year, the rivers supplied sufficient water.  Perhaps any
subsequent rain, accordingly, had a positive impact and was especially appreciated.[510]  On the other hand, in the land of Israel,
which stored up less water, people to a greater degree depended
directly on the rain.  Consequently, people would need a substan-
tial amount of rain to experience a "good" or a bounty.[511]

Samuel's comment undoubtedly did not originate as part of
a tripartite dispute--surely not with two Palestinians.  Judah
transmits the tradition and Yonah cites it.  Yonah may emphasize
that Judah transmits it not in his own name but in that of Samuel.[512]  In addition, the tradition in form differs from the other
two.  The distinctive element of Samuel's comment, the second
part, employs the preposition, "even."  This word serves to extend
the principle of Mishnah or, tacitly, to differ with a more
restricted view, as in the other masters' traditions.[513]  "Even,"
accordingly, either glosses Mishnah or responds to the other comments; in either case Samuel's tradition functions differently
from the latter two.  The use of the overall similar structure,
however, may indicate that his tradition has been shaped to fit
the pattern of the other teachings.  If so, it may have originally
responded directly to Mishnah, supplied a criterion to Mishnah's
undefined referents, and thereby provided information integral to
a commentary.

### 135, 136 [and 137].

#### M. Ber. 9:3A

[One who] built a new house or bought new utensils
(KLYM)--says the blessing, "Blessed [. . .] who brought us[514]
to this time."

(M. Ber. 9:3A)

A.  *Misvot*--when does one say a blessing over them?

B.  R. Yohanan says, Before (ᶜWBR) doing them.

C.  R. Huna says, While doing them.[515]

D.1.  R. Huna accords with Samuel,

D.2.  For said R. Yose b. R. Bun in the name of
Samuel, All *misvot* require a blessing while doing them,

D.3.  except for blowing [the *shofar*] and immersion
[in *miqvah*].[516]

E.  And some say ["even" = S and V MSS][517] sanctification [of marriage] through intercourse.

F.   Said R. Yonah, there is another, *tefillin* . . .
[= attests the principle in C].[518]
(y. Ber. 9:3, 14a)

G.   (*For*) said R. Judah said Samuel, All the *misvot*
one says a blessing over them before (*CWBR*) one does them.

H.   *How do we know that the word CWBR means "before"?*

I.   . . . [exegetical answers for H].

J.   The disciple circle of Rav says, Except for immersion and *shofar*.

K.   As to immersion, *it is understandable, for the
person is not fit, but what is the reason for shofar? . . .*

L.   Rather said R. Hisda, "Except for immersion" only
[= the sole exception to G].
(b. Pes. 7b)[519]

i

Y. Ber. 9:3, 14a, and b. Pes. 7b present a tradition of
Samuel on the saying of blessings.  In y. the *sugya* as a whole
focuses on this problem and introduces A-F as an extension of the
subject.  The issue is relevant to M. Ber. 9 as that chapter deals
with special blessings said on special occasions.  T. Berakhot in
its structural analogue to chapter nine, like y. Ber. 9:3, devotes
space to this problem.  T. Ber. 6:9 opens with a general principle,
and then provides a series of examples.  Some involve making and
using an object and others doing something to an existent object.
At times, Tosefta comments as to the frequency of the blessing's
recitation.  For example:

One who does all the *misvot*--says a blessing over them.

One who makes a *sukkah* for himself--says, "Blessed
[. . .] who brought us to this time."

[When] one enters to reside in it--one says, "Blessed
[. . .] who sanctified us with his commandments and commanded
us to reside in a *sukkah*."

Once he said the blessing over it the first day--he no
longer has to say a blessing [over it].
(T. Ber. 6:9, p. 36, ls. 49-51)

Tosefta applies the first of the above blessings, the one mentioned in M. Ber. 9:3A, to five additional cases in which one
prepares oneself or an object for a *misvah*.  It prescribes a
second blessing, tailored to the particular act, to be said while
doing the *misvah*.  Tosefta thus indicates that the subject of

blessings and the frequency of their recitation appropriately
supplement M. Ber. chapter nine.[520]

In b. Pes. 7b, the larger *sugya* does not deal with the
general issue of blessings. Rather, it focuses on the blessing
said when one searches for leavened bread, a rule integral to
Passover.[521] Samuel's principle assumably would apply to this
latter case.


ii


The two traditions, D.2 and G, not only appear in different contexts but also contradict each other. A careful examination of the materials may throw light on this inconsistency. In
y., Yohanan and Huna address the general principle and they dispute. The first claims a blessing precedes the performance of the
act, perhaps to help one prepare for it and to shape one's experience by doing it. The latter requires the blessing and act to be
simultaneous, evidently avering that the words and the act influence each other and make up an integral unit. *Gemara* cites
Samuel's view which accords with Huna's. As Huna studied with
Samuel, it is understandable that they share the same position.
Yonah, in F, apparently attests Samuel's opinion. D.3 presents
exceptions which make sense. One is physically unable to recite
a blessing while one blows a *shofar* or immerses oneself in water.
These caveats may be fundamental to the tradition or additions,
added by the tradent, i.e., Yose b. R. Bun.

In the b. Pes. version, the authority who cites Samuel's
rule, G, does not spell out its connection with what precedes.
The tradition is thus not shaped specifically to address Passover.
As in y., we find an exception, J, here attribted to the
disciple circle of Rav.[522] The exception is formulated as a gloss
and depends upon its referent for comprehension. Accordingly, J
assumes the existence of the tradition, but it does not attest
the tradition's formulation. As we have seen elsewhere, the
referent of a gloss can be shifted; in the process of transmission
a gloss may be presented on a version of the materials different
from that on which it originated.[523] This observation becomes
important due to the presence of several versions of the tradition and the question in K. As Yellin and Rabinovitz point out,
the difficulty posed by J as an exception applies only to *bavli*'s
version of Samuel, G. It would not, however, apply if J glossed
y.'s version of Samuel's tradition. If this in fact represents
the original state of the materials, we would not have to impose

a difficult rendering onto J.  Consequently, it is possible that
y.'s version may have circulated in the disciple circle of Rav and
it is that version which they glossed but for whatever reason the
gloss later became associated with the wrong version.[524]

    We find support for our suggestion from a third but
related Samuel tradition:

>    M.  Said R. Samuel bar Bidri said Rav; And some way it
>  [thus]: Said R. Aba Arika said R. Huna; And some say it [thus]:
>  Said R. Menashia [bar Yermiah] said Samuel,
>    *tefillin*--from whence does a person say a blessing over
>  them?  From the time of putting them on (MŠ$^C$T HNHTN).
>    N.  Really.  And lo, said R. Judah said Samuel, All
>  the *misvot*--one blesses over them before ($^C$WBR) one does them.
>    O.  Abaye and Rava both said, From the time of putting
>  them on--and until one ties them.[525]
>                  (b. Menahot 35b)

The third tradition, in M, has several attributions.  Since it is
challenged by citing the tradition in N, which we are familiar
with from G, the proposed contradiction attests the assignment to
Samuel.

    *Gemara* perceives an inconsistency between M and N (= G).
If one assumes this contradiction, M must refer to a time other
than "before one does" the action.  Even O's harmonization and in
effect revision of M does not prescribe a time "before one does"
the *misvah*.  But while the principle in M does not accord with N
(= G), it does accord with Samuel's tradition in y. Ber. 9:3,
line D.2.  M may, therefore, assume that principle, i.e., that one
says a blessing while performing the *misvah*.  Hence, b. Men. 35b
indicates that the principle in N (= G) does not represent the
only version of Samuel's position known in Babylonia and that it
is plausible that the version in D.2 may have been known in Babylonia.  Accordingly, the latter version may make up the text known
to the *be Rav* circle and referred to in J.[526]


                                iii

    Mishnah provides the context for teachings on subjects
related to its theme and principles.  In y., the pericope is
initially structured around Huna's and Yohanan's comments.  They
are presented as if directly addressing a topic relevant to M.
Ber. 9:3, when is the blessing to be said.  An anonymous author
cites Samuel's teaching as it accords with Huna's tradition.

Samuel's tradition employs Huna's phraising, "while doing them."
But it does not directly gloss or explain Mishnah and is not
formulated as a direct commentary.  Nevertheless, it does supplement Mishnah.  As evidenced by the example of Tosefta, such independently formulated, supplementary materials can find an appropriate place in a Mishnah commentary.  For toseftan pericopae
which supplement Mishnah employ literary forms different from
Mishnah and often are presented in discrete groupings within
Tosefta.  From a literary perspective, therefore, Tosefta again
sets a paradigm for the contents of *Gemara* and early amoraic
teaching.[527]

       Although Tosefta and Samuel's comments employ a similar
literary pattern, they differ in function.  The concern of Tosefta
is close to that of Mishnah.  It is to rule that the several phenomena and actions require blessings.  Its contribution lies in
delineating additional examples or stages in the performance of a
*miṣvah* which requires a blessing.  Hence Tosefta mentions blessings
in addition to those in Mishnah.  Since it refers to two types of
blessings, it must indicate when, in general, each applies.  But
it does not explicitly focus upon the moment at which the blessing
is recited, though one can try to deduce it from the formulation
of the rules.  On the other hand, Samuel's tradition addresses
this issue.  His concern assumes Mishnah's and Tosefta's point
that a liability exists.  He wants to provide a practical guide
to apply that principle.  While we cannot be sure which version of
Samuel's teaching is fundamental, both preclude reciting a blessing after the action and both are formulated as a comprehensive
principle.  As in the earlier teaching on "rain," Samuel's comment
deals with a pragmatic concern central to commentary on a work
like Mishnah.  Precisely when does one say the blessing?[528]

140.

## M. Ber. 9:5A

       A.  [A person] is obligated to say a blessing over
misfortune as he says a blessing over good fortune.

       B.  As it is said, "And you shall love the Lord your
God with all your heart, and with all your soul, and with all
your might (M'DK)" (Deut. 6:5).

       C.1.  "With all your heart"--with both your inclina-
tions (YSYRYK)--with the good inclination and with the evil
inclination.

C.2.    "With all your soul"--even if He takes your
soul.

C.3.    "And with all *meodeka* [usually rendered as "your
might" but here as:]--with all your wealth.[529]

C.4.    Another matter:

"With all your might" (M⁻DK)--with whatever measure
(MDH) that He metes out to you, with whatever [it is], give
thanks to Him greatly (M⁻WD M⁻WD).[530]

(M. Ber. 9:5[A])

A.    Said Rav, The evil inclination resembles a fly and
it sits between entrances of the heart,

as it is said, "Dead flies turn the perfumer's ointment fetid and putrid [so a little folly outweighs wisdom and
honor.  A wise man's heart tends toward the right, and the
fool's toward the left]" (Kohelet 10:1 [-2]).  [Folly is thus
compared to a fly and there are two locations for the heart,
the right and left.][531]

B.    And Samuel said, It [the evil inclination] resembles a grain (HTH),

as it is said, "Sin (HT⁻T) couches [alt., "is a demon"]
at the door" (Gen. 4:7).[532]

(b. Ber. 61a)

Samuel comments on an item mentioned in an exegesis of
Deut. 6:5, a text cited in M. Ber. 9:5.  Mishnah (A, C.4) rules
one must accept and be thankful for whatever God metes out,
whether perceived as good or evil.  B and C.4 (and perhaps by
implication C.2 and C.3) provide biblical support for this notion.
As C.3 forms a unit with the preceding parts, it is cited along
with them.[533]

Rav and Samuel offer similes for the evil inclination.
The comments are formulated in a variation of the dispute form.
Rav in A--and not Samuel in B--mentions the "evil inclination,"
the item subject to the comparisons.  Both comments, though,
employ the phrase, "it resembles,"[534] and both include a proof
text.

The comments are not balanced.  Rav specifies two elements
("resembles a fly" and "sits . . .").  While the cited part of his
proof text supports only the first element, perhaps the next verse,
Koh. 10:2, not cited, relates to the second one, the location,
viz. "tends . . . toward the left."  Note how Koh. 10:1B makes
the point of the comparison explicit, "so does a little folly.
. . ."  Samuel's comment, on the other hand, mentions only the

item of comparison, though his proof text supplies a reference to
its sphere of activity.[535]

Rav and Samuel consider the evil inclination a small thing
in size but not impact.  For Rav it is like a fly which spoils
perfume or food and thus something which moves on its own.  For
Samuel it is like a piece of grain which is an inanimate object.
But the latter grows by itself, awaits at the door, and creeps up
on the unaware individual.[536]  The rest of Samuel's verse suggests
the person may yet master it, "and you can master it."  This verse
apparently had become a standard reference to the evil inclination.
Sifre Deut. #45, for example, uses it and suggests that the evil
inclination awaits to attack a person, who can be saved only by
the medicinal value offered by the Torah.  Sin and the evil
inclination accordingly encroach on a person.  Samuel's simile
describes how it springs up like the grain.[537]

Each master thus focuses on a different aspect of the evil
inclination and may not actually dispute one another.  Rav speaks
of the spoiling effect of the evil inclination, while Samuel deals
with its growth from a small seed into something of substance.[538]

We remain unsure if Samuel's and Rav's remarks are generated by Mishnah's mention of the evil inclination in M. Ber. 9:5
or if by some other text--and secondarily cited here due to their
relevance.  As already mentioned, the pericope forms part of a
larger *sugya* on "evil inclination" structured on M. Ber. 9:5's
mention of that item.[539]  In any event the pericope exemplifies
one aspect of *Gemara*.  *Gemara* as commentary on Mishnah does not
deal just with the problematic and main themes of Mishnah.  Rather,
what may be secondary to Mishnah, here clause C.1, later becomes
fully subject to a discrete discussion.  This phenomenon is
repeated by the medieval and modern commentaries on M. Ber. 9:5
who focus on clause C.1 and offer explanations how to serve God
with both inclinations.[540]  The mention of evil inclination,
therefore, properly becomes the object of similes and this
scrutiny makes up an integral part of a Mishnah commentary.

NOTES TO CHAPTER TWO

[1] See Lieberman, *TK*, 1:1, n. 2; Ginzerg, *Commentary*, 1:3, n. 1; and cp. Albeck, 1:326.

[2] See Lieberman, *TK*, 1:1; and H. Bornstein, "Sidre Zemanim veHitpathutam BiYisrael," *Hatkufah* 6 (1920):280. On the Mishnah, in general, see b. 4b and 9a, *Makhon-Mishnah*, pp. 1-4, esp. nn. 11-19; D. Weiss, *ST*, 1:11; *TK*, 1:1; and Neusner, *Eliezer*, pp. 18-20.

[3] See also M. Ber. 1:2; Urbach, *The Sages* (Jerusalem, 1969), pp. 15-16, Elbogen, pp. 16-20; *EJ*, 14:1370-1374, s.v. *Shema*[C], by L. Jacobs; and Gilat, pp. 89-92.

[4] Theoretically a master could have ruled in favor of one of the other positions in Mishnah, a fact made evident by a decision, cited in y., in the name of Yohanan, that the law follows the Sages.

One area in which *Gemara*, commentators, and recent writers have differed is whether Gamaliel, in Mishnah, permits a person to recite the *Shema*[C] intentionally after midnight, or whether he provides only a means of redress for one who has forgotten to say it earlier, during its proper time. We do not deal with this issue, as it only indirectly affects the import of Samuel's tradition. See b. Ber. 4b and 8b-9a and *DS*; y. Ber. 1:1, 4d; *OG*, RH, p. 7, #20; Rosh and Yom Tov Lipmann Heller "Divre Hamudot," [on Rosh], #45; Meiri, pp. 2f., Rashba to b.9a; Mareh HaPanim to y. Ber. 1:1, s.v, HLKH KHKMYM, and WRBN GMLY[D]L PLYG: Ginzberg, *Commentary*, 1:61, 75-76, 94; and esp. *TK*, 1:1. Cp. Albeck, 1:325-26.

[5] PT may provide an attestation of the substance of Samuel's opinion. Though the tradition is presented anonymously, we may be able to reconstruct its attribution. In y.'s discussion of the law in M. Ber. 1:2, we find one view attributed to Rav that we follow Joshua after the fact, (BŠKH). Then follows a report of two opposing anonymous amoraic views. One is similar to Rav's and one to Samuel's, as found in b.

    A'. R. Joshua says, Until the third hour of the day.
    B'. R. Idi and R. Hamnunah and R. Ada bar Aha in the name of Rav, The *halakhah* follows R. Joshua when one forgets. [BŠWKH = L and S MSS; or preferably BŠKH, as in V MS, *GYF*, p. 4. See K MS Š to M. Miq. 4:1.]
    C'. R. Huna [= Venice p.e.'s "Rabbi Hunah" is the result of incorrect filling in of L MS's "R'," also found in S and V MSS] says, Two Amoraim [dispute the matter]:
One says, when one forgets.
His fellow reacted to him. And is there a *halakhah* "When one forgets"? [No]. Thus is the *halakhah*, and why did they say (LMH [D]MRW) "when one forgets"? In order that a person be conscientious to read it at its proper time. [See the end of M. Ber. 1:1.]

If we take into account the b. parallel and y.'s style, C' does not dispute the meaning of B'. It is not uncommon for y. to present a tradition and then a pericope which incorporates or reflects that preceding tradition. In this case, accordingly, Huna reports the teachings which he brought to Palestine, those of his two masters, Rav and Samuel. Moreover, the phrase, "why did they say," LMH [D]MRW, in the plural, is appropriate less to an individual Amora, like Rav, than to an earlier pre-amoraic, general view, as in a Mishnah. See Rabiah 1:15-16, #25; Luncz; Goren; *GYF*, p. 4; and esp. Lieberman, *HY*, p. 21, n. 70, and references there, esp. to Engel; and cp. Ginzberg, *Commentary*, 1:124-125. On Mishnah's issue, see Gilat, pp. 92-94.

[6] See *Makhon-Mishnah*.

[7]See Albeck, 1:327, and *TK*, 1:5-6.

[8]See *DS* 48:200.

[9]See *DS* 49:2.

[10]See *DS* 49:2, Flr MS [which has F then G]; Rid; Rabiah, 1:21, #34.   Cp. *HaEshkol*, Ehrnerich ed., 1:9, text to nn. 5-8, with Albeck ed. 1:13.   See nn. 11, 16, 20, below.

[11]As the *baraita* is formulated as a support for an antecedent text, "it was taught likewise," its location varies depending on the comment it supports. In the first version, G comes after F, and in the second version, F' after D-E. Scholars have discussed whether or not the two versions reflect Palestinian vis-à-vis Babylonian practices.   See Mann, *HUCA* 2 (1925):291 [= Jacob Mann, *The Collected Articles of Jacob Mann*, 3 vols. (Gedera, Israel, 1971), 3:374]; Rabiah, 1:21, nn. 16-18, p. 475, note; Ginzberg, *Commentary*, 1:165, 168, 170; and, especially, Beuchler, *REJ* 50 (1905):177-181.   Note Beuchler's reference to Midrash Tehillim 6:1.   See now Lawrence A. Hoffman, *The Canonization of the Synagogue Service* (Notre Dame, 1979), pp. 30-39, 152-156.
     Moreover, Gaonim differed on the matter.   Different locations had different practices.   See *OhG*, "Responsa," pp. 29-31, *Teshuvot Rav Sar Shalom Gaon*, ed. R. S. Weinberg (Jerusalem, 1975), pp. 57-58 and nn., and Hoffman. The different versions of the *baraita* may thus actually be the result of, or at least, the reflection of, different practices.   The text may have been altered so that the thrust of the pericope, viz., the authority of the *baraita*, would conform to the practice.   See Rif, loc. cit; GRA, *Hiddushe*, s.v. WRBNN ᵓMRY; *HG,* III, pp. 6-7, n. 13.   See *HaEshkol*, Ehrenrich ed., nn. 7-8; Abramson, *Inyanut*, p. 224, especially n. 16; and especially *EJ*, 2:454-455, s.v., "Ahava Rabbah," by R. Posner; and Beuchler; and cp. B. M. Lewin, in *Methiboth* (Jerusalem, 1933, Repr. 1973), pp. iv-v.   Significantly, certain anonymous parts of the larger *sugya*, in which A-H is embedded, refer to the prayer as "With great love," and not as "With eternal love."   *OhG*, RH, p. 11, Rif, and others noted this.   This phenomenon might reflect the fact that the earlier stage of the pericope had supported Samuel's position.   If so, version 2 of the *baraita*, F'-G', might represent the earliest formulation of the materials.   See nn. 16, 20, below.

[12]Further complications include the text of Saadiah's *Siddur* (tenth century) which presents both versions with an identical opening phrase, "With eternal love."   See Davidson, ed., pp.13f., 26, and introduction, p. 25.   See also Heinemann, *Prayer*, p. 43, n. 34; Elbogen, p. 15; J. Liebrach, "The Benediction Immediately Preceding and the One Following the Recital of the Shema," *REJ* 125 (1966):151-165, esp. 157f., 159-161, 165; and esp. Posner and Hoffman. Note Liebrach's reference, p. 165, to the text published by Schechter.

[13]See *DS* 51:50, to which add Flr MS, which reads, "Abba."

[14]YWSY BR ᵓBᵓ is an alternative spelling for YWSP BR ᵓBᵓ, the reading found in M MS and some citations.   See *DS* 51:50.   [The Flor MS's reading is unclear.]   This accords with chronological considerations.   See Albeck, *Introduction*, p. 291, and Hyman, pp. 717, 750, to which cp. Margalioth, col. 530, and Albeck, *Introduction*, p. 168.

[15]See *DS* 51:60-70 and Flr MS = "They came before R. . . ."

[16]It is possible that y. preserves the original formulation of Samuel's teaching, i.e., "the blessing over the Torah," which someone later in Babylonia reformulated as "With great love," and thereby incorporated a definition of the original teaching into the teaching itself.   See nn. 11 and 20.   David Weiss Halivni points to numerous examples of this phenomenon; see *ST*, 1: Introduction.

[17] See Margalioth, cols. 1-3, 657-658; Albeck, *Introduction*, pp. 210, 204, 291; and Hyman, pp. 3-8, 915-917, and 717, 750. Cp. S. Zeitlin, "The Morning Benediction and the Reading in the Temple," *JQR* 44 (1953-54):330-331.

[18] That is, though possibly revised. See n. 16.

[19] In y., just below Mattena's [- Matnah's] citation of Samuel, R. Abba, a Babylonian who traveled to Palestine, cites a statement of R. Mattena's (and R. Samuel b. Nahman), without attribution to Samuel, which makes up an analogue to the b. tradition on the Ten Commandments. Perhaps here also the master represents Samuel. Cp. Weiss, *ST*, 1: 138-139, n. 1, and 586, n. 5. Note the role of these two masters in K. On the y, see Lieberman, *HY*, p. 22 and nn. 4-5.

[20] The Ven. p.e. includes a purpose clause appended onto Samuel's tradition, "because he has already exempted himself with the "With great love" [blessing]." If this was part of the tradition, it would provide further confirmation as to the attribution of this version to Samuel. But the latter clause undoubtedly is an explanation added by *Gemara* and not part of Samuel's comment. The correct reading of the clause in MSS and citations places before the purpose clause an Aramaic question, "What is the reason (M⁾Y TͨM⁾). See *DS* 49:3; Flr MS; OhG, "Responsa," p. 31; *SRAG*, p. 7, #8; and Rid. *Gemara* often employs such questions to supply a reason to previous traditions. Moreover, y.'s version of this tradition lacks the purpose clause. Cp. Ginzberg, *Commentary*, 1:170; *OhG*, "Responsa," p. 30; Rif, to b.; Rashba; Rashbas, p. 62b; and Ratner.

[21] See *HY*, p. 22, and n. 6.

[22] So = S MS: *SRAG*, p. 17; Tosf. R. Judah 1:168-169. The names in the attributive formula vary in the MSS, citations, and parallels in Palestinian midrashic works. L MS has ⁾WRY instead of ⁾YDY. See Tanhuma, *Lek Lekha*, #3, Constantinople, 1520-1522 edition, Mantua, 1563 edition, and in Buber ed., 1:57. See also V MS; Rid to b. Ber. 13b [p. 30]; Deut. R.2, #31 [on which see E. Urbach, *Arugat Habosem*, 4 vols. (Jerusalem, 1939-63), 2:20, and n. 12]; and esp. Buber, in Tanhuma, 1:57, n. 3; Luncz; Ginzberg, *Commentary*, 1:229-290.

[23] The reading of this anonymous clarification of A is unclear. We have followed the reading in the MSS, which in substance is supported by the citations. See Luncz, and Ratner, p. 37, to which add *OhG*, RH, p. 14; *SRAG*, p. 17; *HaEshkol*, ed. Albeck, 1:15; Rid to b. Ber. 13b [p. 30]; and Tosf. R. Judah, 1:168-169. Cp. L. Ginzberg, *Genizah Studies*, 3 vols. (N.Y., 1928, reprint ed., 1969), 1:456, and B. M. Lewin, *Otzar Hilluf Minhagim* (Jerusalem, 1942), pp. 1-6, with M. Margulies, *The Differences Between Babylonian and Palestinian Jews* (Jerusalem, 1937), pp. 91-99, Rabinowitz, *Halakha and Aggada in the Liturgical Poetry of Yannai* (Tel Aviv, 1965), p. 129, n. 22. See also the versions in Midrash Tanhuma, *Lek Lekha*, and Deut. R. 2, #31, and below n. 4. See also Ginzberg, *Commentary*, 1:229-230; and L. A. Hoffman, pp. 46-48.

[24] See below, chapter six, category F.

[25] See T. San. 6:2, p. 423, l. 3 to 424, l. 6; b. Shevuot 30a-b; and y. Shevuot, 3:1, 34a. See also Margulies's list of instances for standing, *Differences*, pp. 92-93.

[26] Pace Ginzberg and not withstanding the reinterpretation of the plain sense of Rabbi's action, y. Ber. 2:1, 4a. See M. Ber. 2:2; Sifre Num. #115, Horowitz ed., p. 126, esp. ls. 3-7; Sifre Deut. #31, Finkelstein ed., p. 53, ls. 2-5; Deut. R., Lieberman ed., p. 66, n. 2; and *Sifra*, *Qedshim*, 11:22, Weiss ed., p. 93d, and *Behar*, 5:3, 4, p. 109c; and *Midrash HaGadol: Deuteronomy* p. 127, l. 33, p. 128, l. 1. See also T. Ber. 2:7, p. 7, l. 18, and *TK*, 1:16-17, especially n. 4, and Albeck, 1:328. We have two traditions which possibly confirm Samuel's interest in this subject. BT, Ber. 13b, contains a tradition

attributed to Judah, without assignment to Samuel, that "'Upon they heart' (Deut. 6:6) is said standing." The anonymous *Gemara* explains that this means "Until 'Upon they heart.'" If Judah represents Samuel's view [see Weiss *ST*, 1: 138-139, n. 1] we have a different version of the tradition. See Lewin, Ginzberg, Frankel, and Margulies. But even if Judah expresses his own view alone, his focus on "standing" indicates that Samuel's immediate followers knew of this principle.

Secondly, we have a tradition which accords with the special evaluation of Deut. 6:4.

> Said R. Judah said Samuel, "Hear O Israel the Lord is our God, the Lord is One" (Deut. 6:4). This is the recitation of the *Shema^c* of R. Judah the Patriarch.
>
> (b. Ber. 13b)

On the attributive formula, see *DS* 60:100 and Flr MS, and citations of *OhG*, RH, p. 14; *OZ*, 1:13a, #31 [cp. 1:13b, #35]; and Yalqut Shimoni to Deut. 6:4, #836. This other instance of a report of the practice of Judah the Patriarch [see Shulsinger, *YE*], b. Pes. 103b, also is cited by Judah in the name of Samuel. See *DS*, Pesaḥim, 315:5, and Columbia MS X893-T14. On the relationship of the two passages, in b. Ber. 13b and y. Ber. 2:1, see Rif; Tosf., s.v. ^CL LBBK; Ashbili, pp. 296-297; Meiri, pp. 41-42 all to b. Ber. 13b, and *TK*, 1:15.

Finally, the language of the tradition following Samuel's likewise supports the reference to Deut. 6:4. After the late explanatory pericope in B, we find a *baraita* (TNY) which similarly employs the ṢRYK L- language and requires special focus on the word "one." "TNY, [One] has to lengthen the 'one.'"

[27]Cp. Gen. R. 65.21, pp. 738-739, and Albeck's notes there. See also J. S. Zuri, *Rav* (Jerusalem, 1925), pp. 258-259.

[28]See *OZ*, 1:23b, #130; Mel. S.; Epstein, *ITM*, pp. 645-646; Lieberman, *HY*, p. 31, the end of n. 300; in general, *TK*, 1:24-26. General usage supports the referent's identification as "urine." See the related toseftan *baraitot*, in which "excrement and urine" are coupled: T. Ber. 2:16, pp. 9-10, ls. 51, 52-53. See also 2:19, p. 10, ls. 61-64, cited below, and below, chapter three, n. 54, to #46.

[29]Printed editions add, "Said R. Yoḥanan," and at the end of the tradition, "And thus said Ulla, So . . . moistens," both of which are missing in *DS* 124 and Flr MS. Flr MS also lacks, "Thus said," at the beginning of C.

[30]= Flr MS and printed editions. For other readings, see *DS* 124:100. Note, *OZ*, 1:23b-c, #131, and Rid, apparently had additional and different readings.

[31]S adds, "Excrement" ["until . . ."].

[32]= V MS. "Hezkiah" = L, S MSS. See Ginzberg, *Commentary* 2:314.

[33]The last two clauses have posed numerous problems to the commentaries. See esp. *Nir*; GRA; Frankel, *PT*; Luncz; Ginzberg, *Commentary*, 2:315-317; and Goren, pp. 130-133. Ginzberg and Goren support the reading in O, of the V MS. "According to his approach the law (as to excrement) is correct. Excrement, even if it has become like a bone, is prohibited, because its essence lasts; urine--its essence does not last." Thus the master relies on logic and not Geniva's report.

[34]See also the application of this notion to the Qumran war camp, *War Scroll* 7:6-7, 10:1, in ed. Yigael Yadin, *The Scroll of the War of the Sons of Light Against the Sons of Darkness* (Oxford, 1962), pp. 291, 303, and Yadin's Introduction, pp. 70-75, and to the Holy Prescients, in the *Temple Scroll*, in Yigael Yadin, ed. *The Temple Scroll*, 3 vols. (Jerusalem, 1977), vol. 2: cols.

45:7-10, p. 135, 46:11-18, pp. 140-141, and his Introduction, vol. 1:221-235, esp. 221-223, 228-229; and in the CD, 11:21-22, 12:1, in Chaim Rabin, ed. *The Zadokite Documents* (Oxford, 1958), p. 58, and nn. there. See also Ginzberg, *An Unknown Jewish Sect* (New York, 1976), pp. 46, nn. 36, 37, 71, pp. 223-224, 285, nn. 40-41.

Various rabbinic sources and later commentaries associate Deut. 23:10-15 with the later application of this notion without, however, seeing it in terms of the historical-religious problematic of Mishnah. See. b. Ber. 26a, and Meiri's formulation, p. 88; Sifre Deut. #248, p. 282; *Halakhot Gedolat*, III, p. 35; Maimonides, *Sefer Ha-Miṣvoth*, ec. Ch. Heller (Jerusalem, 1946), Positive, #31, and Negative, #78, especially in *MT*, *Tefillah* 4:8, in *Guide* 3:41, Pinus ed., pp. 566-567; Nahmanides, *Commentary on the Torah*, ed. H. D. Chavel, 2 vols. (Jerusalem, 1962-63), to Deut. 23:10, p. 458; *Sefer HaḤinukh*, ed H. D. Chavel (Jerusalem, 1956), #362, 542; David Hoffman, *Sefer Devarim*, 2 vols. (Tel Aviv, 1959-1961), vol. 2:448-451 to Deut. 23:10-15, and cp. Ginzberg, *Commentary*, 2:209, n. 11, 170, n. 77, 269.

[35] Goren, for example, believes that one of the two citations of Samuel's tradition is the result of a scribal mistake.

[36] In y. the pericope, G-O, forms part of the *Gemara* on the last clause of Mishnah, while in b., A-F, appears on an earlier portion. But this undoubtedly reflects the later use of the materials. Note the related tradition of Samuel in b. Meg. 27b and the citation of the mishnaic clause, "And how far . . ."; and the formulation of the tradition in *Semag*, Positive Precepts, #18, p. 100b.

[37] See *TK*, 1:25-26.

[38] "For said" = M MS; Venice p.e.; Rosh; Rid; and others. "Said" = Flr MS; BT fragment in *Sinai* 37 (73) (1973):228; Rif; *OZ*, 1:17c, #87; and cp. *SRAG* p. 62.

[39] Printed editions only have HLKHTᵓ, the Aramaic, and not the Hebrew form of the word.

[40] The readings vary as to the attributions in B and C. See Rabbinovicz *DS* 139-140:30, to which add, supporting what we printed: Flr MS; *Sinai* fragment; Tos. R. Judah, 1:321 (see n. 125); Rashba; and Meiri, p. 94. Other sources read Abaye in B, and Rava in C. In addition to Rabbinovicz's list see: *HG*, II and III, pp. 21-22 [the discussion in which, however, assumes the reading "Rav"); S. Assaf, *Gaonica*, 1 (Jerusalem, 1933), pp. 73, 172; and *HaEshkol*, ed. Albeck, 1:93, 107 (= C only and attributed to "Rava"). The *Sinai* fragment includes a second attributive formula, "Judah . . . Samuel," at the beginning of B, but it is dotted to indicate that it be deleted. See Rabbinovicz's important reference to b. Yoma 87b which attests Rav's association with C and the existence of a disputant to his position [on which see *DS* Yoma 311: 200]; y. Ber. 4:1, 7c, cited below, text to n. 42, which apparently supports the association of A with Samuel.

[41] See Ginzberg, *Commentary*, 3:28-33, and especially *TK*, 1:27-28; Heinemann, *Prayer*, pp. 22-23, and "On the Meaning of Some Mishnayot," *BIA* 3(1965):10-11; and Elbogen, p. 67.

[42] Epstein, *ITM*, pp. 892-897, and commentaries to b. Ber. 4:1.

[43] Epstein, *ITM*, pp. 892-893 and especially his reference to Zuri. Cp. *ITM*, pp. 212-213; Higger, 7:34-39, 1:153, Ginzberg, *Commentary*, 3:168-169; *Thes. Tal.* 7:298; and Bokser, *Samuel's Commentary*, pp. 199-200, and references. See also Urbach, *The Sages*, p. 297, no. 76, for additional support that A represents (part of) Samuel's formulation.

[44] See n. 43 and chapter nine, nn. 85-86 and text thereto.

[45] *Samuel's Commentary*, pp. 196-197, 236-237.

[46] We do not go into the history of Rav's comment, C. We note, b. and y. after the *sugya* containing A-C and A'-C' present narratives of the deposition of Rabban Gamaliel which refer to Gamaliel's and Joshua's differing views as to the obligatory nature of the evening *Tefillah*. Rav may accordingly have referred to the views in that narrative and someone later appended it to Samuel's adjudication. Alternatively he may have referred to a different version. Naturally, if Samuel did not formulate the dispute in A but it predated him, that text could constitute Rav's referent. Finally, Judah, who is known to transmit Rav's traditions as well as Samuel's, may have presented Rav's ruling after Samuel's, and thus created the variation of the dispute form (B-C).

[47] = M and L MSS and apparently *Aruch*, 6:103. Venice p.e. adds "etc." Cp. Solomon Luria, *Hochmat Shelomo HaShalem* (Cracow, 1541 or 1547, Repr. Jerusalem, 1972), loc. cit.

[48] So in all readings except one, which apparently contains an explanatory geonic gloss. See *DS* 149:20, *HG*, I:4c, II:129; *SRAG*, pp. 183-184; and especially *HY*, p. 7, n. 31, and *TK*, 1:33.

[49] See *DS* 150:30; *HG*, II:129, III:26, *SRAG*, 183-184; Rid; Riaz; and Maimonides, *MT*, *Tefillah*, 2:3. I do not indicate all the slight variations in the text of *havinenu*. Besides the aforementioned witnesses to the readings, see *OhG*, RH and "Commentaries," loc. cit.; *OZ*, I: 18a, #90; Rif; Aaron b. R. Yosef Halevi, on Hilkhot HaRif, ed. M. Blau (New York, 1957, reprint of 1874), pp. 72-73.

[50] This clause has several variant readings and explanations (e.g., BD^CTK; ^CL D^CTK), some of which are motivated by the desire to make the phrase fit what was believed to be its analogue in the longer version of the *Tefillah*. See Rashi; *OhG*, RH, R. Yonah on Rif; *HG*, I, II, and III:26, n. 17, *SRAG* (cp. Maharsha); *OZ*, #90; R. Jonathan of Lunel, Blau, ed. (New York, 1957), p. 65; Aaron Hakohen of Lunel, *Orhot Hayyim* (reprint ed., Jerusalem, 1956), *Tefillah*, #111, p. 44a. Shitah Mequbeset, in *Berakhah Meshuleshet* (New York, 1947); Rashbas; Aaron HaLevi on Rif, p. 73; and *DS* 150:30. But the commentaries incorrectly assumed that their version of the full blessing was the "original" one which is being digested. But the analogue in the *Tefillah* in the stage apparently assumed here and confirmed in several other texts referred to a universal messianic judgment and not a hope for a return of national judges. See the y. parallel, below, D', and K. Kohler, "The Origin and Composition of the Eighteen Benedictions," in *Contributions to the Scientific Study of the Jewish Liturgy*, ed. J. J. Petuchowski (New York, 1970), pp. 65-66 [= *HUCA* I (1924)]; Elbogen, pp. 25-26, 39-40, 47; Heinemann, *Tefillot HaQeva*, p. 63. Cp. L. Finkelstein, "The Development of the Amidah," in Petuchowski, op. cit., pp. 161-162 [= *JQR*, n.s. 16 (1925-1926) to which see *SRAG*, p. 25 and variants for l. 7. The commentators, moreover, disregard the distinctive reinterpretation involved in Samuel's reformulation of the prayer. See Neusner, *History*, 2:159f. Accordingly, one should follow the simple and usual meaning of D^CT, ŠPT, T^CH, and T^CH. T^CH follows biblical usage of to "go astray," to "sin" or "err." See Mandelkern, p. 1250c, esp. Ezek. 14:11, and 44:10 and 15. Under the influence of Aramaic, in Middle Hebrew T^CH had a tendency to drive out T^CH. But it is not surprising that the latter appears here, in a liturgical text, a genre which characteristically preserves "old" forms. See *Thes. Mis.* 2:798; Abba Bendavid, *Biblical Hebrew and Mishnaic Hebrew*, 1- (Tel Aviv, 1967- ), 2:441 and 1:82; *Thes. Tos.* 6:652-653, and note the variant readings in T. B.M. 2:28, p. 376, l. 19, and T. B.Q. 8:6, p. 361, l. 15, wherein Zuckermandel's text, Erfurt MS, has T^CH, while Vienna and p.e. have T^CH. Cp. Kutscher, *Archive of the New Dictionary of Rabbinical Literature*, 1- (Ramat-Gan, 1972- ), 1:24-25, cp. 96; G. Sarfatti, "Addition to T^CH = ŠKH," *Lesonenu* 32 (1968):338; A. J. Sanders, *The Dead Sea Psalm Scroll* (Ithaca, 1967), pp. 54-55, IXQPs, col. XI, Ps. 119:110. The various possible renderings of the

prayer are reflected in the Palestinian *piyyutim* of abridged *Tefillot*; see A. M.
Habermann, *Tefillot Me$^C$en Shemoneh Esreh* (Berlin, 1943), p. 46, ls. 4-5, KLH
BMŠPT ŚWN ⊃Y ṢYWN WŠPṬYNW BRHMYM BYRWŠLYM, and cp. p. 47, l. 11.

[51]Some texts include an apparent geonic explanatory gloss, "in a city,"
BM⊃T⊃. See *DS* 150:40; Rif; M MS; Flr MS between the lines; Aaron HaLevi on
Rif; and esp. *TK*, 1:33.

[52]See *DS* 150:50.

[53]See *DS* 150:60; Flr MS; and Albeck, *Introduction*, p. 420. Though the
Flr MS has Rabbah (RBH), it has, for the second name, Ishmael.

[54]The citation of Mishnah is crossed out in L MS and lacking in V MS.
It is, however, in S, without the first word. See *IAL*, p. 356, n. 21, and *ITM*,
p. 90, n. 1, and 932-945. In addition to the MSS, and the items mentioned in
n.55, the following provide evidence for the reading: *OhG*, RH, p. 37, and *OZ*, I:
18a, #90. For the parallel in y. Taan. 2:2; 65c, there is *GŸF*, p. 175.

[55]See Luncz; Ginzberg, *Commentary*, 3:315; Frankel, *PT*; Epstein, *ITM*,
pp. 89-90, on which see S; and Lieberman, *HY*, "Introduction," p. 7, and p. 32,
n. 20a, wherein Lieberman places the "seven" in parenthesis and thereby apparently deletes the number. V MS includes the term HM⊃WR$^C$, "the event," before
the word "eighteen." *Aruch*, 6:193's citation of the pericope starts with line
C' and thus "Ma$^C$arekhet HaArukh" on y. [in modern editions of PT] suggests that
C' and D' directly refer to Mishnah and that the question is an addition. This
receives support from Sirillo's reading which deletes B'. See Meir Halevi
Lehmann, "Meir Netiv" on S, and below text to nn. 86-87.

[56]= Ven. p.e. and L and S MSS and *OhG*, "Commentaries," p. 115. "Tanhum"
= V MS: "Nisim" (NŠYM), perhaps a corruption of "Nahum" = *OZ*. See Ginzberg,
*Commentary*, 3:321. On the attributive formula, see Ginzberg, *Commentary*,
3:320-321 and 1:377, and E. Z. Malammed, *An Introduction to Talmudic Literature*
(Jerusalem, 1973), p. 625. Cp. V MS, however, which has LGBY and not GBY.
Previously commentators had generally rendered the phrase as, "R. Ze$^C$ira sent
R. Nahum to R. Yannai b. R. Ishmael."

[57]L MS and Ven. p.e. mistakenly have M$^C$YN, "The substance of" before the
word "seven," a reading not in V MS or *OZ*. See *IAL*, p. 356, n. 22. V MS
alone--and mistakenly--does not read ŠMW⊃L.

[58]Explicit in S MS = YMWT. See Ginzberg, *Commentary*, 3:331-333.

[59]= V and S MSS, here, and Ven. p.e., L MS and *GYF*, p. 175 to y. Tan.
L MS and Ven. p.e. here mistakenly have "dews of," a corruption from the next
line. See Ginzberg, *Commentary*. Some readings lack the prefix, B-.

[60]S MS reads, "the summer," YMWT HHMH.

[61]The participle is used to convey the future, a common usage in Middle
Hebrew. See Kutscher, "Hebrew Language. Mishnaic," *EJ*, 16:1600. Cp. Ginzberg, *Commentary*, 3:324-325, and Heinemann, *Prayer*, p. 37, n. 24, and pp. 150-
151.

[62]See n. 50, above.

[63]Cp. Ginzberg, *Commentary*, 3:329.

[64]See Elbogen, pp. 31-32; Sacks, p. 25, n. 5; Epstein, *IAL*, p. 356, n.
23; Lieberman, *TK*, 1:55; and cp. Ginzberg, *Commentary*, 3:329-330; and below,
n. 79.

[65]The sequence of J', K', L' = in y. Ber., V MS; in y. Tan., L MS, Ven.
p.e. and *GYF*. K', L', J' = in y. Ber., L MS and Ven. p.e. See Luncz and
Ginzberg, *Commentary*, 3:330-331, who believes J' is a marginal note added to
the text on the basis of y. Ber. 4:4, 8b, as one version of a "brief Tefillah."
J' is not found in the various citations or references by Rishonim who cite
y.'s version of *havinenu*. As to the last point, however, it is unclear to
what degree the authorities cite the whole text and do not abbreviate or adapt
it. Moreover, the y. Ber. 4:4 passage has parallels in Tos. Ber. 3:7, p. 13,
ls. 33-34, and b. Ber. 29b, both of which lack an analogue to J'. Consequently, the presence of J' in both y. pericopae may reflect an actual Palestinian tradition. The matter, therefore, remains unclear. Finally, even if
the line is original to y., it may not accurately represent a prayer composed
or reported by Samuel. Rather, it would be the Palestinian rendering of
Samuel's opinion.

[66]See Heinemann, *Prayer*, pp. 150-151; and, in general, Elbogen, pp. 20-
32, especially 31-32; Heinemann, "On the Meaning of Some Misnhayot," pp. 9-11,
and *Prayer*, p. 29; Lieberman, *TK*, 1:31-32; Neusner, *Eliezer*, 1:23, 24; and
Gilat, pp. 83-84.

[67]See, however, below, text to nn. 77, 86.

[68]This is so if we follow the MSS and citations which contain the text
of the benediction. But we cannot know whether or not a given liturgical text
in *Gemara* is a post-Talmudic scribal expansion of an initial key word, as here,
e.g., "Give us discernment." Moreover, variant readings abound for liturgical
texts which scribes often revised or adapted on the basis of their own knowledge of contemporary practice. On the other hand, specifically in the case of
individual, less frequently used, and abbreviated prayers, *Gemara* apparently
often spells out the text. See Heinemann, *Prayer*, pp. 45-46. This would seem
to be the case here, especially so as the variant readings are slight. See S.
Friedman, "Critical Study," pp. 305-307.

[69]See Elbogen, pp. 29-30, 42, and esp. 31-32; T. Ber. 3:25, p. 17, ls.
95-97; and Lieberman, *TK*, 1:55; and Epstein, *IAL*, p. 356, n. 22; Heinemann,
*Prayer*, pp. 46, 140.

[70]Neusner, *History*, 2:160.

[71]See Ginzberg, *Commentary*, 3:323-324.

[72]E.g., Rashba; *Beth Nathan*, pp. 15a-b; PM; and see Ginzberg, *Commentary*.

[73]E.g., b. Pes. 104a and M.Q. 12b, and see *Thes. Tal.* 21:659-660.
Geonic and later commentators and codifiers held that E referred only to
unnecessary use of the prayer. See *OhG*; *HG*, I and II; Rif; RH in *OhG*, and in
*OZ*; Tosf.; Rid; Meiri; Shitah Mequbeset, in *Berakhah Meshuleshet*; DS 150:40;
and *TK*, 1:33. Cp. Tosf. R. Judah, 1:12 f. and n. 132.

[74]See Heinemann, *Prayer*, p. 25.

[75]See Aaron HaKohen, *Orhot Hayyim*; and Ginzberg, 3:323-324. Moreover,
the other exception apparently would not be required according to the practice
of those who recited the *havdalah* in the "thanksgiving prayer," one of the
last three benedictions and thus not one of those abridged. See M. Ber. 5:2;
E. Fleischer, "Havdalah Shiv^catot According to Palestinian Ritual," *Tarbiz* 36
(1967): 342; J. Wieder, "The Old Palestinian Ritual-New Sources," *JJS*: 4
(1953):30f., 71-72; *TK*, 1:40-41; and cp. Gilat, pp. 87f. See also the questions posed by Eleazar Havizdorf, "Haqirah Bā^cinyan Seluta Dehavinenu," *Bet
Talmud* 3 (1883): 279 [reprint ed., Jerusalem, 1969] that the contrast of M.
Ber. 4:3 with 4:4, wherein a dangerous situation is spelled out, would argue

that M. 4:3--including the opinion of Joshua--speaks not just about a "dangerous situation."

[76]See *IAL*, p. 356, n. 21, and *ITM*, p. 90, n. 1.

[77]Epstein builds upon the suggestion of Frankel, *PT*, and argues for a "Palestinian reading of Mishnah." But there are several problems with this reconstruction. First, the three relevant pericopae elsewhere in b., viz., Pes. 3a (see *DS* 5:10), Yoma 87b, and Nid. 8a, which speak of an individual who on the outgoing of Yom Kippur prays "Seven the substance of (ŠB$^C$ M$^C$YN) eighteen," are all b. pericopae. Epstein uses these sources to demonstrate that there circulated a tradition, i.e., reading of M. Ber. 4:3, which spoke of "seven the substance of eighteen." Thus one cannot speak of only a Palestinian Mishnah reading. Secondly, those who cited or were responsible for E'2, the *baraita* that reads, "Eighteen the substance of eighteen," undoubtedly read so in their Mishnah, as Epstein himself implies. This indicates that one cannot characterize any single reading as the one universal to all Palestinians. Thirdly, according to Palestinian type MSS to M. Ber. 4:4, one who goes in a dangerous place would pray a "brief *Tefillah* the substance of (M$^C$YN) eighteen," which is a reading closer to Rav's position than Samuel's; see *TK*, 1:33 and n. 19, but see Neusner, *Eliezer*, pp. 23f. Fourthly, if Epstein is correct that "seven the substance of eighteen" represents the "Palestinian" M. text, this would be inconsistent with one general assumption and one fact. It would not accord with the position of Rav, who, supposedly, due to his Palestinian training, taught materials in harmony with the Palestinian tradition; see Neusner, *History*, 2:232-236, and cp. Gordis. Moreover, it does not accord with what is known to have been the actual Palestinian practice and which agrees with Rav's opinion. Many Palestinian liturgical poems (*piyyutim*) indicate that individuals abbreviated each of the blessings, not just the middle section, and recited for each a seal of the blessing. See *TK*, 1:32-33, and Habermann, *Tefillot*, esp. pp. 51-53.

[78]See Margalioth, cols. 275-277; Albeck, *Introduction*, p. 323; Frankel, *Introduction*, pp. 79b-80b; and Hyman, p. 410. The master, whether considered Hagai I or II, is the one who was associated with Zeira.

[79]Some texts contain the reference to David, which derives from an addition based upon b. Thus Venice p.e. adds it on the basis of a marginal addition in the L MS. See above, n. 64.

[80]See n. 65.

[81]Various versions of *tefillot qesarot*, "brief *tefillot*," circulated before Samuel's time, as proven by their presence in M. and T. Ber., e.g., M. Ber. 4:4, and T. Ber. 3:7, on which see Zahavy. On the role of Samuel, see Elbogen, p. 47; Ginzberg, *Commentary*, 3:320-321; Heinemann, *Prayer*, pp. 37, n. 1, 46, and 151; and especially Neuser, *History*, 2:159-161.

[82]Various extant examples contain abridgements of all eighteen benedictions and not just the middle ones. See *TK*, 1:32-33; Habermann, *Tefillot*; and Ginzberg, *Commentary*, 3:317-318.

[83]See Ginzberg, *Commentary*, 3:322; and Neusner, *History*, 2:160.

[84]See Bokser, *Samuel's Commentary*, pp. 213-215, and below, chapter seven. See, however, Lieberman's remarks, *TK*, 1:33, that Rav's opinion was the "standard" position, the validity with which all might agree, while Samuel's constituted an extension thereof. Accordingly, Samuel's tradition from its earliest stage could have employed the present formulation.

[85]*Samuel's Commentary*, p. 224. See chapter eight, subsections 2.F and 4.A.

[86]Our argument holds even if the questions are later added to introduce the traditions. See above, n. 55.

[87]As indicated BT's version of Samuel's comment would not have met Palestinian acceptance due to differences in their *Tefillah*. The y. version of Samuel's comment, D', in effect enabled it to be adapted by Palestinians to fit their liturgical practices, as spelled out in G. See above nn. 64, 65, 66, 69, and 79, and the text thereto. For analogous instances in which Zeira may have formulated Samuel's teachings so that Palestinians would have accepted them, see Goldberg, "R. Ze$^c$ira and Babylonian Custom in Palestine," *Tarbiz* 36 (1967):319-341; and below, chapter eight, category F.

[88]See Elbogen, pp. 88, 414; Lieberman, "Martyrs of Caesarea," pp. 441-443; T. B. B. 6:13, l. 13; T. Meg. 3:29; *TK,* 1:190, 2:574, 5:1212; Ginzberg, *Commentary*, 3:410-428, esp. 421-428; Uri Rappaport, "On the Meaning of *Heber Ha-Yehudim*," *Studies in the History of the Jewish People and the Land of Israel*, 3, ed. B. Oded et al. (Haifa, 1974), pp. 59-67; and especially Geza Vermes and F. Millar, Emil Schurer's *History of the Jewish People, New English Edition*, pp. 211, nn. 603-606, and Harry Freedman, "Haver Ir or Hever Ir," *EJ,* 12:1492-1493 and the additional literature cited there. See also Tzvee Zahavy, *The Traditions of Eleazar Ben Azariah* [Brown Judaic Studies, 2] (Missoula, 1977), pp. 14-15, esp. 15.

[89]See *DS* 156:30. Note, the Flr MS reads like the printed editions, which is also, in part, attested by *OhG*, "Commentaries," p. 42, l. 17.

[90]= Printed editions; Flr MS; *Beth Nathan*, p. 16b; *OhG*, "Commentaries," p. 42; and *OZ*, 1:17d, #89. M MS lacks "in Nehardea," but below, instead of "to the city," has "in Nehardea." See *DS* 156:40.

[91]See *DS* 156:40.

[92]See Neusner, *History*, 2:141-142, and references in *Thes. Tal.* 13: 197b-c, and in E. Hatch and H. Redpath, *Concordance to the Septuagint* (reprint ed., Greg-Austria, 1954), 2:1172-1173, especially LXX to Deut. 24:5, Josh, 22: 33, 1 Sam. 28:1, 2 Sam. 5:24, 2 Ch. 28:12.

[93]This clause is deleted in M and Flr MSS and other readings. See 156:40, and below, text to n. 11. On the b. *sugya*, cp. S. Krauss, "HBR $^c$YR, ein Kapitel aus altjudisch et Kommenalverfussung," *JJLG* 17 (1926):214-215; and J. Horovitz, "Nachmals HBR $^c$YR," *JJLG* 17(1926):264-266.

[94]"Hanina," HNYN$^{\ni}$ = V MS. HNH$^{\ni}$ = L MS. HWN$^{\ni}$= S MS. "Hanina" undoubtedly is the correct reading in that elsewhere R. Bibi transmits in the name of a master of that name and not Hunah or Huna. The latter two may relect an incorrect filling in of an abbreviation of the name, e.g., HN`. See Bacher, *Tradition*, pp. 421-422; Hyman, pp. 264-265; and Goren, loc cit.

[95]See Frankel, *Introduction*, p. 16a; Bacher, *EM,* 2:224-225, contra Ginzberg, *Commentary*, 3:433, who fails to take into account the patterned phrasing of *Gemara*'s clause and, in his interpretation, the context of the Mishnah, which focuses on the *individual*'s responsibility and not the community's. Finally, see Epstein, "Mediqduqe HaYerushalmi," *Tarbiz* 6 (1934):50, who takes a variation of this term as a statement of a legal decision, viz., "the *halakhah* accords with the following amoraic statement." On the deleted portion of the pericope, see M. R. H. 4:9, b. R. H. 35a; and *Nir* to y. Ber. 4:7; Ginzberg, *Commentary*, 3:429, Weiss, *ST* 2:426; Bokser, *Samuel's Commentary*, pp. 194,196.

[96]See Epstein, "Some Variae Lectiones in Jerushalmi," *Tarbiz* 5 (1934): 269, *IAL*, p. 357; Lieberman, *YK*, p. xx, *TK,* 2:500; and Goren. Whether the "they" in this clause refers to sages of Mishnah or to later amoraic

authorities, the point is clear that an individual prays *Musaf*.  Cp Ginzberg, *Commentary*, 3:432-433, and Goren.

[97]On the changes after 70 C.E., see Heinemann, *Prayer*, pp. 18-19, 67. See also Albeck, 2:491; G. Alon, *History of the Jews in the Land of Israel in the Period of Mishnah and the Talmud*, 2 vols., 1:169, and Zeitlin, "The Tefillah," *JQR* 54 (1964):212-223, 236-238 [while various of his specific interpretations and details must be revised in terms of Heinemann, Zeitlin recognizes the transitions after 70]; Elbogen, 364, 369-372. See M. R.H. 4:9 and T. R.H. 2:18, p. 321, ls. 96-103; and below, chapter nine, n. 9, and chapter ten, n. 64, and texts thereto.

Scholars agree as to the *Musaf*'s connection to the sacrificial system, but differ in its specific genesis. *Musaf* either replaced the "additional" sacrifices offered in the Temple or is a remnant of procedures at the Israelite Second Temple regional assemblies in cities. In Second Temple sources, the priests and Levites are divided into 24 regional groups so as weekly to divide up the service in the Temple. Rabbinic sources speak of additional analogous Israelite divisions. Israelite donations in the treasury paid for the communal daily sacrifices. Some individuals from the appropriate weekly group would go to Jerusalem and stand by during the slaughter of the sacrifices and thereby represent all the people. Those individuals who did not go up to Jerusalem met locally, read portions of the Bible, and, apparently, recited some prayers. This latter institution provided the people with a sense of personal involvement.

Specifically on *Musaf*, see, in addition to the above references, Elbogen, pp. 88-89, 95, 180-185, especially 180, 182, 188, 198, 442, n. 17, 442, n. 26; Elijah of London, p. 68; Jacob Joshua Falk, *Pennei Yehoshua* (reprinted, Jerusalem, 1970), to b. Ber. 30a; Albeck 2:495-496; *TK*, 1:41, l. 58, 5:1062, 1102, 1104-1111 (Pace Ginzberg, *Commentary*, 3:428); M. Liber, "Structure and History of the Tefillah," *JQR* 40 (1950): 331-358, esp. 344, 352; Jacob Meyers, *The Anchor Bible. I Chronicles* (Garden City, New York, 1965), pp. 167-177; J. Licht and D. Sperber, "Mismarot and Ma^camadot," *EJ* 12:89-93; L. Finkelstein, *New Light from the Prophets* (New York, 1969), pp. 131-132.

[98]Cp. Ginzberg, 3:410-411. See Zahavy, *Eleazar*, p. 15.

[99]On the *sugya*, see *DS* 156-157; *OhG*, "Commentaries," pp. 42-43, RH, p. 39; *HG*, I:49, III:31; Rashi; and especially Ashbili, p. 370; Tosf., s.v. ꜣYN HLKH: Yellin; and especially Jacob Mosafiah, ed. *Teshuvot HaGaonim* (Lyk, 1864), #101, pp. 32-33. Cp. A. Weiss, *Notes*, p. 8; *DS* 31:9; Albeck, *Introduction*, p. 575. See also Hyman, 2:784-786, and especially b. Ket. 56a; Goldberg, "R. Ze^cira," *Tarbiz* 36 (1967):336. See also below n. 100.

[100]Goldberg, "R. Ze^cira," pp. 319-341, esp. 337-341. In addition to the items in n. 99, see Rabiah, 1:66, #88; Agamati, pp. 58-59; Tosf. R. Judah, 1:338; *OZ*, 1:17d-18a, #89; Raaban, 1:96c, #177; Meiri, p. 108; Maharsha, s.v., GMRꜣ ꜣꜥL.

See Y. R.H. 4, end, 59d, concerning the *Tefillah* on Rosh HaShanah, where y. "reports" the actions of R. Zeira and R. Hisda and their response to a report of a Palestinian tradition on the matter. The appropriateness of the analogy is reflected in the transference of the pericope to y. Ber. 4:6 (7), 8c, which appears below A'-E'. See Nissim b. Reuben Gerondi, *Ḥidushe HaRan* (reprint ed., Jerusalem, n.d.), p. 54b, and Epstein, *IAL*, pp. 312-313.

[101]See n. 96.

[102]Bokser, *Samuel's Commentary*, pp. 152, n. 467, 156, nn. 475, 476. See also Bokser, "A Minor for Zimmun and Recensions of Yerushalmi," *AJS Review* 4 (1979):1-25; and "Redaction Criticism of the Talmud: The Case of Ḥanina Ben Dosa" (forthcoming).

[103]See Sirillo.

[104]See n. 90.

[105]See *Thes. Tal.* 31:197b-c, especially the reference to b. A.Z. 70b, and the instances of thieves, cited 70a [on which see *DS*, A.Z. 139-140, and S. Abramson, ed. *Tractate Abodah Zarah, MS. Jewish Theological Seminary of America* (New York, 1957), Notes, pp. 113-114].

[106]In A, R. Bibi, a third-generation master, transmits the decision and a colleague cites Samuel's tradition. See Frankel, *Introduction*, p. 68b, and Hyman, pp. 264b-265. Of note, R. Aba (apparently the third- to fourth-generation Palestinian Amora of that name), in the pericope which immediately follows E', attests E', whether or not as part of the *sugya*.

[107]Cp. *NY*, to which cp. Epstein, *Tarbiz* 6 (1934):50.

[108]This applies even to y., where the tradition opens with "For Samuel says." The anonymous editor of the pericope, who presents B', D', and E', cites the tradition. See n. 106.

[109]The ꜣYN is missing in V MS.

[110]The question focuses upon A and does not inquire whether one follows A or B (contra Azikri). See Rabad, cited in Rashba to b. Ber. 31a; *Sedeh Yehoshua*; Frankel, *PT*; cp. PM and Luncz. This is so because, first the answer constitutes an explanation of "innovation" and not an adjudication. Secondly, the alternative interpretation of C is motivated by an incorrect assumption that the simple formula in D could not constitute an ample answer. See Ridbaz. This anachronistically assumes that the *Musaf Tefillah* should mention various sacrifices. Originally, however, *Musaf Tefillah* was exactly like that of *Shaharit*. See *Nir*, Ginzberg, *Commentary*, 3:433; and Elbogen, pp. 88, 100-101, 184-185, 441-442. The clause suggested in D thus constitutes the first known formula distinctive to *Musaf* while the mention of different sacrifices make up later additions. See *OhG*, "Responsa," p. 52. Thirdly, numerous citations of the y. pericope cite A and then C-D and thereby take C-D as a comment on A. See Meiri, p. 75, and Ratner, pp. 114f.

[111]B = V MS; Meiri, p. 75; Rashba to b. R. H. 35a, Dimitrovsky ed., p. 215; and other citations, presented in Ratner, pp. 114-115. Some readings, e.g., Rabad in Rashba to b. Ber. 21a that do not employ the B- in the second clause have it in the first.

[112]The issue concerns any *Musaf*, whether Sabbath, holiday, or New Moon. See T. Ber. 3:10, pp. 14-15, ls. 49-52. Cp. Goren. Some commentators, e.g., Fulda and Luncz, follow an apparent referent in a subsequent pericope and incorrectly limit the context. But that referent forms part of a pericope transferred or misplaced from elsewhere. See *Nir*; Frankel, *PT*, p. 30b, top, s.v., WHRNH; Ratner, pp. 116-117; Ginzberg, *Commentary*, 3:440; and especially Lieberman, *OY*, pp. 17-18. See also *TK*, 1:33, n. 60.

A separate issue is why an individual must innovate or vary the *Tefillah*. Some commentators, e.g., Sirillo and Rabenu Meir of Narbonne *Sefer HaMoroth . . . on Brachoth*, to b. Ber. 21a-b, ed. M. Blau (New York, 1964), p. 74, and *OhG*, "Responsa," p. 51, speak of assuring the proper intent. That interpretation may be connected to the incorrect definition of the context in terms of the preceding pericope, which deals with an individual who prays *Musaf* soon after *Shaharit*, the morning *Tefillah*. See below, n. 114 and text to nn. 113-114. But considering that the text of *Musaf* originally was identical to *Shaharit*, a more appropriate issue is, whether or not to provide a distinctive character to the *Musaf Tefillah*. Note the analogous usage of LHDŠ BH DBR in b. Suk. 46a. The latter passage apparently makes up an addition to an earlier *baraita*, a version of which appears in T. Ber. 6:9, p. 36, ls. 49-51. The text suggests that one who changes or improves or adds something to an existing *sukkah* may be considered to have thus distinctively built it for the occasion, a context where the issue of attention is clearly secondary. See *DS.Sukkah*

144:200, *OhG.Sukkah*, "Commentaries," p. 102; Meiri, *Beth HaBehirah.Massekhet Sukkah* (Jerusalem, 1966), p. 163, and to b. Berakhot, p. 75; and Zuri, *Rav*, pp. 281-283. This is not to say that "variation" may not constitute a prime means to facilitate proper ferver and attention. See y. Ber. 4:4, 8a, and *HY*, pp. 32-33, n. 30, and especially n. 70.

[113] See Ridbaz and Azikri. On SRYK L-, see n. 118.

[114] As mentioned in n. 112, some commentators identify Samuel's and Rav's referent on the basis of the preceding pericope. But Samuel and Rav could not have referred to that material, as they lived before the circles responsible for those comments. In part it is attributed to the anonymous pericope's editor and in part to R. Abba, a third- or fifth-generation master of that name. See Frankel, *Introduction*, p. 65b; Hyman, pp. 3-9; Margalioth, cols. 1-3; PM; Frankel, *PT*, p. 30; and cp. Sirillo. The incorrect identification may also be assumed in those medieval authorities who cite A after the mention of the preceding text of R. Abba. See Rabad in Rashba, Meiri, and others cited in Ratner, pp. 114-115.

[115] Bokser, *Samuel's Commentary*, p. 224. See Goldberg, "R. Ze$^c$ira"; above, n. 85 and text thereto; and n. 117.

[116] See Neusner, *History*, 2:159-160, and above, n. 100.

[117] Cp. *Nir*. For an alternative reason appropriate to Rav's position, see Sirillo; Lehmann, Meir Netiv, note "B"; and Ginzberg, *Commentary*, 3:433-436. See also Zuri, *Rav*, pp. 281-283.

[118] See chapter six, category F.

[119] See also the other tradition in y. Ber. 4:4, 8a, whether or not one should "break off" when one inadvertently or mistakenly repeats a *Tefillah* which one earlier had said. See the readings in V and S MSS, the citation in Rid, p. 53, and cp. the version in b. Ber. 21a, and the comments of Ginzberg, *Commentary*, 3:339-342, and of Lieberman, *HY*, p. 19, n. 4, and p. 33, especially n. 60. See also, *OhG*, "Responsa," pp. 50-51, RH, p. 21; Rid to b. Ber. 21a-b, pp. 52-53; Meiri, p. 75; and *TK* 1:28.

[120] See M. Ter. 8:8 [MSS read YHDŠ BH *KL* DBR: see *Makhon-Mishnah*] = "make no change'; T. Ket. 9:7, p. 89, ls. 39-43, and 10:1, p. 90, l. 2, especially T. Sot. 7:18, p. 198, ls. 170-174, $^{\circ}$M HYDŠ BW DBR [to which cf. *TK*, 8:687, and esp. 689] = "make some change" or "variation"; Sifre Deut. #61, p. 127; and M.A.Z. 3:7. Cp. b. Ber. 29b, *DS* 152:5 and Lieberman, *HY*, op. cit., where the procedure of variation is *used* so as to insure attentive prayer. See also b. Sot. 3a and B.Q. 64b, and Eruv. 53a.

[121] The appropriate verb used with *havdalah* is "say," $^{\circ}$MR. Accordingly, the reader should not transfer one of the verbs from clauses 1 or 2, but rather supply the missing verb. See the usages: T. Ber. 3:9, p. 14, ls. 45-46; T. Ber. 5:30, p. 31, ls. 76, 77, 79. On the Mishnah, see Heinemann, *Prayer*, p. 142, n. 19; Neusner, *Eliezer*, pp. 29-31; *TK* 1:37-38; and also B. Z. Bokser, *Pharisaic Judaism in Transition* (New York, 1935), pp. 68-69; Gilat, pp. 87-88; and n. 130, below.

[122] Commentators have variously rendered the phrase, NHWG WB$^{\circ}$: as "present," "ongoing," or "widespread (and known) practice," so Sirillo, Fulda, Sefer Haredim, Frankel, *PT*, and Luncz; and as "longstanding," so PM. Both interpretations assume the "sages in dispute," mentioned in the next clause, means they are in dispute among themselves or dispute an accepted authority like Mishnah (see PM). *Sedah Yehoshua* has a variation of the first alternative: if the general practice is "on the cup" why do the authorities in M. Ber. 5:2, as a group, dispute it by prescribing *havdalah* in *Tefillah*? While this is highly suggestive it does not simply accord with clause D. The usage supports the

rendering of "present custom": M. Git. 7:7, HWLK WB⊃, = T. Git. 5:8, p. 267,
l. 57--see T. B.M. 10:10, p. 394, l. 15, and Sifre Deut. #281, p. 298; M.
Tamid 5:6, RS WB⊃; Sifre Deut. #343, p. 399, = WHZR WB⊃; and Sifre Deut. #355,
p. 421, WHYH MMŠMŠ WB⊃. See 1 Sam. 18:16; 1 Kings 15:17 = 2 Chron. 16:1; and
Ginzberg, *Commentary*, 4:271.

[123]V and S MSS = HLWQYN/M; L MS and Ven. p.e. = HWLQYN. See H. Yalon,
*Studies in the Hebrew Language* (Jerusalem, 1971), pp. 322-324, 437, and Abba
Bendavid, 2:484.

[124]See Ginzberg, *Commentary* 4:271. Commentators, based on b. analogue,
have generally read in a three-step development. But see Ginzberg, *Commentary*,
4:271, who aptly points out that one should not read in *bavli* perceptions of
the history of the liturgy and ceremonies. See also *Śedeh Yehoshua*; M. Narkiss,
"The Origin of the Spice Box Known as the Hadass," *EI* 6 (1960-1961):189-198;
and Ira J. Schiffer, "The Men of the Great Assembly," in *Persons and Institutions in Early Rabbinic Judaism* [Brown Judaic Studies, 3], ed. W. S. Green
(Missoula, 1977), pp. 237-273, esp. 269-270; and the items in n. 130.

[125]This passage has posed difficulties. Interpretations include: (a) The
final clause refers to *havdalah* in *Tefillah*. See S; *Śedeh Yehoshua*; and Fulda:
children are accustomed to and, therefore, easily advised as to *Tefillah* and
not a separate ceremony of *havdalah*. Alternatively, *havdalah* is included in
*havdalah* so as to teach children. The latter fits the usage of LZKWT as to
"involve." While these renderings fit the sequence of clauses, it is inconsistent with F. (b) The final clause refers to the ceremony over a cup and the
sense then accords with the assumption that children do not know the *Tefillah*.
One then must assume an elliptical usage (PM), a requirement that induces
Frankel, *PT*, and Luncz to switch the words "over a cup" (BKWS) with "in the
*Tefillah*" (BTPYLH). We then read, "[If] he said it in the *Tefillah* he says it
over a cup so as to involve the children." In a similar vein, Ginzberg,
*Commentary*, 4:271, and Goldberg, *Tarbiz* 36 (1967), p. 337, n. 32, fill in y.
with another set of clauses: "said it in *Tefillah*, he says it over a cup."
[Ginzberg makes all the verbs past tense, viz., "said it," which, however,
loses the verbal form's identification with that of Mishnah.] The ceremony
over the cup would provide a likely setting for involvement of children, a
point made by Rabiah, 1:243. The latter indeed reads "says it over a cup, so
as to. . . ." See nn. 12, 14, and pp. 511f. But cp. the citations, 1:154
and 2:141, both of which cite E, "[If] he . . . over a cup, he says . . . in
the *Tefillah* so as to involve the children," and then F. See Goren, pp. 204-
205.

[126]V MS reads, "he *says* it."

[127]V MS, probably from a homoioteleuton, lacks the clause.

[128]See PM, *s.v.* the first MYLTYH ⊃MRH.

[129]E.g., T. Ber. 3:9 and M. Ber. 8:5-8.

[130]See "Habdalah," s.v. *JE*, 6:120; Elbogen, "Eingeng and Ausgand des
Sabbats," *Festschrift zu Israel Lewy's Siebzigstem Geburtstag*, ed. M. Brann
and J. Elbogen (Breslaw, 1911), pp. 183-185; Elbogen, pp. 36f., 91-93, 103,
184; Heinemann, *Prayer*, passim, especially pp. 25, 138, 142, n. 19, and see
74-77; and ibid., "Tefillot HaShabbat," *Mahanayim* 85-86 (1964):54; Daniel
Goldschmidt, "Qiddush VeHavdalah," *Mahanayim* 85-86 (1964):52f.; M. Narkiss,
"The Origin of the Spice Box Known as the 'Hadass,'" *EI* 6 (1960-61):189-198;
Goldberg (1967):335, nn. 26, 27, and 338, n. 33; Neusner, *Pharisees*, 2:44-48,
50-52, 296-300; "Haver, Haverim," s.v. *EJ*, 7:1489-1492; Richard S. Sarason, *A
History of the Mishnaic Law of Agriculture*. *Demai*, Part One (Leiden, 1979),
"Introduction"; and below, chapter four, nn. 17-18 and text thereto. Cp.
*HaNer* to b. Ber. 33a, s.v. BTHLH.

In the light of the above, Tosefta's mention of *havdalah* may form part of Mishnah's and Tosefta's emphasis on the importance of *Tefillah* as an effective means of worship and prayer.

[131]See *TK,* 1:37-38, ls. 45, 46, and below, n. 141.

[132]Goldberg (1967), p. 337. See Frankel, *Introduction*, pp. 105b-106a.

[133]The necessity for an antecedent is reflected in other usages of "say it," WᵓMRH, in y. where some type of referent precedes the comment. See the six instances earlier in y. Ber. 5:2, 9b. Note thus the appropriateness of "say it" in the context of M. Ber. 5:2.

[134]On the text, see *DS. Shab.* 363:200; *IAL*, p. 301; Rid to Shab., p. 537. This passage may be the source for the readings which *DS. Ber.* 177:100 cites for b. Ber. 33a.

The passage, as presented, attests the tradition. We, however, cannot be certain that the cited responses originate as responses and were not merely so arranged by the editor or compiler of the *sugya*. Either way, the named masters, R. Nathan b. Ami and Rava [note his use of the term ŠNW, "they learn," which might suggest that the comment originally directly related to M.; see Bokser, *Samuel's Commentary*, p. 23, n. 48 and references there], and then R. Abba and R. Ashi are "late," from the fourth generation on and thus provide no early attestation; see Margalioth, cols. 3, 683.

[135]See b. Pes. 100a (*havadalah* over a cup), 102b (over a cup), 104a twice [but for the first instance, see *DS* 315:8]; 106b (cup) twice [see *DS* 322:400], 107a (cup) [but see *DS* 323:40], and possibly 103b [see *DS* 315:5]. Samuel thus appears concerned with the formulae and procedures of *havdalah*.

[136]See Bokser, *Samuel's Commentary*, pp. 236-237.

[137]See Goldberg, "R. Zeᶜira," pp. 337f.

[138]The clause, "and they said . . . cup," is added from later in the pericope. See A Weiss, *The Talmud in its Development*, p. 87, and Goldberg, "R. Zeᶜira," p. 338. This solves an exegetical problem, how to relate this last clause to the question, and thereby obviates the difficulty recognized by Rashi and Falk, *Penei Yehoshua*, s.v. PYSQᵓ. The *sugya* thus contains five minus one instances of the text of I, without attribution to Samuel.

[139]See Margalioth, col. 291; A. Weiss, *Development*, pp. 88-89; especially Goldberg, "R. Zeᶜira," p. 336; and the master's role in the *sugya* on b. Ber. 33b.

See also b. Shevu. 18b, where Yohanan, in a didactically formulated tradition supports *havdalah* over a cup of wine.

[140]See *DS* 177:90; Goldberg, "R. Zeᶜira," p. 338; and Margalioth, col. 158.

[141]Rabbah is the correct reading. See *DS* 177:70; Flr MS; *OhG*, "Commentaries," p. 45; N.B. M MS lacks the word "Said," ᵓMR, and has Rabbah's name added between the lines. As to Rabbah's comment, generally one cannot automatically know if such an action emends or, through the question, evalutes different versions of the *baraita* and selects the correct text. See *ITM*, pp. 439-440; and cp. Weiss, *ST* 2:90-91. In this case, though, we undoubtedly deal with a revision in the *baraita* once we consider the nature of the pericope in b. 33a, and the version in T. Ber. 3:9, mentioned above, and cited also in b. Ber. 26b and twice in 29a. [Of note, the latter (29a) instances may be the result of transference. The first instance there is missing in MSS (see *DS* 150:80 and Flr MS) and the second instance, while in some citations, e.g., Rashbaṣ and M MS, is lacking in Flr MS.]

[142]There is an additional revision of a comment attributed to R. Aḥa
Arika, a third-generation Babylonian emigré to Palestine, before Huna.  See
*DS* 177; 200 and Flr Ms [which reads Aḥa . . . Huna], and Margalioth, col. 70.
   On the whole b. pericope see *DS* 176-179.  Add to *DS*'s n. 50: Flr MS;
Ashbili, p. 380; especially Tosefot R. Judah, p. 351; *TK*, 1:37f., A. Weiss,
pp. 86-89; N. Wieder, pp. 30-35; E. Fleischer, "Havdalah," pp. 342-365; and A.
Goldberg, Rabbi Ze$^C$ira," pp. 319-341.

[143]If our analysis is correct, Samuel's position is not determined by
Mishnah's overall concern to emphasize the role of *Tefillah*.  See n. 130, and
chapter ten, subsection 3.

[144]V and S MSS, which are supported by b. Nid. 8a, contra L MS and Ven.
p.e. which mistakenly have Eleazar.

[145]A seemingly mistaken gloss appears at the end of the clause.  In B:
V MS = MYYR; L MS and Ven. p.e. = MYD.  In C: V MS = MRY.  S lacks the word in
both, and L MS in C.  See Azikri; Luncz; Ginzberg, *Commentary*, 4:271; and cp.
PM.

[146]HNNYH and not HNYN$^Ɔ$ is the correct vocalization.  It is found in Vat
MS, here, and in Kaufmann MS to all instances of the name in M.: M. Qid. 3:4;
B.B. 10:1; Mak. 3:15 twice, Men. 5:8 [slightly corrupted, see Parma MS]; Bekr.
6:9.

[147]See *Śedeh Yehoshua*; Azikri; Frankel, *PT*; Ginzberg, *Commentary*, 4:272;
and especially *Nir*.  Cp. S and Luncz.

[148]Only Ven. p.e., by mistake, has DRBY HKM̆.  L MS and Ven. p.e. have
an additional two clauses, one before G and one before H, which are to be
deleted.  They probably are marginal additions.  S lacks them along with G,
while V MS has just G and H.  See Epstein, *Tarbiẓ* 6 (1934):49f.; Weiss, *ST*,
1:360, n. 11; and cp. *Nir*.

[149]See text to n. 158.  "He says it," $^Ɔ$WMRH = Vat and S MSS.  "He says,"
$^Ɔ$WMR = Ven. p.e., but probably is an inexact filling in of L MS' $^Ɔ$W$^ᐟ$.  See
Sefer Haredim.

[150]See *DS* 180:8 and Flr MS, and Goldberg, "R. Ze$^C$ira," p. 334, n. 24.

[151]See Goldberg, "R. Ze$^C$ira," p. 336; and Frankel, *Introduction*, p. 106a.

[152]The referent is Rabbi and not Rav.  See Goldberg, "R. Ze$^C$ira," p. 334,
and line B in the y. analogue, in which Yohanan surely does not refer to Rav.
This obviates the difficulty of Jacob Tzvi Yellin, Masa HaRo$^C$im [printed in
back of Vilna BT].

[153]See *DS* 180-181: especially 8-9, Goldberg, "R. Ze$^C$ira," pp. 334-336;
*OhG*, "Commentairies," p. 46, and RH, p. 41; Tosefot R. Judah, p. 353; Wieder,
"Ritual," p. 33.  Cp. Weiss, *ST*, 2:425.
   The comments' referent emerges from the context and the y. analogue.  The
latter explicitly includes the subject in the traditions, B'-C'.

[154]See *DS* 181:30.  While the overall meaning is clear, we are uncertain
as to the exact rendering.  The clause may refer to the alternatives in the
construction of Yohanan's position; so M. Simon, *The BT. Berakoth, 1* (London:
Soncino, 1948), p. 208, n. 10.  But unless the language employs stereotyped
phrasing, it does not fit the readings of the MSS and citations, for they
include more than two versions of Yohanan's comment.  This would seem to be
the logic of Azulai, *Petaḥ Enayim* 1:29b [also cited in *Beth Nathan*, p. 20b],
who specifically mentions the three basic versions.  Hs further renders the
contrast as between those three and the position of anonymous rabbis.  A less
likely, though possible, rendering is, "neither this, R. Eliezer, nor that, R.

Aqiva, rather . . ." See the two somewhat similar phrasings, b. Ber. 53b and b. Hul. 19a, appropriately cited by E. Shulsinger, *YE*.

[155]*DS* 181:30, *SRAG*, p. 129; Rid; Ashbili, p. 381.

[156]While most readings include the full text of "And You Informed Us" prayer, the Flr MS has only this opening, and certain citations, e.g., Ashbili, p. 381, only the first phrase. See *DS* 181. In general, texts of prayers often vary in citations and MSS. Scribes may abbreviate or "correct" a commonly known text, or on the other hand, fill in a text to which *Gemara* just alludes.

[157]See Margalioth, cols. 25, 116, 337, 571, 590.

[158]See Bokser, "Guide," IV.C.

[159]See Abba Bendavid, 1; 69, 71, 142; 2:454. Cp. Yalon, *Studies*, p. 157. This is especially common in Syriac. See esp. David M. Goodblatt, *Rabbinic Instruction in Sasanian Babylonia* (Leiden, 1975), p. 99, who suggests an identical phenomenon in a different talmudic text.

[160]Yellin to b. Ber. 33b. This latter interpretation might find support from the comment of R. Yudan in the pericope that follows. See S and Goren. Cp. Ginzberg, *Commentary*, 4:272-273; Engel to y. Ber. 5:2 (= p. 60 = 30d); Fulda; Beure HaGRA to *SA*, OH, #294, cited in GRA, *Hiddushe*, pp. 44-45f.; and *Nir*.

[161]Zuri, *Rav*, pp. 291-292, believes that the language is distinctive to Rav, who accordingly is responsible for the formulation.

[162]See Rashbas, loc. cit., pp. 201-202, and especially Wieder, "Ritual," pp. 34f.

[163]R. Isaac ben Judah ibn Gayyat, *Lekutay to Tractage Berachot*, ed. C. Z. Taubes (Zurick, 1952), p. 57, and in Sharei Shimhah, ed. I. Bamberger Pirtah (1860, reprint ed., Israel, n.d.), p. 14; Ashbili, p. 381; Shitah Mequbeset, in *Berakhah Meshuleshet*, loc. cit., s.v. "R. Hiyya"; Tos. Anshe Shem to M. Ber. 5:2; and Azulai, *Petah Enayim*, ibid.

[164]Wieder, "Ritual," p. 32.

[165]Wieder, "Ritual," and Fleischer, "Havdalah."

[166]M MS alone deletes the repetition of "from this world."

[167]Flr MS, in place of this clause, has ᵓLᵓ, "rather," as if B continues the thought in A. The style of the "question" and the considerations raised below suggest that B is added by an anonymous authority. Cp. Albeck, *Studies*, p. 95, and below. See also *DS* 191:60.

[168]M MS alone has "in this world." See *DS* 191; Flr MS; *Yalqut HaMakhiri* to Ps. 24:1, p. 161; *Yalqut Shimoni*, to Ps. 24, #696, and to Ps. 115, #873, and citations, e.g., *OhG*, "Commentaries," p. 65; and Rif.
Rosh and Raaban, p. 97c, #190, mistakenly attribute the comment to R. Judah in the name of Rav. That literary tradition probably originally had just "R. Judah," and a later hand incorrectly supplied the name of one of the two masters which Judah regularly cites. See Weiss, *ST*, 1:138-139, n. 1.

[169]See *DS* 191-192:80. Some texts, including M and Flr MSS present first a different tradition of Hanina b. Papa and then E.

[170]On the *sugya* see *OhG*, "Commentaries," pp. 49, 65, 111, RH, p. 43; Tosf. R. Judah, pp. 361f., 371f.; Meiri, pp. 126-128; Coronel, pp. 21d-22a; esp. the comments of A. Weiss, *Notes*, pp. 9-14; and see Albeck, *Introduction*, p. 588,

n. 10; David Hoffmann, *Sefer Vayiqra* [Hebrew translation] (Jerusalem, 1953-54), 2:42; and Baruch M. Bokser, "Ma[c]al and Blessings Over Food: Rabbinic Transformation of Cultic Terminology and Alternative Modes of Piety," (in press).

[171] See David Pardo, *Hasde David to Tosefta*, 6 vols. (Livorno, 1776-90, and Jerusalem, 1880, reprint ed., Jerusalem, 1970-71; Jerusalem, 1970, 1971, 1977), to T. Ber. 4:1.

[172] "Brief Commentary," ad. loc., and *TK*, 1:55-56. See below.

[173] See Rashba to b. Ber. 35a and *TK*, 1:56.

[174] Cp. Albeck, *Studies*, p. 95. Thus once the b. *baraita*, A, contained both the prescription and result and used the language of "benefit" in both, that is, even in the first, it no longer needed a clause analogous to 2b.

[175] Note how the printed editions for the statement of the principle that immediately precedes A employs the second formulation, while the MSS, the first. See *DS* 191:50.

[176] See Max Kadushin, *Worship and Ethics* (New York, 1963), p. 66, and Bokser. "Ma[c]al."

[177] See *DS* 189:2 and Bokser, "Ma[c]al."

[178] See A Weiss, *Notes*, p. 14.

[179] 4 Syb. 24-26. See Aristeas, #158; Philo, *Special Laws*, 4:99; N. B. Johnson, *Prayer in the Apocrypha and Pseudepigrapha* (Philadelphia, 1948) [JBL Monograph Series, 2], pp. 15-16; on New Testament materials, Kittel, *Theological Dictionary*, 2:762-763; Albeck, *Studies*, p.95, n. 3; and, in general, M. Cassuto, BRKH, s.v. *EM*, 2:354-356. Cp. Louis Jacobs, *Studies in Talmudic Logic and Methodology* (London, 1961), pp. 18-19. Josephus claims the Essenes said a blessing before eating, *Wars*, 2:131, a matter found in the DSS, *The Scroll of the Rule*, 6:4-5, and 10:14-15. See also Ezek. 44:30; Sir. 35:8-11; Jacob Milgrom, First Fruits, OT," *IDBSup*. pp. 336-337; and Bokser, "Ma[c]al," n. 13.

[180] This surely is the motivation behind Rava's comment, b. Ber. 35a, clause B. See Heinemann, *Prayer*, p. 30, and Bokser, "Ma[c]al," n. 33 and text thereto.

[181] Elsewhere we also find that Samuel extends a law or notion which responds to Mishnah and which presently is found in Tosefta. See chapter four, especially chart 9.

[182] The point is that Samuel could have used the term M[C]L, as proven by his employment of the term in tradition #114, presented in chapter three, below, and in his discussion of its characteristics in b. Men. 31b, Meil. 14a (= B.M. 57b), and Meil. 20b, with a different version cited in b. B.Q. 20a. The last two references contain different traditions of Samuel which concern the law of M[C]L in the same mishnah; see now Gordis, analysis of texts nos. 174 and 228.

[183] See also Joshua 7:1, and 22:20. See Bernard S. Jackson, *Theft in Early Jewish Law* (Oxford, 1972), pp. 64f., 66, 76-82, 94-99, 110-113, 164-170; especially Jacob Milgrom, *Cult and Conscience* (Leiden, 1976), 16-35 [= *JAOS* 96 (1976):236-247], and 84-102. On the usages in rabbinic literature, see, e.g., *Thes.Mis.*3:1151f., and *Thes. Tos.* 4:470-472; Bendavid, 1:107. See also Albeck, 5:271. The tractate Me[c]ilah is based upon the usage in Lev. 5:15f.

[184] See also Lev. 26:40; Num. 5:6; Jos. 22:16, 22, 31; Ezek. 15:15, 18:24, 20:27, 39:26; Ezra 9:4, 10:6; and 2 Chron. 33:19; and Milgrom, p. 21.

One passage, Lev. 5:21, uses "trespass," M^CL, in the context of robbery. But Milgrom, pp. 84-104, cogently argues that this usage involves the violation of an oath, mentioned in Lev. 5:22. Many readers, though, have understood the usage without reference to the next sentence. If, as we argue, Ḥanina's comment revises Samuel's definition of M^CL, in C, it is possible that Ḥanina likewise assumed the latter interpretation of Lev. 5:21. See ad. Lev. 5:21, Sifra, Vayiqra, #22, 3-4, p. 27d, Rashi, Ibn Ezra, and especially Hoffmann, Vayiqra, 1:152; Job, 21:34, and ad. loc. Pesiqta Rabbati, 29-30/B, Friedmann ed., pp. 138a-b, and M. Pope, The Anchor Bible. Job (Garden City, 1965), p. 144, who renders M^CL, here, as "fraud"; and Lieberman, HJP, p. 49. See also Zech. 5:3-4. In any event, the application of M^CL to theft would be a unique usage. Moreover, Ḥanina's formulation is patterned after Samuel's language, who had already deleted explicit mention of M^CL. Hence, we should not rely upon his comment for an assumed definition of M^CL. See below, text to n. 190, and Bokser, "Ma^Cal." Cp. Jackson, pp. 76-82. On Numbers 5:12, 17, cp. Milgrom, pp. 133-136, and n. 486.

[185] See M. Besah 5:5; Naz. 4:4 = Meil. 3:2; Naz. 4:6; A.Z. 2:5; Tem. 4:1; Meil. 3:1, 2, 4, 5, 7, 8; and T. Sheq. 3:4 [NY^ƆWTYN], p. 213, l. 10; T.Y.T. 4:7, p. 302, l. 36; T. Naz. 3:16, p. 133, l. 41; T. Zav. 5:6, p. 489, l. 9; T. Men. 6:4, p. 519, l. 29; Meil. 1:10, 15, 18, 24, pp. 556, l. 31, and 558, 1s. 18f., 32, and 2:1, 2, 3, 6, p. 559, 1s. 20-26, 28, 34-36. See Jackson, pp. 80, 94-99; Milgrom, pp. 23-24, and nn. 75, 81, and 112; and Gordis, analysis of text #174, concerning Samuel's use of the criterion of "benefit," in b. Meil. 20a.

[186] In "Ma^Cal," we evaluated the degree to which the various agricultural dues could be considered liable to ma^Cal. Misuse of terumah or produce which contains undesignated terumah certainly does. See Num. 18:8, 11-13, 19, 26-32; Lev. 22:1-16, 27, 30; and Milgrom, p. 70, n. 253. While according to P, tithes do not, according to the plain sense of Deut. 26:11-15 they do. See Milgrom, pp. 35-44, 54, n. 189, 55-63. The rabbinic sources do not follow the plain sense of Deuteronomy and they understand the section primarily to refer to second tithes. See, e.g., M. M.S. 5:10-12, and Milgrom, p. 57. On the other hand, various Second Temple sources require tithes to be brought to Jerusalem and some require it to be given to priests alone or in addition to the Levites. See Neh. 10:30; Jdt. 11:11-13, and 1 Mac. 3:48-51. Moreover, according to Neh. 10, Jews took an oath to observe the several agricultural rules. Hence, noncompliance with any one would entail violation of the oath, an act which is one of the definitions for ma^Cal. See above n. 184 and text thereto.

The loss of the Temple and then access to the city of Jerusalem posed problems in different ways for the customary practice of the regulations.

The law of bikkurim could not be fulfilled at all and this stands out especially in light of the great emphasis on it in Second Temple sources. Fourth-year produce elicited various solutions, including redeeming the produce or renouncing its ownership. Terumah remained in effect by ruling, perhaps by extending an earlier Pharisaic notion, that a person could give the heave-offering to any priest at any place. Second tithes also found a solution in its redemption with money.

While some rabbis and Jews found ways to observe certain of these rules and thereby express their piety, they could not observe all of the regulations. The other individuals clearly found difficulties in fulfilling most of them. Unfilled expression of piety thus existed. Moreover, the desire to avoid ma^Cal could literally apply at least in regard to heave-offerings and possibly to first fruits. In addition, someone might assume, be it in error, that tithes had a dimension of holiness. Hence, certain rabbinic authorities may have drawn upon this sentiment to bolster the requirement to say a blessing before eating food.

See T. Ter. 7:8, p. 143, l. 26, p. 144, l. 27; M. Bik. 2:1-3; M. MS. 5:2-3, 12-13; T. MS. 2:8-9, p. 251, l. 39 - p. 252, l. 47, 3:13-14, p. 160, 1s. 44-50, 5:14-16, p. 271, l. 44 - p. 272, l. 54; M. Sheq. 8:8; T. Sheq. 3:24, p. 218, 1s. 65-68; T. Sot. 13:10, p. 235, 1s. 125-131. See also Moshe Weinfeld,

"Tithe," s.v. *EJ*, 15:1156-1172, and A. Oppenheimer, "Terumot and Ma$^C$aserot," *EJ*, 15:1025-1028, and the literature cited in both to which add: Milgrom; Milgrom, "First Fruits"; and Jacob Milgrom, "Heave Offering," *IDBSup*, pp. 391-392; Lieberman, *TK*, 2:783-785, 8:748-750; Sarason, *Demai*, preface; Gereboff, pp. 248-250, 383, 389, 443-450; Yadin, *Temple Scroll*, 19:10, col. 43, esp. ls. 11-12, 16-17, 60:2-11, and vol. 1: 81-99, 124-130; and Bokser, "*Ma$^C$al*."

[187] See Urbach, pp. 54-64, and Japhet, pp. 57-60, 75-78; and, e.g., 2 Chron. 20:6.

ŠMYM appears in phrases with QDŠ in two basic variations. In the first, "Heaven" is the subject, viz., Heaven sanctifies the new moon. See M. R.H. 2:7 and T. R.H. 1:17, p. 311, l. 75, and 2:9, p. 315, l. 34. In the second usage, "Heaven" appears in a construct or as the object of a preposition, e.g., QDŠY ŠMYM or HYQDYŠWHW LŠMYM. The phrase refers to items dedicated or belonging to God. See M. Ned. 5:6, T. Zev. 11:16, p. 497, l. 4; and T. Men. 13:19, p. 533, l. 26. These items can suffer desecration (ḤLL or MBZH). See b. Pes. 57a; b. Ker. 28a; b. Shab. 116b = b. Zev. 85b; b. Zev. 101a and b; and esp. Sifre Deut. #306, Finkelstein ed., p. 342. The lattern pattern is not the standard phraseology to denote dedicated objects. Indeed the above references make up practically all of the instances.

[188] See the association of Samuel with Ps. 24:1 in b. Hul. 139a [on which see *DS* 198a:400]. Considering our argument, Ps. 24:1 fits Samuel's perspective better than one of those verses which come from cultic-related contexts, as Lev. 19:24. On the metaphoric usage and reinterpretation of M$^C$L, here in b. Ber., see Tosf. R. Judah, p. 372; Ribban, p. 163; and especially Hirsch Tewel, *Ṣion LeNefesh* (New York, 1957), pp. 101-102; A Weiss, *Notes*, p. 14; and Zahavy.

[189] See Frankel, *Introduction*, pp. 84b-85a; Hyman, pp. 494-497; Margalioth, col. 346.

[190] We note, the verb T$^C$M, used in one clause of Tosefta's formulation of the law, would have provided Ḥanina with a more viable alternative verb. Since E could have employed that formulation but did not do so, the coincidence in wording with Samuel's tradition would not seem to be a coincidence. On Hanina's comment see Maharsha; Jackson, p. 96; and Bokser, "*Ma$^C$al*." On its occurrrence in b. San. 102a, see *DS* 319:60 and especially Meir Todros HaLevi Abulafia ["Ramah"], *Ḥidushe HaRamah* (Warsaw, 1895), ad. loc.

Neusner, *Purities*, vol. 22, notes that in Mishnah-Tosefta the initial transference of cultic language and purity to outside the Temple by the mid-end of the second century loses its momentum and is replaced by the new metaphor or value term of the community. Ḥanina's comment belongs to a later development of this approach. Cp. Kadushin, pp. 251-252, n. 22, and see Bokser, "*Ma$^C$al*."

[191] See chapter ten, below.

[192] *DS* 193 and Flr MS.

[193] *DS* 193:5, Flr MS, and Rid contain the word "olive," not found in printed editions.

[194] *DS* 194:7 and Flr MS.

[195] See the usage in T. Ter. 9:11, p. 158, l. 51; Lieberman, "Brief Commentary" to T. Ter. 9:12, p. 159, l. 53, and *TK*, 1:458-459, 460-461, and cp. 395-396.

Commentaries vary whether or not in the last sentence the "huge" amount is necessary. Moreover, while the question in H is a valid one, *Gemara's* answer need not represent the simple meaning of G. The commentaries follow H, agree that the blessing, "Who createst the fruit of the tree," applies only when the consumption of the oil involves no ill effect, but differ as to additional aspects of H's implication. The tradition itself, G, lacks any qualification, and y.'s analogue is not even glossed by a clarifying pericope. One must, therefore, assume that the tradition refers to any of the diverse normal ways by which a person consumed the olive oil. Cp. Yellin. This stricture would apply to an even greater degree if, as we suggest below, C and G are late citations of the tradition and K represents the first or "original" citation.

Perhaps in Babylonia people used olive oil less frequently or widely than in Palestine where it was plentiful and a noted commodity. If so, Samuel's comment emerges as a comment generated by Mishnah and not necessarily as a statement of Babylonian practice superimposed upon Mishnah. This accords with the coattribution to Yohanan, a Palestinian, who surely would not be projecting Babylonian practice.

See Maimonides, *MT*, *Berakhot*, 8:2, and Kesef Mishnah, loc. cit.; Meiri, p. 130; Tewel, *Sion LeNefesh*, pp. 102a-103a; Rashbas, pp. 210-211; and especially *TurSA*, OH, #202, and BH, loc. cit., s.v. WM"Š WPY\ H"R YWSP, and WM"Š BŠM HRMB"M; and cp. GRA to *SA*, OH, #202.4. See below, nn. 200, 207, and text thereto, and 290.

On olive oil, see Pliny, 15:4-19; Felix Goldman, "Der Olbau in Palästina in der tannaitischen Zeit," *MGWJ* 50 (1906):563-580, 707-728, and 51 (1907): 17-40, 129-141; Loew, 2:287-295; Feldman, pp. 259-263, 267-268; Feliks, *Plant World*, pp. 25-27, 32, and "ZYT," s.v. *EM*, 2:913; and M. Avi-Yonah, "Trade and Industry in the Land of Israel in the Roman-Byzantine Period," in *Trade, Industry and Crafts in Ancient Palestine* [= Library of Palestinology of the Jewish Palestine Exploration Society 9/10], ed. S. Yeivin (Jerusalem, 1937), pp. 88-89.

[196] See *DS* 196:200, and A. Weiss, *Notes*, p. 17. Commentators dispute the nature of the grain and speak of several principles as criteria. For example, whether or not one can taste grain; whether or not it is edible; and whether or not it is normally eaten. Some, in their citations of BT, include an explanatory gloss which fits one of the approaches. See Rashi; Maimonides, *MT*, *Ber*. 3:2; Tosef; Agamati; Rashba; Shiṭah Mequbeset; Ashbili, p. 394; Tosf. HaRosh; *TurSA*, OH, #208; and Yellin; and cp. Meiri, p. 131 [whose resolution, however, is inconsistent with Rava's comment in J]. Considerations external to the *sugya* may affect the approaches. See n. 195.

[197] See *DS* 196:300.

[198] Found in P MS and Rid. See *DS* 196-197:300 and n. 203, below.

[199] See *DS* 197:400; Flr MS which reads QR⁾ HY⁾; and Rabiah, 1:78, #99. On the "gourd," see J. Feliks, s.v. *EJ*, 7:832, and the literature cited there, and Bokser, *Samuel's Commentary*, pp. 35-36.

Mattena's name is missing in the Flr MS, while it is replaced by "R. Huna," in Tosf. HaRosh.

[200] Perhaps Mar Zutra, a sixth-generation master, attests part of the *sugya*. See Hyman, pp. 382-384, and Margalioth, cols. 645-646. But many texts lack even that attribution. See *DS* 194:6 and Flr MS; A. Weiss, *Notes*, pp. 15-16. Nor can we assume that the last-named masters in the *sugya*, Rava and Nahman b. Yishaq [see *DS* 194:20], whom we do not cite, knew the anonymous material which precedes their comments. For the latter may have been interpolated later. See A. Weiss, *Notes*, pp. 15-16; DeVries, *Studies in Talmudic Literature* (Jerusalem, 1968), p. 208; especially the analogous phenomenon on b. Ber. 36a concerning which see D. Weiss, *ST* 2: "Introduction," pp. 2-3, and S. Frideman, "A Critical Study," p. 295; and below, n. 16 and text thereto.

[201] See A. Weiss, *Development*, p. 90, and *Notes*, p. 16; D. Weiss, *ST*, 3 (in press), and below, nn. 258-260 and text thereto.

[202] See Sussmann, pp. 81-83, n. 75, 100-101, 140-151, especially 143-144, 161, n.b. n. 111; contra A. Weiss, *Leqorot*, pp. 45, 64, 126, and *Studies*, p. 134, n. 58.

[203]Though one might want to construe J-R as a dialogue, wherever a series of comments appear, only the first set of traditions--and not the second and successive ones--can be assigned to named masters. See n. 200, text to nn. 200, 207, and 213.

[204]See Hyman, pp. 915-917; and Margalioth, cols. 657-658.

[205]See n. 199 and b. Shab. 18a. On the barley, see J. Feliks, s.v., *EJ*, 4:241-242, and the literature cited there, to which add Feldman, p. 61, and note Num. 5:15 and M. Sot 2:1.

[206]See Zwi Moshe Dor, *The Teachings of Eretz Israel in Babylon* (Tel Aviv, 1971), pp. 13-14.

[207]See nn. 195 and 200.

[208]If our suggestion is correct, the tradition in I need not have known the principle of "ill effect" which is presented in H and with which it might be construed to conflict. See BH to *SA*, OH, #202. See n. 195.

[209]T. Ber. 4:2, p. 18, ls. 4-5. See Lieberman, "Brief Commentary," loc. cit., and *TK*, 1:56-57.

[210]See, e.g., M. Ter. 1:4; M. Tamid 2:3; and T. Ber. 5:29, p. 30, ls. 68-70; T. Ter. 3:13, p. 119, ls. 49-50; T. Shev. 1:3, p. 166, 1. 16; T.M.S. 1:2, p. 243, ls. 7-9; and T. Eruv. 5:9, pp. 112-113, ls. 22-24. Numerous examples can be gleaned from *Thes. Mis.* 2:609-611, s.v. ZYT, 2:852-857, s.v. YYN, and 4:1785-1786, s.v. ŠMN: and from *Thes. Tos.* 3:50-51, s.v. ZYT, 3:514-519, s.v. YYN, and 6:489-492, s.v. ŠMN. See also Elijah of London, p. 75.

[211]T. Ber. 4:3, p. 18, ls. 5-6. See also n. 209, and the rest of 4:3, and 4:4, 6-7, pp. 18-19, ls. 6, 7-8, 9, 16-21. See also M. Ber. 6:3, end.

[212]Indeed T. Ber. 4:4, p. 19, ls. 8-12, contains both formulations.

[213]T. Ber. 4:2-7, pp. 18-20, ls. 4-22.

[214]As once the palm-heart is picked the tree eventually dries up, the heart, though edible, is not generally eaten. See M. Uqs. 3:7; Pliny, 13:39; Loew, 2:325-326; Feldman, p. 152; Feliks, *Plant World*, p. 42, esp. n. 60; T. Shev. 3:21, p. 179, 1. 50; Lieberman, "Brief Commentary," and *TK*, 2:525, 725.

[215]See *DS* 197 and Rid. See, e.g., David b. Levi, p. 57, who suggests that since the palm-heart is part of the tree which comes from the ground, the blessing is ". . . of the earth." See *TK*, 2:526, top [to 1. 50], and Feliks, *Plant World*, p. 42.

[216]See *DS* 197:4 and Rid.

[217]See *OhG*, "Responsa," p. 85; *Aruch*, 8:113; Payne Smith, p. 587, s.v. ŠNYN⁾, and Levy, p. 587.

[218]See *Aruch*, 7:291, and *Sup.*, p. 319; Loew, 1:511-515; Feldman, pp. 207-208; Feliks, *Marot*, p. 120, and *Mixed Sowing*, p. 78, n. 20. The radish, *raphanus sativus*, becomes hard when it emerges above ground. See Columella, 11:47 [vol. 3, p. 159]; and Pliny, 19:78-87, and 20:23-28.

[219]See nn. 229-230 and text thereto.

[220]Following V MS and Lieberman, *TK*, 2:630, 634, and nn. 69-70, contra "Joshua" of S and L MSS and Venice p.e. Lieberman further suggests that we should perhaps read ⁾MR, "Said," in place of TNY, "Taught." See also *YK*, pp. 32, 440, and nn. 235 and 236, and the text thereto.

221 On the identification of these items, see Lieberman, *TK*, 2:507, 630; as well as Loew, 1:408, 411, 293-294, 284; Levy, 1:414; *Aruch, Sup.*, p. 144; and Feliks, *Plant World*, pp. 134, 188.

222 See n. 214 and references there.

223 See *Samuel's Commentary*, pp. 213-215; above n. 84 and text thereto; and chapter seven.

224 Earlier on the page, *Gemara* cites the two tannaitic views in the form of a *baraita*, which is also found in T.M.S. 1:14, p. 246, ls. 44-46. See *TK*, 2:725-726.

225 For the logic, see Rashi, Tosf., and RH [before the copy editor's correction], and Ritba.

226 Rava is the reading in the printed editions; Vatican BT 109 MS, Makor, 1:33; Ritba, and perhaps RH. While RH has Rabbah (RBH) in this line, in its preceding clause, for the name of the master who rejects the first attempted differentiation, it has Rava (RBᵓ). As both references make up parts of a standard structure, both are to be assigned to the same master. Accordingly, the reading for the second name may be a mistake. See, *ST*, 2:508, n. 2. M MS, however, has Rabbah and lacks a name for the first instance of the name, the rejection of the first differentiation. See *DS* 108:400.

227 The prefix, D-, appears in printed editions and Vatican MS 109, but not in M MS. See *DS* 108:1 and below, n. 232.

228 The main variation, which occurs in only certain texts of the b. Eruv. analogue to T, is an additional gloss appended to the reason supplied for Samuel's opinion. The M and Vatican BT 108 MSS lack this gloss. See *DS* 108:2 and in general, *DS* 108-109.

229 As already pointed out by A. Weiss, *Notes*, p. 18, and, differently, by D. Weiss, *ST*, 2: "Introduction, pp. 2-3. Nahman b. Yishaq does not attest the full *sugya*. Rather, his comment has been used within the *sugya*. See A. Weiss, *Notes*, pp. 17-20, and D. Weiss, and cp. Albeck, *Introduction*, pp. 581-582. Against Albeck's argument that the anonymous material is early, see D. Weiss, *ST* 2:21, 291, especially "Introduction," and 108-109, n. 2; S. Friedman, "Critical Study," pp. 293-299, esp. 295; and the literature cited in Bokser, "Talmudic Form Criticism," *JJS* 31 (1980):46, n.1.

See also b. Git 91 [on which see *TK* 1:146 and *ST* 1:490-493], and b. B.B. 176a which contain analogues to V.4 without an analogue to V.1.

230 See Lehmann, notes to Sirillo.

231 See A. Weiss, *Notes*, p. 18. M MS lacks a D-, "For," to introduce the cited pericope. See. n. 228. This reading may reflect the stage of the tradition at which the pericope was initially transferred to b. Eruv. At a later date someone wanted to smoothen the transition and supplied the D-. Cp. Bokser, "Two Traditions of Samuel: Evaluating Alternative Versions," *Christianity, Judaism and Other Greco-Roman Cults. Studies for Morton Smith at Sixty*, ed. Jacob Neusner, vol. 4 (Leiden, 1975), pp. 53, 55.

232 See Higger, 4:249.

233 See Bokser, "Guide," chapter four, C.

234 See Margalioth, col. 571, and Bacher, *Tradition*, p. 487.

235 The blessing Hoshia requires is mentioned in M. Ber. 6:1, attributed to R. Judah, and also found in T. Ber. 4:4, p. 19, ls. 8-12. See T. Ber. 4:5, p. 19, ls. 15-16, and *TK*, 1:59, 2:634. If Lieberman is correct, one of the

traditions might not actually constitute a *baraita*.  See nn. 220 and 236 and
text thereto.

236<sub></sub>This applies especially following the reading TNY and not TNˀ.  See
n. 220.

237<sub></sub>See above, 71=73=74, Samuel's comment as to the blessing on olive oil,
and nn. 195 and 209, and text thereto.  Cp. Yellin, to b. Ber. 36a and Lehmann,
note A, to Sirillo on the y. pericope.

238<sub></sub>Our analysis depends upon S's representation of Judah's opinion.  If
for some reason the one who placed his and Samuel's opinions into the dispute
form did not accurately represent Judah's position, the ostensible reading of
Samuel's retraction, in U, would result in a different rendering.  If so,
Judah's view and U's assumed position of Samuel might to identical to y.'s version of Samuel.  While this observation is speculation, it serves to underline
the point that those responsible for y.'s version of Samuel did not have access
to--or rely upon--b.'s presentation of Samuel as represented by the dispute in
S.  This supports the notion that the dispute form is secondary.  See above,
n. 223.

239<sub></sub>See n. 215.

240<sub></sub>See above, text to n. 211, for a citation of this text.

241<sub></sub>On these items, see Krauss, *QT*, 2.1, 200, 201, and especially 203;
*Aruch*, 3:335, and *Sup.*, p. 178; Ginzberg, *Genizah Studies*, 2:30; *OhG*, RḤ, p.
44; Maimonides, *MT*, *Ber*. 3:4, Telegedi, *JA*  226/227 (1935):219, 225; and *TK*,
3:194, 1. 49.

242<sub></sub>While M MS lacks the text of the blessing, Flr MS; *OZ*, 1:28a, #165;
and other readings contain it.  See *DS* 201.

243<sub></sub>Rif; *OhG*, RH, p. 44; *HaEshkol*, 1:111; Rashi; Agamati; and others
understand this as mixed with honey, while RN takes it as crushed up.  See Rid.

244<sub></sub>The phrase "Seize . . . Kahana" = *DS* 201:6, to which add Flr MS;
*HaEshkol*, 1:111; Rabiah, 1:80, #102; Aaron HaLevi, Blau ed., p. 108; and Tosf.
R. Judah, 2:404.  "Said R. Joseph, It makes sense like R. Kahana" = printed
editions.  M and Flr MSS contain an additional clause after Kahana's name:
"who is exact in learning his traditions from his master."  See, however, *DS*.

245<sub></sub>The Flr MS twice lacks the tradition KL ŠYŠ BW.  As it is in line FF,
the deletion apparently is a mistake.

246<sub></sub>See *DS* 201-204.  On rice see, Yehuda Feliks, "Rice in Rabbinic Literature," *BIA* 1 [= *Pinkhos Churgin Memorial Volume*] (1963):177-189, and xxxix-xli,
and s.v., *EJ*, 14:155-156; and as to millet, i.e., "Durra," "Sorghum vulgare,"
or "sorghum cernuum," see Feliks, *Mixed Sowing*, pp. 194, 195, *Plant World*,
p. 154, and "Sorghum," s.v. *EJ*, 15:164-165; and cp. Feldman, pp. 44f.

247<sub></sub>On the object of the refutation, see below, nn. 254-257, and text
thereto.

248<sub></sub>Commentators, e.g., Rid, either identify *rihata* with cooked *havis*,
or, e.g., RN, slightly distinguish between the two.  The latter are probably
motivated by a desire to account for the presence of two pericopae.  See *OhG*,
"Lequte Gaonim," p. 112; Judah b. Benjamin, p. 165; Ashbili, p. 400; Aaron
HaLevi, Blau, ed.; and Shiṭah Mequbeṣet.

249<sub></sub>See *HaEshkol*, 1:113, n. 4.

[250] See *DS* 204:200.  "And Rava returned and said" [= retracted] is found in printed editions and Flr MS.  The latter, though, lacks the initial conjunctive W-.  See n. 256, below.

[251] M and Flr MSS contain an additional clause which specifies the *halakhah*.  See *DS* 204:300 and A. Weiss, *Notes*, p. 26.

[252] See *DS* 115:100, to which add Vatican BT 109 MS, which likewise reads MYM before MLH.

[253] *DS* 115:200 and Vatican BT 109 MS.

[254] *DS* 115:300.

[255] See M. Hal. 1:1-2, and M. Ned. 3:7, and T. Ned. 4:3, p. 111, ls. 7-9. Scholars differ in their identification of the five items.  See *TK*, 7:456, ls. 7-8; J. Feliks, "Five Species," *EJ*, 6:1332-1333; and Bokser, *Samuel's Commentary*, p. 116, and n. 329.  Cp. Albeck, 1:271f.

[256] Note the reading of WLᵓ HYᵓ, in II.  See n. 250 and A. Weiss's comments, *Studies* (1975), pp. 245, 246, and *Development*, pp. 40, n. 16, 297, n. 54.

[257] See *OhG*, "Responsa," p. 86, "Commentaries," p. 51; and Rosh, s.v. HBYS.  Cp. *OhG*, RH, p. 44, Rif, Zedekiah b. R. Abraham Anav, *Shibbolei Haleqet HaShalem*, ed. S. Buber (reprint ed., New York, 1959), #159, p. 125, and Abramson, *Inyanut*, p. 146.  See also *HG* I:7a-b, III:86-87 and notes; R. Jehudai Gaon, *Sefer Halachot Pesuqot*, ed. S. Sasoon (Jerusalem, 1950), p. 191; Maimonides, *MT*, *Ber*. 3:10, and Kesef Mishneh, loc. cit.; and Samuel b. Joseph Strashun, "Annotations," in Vilna BT; and especially Rashba [cp. Falk], GRA on *SA*, OH, "202, and in *Ḥiddushe*, p. 51, Rashbas, pp. 220-221, Aptowitzer, in Rabiah, 1:487f., and Albeck, in *HaEshkol*, 1:111, n. 12.

On the nature of the "refutation," see Epstein, *IAL*, p. 49, and especially *ST*, 2:209, n. 2*, 134, n. 3*, and cp. pp. 125, n. 1, and 320f.  On the "late" date of pericopae which delineate, "It is necessary . . . ," see A. Weiss, *Studies* (1975), pp. 245, 248-250, and cp. *Development*, p. 354.

In general cp. A. Weiss, *Development*, p. 90, and *Notes*, p. 16, and below, n. 258.

[258] See Sussmann, p. 173, n. 26, lines 10 through 8 from the end of the footnote.  Cp. A Weiss, who apparently perceives the reference to Huna as central to the *sugya* and proof of its supposed origin in Sura.  See below.  But if the pericope was presented as a backdrop to Huna's comment, his name does not indicate the pericope's date and origin.  The following comments further vitiate Weiss's analysis.  The question, KK, is based on an extended implication.  It mistakenly assumes that "food" is used in the same sense in Mishnah, in an oath, and in the tradition of Rav and Samuel.  But as y. Eruv. 3:1, 20d, recognizes, and to which Yellin points, there are different uses of the word "food," and, accordingly, the question is out of place.  Elsewhere BT notes the distinctive usages of language in vows.  See b. Yoma 76b and b. Ned. 49a (to which see *ST*, 1:315, n. 8).  For a full list, see Kasowsky, *Thes. Tal.* 25: 1093, cols 2-3.  Cp., however, the question asked against Yohanan, y. Eruv. 3:1, p. 20d, and Albeck, in *Bereschit Rabba* (Jerusalem, 1965²), 3:1172, n. 2.

Significantly, Huna's interpretation, which is in Hebrew, is spelled out in Aramaic, "*Water and salt . . . supports*," a measure typical of a later explanatory gloss.  Moreover, b. Ber. 35b, as already indicated, does not quote this as part of the *sugya* from Eruv.  If Huna had presented his remarks in response to the suggested refutation, would he not have expressed himself in a sufficiently clear manner?  This contrasts with the appropriate use of the B-form for a comment directly on M.  PT, too, apparently takes "food," MZWN, not in the sense of food, but as "support."  It uses the word NYZWN which has the same root as HZN.  See Lieberman, *YK*, p. 257.  The pericope's arranger thus put Huna's comment to his own use, and either employed it as an answer to the refutation, or, from a different perspective, supplied it with a backdrop.

[259] The language of KL ŠHWƆ, as discussed below, focuses on the amount of the item.  While one might want to deduce the identity of the items from this formulation--as FF evidently attempts--the point comes across more directly by the formulation of, ƆYN . . . ƆLƆ . . . BLBD, "There is only . . ."

[260] See above, text to n. 201, and A. Weiss, *Development*, p. 90, and *Notes*, pp. 15-16.  [As to p. 16, n. 2, Weiss's suggestion that the reference in Rashi was incorrectly supplied, that observation is made plausible as Ven. p.e. lacks references; they are thus secondary to the text of Rashi.  Cp. I. Levy, *Mavo UPerush LaTalmud Yerushalmi.  BQ Chs. 1-6* (reprint ed., Jerusalem, 1970), p. 14, n. 1.]  Cp. DeVries, *Studies* (1968), p. 208, who suggests that b. Ber. 35b deleted MM-NN, as it was not needed, with, however, Albeck, *Introduction*, p. 564, bottom; Sussmann, pp. 172-175, esp. n. 26, 178-179; Frankel, *Introduction*, p. 47b, Weiss Halivni, *ST*, 2:125, n. 1; and Goodblatt, "The Babylonian Talmud," *ANRW*, IV. 1,b., "Quotations."

[261] See T. Hal. 2:1, pp. 278f., 11. 1-3, and *TK*, 2:803-804.

[262] See also M. Ber. 6:3, 7: M. Kil. 2:1, 10; M. M.S. 1:7; and especially M. Pes. 3:1; b. Shab. 20a; and b. Eruv. 16a.  See Kasowsky, *Thes. Tal.* 18:289-291, and *Thes. Mis.* 2:591f.

[263] PT places an attribution between ZH HKLL and KL ŠHWƆ . . .

[264] See *DS* 235:2, and Flr MS.

[265] See, e.g., Luncz.

[266] See the references to Weiss Halivni, in n. 257.

[267] See T. Ber. 4:6, cited immediately below, which deals with grain and whether or not its pieces are extant.  This concern is analogous to that of KL ŠHWƆ.

[268] See text to nn. 261 and 269.

[269] See *TK*, 1:61.

[270] "Or" = W-, found in Erfurt MS.

[271] On Tosefta's forms, see Neusner, *Purities*, 21:247-297.  On the comment's relationship to Mishnah, cp. Falk, *Penei Yehoshua*, to b. Ber. 35b, s.v. ŠM.

[272] See Rashi, and, especially, Agamati, p. 77, Meiri, pp. 130-140, and *Aruch*, 8:187f., and Krauss, *QT*, 2:165-166.  See also n. 197.

[273] Certain texts append each of the blessing texts, drawn from PP, onto their appropriate places in QQ.2.  See *DS* 207:80.  M and Flr MSS lack this. Certain texts combine QQ.1 and QQ.2, but, as A. Weiss, *Notes*, pp. 29-33, argues, both clauses may actually represent different strata.  QQ.2 may gloss QQ.1 or even provide a separate reason.  This suggestion is supported by the use of the phrasing in QQ.1 ("This one B- thick, and this one B- thin") elsewhere.  It appears--by itself--in M. Ned. 6:1 (. . . RK . . . BᶜBH), M. Men. 3:2 (. . . ᶜBH . . . RKH), and T. Men. 4:3, as criteria by which to differentiate between types of foods; the light one may be considered a *tavshil qederah*, cooked in a pot.  See also T. Ned. 3:1, p. 107, 1s. 1-2, and *TK*, 7:440; M. Men. 5:8 and *TK*, 7:440, n. 1; and cp. M. Kel. 28:8.  Likewise in b. Shab. 156a and b. Bes. 39a it serves to distinguish between two cases or texts.  The usage in the tannaitic sources may have been the pattern for the later instances.  Even if b. Ber. 38a, the only one of the three amoraic instances attributed to a named master, served as the source for the (later anonymous) usage in b. Shab. 156a and b. Bes. 39a, the latter two indicate that the clause in QQ.2, is not

necessary for the differentiation.  Indeed, the comments of Joseph and Abaye, in RR-SS, may have generated QQ.2.  Finally, if the phrasing of QQ.1 constitutes some type of fixed, stereotyped pattern, this would account for the sequence.  Commentators assume the "thick" refers to Samuel and the "thin" to Rav.  If so, following normal sequence one would expect that "thin" precede "thick" in QQ.1-2.  For further comments on the *sugya* see *DS* notes; Maimonides, *MT*, *Ber*. 3:10, and Kesef Mishnah, loc. cit.; Beit Yosef, to *SA*, OH 208, s.v. ŠTYT⊃, end; Meiri, p. 140; *Ginze Rishonim.Berakhot*, p. 400, n. 153; Blau's n. in Meir of Narbonne, *Sefer HaMoroth*, ed. Blau (New York, 1964), p. 117, n. 57; Rashbas, p. 228; GRA, *Ḥiddushe*, p. 52 [26d], s.v. LYŠN⊃; and Falk.

[274] See *DS* 207:90.  Coronel, p. 23d; *OZ*, 1:28a, #167; and Rashba, s.v. ⊃Y S"D, all have "Joseph," the reading also of Flr MS.  Earlier on b. Ber. 37b-38a, Joseph and Abaye figure in several *sugyot*.  See the observations of A. Weiss, *Notes*, pp. 20f.

[275] Cp. Falk.

[276] See n. 273.

[277] See Columella, 6.17:3-4, 8; Pliny, 18:71-75, especially 75 and 78; 24:1, 3; 27:59; Julius Preuss, *Biblisch-Talmudische Medizin* (Berlin, 1911, reprint ed., Westmead, 1969), pp. 660-661; Krauss, *QT*, 2:1, 165-166, and Feliks, *Plant World*, pp. 146-148.

[278] Cp. Falk.

[279] See Yellin to b. Ber. 38a; and Azikri, Mareh HaPanim, and Luncz to PT.

[280] See Bokser, *Samuel's Commentary*, pp. 213-215, and below, chapter seven.

[281] See n. 277.

[282] See *OhG*, RH, p. 46, R. Yohan on Rif; A. Weiss, *Notes*, pp. 52, 71f.

[283] See *OhG*, "Commentaries," p. 52; Rashba, s.v. L⊃ HY⊃: Eliyahu Gutmakhar [in back of Vilna BT, p. 23a]; A. Weiss, *Notes*, p. 52.

[284] See *DS* 210:9.  Certain texts, including P MS and Rid, add "said Ulla," ⊃MR ᶜWL⊃, a clause perhaps generated from the next line.

[285] See *DS* 210:9.

[286] YY may have originally referred to TT and/or possibly a tradition which precedes it and in which Hisda presents the identical comment of Ulla though he [Ḥisda] offers an interpretation different from that in UU.  See the text, cited below, A'-B'.  Cp. A. Weiss, *Notes*, pp. 77-78, 129, n. 3, *Development*, p. 68, and *Studies* (1975), p. 150.

[287] Sirillo has ŠLWQH and then ŠŠLWQYN, "steamed," probably emendations, which in fact Fulda advocates, generated by a desire to render the passage smoother and based upon BT's *sugya*.  See below text to n. 311.

[288] See *TK*, 1:446, n. 60, 4:577, n. 15 and the references there, and Albeck, 3:363-364.  On A. Weiss, *Notes*, pp. 61-70, compare, e.g., *TK*, 2:670-672, and Epstein, *ITM*, p. 263.

[289] See *Thes. Tal.* 23:159-161, for additional instances of this type of gloss.  As it does not commonly refer to Samuel, the likelihood of automatic--and unreliable--identification is not likely.

[290] See n. 286.

291 See Hyman, pp. 941-945, and Margalioth, cols. 872-875.

292 See *DS* 209:7.

293 We follow the MSS for the sequence of the two clauses: a, "Whatever
. . . 'By whose . . . ,' when steamed 'Who createst . . .'"; and then b, "And
whatever . . . 'Who createst . . . ,' when steamed 'By whose word . . .'"
See *DS* 210:7 and Flr MS. The printed editions have the clauses in reverse
order. See also *OZ*, 1:280, #168, and A. Weiss, *Notes*, p. 52.

294 That is, in this context. We do *not* speak of a wider stereotyped
"exposition" form. See the instances of "R. X. DRŠ," in *Thes. Tal.* 9:441-446,
which lists only one other case each of the verb with Naḥman and Ḥisda.

295 A. Weiss, *Notes*, pp. 35-72 [= *Horeb*, 1951], and 129-134 [= *Sefer
Cassuto*, *EI* 3 (1954)], and A. Goldberg, *Tarbiẓ* 36 (1967), pp. 330-334.

296 For example, on differences in an incident associated with Yoḥanan,
see *OhG*, RH, p. 46; especially R. Nissim Gaon, in *Libelli Quinque*, ed. S.
Abramson (Jerusalem, 1965), pp. 311-313, and Abramson's notes, p. 550; Tosf.;
Rashba, s.v. HHWᵓ DᵓYYTHW: R. Yonah [the latter three practically speak of
redactional and/or independent and separate developments in BT and PT]. Cp.
Aaron HaLevi, pp. 115-116; Tosf. R. Judah, 2:426-427, and nn. there; Rosh;
Rabiah, 1:87-98, #106-107; and Rashbaṣ, p. 230. See also the rather explicit
suggestions as to varied conceptual approaches in Tewel, pp. 109-110; esp.
Mareh HaPanim, and *NY*; and cp. A. Weiss, *Notes*, p. 70, and Lieberman, *HY*, p.
38, n. 300. Undoubtedly natural, independent developments of originally mutual
materials played a role, as well. Moreover, it is possible that those in b.
who supplied the reference, perhaps for lack of knowledge of the appropriate
incident, included the wrong one. See, Weiss, *ST*, passim, for such instances,
esp. 1:541-542 to b. Git. 36a, to which n.b. Rashi, s.v. BŠBYᶜYT BZMN HZH, and
cp. A. Weiss, *Notes*, p. 71.

297 On mention of Rav, see Goldberg, p. 333, n. 20. See below for a possible emendation and alternative interpretation of this tradition.

298 See, e.g., Beit Yosef to *TurSA*, OH, #205, s.v. WHRYP, and GRA, SE to
M. Ber. 6:1.

299 See Pliny, 18:127-130; Krauss, *QT*, 2, 1:235-36. See also Feldman,
pp. 192-193; Feliks, *Marot*, p. 84, and *Mixed Seeding*, p. 78, n. 15 (and the
reference to Sifre Deut. #317, p. 360); Loew, 1:487-489; *TK*, 4:542-543; and
Columella, 22:56, who describes the preparation of turnips. By our reference
to a PT passage "similar to Ḥisda," we mean a tradition which is attributed to
Yose b. R. Bun and which appears at the end of the larger *sugya*.

300 The criterion as to "the original state or form of an item" apparently
represents a distinct approach. It appears elsewhere in BT, as BMLTYYHW QYYMY
in anonymous material at 38b, bottom, and at 38a, and attributed to an Amora
[or glossed onto his words] in reference to Samuel, at b. 36a; and as WᶜL
HTBŠYL ŠᶜYBRH ṢWRTH, in a *baraita* at b. Ber. 40b [according to the formulation
in *DS* 219:4; *HG*, I:86, II:58, III:99; Jehudai Gaon, *Halachot Pesuqot*, p. 189;
and Rif]. We may be dealing with a case in which later masters tried to
develop or derive general principles from comments of earlier masters. Cp.
Weiss, *ST*, 2: "Introduction," pp. 2-3, n. 3.

301 See *DS* 212:2. The printed editions read, "he said to us," but the M
and Flr MSS and citations have "we used to say" or "we said." See *DS*. Some
texts, including Flr MS, have "Kahana" instead of "Huna." See, however, *DS*.
On the terminology, see also Goodblatt, *Rabbinic Instruction*, pp. 146, 148.

302 See *DS* 212:2, and 308:50; *HG*, II:59, III:102f. and n. 79; and Krauss,
*LW*, p. 183.

[303] See *DS* 212:3 and Flr MS.

[304] See A. Weiss, *Notes*, p. 67.  On Judah, See Bokser, *Samuel's Commentary*, pp. 216-217, and below, chapter eight, esp. subsections 2.A, and 6.ii.A, and text to n. 41; and Weiss, *ST*, 1:138-139, n. 1.

[305] We thus reject A Weiss's mistaken argument, *Notes*, pp. 61-70, that ŠLWQ can mean chopped up.  See the reference in n. 288.

[306] We emphasize "adapted" and thus leave room open for A. Goldberg's suggestion as to Zeira's role.  As far as Yohanan, Goldberg and A. Weiss, *Notes*, p. 70, agree that an incident probably constituted the original "Yohanan position" and that masters diversely interpreted that event.  Cp. Albeck, *Introduction*, p. 523.

[307] We do not consider PM's suggestion which splits BBB into two parts, first, a question ending in ". . . ground," and second, an answer opening with, "It only says . . ."  This is out of phase with an analogous clause which has an identical formulation and which we discuss below.

[308] This then would fit: either the principle of "regular edible state," as set out in the end of the larger *sugya* in a tradition attributed to Yose B. R. Bun and in Ḥisda's exposition in b.--see Goldberg, p. 332; or a general rule without limitations, like that of Naḥman's rendering of Samuel.  Cp. Luncz, and see below.

[309] Vat MS reads ". . . said R. Ze^Cira," that is, not before but "in the name of Ze^Cira."

[310] GRA, in SE to M. Ber. 6:1, cited also by Ridbaz to y., loc. cit.

[311] See n. 289.

[312] See Bokser, "Guide," IX.B.  See also Bokser, "Talmudic Form Criticism," n. 23.

[313] A variation of our last suggestion involves an identification of BBB's referent as Zeira's version of Yohanan's opinion, which is extant in PT.  If so, BBB was misplaced within the *sugya* and should follow that tradition.  The misplacement of such traditions is not uncommon in y.  See "Guide," IX.B.

[314] See Falk, and A. Weiss, *Notes*, pp. 49, 51, who point to connections with Mishnah.

[315] See Goldberg, pp. 332-333.

[316] Cp. also, for example, the Commentary of R. Elijah of London and how he weaves in the traditions of Samuel and many other masters.

[317] See chapter ten, subsection 3.

[318] See Mel. S.; T. Ber. 6:1, p. 22, 1. 1; *TK*, 1:100; and Goldberg, "R. Ze^Cira," *Tarbiz*  36 (1967):327-330.

[319] The identification of the referents follows the sequence in A and apparently y.'s understanding of M. Ber. 7:1 and 4.  The latter is reflected in what y. presents as its *Gemara* on the two *mishnayot*.  See below, n. 12 and text thereto; R. Johan Gerondi on Rif to BT; Azikri; Frankel, PT; Luncz; and cp. PM.

[320] Some MSS and citations lack this clause.  See *DS* 266, and Flr MS.

[321]= Printed editions and many citations.  The latter include works
which support one or the other of both textual versions in B-C.  See n. 322.
For example, Ashbili; Tosf. R. Judah; Rid; Agamati; and in *OhG*, RH, p. 60.
"Rava" = M MS and some citations, e.g., *OZ*, 1:31d, #203.  As "Rava" is an
abbreviation for "R. Abba," the former may have been generated by the latter.
Though, for sure, in this instance, "R. Abba" refers to the second-third-
generation Babylonian Amora of that name who traveled to Palestine.  See
Hyman, p. 3, and R. Abba's role in y. Ber. 7:1, 11a.  The reading, in Rif, JTS
MS, of "Rav Papa" (RB PP⁾), clearly is a mistake, but surely not for "Rava."

[322]While printed editions contain two versions of Samuel's comment, MSS
and early citations contain only one or the other, F or G.2.  The first, in
part or in toto, is in Flr MS; Tosf. R. Judah; R. Jonah; Elijah of London, p.
97; and Rabiah, 1:133.  G.2. alone appears in M MS and other citations, e.g.,
Rif.  See *DS* 266:70, and below, nn. 331-334, and text thereto.

[323]See the discussion of these two alternatives, below text to n. 335,
and *DS* 266-267:80.  While Rif printed editions, including the first one,
present a conflated reading of both versions, L$^C$SMW alone appears in Rif JTS
MS, p. 8, and citations of Rif in, e.g., Rosh, R. Jonah, and David b. Levi, p.
98.  "From his own plate" = M MS.

[324]See *DS* 267:90.

[325]On the meaning of I-J, see Rashi and cp. Rashba; *OhG*, "Commentaries,"
p. 84; and Agamati, p. 104.

[326]On Grace After Meals and the "Summons," see, *EJ*, 7:838-841, s.v.
"Grace After Meals," by Editor, and the literature cited there; M. Ber. 7:3;
J. N. Epstein, *ITM*, pp. 430-431; Albeck, 1:27, 336-337; Lieberman, *TK*, 1:8-9;
Heinemann, *Prayer*, Ch. 4, pp. 67-77, esp. 73-77; Gary G. Porton, *The Traditions
of Rabbi Ishmael.  Part One* (Leiden, 1976), pp. 13-15; and Hoffman, pp. 145-
146.

[327]While source critics might conclude that these two texts derive from
two different sources, evidently this is not the interpretation offered by
Samuel and the anonymous *Gemara* in the b. on Ber. 7:4 or in the y. on Ber. 7:1.
See Chanoch Albeck, *Untersuchungen Über Die Redaktion der Mischna* (Berlin,
1936), p. 40, and *Mishnah*, 1:337.

[328]See Bokser, "Guide," Ch. IX.

[329]See *OZ*, 1:31d, #203; R. Jonah Gerondi on Rif to b. Ber. 50a; Azikri
to y.; GRA, SE to M. Ber. 7:1; Frankel and Luncz to y. contra PM and Šedeh
Yehoshua.  Cp. *STEI*, p. 15.
   Our rendering also fits the overall conception of *Gemara* as reflected in
the selection and presentation of materials.  PT to M. Ber. 7:1 contains
several pericopae which reflect the notion that M. Ber. 7:1 deals with three
people who have eaten something if not even completely finished eating and
thus examples of BSWP.  This includes: first, a tradition attributed to Yosah
who responds to Zeira and which cites M. Ber. 7:1.  See commentaries, including
Sirillo and b. Ber. 45a-b analogues, which also are on M. Ber. 7:1.  Secondly,
the traditions attributed to Huna and Ḥisda, as to "three who came from a
group" (cited below text to n. 20).  N.B. the apodosis, "They summon Grace,"
MZMNYM.  While b. presents a version of this tradition on M. Ber. 7:4, y. does
not.  As we shall see, y. Ber. 7:4 in fact contains in its stead something that
expresses the opposite point of view.  Thirdly, a tradition which the anonymous
*Gemara* associates with Zeira, "Where all three ate together," WHN Š ⁾KLW ŠLŠ
K⁾HT.  PT Ber. 7:1, 11a-b, later in the *Gemara*, may provide an attributed
instance of the tradition.  In the analysis of the blessings on the Torah, it
is presented in the form of a question, whether or not the Torah blessings are
similar to those of Grace, and it states that three who eat separately--and
presumably who come together--do not summon Grace.  On the initial instance

see Frankel, *PT*, and Luncz, and cp. Fulda, Fourthly, Yonah's analogue to the comments of Zeira, Hisda, and Huna. Fifthly, the *sugya* which deals with "three who ate and one wants to leave" and which focuses on the point in Grace until which he must wait. These passages assume that Mishnah is not based upon the principle that the initial intent determines the situation.

On the other hand, y., as mentioned above, does not have the Huna-Hisda tradition, cited in b. Ber. 50a-b, on M. Ber. 7:4, i.e., as part of y. Ber. 7:4, but in its *Gemara* on M. Ber. 7:1, which deals with a situation of three who ate in three groups and then came together. In its place, y. Ber. 7:4 contains a *baraita* (= T. Ber. 5:23), cited below, which makes the initial intent crucial, and y. understands that it refers to summoning Grace. See *TK*, 1:89, and below, our comparison of the b. and y. versions.

Our rendering, furthermore, fits the usage elsewhere for the doublet, BTHYLH and BSWP. The terms are used to refer to something which precedes or follows, as the beginning and end of a time period or of a geographic place. See, e.g., M. Peᵓah 1:3, T. Peᵓah 1:5, p. 42, ls. 13-17, esp. *TK*, 1:127-129, ls. 13-14; M. Neg. 1:15, 16, and 4:1.

330 See Tosf. R. Judah.

331 See Maharsha; GRA, Haggahot, and Notes to *SA*, OH, #193; and Joel Sirkes, "Haggahot," in Vilna BT editions.

332 Noted by R. Jonah on the Rif, reflected in Rosh, and pointed out by A. Weiss, *Notes*, p. 141.

333 See *Thes. Tal.*, 1:485c, 22:1160; and D. Weiss, *ST*, 1:504-506, 524, 41, and cp. Epstein, *IAL*, pp. 137-144.

334 See *HG*, III:132, and Hai Gaon, in *OhG*, "Commentaries," p. 84.

335 T. Ber. 5:23, pp. 28-29, ls. 47-49. See *TK*, 1:89.

336 See GRA on *SA*, OH, #193, M. Ber. 6:2, and b. Ber. 42b-43a, and *HG*, III.

337 See Bokser, *Samuel's Commentary*, pp. 190-191.

338 For textual notes to this passage, see chapter three, n. 93.

339 See Sirillo to y. Ber. 7:1, who already associated b. Ber. 47a with the Samuel tradition in y. Ber. 7:1.

340 Above, in n. 329, we focused on the ways in which the *sugyot* reflect overall redactional considerations.

341 Frankel; Ratner, pp. 166-167; and Albeck, in *Bereschit Rabba*, 3:1112, cite early medieval authorities who apparently do not include B. Some of their references need revision in light of improved editions of the medieval works; for example, R. Meshulam in *Ginze Rishonim*, p. 245, in contrast to Ratner, contains a version of B. Other recent critical editions confirm their citations; e.g., *Yalqut Shimoni*, ed. Shiloni, 2:783, to Gn. 42, #247, lacks B. While we remain unsure whether or not the y. text used by each author contained the clause, some explicitly state that different readings exist. Perhaps one of the variants consisted of the use of single or plural forms of the pronoun (ᵓWTW or ᵓWTN) and object, *snif*, "adjunct," (SNYP or SNYPYN). See Tosf. R. Judah 2:533-534, and Rosh, to Ber. Ch. 7, #20, in Vilna edition of Babylonian Talmud [against which we checked the first edition (Venice, 1520)], and cp. Tosf. R. Judah, 2:524, n. 452. The difference might imply whether or not the *vav*, "and," is disjunctive, conjunctive, or explicative. See below, n. 349, and the text thereto. In "A Minor for *Zimmun* and Recensions of Yerushalmi," *AJSReview* 4 (1979):1-25, we extensively analyze this pericope.

[342] So = L, V, S, and others; $^C$D MTY $^C$WŚYN $^Ɔ$WTW SNYP = *GYF*, p. 293. Some early medieval authorities including R. Meshullam, p. 245, lack this line. See below nn. 345 and 357, and the texts thereto.

[343] So = L, V, S, *GYF*, and *OZ*, 1:30d, #197 (who supposedly cites R. Judah); KDY ŠYHYH . . . = Rabad in Ramban, *Novellae* to b. Ber. 48a; KŠYD$^C$ = R. Meshulam; KDY ŠYD$^C$ = Tosf. R. Judah.

[344] So = L, S, and Rabad cited in Ramban; KŠYD$^C$ = R. Meshulam; KDY ŠYH$^Ɔ$ . . . = *GYF*, V MS, and *OZ*; KDY ŠYD$^C$ = Tosf. R. Judah. On the PT, see also Mordecai Sacks, *Diqduqe Sofrim LeTalmud Yerushalmi I. Masekhet Berakhot* (Jerusalem, 1943), p. 33, and Epstein, *IAL*, p. 364.

[345] Our discussion is based upon *Midrash Bereschit Rabba, Codex Vatican 60*. A page index by A. P. Sherry (Jerusalem: Makor, 1972). Albeck, in *Bereschit Rabba*, 3:1111-1118, prints the London MS and records variants from other MSS [but not Vatican 60] and early printed editions. Vatican 30, generally today considered the best MS to Gen. R. includes only the opening and closing phrases of the *sugya* and notes that the section in extension is in y. Ber. See Albeck's notes, ad loc., and his "Introduction," *Einleitung und Register zum Bereschit Rabba* (Berlin, 1931-36), printed in *Bereschit Rabba* (Jerusalem, 1965$^2$), 3: Introduction, 107f.; E. S. Rosenthal, "Leshonot Soferim," in *Yuval Shay*. A Jubilee Volume dedicated to S. Y. Agnon, ed. B. Kurzweil (Ramat Gan, 1958), pp. 293-324, especially 312f. As the *sugya* in a recension different from PT appears in Vat 60 MS and substantively in the remaining MSS other than Vat 30, the section represents not merely a late addition to the text. See "Minor for *Zimmun*," nn. 21, 58-66, and texts thereto. Vat MS 60 is considered an important early witness to the text of Gen. R., inferior to Vat 30 but superior to the London and other MSS. See E. Y. Kutscher, *Studies in Galilean Aramaic. Bar Ilan Studies in Near Eastern Languages and Culture* (Ramat Gan, 1976), pp. 12-13, n. 6; L. Barth, *An Analysis of Vatican 30* (Cincinnati, 1973), pp. 83-84; and M. Sokoloff, *The Geniza Fragments of Genesis Rabba and Ms. Vat. Ebr. 60 of Genesis Rabba*, Hebrew University Dissertation (Jerusalem, 1971), revised edition (in press). The first edition, Constantinople, 1512, and the printed editions, based upon Venice, 1545 edition, on the basis of the PT add C-D after Gen. R.'s version of A-B and "correct" Gen. R.'s actual citations or analogues of A-B, where they later appear in Gen. R. See the list of variants in Albeck, and "Introduction," pp. 113, 126, especially 128. A Yemenite MS which accords with the readings in the printed editions, does not represent a manuscript support for these readings, as the MS copies the Venice, 1545, edition. See Albeck, "Introduction," pp. 115-117, and 117, n. 2, Albeck's variants to the pericope, and "Minor for *Zimmun*," esp. nn. 26-29, where we analyze the various Gen. R. variants and suggest how they evolved. Note the reading in Zedqiah b. Abraham Anav, *Shibbolei HaLeqet HaShalem*, #153, p. 60 [= p. 119], $^C$D KMH YHYH NQR$^Ɔ$ QTN, "Until when is he called a 'minor'?" The latter's sequence and wording of the whole *sugya* indicate that it cites Gen. R. and not PT.

[346] So Vat 60. London and other witnesses have variations thereof, all with $^C$D Š-.

[347] See Azikri; Benvenisti, *Śedeh Yehoshua*; Tosf. R. Judah to b. Ber. 47b-48a; and Albeck, in *Bereschit Rabba*, 3:1112, notes. At one point in the *sugya*, an anonymous authority compares the cases of "three" and "ten," and for the sake of the discussion employs the regular usage of "adjunct to ten" and then "adjunct to three." The former usage has generated the latter formulation.

[348] See Z. Frankel, *Introduction*, p. 95a; Hyman, pp. 616-617; Higger, 4:418f.; Margalioth, cols. 476f.; and Albeck, *Introduction*, 332.

[349] See Bokser, *Samuel's Commentary*, p. 27, n. 56, and the references there to Epstein, Kutscher, and especially Lieberman. [The page reference to

Kutscher should be to p. 1602 and not 1595.]   See also *TK*, 5:1273.   Yudan,
therefore, excludes a conjunctive or disjunctive usage of the *vav*.

[350]See, e.g., Sirillo, Tosf. R. Judah, and Benvenisti.

[351]Cp. Albeck, *Introduction*, p. 524.

On Huna and Judah, see Bokser, *Samuel's Commentary*, pp. 216-217.   That
Huna = Huna, see Frankel, *Introduction*, p. 73a, and Kutscher, *Studies*, pp. 67-
96, 103-105, especially p. 70.

On Avina, see Frankel, *Introduction*, p. 61b; Hyman, 1:97f.; Margalioth,
col. 41; and Albeck, *Introduction*, pp. 274f.

[352]See the usage of TYB elsewhere; *Thes. Mis.* 2:766, e.g., M. Ket. 1:8
and B. M. 1:8; *Thes. Tos.* 3:350, e.g., T. Sot. 4:7, Lieberman, ed., p. 173,
1. 146; and *Thes. Tal.* 15:85-86, and especially note the instances in B. B. B.
155b and A. Z. 57a-b [for which see *DS* 120:6] both preceded by the verb YD$^C$,
"to know," and used to define a "minor" in terms of certain matters: business--
knowledge of the practices of business; idolatry--knowledge of the practices
of idolatry.   See also Frankel, *Ahavat Ṣion*, ad loc., and cp. Benvenisti,
Fulda, and Albeck in *Bereschit Rabba*, 3:1113-1114, note to 1. 4.

[353]See below nn. 366 and 374-376, and the texts thereto.   See Lieberman,
*Siphre Zutta*, pp. 15-16, *TK*, 1:84.   Cp. Ritba to b. Suk. 29a, Lichtenstein ed.,
cols. 260-261.

[354]Naturally if B is not original to the text, we would have an additional
factor precluding it as Samuel's referent.   See above, n. 342.

[355]If D concerns "Grace," that would accord with the use of the word
*snif*, "adjunct," which in our context is used to refer to the expanded Summons
to Grace, when ten people are present.   See above, n. 347 and the text thereto.
Among the several reasons which preclude the view that Samuel refers to A
includes the observation that only Palestinians are associated with the term
*snif*, "adjunct."   The fact that A-B immediately precedes C-D does not pose a
problem.   In y., traditions often do not refer to their immediately preceding
pericopae.   See Bokser, "Guide," Ch. IX, B, and the literature cited there.
Accordingly, there is the possibility that the formulation, if not the teaching,
of the *baraita* is amoraic.   On amoraic *baraitot*, see Benjamin De-Vries,
"Baraita," *EJ*, 4:189-193; Goodblatt, "Babylonian Talmud," Ch. IV, 1a; and
Bokser, "Guide," Ch. VIII, D.3, and the literature cited there, especially
Lieberman, Higger, Epstein, Goodblatt (1975), and Moreshet.   On our passage
see further below, n. 372 and the text thereto.

[356]See Bokser, *Samuel's Commentary*, pp. 107, 116, and A. Weiss, *Literature*, pp. 33-34, esp. *Studies* (1974), pp. 236-237, Weiss Halivni, *ST*, 2:i-xii;
Friedman, "A Critical Study," esp. pp. 294-299.

[357]R. Meshullam in "Sefer HaHashlamah," and Abraham ben David, in *Temim
De⁾im* (Warsaw, 1897), #1, p. 1a.   Nahmanides in his "Milhamot HaShem" on Rif
lacks B and C, though in his Novellae to b. Ber. 40a we find C--and interestingly enough that reference is a citation of Abraham ben David.

[358]Maimonides to M. Ber. 7:2, Qapiah ed., 1:82.   See also *MT*, *Berakhot*,
5:7.   Sirillo comments on Mishnah as part of his commentary on y.

[359]As to recensions of y., and the bibliography thereto, see "Minor for
*Zimmun*," nn. 54-57, and n. 345, above, the reference to Barth.   Albeck in his
notes to the passage, 3:1111-1112, 1. 3, and 1112f., 1. 3 [especially top of
p. 1113], specifically relates several of the differences to differences in
recensions.

[360]For variants in the names, see Albeck, in *Bereschit Rabba*, 3:1113,
1. 3, note.

[361]See Sacks, *Diqduqe*, p. 32, n. 2; Albeck, in *Bereschit Rabba*, 3:1112, n. 2; Epstein, *IAL*, p. 364, n. 7; and Z. M. Rabinowitz, "Sepher Ha-Ma[c]aśim Livnei Erez Yisrael--New Fragments," *Tarbiz* 41 (1972):275-305,286.

[362]See Albeck, *Bereschit Rabba*, 3:1112f., n. 3; see also Sacks, *Diqduqe*, p. 32, n. 4, and Epstein, *IAL*, p. 364, n. 10.

[363]Moreover, Gen. R.'s placement of Samuel's comment at the end may accord with our observation elsewhere. In y., Babylonian traditions sometimes are appended at the end and thus do not make up an integral part of the y. *sugya*; *Samuel's Commentary*, pp. 77-80, esp. 79-80 and n. 216. The Palestinian circles who placed C before Samuel's tradition and placed both, C-D, in the midst of the *sugya*, apparently see the issues through what may be called a Palestinian perspective: "A minor cannot serve as an adjunct to three." See Saul Lieberman, *Talmud of Caesarea* [*Supplement* to *Tarbiz*, 2] (Jerusalem, 1931), pp. 20-25, especially 22-23. See also Bokser, *Samuel's Commentary*, pp. 152, n. 467, 156, nn. 475-476, and "Guide," Ch. XII. On the presence in our context of a "Palestinian approach" see below nn. 372 and 380 and the texts thereto; the fragment of the Ma[c]aśim Livne Erets Yisrael, published in M. Margalioth, *Hilkhot Ereẓ Yisrael Min HaGenizah* (Jerusalem, 1973), p. 44, ls. 13-15, and in Rabinowitz, *Tarbiz* (1972):285, especially Rabinowitz's footnote, pp. 285-286; and the reference in n. 372 to Goldberg. As to implications of this suggestion, see "Minor for *Zimmun*," nn. 54-57 and text thereto.

[364]That is, disregarding the "corrected," i.e., corrupted, Yemenite MS and printed editions.

[365]The argument in the text holds unless one understands TYB in a different way. See Maimonides to M. Ber. 7:2, presented below, and Albeck, in *Bereschit Rabba*, 3:1114, notes. The usage elsewhere of TYB, however, supports our comments. See above, n. 352, and the text thereto.

Moreover, as we shall see, D.2 accords with a tradition in b. attributed to Naḥman, a master who had access to Samuel's traditions. It requires a minor "to know to whom they bless" before he can be counted, YWD[c] LMY MBRKYM. See below nn. 369-371, and the text thereto. Of course, the b. tradition may have generated the "correction" of y. If so, the version in Gen. R. would constitute the original reading. See our analysis of Tos. Ber. 5:18, which relates to M. Ber. 7:2, text to nn. 377-378.

[366]See n. 353.

[367]See *TK*, 1:84, and n. 38.

[368]See Samuel Jaffe b. Isaac Ashkenazi, "Yefeh To³ar," digested in *Mishrash Rabba* (Vilna: Romm, 1878, reprint ed., Jerusalem, 1961), loc. cit., Sirillo's aforementioned comment to M. Ber. 7:2, and Maimonides, cited above, n. 358.

We note it is not unprecedented for a tradition to be formulated in terms of "Until . . ." See chapter six, cateogry D; b. Yev. 107b, where a tradition attributed to Samuel opens with [c]D Ś-, "Until"; and a purported citation of y., which Lieberman argues is a Ganoic Gloss, *TK*, 5:1273-74, and which has "'A minor, QTN, does not . . .' Until when, [c]D ³YMTY, . . ."

[369]In addition to Rashi and Tosf., ad loc., see *OhG*, "Commentaries," pp. 82-83; Rif; Maimonides, *MT*, *Berakhot*, 5:7; Ramban to b. 48a; especially Rid; and Lieberman, *TK*, 1:84-86. See *Talmudic Encyclopedia*, s.v. ZMWN, 12:284-290, especially 286, for a survey of authorities who discuss the *sugya* and Nahman's comment, and especially Albeck in *HaEshkol*, 1:41, n. 3.

[370]See Bokser, *Samuel's Commentary*, p. 328 and nn. 3-5, and below, chapter eight, subsection 2.E.

[371]On the association of the comments of Samuel and Naḥman and M. Ber. 7:2, see R. Meshullam, pp. 244-245; R. David B. Levi of Narbonne, pp. 91-92; Rid, cols. 140-142; Dinglas, "Emunat Yosef," in his edition of Sirillo, to y.

Ber. 7:2, s.v. NŠYM W<sup>C</sup>BDYM; Sacks's notes to R. Judah, 2:517, n. 398; and see
Ramban and *Shibbolei HaLeqet*, #153, p. 118.

[372]The possibility that the sources reflect Babylonian and Palestinian
perspectives may correlate with the place of a story in the b. and y. *sugyot*.
BT to conclude the *sugya* presents after Nahman's comment a story about Rabbah,
Abaye, and Rava bar R. Ḥanan. [On the last name see *DS* 253:6, to which add Flr
MS, and Azulai, *Petaḥ Enayim*, 1:35, col. b.] That story employs the language
of Nahman's tradition and apparently attests its point. See commentaries, ad
loc., e.g., Meiri, p. 180. As mentioned above, PT ends with a story which con-
veys the point that we count only a "minor" with two hairs, i.e., who has
reached physical maturity. Thus b. and y. each end with a story which reflects
its perspective. This agrees with the general observation that *Gemara*'s choice
and formulation of stories forms part of its arrangement and is shaped by redactional considerations. See nn. 380 and 363, to which add, A. Goldberg, "R.
Ze<sup>C</sup>ira," *Tarbiz* 36 (1967): 319-341, especially pp. 327-330, and our discussion
below, chapter ten, subsection 2. See also the reference, immediately below,
to *TK*, 5:1275, ls. 18-19; and our forthcoming article, "Redaction Criticism of
the Talmud: The Case of Ḥanina ben Dosa."
 On b. Ber. 47b-48a, in addition to the aforementioned works, especially
Ramban, Rid, and *TK*, see also *Rabiah*, 1:112-115, #128, and note, p. 490; Jonah
Gerondi, Novellae to Rif; Aaron b. Joseph HaLevi of Barcelona, ed. Blau, p. 151;
and Aaron HaKohen, *Orhot Hayyim* [Part One], *Birkat HaMazon*, #39-43, pp. 76-77;
and Abraham Baer Dobsevage, *Sefer HaMesaref* (Odessa, 1871, reprint ed., Jerusalem, 1970), pp. 16-17. See also *DS* 251:100-253:8; especially the readings in
Flr MS; Albeck, *Studies*, pp. 96-97, and *Introduction*, pp. 524, and 565, n. 27;
and esp. Albeck in *HaEshkol*, 1:41, n. 3.

[373]See below on M. Ber. 7:3, and Samuel's comment thereto.
 We note that Samuel's comment does not reflect an exceptional interest in
"youth." See b. Nid. 52b, where Samuel takes a lenient position in the very
definition of "two hairs," the signs of "physical maturity;" b. Shab. 137b, to
which see *TK*, 3:252 and the alternative version of the pericope in a fragment
of the Sheiltot, J. N. Epstein, "Sheiltot Fragments. B," *Tarbiz* 7 (1938):15,
ls. 12-14; b. M. Q. 14b, and b. San. 54b.

[374]The reference often forms part of a list of "women, minors, and
slaves," as in M. Ber. 7:2. See *Thes. Mis.* 4:1574a-b.

[375]See y. Suk. 3:15, 54a, *TK*, 5:1273, and the formulation in T. Hag. 1:2,
pp. 374-375, ls. 6-7.

[376]See the use of this criterion in T. Eruv. 6:12, p. 121, ls. 38-41; and
*TK*, 3:425, and 5:1268f. See also M. Hag. 1:1, T. Hag. 1:2-3, pp. 374-376, ls.
5-22; Sifre Zutta, *Shelaḥ*, ed. Horovitz, p. 288, l. 20 to p. 289, l. 1 [which,
like T. Hag. 1:2-3, has a cluster of references with the pattern, "Whoever
knows to . . . , is responsible . . . ," KL ŠYWD<sup>C</sup> L- HYYB L-, and "Whoever knows
to . . . , is responsible . . . ," KL ŠHW<sup>ɔ</sup> YWD<sup>C</sup> L- . . . <sup>C</sup>LYW; Lieberman, *SZ*,
pp. 15-16; y. Sheq. 1:3, 46a; y. Meg. 4:6, 75b; b. Eruv. 82a [to which see *DS*
325:5]; b. Suk. 28b [to which see *DS* 84:2]; and the additional instances cited in
"Minor For *Zimmun*," nn. 46-48 and texts thereto.

[377]See *The Tosefta*, 1:29, Brief Commentary, l. 38; *TK*, 1:85-86, and Lieberman's reference to Sirkes, and below, n. 379.

[378]See *The Tosefta*, 1:29, Brief Commentary; *TK*, 1:85, to which cp. Albeck,
*Studies*, p. 96. See also Ashbili, p. 502, and Mareh HaPanim, to y. Ber. 7:3.

[379]See *TK*, 1:84, l. 36, where Lieberman suggests that the definition in
clause 1 deals with the youth's "knowledge." Lieberman further explains that
clause 2 is a general principle. If so, it applies also to the Summons to Grace.

[380]We may be able to correlate two readings of the toseftan *baraita* with
the two basic positions as to a "minor" and thus throw light on the b. and y.
*sugyot*. See "Minor for *Zimmun*," n. 52.

381 See *Makhon-Mishnah*, esp. n. 32.

382 See Epstein, *ITM*, p. 511, n. 1, and Ratner, pp. 172-173. On the usage of KLL, see Mekilta, *Bo*, #18, Horowitz edition, p. 73, Lauterbach ed. 1:167.

383 See Epstein, *ITM*, pp. 430-431, 510-511; Heinemann, *Prayer*, pp. 73-77; Porton, *Ishmael*, pp. 13-15; and cp. Albeck, 1:27, and 336-337.

384 BT 50a cites a tradition attributed to R. Adda b. Ahavah in the name of Rav's disciple circle, be Rab, which would seem to attest Samuel's tradition. On the formula, see Goodblatt, *Rabbinic Instruction*, pp. 125, 154. But the comment actually makes up an independent teaching and is used by *Gemara* to deduce a principle which accords with its understanding of Samuel's tradition. See *DS* 263-264:100 and Flr MS, and cp. Agamati and *OZ*, 1:31c, #202.

385 The anomaly of the pattern for the Summons for three people may necessitate the ruling. See Heinemann, pp. 73-77, esp. 73 and 77, On the anomaly itself, see, e.g., David b. Levi of Narbonne, p. 97.

386 Though y. texts contain different readings, they all agree with b. in this manner.

387 See Bokser, *Samuel's Commentary*, 1:220. Our passage may provide an additional example of a traveler who cites Samuel's tradition and analyzes or glosses it. Note the role of R. Zeira in the previous pericope, and see *Samuel's Commentary*, 1:224-225, and below, chapter eight, subsections 2.F and 4.A.

388 So = *GYF*, p. 295, and S and V MSS and L MS' margin [the text of which apparently deleted the passage in a homoteleuton], and several citations. As to the other apparently secondary readings, see Ratner, pp. 172-173, to which add, e.g., Tosf. R. Judah, Ashbili, p. 461, and Rabiah, 1:122. In substance the latter readings do not differ from the "primary" reading.

389 Ashbili, p. 462, Fulda, and Luncz noticed this correlation. On the principle, cp. b. Ber. 29b-30a. On the relationship of Samuel's teachings with Ishmaelite opinions, see A. Goldberg, "On the Use," *Tarbiz* 40 (1971): 144-157; below, chapter nine, n. 87; and Gordis, "Summary and Conclusions.

390 See Bokser, "Two Traditions," pp. 48-52 for an earlier version of the analysis of the pericope and its parallels.

391 "Over the fire" = L and S MSS: "Over it" = V MS and several citations. See Ratner, p. 188, to which add, *SRAG*, p. 85. As pointed out below, the latter reading may reflect an attempt further to integrate Samuel's comment into the *sugya* and accordingly to mention the subject through a reference to the preceding pericope. See below n. 397.

392 *SRAG*'s citation, p. 85. This accords with the version in Gen. R. #11, p. 90, discussed below, Gen. R. #12, p. 103, and Vat MS 60 to Gen. R. #82 [Makor ed., p. 307]. See Albeck in Theodor and Albeck, *Bereschit Rabba*, 2:996, notes.

393 "That whole day"--and not, "the whole day"--represents the best reading. See in addition to the y. variants, the readings in Gen. R.: first, note Gen. R. #11, p. 90, on which see Albeck's notes and MS Vat 60 [Makor ed., p. 33]. Secondly, cp. Gen. R. #12, pp. 103-104, and variants. Although MS Vat 60 to #12 [Makor ed., p. 38] refers the reader to the previous section, #11, for the entire pericope, the MS closes its notational cross-referent with KL ƆWTW HYWM. Vat MS 30 provides no evidence for sections #11-12, as a lacunae runs from section #7-16. Thirdly, at Gen. R. #82, Vat MS 30 [Makor ed., p 147] has a GRS notation that the portion is deleted but ends the notation with a citation of the close of the deleted section, KL ƆWTW HYWM. MS Vat 60 [Makor, p. 307], which contains the whole pericope, reads KL ƆWTW HYWM.

[394] See *Samuel's Commentary*, pp. 192-193.

[395] The text reads: "Rabbi Levi in the name of Rabbi Nezira, '. . . As soon as the Sabbath departed it started to get dark.  Man became frightened and said, . . .'  Said Rabbi Levi, 'At that very hour God prepared for him two flints, and he struck them against each other, and from them came out fire, as it is written. . . .'  And he said over it the blessing, 'Who createst the lights of the fire.'"

[396] See Bokser, "Two Traditions," p. 49, n. 9, and Hyman, 3:851-852 and 859-860.

[397] This applies likewise to the reading "over it" cited in n. 2, above. "Over the fire" is primary, and "over it" represents an attempt further to integrate the tradition into the *sugya*.

[398] Some of the material in the Midrashim has been altered or adapted to the context.  See esp. M. Friedmann, *Pesikta Rabbati* (Vienne, 1880; reprint ed., Tel Aviv, 1963), pp. 118a-b, nn. 51-52, who discusses the parallels; Theodor and Albeck, in *Bereschit Rabba*, 1:89-90, notes; and Bokser, "Two Traditions," pp. 49-50.

Note the formulation in Midrash Tehillim, #92. 4, in Salomon Buber ed., *Midrasch Tehillim* (Vilna, 1891), p. 405.  While it lacks the attribution to Samuel and includes the LPYKK, it does not contain the repetition of the reason, "since it is the beginning of its creation."  The reading thus supports our sensitivity as to what constitutes a smooth reading.

[399] We translate Pesiqta Rabbati from Friedman's text, against which we checked the Prague first edition.  MSS and editions of Gen. R. all lack the LPYKK, "therefore," though they slightly vary in the opening formulation.  The passage appears in several locations in Gen. R.  We find it in:

First, Gen. R. #11.  *Yalqut HaMakhiri*, Psalms, p. 266, citation of Gen. R., and printed editions, as cited in Theodor and Albeck, have ᵓTYᵓ KŠMWᵓL. *Midrash Bereschit Rabba*, *Codex Vatican 60*, p. 33, a MS second in importance only to Vat MS 30 [the latter is missing section #11], reflects this reading. It has ᵓTYH KHHYYᵓ DTNY R. YŠMᶜ.  The attribution to Ishmael instead of Samuel may be the result of a common interchange between the names of these two masters.  See Epstein, *ITM*, pp. 213-214.  Cp. Yellin to b. Pes. 54a, and Higger, 9:291, #133.  If the notation as to a *baraita*, DTNY, is not a mistake, this reading may reflect a stage of the tradition in which Samuel's comment circulated as a *baraita* which explains Mishnah.  See below, the reference to Vatican MS 60 at #82, which reads, . . . KDŠMWᵓL.  A slightly different reading of #11, found in London MS and Yalqut Shimoni's citation of the text, has KŠMWᵓL without the ᵓTYᵓ.  Moreover, *Yalqut Shimoni* [based on Oxford MS] (Jerusalem, 1973), 1:51, while it lacks the attributive formula, presents the tradition as an independent statement.  Cp. Theodor and Albeck, p. 89, n. to line 6, and Luncz, p. 76b, note 27.

Secondly, Gen. R. #12, pp. 103-104, text and variants to ls. 6-14, esp. ls. 12-13.  Vatican MS 30 lacks the entire section of #12, while Vatican MS 60 abbreviates and deletes the pericope and refers the reader to the previous section, #11.

Thirdly, Gen. R. #82.  All texts and MSS that Albeck, in Theodor and Albeck, *Bereschit Rabba*, p. 996, cites, in addition to Vatican MS 60 [Makor ed., p. 307], have ᵓTYYH KDŠMWᵓL.  Of note, Vat MS 60, in contrast to Section #11, here attributes the tradition to Samuel, ᵓTYYH KDŠMWᵓL ŠMWᵓ ᵓ\ . . .

[400] This applies as well to the pattern without the word ᵓTYYH, and just with KŠMWᵓL, "like Samuel," though the former is the standard formulation. See n. 399.

[401] See the literature cited above, to tradition #101, n. 19 and text thereto.  Cp. Edward A. Goldman, *Parallel Texts in the PT to Gen. R.* (Chs. I-V) (Cinn: HUC-JIR, 1969), pp. 84-91, who analyzes the parallel material that precedes Samuel's comment.

[402]See *DS* 155:300.  Col MS has space for a second YŠR but lacks the word.
In its place we find dots, which may indicate that the word has been erased.

[403]See *DS* 155:400 and Col MS, which likewise lacks, "Ulla turned."  We
have basically followed Rashi's rendering of D through H.  Certain difficulties,
however, remain.  Their elucidation must await separate study.  Meanwhile see
Meir b. Gedaliah Lublin [= Meharam], "Me³ir Einei Ḥakhamim," in back of standard BT, and A. Goldberg, "R. Ze^cira," *Tarbiẓ* 36 (1967):336-337.

[404]See *DS* 155:1.  Col MS has "I did not speak [about] this but [about]
the other [teaching] of R. Yohanan."  Cp. Jacob Emden, "Novellae," to b. Pes.
53b [in back of standard BT editions].

[405]See *DS* 155.

[406]See *DS* 155; *OhG. Pesaḥim*, p. 73; and *SRAG*, pp. 85, 172.  Some sources
including Col MS read, "And they follow whom?  In accord with . . ."

[407]Goldberg, "R. Ze^cira," *Tarbiẓ* 36 (1967):336-337, cogently argues that
in D, R. Abba, a Babylonian, follows the practice common to Babylonians,
especially R. Zeira, of attributing Babylonian traditions, here Samuel's, to
Yohanan.

[408]See Shmuel Isaac Hillman, *Sefer Or HaYashar ^cal Yerushalmi* (Jerusalem,
1947), p. 10, to y. Ber. 8:5.  See also Moshe Ḥalavah ^cal *Masekhet Pesaḥim*
(Jerusalem, 1873; reprint ed., 1972), pp. 130b-131a; cp. the comments of
Solomon Luria, *Hokhmat Shelomo HaShalem*; Maharam to b. Pes. 53b; and Eleazer
Moseh HaLevi Horowitz, "Haggahot Veḥiddushim" [in Standard BT editions].

[409]And we should read "over the fire," and not "over it."

[410]See, for example, R. Yom Tov Ashbili to b. Pes. 54a; Moshe Ḥalavah
[p. 131a, top]; Meiri, esp. to b. Ber. 53b, s.v. PRWŠW BTLMWD PSHYM, ed. Daik-
man, p. 200, and to b. Pes. 54a, ed. Yosef Klein (Jerusalem, 1967²), pp. 193-
194.

[411]In addition to L, V, and S MSS, we have Geniza fragments published by
J. N. Epstein, "Geniza Fragments to the Yerushalmi, 4-6," *Tarbiẓ* 3 (1932):
237-238.  See also Lieberman, *YK*, pp. 288-289, *TK*, 3:366f., and Epstein, *ITM*,
pp. 8-10, 43, 183-185.  We rely also on the author's class notes of Saul
Lieberman, in Talmud A, Jewish Theological Seminary of American, New York, New
York, October 3, 1970 [wherein Lieberman revises aspects of *YK*, pp. 288-290].
We primarily cite variants which affect the comments on M. Ber. 8:6.  Additional data appear in our studies of Samuel on M. Eruv. 5:1 and M. A.Z. 1:1-2.
    In each of the two parallels in y., the portion relevant to the location
and its Mishnah appears first.  Y. A.Z. 1:2 includes the comments of Rav and
Samuel and the explanations thereto, but neither the citations of the *mishnayot*
to which the masters refer nor J.  See Epstein, *ITM*, pp. 183-185.

[412]On A-B, see also *Yalqut HaMakhiri* to Is. 50:4, p. 184, and *Aruch*,
1:330, s.v. ³T (second entry) and especially Epstein, *ITM*, p. 185.  We transliterate the substance of the comments of Rav and Samuel.  As discussed below,
the two masters dispute whether Mishnah employs an *alef* or an *ayin*.  Since the
gutturals had weakened, the pronunciation did not provide proof as to the
correct orthography.  See E. Y. Kutscher, *Studies in Galilean Aramaic* (Ramat
Gan, 1976), pp. 67-96, 104f., esp. 69, 83-85, 89-92.  Cp. Kutscher, *Archive*,
pp. 83-89.  The anonymous *Gemara* assumes the differences in spelling reflect
a dispute as to the correct root and thus the meaning of the words.  As analogous pericopae in b. and y. assume that the dispute has exegetical implications,
they must derive from a relatively early date.  See y. Ber. 8:6, y. Eruv. 5:1,
and y. A.Z. 1:2, and b. Eruv. 53a-b, and b. A.Z. 2a, as well as the materials
cited in Engel, *Giljonei*, 1:19b, to Ber. 53b, s.v. ³YB^cY' LHW.  Commentators
generally do not distinguish between these two levels.  But their remarks

remain useful so as to understand the anonymous interpretations and clarifica-
tions of the earlier amoraic comments. See, e.g., PM. Qorban Haedah to y.
Eruv; S [on which see, in Vilna ed., note 2; and Samuel D. Luzzatto, *Ohev Ger*
(Cracow, 1895), pp. 41-43], Samuel D. Luzzatto, *Perush $^c$al Ḥamishah Ḥumshe
Torah*, ed. P. Schlesinger (Tel Aviv, 1965), to Gen. 34:15; and Dinglas to
Sirillo, loc. cit. Once we distinguish between the import of Rav's and
Samuel's comments and their interpretations we may solve several exegetical
problems in the *sugya*. See, e.g., n. 419, below, and the correlation of B
with both L, below, and with tradition #115 (that the blessing over the fire
is said Saturday night), from y. Ber. 8:5, 12b, above. Cp. Emunat Yosef, and
H. Albeck, "Variants in the Mishnah of Amoraim," in *Abhandlungen zur Erinnerung
an Hirsch Perez Chajes* (Vienne, 1933), Hebrew Section, pp. 1-28, esp. 14, 19,
and 26.

[413]See *TK*, 3:366-367; Epstein, *ITM*, pp. 8-10, 43, 183-184; Hanoch Yalon,
*Introduction to the Vocalization of the Mishnah* (Jerusalem, 1964), pp. 85-87.
Cp. Kutscher, *Archive*, 83-89.

[414]In y. Eruv., L MS and RH citation, at b. Eruv. 53a, read Rav/Samuel
teaches (TNY), *edehen*. The presentation as a *baraita* accords with the analogue
in b. A.Z. 2a. But of note, y. A.Z. 1:2, like y. Ber. 8:6 has ᵓmr, "Said."
See also Higger, 1:151-159; 2:253, #51; and 4:449-464; and Epstein, *ITM*.

[415]V MS; *Yalqut HaMakhiri* to Is. 44:9, p. 147; and L MS and RH citation
[at b. Eruv. 53a] to y. Eruv. have ᵓedehen, with an *alef*, for Rav, and $^c$edehen,
with an *ayin*, for Samuel and thus attribute to each a consistent position as to
the *alef* or *ayin* in all three cases. L MS in y. Ber. and A.Z., Venice p.e., S,
and Epstein, "Fragments," have $^c$edehen with an *ayin* for Rav, and ᵓedehen with
an *alef* for Samuel. See Epstein, *ITM*, 183-185, Ratner, *Ber.*, p. 190, and
Kutscher, esp. pp. 79-80. Cp. Lieberman, *YK*, pp. 288-289, which, as mentioned,
the author has revised in part. His argument in *YK* is based upon clause J,
which, Epstein, however, suggests is secondary.

[416]Lieberman, class notes, and *ITM*, p. 184.

[417]MH = Epstein, "Fragments," and L MS to y. Eruv. See Luncz. The reading of MᵓN, "Who," or "The one who," in L MS undoubtedly is influenced by the
instances of MᵓN throughout the *sugya*.

[418]See n. 419 and text to n. 429.

[419]See Epstein, *ITM*, pp. 184-185, Lieberman class notes, and below, text
to n. 432. The items in Epstein and the texts cited in n. 415, above, provide
textual witnesses to this pericope.

Epstein notes that J.1. is not in y. A.Z. 1:2, the clause's "natural" or
"original" location, on M.A.Z., nor in the RH citation of y. Eruv. 5:1. V MS
to y. Ber. 8:6 contains a remnant of a reading which deletes J.1. and includes
only J.2. It opens with J.2. and reverts to J.1. See Epstein, *ITM*, p. 184, n.
4. If we assume J.1. postdates I, we may without difficulty explain the use
of Is. 44:9. As Emunat Yosef asked, if J.2. is projected as Samuel's understanding of Is. 44:9, how does that rendering preclude the use of the verse as
a proof text for the "alternative" derivation of *edehen* which Samuel had
rejected? Moreover, how did Rav understand the verse? Commentators have
struggled with this. See, e.g., S; Azikri: Samuel Yafeh b. Isaac Ashkenazi,
*Yefeh Mareh* (reprint ed., in *Yer. Zera$^c$im*); and Luncz. One such "solution"
suggests that J.2. indicates that the verse's subject is a judgment day and,
therefore, the verse is irrelevant to the usage in M, where the subject is
idols.

[420]Lines L. 1-3 are found also in *Responsa Rashi* (Solomon ben Isaac),
ed. Israel Elfenbein (New York, 1943), #98, p. 224.

[421]So Ven. p.e.; L and V MSS; Epstein, "Fragments"; and citation in
*Responsa Rashi*. "And R. Yoḥanan said," = S MS.

[422]See Epstein, "Fragments," p. 238, n. to l. 12.

[423]HYNNH = S and L MS.  HNYNH = Ven. p.e. and Epstein, "Fragments."  On the possible identification of these two names, see n. 436.

[424]The word, *triclinium*, literally means a large dining room.  Rabbinic sources extend its definition to a large room.  See Frankel, *PT*; Luncz, 1:35b, n. 1; and Krauss, *QT*, 1.2:412, 437-438.  See, e.g., T. Ber. 6:21, p. 39, ls. 100-101; M. Eruv. 6:6; and M. B.B. 6:4, which refers in increasing size to rooms, and places TRQLYN last, "after a large room," and defines it as "ten by ten."

[425]As to the possible significance to the presence of Zeira in the first pericope in the *sugya*, see text to n. 432.  The reference to Zeira, while only a marginal addition in L MS, appears in V and S MSS and in Epstein, "Fragments." See Epstein, *IAL*, p. 368, n. 21, and Sacks, *Diqduqe*, p. 37, n. 2.

[426]The *sugya* that precedes A-N deals with the requirement to use the light.  As indicated below, text to n. 432, it opens with a tradition which is attributed to Zeira and which implies that one must make use of the light before one may say the blessing.  See, e.g., Luncz, ad loc. and n. 425.

[427]See n. 2, above.
Epstein, *ITM*, pp. 183-185, suggests that the *ayin* derives from an etymological spelling and the *alef* from a Galilean pronunciation, and that Rav, who had studied in Palestine, consistently follows the latter.  But see Kutscher, *Studies* and *Archive*.

[428]See n. 412.  We follow Epstein's philological and textual analysis, focus on the comments to M. Ber. 8:6, and leave more extensive treatment of the other *mishnayot* and their comments to our study of those tractates.
An alternative explanation for the motivation for C is that the anonymous circles used the variations in spelling as a point of departure for an exposition.  See especially the use of the tradition in b. A.Z. 2a.

[429]See nn. 418-419 and texts thereto.

[430]Cp. Lieberman, *YK*, p. 288.  [Lieberman no longer holds that the *sugya* in y. A.Z. should be on M.A.Z. 1:1 and not 1:2, as found in the L MS.]
Our analysis assumes that masters actually commented on each separate text and that someone did not merely apply the dispute which originated in one text to other instances of words with weakened gutturals.

[431]Class notes to October 3, 1970, lecture.

[432]See nn. 425-426 and cp. Goldberg, "R. Ze$^c$ira," *Tarbiz* 36 (1967).

[433]See *Samuel's Commentary*, pp. 192-193.  Note the observations in Rashba to b. ber. 53b, s.v. RB HW$^⊃$ . . . , as to the plain sense of M. and Mel. S. to M. Ber. 8:6.

[434]See n. 424.

[435]This is how *Gemara* understands line M.  For in N, as indicated in text to n. 432, students cite line M as a challenge to the action of Zeira, who had drawn the light close to himself.  See Rashba and Yellin to b. Ber. 53b, and, in general, cp. Azikri.
An analysis of the analogous *sugya* in b. Ber. 53a-b, reveals several different criteria.  [BT does not contain a dispute as to the correct orthography of *yeoto* in M. Ber. 8:6B.]  See the *baraita* and traditions there; *DS* 284, especially notes 200, 2, and 3, and Florence MS; and RH, *OhG*, p. 88; David b. Levi of Narbonne, pp. 107-108; Meshulam of Beziers, "Sefer HaHashlamah, in *Ginze Rishonim. Berakhot*, p. 249, Ashbili, p. 483; Rashbas, pp. 203-204; and

especially Rashba, *TK*, 1:98, the comments of Rashi in *Responsa*, #98, pp. 123-
124, *DS* 284:2 and note [to which add Florence MS] and A. Weiss, *Literature*,
pp. 69-74, especially 69, n. 37, 71, n. 46, and 73-74.

[436] Zeira is a Babylonian while Yohanan and Hoshiah are Palestinians. The
identity of the master in L.3. is not clear; see n. 423. The possibilities
include: (1) a third-generation Palestinian Amora by the name of Hinana;
Margalioth, col. 308. (2) Haninah, a first-generation Babylonian who traveled
to Palestine. He apparently was Yohanan's senior. See Hyman, pp. 484-488;
and Frankel, *Introduction*, pp. 86b-87. (3) A later Palestinian master,
colleague of R. Mana; Hyman 2:497-498, and Lieberman, *Caesarea*, p. 94. See
also the reading in *Aruch*, 5:151, s.v. MLZMH, HNYNH CNTWNYTYH, a fourth-
generation Palestinian; Hyman, p. 499. Cp. *Aruch*, *Sup.*, p. 256. The problem
is compounded by the fact that texts throughout *Gemara* interchangeably use
Haninah and Hinanah. See, e.g., J. N. Epstein, "Leiden MS," *Tarbiz* 6
(1944), p. 44. Only by way of a guess, would we assume that the reading in
L.3. refers to the late master by that name.

[437] T. Ber. 5:31's rule mentions seeing and using the light but does not
define those terms, something which Samuel, for one, does clarify.

[438] "Hiyya = L and S MSS. "Aha" = V MS and Epstein, "Fragments," p. 238,
l. 2. The former refers to the third-generation Babylonian Amora who emigrated
to Palestine where he studied with R. Yohanan. He apparently had access to
Samuel traditions, perhaps through R. Huna. See Frankel, *Introduction*, pp.
81b-82b, especially 82a-82b; Margalioth, cols. 291-295; Albeck, *Introduction*,
pp. 236-237. "Aha," on the other hand, refers to a fourth-generation Palestinian Amora. See Frankel, *Introduction*, pp. 82a-82b; Margalioth, cols. 67-70.
Albeck, *Introduction*, pp. 316-318. Due to the connections with Babylonian
traditions and R. Yohanan, R. Hiyya is more likely to be Samuel's tradent.
See n. 442.

[439] We follow the reading in Epstein, "Fragments," p. 238, which substantively = L and S MSS. The Venice and most printed editions include a marginal
addition to the L MS which attributes M. Ber. 8:7 B'.2 to Samuel and assigns
Samuel's comment to sages, as "And sages say." On the variants see Epstein,
"Fragments," p. 238, footnotes to ls 2-3, *IAL*, p. 369, n. 23 [which was written
before Epstein," Fragments," though published after it]; and cp. Sacks,
*Diqduqe*, p. 37, n. 4.
    The text of the L MS presents M. Ber. 8:7 B'.1 as A and then the two
traditions found in B. The marginal addition in L MS along with the text of
the L MS accords with the reading in V MS. It cites M. Ber. 8:7 B'.2, the
second half of the lemma and then the phrase, "And sages say," which Epstein
suggests represents the corruption of the y. terminology, "[Words of] Sages."
The latter phrase is used to aver that the coming clause represents the
*halakhah*. See also Epstein, *Tarbiz* 6 (1934):49-50. Cp. Sacks, *Diqduqe*, pp.
37-38, n. 4, for an alternative explanation of the corruption.
    S contains M. Ber. 8:7 B'.2 as the lemma, then M. Ber. 8:7 B'.1 as the
introduction to B, and thereby presents the two traditions as replacements of
B'.2 of Mishnah. The two traditions would have originated as glosses to
Mishnah, which then entered its text. S lacks, "And sages say,"
    Perhaps the function of Samuel's (and Yohanan's) comment as a gloss to
Mishnah contributed to the confusion or corruption in the tradition. See
below, and also Azikri; Israel Eisenstein, "Amude Yerushalayim," in standard
editions of PT; Fulda [and the reading in the Amsterdam edition of PT printed
along with Fulda]; Meir Netiv, n. 4; Luncz, p. 78a, note 17; Ratner, p. 190,
and the reference to our y. in *OZ*, 1:32b, #212.

[430] "Until" = V and S MSS, Epstein, "Fragments," and correction in L MS.
"As long as (he is hungry)" = text of L MS. The latter constitutes an inappropriate definition of satiation from a meal and liability to say Grace. While
b.'s version of Yohanan's tradition employs this opening formulation, it
includes a negative, "As long as he is *not* hungry." See n. 442. Accordingly,

Samuel's comment, which appropriately employs the "as long as" language, and/
or b.'s version may have generated the latter reading.  See Sacks, *Diqduqe*,
p. 38, n. 1.

[441]See n. 440 for an unsuccessful attampt to make Yohanan's comment
balance Samuel's.

[442]See *DS* 286:30.  The FL MS reads like the printed editions.
The comparison of the b. and y. pericopae deserves further comment as it
may throw light on the transmission of Samuel's tradition.  BT cites a second
tradition, after Yohanan's which is attributed to R. Simeon b. Laqish and which
is identical to Samuel's.  BT then includes a second pericope which analyzes
Simeon b. Laqish's criterion in light of a different tradition attributed to
that master and harmonizes the two.
    If the transmission of the several traditions have not been corrupted,
two possibilities explain the diverse attribution of the criterion of "thirst"
to Samuel and to Simeon b. Laqish.  First, the b. circle which transmitted and
cited Samuel's tradition in Palestine did not stand behind the tradition in
b. Ber. 53b.  Hiyya, Samuel's tradent in y., may have played a central role in
the pericope.  A third-generation master, he studied with Huna and may thereby
have had access to Samuel's traditions.  He emigrated to Palestine, where he
studied with Yohanan.  See above, n. 438.  Accordingly, perhaps we have an
additional example of the inroad or Babylonization of traditions in Palestine.
See above, to traditions #56, 65, and 67.  If Simeon b. Laqish's attribution
was known, perhaps the Babylonian Hiyya preferred to cite his tradition in the
name of Babylonian.  This would be especially true if Hiyya knew Samuel's tradition in the form of a gloss to Mishnah.  On the other hand, the b. pericope
on Simeon b. Laqish's tradition has fifth- and sixth-generation masters, a R.
Yeemar [b. Shelamiah, or someone else, See *DS* 286:30, and Flr MS] before Mar
Zutra.  See Margalioth, cols. 563, 645-646; Albeck, *Introduction*, pp. 411-412,
435-436.  This circle either did not know or choose to cite Samuel's tradition.
They preferred to cite Simeon b. Laqish, Yohanan's regular disputant.  Significantly, Yohanan's and Simeon b. Laqish's opinions, in contrast to those of
Yohanan and Samuel, make up a balanced dispute form and may have circulated as
a unit.
    An alternative explanation approaches the problem differently.  As far
as the y. traditions, the role of Hiyya remains the same.  But as to the b.
ones, perhaps we should not follow b.'s harmonization of the two Simeon b.
Laqish traditions.  If so, we should assign the second Simeon tradition to that
master but not the first, i.e., the one which accords with Samuel's teaching.
We might then hypothesize that Samuel actually stood behind the latter tradition but for some reason was not given the attribution.  On the b. *sugya*, see
*DS* 286, especially note to line 30; Flr MS; Ashbili, p. 484, esp. n. 131, to
which see *DS* 67:7 [to b. Ber. 15a]; Rashi; *OhG*, RH, p. 62; Tosafot; and
Yellin.
    While we remain unsure which, if any, of the two alternatives account
for the diverse attributions, our analysis underscores the transmission's
impact on the tradition and the significance of the forms employed.

[443]So Epstein, *IAL*, p. 369, n. 3.  Cp. E. Shulsinger, *YE*.

[444]Most commentators thus suggest that Samuel and Yohanan provide signs
for the digestion of food.  See, e.g., Sirillo; Śedeh Yehoshua; Fulda; PM;
Luncz; Bertinoro; and esp. Mel. S. and GRA, SE.

[445]E.g., Sirillo and Luncz.  Dr. Gene Weininger advises me that the
duration of satiation, presence of thirst, and recurrence of hunger depends to
a great degree on the body functions of each individual, cultural habits of
eating, and types of foods consumed.

[446]The identical text appears in T. Ber. 3:26, p. 18, ls. 97-99.  Mishnah's context is blessings over things which a person enjoys, while that of
Tosefta is the blessings of the *Tefillah*.  See *TK*, 1:55, and also T. Ber.
5:21, p. 28, ls. 42-43.

447See *DS* 286-287:100; Florence MS. See the full citation of Beth Nathan, cited in *DS*, in Coronel ed., p. 32d; and *HG*, II, p. 43.

448See *DS*; Mel. S.; Rashbas; and Higger, 6:492.

449On the term, see Goodblatt, *Rabbinic Instruction*, pp. 111-114.

450On the interpretation of this clause, see Rashba; Rosh; Rabiah, 1:133, #144; David b. Levi of Narbonne, p. 110; Ashbili, p. 485; and Meiri, p. 201. Considering that the clause is missing in Flr MS, that it has several variant readings, and is subject to diverse interpretations, it may be secondary to the text. See the formulation in Agamati.

451On the meaning of Mishnah, see *TK*, 1:55, 86-87.

452See Higger's remarks, 2:11-12.

453See, e.g., the reference in Mel. S. It is possible, as well, that the question serves to clarify the principle in Mishnah, viz.: Is the special situation caused by Samaritans due to their status and character or due to their ability to say the blessing?

454L MS and Venice first edition. This reading finds support in the version in Midrash Tehillim, 16.#8, pp. 122-123, variants cited in n. 32, supported by the citation in *Yalqut HaMakhiri* to Psalms, p. 90; and Zedekiah b. Abraham Anav, *Shibbolei HaLeqet*, ed. Buber, #165, p. 66a, cited by Buber, n. 32, and Lieberman, *TK*, 1:60.

Ratner cites Tosf. RY"H as a witness to this reading, but in a new critical edition of this work, as Tosf. R. Judah Sir Leon, 2:603, we find the second version. See n. 455. On the readings, as well as the import of the two positions and the rationale for the dispute, cp. the treatment of Louis Finkelstein, "The Prayer of King David According to the Chronciler," *EI* 14 (1978):126*-127*, 110-116.

455V and S MSS. [In the text of S we find the addition of a conjunctive "and," W-, "And (a person) has to . . ."] Citations include Rosh to b. Ber. 54a [on which see Heller, "Divre Ḥamudot," note 7, loc. cit.]; Tosf. HaRosh, in *Berakhah Meshuleshet*, p. 38; Tosf. R. Judah, 2:603; Ashbili, p. 487; Elijah of London on M. Ber. 9:1, p. 119; Rashba to b. Ber. 54a; Rabiah, #114, 1:96; and Aaron HaKohen of Lunel, *Orhot Ḥayyim*, 1, *Hilkhot Berakhot*, #68 [= p. 90a]. See also Ratner, p. 195; J. Heinemann, "The Formula Melekh Ha-Colam," *JJS* 11 (1960): 179; and E. J. Wiesenberg, "The Liturgical Term Melekh Ha-Colam," *JJS* 15 (1964): 18-19, 33-35.

456See *TK*, 1:59-60, 103; Heinemann, *Prayer*, Ch. 3, pp. 52-55, 57-59, esp. p. 57, n. 14, 61-63, Ch. 7, pp. 99-101, 102, 111, 112; Elbogen, pp. 3, 197-199, and esp. Heinemann's notes, pp. 383-384. See also A. Spanier, "Zur Formengeschichte des altjudischen Gebetes," *MGWJ* 78 (1934): 438-447, esp. 442-446; and W. S. Towner, "'Blessed be YHWH' and "Blessed art Thou, YHWH': The Modulation of a Biblical Formula," *CBQ* 30 (1968): 386-399. Cp. the discussion by J. Weiss, C. Roth, J. Heinemann, and E. J. Wiesenberg, in *JJS* 10 (1959): 169-170; 11 (1960): 173-175, esp. 177-179, n.b. 179; especially 15 (1964): 1-56, and 149-154, n.b. 150, 152, as well as Heinemann's revised views in the English edition of *Prayer* (Berlin, 1977), pp. 94-96, n. 26.

457See Rashba and Meiri, p. 202, to b. Ber. 54a; Lieberman, *TK*, 1:60, 103; Heinemann, *Prayer*, pp. 54-55, 102, n. 10. For sure, the lack of a "full" formula may mean that the blessing actually lacks it and we, therefore, do not always deal with an abbreviated text. See the Dura Europos fragment presented in Lieberman, *Yemenite Midrashim* (Jerusalem, 1940), p. 40; y. Ber. 6:2, 10b, the incident of a Persian before Rav; Lieberman's comments, *TK*, 1:60, which revises his remarks in *Yemenite Midrashim*, and *HY*, p. 40, n. 8. See also, Weisenberg, pp. 46-51.

[458] See Heinemann, *Prayer*, p. 57, n. 14; *TK*, 1:60; and below.

[459] See Sirillo; Zedekiah b. Abraham Anav; Buber in *Midrasch Tehillim*, p. 122, n. 32; Sacks, in Tosf. R. Judah, 2:603, n. 15; and Lieberman, *TK*, 1:60, especially n. 10. Cp. Rabiah, 1:97, n. 2; Wiesenberg, pp. 47-48, and 50, n. 232, who argues that the two masters may not dispute; and below, n. 465 and text thereto.

[460] See, e.g., Tosf. and Rashba to M. Ber. 9:1 on b. Ber. 54a.

[461] See n. 457. Note especially the traditions attributed to Rav and Samuel in y. Ber. 9:3, both of which open with the work WṢRYK, the same term used in y. Ber. 9:1's traditions, and one of the former has the same wording as that of Samuel's tradition in the latter. If the former usage applies in the latter case, the traditions may be formulated as glosses.

[462] We cite this example as b. Ber. 54a presents a tradition which employs it as a proof text for M. Ber. 9:1.
        See Heinemann, especially the list, p. 55, n. 9, and the literature which he cites, to which add, Towner, and Moshe Greenberg, "on the Refinement of the Conception of Prayer in Hebrew Scriptures," *AJS Review* 1 (1976):71-74. The two biblical instances of the "Thou" pattern are in Ps. 119:12, and 1 Chron. 29:10. See Heinemann, *Prayer*, pp. 58-59, and Finkelstein.

[463] See Heinemann and the literature there and the observations in Finkelstein.

[464] Heinemann, *Prayer*. Some medieval commentators, e.g., Abraham ben David, Rashba (who cites R. Abraham b. David), Meiri, pp. 202, 204, classified rabinic prayers into different types and argued that certain formulae applied to only certain categories. See also *EJ*, 4:484-488, s.v. "Benedictions," by Ed.

[465] See Heinemann, *Prayer*, pp. 53-54, and cp. Finkelstein. We may be able to correlate Lieberman's comments, *TK*, 1:60, with our text. He suggests that the phrase, ". . . *enah berakhah*," ". . . is not a blessing," means the pattern is not a proper one to be preferred but after the fact is accepted. Cp. the use here of the formulation, ṢRYK, "[one] has to say . . . ," and not a stronger language, as "does not fulfill one's requirement." On Samuel's view, see also Zedekiah b. Abraham Anav; Sirillo; *TK*, 1:60; the possibly related view from y. Ber.6:2, 10b, #92, in chapter three, which supports Meiri's position as to the use of nonstandardized versions of the blessing over bread, a version of which appears in b. Ber. 40b (see chapter three, n. 87). Cp. Rav's view at b. Ber. 40b, and y. Ber. 6:3, 10b, to which see *HY*, p. 40, n. 8, and *TK*, 1:60-61; and below, n. 14. A comparison of our *sugya* with b. Ber. 40b deserves further attention. See Rabiah, 1:97, n. 2, and Weiss, *Notes*, pp. 44-45, and 95-98. Note Rav's view at b. Ber. 40b and the version in Ginzberg, *Genizah Studies*, 2:39, and in *OhG*, which A. Weiss discusses. Finally, see Zuri, *Rav*, pp. 248, 258, 267, and esp. 283, who tries to place Rav's view within his general theology.
        To reemphasize our earlier analysis, Samuel may be allowing a nonstandardized but popular version and this may be reflected in the Dura version of Grace After Meals. See Lieberman's presentation of the text, in *Yemenite Midrashim*. The fragment lacks the "Thou" and God's name. See n. 457 above.

[466] We note the preceding tradition which is attributed to Rav is transmitted by Zeira. Following our suggestion elsewhere, it is possible that he is also the tradent for Samuel's comment. See chapter eight, subsections 2.F and 4.A.

[467] See Meiri's language, p. 202, that the issues of nonmandatory blessings appears "right near the Mishnah," TKP LMŠNH; Fulda's explicit observation; and cp. Šedeh Yehoshua, and Ginzberg, *Genizah Studies*, 2:11-12. But see n. 461.

[468]See *Makhon-Mishnah* for varients.

[469]Flr MS = "Said R. Judah said Samuel."

[470]Immanuel Loew suggests a vocalization of *kokhba deshavet*. See I. Loew, "Lexikalische Miszellen," *Festschrift zum Siebigstem Geburstage David Hoffmann's*, ed. S. Eppenstein, et al. (Berlin, 1914; reprint ed., Jerusalem, 1970), p. 138. See also J. N. Epstein, "ZYQYN und RWḤWT," *MGWJ* 63 (1920): 15-19.

[471]"Firmament," = M and Flr MSS and others, including *Midrash HaGadol* to Ex. 10:2, p. 147. See *DS* 332:20.

"Heavens" = printed edition. On the phrase, "paths" or "roads of the sky" for stars, see A. Leo Oppenheim, *Ancient Mesopotamia* (Chicago, 1964, 1968), p. 308.

[472]KSLᵓ. On the identification with Orion, see *EM*, 3:103, s.v., KYMᵓ WKSYL, by "Ed."

[473]*Gemara* contains two additional traditions which focus on astronomical matters and which form part of the same *sugya* with A-E. Both may provide further explanations for the visual mistake. Some commentators believe that the first one refers to Mishnah and thus represents an alternative definition of *ziqim*. Cp., Rashi, Meiri, p. 208, and Elijah of London, pp. 120-121, with Tosf., s.v., WYLWN.

[474]The lemma is found in V and S MS. L and V MSS place before Samuel's initial tradition a teaching of Bar Qappara on earthquakes [in V, after the lemma]. Sirillo logically places it after the end of the *sugya* on *ziqim* and as an introduction to the *Gemara* on "earthquakes." It is difficult to know if this sequence constituted S's reading or his rearranging of the materials.

For citations of y., see Ratner, p. 199, and *Ginze Kedem* 5 (1934):31-32.

[475]HHN = L and S MSS and Venice p.e. HDYN - V MS. See *EJ*, 3:272, s.v. "Aramaic, 'Western Aramaic,'" by Kulscher.

[476]L and S have ZYQᵓ a more Aramaized form than V MS' ZYQH.

[477]V MS and S add ᵓLᵓ, "rather." [For S, the word is in the text of the British Mus. MS, and added between the lines in the Paris MS.]

[478]ŠQQY = "alleys." Samuel is thus familiar with not only the public areas but also the small ways. See *Aruch*, 8:146b; J. Payne Smith, *A Compenious Syriac Dictionary* (Oxford, 1903, 1967), s.v.; and Fulda. For "heavens," V has PYMH, an apparent corruption of ŠMYᵓ.

[479]QRTY = L and S MSS. QRTYM = V MS.

[480]MH HWᵓ = L MS and Venice. MH ᶜSQYH = V MS. MH HWᵓ [in Paris MS of S = MHW] ᶜYSQYH = S MS. I do not include the following pericope which inquires as to the source of Samuel's astronomical knowledge. Cp. Deut. R. 8:8, Lieberman ed. *Neṣavim*, #6, pp. 118-119. See Shulsinger, *YE*, p. 18a, to y. Ber. 9:2.

[481]See, e.g., GRA, SE for a suggestion why Mishnah specifies these five items. On the theology here see, e.g., Max Kadushin, *Worship and Ethics* (New York, 1963).

[482]See, e.g., *OhG*, "Commentaries," p. 91, especially n. 5; Rashi; Maimonides *MT*, *Berakhot* 10:14; *Aruch*, 3:313, s.v. ZQ; 4:220, s.v. KKB; especially Loew [see n. 470]; especially J. N. Epstein, "ZYQYN und RWHWT." See also Stephen A. Kaufman, *The Akkadian Influences on Aramaic* (Chicago, 1974) pp. 113-114. On the possible biblical reference to ŠBT, in Num. 24:17, see

*OhG*, "Commentaries," p. 91, Harry M. Orlinsky, ed., *Notes on the New Translation of The Torah* (Philadelphia, 1969), p. 238, and especially Stanley Gevirtz, "A New Look at an Old Crux: Amos 5:26," *JBL* 87 (1968):267-276, especially 269-271. As to the Aramaic word ZYQ, which means "wind," see below n. 489 and text thereto.

On the astronomical issues, see W. M. Feldman, *Rabbinical Mathematics and Astronomy* (London, 1931, New York, 1965[2]), p. 216, and his references, and especially Lloyd Motz, *This Is Astronomy* (New York, 1958, 1963), pp. 126-130. Meteors and especially comets had ominous meanings to ancients. Ms. Sara Beck, in consultation with her colleagues in the Townes Group in Astrophysics, University of California, Berkeley, informs me that given the distance of Orion, it is highly unlikely a comet would go through it. To be seen, it would have to appear just before sunrise or just after sunset and it would have to be very bright. As to a meteor, there are no showers (= groups) of meteors in Orion. At most, there might be a random meteor.

[483] See Motz, Feldman, and cp. Tosf. Y.T. to M. Ber. 9:2.

[484] On the ominous nature see Feldman, pp. 12, 192, 216; Oppenheim, p. 219.

[485] See n. 474.

[486] This earlier pericope became subject to further additions. See n. 473.

[487] Cp. Ashkenazi, *Yefeh Mareh*. On the significance of Samuel's knowledge of astronomy, see Neusner, *History*, 2:141-145, and Goodblatt, *Rabbinic Instruction*, pp. 283-285.

[488] Epstein, "ZYQYN und RWHWT."

[489] See also *Aruch*, 3:313, s.v., ZQ; E. S. Drower and R. Macuch, *A Mandaic Dictionary* (Oxford, 1963); Kaufman; and *Chicago Assyrian Dictionary* (Chicago, 1956-), Vol. "Z," p. 64, s.v., zâqu. In the b., this usage generally is in the singular, though occasionally in the plural. See *Thes. Tal.* 12:215-216.

[490] In this light, see Engel, *Giljonei Haschass*, 1:38a, bottom [to b. Ber. 54a].

[491] See *DS* 334:10, Flr MS, and *Yalqut HaMakhiri* to Ps. 77, p. 20. While the printed text has "clouds in a circle," many MSS and texts have "clouds which come into a circle." On the interpretation of the passage, see Elijah of London, p. 121, and *Tur*, OH, #127, and cp. Maimonides, *MT*, *Berakhot*.

[492] Rav = M MS and probably behind Flr MS's RB? ?. See *DS* 334:10, *Yalqut HaMakhiri*, and *OhG*, RH, p. 64.

[493] See *DS* 334:20. Flr MS places G after E, which accords with the reading in RH and perhaps *Yalqut HaMakhiri*. Flr MS, though, includes more than one version of R. Aha's comment. The fact that clause G is found in more than one place may reflect that it is secondary to the text and perhaps originated as a gloss. See Friedman, "Critical Study," pp. 305-306. Note, R. Elijah of London, p. 121, may not have had it. Cp. n. 36 there.

[494] See n. 493.

[495] See n. 493 and *DS* 334:20-30.

[496] See Francis Brown, S. R. Driver, and Charles A. Briggs, *A Hebrew and English Lexicon of the Old Testament. Based Upon the Lexicon of William Gesenius* (Oxford, 1907, 1966), and Jastrow, s.v. R[C]M; and Pope, *The Anchor Bible. Job*, pp. 240-241.

[497] See *TK*, 3:91.

[498] See Rashi, Elijah of London, and Maharsha. Note as to the explanation in D, Jer. 10:13 makes clear that God makes noise in the clouds when filling them with water before a storm. If we understand *reamim* as "thunder," E's association of lightning with thunder accords with modern science's explanation of thunder. For example, William Morris, ed., *The American Heritage Dictionary of the English Language* (Boston, 1969), defines "thunder," as, "the sound emitted by rapidly expanding gases along the path of the electrical discharge of lightning." On the formulations, see chapter six, categories H and O.

[499] Huna refers to Job 26:14 which expresses the sentiment that no one understands God's roar.

[500] See Pliny, *Natural History*, 2:131-145, esp. 142-144.

[501] Some commentators, e.g., S and PM, perhaps influenced by the analogous tradition in b. Taan. 6b, which is attributed to R. Abbahu and which speaks of "the first rain" and "the second rain," define "in the beginning" as the "time of the first rain" and "afterwards," as "the time of the second rain." The usage of the two phrases precludes this. See *Thes. Mish.* 3:1267 and *Thes. Tos* 5:179. We thus follow Qorban Haedah in y. Taan, Luncz and Frankel in by. Ber., and Ze[c]ev Wolf Einhorn, "Meharzu" (in Vilna editions of Gen. R.) to Gen. R. Cp. Azikri and E. E. HaLevi, in *Midrash Rabbah* (Tel Aviv, 1956), p. 199. See also Lieberman's careful formulation, *TK*, 5:1068, top.

[502] The word for "tiles," QRMYD, appears in Vat and S MSS, in y. Ber.; in L MS in y. Taan [i.e., but not in y. Ber.]; and in Gen. R. See *Aruch, Sup.*, p. 376; Luncz; Albeck on Gen. R. 13:15, p. 123, note to l. 5; Krauss, *QT*, 1.2:257-258, and *LW*, p. 569, and Henry George Liddell and Robert Scott, *A Greek-English Lexicon*, revised and augmented throughout by Henry Stuart Jones, with a Supplement, ed. E. A. Barber (Oxford, 1968), p. 540b.

[503] See Shulsinger, *YE*, p. 18b, on the attribution.

[504] Commentators differ as to the meaning of this phrase and the clarification-revision in D. See PM, Luncz, and Albeck to Gen. R. Our rendering is guided by the general usage of ŠRY/H "to soak," in particular the usage and the close parallel in T. B.M. 11:6, p. 395, ls. 8-9, "A person brings dirt, and piles it up upon [= before] the entrance to his house, in the public domain, so as to soak it into clay (LŠRWTW LTYṬ), to which see M. B.M. 10:5; the realia, concerning which see Brand, *Ceramics in Talmudic Literature* (Jerusalem, 1953), p. 366; cp., however, Y. Yadin, *Judean Desert Studies, The Finds from the Bar-Kokhba Period in the "Cave of Letters"* (Jerusalem, 1963), p. 118; the analogue in b. Taan, 6a; and finally the context here, as an instance of "the good" derived from rain. The suggested alternative, "dissolving a stopper" does not involve a bounty. See also M. Shab. 1:5 and Moreshet, *Lexicon*, p. 258.

[505] See n. 504, Azikri, especially PM, and Qorban Haedah in y. Taan.

[506] See *EJ*, 13:1520-1523, s.v. "Rain," by J. Katsnelson; and Elbogen, p. 96.

[507] See *TK*, 5:1067, ls. 17-18, and below n. 508.

[508] In PT, the *baraita* follows A-E, while in Gen. R. it precedes it. The definition of "sufficient for fructification" is assumed in b. Taan. 25b, where the definition has replaced the item defined, (T"R, Until when . . . the community . . .).

[509] On the relationship betweeen the criteria, see Samuel Jaffe Ashkenazi "Yefe To[ᵓ]ar," in Vilna Gen. R. eds., to Gen. R. 13:15; Albeck, in Gen. R. , p. 127, note to 1:7; and Lieberman, *TK*, 5:1068, top, and the references there.

[510]Note the several liturgical texts of prayers over rain which make up alternatives to M. Ber. 9:2's "One who is good and does good." They speak of the miracle of every drop of rain. See Weiss, *ST*, 2:439, and n. 9 there, and cp. Albeck, *Introduction*, pp. 47-48, n. 73.

[511]An analogue to Simeon b. Laqish's tradition in b. Taan. 6b and 25b, attributed to R. Abbahu, might indicate that his tradition originated in the context of ceasing a rain fast. Yet a separate tradition also attributed to R. Abbahu provides a single criterion as an answer to the question, "When do they bless over rain," i.e., our context. In any event Samuel's comment lacks any analogue and Simeon b. Laqish's tradition may not be probative. Rain fasts occurred among Palestinians and not Babylonians and therefore it is less likely to have elicited Samuel's response than would a blessing over rain. Cp. Aaron HaKohen, *Orḥot Ḥayyim*, *Hilkhot Berakhot*, #55. The problem as to the correct context, though, forms part of the wider issue as to the referent of a different dispute.

The *sugya* after A-E includes a dispute as to the context of a rule. The rule applies either to "ceasing a fast for rain" or to "saying a blessing for rain." The pericope, however, does not make explicit which rule. Some commentators follow the sequence in PT and explain that the dispute refers to B-D, that is, the parties differ as to the subject of the three definitions. But according to an alternative and better identification, the dispute refers to a *baraita* which *Gemara* cites below the dispute and which defines the term "sufficient for fructification." The masters would then differ as to the application of the definition of "sufficient for fructification." As each of the three opinions in B, C, and E employ this phrase, they make up one example of the phrase's use. We, accordingly, can understand why someone placed the dispute after E. The alternative use of the phrase is reflected in the aforementioned text in b. Taan. 25b (see n. 508) and T. Taan. 1:4. Lieberman, *TK*, 5:1067, apparently associates the amoraic dispute in this manner with the application of the definition of "sufficient for fructification," something explicitly claimed by Azikri and various commentaries to Gen. R. 13:13-15. See Pseudo-Rashi, in Vilna Gen. R., s.v. KMH GŠMYM . . . RBY[C]H; Issachar Berman b. Naphtali HaKohen, "Mattenot Kehunah," in Vilna Gen. R., s.v. KDY RBY[C]H, and s.v., BMDH; and Einhorn, "Meharzu," s.v. KDY RBY[C]H: and E. E. HaLevi. Cp. Sirillo and Emunat Yosef to y. Ber. The Gen. R. parallel places the *baraita*, which defines "sufficient for fructification," before its analogue to A-E and lacks the dispute as to the context of the unspecified rule.

[512]See Fulda and Frankel, *PT*.

[513]See Bokser, *Samuel's Commentary*, pp. 192-193. We can, moreover, understand Samuel's logic if he holds that any amount of rain is worthy of a blessing. See above n. 510. Note, Judah, who transmits Samuel's teaching, presents one of the liturgical texts for a prayer over rain and it expresses thanks for *every drop* of rain.

[514]See *Makhon-Mishnah*.

[515]For variants see Luncz and Ratner. While V MS has "Resh Laqish" in C, it has "Huna" in D. Likewise, while Eleazar b. Judah of Worms, *HaRoqeaḥ HaGadol*, #340, p. 238, reads "Resh Laqish," in #219, p. 121, it reads "Huna." As to the supposed variant of "Aha" for "Yohanan," "Haggahot Maimuniyyot" (on *MT*, *Lulav*, 7:6), in the Constantinople, 1590 ed., has "Yohanan." On the whole *sugya*, see Azikri; Fulda; *Nir*; *STEI*, pp. 598-599; and Yellin to b. Pes. 7b; and cp. *NY*, and Shulsinger, *YE*, p. 18.

[516]See S; Azikri; Fulda; Luncz; and Frankel, *PT*.

[517]See *OZ*, 1:79a, #581; Luncz; and cp. Weiss, *ST*, 1:55, n. 6, and 570, and vol. 2:263.

[518] Many of the early commentators to b. Pes. 7b, who are the sources for the variant readings cited in Luncz and Ratner, appear in critical editions in Baruch Naeh, *Gemara Shelemah* (Jerusalem, 1960), Section: "Thesarus of Rishonim," pp. 118-119, 123, 128, 132-134, 135, 138, 140.   See the notes to these pages.

[519] For variants to this pericope see *DS* 18, and Naeh, Section: "Variant Readings," 1s. 23-24.   Several MSS, including the Columbia MS, delete the opening "for."   See also *OhG*, "Responsa," pp. 8-9; Epstein, *IAL*, p. 155; Weiss, *ST*, vol. 3 (in press).   See n. 521 for other instances of clause G.   Lines H and I may constitute later additions to the *sugya*.   See Naeh, Section: "Explanation of Readings," p. 40, to l. 26, and esp. Weiss, *ST*, 3.   The three dots in K represent two anonymous lines which gloss and support the question.

[520] T. Ber. 6:9-14, pp. 36-37, 1s. 49-68.   See *TK* , 1:112-115.   Elijah of London, pp. 124-125, provides an example of a Mishnah-commentary's inclusion of these types of materials.

[521] Samuel's tradition in clause G without the full *sugya* appears in b. Pes. 119b, b. Meg. 21a, b. Suk. 39a, and b. Men. 35b.   See n. 525, below, and the text thereto, n. 528, below, and cp. Weiss, *Studies* (1975), pp. 116-119. On the tradition, see also Hoffman, p. 223, n. 15.

[522] On this term, see Goodblatt, *Rabbinic Instruction*, p. 125.

[523] See, e.g., Bokser, *Samuel's Commentary*, pp. 157-162, and "Guide," VIII.D; and Weiss, *ST*, 1-2, passim.

[524] Yellin, to b. Pes. 7b, and Men. 35b; *STEI*, pp. 598-599, and cp. Fulda, and R. Nissim b. Reuben Gerondi on Alfasi to b. Pes. 7b.
For sure, we do not know if and to what degree Yonah's exception in F represents Samuel's opinion.   Significantly it is represented as his (Yonah's) additional exception.   On the meaning of this difficult clause, see the commentaries in n. 515  and the reading in Vatican MS.

[525] See *DS* 87:300-400, and Vatican BT 113 MS [Makor ed., B. 4:161].

[526] Yellin, to b. Men. 35b, may have sensed this.

[527] See Neusner, *Purities*, 21-22; and above, to tradition #101, and below, chapter four, chart 9, and chapter ten, subsection 3.

[528] See above, n. 520, and text thereto.   Tosefta's focus thus remains the liability to say the blessings and the content of the benedictions.   See esp. T. Berakhot 6:10, p. 36, 1s. 53-54, 55-56, 57-58, and 6:15, p. 37, 1s. 68-72; *TK*, 1:112, and esp. the reference there to *Tashlum Tosefta*, p. 33; and *TK*, 1:116-117, for examples of the types of deductions necessary if one relies upon Tosefta's formulation.
The relationship of Samuel's comment to Mishnah and Tosefta is reflected in the placement of the Toseftan materials in both *Gemarot*.   It is cited in y. immediately preceding A-F and the *sugya* thus appears to focus on these rules. In b. Pes. 7b, a version of T. Ber. 6:9 is presented earler on the page and the *sugya* treats the rules as subjects in their own right.   Hence it constitutes a further refinement and development in the interest in these laws.

[529] On the usage of M$^C$D as "means" or "possessions" see Louis Ginzberg, *An Unknown Jewish Sect* (New York, 1976), pp. 290-291.

[530] See *Makhon-Mishnah* for variants.

[531] See *DS* 353:60.   On the rendering, see below, nn. 535-537 and text thereto.

[532]See DS 353:60. M MS and *Yalqut Shimoni*, #38, Lerner and Shiloni ed., 1:125, lack the word, DWMH, though include the comparative prefix, K-, "like." On the rendering, see commentaries on Gen. 4:7, especially Orlinsky, pp. 67-68, and E. A. Speiser, *The Anchor Bible. Genesis* (Garden City, 1964), pp. 32-33; and below, nn. 535-537 and the text thereto.

[533]See Meiri, p. 213. On the exegetical text, see Tos. Ber. 6:1, pp. 32-33, ls. 8-10, and 6:7, p. 35, ls. 35-40, and *TK*, 1:102-103, 111; Mekilta, *Bo*, #16, Horowitz ed., p. 60, l. 20 - p. 61, l. 1; Sifre Deut. to 6:5, #32, Finkelstein ed., p. 55; Midrash Tannaim to Deut. 6:5, Hoffman ed., pp. 25-26; Deut. R., Lieberman ed., p. 70, especially n. 3. Cp. Ginzberg, *Unknown*, pp. 202-204.

[534]See n. 532. All the texts include in A the word "resembles," DWMH. Of those that include it in B, some place it before the subject of the comparison and some at the end of the clause.

[535]See *OhG*, RḤ, p. 68. The proof text thus supplies a substantive analogue to Rav's second part. Note how some circles understand the word, "the door," LPTH, in Gen. 4:7, as the entrance to the heart; *Targum Neofiti*, Makor ed. (Jerusalem, 1970), 1:9; *Targum Jonathan Ben Uziel* on the Pentateuch, ed. David Rieder (Jerusalem, 1974), p. 6; *Das Fragmententhargum: Thargum Jeruschalmi zum Pentateuch*, ed. Moses Ginzburger (Berlin, 1899; reprint ed., Jerusalem, 1969), p. 6.

[536]See Maharsha and GRA, *Ḥiddushe*, p. 77 [= 39a], and Judah of Barcelona, cited in Kasher, *Torah Shelemah*, 1- (Jerusalem, 1929-), 1:315, n. 55. See there n. 56, and cp. Rashi and Z. W. Rabinowitz, *Sha^c are Torath Babel* (Jerusalem, 1961), pp. 13-14, both to b. Ber. 61a. See also the commentaries of Joseph Bekhor Shor, *Perusah ^c al HaTorah*, 3 vols. (Jerusalem, 1957-60, and London, 1960), 1:8, loc. cit.; Rabbi Meyuhas B. Elijah, *Commentary on the Pentateuch. Genesis* (London, 1909; reprint ed., Jerusalem, 1968), p. 19, ls. 2-3; and S. D. Luzzato, *Perush Shadal* (Tel Aviv, 1965), p. 34. See the usage of Koh. 10:1, at y. Qid. 1:10, 61d.

[537]Sifre Deut. #45, Finkelstein ed., pp. 103-104. See the references to the several Targumim, above n. 535, b. Qid. 30b; and Gen. R. to Gen. 8:21, #34, 10, Theodore and Albeck ed., p. 320, which calls the inclination of a person's heart "evil" and which may assume a different comparison of the evil inclination. Gen. R. to 4:7, #22.6, pp. 210-213, provides several parables and similes of the evil inclination which focus on the dynamics of its enticement and protection from it. See also the commentaries in n. 536, to which add Speiser, pp. 32-33, and cp. Moshe Zucker, *Rav Saadya Gaon's Translation of the Torah* (New York, 1959), pp. 140-141, esp. n. 573.

[538]As seen by the presence of B alone in *Yalqut Shimoni* to Gen. 4:7, #38, Lerner and Shiloni ed., 1:125, Samuel's comment can circulate without Rav's.

[539]See Eleazar Horowitz, "Novellae," in back of BT to b. Ber. 61a, s.v. GM', and A. Weiss, *Studies* (1962), p. 123.

[540]E.g., Rambam on M. Ber. 9:5; GRA, SE; Tosf. Y.T.; and Mel. S. to Mishnah.

PART TWO

CHAPTER THREE

THE FULL CORPUS

The present chapter lists all the traditions of Samuel in
the two *Gemarot* on Berakhot and those found elsewhere which
directly deal with Mishnah Berakhot and its themes.  They are
presented under the rubric of their appropriate Mishnah.  We present the full text of the traditions along with the essential
parts of their surrounding context, though we at times abridge
the texts of Mishnah.  We number the traditions for easy identification and discussion in the rest of our study.

The question of the present part of our study is the
relative relationship of Samuel's teachings to Mishnah.  Accordingly, we review all of Samuel's teachings, not just those which
directly comment on Mishnah, i.e., those analyzed in Part One.
Earlier in Volume One we demonstrated the importance of Mishnah
to Samuel's study.  We employed several criteria in our analysis.
We found, among other things, that a significant portion of his
teachings on Mishnah Zera$^C$im are so formulated to have once circulated along with Mishnah, even though they now may appear in the
literary work Talmud and be embedded in a *sugya* or cast into a
dispute with another Amora.  Moreover, the spread of the Mishnah
comments throughout *Gemara* and on many and diverse *mishnayot* in
Zera$^C$im indicates that we deal with more than a limited focus on
Mishnah.

We pursue this point in this and the following chapter,
and discover that this extended focus applies to Samuel in Berakhot
as well.  In subsequent chapters we focus on the other criteria
and analyze other aspects of the question, including the literary
forumulation and presentation of the traditions.  But combining
our earlier results with our present findings we approach the next
logical question, as well.  How important is the Mishnah and to
what degree does it shape Samuel's concerns and focus.  For example: what is the relationship of this scrutiny on Mishnah to the
other teachings which do not directly comment on Mishnah and which
therefore do not properly belong to a "Mishnah Commentary"?  Does
Mishnah in any way prompt these comments?  Accordingly, wherever
appropriate at each stage of our analysis we also take into account
the non-"Mishnah Commentary" comments.

In the presentation of the data we classify the sources as
to their relationship to Mishnah.[1]  We have employed several

categories, each of which is indicated by an abbreviation on the
margin to the right of the tradition.

> MC = Mishnah Commentary.
>
> R = Related to Mishnah.
>
> MES = Mishnah Explicative Supplements.  These com-
> ments closely relate to Mishnah.  While at
> times they appear as supplements, they focus
> on and explicate Mishnah's principle or a
> specific clause of its text.
>
> RC = Related and Complements Mishnah.  The scrutiny
> is shaped by the way in which Mishnah presents
> the topic.  These traditions differ from the
> MES items in that they do not formally expli-
> cate something in Mishnah.
>
> RS [or "MRS"] = Related and Supplements Mishnah.  These treat
> an item which Mishnah mentions even in passing
> and which is not shaped by the perspective of
> Mishnah's problematic.
>
> TC = Tosefta Commentary.  Comments on a toseftan
> passage which relates to Mishnah and thus in
> effect assumes Mishnah or its law.
>
> UR = Unrelated to Mishnah.
>
> UR-E = Unrelated Extensions.  These are unrelated to
> Mishnah though they form part of an extended
> *sugya* which may have originated in response to
> Mishnah.

Following the list of the traditions, presented as the
bulk of chapter three, we comment upon the spread of the traditions in chapter four and make other related observations.  We
separate our discussion from the traditions in order to facilitate
consultation, for we refer to them in other chapters as well.

ii

M. Ber. 1:1A

From what time do they recite the *Shema$^c$* in the evening?
From the time that the priests start to eat their heave-
offerings.
[And they read the *Shema$^c$* until . . . .  --the words of R.
Eliezer.
And Sages say, Until midnight,

Rabban Gamaliel says, Until the first light from the East appears [literally, "until the pillar of morning rises," which precedes sunrise].

1.        Said R. Judah said Samuel, The *halakhah*    MC
   follows (HLKH K-) R. Gamaliel.
                      (b. Ber. 8b)

2.        And teaches Samuel likewise, The moon      RS
   does not shine while the sun sets, and it does
   not set while the sun shines.
                      (y. Ber. 1:1, 2b)

3.        A.  Rabbi said, [There are] four
   watches . . . The "term" (H$^C$WNH) is . . . ,
   the "second" (RG$^C$) is 1/24 of the "moment"
   ($^C$T).

          B.  How much is the "second"?
          . . . . .
          Teaches (TNY) Samuel, The second is        RC-TC
   1/56,848 of the hour.[1a]
          C.  R. Nathan says, [There are] three
   watches.
                      (y. Ber. 1:1, 2d)


M. Ber. 1:2

From what time does one recite the *Shema*$^C$ in the morning?
From . . . ; R. Eliezer says, . . .
Until the sun rises.
R. Joshua says, Until the third hour of the day, for such
is the custom of kings to rise at the third hour.
One who recites the *Shema*$^C$ from then on has not lost. . . .

4.        For said Samuel, [They] do not inter-      UR-E
   calate [an extra month into] the year on the
   thirtieth day of Adar, as it [that day] is
   worthy to be designated as [part of] Nisan.
                      (b. Ber. 10b)

5.        "Let us make, please, a little walled
   upper chamber" (2 Kings 4:10).
          Rav and Samuel,                            UR-E
          One said, It was an open upper chamber
   and they roofed it.

And one said, It was a large veranda
and they divided it into two [viz., with a
wall].

> (b. Ber. 10b)

6.        "And she said to her husband, Lo, now
I know that he is a holy man of God" (2 Kings
4:9).

    Rav and Samuel,                                    UR-E

    One said, She did not [ever] see a fly
pass over his table.

    And one said, She spread a linen sheet
on his bed and she never saw a nocturnal emission (QRY) on it.[2]

> (b. Ber. 10b)

7.        Said R. Judah said Samuel, The *halakhah*    MC
follows R. Joshua.[3]

> (b. Ber. 10b)

## M. Ber. 1:3

The House of Shammai say, In the evening all should
recline and recite [the *Shema*$^c$], and in the morning all should
stand, as it is said, "When you lie down and when you get up"
(Deut. 6:7). The House of Hillel say, All read the way they are,
as it is said, "When you walk by the way" (ibid.). If so, . . .
Said R. Tarfon, I was going on the way and I reclined to recite
[the *Shema*$^c$] in accordance with the House of Shammai, and I
endangered myself because of bandits. They said to him, You
deserved to lose your life because you transgressed the words of
the House of Hillel.

## M. Ber. 1:4

[As to] the morning [*Shema*$^c$], one blesses two [blessings]
before it and one after it. And [as to] the evening *Shema*$^c$, one
blesses two before it and two after it, one long and one short.

Where they said "to lengthen" one is not permitted to
shorten; "to shorten" one is not permitted to lengthen; "to seal"
one is not permitted not to seal; "not to seal" one is not permitted to seal.

8.        What is the other one [before the
*Shema*$^c$]?

Said R. Judah said Samuel, "With great    MC
love" (ᵓHBH RBH).

(b. Ber. 11b)

9.        Said R. Judah said Samuel, If one    RS
awoke early to study--before one recited the
*Shema*[c], one is required to say a blessing
[over Torah study]; after one recited the
*Shema*[c], one is not required to say a blessing.[4]

(b. Ber. 11b)

10.       What does one say [over study]?
Said R. Judah said Samuel,[5] "[Blessed    UR-E
. . .] who sanctified us with His commandments
and commanded us to engage in the words of
Torah."

(b. Ber. 11b)

[M. Tamid 5:1, items #11-12, 15-16]

[The appointed one said to them [i.e.,
to the priests, in the morning], Say a blessing.  And they said the blessing and read the
Ten Commandments, *Shema*[c], . . .]  [= M. Tamid
5:1.]

11.       What is "a blessing"?
Like that of R. Abba and R. Yosi bar
Abba[6] who chanced to be in a certain place,
. . . What is "a blessing"? . . . They came,
asked R. Matnah.  He did not know.  They came,
asked R. Judah, He said to them, Thus said
Samuel, "With great love."[7]                  RC
                                               [M. Tamid:
(b. Ber. 11b)                                  MC]

12.       Said R. Judah said Samuel, Also in the   UR-E
country (BGBWLYN) they wanted to read them        [M. Tamid:
[the Ten Commandments] but it had already been    MC]
abolished because of the jealousy of the
sectarians.[8]

(b. Ber. 12a)

(13-14)

And said Rava b. Hinenah the Elder in
the name of Rav, One who says the *Tefillah*--
when he bows, he bows at [the word] "Blessed"

[which opens the blessing], and when he rises
he rises at the Name [of God].

13.         Said Samuel, What is Rav's reason?          RS
Because it is written, "The Lord raises up          [TC-S]
those that are bowed down" (Ps. 146:8).
            . . . [= Question.][9]

14.         Said Samuel to Hiyya the son of Rav,        RS
O, son of the Law, Come and I will tell you a       [TC-S]
fine thing that your father used to do.  When
he bows, he bows (KWR[C]) at [the word] "Blessed."
When he rises, he rises at the Name.[10]
                (b. Ber. 12a-b)

[M. Tamid 5:1]

15.         There we learnt, The appointed one said
to them, Say a blessing and they blessed [= M.
Tamid 5:1.]  What did they bless?
            R. Matnah in the name of Samuel, This     RC
is (ZW) the blessing over the Torah.[11]             [M. Tamid:
                                                     MC]
            (y. Ber. 1:8; 3c) [= y. on M. Ber. 1:4]

16.         The appointed one. . . . What . . .
            R. Matnah in the name of Samuel, This     RC
is the blessing over the Torah.   [= #15 cited       [M. Tamid:
for separate analysis.][12]                          MC]
                (y. Ber. 1:8, 3c)

17.         Samuel said, One who awoke early to        RS
study--before recitation of *Shema[c]*, he is
required to say a blessing [over Torah study];
after recitation of *Shema[c]*, he is not required
to say a blessing [over Torah study].[13]
                (y. Ber. 1:8, 3c)

(18-19)

18.         For Hannan bar Ba told his fellows
(HBRY[ɔ]) I will tell you a good thing which I saw
Rav do, and I told it to Samuel, and he rose and     RS
kissed me on my mouth: "Blessed art Thou (BRWK        [TC-S]
ɔTH)--bend down (ŠWHH); when one is about to
mention the [divine] Name--Rise (ZWQP).

19.         Samuel said, I will say the reason,        RS
"The Lord raises those who are bowed down"            [TC-S]
(Ps. 146:8).[14]
            (y. Ber. 1:8, 3d = y. Ber. 4:1, 7a)

## M. Ber. 1:5

They mention the Exodus from Egypt at night.  Said R.
Eleazar b. Azariah, Lo I am not like a seventy year old and I did
not understand why the Exodus from Egypt should be said at night
until Ben Zoma expounded. . . .

## M. Ber. 2:1

[If] one reads the Torah and the time of recitation [of
*Shema*$^c$] came--if he directed his heart, he fulfilled [his obligation to say *Shema*$^c$] and if not, he did not fulfill [his obligation].

Between the sections he inquires out of respect and he
replies, . . .

20.           Said R. Judah said Samuel,[15] "Hear, O          RC
        Israel, the Lord is our God the Lord is One"
        (Deut. 6:4).  This is (ZW) the recitation of
        the *Shema*$^c$ of R. Judah the Patriarch.
                        (b. Ber. 13b)

21.           R. Huna, R. Idi, R. Joseph, R. Judah
        in the name of Samuel, [One] has to take upon          MC
        oneself the Kingdom of Heaven--standing.[16]
                        (y. Ber. 2:1, 4a)

22.           Said Rav, One who gives greetings to
        his fellow before he prays the *Tefillah*, is as
        if he made it [or "him"] a "high place" (BMH),
                as it says, "Cease ye from the man in
        whose nostrils is a breadth, for how little (BMH)
        is he to be accounted" (Is. 2:22).  Read not
        *bammeh* [= "how little"], but *bammah* [= high
        place"].[17]
                And Samuel said, For what reason (BMH)      RS
        have you regarded this one and not God?[18]
                        (b. Ber. 14a)

## M. Ber. 2:2

These are "between the sections": . . . Said R. Joshua b.
Qorhah, Why does "Hear" (Deut. 6:4) precede "And if you hear"
(Deut. 11:13)?

## M. Ber. 2:3

One who reads the *Shema*$^c$but does not make it audible to
his ear, fulfills his obligation. . . [If] he read but but was not

exacting as to its letters, . . . One who reads in reverse order.
. . . [If] one read and erred, he should return to the place at
which he erred.

23.              Samuel said, [When I prayed] I counted        RC
        the *parohayya* [= "floating clouds"].[19]

                (y. Ber. 2:4, 5a [= *Gemara* on M. Ber. 2:3])


## M. Ber. 2:4

        Workers recite [*Shema^C*] on top of a tree. . . .


## M. Ber. 2:5

        A bridegroom is exempt from recitation of *Shema^C* the first
night [of marriage] until the expiration of the Sabbath, if he did
not consummate the marriage.  Case concerning R. Gamaliel . . .
(24-27)

                A.  Benjamin of Ginzak went out and
        said in the name of Rav, It [= the first act of
        intercourse on the Sabbath] is permitted.

24.              B.  Samuel heard and became angry at        RS
        him [= at Benjamin] and he died.

25.              C.  And he [Samuel] said about him,        RS/[UR-E]
        Blessed [is He][20]who struck him [= Benjamin,
        because of his sin], and about Rav he read,
        "Ill will not come to a righteous person"
        (Prov. 12:21).

26.              D.  Samuel said, That whole *halakhah*        UR-E
        which begins the last chapter of Niddah--is
        *halakhah* [= theoretical law], but is not for
        practice.

                E.  . . .

                F.  Said R. Abbahu, . . . I asked R.
        Eleazar, Is it permitted to have a second act
        of intercourse [on the Sabbath]?  And he per-
        mitted me, for he holds like that of Samuel,

27.              For Samuel said, A confined opening is        UR-E
        entered on Sabbath even if one loosens [= dis-
        lodges] pebbles.[21]

                (y. Ber. 2:4, 5b [= y. on M. Ber. 2:5])


## M. Ber. 2:6

        He [R. Gamaliel] washed the first night after his wife
died, . . .

28          . . . but bathing which is not for
      pleasure is permitted, Like that of Samuel bar      UR-E [RC]
      Abba.  Scabs appeared on him.  They came, asked
      R. Yosa [= Asi], Is he permitted to bathe?  He
      said . . .[22]

            (y. Ber. 2:7, 5b [= *Gemara* on M. Ber. 2:6]
                  = y. M.Q. 3:5, 82d)


## M. Ber. 2:7

      And when Tabi his slave [R. Gamaliel's] died, he accepted
condolances, . . .
(29-30)
            What is "We are instructed, we are
      well laden" (Ps. 144:14)?[23]
29.             Rav and Samuel, and some say, R.            UR
      Yohanan and R. Eleazar [differ in the verse's
      interpretation]:
            One said, "We are instructed" in
      Torah, "and we are well laden" with precepts.
            And one said, "We are instructed" in
      Torah and precepts, "and we are well laden"
      with suffering (YSWRYN).

            . . . . .
            "Listen to me you stubborn of heart,
      you who are far from victory" (Is. 46:12).
30.             Rav and Samuel, and some say R.             UR
      Yohanan and R. Eleazar,
            One said, The whole world is supported
      by charity and they are supported by force.
            And one said, The whole world is
      supported by their merit, and they, even with
      their own merit, are not sustained.[24]
                  (b. Ber. 17a-b)


## M. Ber. 3:1

      Whoever's dead is lying unburied before him is exempt from
*Shema*[c] . . .
31.             A.  Come and hear,[25] for the father of
      Samuel had some *zuzim* belonging to orphans
      deposited with him.  When he died, [his son]
      Samuel was not with him.

They would call him [= Samuel], "The
son who consumes the money of orphans."

He went[26] to the cemetery, He said to        UR
them, I want my Abba [= "my father"].

They said to him, There are many Abba's
here.

He said to them, I want Abba bar Abba.

They said to him, There are also many
Abba bar Abba's here.

He said to them, I want Abba bar Abba,
the father of Samuel.

They said to him, Go up to the heavenly
*metivta*.[27]

Meanwhile he saw R. Levi sitting outside.  He said to him, Why do you sit outside?

He said to him, Because they said to
me, "For as many years that you did not enter[28]
the sessions of R. ꜢEfes[29] and did hurt his
feelings, we will not let you enter the heavenly *metivta*."

Meanwhile, his father came.  He saw
that he was crying and laughing.  He said to
him, Why do you cry?

He said to him, Because you will soon
come [here].

And why do you laugh?

He said to him, Because you are
esteemed in "this world."

He said to him, If I am so esteemed,
Let them take in Levi.

They led Levi in.[30]

He said to him, Where are the orphans'
*zuzim*?

In the base of the millstones.  The
top is ours and the bottom is ours, and the
middle is the orphans; for if thieves steal,
let them steal ours and if the earth consumes
[*zuzim*], let it consume ours.

Thus [this shows] that they [the dead]
do know [what occurs among the living, e.g.,
that Samuel will soon die]?  [The passage thus
makes up a question against the notion that

the dead do *not* know what occurs among the
living.]

   B.   It is different with Samuel, for
as he is an esteemed person, they proclaimed
[to the dead] beforehand [that he is
coming].[31]

                    (b. Ber. 18b)

32.          A.   Really?  And lo,
   R. Papa[32] spoke (negatively) about Mar
Samuel,[33] and a reed from the roof fell and          UR
was about to split the membrane of his brains
[= skull].

             B.   It is different with a rabbinic
student, for the Holy One Blessed Be he avenges
his insult.

                    (b. Ber. 19a)

[M. Kel. 5:10]

33.          A.   For we have learnt, [If] one cuts
it [an earthenware oven which has been declared
unclean] up into rings and puts sand between
the rings--R. Eliezer declares [it] clean, and
the Sages declare [it] unclean.  And this is
the oven of Akhnai.  [= M. Kel. 5:10.]

             B.   What is Akhnai?
             Said R. Judah said Samuel, Because          UR
they surround it with *halakhot* as a serpent
(K$^C$N$^)$Y) and declared it unclean.[34]

             C.   And it was taught (WTNY$^)$). . . .
                    (b. Ber. 19a = b. B.M. 51a-b)


M. Ber. 3:2

   [If] they buried the dead and returned, if they are able
to start and finish [the *Shema*$^e$] before they reach the row [for
condolences], they should start. . . .

34.          A.   R. Abba explained that it [= a preceding *baraita* which avers that a priest
returns with mourners and which forms a question against a tradition Judah transmits in
the name of Rav] refers to a rabbinic *bet
haperes* [= a ploughed up field that had contained a grave whose bones are now scattered
about and which the rabbis declared unclean],

B.   for said R. Judah said Samuel, A          UR-E
person plows in a *bet haperes* and proceeds.

And R. Judah bar Ami in the name of R.
Judah said, A *bet haperes* which has been well
trodden is clean.[35]

(b. Ber. 19b)

35.          Said R. Papa to Abaye, . . . In the
days of R. Judah all their study was in Neziqin
[the fourth Order of Mishnah, "Torts"], while
we teach [all] six Orders.  And when R. Judah
came to [Tractate] ᶜUqsin, . . . he said, We
see here the debates (ḤWYYᵓ)[36] of Rav and
Samuel, while we teach thirteen lessons in          UR
ᶜUqsin.[37]

(b. Ber. 20a = Taan. 24a-b = San. 106b)

## M. Ber. 3:3

Women, slaves, and minors are exempt from the recitation
of the *Shemaᶜ* and from *tefillin*, and obligated as to *Tefillah*, and
*mezuzah*, and Grace After Meals.

## M. Ber. 3:4

One who had a nocturnal emission--thinks ["of the *Shemaᶜ*";
alternatively: "of the *Shemaᶜ* blessings"[37a]] in his heart and does
not say the blessing before or after it, and over food he says the
blessing after it [= Grace] and does not say the blessing before
it.   R. Judah says, He says the blessing before them and after
them.[37a]

36.          Said R. Judah said Samuel,[38] [If one          RS
is in] doubt whether or not he recited the
*Shemaᶜ*--he does not recite [it] again.   [If
one is in] doubt whether or not he said,
"True and Firm" [= the blessing following
the recitation of the *Shemaᶜ*]--he says [it]
again.[39]

(b. Ber. 21a)

37.          Said R. Judah said Samuel, If one was          RS
standing saying the *Tefillah* and remembers
that he had already said it--one breaks off
even in the middle of a blessing.[40]

(b. Ber. 21a)

38.          And said R. Judah said Samuel, If one          RS
had already said the *Tefillah* and entered into
a synagogue and found the congregation saying
the *Tefillah*--if he can innovate something in
the *Tefillah*,[41] he should say the *Tefillah*,
and if not, he should not say it.[42]

                    (b. Ber. 21a)


## M. Ber. 3:5

    [If] one is engaged in the *Tefillah* and remembers that he
had had a nocturnal emission--he should not terminate [his prayer]
but rather shorten [it].

    [If] one goes down to immerse oneself--if he can come up,
cover himself, and recite [the *Shema*[c]] before the sun rises, he
should come up, cover himself, and recite [it]; and if not, he
should cover himself with water and recite [it], but he should not
cover himself with foul water or soaking water [for flax] . . .

    And how far should one distance oneself from them and
excrement?  Four cubits.[42a]

39.          Our rabbis taught, A man should not
hold *tefillin* in his hand or a Torah scroll in
his arm while saying the *Tefillah*; nor should
he urinate with them (BHN), nor sleep with
them, whether a regular sleep or a temporary
nap.

          Said Samuel, A knife, money, a dish,          RS
and a loaf of bread--these are like them (HRY
ꜢLW KYWSꜢ BHN).[43]

          (b. Ber. 23b = b. Suk. 41b)

(40-41)

          R. Joseph the son of R. Nehuniah[44]
asked R. Judah, Is it permitted for a man to
place his *tefillin* under his pillow? . . . [a
later explanatory gloss].

40.          Said he to him, Thus said Samuel, It          RS
is permitted, and[45] even if his wife is with
him.

          They retorted . . . Is this not a
refutation of Samuel?  It is a refutation.

          Said Rava, Even though a refutation of
Samuel was taught, the *halakhah* follows him.

          . . .

R. Joseph the son of R. Nehuniah[44] asked
R. Judah, [If] two persons are sleeping in one
bed [alternatively "one garment"],[46] is it permitted for one to turn one's face away and
recite the *Shema*[c] and for the other one to
turn his face away and to recite the *Shema*[c]?

41.          He said to him, Thus said Samuel, It          RS
is permitted,[47] and even if his wife is with
him.

R. Joseph attacked . . . An objection
. . . But if we accept Samuel's view there is
a difficulty?  Samuel can reply, . . .[48]

Said R. Kahana to R. Papa,[49] There
Rava said that although there is a refutation
of Samuel, the *halakhah* follows Samuel.  Here
what is the case? . . .[50]

(b. Ber. 23b)

42.          Said Samuel, The voice of a woman is          RS
"unseemly" [i.e., has sexual attraction]
([c]RWH),

for it is said, "For your voice is
sweet and your appearance is pleasant" (Cant.
2:14).[51]

(b. Ber. 24a)

43.          Samuel said, The voice of a woman is          RS
unseemly.

What is the reason?  "Indeed, the land
was defiled by the voice of her immorality, as
she committed adultery with stone and with
wood" (Jer. 3:9).[52]

(y. Hal. 2:4, 48c)

44.          And in the case of certainty [that
urine is present] how long [is it prohibited]?

Said R. Judah said Samuel, So long as          MC
they [= "urine," mentioned in last clause of
Mishnah] moisten.[53]

(b. Ber. 25a)

(45-46)

45.          Samuel said, Until its top has dried.          MC
        . . . . .

46.              Samuel said, Until its top has dried.[54]   MC
                      (y. Ber. 3:5, 6d)

47.              Said R. Judah said Samuel, A person is    RS
         permitted to urinate within four cubits of
         *Tefillah*.[55]
                          (b. Meg. 27b)


M. Ber. 3:6

         A *zav* who had an emission and . . . require   immersion; R.
Judah exempts [them].


M. Ber. 4:1

         The morning *Tefillah* [is said] until noon; R. Judah says,
. . .
         The afternoon *Tefillah* [is said] until the evening.   R.
Judah says Until the second half of Minhah (PLG MNHH) [= one and
one-half hours before nightfall].
         The evening *Tefillah* has no fixity [= has no fixed time],
and that of the extra service (WŠLMWSPYN) [is said] the whole day.
R. Judah says, Until the seventh hour.[55a]

48.              For said R. Judah said Samuel, A         RS-E
         person prays the *Tefillah* of the Sabbath
         before the Sabbath and says the Sanctification
         over the cup.[56]
                          (b. Ber. 27b)

49.              For said R. Judah [or "Nahman"] said
         Samuel, One prays the end of the Sabbath    RS
         *Tefillah* on the Sabbath and says *havdalah* over
         the cup.[56]
                          (b. Ber. 27b)

50.              It was said also: Said R. Tahlifa bar
         Avdumi[57] said Samuel, One prays the end of the   RS-E
         Sabbath *Tefillah* on the Sabbath and says
         *havdalah* over the cup.[56]
                          (b. Ber. 27b)

51.              A.  For [deleted in certain read-
         ings],[58] said R. Judah said Samuel, The evening   MC
         *Tefillah*--R. Gamaliel says, [It is] compulsory.
         R. Joshua says, [It is] optional.

B.   and the *halakhah*[59] follows the
words of the one who says, "Compulsory."[60]

C.   Rav[60] said, The *halakhah* follows
the words of the one who says, "Optional."

(b. Ber. 27b)

(52-53)

52.          For Hannan bar Ba told his fellows, I
will tell you a good thing which I saw Rav do,
and I told it to Samuel, and he rose and kissed      UR-E
me on my mouth, "Blessed art Thou"--bend down;       [RS]
when one is about to mention the [divine] name
--rise.

53.          Samuel said, I will say the reason,      UR-E [RS]
"The Lord raises those who are bowed down" (Ps.
146:8).[61]

(y. Ber. 4:1, 7a = y. Ber. 1:8, 3c)

## M. Ber. 4:2

R. Nehuniah b. Haqanah used to pray a brief *Tefillah* when
he entered the house of study and when he exited.  They said to
him, What is the nature of this *Tefillah*?  He said to them, . . .

## M. Ber. 4:3

Rabban Gamaliel says, Every day a person prays eighteen
[prayers].  R. Joshua says, The substance of (M$^C$YN) eighteen.  R.
Aqivah says, If his *Tefillah* is fluent in his mouth, he prays
eighteen; and if not, the substance of eighteen.

(54-55)

A.   R. Joshua says, . . .

B.   What is "the substance of
eighteen"?

C.   Rav says, The substance of each
blessing (M$^C$YN KL BRKH WBRKH).

54.          D.   And Samuel said, Give us discern-       MC
ment (HBYNNW), Lord our God, to know Thy ways;
and circumscribe our hearts to fear Thee, so
that we may be forgiven and redeemed, and keep
us far from agony, and fatten us in the pastures of Your land; and the [alternatively
"our"] dispersed from the four [corners of the

earth] gather; and those who go astray by
[alternatively "in" or "from"] Your knowledge
judge, and against the wicked raise Your hand;
and let the righteous rejoice, in the building
of Your city and establishment of Your Temple,
and in the growth of the horn of David, Your
servant, and in the preparation of a light for
the son of Yishai, Your anointed one.  Before
we call, may You answer.  Praised are You,
Lord, who hearest prayer.

    E. Abaye cursed (LYTT ᵓBYY) anyone
who prayed, "Give us discernment" (HBYNNW).

55.    F. Said R. Naḥman said Samuel,   MES
Throughout the year a person prays, "Give us
discernment" except on the outgoing of Sabbath
and festivals because [one] has to say *havdalah*
in [the prayer which opens with the phrase]
"Who graciously gives knowledge."  [= The
fourth blessing of the *Tefillah*, which, when
abridged, cannot take the addition.][62]

     (b. Ber. 29a)

    A. R. Joshua says, . . .
    B. What is "(Seven)[63] the substance
of eighteen."
    C. Rav said, The end of (SWP) each
blessing.
56.    D. And Samuel said, The beginning  MC
(RᵓŠ) of each blessing.
    E. There are teachers who teach,
"Seven the substance of eighteen"; and there
are teachers who teach, "Eighteen the substance
of eighteeen."  The one who says, "Seven the
substance of eighteen" supports Samuel.  The
one who says, "Eighteen the substance of
eighteen" supports Rav.
    F. R. Zeᶜira sent to R. Nahum via R.
Yannai b. R. Ishmael, What is "Seven the substance of eighteen" of Samuel?    RC/MES
(56a)                  explanation

    G. He said to him, Give us discernment
(HBYNNW); Desire our repentence; Forgive us;
Redeem us; Heal our sickness; Bless our years.

H.   (Said R. Hagai, If it was [the time
of the] rains, they say, "In rains of blessing."   If it was [the period of] dews, they
say, "In dews of blessing.")

I.   For, the dispersed You [hopefully
will] gather; And those who go astray against
You [alternatively "for you to"] judge; And
upon the wicked place Your hand; and let all
those who rely upon You rejoice, In the
building of Your city and in the renewal of
Your holy-house; For before we call, may You
answer, As it is said, "And it shall be, before
they call I will answer; while they are yet
speaking, I will hear" (Is. 65:24).

J.   And he says, Praised Lord, for You
hear the voice of my supplication.

K.   Praised be Thou Lord, who hears
prayer.

L.   And he says the first three blessings and the last three.[64]

(y. Ber. 4:3; 8a = y. Taan. 2:2; 85c)


## M. Ber. 4:4

R. Eliezer says, One who makes his prayer fixed, his
prayer is not a supplication.   [= Relates to M. Ber. 4:3.]

R. Joshua says, One who goes in a dangerous place, prays
a brief *Tefillah*, and [he] says, Save . . . Blessed are Thou who
hears prayer.[65]

57.          [If] one was standing and praying[66]
[the *Tefillah*] and remembered that he had
already prayed--

Rav said, He cuts off (HWTK).

And Samuel said, He does not cut off          RS
[= L MS.   "He cuts off" = S and V MSS].[67]

(y. Ber. 4:4, 8a)


## M. Ber. 4:5

If one was riding on an ass--he should dismount, and if
he cannot dismount, he should turn his face, and if he cannot
turn his face, he should direct his heart to the House of the
Holy of Holies.

## M. Ber. 4:6

If one was sitting on a ship or on a raft--he should
direct his heart toward the House of the Holy of Holies.

## M. Ber. 4:7

R. Eleazar b. Azariah says, There is *Tefillah* of *Musafim*
[= the additional *Tefillah*] only where there is a *hever* $^c$*ir* [=
town congregation?]. And Sages say, Whether there is a *hever* $^c$*ir*
or whether there is no *hever* $^c$*ir*. R. Judah says in his name [= of
R. Eleazar b. Azariah], Wherever there is a *hever* $^c$*ir* an individual
is exempt from the *Tefillah* of *Musafim*.

58.              . . . The *halakhah* follows R. Judah
       . . .

            Said to him R. Hiyya bar Abin, You are
     right, For said Samuel, During my days I                 MC
     individually in Nehardea never prayed the
     *Tefillah* of *Musafim* except on the day in which
     the king's force came to the city and the
     rabbis became terrified and did not pray, and I
     individually prayed (and I was an individual,
     not in the context of a *hever* $^c$*ir*).[68]
                 (b. Ber. 30a-b)

59.              . . . The *halakhah* follows R. Judah
       . . .

            The matter of Samuel said thus [=              MC
     accords with the previous decision]. For said
     Samuel, I never prayed that of *Musaf* except
     once when the son of the exilarch died and the
     community did not pray [it] and I prayed it.[69]
                 (y. Ber. 4:7 [6], 8c)

60.          Rav said, [One] has to innovate some-
     thing in it (LHDŠ BH DBR) [= in *Musaf*].
            Samuel said, One does not have to              MC
     innovate something in it.[70]
                 (y. Ber. 4:6 [7], 8c)


## M. Ber. 5:1

They do not stand up to pray the *Tefillah* except in a
serious manner. The early pious ones . . . in order to direct
their hearts. . . . Even if a king greets him, he should not

respond, even if a snake encircled around his
heel, he should not interrupt [his prayer].

61.          "And You shall give to Your handmaiden
a seed of men (ZR^C ꜣNŠYM)" (1 Sam. 1:11).

          Said Rav, A man among men.

          And Samuel said, A seed (ZR^C) which          UR-E
annoints two men.

          And who are they?  Saul and David.

          And Y. Yohanan said, A seed equal to
two men.

          And who . . .

          And rabbis say, Seed which is merged
among men. [71]

                    (b. Ber. 31b)

62.          "And Moses besought (WYHL) the Lord"
(Ex. 32:11). . . .

          Samuel [alternatively "Yohanan"] says,          UR-E
[This] teaches that he risked his life for
them,

          as it says, "And if not, please, blot
me out of Your book" (Ex. 32:32). [72]

                    (b. Ber. 32a)

63.          Said R. Isaac the son of Judah, If one
saw oxen, he interrupts (PWSQ).  For teaches
R. Hoshaia, One removes oneself from a *tam* 50
cubits and from a *mu^cad*, as far as one can see.

          Said Samuel, In these situations: With          UR-E
a black ox and in the days of Nisan [some add:          [adapted:
"when it is coming up from the marsh"] because          RS]
the devil dances between his horns.

          It was taught in the name of R. Meir
. . . [73]

                    (b. Ber. 33a ≈ b. Pes. 112b)

## M. Ber. 5:2

          They mention the "Powers of Rain" in [the blessing]
"Resurrection of the Dead," and ask for rain in the "Blessing of
the Years."  And *havdalah* [they say] in "Favors [a person with]
knowledge."  R. Aqivah says, He says it (ꜣWMRH) as a fourth blessing by itself.  R. Eliezer says, In "Thanksgiving."

64.         And Rav and Samuel both say, and some          RS
say it [thus]: R. Yohanan and R. Eleazar
[alternatively "Resh Laqish"] both say,
         Whoever says a blessing which is not
needed, violates the prohibition, "Thou shall
not take [the name of the Lord, your God, in
vain]" (Ex. 20:7).[74]
                  (b. Ber. 33a)

65.         R. Ze$^c$ira, R. Judah in the name of
Samuel, [If] he said it over a cup, he says it          MC
in the *Tefillah*.  [If] he said it in the              [RC]
*Tefillah*, he says it over a cup.
         That indicates that its essence is in
both.[75]
                  (y. Ber. 5:2, 9b)

66.         And did not say R. Judah said Samuel,          MC
         And the one who says *havdalah* in              [RC]
*Tefillah* must say *havdalah* over a cup?[76]
                  (b. Shab. 150b)

67.         The words of the sages: [i.e., the
following tradition represents the *halakhah*:]
         R. Yaaqov b. Aha in the name of
Samuel, [He] says it ["as" or "in"] the fourth          MES
blessing.[77]
                  (y. Ber. 5:2, 9b)

68.         [As to R. Eliezer's position on the
outgoing of the Sabbath which coincides with a
holiday:]
         Said R. Joseph, We [= I] know neither
this nor that.  Rav and Samuel already arranged          MES
for us a "pearl" in Babylonia.
         "And you informed us, O Lord, our God,
Your righteous judgments, and taught us to do
Your desired statutes, and You caused us to
inherit occasions of gladness and celebrations
of free will offerings, and You transmitted to
us the holiness of the Sabbath and the glory of
the festival days and the celebration of the
festival, You divided between the holiness of
the Sabbath and that of the holiday, and You
sanctified the seventh day above the six days

of creation, You separated and sanctified Your
people Israel with Your holiness."

"And You have given us" etc. [= The
regular festival prayer.][78]

(b. Ber. 33b)

## M. Ber. 5:3

One who says, "Over the 'bird's nest' may your mercies
reach . . ." and "We give thanks, we give thanks" [= doubling the
opening of the third-to-last blessing in *Tefillah*]--they silence
him.

## M. Ber. 5:4 [or continuation of 5:3]

One who goes before the ark [to lead in prayer] and errs--
another should go in his place. . . .

[According to the alternative division, the beginning of
M. Ber. 5:4:] One who goes before the ark should not answer Amen
after the priests. . . .

## M. Ber. 5:5

One who prays and errs--it is a bad sign for him . . .
They tell of R. Hanina ben Dosa . . .

69.            And [this preceding tradition] is in
dispute with Samuel.                                    UR-E

For said Samuel, The only difference
between this world and the days of the messiah,
is subjugation to the nations,

as it is said, "for there will never
cease to be needy ones in your land" (Deut.
15:11).[79]

(b. Ber. 34b)

## M. Ber. 6:1

How do they say blessings over fruit? Over fruit of the
tree one says, "Who createst the fruit of the tree"; except for
wine, for over wine one says, "Who createst the fruit of the
vine." And over fruit of the earth one says, "Who createst the
fruit of the earth"; except for bread, for over bread one says,
"Who bringest forth bread from the earth." And over vegetables
one says, "Who createst the fruit of the earth." R. Judah says,
"Who createst various types of grasses."

70.        Said R. Judah said Samuel, Whoever          MC
benefits from this world without a blessing is
as if he benefits from items dedicated to
heaven, as it is said, "The earth is the
Lord's and all that it contains" (Ps. 24:1).[80]
                    (b. Ber. 35a)

(71-72)

71.        For said R. Judah said Samuel, and          MES
thus said R. Yishaq said R. Yohanan, Olive oil
--over it they say the blessing, "Who createst
the fruit of the tree."[80]

72.        *Let us say that it constitutes a refu-*
*tation of Rav and Samuel who both say* that,
They say the blessing, "Who createst various
kinds of foods," only over the five kinds [of
grains distinctive to the land of Israel].[81]
                    (b. Ber. 35b)

73.        GWP⊃: Said R. Judah said Samuel, and        MES
thus said R. Yishaq said R. Yohanan, Olive oil
--over it they say the blessing, "Who createst
the fruit of the tree."[80]
                    (b. Ber. 35b)

74.        *Said Rava to R. Nahman, Do not dispute*
*R. Judah, for Samuel and R. Yohanan hold like him,*
          *For said* R. Judah said Samuel, and        MES
thus said R. Yishaq said R. Yohanan, Olive oil
--over it they say the blessing, "Who createst
the fruit of the tree."[80]
                    (b. Ber. 36a)

75.        And did not say R. Zera said R. Mattena
said Samuel, *Over raw bottle-gourd and barley-*      MES
*flour--over them we say the blessing,* "By whose
word all things come into existence."[80]
                    (b. Ber. 36a)

(76-77=79-80)

76=79.     Palm-heart--R. Judah said, . . . Samuel     MES
said, "By whose word all things come into existence."[80, 82]

                    . . .

77=80      Said Samuel to R. Judah, *Shinena,*         MES
*Your opinion makes sense.  For behold,*

A radish which eventually hardens and
*over it we say the blessing*, "Who createst the
fruit of the earth."

And even though Samuel *praised* R. Judah
*the halakhah follows* Samuel.[80]

(b. Ber. 36a = b. Eruv. 28b)

78.          Palm-heart--R. Yaaqov bar Aha in the
name of Samuel, Over it one says, "Who createst          MES
the fruit of the tree,"[80, 83]

(y. Ber. 6:1, 10b)

(81-83)

          Said R. Joseph, Seize that of R. Kahana,
81.          *for Rav and Samuel both say*, "Whatever          MES
contains anything of the five kinds--over it
they say the blessing, "Who createst various
kinds of foods."

82.          GWP⊃. *Rav and Samuel both say*, What-          MES
ever contains anything of the five kinds--
over it they say the blessing, "Who createst
various kinds of foods."

          And it was said also,

83.          *Rav and Samuel both say*, "Whatever of          MES
the five kinds--over it they say the blessing,
"Who createst various kinds of foods."

          . . .

          *And it is a refutation of Rav and*
*Samuel, a refutation.*[80]

(b. Ber. 36b-37a)

84.          *And it is not so* [alternatively "And
Rava returned and said" = retracted], *Both*
*require*, "Who createst various kinds of food,"
          *for Rav and Samuel both say*, Whatever          MES
contains anything of the five kinds--over it
they say the blessing, "Who createst various
kinds of foods.[80]

(b. Ber. 37b)

85.          *Let us say that it constitutes a*
*refutation of Rav and Samuel who both say*,          MES
They say the blessing, "Who createst various
kinds of foods," only over the five kinds?"[80]

(b. Eruv. 30a)

86.          *Shatita* [= roasted barley porridge]--
Rav said, . . . Samuel said, "Who createst        MES
various kinds of foods."[80]

(b. Ber. 38a)

87.          Taught R. Nahman in the name of our
Rabbi--and who is he?  Samuel--Steamed foods,     MES
over them they say the blessing, "Who createst
the fruit of the earth." . . .[80]

(b. Ber. 38b)

(88-89)

88.          R. Abba said, *Rav and Samuel both say*,   MES
Steamed vegetables--over it one says, "By
whose word all things come into existence."[84]

89.          R. Ze[c]ira in the name of Samuel, Turnip   MES
heads that have been steamed--if they are in
their original state, over them one says, "Who
createst the fruit of the earth"; that have
been ground, over them one says, "By whose word
all things come into existence."[80]

(y. Ber. 6:1, 10a)

## M. Ber. 6:2

[If] one said the blessing over fruit of the tree, "Who
createst the fruit of the earth," he fulfills [his requirement];
and [if] over fruit of the earth [he says the blessing] "Who
createst fruit of the tree," he does not fulfill [his requirement];
and over all of them he says, "By whose word all things come into
existence," he fulfills [his requirement].

(90-91)

A.   [Those in response to a question of
R. Judah, tell him:]

B.   They said to him, Yes.  For it was
taught, R. Muna said in the name of R. Judah,
Breaded-*kisnim* [= dried fruits with honey and
nuts baked with bread][85]--over it they say the
blessing, "Who bringest forth [bread from the
earth]."

90.  (a)      C.  And said Samuel, The *halakhah* fol-     RS
lows R. Muna,                                              [TC]

(b)      D.  He said to them, *The halakhah is
not* [like R. Muna] *it was said.*

91.            E.  *They said to him, And behold, it*
*is the master [= you] who said in the name of*
*Samuel,* Unleavened cakes (LHMNYWT)--they make        RS
an *eruv* with them, and they say over them the
blessing, "Who bringest forth," and [for grace]
"three blessings."
               F.  There . . . [= harmonization of
the two traditions].[86]
                    (b. Ber. 42a)

92.            R. Meir says, Even [if] one said,
"Blessed [art Thou . . .] who created this
thing, How pleasant this is"--He has fulfilled
[his obligation].
               R. Yaaqov bar Aha in the name of
Samuel, The *halakhah* follows R. Meir.[87]          RS
                    (y. Ber. 6:2, 10b)                [TC]

## M. Ber. 6:3

     Over an item whose growth is not from the earth--[one]
says, "By whose word all things come into existence."  Over vinegar, unripe and fallen fruit, and locusts--[one] says, "By whose
word all things come into existence."  R. Judah says, Whatever is
in the nature of a curse, they do not say a blessing over it.

## M. Ber. 6:4

     [If] various kinds were before him.  R. Judah says--If
one of the seven kinds is among them, over it one says the blessing.  And sages say, One says the blessing over whichever of them
one wants.

## M. Ber. 6:5

     [If] one said the blessing over wine before the meal--one
exempted the wine after the meal.  [If] one said the blessing over
the savory before the meal--one exempted the savory after the meal.
[If] one said the blessing over bread--one exempted the savory;
over the savory--one has not exempted the bread.  The House of
Shammai say, Even a cooked food one does not [exempt].

93.            They asked, If wine came before them
in the midst of the meal, Does [the blessing
over] it exempt that after the meal?

Rav said, One exempts.  R. Kahana says,
One does not exempt.

["And Samuel said, One does not exempt"    RC/S
= M MS.]<sup>88</sup>                                         [MC
revision?]

R. Nahman says, One exempts.  And R.
Sheshet says, One does not exempt.

R. Huna and R. Judah and all the students of Rav say, One does not exempt.<sup>89</sup>

(b. Ber. 42b)

## M. Ber. 6:6

[If] they were sitting, each one says the blessing to
oneself.  [If] they reclined, one says the blessing for all of
them.  [If] wine came to them--in the midst of the meal, each one
says the blessing to oneself; after the meal, one says the blessing for all of them.  And one says [the blessing] over the burning
spices, even though they do not bring the burning spices until
after the meal.

94.            We learned there . . .
R. Yaaqov bar Aha in the name of
Samuel, [If] one said Sanctification in this      UR-E
house and changed one's mind to eat in another    [RS-E]
house--one must say Sanctification [again].

Said R. Avun, And they are not in
dispute, . . . And what Samuel says applies
when (B-) one intended to eat in one house.

Said R. Mana, Samuel's position accords
with R. Hiyya [whose view is cited earlier in
the pericope], . . .<sup>90</sup>

(y. Ber. 6:6, 10d = y. Suk. 4:5, 54c)

## M. Ber. 6:7

[If] they brought him a salted [relish] together with
bread, one says the blessing over the salted [relish] and exempts
the bread, because the bread is secondary to it.  This is the
principle: Whatever is the main [food] together with a secondary
[food], one says the blessing over the main [food] and exempts
the secondary.

## M. Ber. 6:8

[If] one ate fits, or grapes, or pomegranates, one says
the "three blessings" [= the full Grace After Meals] after them--
words of R. Gamaliel.  And sages say, One blessing.[91]  R. Aqivah
says, Even if he ate [only] steamed [vegetables] and it is his
meal, he says three blessings after it.  One who drinks water to
[quench] his thirst, says "By whose word all things come into
existence."  R. Tarfon says, "Who createst many living beings and
their needs."

95.          Woe to the house into which turnip
        passes. . . .
             It was said, Rav said, Without meat.
        And Samuel said, Without branches [to make a        UR-E
        hot fire to cook them well].  And R. Yohanan
        said, Without wine.[92]
                    (b. Ber. 44b)


## M. Ber. 7:1-2

Three who ate together are obligated to summon [Grace =
to have one person invite the others].  [If] one ate *Dem ai*, or
First Tithe from which heave-offering has been taken, or Second
Tithe, or consecrated produce that has been redeemed; or the
waiter who ate an olive's amount of food; or a Samaritan--they
summon Grace over them.  But [if] one ate untithed produce, or
First Tithe from which heave-offering has not been taken, or
Second Tithe, or consecrated produce that has not been redeemed;
or the waiter who ate less than an olive's amount of food; or a
gentile--they do not summon grace over them.

Women, or slaves, or minors--they do not summon Grace over
them.  From what amount [of food] do they summon Grace?  The size
of an olive.  R. Judah says, The size of an egg.

96.          Rav and Samuel sat at a meal.  R. Shimi
        bar Hiyya entered and started to eat quickly.
             Said to him Rav, What is your inten-
        tion, to join us [so as to say Grace together
        with a "Summons"]?  We have already eaten.
             Said to him Samuel, If they bring me        RC
        mushrooms and pigeons to Abba [= Rav] would we
        not eat them?[93]
                    (b. Ber. 47a)

97.          "As soon as you enter the town, you
will find him before he goes up to the shrine
to eat; the people will not eat until he comes;
for he must first bless the sacrifice and only
then will the guests eat" (1 Sam. 9:13).

          Why so much [verbosity]?

          Said Rav, From here [we learn] that
women are talkers.

          And Samuel said, So that they might          UR-E
look (LHSTKL) at Saul's beauty,

          for it is written, "he was a head
taller than any of the people" (1 Sam. 9:2).

          And R. Yohanan said, Because one
kingdom cannot intrude upon another even a
hair's breadth. [94]

                    (b. Ber. 48b)

98.          A.   Said R. Idi bar Abin said R. Amram
said R. Nahman said Samuel, [If] one errs and          RS
did not mention the New Moon--in the *Tefillah*,
they make him return; in the Blessing After
Food, they do not make him return.

          B.   Said to him [= R. Idi bar Abin to
R. Amram], How does the former differ from the
latter?

          C.   Said to him [R. Amram, presumably],
I also found this difficult and I asked R.
Nahman and he said to me, I have not heard from
Samuel [the reason],

          D.   but let us see [alternatively "it
is a matter of logic"]. . . . [95]

                    (b. Ber. 49b)

99.          A. Here [= M. Ber. 7:4] it says, "They
are not permitted to separate." Here [= M.
Ber. 7:1] it says, "They are required to
summon" [Grace = a redundancy]?

          B.   Samuel said, Here [M. Ber. 7:4,          MC
speaks of a case in which] (B-) it is in the
beginning" (K^2N BTHYLH).

          And here [M. Ber. 7:1, speaks of a case
in which] (B-) it is in the end (K^2N BSWP). [96]

                    (y. Ber. 7:1, 11a)

100.            A.  Rabbis from here [= Palestine]
        follow their approach and the rabbis from
        there [= Babylonia] follow their approach:
                B.  Samuel said, Two who judged, their        UR-E
        judgment is the law, but it [= that "court"
        which should consist of three people] is called
        a presumptuous court.
                R. Yohanan and R. Simeon b. Levi both
        said, Even if two judged, their judgment is
        not the law.[97]
            (y. Ber. 7:1, 11a; Clause B = y. San. 1:1, 18a)

101.    (a)     From when do they start to consider him
        as an adjunct [to make up the ten]?
                R. Avina said, *R. Huna and R. Judah,*
        *both of them in the name of Samuel, dispute*        MC
        [the matter]: *One said*, When he knows the
        character of the blessing. *And the other said*,
        When he knows to whom he says a blessing.
                        (y. Ber. 7:2, 11b)

        (b)     And until when is he considered a
        minor?
                Said R. Avina, *R. Huna and R. Judah,*
        *both of them in the name of Samuel* [dispute        MC
        the matter]: *One said*--Until he knows how to
        say a blessing. *And the other said*--Until he
        knows the character of the blessing.[98]
        (Gen. R. 91.4 = an earlier recension of y. Ber. 7:2)


## M. Ber. 7:3

        How do they summon [people to Grace]?  In the case of
three--he says, "Let us bless," in the case of three and himself
--he says, "Bless." . . . R. Yose the Galilean says, According to
the size of the congregation they bless. . . . Said R. Aqivah,
What do we find the house of assembly?  Whether many or whether
few, [the person] says, "Bless the Lord."  R. Ishmael says, "Bless
the Lord, who is blessed."

102.            Said Samuel, Let a person never exclude     MC
        himself from the group.[99]
                    (b. Ber. 49b)

103.            Samuel said, I do not exclude myself       MC
        from the group.[99]

                    (y. Ber. 7:3, 11c)


M. Ber. 7:4

     Three who ate together are not permitted to separate.  And
thus four and thus five; six until ten separate, and ten until
twenty do not separate.

104.            It was taught (TNY), [If] one was
        sitting and eating on the Sabbath and forgot
        and did not mention the Sabbath [in Grace
        After Meals]--
                Rav said, [One] returns.
                And Samuel said, [One] does not return.    RS
                . . .
                There is a teaching which disputes
            [Samuel] . . .[100]

                    (y. Ber. 7:4, 11c)


105.            What does [M. Ber. 7:4] teach us?  We
        have learned [it already] one time: "Three who
        ate together are required to summon [Grace]:
        (M. Ber. 7:1).
                This [M. Ber. 7:4] teaches us in
        accordance with that which
                    said R. Abba said Samuel, Three who     MC
        sat to eat together and still have not eaten,
        are not permitted to separate.
                    An alternative version: Said R. Abba
        said Samuel, Thus it is taught, Three who sat
        to eat together, even though each one eats by
        himself [alternatively "each one eats from his
        own plate"] are not permitted to separate.[101]

                    (b. Ber. 50a)


M. Ber. 7:5

     [As to] two groups who were eating together--when some of
each see each other, Lo, these join together for the Summons [to
Grace]; and if not, they each individually summon Grace.  They do
not say the blessing over wine until [the waiter] dilutes it with
water--the words of R. Eliezer.  And sages say, They say the
blessing [even if it is not diluted].

106.        *According to whom does this which*
        *Samuel said follow* (KM⁾N ⁾ZL⁾ H⁾ D⁾MR ŠMW⁾L)?        UR-E
                A person does whatever he wants with
    bread.
            *According to whom?  According to* R.
    Eliezer.[102]
                        (b. Ber. 50b)


## M. Ber. 8:1

    These are the things wherein the House of Shammai and the
House of Hillel differ concerning a meal:
    House of Shammai say, One says the blessing over the day
and then one says the blessing over the wine.  And the House of
Hillel say, One says the blessing over the wine and then one says
the blessing over the day.

107.        [As to the beginning of] a festival
    which falls at the outgoing of the Sabbath:
                R. Yohanan says,  . . .
                Hanan bar Ba in the name of Rav, . . .
                R. Hanina says, YNH"Q. [= Wine, (YYN),
    candle (NR), *havdalah* (HBDLH), Sanctification
    (QYDWŠ).[103]  *Havdalah* precedes Sanctification--
    in contrast to the sequence in the two previous
    comments.]
                Samuel follows R. Hanina, for said R.        RS
    Aha in the name of Samuel, A king departs and
    a governor enters--They escort out the king
    and afterwards usher in the governor.  [So one
    ushers out the Sabbath, of supreme importance,
    with *havdalah*, before one escorts in the
    festival with Sanctification.]
                R. Levi said, . . .[104]
                    (Y. Ber. 8:1, 12a)

108.        GWP⁾:[105] [As to the beginning of] a
    festival which falls [immediately] after the
    Sabbath--
                Rav said, YQNH.
                And Samuel said, YNHQ.[106]        RS
                . . .
                Samuel's father sent to Rabbi, May the
    master teach us, What is the order of the
    *havdalot*?

He sent him, . . .

Said R. Hanina, a parable. . . .[107]

(b. Pes. 102b)

## M. Ber. 8:2

The House of Shammai say, They wash the hands and then mix the cup. And the House of Hillel say, They mix the cup and then wash the hands.

(109-110)

109.            Samuel went up to Rav.                                    RS

He saw him eating [bread] in a sack [alternatively "eating" as (they eat) there].[108]

He said to him [= to Rav], What is [the law], thus?

He [= Rav] said to him, [S MS adds: "No"],

I am sensitive [= I eat thus as a personal practice].[109]

R. Ze[c]ira when he came up to here [= to Palestine], saw priests eating with a sack [alternatively "as there"].[110]

He said to them, Is that [teaching] of Rav and Samuel to be disregarded?[111]

110.            R. Yose [in the name of] bar Ba Huna [= R. Yose BŠM (Ab)ba bar R. Huna, in the name of] Kahana in the name of Samuel,[112]                RS

Washing the hands applies to unconse-crated food. Washing of hands does not apply to heave-offering. [The former requires greater institutionalized precautions.][113]

R. Yose says, It applies to heave-offering and unconsecrated food.[114]

(y. Ber. 8:2, 12a)

(111-112)

They asked, Is it permitted to eat [holding the food] in a napkin [without first washing one's hands]?

. . . . .

Come and hear [the following as an answer]: For

111.             Samuel found Rav eating with a napkin.      RS
                 He said to him, We act thus?
                 He [Rav] said to him, I am agitated
        [or "preoccupied"].[115]
                 When R. Zeira came up [to Palestine]
        he found R. Ami and R. Asi eating with frag-
        ments of wine bags.
                 He said, Two great masters like you
        [alternatively "like our rabbis"] disregard
        [literally "curse"] Rav and Samuel?  He [Rav]
        had said to him [Samuel], "I am agitated."
        [Therefore, holding food in a garment is not
        the regular procedure.]

112.             He forgot the following which said R.
        Tahifah bar Abimi said Samuel, They permitted
        a napkin to those who eat heave-offering, and
        they did not permit a napkin to those who eat
        [unconsecrated foods] in a ritual state of
        purity.  --And R. Ami and R. Asi were priests
        [and therefore for them the napkin sufficed].[116]
                      (b. Hul. 107a-b)


## M. Ber. 8:3-4

        The House of Shammai say, One wipes one's hands with a
napkin and lays it on the table.  And the House of Hillel say,
[One lays it] on a cushion.
        The House of Shammai say, They sweep the house and then
wash the hands.  And the House of Hillel say, They wash the hands
and then sweep the House.[117]


## M. Ber. 8:5

        The House of Shammai say, [The order of the blessings at
the outgoing of the Sabbath is], lamp, and food, and spices, and
*havdalah*.  And the House of Hillel say, Lamp, and spices, and
food, and *havdalah*.
        The House of Shammai say, [The blessing over the lamp is,
"Blessed art Thou] who did create the light of fire."  And the
House of Hillel say, [. . .] who createst the lights of fire.

(113-114)

             Abba bar R. Huna and R. Huna . . .[118]

Said Abba bar R. Huna to him [= to R.
Ze$^c$ira], . . . And his father [= Huna] became
angry at him [= at his son].

113.          He [Huna] said to him, . . . and said          UR-E
     Samuel, Whoever makes use of the priesthood,
     performs a sacrilege (M$^C$L). . . .

              From where do we learn that one who
     makes use of the priesthood performs a sacri-
     lege?

114.          R. Aha[119] in the name of Samuel said,          UR-E
     "And I said to them, you are holy unto God and
     the utensils are holy" (Ex. 8:28)--just as with
     the [Temple] utensils one who makes use of them
     performs a sacrilege, so one who makes use of
     the priests performs a sacrilege.[120]

                    (y. Ber. 8:5, 12b)

115.  (a)     Samuel said, Therefore we say a bless-     MC
     ing over the fire on the outgoing of the
     Sabbath since it is the beginning of its
     creation.[121]

              R. Huna in the name of [Rav,] Rabbi
     Abbahu in the name of R. Yohanan, Even at the
     outgoing of Yom Kippur one says the blessing
     over it, since the fire rested that whole
     day.[121]

                    (y. Ber. 8:5, 12b)

     (b)     This follows Samuel for Samuel says,     MC
     Why do they say the blessing over the lamp at
     the outgoing of the Sabbath?  Because it is
     the beginning of its creation.[121]

          (Gen. R. #11, p. 89 = Pesiqta Rabbati, #23,
                    Friedman ed., p. 118b)

116.          Said R. Judah said Samuel, They do not     MC
     say the blessing over the fire except at the
     outgoing of the Sabbath since it is the begin-
     ning of its creation.[121]

                    (b. Pes. 53b)


M. Ber. 8:6

     They do not say the blessing over the lamp or over the
spices of Gentiles, nor over the lamp or spices of the dead, nor
over the lamp or spices [placed] before idols.

They do not say the blessing over the lamp until they
enjoy (ŠY⊃WTW) its light.

(117-120)

        A.   They do not say the blessing over
the lamp until they enjoy (ŠY⊃WTW) its light.
[= M. Ber. 8:6B.]

        B.   Rav said, *yeoto* (Y⊃WTW).  [= With
an *alef.*]

117.        And Samuel said, *yeoto* (Y^C WTW).  [=      MC
With an *ayin.*]

        C.  . . .

        D.   There we learnt, How do they extend
the [Sabbath] limits of cities?  [= M. Eruv.
5:1.]

        E.   Rav said, *Me⊃abrin* (M⊃BRYN).  [=
With an *ayin.*]

118.        And Samuel said, Me^C abrin (M^C BRYN).     UR-E/S
[= With an *ayin.*]                               [M. Eruv.:
                                                          MC]

        F.  . . .

        G.   There we learnt, Before the festi-
vals of the nations.  [= M.A.Z. 1:1.]

        H.   Rav said *edehen* (⊃YDYHN). [= With
an *alef*, though many texts read with an
*ayin.*][122]

119.        And Samuel said, *edehen* (^C YDYHN).    UR-E/S
[= With an *ayin*, though many texts read with     [M.A.Z.:
an *alef.*][122]                                                       MC]

        J.1.  How does Samuel deal with the
reason [= verse] of Rav. . . .[123]

        J.2.  . . .

        K.   They do not say the blessing over
the lamp until they enjoy its light [= M. Ber.
8:6].

120.        L.1.  R. Judah in the name of Samuel,    MC
Sufficient that women spin by its light.

        L.2.  Said R. Yohanan, Sufficient . . .

        L.3.  Said R. Hanina, Sufficient . . .

        M.   Teaches R. Hoshiah, Even . . .

        N.   R. Ze^C ira . . .[124]

        (y. Ber. 8:6, 12c [A-J = y. Eruv. 5:1, 22b.
            A-I = y. A.Z. 1:2, 39c]

## M. Ber. 8:7

[As to] whoever ate and forgot to say the blessing [of Grace After Meals]--The House of Shammai say, He should return to his place and say the blessing. And the House of Hillel say, He should say the blessing in the place where he remembers.

And until when [after eating] does he say the blessing? Until the food in his bowels is digested.

121.                 Until when does he say the blessing?
          Until the food in his stomach is digested.
                   R. Hiyya in the name of Samuel, As          MC
          long as he is thirsty from that meal.
                   R. Yohanan said, . . .[125]
                        (y. Ber. 8:7, 12c)


## M. Ber. 8:8

If wine is brought to them after the meal and there is only that [one] cup--The House of Shammai say, One says the blessing over the wine and then says the blessing over the food. And the House of Hillel say, One says the blessing over the food and then says the blessing over the wine.

They respond "Amen" after an Israelite who says a blessing. And they do not respond "Amen" after a Samaritan who says a blessing--until one hears the whole blessing.

122.                 *Samuel asked Rav*, Should a person          MC
          respond "Amen" after school children?
                   He [= Rav] said to him, . . .[126]
                        (b. Ber. 53b)


## M. Ber. 9:1

Whoever sees a place in which miracles were wrought for Israel says, "Blessed [is He] who wrought miracles for our ancestors in this place." [Whoever sees] a place from which idolatry has been uprooted says, "Blessed [is He] who uprooted idolatry from our land."

123.                 Samuel, when he dreamt a bad dream,          UR-E
          said, "Dreams speak lies" (Zech. 10:2). When
          he dreamt a good dream, he would ask,[127] Do
          "dreams speak lies" [Zech. 10:2, taken as a
          question]? Is it not written, "I will speak
          with him [a prophet] in a dream" (Num. 12:6).[128]
                        (b. Ber. 55b)

124.            King Shapur said to Samuel, They say
         that you are very wise.  Tell me, what will I
         see in my dream?

                  He said to him, You will see that the        UR-E
         Romans[129] press you into service, rob you, and
         make you graze pigs with a golden rod.

                  He thought [about that] the whole day
         and at night saw [it in his dream].[130]
                        (b. Ber. 56a)

125.            Rav said, [One] has to say "Thou"
         (ᵓTH).

                  And Samuel said, [One]                        MC
         [L MS:' does not have        [V and S MSS and many
         to say "Thou."               citations:] has to say
                                      "our God."[131]
                  (y. Ber. 9:1, 12d)


## M. Ber. 9:2

         Over [= upon seeing] *ziqim* [= comet or meteor],[132] and
over earthquakes, and over lightning, and over *reamim* [= thunder]
and over tempests--He says, "Blessed [. . .] whose strengh fills
the world"

         Over mountains, and over hills, and over seas, and over
rivers, and over deserts--He says, "Blessed [. . .] Maker of
creation."  R. Judah said, Whoever sees the Great Sea says,
"Blessed [. . .] who made the Great Sea"--when he sees it at
intervals.

         Over rain and over good tidings--He says, "Blessed [. . .]
who is good and does good."  And over bad tidings--He says,
"Blessed [. . .] the true Judge."

(126-127)

                  What is *ziqin*?
126.            Said Samuel, *kokhba deshevit* [= "shoot-      MC
         ing star" or "comet"].
127.  (a)       And said Samuel, I am as familiar with         MES
         the paths of the firmament as with the paths
         of Nehardea--

                  Except for *kokhba deshevit*, which I do
         not know what it is,

         (b)       though I have learnt that it does not
         pass through the constellation of Orion, and

if it passes through Orion, it destroys the
world.

    And lo, we see that it passes through
[Orion]?

(c[?])   Its brightness passes through and it
appears as if it itself passes through.[133]
           (b. Ber. 58b)

(128-129)

      Over *ziqim*.

128.  (a)    Samuel said, If this *ziqa* passes      MES
through Orion, it will destroy the world.

    They challenged Samuel, And we saw it
pass through.

(b[?])  He said to them, It is not possible.
It either [passed] above it or below it.

129.       Samuel said, I am as familiar with the   MES
alleys of the heavens as with the alleys of
Nehardea my city--

    Except for this *ziqa*, which I do not
know what it is.[134]
          (y. Ber. 9:2, 13c)

(130-131)

130.  (a)    Samuel contrasts, It is written, "Who    UR-E
makes the Bear, Orion, and Pleiades" (Job 9:9).
And it is [also] written, "Who makes Pleiades
and Orion" (Amos 5:8)--

    How so?

    If it were not for the heat of Orion,
the world would not endure because of the cold
of Pleiades.  And if it were not for the cold
of Pleiades, the world would not endure because
of the heat of Orion.

(b)    And I have learnt, Were it not for that
the tail of Scorpio [which is the sign of
Pleiades] rests in the Fire River, whoever was
bitten by a scorpion would not live.[135]

    And thus is what the Merciful One[136]
said to Job, "Can you tie the Pleiades' fetters,
or loosen Orion's bands" (Job. 38:31)?

131.       What is *kimah* [= Pleiades]?

Samuel said, *kimeah* [= like 100                    UR-E
stars].[137]

(b. Ber. 58b)

132.          And over *reamim* [= M. Ber. 9:2].

What is *reamim*?

Said Samuel, Clouds joining in a circle      MC
[= a "whirlwind," or the noise of thunder
caused by clouds joining], as it is said, "The
sound of Thy *reamim* in the whirlwind, the
lightning illuminating the world, the earth
trembled and shook" (Ps. 77:19).

Rav said, . . .[138]

(b. Ber. 59a)

133.          And in *Tefillah*.

R. Yosi bar Nehorai said, "Who sanctifies Israel and makes new the months."

R. Hiyya bar Ashi said, "Who sanctifies
Israel and the new months."

Samuel said, [A person][139] has to say,      UR-E
"And he has raised us (WHŚYꜛNW)."

Rav said, [A person] has to say the
"time" (ZMN) [= mention the special day in it].

Teaches R. Hoshayia, . . .[140]

(y. Ber. 9:2, 13d)

134.          And how much rain must fall so that a
person will have to bless [the benediction
over rain]?

. . .

R. Yose in the name of R. Judah, and
R. Yonah and R. Judah in the name of Samuel,      MC
In the beginning--sufficient for fructifica-
tion; and afterwards--even any amount.[141]

(y. Ber. 9:3, 13d-14a = y. Taan. 1:3, 64b
= Gen. R. 13.13; pp. 122-123, in which
Samuel's comment immediately
follows the question)


## M. Ber. 9:3

[One who] built a new house or bought new utensils--says
the blessing, "Blessed [. . .] who brought us to this time."

One says a blessing over misfortune just like over good
fortune, and over good fortune just like over misfortune.

One who cries out for what is past--Lo this is a vain prayer. How so? [If] one's wife was pregnant and one says, "Let it be Thy will [. . .] that my wife give birth to a male"--Lo this is a vain prayer. [If] one was journeying home and heard the sound of cries in the city, and says, "Let it be Thy will [. . .] that these [shouts] not be in my house"--Lo this is a vain prayer.[142]

135.        *Misvot*--when does one say a blessing over them?

R. Yohanan says, Before doing them.

R. Huna says, While doing them.

R. Huna accords with Samuel.

For said R. Yose b. R. Bun in the name of Samuel, All *misvot* require a blessing while        MC doing them,

except for blowing [the *shofar*] and immersion [in *miqvah*].[143]

(y. Ber. 9:3, 14a)

136.        (For) said R. Judah said Samuel, All        MC the *misvot*--one says a blessing over them before one does them.

. . .

The disciple circle of Rav say, Except for immersion and *shofar*.[144]

(b. Pes. 7b)

137.        Said R. Samuel bar Bidri said Rav; And        RS some say it [thus]: Said R. Aha Arika said R. Huna; And some say it [thus]: Said R. Menashia [bar Yermiah] said Samuel,

*tefillin*--from whence does a person say a blessing over them? From the time of putting them on.

(= 136)

Really. And lo, said R. Judah said Samuel, All the *misvot*--one blesses over them before one does them.[145]

(b. Men. 35b)


## M. Ber. 9:4

One who enters a city--prays two [prayers], one on his entering and one on his leaving. Ben Azai says, Four, two on his

entering and two on his leaving, and he gives thanks over the past
and cries out for the future.[146]

138.              Our rabbis taught: One who enters the
       bathroom says, . . .
              When he leaves--he says, "Blessed [is
       the One] who has formed man in wisdom and
       created in him cavities and orifices.  It is
       revealed and known before the seat of Your
       throne that if one of them opens up or closes
       up it is impossible to stand before You."[147]
              What does he seal [the blessing with]?
              Rav said, "Heals the sick."
              Said Samuel, You have made, Abba
       [= Rav], the whole world into invalids.  Rather
       say thus--"Blessed[148] [. . .] healer of all
       flesh."
              R. Sheshet said, . . .[149]
                   (b. Ber. 60b)


## M. Ber. 9:5A [= 9:5]

       [A person] is obligated to say a blessing over misfortune
as he says a blessing over good fortune.  As it is said, "And you
shall love the Lord your God with all your heart, and with all
your soul, and with all your might (M'DK)" (Deut. 6:5).  "With all
your heart"--with both your inclinations (YSRYK)--with the good
inclination and with the evil inclination.  "With all your soul"
--even if He takes your soul.  "And with all your *meodeka*" [usu-
ally rendered as "your might"]--with all your wealth.[150]  Another
matter: "With all your *meodeka*--with whatever measure that He
metes out to you, with whatever [it is], give thanks to Him
greatly.[151]

139       "And the Lord God fashioned the rib"
       (Gen. 2:22)--Rav and Samuel [differed as to        UR-E
       the meaning of the "rib"].  One said, [It
       refers to] a face [= Adam's second face].  And
       one said, [It refers to] a tail.[152]
                   (b. Ber. 61a = Eruv. 18a)

140       Said Rav, The evil inclination resem-
       bles a fly and it sits between entrances of
       the heart,

as it is said, "Dead flies turn the
perfumer's ointment fetid and putrid [so a
little folly outweighs wisdom and honor.  A
wise man's heart tends toward the right, and
the fool's toward the left]" (Kohelet 10:1
[-2]).

And Samuel said, It [the evil inclina-     MC
tion] resembles a grain (HTH),
.
as it is said, "Sin (HT$^\text{Ɔ}$T) couches at
the door" (Gen. 4:7).$^{153}$      ..

(b. Ber. 61a)

## M. Ber. 9:5B [= 6]

A person should not behave lightly opposite the Eastern
gate, since it faces toward the Holy of Holies; nor should [one]
enter the Temple mount with his staff, or his shoes, or his money-
bag,$^{154}$ or with dust upon his feet; nor should [one] use it as a
short cut, and all the more so spitting [is forbidden there].

141.          Said Samuel, Urinating [alternatively,     UR-E
"study" or "sleep"] (ŠYNH) at morning dawn is
like the steel edge is to iron,
and$^{155}$ relieving oneself at morning
dawn is like the steel edge is to iron.$^{156}$

(b. Ber. 62b)

142.          "And as he was about to destroy, the
Lord saw, and He repented" (1 Chron. 21:15).
What did He see?
Said Rav, He saw Jacob your father,
as it is written, "And Jacob said when
he saw them" (Gen. 32:3).
And Samuel said, He saw the ashes of     UR-E
Isaac,
as it is said, "God will see for Him
the lamb" (Gen. 22:8).
R. Isaac Nappaha$^{157}$ said, He saw the
money of expiation,
.
As it is said, "And you shall take the
expiation money from the Israelites [. . . it
shall serve the Israelites as a reminder before
the Lord, as expiation for your persons]" (Ex.
30:16).$^{158}$

And R. Yohanan said, He saw the Temple,
as it is written, "In the mountain
where the Lord will be seen" (Gen. 22:14).[159]

(b. Ber. 62b)

## M. Ber. 9:5C [= 7]

Every seal of the blessings which were [said] in the
Temple were "from the world."[160]  After the sectarians had corrupted and said, "There is only one world," they ordained that
[people] should say, "From the world and until the world."

They ordained that a person greet his fellow with the Name
[of God], as it is said, "Presently Boaz arrived from Bethlehem
and he said to the reapers, 'The Lord be with you.' And they
responded to him, 'The Lord bless you'" (Ruth 2:4). And [it]
says, "[The angel of the Lord . . . said to him,] The Lord is with
you, valiant warrior" (Jud. 6:12). [= The divine confirms the
usage.] And [it] says, "Do not despise your mother when she is
old" (Prov. 23:22). [= Learn from the practice of enactments of
the ancients.] It is a time to act for the Lord, violate the
Torah" (Ps. 119:126) [e.g., require the use of God's name].[161]

143.          A.  Said R. Tabi [alternatively "Samuel
     bar Mattenah"] said R. Joshiah, Whoever makes
     himself faint in the words of the Torah will
     not have strength to stand in the day of
     trouble,

          as it is said, "If you are faint in the
     day of trouble your strength will be small"
     (Prov. 24:10).[162]

          B.  Said R. Ami [alternatively "Tabi"]
     bar Mattenah said Samuel, And even [in perform-          RS
     ance of] one *misvah*,

          as it is said, "If you are faint"--in
     any case.[163]

          (b. Ber. 63a)

[1]The footnotes discuss any problem in classification.

[1a]Samuel's *baraita* and the rest of B, additional definitions of the word "second," are interpolated between Rabbi's comment, A, and C. The latter two form a unit in T. Ber. 1:1, p. 1, ls. 7-10. Samuel's teaching, in contrast to the other definitions in B, includes a subject and predicate object and thereby does not just respond to the question that opens B. This accords with the fact that Samuel's *baraita*, though not attributed to Samuel, appears in b. Ber. 7a and b. A.Z. 4a. See *DS*; *Yalqut HaMakhiri* to Ps. 7:22, p. 45; and *Aggadot HaTalmud*, p. 2d. It, moreover, provides a Babylonian system of calculation. See Bornstein, pp. 268-272; Ginzberg, *Commentary*, 1:59-60; Epstein, *ITM*, p. 212; Lieberman, *HY*, pp. 19-20, n. 8, *TK*, 1:2-3, and "Brief Commentary" to T. Ber. 1:1, l. 7. Samuel's commentary makes up part of an extended analysis of Mishnah. Mishnah, in its initial standardization of the liturgy and application of it to all of Israel, requires fixed times for *Shemaᶜ*. *Gemara* takes up the notion of fixed time and focuses on the divisions of the day and hour. As T. Ber. 1:1's *baraita* (the analogue to A and C) indicates, this interest is a logical scrutiny or response to M. Ber. 1:1.

[2]See *DS* 45:20, Flr MS, and the version in y. Yev. 2:4, 3d, and y. San. 11 (17):2, 29b.

[3]See y. Ber. 1:2, 3a, the traditions of Rav and the two views which Huna reports, the first of which may represent Rav's opinion and the second Samuel's. See above, chapter two.

[4]The reason appended in printed editions to the end of the tradition is an addition. MSS include an amoraic question, "What is the reason," before the clause. See *DS* 49:3; Flr MS; *OhG*, "Responsa," p. 31; *SRAG*, p. 7, #8; Rid; the y. version below, item #17; chapter two, n. 20; and Hoffman, pp. 30-39,128,152-56.

[5]"Said Samuel," lacking in Flr MS. Where a tradent transmits a series of two or more traditions all in the name of the same master, we occasionally find the second instance of the master's name deleted. See Weiss, *ST*, 1:138-139, n. 1, and 586, n. 5.

[6]This is an alternative spelling for Yosef Bar Abba, the reading found in M MS and some citations. See *DS* 51:50; Albeck, *Introduction*, p. 291; and Hyman, pp. 717, 750. As to other variants, see *DS* 51.

[7]Thus #8 and #11 form alternative contexts for Samuel's gloss. In chapter two, we evaluate the appropriateness and originality of each location.

[8]M MS reads, " . . . wanted to *do it* . . . "; Flr MS, " . . . to *say it* . . . " See *DS* 52. On the passage, see Lieberman, *YK*, p. 526, *HY*, p. 22, note 6 and n. 25; Ginzberg, *Commentary*; 1:166-169; Geza Vermes, "The Decalogue and the Minim," in *In Memoriam Paul Kahle*, ed. Matthew Black, et al. (Berlin, 1968), pp. 232-240. Cp. S. Zeitlin, "The Morning Benediction," pp. 330, 334-336; Urbach, *The Sages*, p. 350; and Ronald Reuven Kimelman, "Rabbi Yoḥanan of Tiberias" (Ph.D. dissertation, Yale University, 1977), chapter five, and the literature cited there, and chapter six, n. 60.

[9]MSS and citations vary in the spelling of the name of Rav's tradent and in the sequence of Samuel's "reason" and the question. See *DS* 54:30-40, 50, and Flr MS.

[10]Additional variants in *DS* 54; *Yalqut HaMakhiri* to Ps. 146, p. 283, and to Mal. 2:5, p. 23; and *OZ*, 1:12d, #28. The pericope is structured around the second in a series of five traditions Rava b. Ḥinenah the Elder transmits

in Rav's name.  Accordingly, it is likely that Samuel's tradition has been
placed after Rava b. Hinenah's report.  This would accord with the y. version,
cited below, #18-19, and might account for the variation in the sequence of
Samuel's explanation and the question.  See nn. 9, and 13-14, on the y.
version.

[11]The lack of "said" in the attributive formula follows V MS and
Epstein, "Mediqduqe Yerushalmi," *Tarbiz* 6 (1934):41.  The word ZW appropriately serves to introduce comments directly generated by a text.  Samuel's
comment may thus directly respond to the Mishnah.  See above n. 7 and #8 and
#11, and chapter two, and cp. Ginzberg, *Commentary*, 1:168-169.

[12]See Sirillo.  Just below this tradition, R. Abba, a third generation
Babylonian who travelled to Palestine, cites a statement of R. Mattena (and
R. Samuel b. Nahman) which is not attributed to Samuel, but which makes up an
analogue to #12, on the Ten Commandments.  See n. to #12.  Perhaps here, as
well, he represents Samuel.  Note the role of the two masters in #11, and
Ba's [= Abba's] role in a  gloss to #17.  Elsewhere we suggest that in such
instances the glossator might constitute the tradent.  See chapter eight,
subsection 4.A, and Azikri, s.v. M⁾Y BRKW.

[13]See *HY*, p. 22, and n. 6; above, n. 4, to #9; and cp. Ginzberg,
*Commentary*, 1:170.  R. Ba, who glosses this tradition, may have transmitted
it.  See n. 12, to #16.

[14]See nn. to #13-14; Sirillo, s.v. ⁾LW BRKWT ŠŠWHHYN; Azikri; Luncz;
and Ginzberg, *Commentary*, 1:185, 188-189; and cp. Zuri, *Rav*, p. 259.  In
addition to MSS to PT, see *Yalqut HaMakhiri* to Mal. 2:5, p. 23.  BT and PT
versions employ different verbs.  The former uses KR$^C$ and the latter ŠHH
(ŠHH).  Following local practices, each uses the term for the mildest type
of prostration.  Palestinians use ŠWHH, bending at waist, an action which
Babylonians did not consider bowing down.  See Ginzberg, *Commentary*, 3:267;
*TK*, 4:696; and Rabinowitz, *Halakha and Aggada*, p. 254, n. 8; and, in general,
G. Blidstein, "Prostration and Mosaics in Talmudic Law," *Bulletin of the
Institute of Jewish Studies* 2 (1971):19-39, especially 19-28, and the litera-
ture cited there.  In this light perhaps we should follow Mayer Irwin Gruber,
*Aspects of Nonverbal Communication in the Ancient Near East* (Ph.D. disserta-
tion, Columbia University, 1977.  Published on demand, Ann Arbor: University
Microfilms, 1977), pp. 123-124, 149-155, who translates KR$^C$ as stoop.
    The two versions share the following characteristics: an Amora reports
Rav's tradition; someone asks and answers a question; Samuel supplies a reason.  If the two are not inconsistent, they reflect the following: Samuel hears
the tradition and expresses his appreciation (a perspective transmitted by
Rav's students).  Subsequently, Samuel tells Hiyya of Rav's practice and
at another occasion offers a reason for the teaching.  In BT this reason
makes up one of a series of teachings of Rava b. Hinenah the Elder in the name
of Rav.  The latter traditions form the larger *sugya*'s structure.  Moreover,
Samuel's comment, #19, is immediately followed by a gloss of R. Ami, a third-
generation Palestinian who was in Babylonia and who, therefore, may be the
one who transmits Samuel's--and Rav's--teaching to Palestine.  See Frankel,
pp. 63a-b, and esp. Hyman, pp. 218-225, and Margalioth, cols. 150-153, and
see chapter eight, subsection 4A.
    The pericope focuses on the proper mode of bowing in the *Tefillah*.
Tosefta had already added to Mishnah's mention of long and short, and sealed
and unsealed benedictions concern for this matter.  Tosefta and Samuel's
tradition thereby indicate that the proper procedures in Benedictions have
become subjects of concern in their own right.

[15]Printed editions present the tradition as a *baraita*.  The attribution
to Samuel appears in MSS and citations of RH, *OhG*, p. 14; *OZ*, 1:13a, #31
[cp. 1:13b, #35]; and *Yalqut Shimoni* to Deut. 6:4, #836.  See *DS* 60:100 and
Flr MS.  The other instance of a report of the practice of Judah the Patriarch
is also cited by Judah in the name of Samuel; b. Pes. 103b, in *DS* 315:5 and
Columbia MS X893- T14.

Samuel's comment may relate to the issue of "intention" required in the *Shema*[c]'s recitation. Tannaitic and amoraic masters differed on whether it is required for only the first verse, Deut. 6:4, or also through 6:6 or 6:9. Samuel would accord with the first position. See b. Ber. 13a-b; T. Ber. 2:2, p. 6, ls. 3-4; and Rif; Ashbili, pp. 296-297; Meiri, pp. 41-42; and *TK*, 1:1-15. See tradition #31, below.

[16] The names in the attributive formula vary. See our discussion in chapter two, and the preceding tradition, #20 and n. 15 thereto.

[17] See *DS* 63. Flr MS reads like the printed edition.

[18] The comment is followed by a question based upon M. Ber. 2:1. A second generation Nehardian [Sheshet in printed editions; R. Naḥman bar Yiṣḥaq in some MSS and citations, including Flr MS, M MS with its marginal addition of bar Yiṣḥaq--see *DS* 63:70] poses the problem, which is answered by R. Abba. See also *DS* 63:80 and Flr MS for additional instances of the same tradition, attributed, though, to other masters; and b. Sot. 4b for a different application of this exegesis. *Yalqut HaMakhiri* to Is. 2:22, p. 25, apparently combines both texts.
The pericope focuses on the importance of prayer said first thing in the morning, something different from Mishnah's issue.

[19] See Saul Lieberman, "Rays From the East," in *Texts and Studies* (New York, 1974), pp. 276-277 [= a revision of "Roman Legal Institutions," ibid., p. 59]. The context makes the referent clear. T. Ber. 2:4, 5, pp. 6-7, ls. 6-8, 10-12, provides further details on Mishnah's issue of erring and applies this principle to *Hallel*, *Megillah*, and *Tefillah*. Samuel's comment is part of a *sugya* on erring in *Shema*[c] and *Tefillah*, and is cited along with other traditions to indicate that rabbis found it difficult to concentrate and some had to resort to a special means in order to prevent distractions. It shares a similar pattern with the following view, attributed to R. Bun bar Hiyya, a third-generation Palestinian. Samuel's tradition thus falls within the full ramifications of Mishnah's text and thereby develops Mishnah's agendum.

[20] S MS actually supplies HMQWM, "the Presence."

[21] The context makes clear Samuel's referent in B. On the text, see V, L, S MSS and especially *GYF*, p. 11. Sirillo, perhaps influenced by the b. Nid. 65a parallel, makes D, #26, into a joint tradition of Rav and Samuel.
The parallel or variant versions include: to #24 - b. Nid. 65a; to #25, Samuel's praise of Rav - b. Nid. 65a, Yev. 121a, Hul. 59a; to #26 - b. Nid. 64b; to #27 - b. Nid. 64b, Ket. 6b. On the *sugya* and the significance of the variations, see Weiss, *ST*, 1:132-135, esp. p. 134, and T. Ket. 1:1, p. 56, ls. 5-6. Note, y.'s version, in effect, has Samuel and Rav in accord with several Palestinian traditions and with the immediately preceding tradition of Asi which likewise prohibits a first act of intercourse on the Sabbath. Perhaps Asi, a third-generation Babylonian emigré to Palestine, presents Babylonian material to accord with the Palestinian position. On Asi, see Volume One, pp. 94-95, n. 262.

[22] The *sugya* appears also in y. M.Q. 3:5, 82d, from where it has been transferred due to its association with M. Ber. 2:6's mention of mourning and bathing. See Luncz; Ginzberg, *Commentary*, 1:375-377, 380-381; Liebermann, *HY*, p. 35, n. 10, ls. 2 and 3 from the botton. The name "Samuel b. Abba" refers to Samuel. While all the MSS here and at y. M.Q., including *GYF*, p. 201, and citations, read Samuel b. Abba [or, in some citations, "Samuel"], the content of the narrative has led some scholars to deny the identification in this instance or to emend the name to "Simeon b. Abba." See Ratner, *Ber*. p. 59, *M.Q.* p. 119; Rabinowitz, *STEI*, pp. 8-9, 592; Sussmann, p. 237, n. 12; and, in general, *TK*, 3:74-75, n. 40, Bokser, *Samuel's Commentary*, pp. 98-99, and n. 275. Cp. Albeck, *Introduction*, pp. 263-264. See b. B.Q. 80b, and below.

[23]The pericope appears at the end of a *sugya* of special individual prayers, the last of which ends with Ps. 144:4. Samuel's comment is thus used to focus on that reference. See *DS* 81:9, and on the terminology of the reference, Goodblatt, *Rabbinic Instruction*, pp. 151, 152, 286-288. The introductory question, "What is" appears in M and Flr MSS and citations. See *DS* 81:9.

[24]On variants in the pericope, see *DS* 81:9, 40; Flr MS; and *Yalqut HaMakhiri* to Ps. 144:12, p. 276 [= p. 138b], and to Is. 46:12, p. 162.

[25]The *sugya* makes up the third in a series of three narratives presented in an attempt to prove that the dead are able to "know" of the happenings on earth. See Jacobs, *Studies*, pp. 65-67. We cite variants primarily where we deviate from the printed text. In general see *DS* 87-88 and Flr MS.

[26]*DS* 87 and Flr MS.

[27]= "academy" or "session(s)." See Goodblatt, *Rabbinic Instruction*, pp. 83, 90-92, and especially 85-86. Cp. Isaiah Gafni, "Yeshiva and Metivta," *Zion* 43 (1978):12-37, esp. 29-30, and n. 87, and see below, chapter ten, n. 5.

[28]See *DS* 88:3 and Flr MS. [The reading ꜥGYSꜥ, in *DS*, n. 3, is found in the margin to the Flr MS.] Cp. Gafni, p. 30, n. 87.

[29]Goodblatt, *Rabbinic Instruction*, p. 83.

[30]*DS* 88:5 and Flr MS.

[31]Printed edition and some texts add, "Make way." In B, the anonymous *Gemara* provides an evaluation of Samuel. On the story, see Neusner, *History*, 2:137-138.

[32]The context is the effect of speaking negatively about the dead. See *DS* 89. In MSS (*DS* 89:9 and Flr MS) Papa apparently does the speaking, while the printed edition has "and lo, said R. Papa, a certain one (ḤD) spoke. . . ." Note, on the other hand, the MSS have "about to split," while the printed edition as "split." It is understandable why the latter reading, "split," fits with the referent of "a certain one," i.e., and not Papa himself. See Kohut, *Aruch*, 1:296, s.v. ꜥRNQ, and note his reference to b. B.B. 10a.

[33]Texts vary as to the name. Printed editions = Mar Samuel; M MS = Samuel; Paris [cited in *DS* 89:9] and Flr MSS = Rav Samuel. See Rabbinovicz's footnote. Some texts have "spoke after the bier of Samuel." See *DS* 89:9. See Hyman, 3:1149-1150; Margalioth, cols. 834-835; Neusner, *History*, 5:55, especially 57, 183, 260; and especially Goodblatt, *Rabbinic Instruction*, pp. 134-135. The term in B, which we translated as "rabbinic student," is *ṣurba merabbanan*. The clarification of the use of this term might indicate at least with whom the anonymous *Gemara* identified the master. Given the pericope's context after the narrative in #30, a reference to Samuel would be plausible. Moreover, one could understand why a scribe might correct the text--namely, so Papa would gossip not about Samuel but about some lesser figure. The reverse of this would be much less likely. Note #24; Hyman, ibid; and Neusner, *History*, 2:137, n. 2.

[34]Samuel's tradition is cited along with M. Kel. 10:5 from b. B.M. 59a-b. The Mishnah and an accompanying *baraita*, A and C, make up a question in b. Ber. 19a concerning masters worthy of excommunication. Cp. R. Nissim, in Vilna editions of BT.
    We cite B according to the printed editions and Flr MS, the reading which accords with the original location in b. B.M. 59a-b. The M and P MSS and some citations [see *DS* 89-90:7 and R. Nissim] incorporate the question into the attributed tradition: "And said R. Judah. . . . Why is it called Akhnai? Because they surrounded . . . ." In pericopae cited from elsewhere we

commonly find the "quote" introduced with an "and," W-, and a slight modification of the language.  On the other hand, while Samuel's comment was
probably mentally generated by such a question it originally was not formulated along with such an introductory clause.  See *Samuel's Commentary* to
*Neziqin* and to *Tehorot* (in progress).  See also Epstein, *ITM*, p. 806; Neusner,
*Eliezer*, 1:422-427, and *Purities*, 1:149-150; and Friedman, "Critical Study,"
pp. 396-399, and 350, and n. 34 there.

[35]See *DS* 92-93, especially n. 2.  M and Paris MSS, but neither Flr MS
nor printed editions, include an explanatory gloss at the end of Judah bar
Ami's tradition.  The two traditions in B appear here and in seven other b.
locations to convey the notion of a *bet haperes* of rabbinic origin.  Twice
they are cited with M. Ohal. 18:4, and once they form part of the *Gemara* on
M. Nid. 7:5, as an explanation of Mishnah.  See Eruv. 30b [*DS* 117:11 and
Weiss, *ST*, 3:ad loc.]; Pes. 92b [*DS* 285:7]; M.Q. 5b [especially *ST*, 2:523,
n. 2**]; Hag. 25b [*DS* 87:100]; Ket. 28b [*ST*, 1:166, n. 4, and *TK*,6:233-234];
Bekr. 29a; Nid. 57a.  In particular: see the correlation of variants from
each location in *Talmud Bavli.  Masekhet Ketubot.  Diqduqe Sofrim HaShalem*
ed. Mosheh Hershler, 1- (Jerusalem, 1972), to b. Ket. 28b, pp. 207-208,
on which see Weiss, *ST*, 1:138-39, n. 1, and 586; Weiss's observation, *ST*,
2:523, n. 2**.  On b. Ber. see Lieberman, *HY*, p. 28, n. 6; Ginzberg,
*Commentary*, 2:101-103; and Bokser, *Samuel's Commentary to Tehorot* (in
progress).

  Samuel defines and explains a type of impurity.  An anonymous authority
cites this comment in b. Ber. to fulfill a need of the *sugya* which is unrelated
to Mishnah.

[36]=MSS.  The printed editions have HWYWT.  See *DS* 95:60 and Flr MS.
See also Henry Malter, *The Treatise Ta$^c$anit of the Babylonian Talmud* (New
York, 1930), to b. Taan. 24a-b, p. 107, variants and note to 1.10.

[37]In the passage R. Papa laments how his effort to bring rain was less
efficacious than that of R. Judah.  See *DS* 95; Sussmann, pp. 55-68;
E. S. Rosenthal, "A Contribution to the Talmudic Lexicon--Elucidation of Words
Based on Textual Variants," *Tarbiz* 40 (1971):193-200, especially 193-196; and
especially Goodblatt, *Rabbinic Instruction*, pp. 77-79, 144, n. 138, and
Gafni, p. 28, n. 76.

[37a]See Lieberman, *TK*, 1:20-21.

[37aa]This and the following *mishnayot* reflect a new application of
purity, holiness and cleanliness rules.  Earlier they had applied to the
Temple or the camp of Israel, where God's presence was assumed to have
dwelled.  Now, since an individual in prayer at any place might relate to
God, the rules potentially applied to any location.  See Deut. 23:8-15; above,
chapter two, to traditions #44-48; and below (chapter three), n. 51.

[38]" . . . said Samuel" = MSS and citations.  See Masoret HaShas, on
margin of Vilna edition, and *DS* 100:3, to which add Flr MS and *HaEshkol*,
1:30.  "Said R. Judah" = printed editions.  As Rabbinovicz points out, this
is the first of three traditions Judah transmits in Samuel's name.

[39]The "True and Firm" prayer reaffirms the notions of *Shema$^c$* and
focuses on redemption.  It is mentioned in M. Tamid 5:1, and T. Ber. 2:1,
p. 6, ls. 1-3.  See Elbogen, pp. 17-18.  The tradition is attested by
R. Joseph, a third-generation Babylonian, and Abaye, a fourth-generation
Babylonian, and is used in a *sugya* which deals with the issue whether the
recitation of *Shema$^c$* and *Tefillah* are biblical or rabbinic obligations.  The
pericope on Samuel's tradition focuses on this problem.  Then there follows
an alternative view, which is attributed to R. Eleazar and which is formulated in a pattern similar to that of Samuel's tradition.  There, however,
the items of doubt are the recitation of *Shema$^c$* and the *Tefillah*.
Eleazar's view is juxtaposed to a comment of Yohanan which deals only with
*Tefillah*.  On the *sugya* see Lieberman, *HY*, p. 19, nn. 4-5; Ginzberg,

*Commentary*, 1:12, 126-128, and cp. Urbach, *Sages*, pp. 15-17; and Y. Gilat, "Binah BaMishnah," *Sinai* 21 [#11-12] (1958):401-418, especially 402. Ginzberg astutely suggests that Samuel's ruling may reflect the different natures of the two liturgical texts. The *Shema^C*, due to its common use, is fixed in a person's mouth and one might, therefore, recite it automatically without paying too much, if any, attention to it. Accordingly, while praying one might find oneself at the beginning of the *Tefillah* without knowing for sure whether or not one had just previously recited the *Shema^C*. But the "True and Firm" blessing is not as frequently said and, consequently, might less likely have been skipped in haste. See above, tradition #23, and the rest of y. Ber. 2:4 end, p. 5a, and b. Ber. 16a for amoraic recognition of the factor of presumption concerning recitation of *Shema^C*. In this light, see T. Ber. 2:4-5, pp. 6-7, ls. 6-8, 10-12, which presents several rulings on erring in the recitation of *Shema^C*. They include: skipping a verse; erring but not knowing exactly where; and erring within or between sections. Samuel's comment thus focuses on an additional stage of the erring, thereby extending Tosefta's concern, and relates the issue of erring to the "True and Firm" prayer. As mentioned above, the contents of the latter text is the subject of T. Ber. 2:1, p. 6, ls. 1-3. Samuel's comment thus does not deal with Mishnah's problematic. Moreover, it has not been generated directly by Mishnah. Nevertheless, it may constitute a further extension of materials which earlier had been added to Mishnah. In any event, *Gemara* has used it for its own purposes and integrated it within its own concerns.

[40]See the version in y. Ber. 4:4, 8a, tradition #57, below, and n. 67, thereon. The content of the tradition more appropriately fits there in the *Gemara* on *mishnayot* which deal with the *Tefillah*. The tradition appears here as the second in three traditions Judah transmits in Samuel's name and the anonymous *Gemara* challenges and defends the tradition.

[41]See DS 101:20; Flr MS; and *HaEshkol*, 1, p. 31.

[42]See the version in y. Ber. 4:6[7], 8c, tradition #60, below, and n. 70 thereon, and *HY*, pp. 32-33, n. 30. As with item #37, the tradition more appropriately fits below in the context of *Tefillah*. Here it makes up the third in the series of three traditions Judah transmits in the name of Samuel. The tradition is analyzed by the anonymous *Gemara* and is followed by a different tradition, which is attributed to a different master, but which employs a similar pattern and deals with the *Tefillah*. Cp. the pattern in T. Ber. 2:4, p. 7, ls. 8-9. While it deals with recitation of *Shema^C*, it is followed by a clause, "thus with *Hallel*, and thus with *Tefillah*, and thus with *Megillah*."

[42a]See n. 37a and chapter two, to traditions #44-46, esp. n. 28.

[43]See DS 115, esp. n. 90; Flr MS; and *DS. Sukkah*, 128:2, for variants in the sequence of the items which Samuel mentions.
In b. Suk. 41b an anonymous *sugya* cites the *baraita* along with Samuel's comment to challenge a different tradition.
While the *baraita's* mention of urinating appropriately belongs to a *Gemara* on M. Ber. 3:5 and fits its surrounding *sugya* [see n. 37a], Samuel's clause relates to the first part--the action of saying the *Tefillah*. Samuel, accordingly, glosses that part (which indeed may have once independently circulated). By providing further examples he makes clear that the principle is to avoid distraction. See Rashi; Meiri's formulation, p. 82, col. 2, bottom; Ginzberg, *Commentary*, 1:353-354, and also T. Ber. 2:20, p. 10, l. 64.

[44]= Flr MS and printed editions. Neḥemiah = M MS and others. See DS 117:3 and 118:9.

[45]"And," W- = MSS. See DS 117 and Flr MS.

[46]Paris and Flr MSS read, BṬLYT, "garment," the reading in the Tosefta passage mentioned below. See Eleazar b. Judah, #345, p. 237.

[47]"It is permitted," lacking in printed editions, is in MSS and readings. See *DS* 118:10 and Flr MS.

[48]The anonymous *Gemara* makes these references to Samuel.

[49]See *DS* 119:60 and Flr MS.

[50]There are thus two alternative or different contexts for Samuel's traditions, in both of which Samuel's words remain identical. Obviously Samuel, however, did not formulate his comment as a response to the question of the later Amora Joseph. The tradition is made up of two parts, viz., "it is permitted," and the gloss or extension, "even his wife," joined by a conjunctive "and," W-. Judah either appropriated an autonomous and independent tradition of Samuel's and formulated his answer to fit the context, or, alternatively, Samuel originally glossed a separate text, which Judah cited for his purpose. In either case, Judah may have added one of the two parts so as to make the answer fit the question. Moreover, it is possible that Judah answered only one question, and sometime before the time of R. Kahana and R. Papa, the second version was generated.

The first version, Ginzberg suggests, might reflect a Babylonian practice to use *tefillin* to protect oneself from evil forces. See Ginzberg, *Commentary*, 2:302-304, and 1:273; b. Ber. 24a and y. Ber. 3:5, 6d; Yellin, to b. Ber. 23b, s.v., THT MR²ŠWTYW. Samuel's "even" then provides the extreme case, in which a man and woman sleep together and possibly have sexual activity. Nevertheless, it is not disrespectful to the *tefillin* to place them under the bed. We note, though the application differs, this text shares Mishnah's principle as to the proper cleanliness and purity in the context of holiness, God's presence, or the mention of God. The *tefillin* contain the biblical text of the *Shema^C* and constitute a symbol or means to experience God in prayer. Mishnah's problematic is tacitly to demonstrate that the earlier application of this notion, e.g., to the Temple, applies to rabbinic, standardized, prayer. See chapter two, to traditions #44-46. While Samuel's tradition lacks that concern, it directly responds to Mishnah. It atomizes Mishnah and, as part of its focus, offers additional cases of Mishnah's principle.

The second version also relates to the theme of Ber. Ch. 3. Indeed T. Ber. 2:15, p. 9, ls. 48-50, includes a *baraita* whose substance, formulated as a statement of law in terms of "in one garment," is very similar to the contents of Joseph's question. Moreover, it is possible that Samuel glossed part of this version of the *baraita*. See the version in y. Qid. 4:11, 66b, and b. Ber. 24a; *TK*, 1:23; and Yellin to b. Ber. 24a, s.v., D²R"H ^CGBWT. In this version, Samuel extends a supplement of Mishnah. The supplement deals with the nighttime recitation of the *Shema^C* in bed, something which Tosefta already discusses. Samuel would therefore be focusing on the extent of one of the laws. Samuel's comment, in addition, reflects the concern for appropriate "holy" or "clean" contexts for the recitation of the *Shema^C* and for the problem of distraction. Both of these interests are found above in items #38, 39, 42-46. Here the "even" provides a more extreme case of both factors. "Even" when a person sleeps with his wife or may be distracted by his wife, one may recite the *Shema^C* if one turns one's face away.

[51]See y. Hal. 2:4 (3), 48c, item #43, for a parallel. There an introductory question elicits the biblical proof text, Jer. 3:9. That verse clearly is not integral to the tradition. Probably the tradition originally circulated without any verse and Babylonian and Palestinian circles associated different verses with it. In b., the presence of the verse fits redactional considerations. Samuel's comment is the second of three traditions which list an item of feminine sexual arousement and which contain a verse. [A fourth, which is separated by a discussion, lacks a verse.]

The context here and in y. is not explicit. In y., it is juxtaposed to a tradition on *Tefillah*. See below n. 52 on item #43. Note Deut. 23:15 uses the word ^CRWH and that passage along with the rest of Deut. 23:10-15 provide the program for M. Ber. 3:4-6. See n. 37, above. Samuel is thus concerned with distraction in prayer and its proper context, matters relevant to M. Ber. See Meiri, p. 84, and Rabiah, 1:52-53, #76.

[52]See item #42 and n. thereto.

The tradition is cited as part of the *Gemara* on M. Hal. 2:3, which has implications as to a woman exposing her buttocks while saying a blessing. *Gemara* takes up that theme and discusses other "unseemly" matters. It presents Samuel's tradition after one which is attributed to Huna and which explicitly deals with *Tefillah* and excrement. Samuel's comment, therefore, probably originated elsewhere, as on M. Ber. 3-4, where it appropriately fits.

[53]Despite the introductory clause, Samuel's tradition glosses Mishnah. See chapter two.

[54]In the course of the transmission of several versions of Rav's tradition on this matter, Samuel's tradition is repeated. Cp. though, Goren, p. 130, who believes that the repetition is due to a scribal mistake.

In both b. and y., Samuel is in dispute with Rav, whose position each *Gemara* reports in more than one version. While Rav's versions are inconsistent, those of Samuel are complementary. BT focuses on "urine," and PT on excrement ("its top"). Samuel's reference to "urine" and to Mishnah accords with the fact that Babylonian circles understood, in the last clause of Mishnah, the "them" to refer to "urine," a meaning which may fit the plain sense. See *OZ*, 1:23b, #130; Mel. S.; *ITM*, 645-646; Lieberman, *HY*, p. 31, n. 300, and, in general, *TK*, 1:24-26; and the usage in the toseftan analogues, T. Ber. 2:16, 19, pp. 9-10, ls. 51, 52-53, 61-64; and chapter two.

[55]Rashi explains that this refers to urinating subsequent to the place's use for prayer. The place, therefore, does not maintain permanent sanctity. See *TK*, 1:25. This notion is consistent with that of #44-45, that the urine or excrement do not permanently disqualify a location from prayer. Cp. Ginzberg, *Commentary*, 2:313. This passage relates to our Mishnah, as reflected in b. Meg. 27b citation of *baraitot* analogous to those in T. Ber. 2:19, p. 10, ls, 61-65, and which relate to M. Ber. 3:5. Samuel thus supplements Mishnah. The tradition, though, is presented in b. Meg. due to the relationship of its assumed principle to M. Meg. 3:3.

[55a]Judah's opinion on the evening *Tefillah* is missing in many MSS and the first edition. See *Makhon-Mishnah*.

[56]Items 48-50 share the notion that the evening *Tefillah* may be said before the night. That is, the afternoon *Tefillah* may be said only until the late afternoon (PLG MNHH), after which comes the evening *Tefillah*. See commentaries and esp. *TK*, 1:28, l. 7. Alternatively, Samuel and the other masters understand the term "no fixity" of the evening *Tefillah* such that it permits them to say it whenever they want, even early. According to the first explanation, Samuel's view accords with Judah's position in M. Ber. 4:1. According to either explanation, Samuel's comment deals with an implication and practical application of M. Ber. 4:1 and relates its principle to other laws and concerns; in #48, to the saying of "Sanctification" so as to usher in the Sabbath, and in #49-50, to *havdalah* so as to escort out the Sabbath.

The textual history of #48-50 is complex. The number of traditions and the identities of the tradents vary in the MSS and citations. The printed editions and some other texts include only two traditions, #48-49, and some MSS add #50. The phrase, "It was said also," which opens #50, constitutes a standard pattern used to repeat an immediately preceding tradition now presented in a discrete formulation. See A. Weiss, *Development*, pp. 70-80, especially 76-78. The variations fall within the following patterns: (1) One instance of the two traditions, but no unanimity as to the tradent ("Judah" or "Nahman" for the first, and "Judah," "Nahman," or "Tahlifa," for the second). (2) One citation of the first tradition and two citations of the second ("Judah . . . Judah, . . . It was said also Tahlifa . . ."; "Judah . . . Nahman . . . It . . . Tahlifa. . . ."). (3) In a discrete discussion of only the second tradition, only the version attributed to Tahlifa. See *DS* 139:8; Flr MS [which for #49 has "Judah said Rav," which must be in error, as indicated by the tradition's use later in the pericope. Where Judah transmits a tradition, the names of Rav and Samuel are often (later)

supplied or mixed-up.  See Weiss, *ST*, 1:138-139, n. 1]; Talmudic Fragment in
*Sinai* 37 (73) (1973):228; *OhG*, "Responsa," p. 64, "Commentaries," pp. 35, 37,
RH, p. 34; Eliezer b. Nathan, *Raaban*, #171a, two different citations; Rid;
*OŽ*,1:10c, before correction; Rosh; *HG*, I:13c-d, III:64, II:28-29 and 45-46;
Coronel, p. 13c; *SRAG*, 2:101, p. 133.

    All three masters had access to Samuel traditions.  Apparently, two
sets of the traditions circulated each with a different set of tradents.  When
the traditions were combined, the analogue to the first tradition was deleted
while that to the second was included.  Alternatively, one of each tradition
was originally cited to answer the question raised in the pericope.  Subsequently, a different hand who had the other set added it to the pericope, but
included the "It was said also" version only to the second tradition.  In any
event, the various versions indicate that two traditions attributed to Samuel
circulated among his students.  Moreover, the variants derive from *Gemara*'s
attempt to present--or combine--the several reports.  In general, see Ginzgerg,
*Commentary*, 2:75-76; Maimonides, *MT*, *Tefillah*, 29:11; *TurSA*, #293, and Joseph
Cairo, "Beit Yosef," loc. cit.; and Mordecai Margalioth, ed., *Hilkhot Hannagid,
A Collection of Extant Halakhic Writings of R. Shmuel Hannagid* (Jerusalem,
1962), pp. 85-90, and notes.  The principle of #49-50 accords with that of
#65 from y. Ber. 5:2, 9b.  See below.

[57]The readings here, as elsewhere in b., vary in the spelling of the
name of Tahlifa's father, ᵓBYMY or ᵓBDYMY, or ᶜBYY.  See Hyman, p. 337;
Margalioth, col. 882; and Albeck, *Introduction*, p. 210.

[58]See above, chapter two.  The pericope is cited to identify "the one
who said, 'The evening *Tefillah* is optional,'" the reference in the anonymous
*Gemara*'s (late) interpretation of Mishnah.  The reading, in A, of "For" makes
explicit this relationship.  If it is secondary, a separate hand juxtaposed
the materials due to their mutual relevance.

[59]Venice p.e. alone has HLKTᵓ, the Aramaic, and not the Hebrew form of
the word.

[60]The readings vary as to the attributions in B and C.  See chapter two
for our analysis of this pericope and its variants.  Judah may be citing a
formulation of the Gamaliel-Joshua dispute, for which he draws on a Samuel
*baraita* which served to supplement Mishnah, and then cites Samuel's decision
as to the law.

[61]The tradition is transferred from above, y. Ber. 1:8, 3c, #18-19.
See Ginzberg, *Commentary*, 3:7-8, and cp. Luncz and Frankel, *PT*.

[62]See chapter two and the y. version, #56.

[63]The word "Seven" either represents a reading or interpretation of
Mishnah, or else is the result of contamination from lines D or E, below.
See above, chapter two.

[64]The sequence of J, K, L vary in the MSS and citations.  See chapter
two for textual and exegetical analyses of the whole passage.  G evidently
represents a Palestinian explanation or rendering of Samuel's opinion.

[65]On the Mishnah, see *Makhon-Mishnah*, variants and notes; *TK*, 1:31-33;
and Neusner, *Eliezer*, 1:4, 23-24.

[66]"And praying" = V and S MSS and citations in Meiri, p. 75, and Rid,
col. 54.

[67]L MS is supported by reading in Meiri; and that of S and V by Rid,
which has "Rav and Samuel say, He cuts off."  See Meir Netiv on Sirillo,
n. 3; Luncz; Ginzberg, *Commentary*, 3:339-342.  The use of the dispute form
(in other than Rid's reading) would support L MS.  The other reading may thus

have been "corrected" to harmonize it with Samuel's tradition in b. Ber. 21a.
Cp. Ginzberg. See above, item #37, and n. 40, thereto.

   Samuel's view, as in #37, is followed by one attributed to Yoḥanan. See
*HY*, p. 19, n. 4, and 33. Samuel's comment properly belongs here on a Mishnah
which deals with *Tefillah*. PT places it within a *sugya* on mistaken praying of
*Tefillah*. Tosefta on M. Ber. Ch. 3 and its topic of *Shema^C* dealt with this
issue and applied Mishnah's rules to other areas, including *Tefillah*.

   [68]This clause, not found in M and Flr MSS, is a late gloss which probably
was generated by the previous pericope. See above, chapter two.

   [69]See above, chapter two.

   [70]See above, chapter two.

   [71]See *DS* 165:50 and 60, and Flr MS. T. Ber. 3:4, pp. 12-13, ls. 21-22,
already drew upon the Ḥanah narrative and her prayer for a child, for a proper
understanding of the practices in prayer, including *Tefillah*. Y. Ber. 4:1,
7a uses it and b. Ber. 31a-b extends this analysis. Item #61 forms one
element structured as part of the running exegesis of the Ḥanah narrative.
Elsewhere, as well, the import of Ḥanah's reference to a "seed of men," or
"man-child," became subjects of discussion. See *Midrash Samuel*, ed. S. Buber
(Vilna, 1925), 2.7, p. 9. See commentaries to the verse, including Abarbanel
*Commentary on Former Prophets* (Jerusalem, 1955), p. 172b; and also Neusner,
*History*, 2:200. On the larger structure of the *sugya* see A. Weiss,
*Literature* (1962), pp. 251-256.

   [72]The master apparently takes WYḤL from the word ḤLL, which means,
"slain." See Rashi. This forms one of several interpretations each set in
the same format," [This] teaches that . . ." The first one is attributed to
R. Eleazar. The pericope makes up part of an extended *sugya* on the power of
prayer and the impact of Moses' prayer, in particular. See A. Weiss,
*Literature* (1962), pp. 251-256.
   "Samuel" = Printed editions; Coronel; *Aggadoth HaTalmud*, p. 5d; and
*Midrash HaGadol* to Ex. 32:11, p. 683. "Yoḥanan" = M and Flr MSS; and *Yalqut
Shimoni* to Ex. 32:11, #392. See *DS* 169-170:3-5, especially 4.

   [73]See *DS* 175. For a full analysis see Bokser, "Two Traditions,"
pp. 52-55 [correct: in pp. 52 and 53, l. 12, "Tefillah" for "Shema^C"].
Samuel's comment has been transferred from b. Pes. 112b, where it glosses a
teaching of Rabbi:

      And do not stand before an ox when it is coming up from the marsh
   because the devil dances between his horns.
      Said Samuel, With (B-) a black ox and in the days of Nisan.

Certain words have been added to the version in b. Ber. to make it comprehensible in the new location. MSS and the printed edition vary in placing
Samuel's comment third or fourth in the pericope. This fluidity reflects the
fact that the tradition has been transferred.

   [74]MSS and citations vary in the names in the attributive formula.
There are three basic patterns with variations: (1) "Rav and Samuel, and some
say it R. Yoḥanan and R. Eleazar" = Paris MS [cited in *DS* 179:1] and Coronel,
*Beth Nathan* [who adds, "both say" after the first pair of names]; and Rid
col. 95, who, however, has "Resh Laqish" instead of "R. Eleazar" for the
fourth name and who places "both say" after the second set of names to apply
to both sets. (2) "Yoḥanan . . . Resh Laqish" and "Rav and Samuel" = M MS
margin [and thus the reverse order of Rid], and Flr MS, who, however, has
"Rav" instead of "Yoḥanan" for the first name. (3) "And said Rav and some
say R. Simeon ben Laqish, and some say it Rav and R. Simeon b. Laqish" =
Printed editions and *HG*, I:14a, II:49, and III:71, which thus lack the attribution to Samuel.
   In b. Yoma 70a and b. Sot. 41a, we find a version of the tradition

attributed to Resh Laqish alone but without the proof text: "Because it is a
blessing which is not needed" and "Because they do not bless a blessing which
is not needed."

As the reading "Resh Laqish" is found in most witnesses, perhaps we
should follow Rid's reading.  On the other hand, elsewhere, at b. Ber. 17a
(twice) [above items 29-30] and b. B.B. 3a, we find the formula "Rav and
Samuel, and some say R. Yoḥanan and R. Eleazar."  Accordingly, the reading of
Resh Laqish may have been generated by or transferred from b. Yoma or B.B.

Mishnah Berakhot emphasizes the saying of the appropriate prayers and
blessings.  Once that concern is developed one of the next issues logically to
arise involves the question of needless repetition of a blessing.  Earlier we
found several traditions and a toseftan passage which dealt with aspects of
the problem.  See #36-38 and nn. thereto.  As all the variants to b. Ber. 33a
in the attribution are of names of early Palestinian and Babylonian masters,
this principle represents an early and, presumably, accepted notion.  We find
a differently formulated application of the notion in Sifra, *Vayiqra*, 2:4
[cp. T. Sot. 7:2, pp. 190-191, ls. 4-8].  In b. Yoma and b. Sotah, the tradition
serves as a reason for a specific rule.  The surrounding traditions attributed
to different masters offer other reasons for the matter.  It is thus possible
that the original thrust of the comment in b. Ber. 33a is to associate the
verse with the principle.  In any event, the tradition is cited by the anonymous author of the *sugya* to make explicit an allusion in an argument and is
thus secondary to the context of M. Ber. 5:2.

[75]See chapter two.  The second clause of the tradition employs Mishnah's
language "he says it," and the indefinite "it" here and in the first clause
refer back to Mishnah.  T. Ber. 3:9, p. 14, ls. 46-47, likewise deals with the
contexts in *Tefillah* and over a cup.  If one forgets *havdalah* in the former,
the latter suffices, and if one does not do it in the latter, one returns to
the *Tefillah*.  Thus Tosefta adds to Mishnah the consideration of the relative
importance of the two contexts and in effect indicates its preference for the
*Tefillah*.  This accords with Mishnah-Tosefta's emphasis of *Tefillah* as an
important and effective means of divine worship and prayer.  Samuel's comment
--and its wider context--further develops the interest which Tosefta exhibits,
though Samuel's view does not follow Tosefta's preference for *Tefillah*.
Moreover, the *sugya*'s editor glosses his comment like those of the two previous
ones with a clause which makes explicit the legal implication.  It is thus used
as a decision.  See the b. version for what an autonomous formulation might
have looked like.

[76]See above, chapter two.

[77]See above, chapter two.

[78]See above, chapter two, and the previous item.

[79]Samuel's comment is interpolated into a series of traditions which
Ḥiyya b. Abba cites in the name of R. Yoḥanan, the first of which, following
the reading of MSS, directly deals with M. Ber.  See *DS* 187:7-8 and
Rabbinovicz' remarks.  But cp. y. Ber. 5:5, p. 9d, and Lev. R. 15.9,
Margulies ed. pp. 366-367 and notes.  The tradition thus forms a secondary
element to an extended *sugya*.  Samuel's tradition is editorially added also
at b. Shab. 63a, 151b; Pes. 68a = San. 91b; San. 99a.  As the last instance
is identical to b. Ber. 33a and is not found in MSS and printed editions, it
is probably a transference from Ber.  See *DS*.  San 296:100.

[80]See chapter two for analyses of items 70-89.  Considering 76-77 are
duplicates of 79 and 80 in a parallel *sugya*, there are a total of 20 comments.
Taking into account, however, the fact that #72 originates elsewhere and thus
duplicates #85 and that some of the remaining items are different versions or
instances of the same tradition, we actually have nine different, distinct
traditions.

1.  #70 provides a conceptual metaphoric basis for Mishnah.

2-9.  The others supplement Mishnah, some of which have been used, recast,
and adapted.

2.  #71, 73, 74.
3.  #72, 85; 81, 82, 84; 83.
4.  #75.
5-6.  #76=79; 77=80; 78.
7.  #86.
8-9.  #87, 89; 88.

[81] This is drawn from b. Eruv. 30a.  See item #85.

[82] The clause following Judah's and Samuel's opinion cites the two traditions and glosses each with a reason.  For Samuel it reads, "And Samuel
said, 'By whose word all things come into existence'--since it eventually
hardens."

[83] Sirillo supplies a different prayer text but this reading probably is
the result of an emendation.  See above, chapter two.

[84] Above we hesitantly suggested a possible emendation of the prayer
text.

[85] See *TK*,1:58-59, 79-80, esp. n. 23, and *DS* 223:40.

[86] For textual matters, see *DS* 223:40-70, Flr MS, Rid, and, in general,
*TK*, 1:79-80.
We comment on the passage as Samuel's ruling may have originally
responded to the version of Muna's opinion presently found in T. Ber. 5:12,
p. 27, 1s. 24-26, and in y. Ber. 6:5, p. 10c: "R. Muna says in the name of
R. Judah, Breaded-*kisnim* after the meal--requires a blessing before and
after."
        Judah's fellows cite the *baraita* along with Samuel's ruling, B-C.  The
former thus appears to circulate with the latter.  Judah claims that the
report of Samuel's position should be reversed.  The fellows respond by
citing a different traditions which Judah himself had cited in Samuel's name,
E.  The latter item makes up an autonomous tradition which, while in part
deals with an issue relevant to Mishnah's concerns, is not presently formulated to supplement Mishnah Berakhot.  On the other hand, the *baraita* makes
up a proper supplement to Mishnah, as indicated by its presence, in a variant
version, in Tosefta.
        As each version of the *baraita* addresses different issues, only B
involves a contradiction with E.  B deals with eating breaded-*kisnim* after
the meal and recitation of Grace, and teaches what constitutes the appropriate
blessing.  The alternative version deals with eating breaded-*kisnim* after the
meal but before Grace, and teaches that a blessing is necessary before and
after it.  As Lieberman shows, in this version the first blessing is not "Who
bringest forth," but rather, "Who createst various kinds of food," or "Who
createst kinds of *kisnim*."  See *TK*.  If we, therefore, do not have to
distinguish between E and Samuel's ruling, we would obviate a forced definition of LHMNYWT, in E.  This word generally means "unleavened cakes," and not
"thin wafers."  But F requires the latter, forced, rendering.  See Tosf. b.
Ber. 42a, s.v. LHMNYWT, and R. Nissim, s.v. "And said R. Judah"; and Krauss,
*QT*, 2.1:204.  Our suggestion receives credence because Babylonians knew the
alternative version of the *baraita*.  It is transmitted in y. Ber. by
R. Helbo, R. Huna in the name of Rav, in Hiyya the Great's name.  In addition,
the several Babylonians in their actions assume the notion or practice of
eating breaded-*kisnim* after the meal but before Grace.  This includes, first,
Huna, who responds to Hiyyah bar Ashi, in y. ibid. and in an analogous Huna
and Nahman incident, in b. Ber. 42a, and secondly, Sheshet, in b. Ber. 41a,
as argued by Tosf. s.v. ᵓLᵓ PT HBᵓH BKYSNYM, and Lieberman, *TK*, 1:80.
        Accordingly, Judah, in D, evidently knew the substance of Samuel's
opinion on breaded-*kisnim* and, therefore, when the ruling was presented in
conjunction with B, he had to reject that tradition.  But his tradition of
Samuel would accord with a gloss of Samuel's on Tosefta's version.  Judah's
fellows or their source, however, associated Samuel's view with the first,
and wrong version.  Elsewhere we find analogous cases in which Samuel's

tradition is tacked onto the wrong version of a teaching and that juxtaposition, as a result, produces problems. See *Samuel's Commentary*, pp. 157-162.

PT's version of the *baraita* appropriately appears in *Gemara* to M. Ber. 6:5 which deals with foods eaten after the meal. Given, however, b.'s understanding of Samuel, we can understand why it does not appear in that context. If our analysis is correct, however, Samuel's ruling would have originally dealt with the issue of M. Ber. 6:5, through the extension of Tosefta.

[87]R. Meir's view forms one part of a *baraita*, which in PT and T. Ber. 4:4-5, p. 19, ls. 11-16, contains three views and in BT, two views. Meir apparently disputes a view attributed to Yosi who requires one to employ the blessing text coined--or standardized--by the rabbis. Meir on the other hand extends the last clause of M. Ber. 6:2. The blessing text, at least in part, is the one used for aesthetic appreciation of natural objects. See *TK*, 1:60-61, and Azikri.

Samuel, in his ruling, thus supports the position that allows the greatest flexibility. PT presents immediately after Samuel's opinion a concurring view of Rav. But Rav's and Samuel's views are not redacted into a single pericope. Rather the editor of the larger pericope introduces an incident and a comment of Rav with the formula, "The matter of Rav says thus [like the above]."

As Meir's opinion makes up an appropriate part of a Mishnah commentary, Samuel's comment does so by extension. Formally, however, it constitutes a gloss on the *baraita*. But as Rav's opinion indicates, an amoraic view on the matter could be formulated in its own terms. See also Huna's view immediately above; b. Ber. 40b; chapter two, analysis of tradition #125. In any event, Samuel focuses on a mishnaic issue.

[88]See *DS* 226:50, and Rashba. Flr MS lacks the added opinion. The references to Tosf. and Tosf. R. Judah may not actually constitute attestations of Samuel's opinion. See also Albeck, *HaEshkol*, 1:67-68, and nn. As Samuel's opinion breaks the pattern of doublets of two opposite positions, the clause is suspect.

[89]M MS deletes "And R. Judah," and the negative, "not." But these words are found in various citations and Flr MS.

The passage focuses on a theme of Mishnah and relates to its problem the practice of drinking wine in the midst of a meal, an item mentioned in M. Ber. 6:6. If the reading with Samuel's position is original, he would thereby attest Mishnah and deal with an extended issue.

It is possible that the subject of the dispute has been revised and it originally dealt with the case of Mishnah. If so, Samuel and the others directly address Mishnah. See y. Ber. 6:5, 10c, and Mareh Hapanim, Frankel, *PT*, and Epstein, *IAL*, p. 314, and cp. Luncz.

[90]Samuel's comment is cited as part of a pericope from y. Suk. 4:5. It serves to make explicit in y. Ber. the principle that the onset of the actual meal [= reclining] ends the applicability of blessings said prior to that moment. See *Pesiqta de Rav Kahana*, Mandelbaum edition, pp. 418, 430; *Pesiqta Rabbati*, p. 202a; Azikri; Ratner, pp. 155-156, to which add R. Nissim Gaon, ed. Abramson, p. 549; especially Lieberman, *HY*, p. 41, n. 60, and in *Pesiqta de Rav Kahana*, Mandelbaum ed., p. 475, n. to p. 430; and the analogous traditions in b. Pes. 100b-102a, and b. Suk. 48a. Avun a traveler, may have played a role in the transmission of the teaching. See Hyman, pp. 89-92, Margalioth, cols. 782-786, and Albeck, *Introduction*, pp. 352-353; and cp. Frankel, *Introduction*, pp. 60b-61a. See also Rabinovitz, *STEI*, pp. 337-338.

[91]See *Makhon-Mishnah*, esp. n. 77.

[92]The initial clause forms the last line of a (Babylonian) *baraita* which *Gemara* cites earlier on the page and then analyzes part by part. See Higger, 6:393-394, #12. J. Feliks suggests that the idiom reflects the fact that turnips, *brassica rapa*, were mainly the food of the poor. See *Mixed*

*Sowing*, p. 78, n. 17, and *EJ*, 16:83, s.v. "Vegetables." Cp. Rashi. The comments of Samuel, Rav, and Yoḥanan and others, not cited, apparently supply means with which to prepare the turnip and, therefore, assume that this variety is not good to eat raw or by itself. See Pliny, 20:78-96, esp. 91, and 96. Cp. Loew, 1:487-88; Feliks; and Feldman, p. 193.

The clause appears in printed editions, Flr MS, and with variants, in P MS, but not in M MS. See *DS* 239:200.

[93]See *DS* 248:400, 249:1. The readings vary for Samuel's comment. The correct text, following Flr and M [before "correction"] MSS and some citations apparently = . . . MYTW LY ꜂RDYY [or: MYYTW ꜂RDYY꜂ LY] . . . WGWZLY꜂ L꜂B꜂. See Lowe, 1:33f.; *Aruch*, 1:273, and *Sup*. p. 64, and Jastrow, s.v. ꜂RDꜛ. See also the citations of Rif [in JTS MS]; David b. Levi; Ribban; and Ashbili; Shiṭah Mequbeṣet; Agamati; Tosf. R. Judah, 2:505; *HG*, I:11b; and *OhG*, "Responsa," p. 111. See also Rashbaṣ, pp. 272-273, and cp. Rid. In general, see Meiri, p. 176.

The pericope assumes that the common summons to Grace can occur even when the parties have not from the onset eaten or intended to eat the whole meal together. This notion accords with our understanding of Samuel's interpretation of M. Ber. 7:1. See below, item #105. The pericope thus presents an incident which throws light on Mishnah. Tosefta itself includes such genres of materials even though they are not formulated to comment on Mishnah.

[94]See *DS* 257:9-10 and notes, and Flr MS. The masters wonder why a simple question, "Is the seer in town," 1 Sam. 9:11, elicited a long answer. Verse 12 supplies the "Yes," and a detailed response, after which v. 13 follows. The comments thus respond to the verse, though each master in formulating his remarks apparently is influenced by previously held notions. Rav generalizes as to the qualities of women; Samuel perhaps draws upon the notion that a (royal) leader is beautiful, which may form part of a political theory of leadership; and Yoḥanan assumes his political-theological theory of world empires. See Wilhelm Bacher, *Agadot Amoraei Eres Yisrael*, Hebrew edition, 3 vols. in 6 parts (Tel Aviv, 1925-1936), 1, 2:25 and n. 3, 76-77, and n. 5, and 21, n. 8; Nahum Glatzer, "The Attitude Toward Rome in Third-Century Judaism," in Alois Dempf et al., eds. *Politische Ordnung und Menschliche Existenz* (Munich, 1962), pp. 243-257; Neusner, *History*, 2:52-53; Reuven Kimelman, "Non-Violence in the Talmud," *Judaism* 17 (1968):316-334. See also the parallel in *Midrash Shemuel*, ed. Buber, p. 44, and Gen. R. #70, p. 810, l. 4.

The pericope employs an exegetical dispute pattern and as a unit is interpolated into a reference in a *baraita* which sets out the basis of Grace After Meals. Versions of the *baraita* appear in T. Ber. 6:1, pp. 32-33, ls. 1-10, y. Ber. 7:1, 11a, and esp. Mekilta, *Bo*, #16, Horowitz ed. pp. 60-61. See also Yellin and Maharsha to b., and *TK*, 1:100-103.

[95]See *DS* 262 and Flr MS. This tradition and an alternative version in y. Ber. 7:4, 11c, item #104 below, deal with a special problem and subtle issue in the laws of Grace After Meals. On the logic of the argument see Jacobs, *Studies*, pp. 47-48.

B-C attest the tradition and the place of Naḥman in its transmission. C indicates that a tradition might circulate without an interpretative explanation. Samuel's comment itself forms a fully comprehensive statement. Though b. elsewhere on the page presents opposing views attributed to Rav and others, the former and latter are not redacted into a dispute form. The pericope following D harmonizes Samuel's and Rav's position and limits Samuel's comment to the Grace of the New Moon only. But Samuel's language lacks any such limitation.

The tradition and its y. variant provide a fine example of how mishnaic supplements turn into independent traditions and discussions. First, the traditions assume the rule of M. Ber. 7:1, that Grace is said, and that on special days, e.g., New Moon and Sabbath, something special is mentioned in the Grace. Mishnah and Tosefta contain several traditions which attest such practices and other uses of interpolations in the *Tefillah* and special mentioning of the Sabbath and holidays. See M. Ber. 5:2-3, 8:1, and esp. T. Ber. 3:8, p. 14, ls. 41-44. Secondly, the traditions apply to Grace the issue of "forgetting," which Mishnah and Tosefta address elsewhere. Indeed the aforementioned Tosefta passage sets out the requirement to say the special "mention" and refers to the New Moon. Tosefta then focuses on *Tefillah* and the issue of forgetting (= T. Ber. 3:9, which relates to M. Ber. 5:2), after which it presents a general principle concerning, first, special days, and, secondly, whether or not one mentions something special for the day (= T. Ber. 3:10, ls. 47-51; see through 3:13, p. 15, l. 63). The text explicitly states that one who errs--repeats, and, of note, it employs the language found in Bavli's version of Samuel's comment, MḤZYRYN ᵓWTW. This part of the *baraita* does not mention Grace After Meals. BT cites and combines different parts of the *baraita*, while PT, following Ginzberg's interpretation, understands or applies that text to Grace After Meals on the New Moon. See Ginzberg, *Commentary*, 3:296, and Friedman, in *Pesikta Rabbati*, #1, p. 1a, n. 3.

Samuel and the other masters thus deal with an issue integrally related to the concerns of Mishnah though not part of its problematic--the make-up and applicability of the Summons to Grace. Tosefta, in its supplement and commentary to Mishnah's focus on *Tefillah*, already included materials which raise relevant matters and apply several rules to Grace After Meals. Samuel's concerns thus extend to an area into which one's thought might logically lead. He and the others may have responded to the aforementioned *baraita* (T. Ber. 3:8-10), and they may differ as to what degree one applies the logic of repeating, found in *Tefillah*, to the case of Grace. The masters, however, may have had different versions of the tannaitic traditions and/or they may draw up distinctive approaches. Finally, in both b. and y., Samuel's comment is challenged and Rav's position appears dominant. See chapter ten, text to n. 69.

Samuel's tradition reflects the growing standardization of the liturgy. He is aware of the principles of Mishnah and *baraitot*, relates the problem of forgetting and the solution of "repeating" found in a related area, to the new matter of Grace. He thereby deals with a subject not earlier addressed. See also b. Ber. 49a and n. 100 to the y. version below.

[96]Following Samuel's comment, y. presents two amoraic interpretations of the terms BTHYLH and BSWP. For a full analysis of this tradition and its b. 50a-b analogue, item #105 below, see above, chapter two.

[97]The *sugya* focuses on whether or not M. Ber. 7:1's requirement of three people for the communal Grace makes up an absolute minimum. The anonymous editor cites the views of Samuel and Yohanan and Simeon b. Laqish which relate to M. San. 1:1 to demonstrate that the former dispute forms part of a wider conceptual difference between the Babylonian and Palestinian circles. See Goldberg, "R. Zeᶜira," pp. 327-330. The opinions of Samuel and other masters appear also in b. San. 3a [see Tosf. s.v. LRBᵓ LYT LYH DŠMWᵓL, and 2b and 6a], 5b, 87b, and b. Ket. 22a.

[98]Samuel defines the category of "minor" listed in M. Ber. 7:2. In y. Ber. 7:2, 11b, as preserved in the MSS and editions of PT, Samuel's comment and the introductory question have been revised and integrated into the *sugya*. See above, chapter two.

[99]See above, chapter two.

[100]In addition to L, V, and S MSS, see Ginzberg, *GYF*, p. 296; Frankel, Luncz, and Elijah David Rabinowitz-Teomim, "Tov Yerushalayim," [in Vilna PT], and cp. *Nir*. The pericope presents a different version of the tradition in b. Ber. 48b, above #98. M. Ber. 7:1 and 4 both set out the principle that an individual is to invite others to Grace, as items #99 and 104 point out. They both, therefore, provide appropriate contexts for laws like 98 and 104 which supplement the basic principle of Grace After Meals. See above n. 95, for a discussion of the issue which Samuel addresses and the tradition's relationship to Mishnah.

In the y. version, Samuel appears in dispute form with Rav and the protasis defines the context as the "Sabbath." This is consistent with b.'s harmonization which claimed the masters agree in such a case. Rav's opinion--

as in BT--emerges dominant, a point reflected in the rest of the *sugya*.
Processes of transmission and redaction may account for some of the variations
between these two versions. E.g., y. circles held that meals were equally
important on all special days, including the New Moon, or they followed the
Tanna Eliezer, regarding special "mentions" in *Tefillah*. Alternatively, BT's
larger *sugya*, with its focus on the New Moon, shaped b.'s particular dispute.
See *TK*, 1:36-37, esp. n. 27; Azikri; *Pesiqta-Rabbati*, #1, esp. Friedman's n. 3.

[101] See the y. Ber. 7:1, 11a version, item #99, above, and chapter two
for our full analysis of both the b. and y. versions. There we reconstruct a
version of the comment which may lie behind both alternatives in BT.

[102] The tradition follows a *baraita* which supplements Mishnah and contains the opinions of an anonymous authority and of R. Eliezer. The latter,
and not the former, permits a person to wash hands with wine. See the version
in T. Ber. 4:3, pp. 18-19, ls. 5-8. An anonymous authority in *Gemara* uses
Samuel's tradition as a gloss on this *baraita*. Samuel and Eliezer hold their
positions apparently irrespective of the disrespect to the food. See Rashi,
especially Ashbili, p. 468; *DS* 266:300; Lieberman's discussion of the
variants, *TK*, 1:57; and note Eliezer's opinion as to the use of bread, in
*Massekhet Soferim*, ed. M. Higger (New York, 1937; reprint ed. Jerusalem,
1970), 3:18, pp. 65-66. Samuel's comment also appears in b. Shab. 50b, 143a,
and b. Bes. 21b. The latter instances may be independent of b. Ber. 50b. See
Tosf. b. Ber. 50b, s.v. KM⁾N ⁾ZL⁾.

[103] So=S MS. YNHYQ=L MS and Venice p.e.; NHYQ=V MS. See Luncz. In all
three readings, in contrast to Yohanan and Ḥanan bar Ba, *havdalah* precedes
Sanctification.

[104] For the references to Samuel and his tradition we follow the correc-
tions offered by various commentaries. V, L, and S MSS have variations of it.
See Azikri; Meir Netiv to Sirillo; Ratner, pp. 182-183; esp. Luncz; Frankel,
*PT*; *STEI*; Shulsinger, *YE*; and Yellin, to b. Pes. 102b [printed after b. Yoma].
On Rashba to b. Pes. 102b, see *DS* 312:6, and n.b. the attributive formula in
tradition #114.
     On the tradition's relationship to Mishnah, see the version in b. Pes.
102b, item #108, and n. 107. Note the role of R. Zeira later in the *sugya*.
and see chapter eight, subsection 4.A.

[105] The GWP⁾, "essence," serves to indicate that an earlier item, Rav's
opinion, is presented in its entirety in the following pericope.

[106] On the sequence see *DS* 312, Columbia MS, and especially Tosf. b. Pes.
103a, s.v. RBH.

[107] See *DS* 312 and Columbia MS.
     PT Ber. 8:1 and b. Pes. 102b-103a contain two related traditions
attributed to Samuel. Each belongs to a pericope which focuses on the
sequence of blessings in *havdalah* and Sanctification (*qiddush*) when a
Saturday night coincides with the beginning of a festival. The masters share
with M. Ber. 8:1 the assumption that blessings mark the beginning and the end
of holy times and that the sequence of the blessings and actions is significant. M. Ber. 8:1 (and its explanation in T. Ber. 5:25, p. 29, ls. 53-57) in
particular deals with the sequence of the wine and the special mention of the
day. M. Ber. 8:5 and T. Ber. 5:30, pp. 30-31, ls. 72-77 treat the sequence of
the *havdalah* blessings when it is combined with the Grace After Meals. Note
Mishnah's use of a list, "lamp, food, spices, and *havdalah*, . . . " a pattern
found in Samuel's tradition. The continuation of the Tosefta text, ls. 77-79,
focuses upon when the *havdalah* is recited and specifically mentions a Saturday
night which coincides with a festival. Samuel's tradition further extends
this concern and raises the problem when *qiddush* is said.
     The issue of M. Ber. 8:1 and Samuel's tradition, therefore, constitutes
the relative importance shown to different items of compelling importance, and
the different criteria employed to establish the preferences. Samuel's tradition, in b., provides the rule, and, in y., a parable which sets out the logic

behind the rule. The opinions are congruent with each other as are the functions of the parables. BT's version of the parable, like the y. version
attributed to Samuel, serves to support a view which avers that the more
important item is attended to before the less important one. Samuel's
traditions thus augment Mishnah and develop its law to a stage beyond his
predecessors.

[108]V MS=ᵓKL BḤTH YDYH; S and L MSS=ᵓKL KHTM. On the former see *Aruch*,
3:517, and Payne Smith, s.v. ḤT=sack, and Luncz, esp. p. 74, n. 2.

[109]The passage is open to several interpretations. Rav wanted to avoid
the cold of the water. Therefore, he did not wash his hands but ate the food
with something separating it from his hands and thereby prevented the transmission of uncleanness. This procedure may accordingly replace washing. Alternatively, Rav washed his hands and wore some type of gloves to keep warm and
to prevent holding food in his hands. In this instance, the procedure makes
up an extra safeguard. Samuel may have understood Rav's action in the first
way and, accordingly, asked his question. Rav, however, answers that this is
a misapprehension for his action was an extra safeguard. See Sirillo and
Śedeh Yehoshua. Zeira may be the one who transmits the narrative (and its
b. parallel, #111) to Palestine.

[110]L MS=KHTM; S MS=KHYTM; V MS=BḤLH. In rendering the passage, the commentaries may have been overly influenced by the b. Ḥul. 107a-b parallel. See
*Nir* and Luncz. Luncz's logical objection that HTM should not be used in two
different ways disregards the change in location. Line B is assumed to
transpire in Babylonia while line E is in Palestine. Note how the latter opens
with the term "here," which refers to Palestine. Accordingly it would not be
inappropriate for Zeᶜira to use "there" when he speaks of Babylonia. See
additional instances in E. Bacher, *Aggadot Amoraei Ereṣ Yisrael*, 3A:11, n. 2.

[111]=ᵓZYLᵓ, which means either "gone" or "light," i.e., devalued or
scorned. See Jastrow, p. 37; *Aruch*, 1:51, and *Sup*. p. 15a and 421b; Levy,
1:50-51; and Hanoch Yalon, *Introduction to the Vocalization of the Mishna*
(Jerusalem, 1964), pp. 173-175.

[112]=V MS and the correction of Epstein, "Mediqduqe Yerushalmi," pp. 43-
44; YWSY BR BR KHNᵓ BŠM ŠMWᵓL=L MS; YWSY BR KHNᵓ = S MS. Cp. Luncz. The
reading which we have adopted must refer to the Yose who was a fourth-generation Palestinian. See Albeck, *Introduction*, pp. 334-346.

[113]See Sirillo; Azikri; Fulda; Luncz; Frankel, *PT*; Jacob Neusner,
*Invitation to the Talmud* (New York, 1973), pp. 193-195. The notion is that
priests who eat heave-offering are naturally careful and, therefore, require
fewer and milder precautions. PM, Ratner, and Sacks, *Diqduqe*, p. 36, n. 2,
on the other hand, suggest that we reverse the apodoses: "Washing hands
applies to heave-offering . . . does not apply to unconsecrated food." In this
case the sequence in which "heave-offering" appears first is identical in
three consecutive comments, here, in Yose's, and in a third adjacent comment.
Moreover, Samuel's comment and one attributed to Rav, which follows Yose's,
would then document Zeira's comment, i.e., that Rav and Samuel require washing
hands for priests. This would accord with the role of R. Yose, a student of
R. Zeira. In this light, see T. Ber. 5:13, and 27, p. 27, 1. 26, and p. 30,
1. 63. If this rendering is correct, those responsible for the present y. text
and its point of view may have been motivated by a desire to harmonize the y.
with the b. See n. 116, below.

[114]Samuel's traditions deal with the requirement to wash hands before
eating. PT Ber. 8:2 and b. Ḥul. 105a-107b contain extended *sugyot* on the subject and as part of their analysis cite similar narratives concerning Samuel
and analogous traditions attributed to him. Mishnah Berakhot treats certain
aspects of washing. Ber. 8:2 concerns the order in which one washes hands and
drinks wine and Ber. 8:3 the sequence in which one drys one's hands. The
latter make up part of a series of Houses disputes. Samuel's traditions thus

focus on washing as a separate subject and not in terms of Mishnah's problematic. But such independent treatment predates Samuel. Tractate Yaddayim,
in part, is devoted to the subject. Moreover T. Berakhot supplements Mishnah's
rules. T. Ber. 5:26, pp. 29-30, ls. 57-61 (and *Gemara*) explain the reason
for the washing and indicate that it serves to prevent impurity which would
render the cup unclean. T. Ber. 5:13, p. 27, ls. 26-27, deals with the basis
and nature of the washing. The latter text is cited in the y. on Ber. 8:2.
See *TK*, 1:80-81.

Accordingly, neither the narrative nor the tradition formally comment on
Mishnah, but they do assume its concerns and principles. Mishnah, as elsewhere, has been atomized and its references thereby become subject to separate
study. We remain unsure, however, if Samuel's comments originated in the
context of, or in response to, M. Ber. 8:2. Even item #110, which could be
formulated as a gloss to a text, could just as well have circulated elsewhere.
Indeed its analogue in b. Hul. 106b [see Epstein, "Mediqduqe," p. 44] presently
appears as a gloss to a *baraita*. See Ramban to b. Hul.; T. Yad. 2:1-4, p. 682,
ls. 13-24, and cp. T. Ber. 5:27, p. 30, l. 63.

In general, see Neusner, *Invitation*, pp. 45-47, 193-195, and *Purities*,
vol. 19: "Yadayim," Introduction, pp. 104-108, and vol. 22: 88-89, 288-289;
Joseph Tabory, "The History of the Order of the Passover Eve" (Ph.D. Thesis,
Bar Ilan University, Ramat Gan, Israel; submitted February, 1977), pp. 97-111,
esp. 102; and see below, n. 119, for items 110-111. See also *TK*, 5:1309-10,
as to priests being less stringent than others in regard to purity.

[115] See Rashi and *TK*, 1:34.

[116] See *DS* 146a:5-8; Rashi; and cp. Meir ben Jacob HaKohen Schiff,
"Ḥiddushe," in BT Vilna editions. The pericope forms part of a long *sugya* on
washing hands. It contains additional traditions attributed to Samuel. See
especially b. Hul. 106b, and *DS* 145a:6, and Epstein, "Mediqduqe," p. 44, who
argues that Samuel's opinion circulated in different versions. See also
Higger, 5:611-612, and 464.

The b. and y. pericopae thus exhibit certain differences but many
similarities. See nn. 113 and 114.

[117] Many MSS reverse the order of these two *mishnayot*. See *Makhon-
Mishnah*, esp. n. 11. Cp. the sequence in T. Ber. 5:27-28, p. 30, ls. 61-67.

[118] V MS preserves the correct names, according to which the reference to
"his father" makes sense, for father and son are mentioned in the beginning.
Considering that "R. Abba" = "Rabbah," various citations support V MS. See
Epstein, "Mediqduqe," p. 43; Rabinovitz, *STEI*, p. 597; R. Judah b. Qalonymous,
*Yeḥuse Tanna^c im VeAmora^c im*, ed. Judah Leib Maimon (Jerusalem, 1963), p. 144,
esp. n. 77; Ratner, p. 187; and Albeck, *Introduction*, p. 306; and esp. cp.
Lieberman, *TK*, 1:95, n. 69.

[119] So=L and S MSS, and Judah b. Qalonymous, p. 144. R HYYH=V MS [twice
as the attribution appears a second time, in a wrong place]. See the attributive formula in #107. As Zeira was a priest, the passage reflects the notion
that Palestinians should or do respect Babylonian priestly pedigrees. See
above, chapter two.

[120] The reference to Samuel appears within a narrative which relates to
Mishnah's issue. Samuel's comment itself, however, is unrelated to Mishnah.
Ḥuna [=Huna] ostensibly cites Samuel's teaching. The second item supplements
the first one and provides a proof text for it.

[121] The tradition appears in two versions, one in y., item #115, and one
in b., #116. The reading in the Midrashim, #115b, may preserve an earlier
stage of the tradition, in which it clearly appears as an independent statement. See above, chapter two.

[122] See chapter two for our full analysis of these traditions. Number 118
has an analogue in b. Eruv. 53a, and #119 in b. A.Z. 2a. See chapter two, to
#117, esp. n. 412.

[123] This clause accords or goes along with the reading, in H, that Rav said *cedehen*, with an *ayin*, and Samuel, *ᵓedehen*, with an *alef*. But the whole clause may constitute a secondary addition to the pericope. See above, chapter two, nn. 418, 419, 429 and texts thereto.

[124] See chapter two, especially our comments as to Zeira's possible role in the *sugya*'s transmission.

[125] See above, chapter two.

[126] See above, chapter two.

[127] See *DS* 304:5, Flr MS, and *Yalqut HaMakhiri* to Zech. 10:2, p. 95. Printed editions have "said," which does not change the meaning.

[128] See *DS* 304:5-6, and other references in n. 127.
The report of Samuel's response to good and bad dreams begins an extended *sugya* on dreams, which forms part of a series of pericopae interconnected and associated by formal and thematic considerations. BT Ber. 54a contains a *baraita* which relates to Mishnah and which lists things for which we give thanks. BT 54b presents a series of pericopae which list items "which need" something, the first of which is "thanks." In 55a's list of such items, the three things "need" mercy. One of the three is a good dream. This leads into a section on dreams. BT 55b has a tripartite *sugya* whose first pericope deals with a "dream." Samuel's comment begins the extended focus on dreams which ends on b. Ber. 57b.

[129] Some texts have, "that the Romans come. . . ." See n. 130.

[130] We follow the MSS and citations listed in *DS* 305:60-70, Flr MS, *Midrash HaGadol* to Gn. 41:1, p. 694, and *Yalqut Shimoni* to Dan. 2, #1060. The printed edition attributes to Samuel and Shapur with one variation, what the immediately preceding pericope attributes to R. Joshua b. Ḥanina and a Caesar, viz., "That the Romans come and take you captive and make you grind date-stones in a golden mill." The variation exists in the name of the plunderers; in the Caesar's dream "Persians" come. What the printed editions assign to Samuel and Shapur, the MSS attribute to the Caesar and Joshua b. Ḥanina with "Persians" replacing "Romans." Thus we have two forecasts and dreams. MSS and citations reverse the printed editions' assignment of each set. See also Jastrow, p. 1551; *Aruch, Sup*. p. 337; and Gafni, p. 28, n. 76.
As both dreams and forecasts employ a similar style, one may copy the other. In any event, both have received a literary formulation. The two incidents thus present a rabbinic sage forecasting what a secular power will dream. This reflects the sagacity of the rabbinic sage in the eye of the secular power. Moreover, the stories reflect the power of suggestion, a notion spelled out in traditions in the immediately preceding *sugya* and reflected in the *sugya* which follows. See also Neusner, *History*, 2:70.
Of note, items #123 and 124 agree that dreams have no inherent power.

[131] See above, chapter two.

[132] Many readings lack the word "tempests," the last item of this clause, and Epstein, accordingly, suggests that we should render *ziqim* as "winds," and thus follow this usage found elsewhere. See above, chapter two, to traditions #126-129, esp. text to n. 488.

[133] See chapter two. We place a question mark next to #126c, as we cannot be sure if this line makes up a Samuel tradition or a later gloss to it. See the version in y. Ber. 9:2, 13c, items #128-129.

[134] See chapter two; the b. version, item #126-127; and above (chapter three), n. 133. Though the formulation here would seem to suggest that Samuel is the attributed author of the response, we cannot be totally definite.

[135]So = printed editions and Flr MS.  Other MSS include an additional
clause.  See *DS* 332:60-80.  On the other hand, Flr MS like M MS has
". . . by a serpent" and not "by a scorpion."  We cannot be sure how much of
the material represents Samuel's tradition and how much later additions.  This
pericope separated by a brief section follows the pericope in which Samuel
deals with *ziqim*, items #126-127.  The structure of both pericopae consists
of a statement and then a comment introduced by, "I have learnt, . . ."  The
phrasing may thus make up a pattern to convey a two-part tradition.  See
n. 136.  On "I have learnt," see Wilhelm Bacher, *Die Agada der babylonischen
Amoräer* (Frankfurt, 1913; reprint ed., Hildesheim, 1967), p. 41, n. 48, and
*EM*, 2:165.

[136]See *DS* 332:80.  Again Flr MS, like M MS, has "his friends" instead of
"The Merciful One."  This reference to Job 38:31 may not have originally made
up an integral part of the tradition.  See n. 135.

[137]This means "in number."  See Feldman, *Rabbinical Mathematics*, p. 214,
and cp. Jastrow, s.v. KYMH.  The clause is glossed by a clarifying clause, on
which see Albeck, *Introduction*, pp. 518-519, n. 118.  On the whole passage see,
e.g., *OhG*, "Responsa," p. 130; Rashi; Samuel ben Nissim Masnuth, *Majan-Gannim,
Commentary on Job*, ed. Salomon Buber (Berlin, 1889), to Job 9:9, p. 31;
Maharsha; Louis Ginzberg, *Legends of the Jews*, 7 vols. (Phil., 1909-1938),
1:162, and 5:183, n. 40, and references there; and especially *Jewish
Encyclopedia*, 9:434-440, "Orion," s.v., by Ludwig Blau, and 10:88-89,
"Pleiades," s.v., by Ludwig Blau.
    The pericope is made up of two discrete, though connected units.  The
first is in two parts [see n. 135].  It opens with a comparison of two
biblical references to *kesil* and *kimah* and argues that the two complement each
other.  It then includes a mythological-astronomical comment concerning the
tail of Scorpio, the sign of Pleiades.  The second tradition defines *kimah*.
The pericope as a whole makes up part of a *sugya* which starts with Samuel's
comment on *ziqim* of M. Ber. 9:2, items #126-127.  That pericope mentions
*kesil*.  The latter reference, accordingly, sets the foundation for a *sugya*
on *kesil* and *kimah*.  But this material, i.e., #130-131, may have originated
elsewhere where it was structured around references to *kimah* and *kesel*, as on
the verses in Job.  Cp. Bacher, *Babylonischen Amoräer*, pp. 41-42, 44, and
n. 68.

[138]See chapter two.

[139]So=L and V MSS.  "And [a person] . . . = S MS.

[140]Samuel's comment concerns the New Moon liturgy and forms part of a
*sugya* on special blessings said on seeing the moon.  The appropriateness of
the pericopae in y. Ber. 9:2 is manifest once one notices that a *baraita*
specifically extends M. Ber. 9:2's mention of a blessing said when one experiences the things created during the days of creation to the cases of the sun
and moon.  The *baraita*, a version of T. Ber. 6:6, p. 34, ls. 32-33, likewise
appears in the b. on M. Ber. 9:2.  The y. thus further extends this reference
to additional special blessings said over the moon.
    Samuel's comment requires a referent.  See above, item #127 for another
instance of the formulation, "[A person] has to . . ." and chapter six, category F.  The opening word, "*Tefillah*," can appropriately function as the
referent, but its place in the pericope may be redactional.  Tosefta, however,
provides an example of another fitting referent.  While Samuel could not gloss
T. Ber. 6:6, mentioned above, as it deals with a simple blessing said over
experiencing the created item, he could refer to a version of T. Ber. 3:10,
pp. 34-35, ls. 49-52.  The latter rules that a special prayer is interpolated
into the *Tefillah* on the New Moon.  Hoshia's teaching supports the inclusion
of special prayers on the New Moon.  See Ratner, PM, and Luncz; Gen. R. #6.1,
p. 41; b. Shab. 24a and b. Eruv. 40b; and especially *TK*, 1:36-37, 39, 109-110.

[141]See chapter two.

142 See *Makhon-Mishnah* and Albeck, 1:338.

143 See chapter two. Tosefta 6:9 provides a first step in the continued
focus on the rule of Mishnah. Tosefta, though, shares with Mishnah the concern for the liability to say the blessing and for the appropriate text of
the blessing. Samuel's comment, like in the instance of rain, item #134,
assumes this liability but focuses on exactly when it takes effect. See the
other versions or related traditions, #136-137.

144 Oxford MS [*DS* 18:90] and Columbia MS delete the opening "For." This
tradition appears also in b. Pes. 119b, b. Meg. 21a, b. Suk. 39a, and b. Men.
35b. See n. 143, and the y. version, item #135. Rav's disciple circle may
attest not the version as printed in b. Pes. 7b, but the one in y. See
chapter two and n. 145, immediately below.

145 See above. While the principle here may be inconsistent with item
#136, it is consistent with the y. version, #135. We, therefore, need not
employ the forced harmonization which b. Men. offers.

146 See *TK*, 1:118, 119.

147 See *DS* 344:3; *OhG*, RH, p. 67; Rishonim, especially Tosf. R. Judah,
2:635, and Sacks' notes there; and GRA, *Ḥiddushe*.

148 On variants, in addition to items in nn. 146-147, see *DS* 345. "Say
thus--Blessed" = M MS.

149 Samuel's comment adds to a *baraita* which supplements Mishnah and
Tosefta. That *baraita* has a formal similarity with a law in M. Ber. 9:4 and
the pericope appropriately appears in the latter's *gemara*. The *baraita*
prescribes prayers to be said on entering and leaving a city, which in late
antiquity was considered a dangerous place. See *TK*, 1:118 and n. 61. T. Ber.
6:16-17, pp. 37-38, ls. 72-83, supplies the text of such a blessing and adds
the case of a bath house, which was also considered a dangerous place. Mishnah
and Tosefta assume that a prayer constitutes an appropriate means both to
beseech God before the potential danger and to express one's thanks on avoiding
it. The Tosefta in different versions appears in the b. and y. on the Mishnah.
BT adds the additional instances of entering a place for bloodletting and
entering a bathroom, while PT has just the latter. The prayer for the bathroom
differs from the others in its form and notion, though its pericope is similar
in its structure, viz., "One who enters. . . . When he leaves. . . ." See *TK*,
1:118-119, esp. to 1.81; and T. Ber. 3:7, pp. 13-14, ls. 28-39, and Krauss, *QT*,
1.2:406-410, and *Tal. Arch.*, 1:48, and nn. 359-361.
    Samuel disputes Rav as to the proper seal to the prayer. His remarks
include a narrative response and the alternative seal. If the comments originally appeared in a dispute form, the narrative leading up to Samuel's formula
may constitute a secondary addition to justify the superiority of Samuel's
position. Sheshet provides a third formula and R. Papa comments on his and
Samuel's views. See n. 148.
    Samuel and the other masters see the functions of human anatomy as
praiseworthy and as an example of God's miraculous hand. Tosefta attests that
Mishnah's prescription for such individual prayers could and should be extended.
Samuel (and the other masters) assumes this requirement, but focuses on the
practical application and, as elsewhere, offers a precise standard and formula.
In this case, Samuel may have been further motivated by the specific issue as
well. The endings of blessings posed a problem, especially to third-century
Babylonians. Palestinian authorities--in contrast to Babylonian ones--
apparently did not require a sealing for such liturgical texts. Accordingly,
to set such seals the Babylonians had to scrutinize and adapt the traditions
which they received from Palestine. See *TK*, 1:60-61; Heinemann, *Prayer*, p. 68;
and cp. Emunat Yosef in Sirillo, to y. Ber. 9:4. On the subject of the prayer,
see Gen. R. 1:3, p. 5, and the Rishonim who cite this text, including David b.
Levi of Narbonne, p. 119 [n.b. n. 55]; Ashbili, p. 495; Tosf. R. Judah, 2:635;
and Elijah of London, p. 126. Cp. GRA, *Ḥiddushe*, p. 76; and below, item #141.

[150] See chapter two, to traditions #135-136, n. 514.

[151] See *Makhon-Mishnah* for variants.

[152] The pericope forms part of an extended *sugya* which developed from the use of Gen. 2:7 for throwing light on Mishnah's reference to a person's "two inclinations." See A. Weiss, *Literature*, p. 123. The support for Mishnah comes from the first of three exegeses of the verse. According to the third one, God originally created Adam with two faces and out of the second face He formed Eve. See Ginzberg, *Legends*, 1:66; 5:88-89. The text is the reason for including Rav's and Samuel's comments on Gen. 2:22, since one of them refers to Adam's "second face." In form, the traditions make up an exegetical dispute and may have originated in response to the verse. See the related view of Samuel in Gen. R. 17.6, Theodor and Albeck, ed., p. 157, and the comments of M. A. Kasher, *Torah Shelemah*, 1- (Jerusalem, 1929-), 1:214, n. 155, 241, n. 275, 242-243, n. 281.

The pericope, and its surrounding material in a somewhat different order, appears in b. Eruv. 18a. There the pericope makes up part of an extended *sugya* whose point of departure is the third of three traditions which are related formally. Each interprets a text with the formulation ". . . it is two (DYW [or DW]) . . ." See *DS*. Eruv. 56:70, and Vatican BT MS 109, Series A, 1:18. The third asserts that God created Adam with two faces DW PRṢWP [or DYW PRṢWPYN]. Next, as in b. Ber. 61a, follows the Rav and Samuel dispute. See A. Weiss, *Literary Unit*, p. 140, and *Literature*, pp. 62-63.

The Samuel tradition in Gen. R. 17.6, as Kasher and Yellin (to b. Eruv. 18a) observed, indicates that the second interpretation ("tail") belongs to Samuel.

For variants, see *DS*. Ber. 350; *DS*. Eruv. 56; *Midrash HaGadol* to Gen. 2:21, Margulies ed. p. 86. See also Hanoch Zundel, "Eṣ Yosef," in *Ein Yaᶜoqov* (reprint ed., New York, 1955), to Ber. 61a; Midrash Tehillim, to Ps. 139, Buber ed. p. 528, #5.

[153] Rav and Samuel provide different similes for the "evil inclination" mentioned in Mishnah. The reference forms part of a text whose other parts directly relate to Mishnah's theme that one must accept whatever God metes out. See chapter two.

[154] See *TK*, 1:121.

[155] M MS repeats the attribution to Samuel. See *DS* 362:9.

[156] On the rendering of ŠYNH, see *Aruch* 8:68, 113, 114; *OhG*, "Responsa," p. 138, "Commentaries," p. 99; Levy, 4:547; and Simon, p. 391, n. 6; and cp. *Thes. Tal.* 17:660. On ᵓSṬMᵓ, "steel edge," see *Aruch*, 1:170, s.v., and *Sup*. p. 42, and Jacob N. Epstein, *Der Gaonaeische Kommentar zur Mischnaordung Teharoth* (Berlin, 1924), p. 31, n. 15.

Samuel's comment focuses on the beneficial value of relieving oneself and forms part of a *sugya* on defecating. The *sugya* extends M. Ber. 9:5B[6]'s concern for respect for the Temple due to its holiness. T. Ber. 6:19, pp. 38-39, ls. 90-96, makes the issue explicit with proof texts. One dimension of the respect involves proper toilet procedures, if not a ban on relieving oneself. See Yadin, *Temple Scroll*, 1:228-235, esp. 230. As in #138, this topic constitutes a proper subject of teaching and thus an aspect of Torah. *Gemara* atomizes Mishnah and makes explicit the application of the notion of respect for the holy Temple to extra- or non-Temple holy places. Due to this extension, M. Ber. 9:6 may have been placed at the end of the tractate. See above, #40, 42-47, and T. Meg. 3:25-26, p. 361, ls. 90-93, and Sifre Deut. #254-258, pp. 280-282; Sifra, *Qedoshim*, 7, 8-9, pp. 90d-91a; M. Meg. 3:4 and esp. T. Meg. 2:18, p. 353, ls. 58-63, which, in effect, is the synagogue application of M. Ber. 9:5B[6]. See also the parallels Lieberman cites for T. Ber. 6:19; and *TK*, 1:121-122.

[157] See *DS* 364:7. *Aggadot HaTalmud*, like the printed edition, includes the name Nappaḥa.

[158] See *DS* 364:8.  The context deals with the collection of ransom money as part of the census of Israel.

[159] On variants see *DS* 363-364.  Samuel's tradition makes up an exegetical dispute form with Rav.  They differ as to what God saw during the plague that afflicted Israel at the time of David's census (1 Chron. 21:15).  The *sugya* focuses on David's sin, which apparently was impertinence and lack of modesty before God.  The section is autonomous and not related to Mishnah, though, through its association of the theme of modesty, it is connected to the preceding *sugya*.  That *sugya* develops Mishnah's reference to avoidance of disrespectful behavior in the Temple area, an example of which is relieving oneself.  It treats various aspects of relieving oneself, including outside the Temple, and ends with the importance of modesty while doing it.  See Meiri, p. 214; Ribban, p. 194; cp. Ashbili, p. 496, and *OhG*, RH, p. 69.

Samuel draws upon an earlier tradition that the binding of Isaac later proved efficacious in helping Israel.  The tradition in different ways was applied to different events and in the third century was associated with David's census and the danger of the plague.  Mekilta, *Pisḥa*, 7.11, Lauterbach ed. 1:57, 88, and Horowitz ed. pp. 24-25, 39, express this in terms of Isaac's blood; Targum to 1 Chron. 21:15 and Samuel, here, expresses this conviction in terms of Isaac's ashes.  The notion regarding the effect of the ashes, in particular, appears in different locations, first explicitly in Sifra, *Beḥukosai*, 8:7, p. 112c.  See the references, notes, and discussions in Gen. R. #94, Theodore and Albeck ed. 3:117; b. Taan. 16a and y. Taan. 2:1, 65a; Lev. R. #36.5, Margulies ed. p. 849; especially Shalom Spiegel, *The Last Trial* (New York, 1967), pp. 38-44, esp. 43-44; G. Vermes, *Scripture and Tradition in Judaism* (Leiden, 1973), pp. 193-227, esp. 212, 204-208; R. Le Déaut and T. Robert in *Targum Des Chroniques* 2 vols. [Analecta Biblica, 51] (Rome, 1971), 1:86-87, n. 5.

[160] Alternatively, "To the world."  According to the latter reading, the unnamed authorities ordained that people add to the seal, "From the world," a reference to whence we came.  This refers to the world to come which was created and prepared from the six days of creation.  See *Makhon-Mishnah* and, especially, *TK*, 1:122-123.

[161] For variants see *Makhon-Mishnah* and *TK*, 1:122-125.

[162] There are several readings for the names in the attributions in A and B.  M MS has "Samuel bar Mattenah," in A, and "Tabi," in B.  Some have Samuel's name in A.  See *DS* 368:3 and n. 163, below.

[163] See n. 162.  Some readings lack the name of "Samuel."  Some of the latter, though, include it in A.  See *DS* 368:4 and also *Yalqut HaMakhiri* to Prov. 24:10, p. 46b.

Prov., Ch. 24, esp. vs. 1-12, speaks of the importance of wisdom and the strength it provides a person.  A follows the standard identification of wisdom as Torah and, accordingly, understands v. 10's reference to the loss of strength as due to the weakness in Torah.  B adds or revises the notion that not only the study of Torah--or its laxity--but even the performance of a commandment has this effect.

A-B do not formally make up a comment on Mishnah or directly respond to it, though we may be able to understand their place with the *Gemara* on M. Ber. 9:5C[7].  As B circulates along with A, together they make up a unit.  But A-B do not constitute a mere extension of the previous *sugya*.  The pericope preceding A deals with the use of God's name and thus supplements Mishnah.  But A and the materials which follow B focus on Torah.  Since the last clause of M. Ber., however, mentions Torah, A-B may therefore take up this reference.  If so, nevertheless, the focus on Torah is not defined by Mishnah's problematic.  Rather Torah has become a subject in its own right.  In part this is paralleled in T. Ber. 6:23-25, pp. 39-40, ls. 106-120, which deal with Torah and *miṣvot*.  Hence we notice, as we did elsewhere, that *Gemara*'s response to Mishnah not only elucidates Mishnah, but employs it as a framework and point of departure

independently to develop the items mentioned in Mishnah.  Due to the variants
for the attributions, however, we remain unsure if this instance derives from
Samuel's circle.

PART THREE

CHAPTER FOUR

THE *PRIMA FACIE* CASE FOR A MISHNAH-COMMENTARY

1. *The Spread and Distribution of Comments*

i

The question before us is: Do Samuel's traditions *prima
facie* represent the remains of a Commentary on Mishnah and to
what degree? Although comments are not extant on every mishnah
and in that sense do not constitute a running commentary on
Mishnah, they may still reflect a sustained effort at commentary.
If so, they would exhibit certain qualities and not others. For
example, the traditions would appear throughout the tractate on
many diverse *mishnayot*. If on the other hand they would make up
only a limited number of teachings about a limited number of
*mishnayot*, the Mishnah as a whole would not have provided the
structure around which Samuel organized his instruction. Accordingly, we evaluate the distribution of Samuel's traditions. Our
specific questions include: How many *mishnayot* provide the rubric
for comments and what portion of the tractate do these *mishnayot*
make up. Likewise, how many traditions appear in the context of
the different *mishnayot* and how many per mishnah. These questions
apply to the Mishnah comments and to the other traditions as well.

Fifty-nine traditions very closely relate to Mishnah and
can be considered part of a primary effort at commentary on
Mishnah. We have divided this category into two parts. The
first includes items which directly explain Mishnah's text,
wording, and law and thus formally belong to a Commentary (MC);
the second are those materials which also explain Mishnah by
focusing on a key element or principle but do so by supplementing
it. We call the latter "Mishnaic Explicative Supplements" (MES).

Whatever criteria we have employed to distinguish the
Mishnaic Explicative Supplements from the comments which complement and supplement Mishnah (RC and RS), neverthelesss the
differences between the two groups may occasionally appear slight
and, therefore, arbitrary. For sure, as we argue below, the
process of commentary inevitably leads into complementing and
supplementing and, thereby, developing Mishnah, and consequently
our classifications inevitably involve some degree of subjectiv-
ity. Nevertheless, as we shall also see when we deal with the

253

function of the traditions, the Mishnaic Explicative Supplements
provide information integrally relevant to a Commentary.   In
addition, as we already found in Volume One of our project, not
all the direct Mishnah comments are presently preserved as tight
glosses on Mishnah.   From their earliest stage the traditions
made up different types of commentary and circulated in different
modes.   Accordingly, for the purposes of this study it remains
useful to include the Mishnaic Explicative Supplements (MES)
along with the direct Mishnah Commentary (MC) items.   In fact, by
doing so we are able to trace the transition to the wider
response to Mishnah.

These fifty-nine traditions relate to twenty-two different
*mishnayot*.[1]  Of these, seven *mishnayot* have only BT comments, six
have only PT ones, and nine have both.   The following chart lists
the specific texts of Mishnah and the location of the comments:

CHART 1

LOCATION OF THE COMMENTS ON *MISHNAYOT*

| *Mishnayot* with Comments | *Mishnayot* with Traditions in: | | | Total *Mishnayot* per chapter |
|---|---|---|---|---|
| | BT Only | PT Only | BT and PT | |
| 1:1, 2, 4 | 1, 2, 4 | | | 3 |
| 2:1 | | 1 | | 1 |
| 3:5 | | | 5 | 1 |
| 4:1, 3, 7 | 1 | | 3, 7 | 3 |
| 5:2 | | | 2 | 1 |
| 6:1 | | | 1 | 1 |
| 7:1, 2, 3, 4 | 4 | 1, 2 | 3 | 4 |
| 8:5, 6, 7, 8 | 8 | 6, 7 | 5 | 4 |
| 9:1, 2, 3, 5 | 5 | 1 | 2, 3 | 4 |
| Total *Mishnayot* per *Gemara* | 7 | 6 | 9 | 22 |

Every chapter of Mishnah is thus subject to Samuel's
scrutiny, though the scope of Samuel's focus apparently is
greater in certain chapters than in others.   We can evaluate the
significance of this scope once we examine the spread from the
perspective of Samuel's traditions.   We will also be able to conclude if an external factor determines which *mishnayot* elicit a
response and which do not.   If such a pattern is discernible,

Samuel's traditions might then constitute remains of a focus on a
single topic and not on Mishnah in general.

ii

The fifty-nine items do not make up fifty-nine separate
and totally different traditions.  Several comments appear in more
than one location.  First, we have a *sugya* or tradition transferred or cited by a later authority and placed in a second
location.  Such an occurrence does not constitute an independent
usage of the tradition.  We generally have not numbered these
additional instances (#117, 134, 136) as distinct items in the
catalogue of the traditions, in chapter three.[2]  On the other
hand, we generally have separately classified duplicated instances
of the exact same tradition independently cited or used in an
adjacent pericope or elsewhere in *Gemara*.  For the purposes of the
present discussion, however, they naturally make up a single
tradition.  These repetitions account for eight items:  45=46;[3]
71=73=74;[4] 72=85; 81=82=84;[5] 76=79; 77=80.  Thirdly, a somewhat
different category consists of the b. and y. analogous versions
of a tradition.  Six items have consistent analogues:  44, 45;[6]
54, 56; 58, 59; 67, 68; 99, 105; 135, 136.  Four have even closer
or practically identical analogues; these yield five "repeated"
traditions:  65, 66; 102, 103; 115, 116; 127, 128-129.[7]  The
fifty-nine items, therefore, represent fifty-one different traditions.  However, this number will be further reduced when we take
account of the b. and y. analogues.

The fifty-nine items, or fifty-one separate traditions,
are found scattered in both *Gemarot*.  Twenty-three appear in PT,
all appear in Berakhot, and thirty-six are in BT, with thirty-two
in Berakhot, and one each in Shabbat (#66) and in [C]Eruvin (#85),
and two in Pesahim (#116, 132).  Chart 2 provides a breakdown in
terms of the type of comment.  The numbers in parentheses represent the total less repeated traditions.

While in several instances several traditions deal with
the same Mishnah and are analogues, alternative versions, repetitions, or complements of each other, a close examination of all
the Mishnah-traditions reveals that, in general, the teachings
are not clustered together.  Chart 3 lists the location of the
traditions with the individual *mishnayot* subject to comment.  The
first number after the citation of the Mishnah represents the
number of items in BT and the second, in PT.

CHART 2

TYPES OF COMMENTS IN EACH *GEMARA*

| Location | MC | MES | Total |
|---|---|---|---|
| BT | | | |
|   Ber. | 14 | 18 (11) | 32 (25) |
|   Elsewhere | 3 | 1 | 4 |
|   Total | 17 | 19 (12) | 36 (29) |
| PT | | | |
|   Ber. | 17 (16) | 6 | 23 (22) |
| Totals | 34 (33) | 25 (18) | 59 (51) |

Twenty-two individual *mishnayot* are presented. Most are
subject to one to three traditions. Chart 4 provides the specific
breakdown in terms of comments per mishnah. We calculate the
totals with and without the repeated traditions. The latter figure is the number in parentheses. Considering there are very few
exceptional *mishnayot* that yielded more than three comments, the
spread is well distributed throughout the tractate. Moreover,
taking into account the presence of the b. and y. analogues further levels the figures, leaving twenty of the twenty-two
*mishnayot* with one to three traditions; one with four items; and
one with thirteen items.[8] While, as stated above, we consider
such analogous comments, even those practically identical, as
separate traditions, nevertheless, this observation underscores
the way in which M. Ber. 9:3 and especially 6:1 are exceptions--
and exceptions which prove the rule.

The correlation between the *mishnayot* and traditions
indicates that the comments do not constitute a focus on only a
few highly selected items in Mishnah. This conclusion is not
disproven by the presence of one or two exceptional *mishnayot*.
Thus the traditions *prima facie* may add up to a response to
Mishnah in general or to a significant part of Mishnah. Moreover,
the scattered distribution of Samuel's comments within each and
both *Gemarot* reflects the fact that his teachings are not organized and preserved as a group on the basis of their content,
literary formulation, or some other aspect inherent to them.
Indeed, the presence of repeated traditions, especially the

b. and y. analogues, supports this contention, for the traditions
had to circulate individually, possibly originally along with the
text of Mishnah.  Otherwise they could not be cited individually,
be they slightly adapted in the transmission, application, and
redaction.

CHART 3

TOTALS AND LOCATION OF COMMENTS ON EACH MISHNAH

| Mishnah Chapter | Passage Number and Sum of Traditions on each (BT, PT) | Total Number of Traditions |
|---|---|---|
| 1 | 1(1,0), 2(1,0), 4(1,0) | 3 |
| 2 | 1(0,1) | 1 |
| 3 | 5(1,2*) | 3* |
| 4 | 1(1,0),   3(2,1), 7(1,2) | 7 |
| 5 | 2(2,2) | 4 |
| 6 | 1(17*,3) | 20* |
| 7 | 1(0**,1), 2(0,1), 3(1,1), 4(1**,0) | 5 |
| 8 | 5(1,1), 6(0,2), 7(0,1), 8(1,0) | 6 |
| 9 | 1(0,1), 2(3,3), 3(1,1), 5(1,0) | 10 |
| | | 59 |

*Includes the eight repeated items, one on 3:5, and seven on 6:1.

**The traditions on 7:1 and 4 originated in response to the same mishnah
though they both deal with both *mishnayot*.

CHART 4

COMMENTS PER MISHNAH

| Number of *Mishnayot* | Comments per Text | Total |
|---|---|---|
| 12 ⎫ 16 (17) ⎫ | 1 | 12 |
| 4 (5) ⎭        ⎬ 19 | 2 | 8 (10) |
| 3 (2)          ⎭ | 3 | 9 ( 6) |
| 1 | 4 | 4 |
| 1 | 6 | 6 |
| 1 | 20 (13) | 20 (13) |
| 22 | | 59 (51) |

Before concluding that we in fact do have a *prima facie*
case for the remains of a Mishnah Commentary, we must evaluate
the twenty-two *mishnayot* which elicit Samuel's response in light
of all the *mishnayot* in Berakhot.  This comparison will enable us
to consider the significance of the exceptional passages, M. Ber.
9:3 and especially 6:1, which elicit a rather large number of
traditions.  As we shall see, Samuel's Mishnah-comments cover the
full range of subjects within M. Berakhot.

### 2.  *Mishnah's Themes vs. Samuel's Themes*

#### i

M. Berakhot contains nine chapters, each of which has
five to eight individual *mishnayot*, totaling fifty-seven texts or
fifty-nine, if one counts M. Ber. 9:5 as three separate units.
Samuel's direct response to twenty-two different *mishnayot* adds
up to a focus on about 39 percent of the texts.  But a comparison
of the specific themes within each chapter with those of Samuel's
teachings reveals that this 39 percent treats the main issues of
each section and thus most of Mishnah.  Below we extend this
inquiry to take into account all of Samuel's teachings and we
demonstrate that he not only focuses on Mishnah's contents but
dwells upon them and develops their concerns and topics.

One can readily make the comparison by reviewing our layout in chapter three and by noting the relationship of the
Mishnah to the relevant traditions, the MC and MES items.  The
topic, however, is worthy of an explicit comparison, to which we
now turn.[8a]

#### ii

We can divide the tractate into six different subjects.

1.  Chs. 1-3 = *Shema*[c]
2.  Chs. 4-5 = *Tefillah*
3.  Ch. 6    = Blessings said before eating food
4.  Ch. 7    = Communal Grace After Meals
5.  Ch. 8    = Procedures and rituals said at a meal
6.  Ch. 9    = Blessings for special experiences

## 1.  Chs. 1-3.  *Shema$^c$*

Chapter 1 deals with three issues.  First are the time periods in which one recites *Shema$^c$* morning and evening.  Masters dispute the latest hour within each period (1:1-2).  These *mishnayot* assume that the Houses' dispute in M. 1:3 follows the House of Hillel.  The second issue centers on this dispute between the Houses with regard to the time for recitation and the proper body posture, views associated with alternative understandings of Deut. 6:7.  The third issue, M. 1:4-5, consists of rules that blessings should encase the recitation of *Shema$^c$* and that the text following *Shema$^c$* mention the Exodus from Egypt.

Samuel deals with the first and third issues.  He rules as to the latest limit for reciting *Shema$^c$* (#1, 7), and defines the blessing which precedes *Shema$^c$* (#18),[9] though he does not deal with the reference to the Exodus.

The lack of focus on the second item, however, does not adversely affect our argument.  First, we claim only that the *Gemara* preserves, be it in an adapted and reused form, the remains of Samuel's Commentary on Mishnah.  Therefore, we should expect that some passages and themes lack extant responses.  Moreover, it may not have been as necessary in the case of M. 1:3 as elsewhere to have--or preserve--a comment on Mishnah, for M. 1:1-2 makes clear that the law follows the Hillelites.  This proposition implies that a law's practical application may affect Samuel's scrutiny.  Below we return to the viability of such a possibility.

Chapter 2 deals with the proper attention in recitation of *Shema$^c$*, specifically how to maintain it, what it involves (2:1, 3, 4), and when it cannot be maintained (2:5, 6).  The chapter includes a subunit on Rabban Gamaliel's peculiar practices (2:6-7) and a pericope (2:2) that defines items mentioned in the preceding text (2:1).

Samuel is aware of the main themes of attention and comments that it entails (or may be achieved through) standing (#21), but he does not directly respond to all the specifics in Mishnah.[10]

Chapter 3 focuses on those who do not recite *Shema$^c$*, whether due to some valid preoccupation which prevents attention (3:1-2), or to a status or lack of knowledge (3:3), or to some temporary unclean condition which would desecrate the holy space wherein *Shema$^c$* and blessings are recited (3:4-7).  As the last concern applies to prayer, as well, this item (3:5) provides a transition to *Tefillah*.

Samuel's direct Mishnah comments define or limit the
principle of unseemly desecration of a prayer site (#44, 45-46).
The items reflect both a practical concern and possibly a development of Mishnah's principle, something found in several other
traditions, as we shall see below.[11]

## 2.  Chs. 4-5.  *Tefillah*

Chapter 4 takes up the number and items of *Tefillah*
(4:1, 7), standardization of its main structure (4:3-4A), and the
proper direction and intention (4:5-6), and presents examples or
precedents of special uses of *Tefillah* (4:2, 4).

Samuel focuses on the requirements of *Tefillah*, specifically in terms of its evening and afternoon versions (#51, 58, 59,
60), and dwells upon its thematic structure (#54-55, 56).[12]
While again he does not directly comment on every text, he does
cover central aspects of Mishnah's rubric in addition to developing them, as we shall see.[13]

Chapter 5 treats proper intent.  It presents the requirement (5:1) and models of ancient pious individuals and of
Hanina b. Dosa who achieved it (5:2, 5), appropriate and inappropriate special interpolations in *Tefillah* (5:2, 3), processes to
avoid losing attention (5:4), and implications if one lacks it
(5:5).[14]

Samuel focuses on one of the special interpolations and
is concerned with its practical application (#65-68).  In contrast to the previous chapters, he deals not with the overall
topic of intent but only with a side issue.  For sure, however,
his scrutiny of chapter three indicates that he is aware of the
principle, there applied to the recitation of *Shema*[c].  Either a
direct comment did not exist or was not transmitted or preserved.
Perhaps this requirement was already sufficiently accepted so
that here it did not elicit a response commensurate to the other
sections.  As we shall see Samuel does deal with highly developed
aspects of the issue.[15]

## 3.  Ch. 6.  Blessings Said Before
## Eating Food

Chapter 6 lists diverse blessings said over food, rules
whether or not one formula said over one food may exempt another
on a different food or the same food at a different part of the
meal.

Samuel's extensive focus includes the overall notion behind the blessings in general (#70), and the elucidation of specific principles guiding the proper blessing. While the latter, which make up nineteen items (seven of which are repetitions and thus represent twelve different comments) are found on M. Ber. 6:1, the comments indirectly focus on and explain M. 6:1, 2, 3, 4, 7, 8.[16] Samuel's focus is therefore not just on M. Ber. 6:1. Nevertheless, the number of traditions needed to elucidate the principles still reflects that he--or those who transmitted and preserved his teachings--had a special interest in this topic. Moreover, we may find secondary factors to help explain the lack of a direct response to several *mishnayot*. M. 6:5 ostensibly is attested by the House of Shammai and thus may represent an early law. In any event, it gives the impression of an "early" law and perhaps by the third century was in less need of direct clarification.[17] The situation assumed in M. 6:5 may be characteristic of *havurot* or Pharisaic meals and therefore typical of a social context no longer as prevalent in Samuel's day.[18] Finally, when we consider the remaining traditions, we shall see an explicit concern with extended aspects of M.6:2 and the subject of 6:5-6.[19]

### 4.  Ch. 7.  Communal Grace After Meals

Chapter 7 requires three or more who eat together to preface Grace with a summons to join in thanking God, defines to which individuals and foods the rules apply (7:1, 2, 3, 5A), provides patterns for the invitation formulae (7:3), and closes (7:5B) with a rule which defines an aspect of M. 6:1 and thereby relates back to the previous chapter as if together they make up a larger unit.[20] M. 7:5B also provides a transition to Ch. 8.

Samuel covers each of the three major subjects of the chapter: the meaning and necessity of both references to the requirement for communal Grace (#99, 105 on M. 7:1, 4), definition of one category of the group excluded from the Summons (#101) and a stricture on the formula (#102B).

### 5.  Ch. 8.  Houses; Disputes Concerning Procedures and Rituals Said at Meals

The chapter contains a collection of disputes as to items that occur at a meal. They include: the sequence of the blessing of the Sanctification and that over the wine (8:1); the order of

the blessings in the *havdalah*, as well as the proper pattern for
the *havdalah* blessing over fire (8:5); the sequence of washing
hands and mixing the wine (8:2) and of sweeping the floor and
washing after the meal (8:4); the place where one places the
napkin (8:3); special problems if one forgot to say Grace,
whether or not one returns to one's eating place, and until when
one is required to say Grace (8:7), and what one does when one
has one cup of wine and needs it for multiple purposes (8:8); and
finally, a non-Houses subunit on *havdalah* and spices (8:6) and on
saying Amen to a person's blessing (8:8B).

       Samuel does not treat all aspects of the Houses' disputes,
especially those integrally tied to the meal context, though he
does focus on elements of several major parts of the chapter.
These include *havdalah*, specifically the reason for the requirement to use fire, the orthography of a word in the criteria of
"use" and a practical definition of it (#115, 117, 120), the criteria as to the duration of the Grace requirement, and the Amen
response to the blessing (#121, 122). Significantly, Samuel's
greater focus on aspects of *havdalah* accords with a comparable
greater focus in Mishnah itself.[21]

6.  Ch. 9.  Blessings for
         Special Experiences

       The chapter requires and specifies blessings over seeing
places of miracles and uprooted idolatry and natural wonders
(9:1-2), over an individual's newly built or acquired home or
utensil (9:3A); and on entering a city (9:4). It includes the
general principle to thank God for what appears good and bad
(9:3B), a ban on inappropriate blessings, with examples (9:3C),
a second reference to thanking God for good and bad (9:5A=9:5),
and an appended proof text contained within a midrashic unit;
and, as a conclusion, rules ostensibly from Temple days. The
first part (9:5B=9:6) concerns the sanctity of sacred area,
implicitly now applicable to the place of prayers and blessings,
a notion which chapter three already made explicit; the second
(9:5C=9:7) refers to a supposed special Temple-days enactment as
to a liturgical formula and the use of the divine name in greetings. This last item with which the tractate appropriately
closes now serves as a precedent for post-70 uses of divine
names in liturgical blessings.

       Samuel covers essential, though not all, elements of the
chapter. He focuses on appropriate formulae for the special
blessings (#125); explains the meaning and applicability of

several of the natural wonders (#126-129, 132, 134); provides a
general principle as to when one recites a private mandatory
blessing (#135, 136); and responds to the *midrashic* text (#140).

iii

We thus see that Samuel focuses on the major issues of
every chapter. While there are *mishnayot* and themes which lack
a comment, his treatment includes all the major topics. Likewise,
while the degree of focus may vary and be affected by factors
other than the activity of commentary itself,[22] these factors do
not account for the extent and diversity of the response. Therefore, we may reasonably conclude that the traditions make up or
represent the remnants of a response to M. Ber. as a whole and
not just a scrutiny of only a few highly selected items which
happen to be in Mishnah. Accordingly, in the following chapters
we examine the characters of this response, especially in terms
of the formulation, form, and function of individual traditions,
and suggest the apparent purposes Samuel had in responding to
Mishnah. We conclude the present chapter with an additional
review of the non-Mishnah commentary traditions to demonstrate
the degree to which Mishnah shaped even these teachings.

### 3. The Place of Mishnah-Comments Within the Full Corpus: The Overall Impact of Mishnah

#### A. The Spread and Classification

i

Chapter three contains all of Samuel's teachings on
Berakhot and in its two *Gemarot*. A review of the spread of the
traditions and attention to their classification by type indicates that Mishnah not only elicited a sustained effort at
commentary but also became the point of departure for the
development and presentation of numerous additional teachings.

ii

There are 143 traditions with 91 in BT and 52 in PT.
This classification can be further refined in terms of location,
instances of repeated traditions, and textual problems in
attributions.

Of the ninety-one b. items, eighty-one are found in
Berakhot and ten in other b. tractates.[23] These ten items may

have  evolved originally in response to M. Ber. and its themes.[24]
Three of the ten have duplicates in b. Ber. but we have separately
numbered them because of the particular use of the traditions in
their second location.  This facilitated their analysis.[25]  An
additional five b. items, not included in the above ten, likewise
are repeated in another b. tractate but they have not been
separately numbered.  Four probably originated in that other location,[26] while the fifth's original context remains unclear.[27]

Among the fifty-two y. items, only #43 appears outside of
Berakhot--in y. Hal.--and as it concerns a Berakhot theme we have
included it.  Seven traditions appear in y. Ber. and in another
y. tractate as well.  Five apparently originated in that second
location,[28] and the other two probably in y. Ber.[29]  A separate
category consists of three y. traditions which have slightly
variant and probably more fundamental recensions in Gen. R.[30] These
repetitions outside of y. Ber. have not been enumerated separately.

The final category, applying to b. and y., consists of
duplicates within Berakhot itself.  As the repetitions are used
within their new location, they have been separately numbered.  In
b., the repetitions involve two traditions and account for four
extra items,[31] and in y., four traditions and four extra items.[32]

Based upon the above calculations, we must subtract 11
items from the 143 to obtain the number of distinct traditions:
four from y. Ber., four from b. Ber., and three from another b.
tractate.  We accordingly have an actual total of 132.[33]  Chart 5
lays this out.

CHART 5

LOCATION OF NUMBERED ITEMS

| | Number of Instances In: | | Duplicated |
| | BT | PT | Items |
| --- | --- | --- | --- |
| Once in Ber. | 77 ⟍ | 47 ⟍ | -- |
| | ⟍ 81 | ⟍ 51 | |
| Repetitions in Ber. | 4 ⟋ | 4 ⟋ | 8 |
| Ber. and Elsewhere | 3 ⟍ | -- | 3 |
| | ⟍ 10 | | |
| Elsewhere Alone | 7 ⟋ | 1 | -- |
| Totals | 91 | + 52 = 143 less | 11 = 132 separate traditions |

Other factors impose additional problems in the classification of traditions. First, some items which are counted as a
single comment have more than one part and may actually represent
multiple traditions.[34] Secondly, in one pericope, a master in
detail spells out the liturgical text wich Samuel mentions. We
cannot definitely know if this interpretation is the product of
the one who presents it or if it dates back to Samuel.[35] Thirdly,
#90 perhaps should be considered as two traditions, one (#90a)
being the opposite of the other (#90b). Fourthly, we should note
that textual variants in the attribution to Samuel poses a question as to the inclusion of one y. tradition and two b. ones.[36]
Therefore, even our revised total of 132 separate traditions--and
not "143 items"--may itself be slightly inexact.

iii

The 143 items, which make up 132 traditions, relate to
Mishnah and function within their *sugyot* in several different
ways. In chapter three to the right of each text we classified
each tradition with a notational abbreviation. There are three
broad categories: those belonging to a Mishnah-commentary (MC and
MES), which are extensively analyzed in chapter two; Mishnah
Complements and Supplements (RC and RS); and those Unrelated to
Mishnah (UR-E and UR). Chart 6 groups them and indicates how
many of each type appear in which *Gemara* and within the structure
of a given Mishnah.

We thus have 34 (33) direct Mishnah Comments, 25 (18)
Mishnaic Explicative Supplements, which together total 59 (51)
Mishnah comments; 8 (7) Related Complements and 38 Related
Supplements, which together total 46 (45) "Related" items; and
32 (30) Unrelated-Extensions of Mishnah and 6 completely Unrelated items, which together total 38 (36) items unconnected in
any way with Mishnah.

In other words, 59 (51) of 143 (132) or 41.3 percent
(38.6 percent) properly belong to a Mishnah Commentary; 46 (45)
of 143 (132) or 32.2 percent (34.1 percent) respond to Mishnah
by complementing or supplementing it and extending its themes but
not in terms of Mishnah's overall concerns and framework; and
only 38 (36) of 143 (132) or 26.6 percent (27.3 percent) fail to
relate to Mishnah. When we take into account the eleven repeated
items, represented by the numbers in parentheses, the percentages
do not substantively differ. We, accordingly, observe the formative role which Mishnah played for 105 (96) of 143 (132) or 73.4
percent (72.3 percent) of the teachings.[37]

CHART 6

TYPES OF TRADITIONS AND THEIR LOCATION

| Type of Tradition | ME | | MES | | RC | | RS | | UR-E | | UR | |
|---|---|---|---|---|---|---|---|---|---|---|---|---|
| | BT | PT | BT | PT | BT | PT | BT | PT | BT | PT | BT | PT |
| Item's Number | 1,7,8, 44,51, 54,58, 66,70, 102,105, 116,122, 126,132, 136,140 | 21,45, 46*,56, 59,60, 65,99, 101,103, 115,117, 120,121, 125,134, 135 | 55,68, 71,72*, 73*,74*, 75,76, 77,79*, 80*,81, 82*,83, 84*,85, 86,87, 127 | 67,78, 88,89, 128,129 | 11,20, 93,96 | 3,15, 16*,23 | 9,13, 14,22, 36,37, 38,39, 40,41, 42,47, 48,49, 50,64, 90,91, 98,108, 111,112, 137,138, 143 | 2,17, 18,19, 24,25, 43,57, 92,104, 107,109, 110 | 4,5,6, 10,12, 34,61, 62,63, 69,95, 97,106, 123,124, 130,131, 139,141, 142 | 26,27, 28,52*, 53*,94, 100,113, 114,118, 119,133 | 29,30, 31,32, 33,35 | |
| Sub-totals** | 17 | 17(16) | 19(12) | 6 | 4 | 4(3) | 25 | 13 | 20 | 12(10) | 6 | 0 |
| Totals** | 34(33) | | 25(18) | | 8(7) | | 38 | | 32(30) | | 6 | |

*One of the eleven repeated traditions.

**A number in parentheses indicates the total less repeated traditions.

When we carefully examine Samuel's comments on each
*Gemara* separately we find that Mishnah has an impact on all the
y. teachings and that that connection in effect may constitute
the determining factor as to which teachings are transmitted in
Palestine.  Chart 6 sets out the various types of teachings by
location.  We can synthesize the various y. "Related" and
"Unrelated" materials.  There are seventeen "Related" items and
sixteen traditions (2, 3, 15=16, 17, 18-19, 23, 24-25, 43, 57,
92, 104, 107, 109, 110) and twelve "Unrelated" items and ten
traditions (26-27, 28, 52*-53*, 94, 100, 113, 114, 118-119, 133).
PT does not ostensibly exhibit a pattern as to what it contains.
But when we examine it more closely we find the opposite.  In
effect every y. item deals with Mishnah in some way.  Numbers
26-27 are part of a unit along with #24-25 and the latter are
integrally related to Mishnah.  Numbers 28, 94, 100, 118, 119
take up *mishnayot* from elsewhere and are cited or transferred
from another location.[38]  Numbers 52-53, "Related" comments,
duplicate #18-19 and are cited later in Berakhot for a secondary
purpose.  Number 133, while "Unrelated" to Mishnah, still deals
with a liturgical matter and in fact responds to an issue raised
in a *baraita* which is found in T. Berakhot and which expands the
concerns of M. Ber. 9:2.[39]  It is thus integrally related to the
larger subject of the tractate.  Finally, #113-114 make up part
of a narrative which relates to Mishnah's issues, though Samuel's
comment itself does not.  In a sense, therefore, it is similar to
the cases of #26-27.  Moreover, the narrative involves Zeira who
had an interest in presenting such incidents which aver that
Palestinians respect Babylonians, here Babylonian priestly pedigrees.[40]  Accordingly, every y. item initially related to Mishnah
or its subject or belongs to a unit that does so.  Later
Palestinian authorities or scribes, though, might revise the
teachings to address a different issue.  This suggests that
Samuel's teachings that relate to Mishnah are the ones found in
y. Traditions that deal with other matters apparently were not
reported, sought out, or cited.  The latter comments would more
naturally appear in b. where Samuel played a role in setting the
agendum for the full range of teachings and where Samuel's
disciples and disciples' disciples might have had an interest in
preserving teachings and stories of Samuel.

While this observation remains tentative we at least must
become sensitive to this dynamic in any subsequent review and
analysis of Babylonian teachings in Palestine.  Moreover, while
in chapters nine and ten we do provide a fuller discussion of

this observation, at this point we may conclude that we have discerned another aspect of Mishnah's impact.  Mishnah played a decisive role for all the y. materials, even beyond the superficial
impression imparted by the number of entries in the several
categories of teachings.  Our hypothesis as to the significant
role of Mishnah thus gains additional credence as it does from an
examination of the number of *mishnayot* and mishnaic themes to
which Samuel responds, to which we now turn.

iv

          The 143 (132) Samuel teachings fall within the *Gemara* on 42
of 59 *mishnayot* in Berakhot and six of the 143 (132) are on three
*mishnayot* not in Berakhot.[41]  On 19 *mishnayot* there are traditions
in both b. and y. Ber. and on 23 there are traditions in one or
the other *Gemara*.  Chart 7 lays out the correlation between traditions and their *mishnaic* rubrics.  We can further break down the
above figures and thereby indicate the spectrum of Samuel's focus
on Mishnah.  Chart 8 indicates which *mishnayot* are subject to a
given category of tradition and which of these are otherwise without a response, that is, are subject to only one type of tradition.
          The breakdown is very revealing.  First, 59 (51) MC and
MES items out of 143 (132), or 41.3 percent (38.6 percent) of all
the traditions deal with 22 distinct *mishnayot* or 37.3 percent of
the *mishnayot*.

CHART 7

TOTAL NUMBER OF DISTINCT *MISHNAYOT*

| Traditions | | Number of Ber. *Mishnayot* Object of Traditions | | |
| | | | With Additional Traditions in other *Gemara* | |
| Location | Sum | Total | Lacking | Extant |
| --- | --- | --- | --- | --- |
| BT | 91 (84) | 34 | 15 | 19 |
| PT | 52 (48) | 27 | 8 | 19 |
| BT & PT | 143 (132) | | 23 | |

Secondly, 46 (45) RC and RS items out of 143 (132), or 32.2 percent (34.1 percent) of all the traditions extend the focus by
complementing and supplementing 19 different *mishnayot*, or 32.2
percent of the tractate.  Ten of these texts lack a MC and MES
item which means that the RC and RS extend Samuel's response by
16.9 percent of the tractate.  Thirdly, 38 (36) of 143 (132)
items, or 26.6 percent (27.3 percent) of all the traditions are
unrelated to Mishnah and its themes.  Mishnah, accordingly, in

one way or another is formative for 73.5 percent (72.7 percent)
of Samuel's teaching.  In turn, Samuel's extant response encompasses 32 out of 59 mishnaic texts, or 54.2 percent of the
tractate.

Samuel's close relationship to Mishnah is confirmed by a
comparison of the overall themes of his traditions with those of
Mishnah.  We now turn to this last piece of evidence.

### B.  *A Comparison of Themes*

i

Above we reviewed the themes of Mishnah and Samuel's
Mishnah comments (MC and MES) and demonstrated the extent of
Samuel's interest in Mishnah and his concern with the main topics
of each section.  We presently expand our analysis to include the
other traditions which relate to Mishnah (RC and RS).  We shall
see that Samuel's scrutiny of Mishnah is enriched and expanded
and to an even greater degree takes up the themes and laws of
Mishnah.  We pay attention to the logical development of Mishnah's
laws and Samuel's place in that development.  In doing so, we
notice that Tosefta often provides a response at an analogous
or intermediate stage in the development.

ii

In the following examination we draw upon the earlier
comparison of themes, in particular, the summary of Mishnah's
contents.

### 1.  Chs. 1-3.  *Shema$^c$*

Ch. 1.  Times and blessings of *Shema$^c$*

Samuel enriches his earlier focus and expands it by
dwelling upon laws and items mentioned in Mishnah and treats
them in their own terms.  Firstly, Mishnah's and Samuel's concern
for the proper time for *Shema$^c$* assumes one can divide time into
various divisions.  T. Ber. 1:1 already makes the division a subject worthy of scrutiny in its own terms.  *Gemara* cites a version
of this *baraita*.  Samuel (#3) glosses it and thereby defines one
of these divisions.[42]  Number 2 also deals with this subject in
terms of the relationship of the setting and rising of the moon
and sun.  Samuel's attested interest in the contents of the
blessing encasing *Shema$^c$* (#8) leads into an independent focus on
these blessings: #9 and 17 in terms of the benediction's use as a

CHART 8

CATEGORY OF TRADITIONS AND *MISHNAYOT*: THE ROLE OF MISHNAH

| Category and Sum of Traditions | On *Mishnayot*[*] | Total Texts and Percent[**] | No. Without Other Traditions | Without MC and/or MES | Total | Without RC and/or RS | Total |
|---|---|---|---|---|---|---|---|
| I. MC 34 (33) | 1:1,2,4; 2:1; 3:5; 4:1,3,7; 5:2; 6:1; 7:1,2,3,4; 8:5,6,7,8; 9:1,2,3,5 | 22 / 37.3% | 5 | All but 4:3; 5:2; 6:1; 9:2 | 18 | 1:2; 4:3,7; 6:1; 7:2,3; 8:5,6,7,8; 9:1,2,5 | 13 |
| MES 25 (18) | 4:3; 5:2; 6:1; 9:2 | 4 / 7.8% | – | – | 0 | 4:3; 6:1; 9:2 | 3 |
| Total MC & MES 59 (51) | | 22 / 37.3% | = 5 | | = 18 | | = 13 |
| II. RC 8 (7) | 1:1,4; 2:1,3; 6:5; 7:1 | 6 / 10.1% | 2 | 2:3; 6:5 | 2 | 2:3; 6:5 | 2 |
| RS 38 | 1:1,4; 2:1,5; 3:4,5; 4:1,4; 5:2; 6:2; 7:1,4; 8:1,2; 9:3,4,7 | 17 / 28.8% | 7 | 2:5; 3:4; 4:4; 6:2; 8:1,2; 9:4,7 | 8 | 2:5; 3:4,5; 4:1, 4; 5:2; 6:2; 7:4; 8:1,2; 9:3,4,7 | 13 |
| Total RC & RS 46 (45) | | 19 / 32.8% | = 9 | | = 10 | | = 15 |
| III. UR-E 32 (30) | 1:2,4; 2:5,6; 3:2; 4:1; 5:1,5; 6:6,8; 7:1,5; 8:5,6; 9:1,2,5,6 | 18 / 30.5% | 8 | 2:5,6; 3:2; 5:1,5; 6:6,8; 7:5; 9:6 | 9 | 1:2; 2:6; 3:2; 5:1,5; 6:6,8; 7:5; 8:5,6; 9:1,2,5,6 | 14 |
| U 6 | 2:7; 3:1,2 | 3 / 5.1% | 2 | 2:7; 3:1 | 2 | 2:7; 3:1 | 2 |
| Total UR-E & U 38 (36) | | 20 / 33.9% | = 10 | | = 11 | | = 16 |

[*]For UR-E and UR, the references are to *mishnayot* which provide a rubric for the traditions.

[**]Percentage is based upon total number of *mishnayot* in M. Ber., i.e.,59.

blessing over Torah study,[43] and #11 and 15=16, the use of the
blessing in the Temple.

Samuel's treatment of blessings, moreover, makes up a
logical extension of a process which M. 1:4 began. Mishnah refers
to long, short, sealed, and unsealed blessings, and T. 1:5-9 adds
additional types including those that involve bowing and not bowing. Samuel in #13-14 and 18-19 discuss this last type.[44]

In Ch. 1, "Related" items (RC and RS) thus take up
in their own terms themes mentioned in Mishnah. Mishnah included
them for its own purposes but Samuel's concern is not just to
explain Mishnah's point. We, accordingly, see that anything in
Mishnah may deserve--or serve--as a subject of study and dis-
course. Samuel thereby extends his handling of fixed times for
*Shema*[c], already subject to a Mishnah comment, into "time
divisions" and, secondly, widens his focus to include M. 1:4B,
not by explaining it, but by dealing with a logical development
of its law.

Ch. 2.   Proper attention in recitation
         of *Shema*[c]

Samuel, in a Mishnah Commentary item (MC) holds that
proper attention entails standing. He enriches this focus, first,
in #20, by indicating, which part of the *Shema*[c] constitutes the
essential portion requiring full attention,[45] and secondly, in
#22, by underscoring the importance of an individual's eagerness
to pray.[46] Samuel, in addition, extends his focus by complementing M. 2:3's remedy for a person's error. In #23 he provides a
way in which to avoid distraction and thereby maintain one's
attention.[47] Moreover, a tradition in the *Gemara* to M. Ch. 3,
#39, provides a rule to prevent distraction in prayer[48] and two
other traditions there, #36-37, treat the issue in terms of a
person who is in doubt whether or not he erred.[49] T. 2:4-5, in
its analogue to M. Ch. 2 already makes liturgical error a subject
in its own terms and explicitly applies the law to *Tefillah*, as
well. Therefore, it is not surprising that Samuel deals with the
subject's application to *Shema*[c], its blessings, and *Tefillah*.[50]

Samuel figures in a focus on M. 2:5-6 on subjects secondary to the chapter's overall concern and mentioned only in
passing; #24-25 make up a report of Samuel's action, and #26 a
narrative concerning Samuel.[51]

Thus on M. Ch. 2, Samuel's "Related" items both enrich a
focus already developed in his direct Mishnah comments and
and expand it to cover specifics of additional mishnaic law.

Ch. 3.  Those who do not recite the *Shema*[c]

        Samuel enriches a concern evidenced in his own direct
Mishnah comments and in Tosefta for "unseemly" disqualifications
from *Shema*[c].  The MC item and the toseftan analogues indicate
that Samuel's teachings form part of a logical development of
Mishnah's themes.  In #47, he treats aspects of unseemliness
from urine and in #41 and 42-43 those from risqué behavior.[52]
One version of a tradition, #40, clarifies the principle itself,
though it is presented not in reference to reciting *Shema*[c] but to
proximity to *tefillin*, which contains the text of the *Shema*[c].[53]
Samuel likewise deals with a different kind of distraction--that
of holding something, #39.  This might suggest that Samuel perceived the issue no longer as just "unseemly" behavior in a holy
place but as distraction in general.

        We also have three items, #36-38, which serve to focus on
the nature of *Shema*[c] and *Tefillah*, though they are formulated in
terms of avoidance of identical repetition of the prayer.  Therefore, in their fundamental stage they may more properly relate to
the themes of M. 2:3 and possibly 4:1.

        Chapter 3's traditions thus enrich Samuel's Mishnah
Commentary concern for disqualification due to "unseemly"
behavior and further apply his interest, perhaps developed elsewhere, in the repetition of *Shema*[c] and *Tefillah*.  In both of
these areas, Tosefta provides analogues for adding examples and
special cases.


2.  Chs. 4-5.  *Tefillah*

Ch. 4.  Number and structure in *Tefillah*
        and proper intention

        In Ch. 4, Samuel covers central aspects of the chapter.
One Mishnah comment, #51, focuses on the law of M. 4:1 and with
Related Supplements, #48, 49, and 50, he assumes that interest
and develops its implications that one may pray the evening
*Tefillah* before the night.[54]  We also find Samuel's teaching,
#57, as to what a person should do when one finds oneself in the
midst of mistakenly repeating the *Tefillah*.  This forms part of
an extended development of the subject of erring.  Earlier we
noticed that M. 2:3 on *Shema*[c] mentions this issue and Tosefta
thereto begins to develop the topic and while doing so applies
it to *Tefillah*.[55]  It is therefore not surprising that we found
several b. traditions, #36-38, in the *Gemara* to the chapter on
*Shema*[c], which treats an aspect of the topic in terms of *Shema*[c]

and *Tefillah*. The concern reflected in #57 may be especially
relevant here as an example of the mindlessness which Eliezer
decries in M. 4:4.[56]

Samuel develops his focus in terms of the implication of
evening *Tefillah* and expands his horizon to include needless
repetition of *Tefillah*. Due to the problem addressed in the
latter text, the application here to *Tefillah* makes up one of
several appropriate contexts for such a tradition. As we shall
see in chapter ten, this fact exemplifies one characteristic of
Samuel's traditions. They respond to issues and problems mentioned in Mishnah and not just its structural themes.

Ch. 5. Proper intent

Samuel's direct response to Mishnah (#65) focuses on one
of the special interpolations and thereby demonstrates a concern
for the saying of the appropriate blessing. He further supplements Mishnah by developing the general principle, #65, as to
needless repetition of a blessing[57] and thus enriches his treatment.

3. Ch. 6. Blessings Said Before
      Eating Food

Samuel supplements his already extensive focus on the
chapter's principles with rulings on additional special cases,
#90 and 92, and with an autonomous teaching, #91, all delinating
appropriate blessings for certain foods. As the two cases appear
in a *baraita* and in Tosefta on M. 6:2, Samuel clearly addresses
logical developments of Mishnah's law.[58] In addition, he apparently expands his focus, in #93, to encompass M. 6:5 (or 6:6) as
to the scope of the blessing said over wine.[59] Samuel thus
supplements his extensive Mishnah comments and possibly expands
his focus.

4. Ch. 7. Grace After Meals

Samuel's Mishnah comments deal with the chapter's three
main topics. The "Related" items enrich the focus with, first,
#97, a narrative reflecting the meaning of M. 7:1, and with,
secondly, #98 and 104, autonomous teachings which develop the
law of Grace by applying to it an issue which earlier circles,
including Tosefta, had applied to *Tefillah*. The question, in
the former, is until when in the meal may three people join
together to form the unit of three to say Grace communally, and

in the latter, does one repeat the prayer if one forgets to add
the special interpolation in *Tefillah* and Grace.[60]  Samuel thus
enriches and develops his focus on Ch. 7.

### 5.  Ch. 8.  Houses; Disputes Concerning Procedures and Rituals Said at Meals

Samuel's Mishnah comments focus on several but not all of
the major parts of the chapter.  The "Related" items, #107 and
108, expand the focus by augmenting M. 8:1 and developing its
issues of the relative importance of different compelling items
and do so in terms of the special case of the sequence of blessings.  We find an earlier stage of this development reflected in
Tosefta.[61]  Items #109-112 may supplement M. 8:2 though they are
not formulated to do so.  They take up the subject of washing,
mentioned in M. 8:2, and treat it in its own terms and not those
of Mishnah.[62]  Samuel thus expands his focus onto M. 8:1-2 by
augmenting and supplementing Mishnah.

### 6.  Ch. 9.  Blessings for Special Experiences

Samuel's Mishnah comments cover essential but not all
the elements of the chapter.  Two "Related" items deal with
aspects of issues developed out of M. 9:3-4.  Number 137 supplements M. 9:3 with an additional case of a blessing said before
an action or *miṣvah*.  T. 6:9-12 already supplements Mishnah with
additional instances of a requirement to say a blessing and with
a general principle on the matter.  Samuel here and in his Mishnah
comments (#135, 136) assumes that liability and deals with the
next logical question, when the liability takes effect.  Number
137, therefore, is an enrichment which addresses a special application of the rule.[63]  Number 138, a delineation of a liturgical
formula for a blessing said on leaving a bathroom, extends the
focus to M. 9:4 by addressing a case structured upon that of
Mishnah.  Tosefta already uses Mishnah's case as a paradigm for
additional cases.[64]  Number 143, if to be attributed to Samuel,
forms part of an independent treatment of the subject mentioned
in M. 9:7 (=M. 9:5C).  Again, Tosefta, in part, parallels this
independent treatment.[65]  Samuel thus enriches his focus and
expands it to an additional one or two *mishnayot*.

iii

Chart 9, on pages 276-277, summarizes our review of
the relationship of the "Related" items to Mishnah and

whether or not Tosefta provides an analogous development.

Consideration of the contents of the "Related" items confirms our analysis of the spread of the comments and our conclusion as to Mishnah's formative role. The traditions enrich the focus on eight chapters of Mishnah by treating additional cases and aspects of Mishnah's law and by developing its principles. They further expand the focus onto additional *mishnayot* in six to seven[66] chapters by developing Mishnah's themes and independently taking up something mentioned in Mishnah. Mishnah, therefore, even when it does not set Samuel's agendum greatly shapes and directs it.

In addition, Samuel's teachings appear within a logical line of development of Mishnah as attested by Tosefta's response to Mishnah. Tosefta repeatedly provides an example of the treatment of similar problems or of problems at the stage immediately prior to that in which Samuel addresses them. In the latter cases, Samuel apparently assumes this earlier development which he further extends. In chapters nine and ten, we discuss the implications of this observation in terms of the nature of commentary and of the dating of Tosefta.

### 4. *Conclusions*

Samuel's response to Mishnah involves a direct commentary on it and, as we argued in Volume One and continue to do so in this Volume, one portion of this commentary originally was to circulate along with the text of Mishnah. Here we have established a *prima facie* case that this applies to M. Berakhot. The response, moreover, entails an amplification and expansion of Mishnah. First, it provides additional examples so as to refine Mishnah's logic, it develops Mishnah's principle to its next logical stage, and it takes up a principle or situation mentioned elsewhere and applies it to the text at hand. Secondly, it focuses upon an item which Mishnah mentions only in passing and amplifies and expands it in all of the above ways. Samuel hence emerges as a master concerned not solely with an explanation of the text of Mishnah, as if it contained everything worth knowing. Rather, he perceives Mishnah as a comprehensive statement of important topics, themes, and laws, and as a point of departure for independent teaching. Below we develop the implications of this proposition and suggest dynamics and processes through which this expansive teaching took shape. But at the present moment we conclude that the consideration of all of Samuel's teachings confirms the results based upon the examination of the

CHART 9

THEMATIC RELATIONSHIP OF RC AND RS TO MISHNAH AND MC ITEMS*

| Mishnah Chapter | Items Which Enrich Focus by: | | Expand Focus to Additional *Mishnayot* by: | |
|---|---|---|---|---|
| | Development | Independent Treatment | Development | Independent Treatment |
| 1 | 2,3: times (T) | 9,17,11,15,16: blessing before *Shema^c* | 13,14,18,19: bowing (T) re M. 1:4B | |
| 2 | 10: essence; 22: eager | | 23 (and 36,37,39) error and distraction re M. 2:3 (T)** | 24: intercourse re M. 2:5; 25: washing re M. 2:6 |
| 3 | Unfit--41-43,47: unseemliness (T); 40: re *tefillin*; 39: holding = distraction | | | (36-38: repeating Cf. on M. 2:3; 4:1) |
| 4 | 48-50: evening *Tefillah* | | | 57: mistaken repetition re M. 4:4 (T) |
| 5 | 65: needless repetition | | | |
| 6 | 90-92: more cases (T)*** | | | 93: wine blessing re M. 6:5 (or 6) |
| 7 | 96: joining together; 98,104: forgets special interpolation (T) | | | |
| 8 | | | 107,108: sequence of blessing re M. 8:1 (T) | 109-112: washing re M. 8:2 |
| 9 | 137: moment to bless over *tefillin* (T) | | 138: leaving bathroom-blessing formula re M. 9:4 (T) | 143: Torah and *miṣvot* re M. 9:7 (T) |

*A "T" in parentheses denotes a treatment begun or already found in Tosefta.

**These traditions in part develop and in part independently treat an additional mishnah.

***Several of the MC items deal with M. Ber. 6:2 though they are not presented within the *Gemara* on this text. See above, chapter four, n. 16.

Mishnah Commentary items.  While by definition our focus is
Mishnah centered our argument is not invalid as self serving.
This is so because Mishnah takes a formative role in the shaping
of the majority of Samuel's teachings and not just of the Mishnah
comments.

          We must now face the problem of proving that the existence
of a Mishnah Commentary is not just a *prima facie* possibility but
an actual reality.  To do so we turn to the types and traits of
the traditions to see if they represent the standard characteristics of a commentary on a work like Mishnah.

[1]We identify the *mishnayot* by the presence of a tradition within its *Gemara* or, for the traditions elsewhere in the Talmud, by its direct relevance to the Mishnah passage. As we see below, consideration of the contents of the traditions indicates that the traditions may actually deal with additional *mishnayot*, as well. See below, text to n. 16.

[2]Note that #101 and 115 have parallels, indeed earlier recensions, in Gen. R., and #134 has a parallel in y. Taan. and Gen. R.

[3]See chapter three, n. 54.

[4]See chapter three, n. 80.

[5]Note, we argue, above, that #72 and 85; 81, 82, 84; and 83 all may ultimately derive from a single tradition. See chapter two, "Analysis of Traditions," #81-85 and 72, subsection vi.

[6]See chapter three, n. 54.

[7]That is #128-129 parallel #127. Cp. also items #76-77=79-80 with #78 and see nn. thereon.

[8]On the analogues see text to nn. 6-7. If we take these analogues into account we would decrease the category of six traditions on M. Ber. 9:4 to four items; four traditions on M. Ber. 5:2 to two items; three traditions each on M. Ber. 4:3 and 7, to two items; and two traditions each on M. Ber. 7:3, 8:5, and 9:3, to one item.

[8a]On the divisions and themes of the tractate cp. Zahavy.

[9]Cp. #11.

[10]As we see below, however, in #20, 23, he does develop the themes of Mishnah.

[11]See chapter three, nn. 54-55 and items #39-43.

[12]See also #60.

[13]In #48, 49, 50.

[14]See also M. Ber. 5:3.

[15]See especially #37, for an example in which Samuel explicitly mentions *Tefillah*.

[16]#71, 73-74 on M. 6:1, 2; 72, 81-85 on M. 6:1; 75 on M. 6:1, 2-3, 8; 76, 78, 79 on M. 6:2-3, 8; 77, 80 on M. 6:2; 86 on M. 6:1, 4, 7; 87, 88 on M. 6:1-2, 8; 89 on M. 6:1-2, 3.

[17]Cp. Neusner, *Pharisees*, 2:42-43.

[18]See e.g., Leiberman, *TK*, 1:62, 95, and cf. 77 as to the decreased use of wine in Babylonia which might affect the focus on mishnaic references to wine; Gedaliahu Alon, *Studies in Jewish History*, vol. 1 (Tel-Aviv, 1958), pp. 286-289; Heinemann, *Prayer*, pp. 73-77, esp. 74-75; Stephen Gero, "The So-called Ointment Prayer in the Coptic Version of the Didache: A Reevaluation," *HTR* 70 (1977): 67-84, esp. 82-84, and n.b. n. 78; above, chapter two, n. 130 and text thereto, and below, chapter nine; and Baruch M. Bokser, *Passover Eve Celebration and Early Rabbinic Judaism* (Chico, 1980). See also

Zahavy's review of the law.  He finds that the pre-70 materials generally deal
with aspects of a meal and make up a "fellowship" type of piety.

[19]Note, #93, according to the readings that include Samuel, deals with
an extension of Mishnah's issue.  See chapter three, nn. 88-89.  While #90-91
are structured and classified not as a direct comment on Mishnah they are very
close in substance and within the purview of the issue of M. 6:1, 2, 8.  See
chapter three, n. 86.

[20]Cp. Albeck, 1:11-12.

[21]Additionally, #107-112 treat extended aspects of Mishnah.  See below.

[22]This applies, as well, to the possibility that the interests of the
transmitters account for the character of the focus.

[23]#47 is in b. Meg.; 66 in b. Shab.; 79-80 (duplicating 76-77) and 85
(duplicated by 72) in b. Eruv.; 111-112 in b. Hul.; 116, 136 in b. Pes.; and
137 (adjacent to which appears an additional instance of #136 which we, however, have not separately numbered) in b. Men.

[24]This applies even to #85 which is a reformulation of a b. Ber.
tradition to fit the Eruv. context.

[25]See n. 23.

[26]#33 in b. B.M.; 35 in b. Taan. and San.; 39 in b. Suk; and 63 in
b. Pes., though it has been adapted to fit its use in b. Ber.; and cp. 136,
from b. Pes., as cited in b. Men.

[27]#137, which is found also in b. Eruv.

[28]#28 in y. M.Q.; 94 in y. Suk.; 100 in y. San. (on which see chapter
three, n. 97); 118 in y. Eruv.; 119 in y. A.Z.

[29]#56 and 134, both duplicated in y. Taan.

[30]#101, 115, 134.  #134 thus has a parallel in y. Taan. and Gen. R.

[31]#71=73=74; and 81=82=84.

[32]#15=16; 18-19=52-53; 45=46.

[33]Even this figure may be too high.  For example, #85=72 probably
represents the reformulation of another tradition.

[34]E.G., #31, 90, 127, 128, 130.

[35]#56a.  See above, chapter two, "Analysis of Traditions," #54, 55, 56.

[36]#28 in y., and 62, 93 in b.

[37]The perspective of M. Ber. and a tradition's use and place within the
*sugya* in b. and y. Ber. determine the above classifications.  A different
perspective, however, would affect the classification of several items and
would reveal an even greater impact of Mishnah.  Immediately below we demonstrate this for y. "Unrelated" items.  It can also apply to "Related"
comments there.  Thus #15=16 are "Mishnah Comments" (MC) in terms of M. Tamid.
The factor of our *perspective* also holds true for b. comments.  Number 11,
like its y. analogues 15=16, is a RC but in terms of M. Tamid it makes up a
MC.  Number 93 presently constitutes a RC but it may possibly represent the
revision of what was once a MC tradition.  On the other hand, #66, like its
y. analogue, is classified as a MC but one could argue that at least in part
it is a RC.  Thus one of the b. UR-E items--and several of the y. ones--in

another location makes up a MC and two b. RC--like at least one y. comment--
make up MC.  Hence, Mishnah's role in *the origin* of the traditions is actually
somewhat greater than that represented in the calculations and percentages in
the text.  The teachings are thus separated from their original contexts by
their later use and by the perspective of M. Ber.  See below chapters nine and
ten.

[38]See chapter three, nn. 22, 90, 97, and chapter two, "Analysis of
Traditions," #117.

[39]See chapter three, n. 140.

[40]See chapter three, nn. 119-120.

[41]See n. 40.  The three are M. Eruv., M.A.Z., and M. Tamid.  See n. 37
and n. 38, and text thereto.

[42]See chapter three, n. 1.

[43]See also #10.

[44]See chapter three, n. 14.

[45]See chapter three, n. 15.

[46]This does not involve *Shema$^C$*, though, as already found in Mishnah
itself, *Shema$^C$*-issues by association often lead into *Tefillah*-issues and vice-
versa.  See chapter three, n. 18.

[47]See chapter three, n. 19.

[48]See chapter three, n. 43.

[49]See #57 and chapter three, n. 67.

[50]See chapter three, n. 39.

[51]See chapter three, n. 22.

[52]The MC items are #44, 45=46.  See chapter three, nn. 37a, 55, and
50-52.  Number 41 deals with reciting *Shema$^C$* while in bed with one's wife, and
#42-43, when in earshot of a woman's voice.  Significantly, the latter item
even employs a term from the biblical paradigmatic text of Deut. 23:15.

[53]See chapter three, n. 50.

[54]See also #65 and chapter three, n. 56.

[55]See chapter three, n. 67, and chapter four, text to nn. 44-47.

[56]Even if M. Ber. 4:4 originally formed part of M. 4:3, which is subject
to a Mishnah Commentary tradition, the clause represented in M. 4:4A is otherwise without a response.

[57]See chapter three, n. 74.

[58]See chapter three, nn. 85-87.

[59]See chapter three, n. 89.

[60]See especially chapter three, nn. 95 and 100.

[61]See chapter three, n. 107.

[62]See chapter three, n. 114.

[63]See chapter three, n. 143.

[64]See chapter three, n. 149.

[65]See chapter three, n. 163.

[66]We say "six or seven chapters" because the number depends on whether or not one considers items #36-38 part of the focus on chapter three.

# CHAPTER FIVE

## THE TYPES OF COMMENTS

### 1. *Introduction*

The present chapter responds to the question: Do the traditions supply the type of information appropriate to a Commentary on a legal work like Mishnah? This inquiry forms the first part of our systematic review of the traditions to see if their traits make up those characteristic of such a commentary. Accordingly, we evaluate the ways in which the traditions relate to Mishnah and thus their functions and purposes, as well. In the following chapters we focus on the formulations and tradents of the traditions and correlate that data with the information developed here.

Samuel's comments fall into seven different categories. They are: A. Definitions of a Word or Referent; B. Definitions of a Case; C. Textual Notes; D. Reasons; E. Decisions; F. Related Rulings on Different Aspects of Mishnah's Issue or Topic; and G. Additional Cases and Applications of Mishnah's Principle.[1]

In the lists of classifications, we number and cite the relevant Mishnah, in an abbreviated form, and then Samuel's tradition. The number in parenthesis adjacent to the latter is the number of the tradition, as found in the full list, in chapter three.

### 2. *The Types of Comments*

#### A. *Definitions of a Word or Referent*

The comments clarify a word or reference in Mishnah with a different word, term, or phrase. There are nine items, six in b. and three in y., though they actually make up seven distinct instances of Definitions, five in b. and two in y., since in two cases two traditions form a unit (#126-127 and 128-129). Moreover, these two form b. and y. analogues of each other and so, in part, do #54 and 56. Accordingly, we have five different Definitions.

The Definitions deal with four different *mishnayot*. Two, #18 and 54/56, supply liturgical texts for Mishnah's references, another two, #126-127/128-129 and 132, render a word, and one presents a simile for an item mentioned in Mishnah.

*1.  M. 1:4.  Shema^c* . . two [blessings] before it.
    (8)  Said R. Judah said Samuel, "With great love."   (b.)

*2.  M. 4:3.*  R. Joshua says, The substance of eighteen.
    (54)  And Samuel said, Give us discernment (HBYNNW),
Lord our God, to know Thy ways; and circumscribe our
hearts to fear Thee, so that we may be forgiven and redeemed, and keep us far from agony, and fatten us in
the pastures of Your land; and the [alt. "our"] dispersed from the four [corners of the earth] gather;
and those who go astray by [alt. "in" or "from"] your
knowledge judge, and against the wicked raise Your hand;
and let the righteous rejoice, in the building of Your
city and establishment of Your Temple and in the growth
of the horn of David, Your servant, and in the preparation of a light for the son of Yishai, Your anointed
one.  Before we call, may You answer.  Praised are You,
Lord, who hearest prayer.                                (b.)
    (56)  And Samuel said, The Beginning of each
blessing.[2]                                             (y.)

*3.  M. 9:2.*  Over *ziqim*, . . . and over *reamim*, . . .
He says . . .
    (126)  What is *ziqin*?  Said Samuel, *kokhba
deshevit*.                                               (b.)
    (127)  And said Samuel, I am as familiar with the
paths of the firmament as with the paths of Nehardea--
except for *kokhba deshevit*, which I do not know what
it is, though I have learnt that it does not pass
through the constellation of Orion, and if it passes
through Orion, it destroys the world.  And lo, we see
that it passes through [Orion]?  Its brightness passes
through and it appears as if it itself passes
through.[3]                                              (b.)
    (128)  Said Samuel, If this *ziqa* passes through
Orion, it will destroy the world.  They challenged
Samuel, And we saw it pass through.  He said to them.
It is not possible.  It either [passed] above it or
below it.                                                (y.)
    (129)  Samuel said, I am as familiar with the
alleys of the heavens as with the alleys of Nehardea
my city--Except for this *ziqa*, which I do not know
what it is.                                              (y.)
    (132)  What is *reamim*?  Said Samuel, Clouds join-
ing in a circle, as it is said, "The sounds of Thy
*reamim*, in the whirlwind, the lightning illuminating
the world, the earth trembled and shook" (Ps. 77:19).   (b.)

*4.  M. 9:5[A].*  "With all your heart"--with both
inclinations--with the good inclination and with the
evil inclination.
    (140)  And Samuel said, It [the evil inclination]
resembles a grain, as it is said, "Sin couches at the
door" (Gen. 4:7).                                        (b.)


B.  *Definitions of a Case*

    The comments specify the circumstances or situation
operative in Mishnah and thereby set out when a certain rule
applies.  There are nine items, two in b. and seven in y.  Since
#46 duplicates 45, they make up eight different traditions, two

in b. and six in y.  Two sets of related b. and y. traditions,
#44 and 45, and 99 and 105, complement each other--though they do
not represent identical analogues.

The traditions deal with six different *mishnayot*.  Four,
#44/45=46, 120, 121, further define and in the process limit cri-
teria in three *mishnayot*.  Number 101b imposes the criterion onto
Mishnah's exclusion of a minor and #134 does so on Mishnah's prescription of a blessing over rain.  Another two, #99 and 105, spell
out the distinctive thrust of two similar *mishnayot*.

*1.  M. 3:5*.  And how far should one distance oneself from
them and excrement?  Four cubits.
　　　　(44)   Said R. Judah said Samuel, So long as they
moisten.                                                      (b.)
　　　　(45=46)   Samuel said, Until its top has dried.        (y.)

*2-3.  M. 7:1*.  Three . . . are required to summon. . . .
Women, or slaves, or minors . . .
　　　　*M. 7:4*.  Three are not permitted to separate.
　　　　(99)   Samuel said, Here [=7:4] it is in the
beginning.  And here it is in the end.                        (y.)
　　　　(101b)   Said R. Avina, *R. Huna and R. Judah,
both of them in the name of Samuel, dispute* [the
matter]:  *One said*--Until he knows how to say a
blessing.  *And the other said*--Until he knows the
character of the blessing.                                    (y.)
　　　　(105)   Said R. Abba said Samuel, Three who sat to
eat together and still have not eaten, are not permitted to separate.  An alternative version: Said
R. Abba said Samuel, Thus it is taught, Three who sat
to eat together, even though each one eats by himself
[alt. "each one eats from his own plate"] are not
permitted to separate.                                       (b.)

*4.  M. 8:6*.  They do not say the blessing over the
lamp until they enjoy its light.
　　　　(120)   R. Judah in the name of Samuel, Sufficient
that women spin by its light.                                (y.)

*5.  M. 8:7*.  And until when [after eating] does he
say the blessing?  Until the food in his bowels is
digested.
　　　　(121)   R. Hiyya in the name of Samuel, As long
as he is thirsty from that meal.                             (y.)

*6.  M. 9:2*.  Over rain . . . He says . . .
　　　　(134)   R. Yose in the name of R. Judah, and
R. Yonah and R. Judah in the name of Samuel, In the
beginning--sufficient for fructification; and after-
wards--even any amount.                                      (y.)

C.  *Textual Notes*

The single instance of this type of comment focuses on
the orthography of a term in one passage of Mishnah.

*1.  M. 8:6*.  . . . until they enjoy (ŠY⁾WTW) its light.
　　　　(117)   And Samuel said, *yeoto*  (Y<sup>c</sup>WTW) [=With an
*ayin*]                                                      (y.)

## D. *Reasons*

The comments explain the reason for a view or
institution mentioned in Mishnah.  There are three items, two
in b. and one in y.  One b. teaching, #116, constitutes an
analogue to one of the y. ones, 115a, which itself has a more
fundamental version in Gen. R., #115b.  We therefore have
two separate instances of Reasons which relate to two different
*mishnayot*.

1.  *M. 6:1*.  How do they say blessings over fruit? . . .
    (70)  Said R. Judah said Samuel, Whoever benefits
from this world without a blessing is as if he benefits
from items dedicated to heaven, as it is said, "The earth
is the Lord's and all that it contains" (Ps. 24:1).        (b.)

2.  *M. 8:5*.  The House of Shammai say, [The blessing
over the lamp is " . . .] who did create the light
of fire." . . .
    (115a)  Samuel said, Therefore we say a blessing
over the fire on the outgoing of the Sabbath since it
is the beginning of its creation.                          (y.)
    (116)  Said R. Judah said Samuel, They do not say
the blessing over the fire except at the outgoing of
the Sabbath since it is the beginning of its creation.     (b.)

## E. *Decisions*

The comments rule as to the legal status of an opinion
in Mishnah and thereby decide between several possible positions.
There are ten items, seven in b. and three in y.  The three y.
traditions are analogues to three of the b. ones and we therefore have seven separate decisions.  These relate to seven distinct *mishnayot*.

In the next chapter we deal with the formulations of the
traditions, but at this point we may observe that all of the y.
items--like their b. analogues--fail to employ the regular decision formula, HLKH K-.  Rather, they use one of the several standard teaching and gloss patterns.  But the HLKH K- form does
appear among the other b. traditions.  Below we discuss whether
or not this may accord with a wider phenomenon as to different
images of Samuel.  While Babylonians may have seem Samuel also
as a legal expert and authority, Palestinians may have focused
on him more exclusively as a teacher.[4]

1.  *M. 1:1*.  [And they read the *Shema*[c]] until . . .
R. Gamaliel says, Until the first light from the
East appears.
    (1)  Said R. Judah said Samuel, The *halakhah*
follows (HLKH K-) R. Gamaliel.                             (b.)

2.  *M. 1:2*.  [One recites *Shema*[c] in the morning]
R. Judah says, Until the third hour. . . .
    (7)  Said R. Judah said Samuel, The *halakhah*
follows R. Joshua.                                         (b.)

*3.  M. 4:1*.  The evening *Tefillah* has no fixity. . . .
     (51)  For said R. Judah said Samuel, The evening
*Tefillah*--R. Gamaliel says, [It is] compulsory.  R. Joshua
says, [It is] optional.  And the *halakhah* follows the
words of the one who says, "Compulsory."                    (b.)

*4.  M. 4:3*.  Rabban Gamaliel says, Every day a person
prays eighteen [prayers].  R. Joshua says, The substance
of eighteen.  R. Aqivah says, If his *Tefillah* is fluent
in his mouth, he prays eighteen; and if not, the substance of eighteen.
     (55)  Said R. Naḥman said Samuel, Throughout the year
a person prays, "Give us discernment" except on the outgoing of Sabbath and festivals because [one] has to say
*havdalah* in [the prayer which opens with the phrase]
"Who graciously gives knowledge."[5]                        (b.)

*5.  M. 4:7*.  R. Judah says in his name, Wherever there is
a *ḥever* *ᶜir* an individual is exempt from the *Tefillah* of
*Musafim*.
     (58)  Said to him R. Ḥiyyah bar Abin, . . . For said
Samuel, During my days I individually in Nehardea never
prayed the *Tefillah* of *Musafim* except on the day in which
the king's force came to the city and the rabbis became
terrified and did not pray, and I individually prayed.  (b.)
     (59)  . . . For said Samuel, I never prayed that
of *Musaf* except once when the son of the exilarch died
and the community did not pray [it] and I prayed it.     (y.)

*6.  M. 5:2*.  And *havdalah* [they say] in "Favors [a person
with] knowledge."  R. Aqivah says, He says it as a fourth
blessing by itself.  R. Eliezer says, "In Thanksgiving."
     (67)  R. Yaaqov b. Aḥa in the name of Samuel, [He]
says it ["as" or "in"] the Fourth blessing.                 (y.)
     (68)  Said R. Joseph, We know neither this nor
that.  Rav and Samuel already arranged for us a "pearl"
in Babylonia.  "And you informed us, O Lord, our God,
Your righteous judgments, and taught us to do your
desired statutes, and You caused us to inherit occasions
of gladness and celebrations of free will offerings,
and You transmitted to us the holiness of the Sabbath
and the glory of the festival days and the celebration
of the festival, You divided between the holiness of the
Sabbath and that of the holiday, and You sanctified the
seventh day above the six days of creation, You separated
and sanctified Your people Israel with Your Holiness."
"And you have given us," etc.                               (b.)

*7.  M. 7:3*.  How do they summon [people to Grace]? . . .
"Let us bless," . . . " Bless." . . .
     (102)  Said Samuel, Let a person never exclude him-
self from the group.                                        (b.)
     (103)  Samuel said, I do not exclude myself from
the group.                                                  (y.)

F.  *Related Rulings*

     The comments take up the subject mentioned in Mishnah
and supplement it with additional rulings.  They focus on
Mishnah's principle or on an essential aspect of its topic,
though they do so not by a simple exegesis of the text.  There
are eight times, three in b. and five in y.[6]  There are two

sets of b. and y. analogues.  In one set, the items, #65 and 66,
are similar, while in the other, the two, #135 and 136, ostensibly differ.[7]  We thus have seven different traditions which
make up six different responses to Mishnah and which offer
related rulings on six different *mishnayot*.

*1.  M. 2:1*.  [If] one reads the Torah and the time of recitation [of *Shema*[c]] came--if he directed his heart, he
fulfilled [his obligation] . . .
        (21)  R. Hunah, R. Idi, R. Joseph, R. Judah in the
name of Samuel, [One] has to take upon oneself the
Kingdom of Heaven--standing.                                 (y.)

*2.  M. 4:7*.  . . . *Tefillah* of *Musafim* . . .
        (60)  Samuel said, [One] does not have to innovate
something in it.                                             (y.)

*3.  M. 5:2*.  And *havdalah* [they say] in . . .
        (65)  R. Ze[c]ira, R. Judah in the name of Samuel,
[If] he said it over a cup, he says it in the *Tefillah*.
[If] he said it in the *Tefillah*, he says it over a
cup.                                                         (y.)
        (66)  And did not say R. Judah said Samuel, And
the one who says *havdalah* in *Tefillah* must say
*havdalah* over a cup?                                       (b.)

*4.  M. 8:8*.  They respond "Amen" after an Israelite
who says a Blessing.  And they do not respond "Amen"
after a Samaritan who says a blessing--until one hears
the whole blessing.
        (122)  Samuel asked Rav, Should a person respond
"Amen" after school children?                                (b.)

*5.  M. 9:1*.  Whoever sees . . . says, "Blessed who . . .
        (125)  And Samuel said, [One] [L MS:] does not
have to say "Thou."  (V and S MSS:] has to say "our
God."                                                        (y.)

*6.  M. 9:3*.  [One who] built a new house or bought
new utensils--says the blessing . . .
        (135)  For said R. Yose b. R. Bun in the name of
Samuel, All *miṣvot* require a blessing while doing
them, except for blowing [the *shofar*] and immersion
(in *miqvah*].                                               (y.)
        (136)  (For) said R. Judah said Samuel, All the
*miṣvot*--one says a blessing over them before one
does them.                                                   (b.)

G.  *Additional Cases and Applications
     of Mishnah's Principle*

        By presenting additional examples, the traditions offer
further applications of Mishnah's principle, which is refined
in the process.  There are nineteen items, seventeen in b. and
two in y.  Since several are repetitions we actually have twelve
different traditions, ten in b. and two in y.  Moreover, as
several of these may constitute different versions of the same
tradition, we may have an even smaller number.[8]

All the comments deal with blessings over food and
formally respond to a single Mishnah, M. 6:1, though in substance
they are informed by several other *mishnayot* in the chapter as
well.[9]

*1. M. 6:1.* How do they say blessings over fruit? Over
fruit of the tree one says, "Who createst the fruit of the
tree"; except for wine, for over wine one says, "Who
createst the fruit of the vine." And over fruit of the
earth one says, "Who createst the fruit of the earth";
except for bread, for over bread . . . And over vegetables
one says, "Who createst the fruit of the earth."
R. Judah says, "Who createst various types of grasses."
     (71, 73, 74)   (For) said R. Judah said Samuel, and
thus said R. Yisḥaq said R. Yoḥanan, Olive oil--over it
they say the blessing, "Who createst the fruit of the
tree."                                                            (b.)
     (72, 85)   *Let us say that it constitutes a refuta-*
*tion of Rav and Samuel who both say* that, They say the
blessing, "Who createst various kinds of foods" only
over the five kinds.                                             (b.)
     (75)   And did not say R. Zera said R. Mattena said
Samuel, *Over raw bottle-gourd and barley-flour--over*
*them we say the blessing,* "By whose word all things
come into existence."                                           (b.)
     (76, 79)   Palm heart-- . . . Samuel said "By whose
word  all things come into existence."                          (b.)
     (77, 80)   Said Samuel to R. Judah, *Shinena,*
*Your opinion makes sense. For behold,* a radish which
eventually hardens and *over it we say the blessing,*
"Who createst the fruit of the earth."                          (b.)
     (78)   Palm heart--R. Yaaqov bar Aha in the name
of Samuel, Over it one says, "Who createst the fruit
of the tree."                                                   (b.)
     (81, 82, 84)   *(for) Rav and Samuel both say,*
Whatever contains anything of the five kinds--over it
they say the blessing, "Who createst various kinds of
foods."                                                         (b.)
     (83)   *Rav and Samuel both say,* Whatever of the
five kinds--over it they say the blessing, "Who createst
various kinds of foods."                                        (b.)
     (86)   *Shatita*-- . . . Samuel said, "Who createst
various kinds of foods."                                        (b.)
     (87)   Taught R. Naḥman in the name of our Rabbi--
and who is he? Samuel--Steamed foods, over them they
say the blessing, "Who createst the fruit of the
earth."                                                         (b.)
     (88)   R. Abba said, *Rav and Samuel both say,*
Steamed vegetables--over it one says, "By whose word
all things come into existence."                                (y.)
     (89)   R. Zeᶜira in the name of Samuel, Turnip
heads that have been steamed--if they are in their
original state, over them one says, "Who createst the
fruit of the earth"; that have been ground, over them
one says, "By whose word all things come into
existence."                                                     (y.)

### 3. Conclusions

Chart 10, on the following page, summarizes the seven detailed lists.

Below we discuss different aspects of these figures. Presently we are interested only in whether or not the types of comments make up the spectrum of interests which we would expect to find in a commentary on Mishnah.[10]

The largest two of the seven categories, G and E, reflect the practical use of Mishnah, and together account for about 49 percent of the items, or, less repeated comments, 43.1 percent of the teachings. The largest unit is G, "Additional Cases." These comments would not have formed glosses on Mishnah. But as we have seen from the toseftan analogues, they do fall within a natural response to Mishnah conceived as a legal work which provides guidelines for practice and which constitutes a point of departure for further legal teaching, including the application and development of the law and its principles. The fact that the entries deal with only blessings over food, a single topic, may indicate that a special interest generated this focus, though we again find that Tosefta likewise provides an analogue for such an extensive response. Earlier we also saw how the process of transmission has affected these items, an observation whose significance we discuss below, after we examine the forms and tradents of the teachings.

The second category, F, "Related Rulings," also reflects the concern for the application of Mishnah. We already noticed that the HLKH K- form appears only among the b. items. When we noticed the identical phenomenon in Volume One, we pointed out that this form, however, does appear elsewhere in y. traditions attributed to Samuel. We therefore concluded that only from a larger sample can we determine if this spread is significant and in what way. Below in chapters nine and ten we deal with this matter.

Categories A and B, the next two largest entries, together account for 30.6 percent of the items or 33.3 percent of the teachings. The rendering of unclear words or terms forms an integral part of any kind of commentary. The definitions of a case, on the other hand, are normal when the commentary is on a legal work; for then the circumstances of a case or ruling become vital.[11] Even if they limit or expand Mishnah's ruling this is expected and inherent in the law's application. That the spread may be so motivated is attested not only by

CHART 10

TYPES OF COMMENTS

| Type | Items | Percent | Less Repeated | Percent | Distinct Instances* | Total *Mishnayot* | Provenance b. | y. |
|------|-------|---------|---------------|---------|---------------------|-------------------|---------------|----|
| A. Definitions of a word | 9 | 15.3 | | 17.6 | 5 | 4 | 6 | 3 |
| B. Definitions of a case | 9 | 15.3 | 8 | 15.7 | 8** | 6 | 2 | 7 |
| C. Textual notes | 1 | 1.7 | | 2.0 | 1 | 1 | | 1 |
| D. Reasons | 3 | 5.1 | | 5.9 | 2 | 2 | 2 | 1 |
| E. Decisions | 10 | 16.9 | | 19.6 | 7 | 7 | 7 | 3 |
| F. Related rulings | 8 | 13.6 | | 15.7 | 6 | 6 | 3 | 5 |
| G. Additional cases | 19 | 32.2 | 12 | 23.5 | 12 | 1*** | 17 | 2 |

*Less b. and y. analogous or contradictory items and two instances in which two traditions, 126-127 and 128-129, form a unit.

**Two sets of related b. and y. traditions complement each other though they are not identical analogues.

***In substance may cover more texts. See n. 9.

Categories G and F, but also by the character of the various
"Related" complementary and supplementary comments (the RC and RS
items) presented in chapter three and analyzed in chapter four,
and by the next largest category, the "Related Rulings," F.  They
account for 13.6 percent of the items, or 15.7 percent of the
teachings.  While they secondarily focus on the nature of the
item in Mishnah, they primarily reflect the interest in applying
something mentioned in Mishnah.  For example they deal with when
and how one may say a certain prayer.

The final two categories account for a small percentage
of the teachings.  D, "Reasons," involve 5.1 percent of 5.9 percent of the focus.  The several items explain an institution as
a whole and not the opinion of one party in a dispute.  At this
point we can only hypothesize why the number is so small.  Either
people in general lacked an interest in the subject of "reasons,"
or else, though they were concerned with it, they believed the
rationale for the other institutions in Berakhot did not pose
difficulties.  Alternatively, perhaps the two areas which
elicited the "reasons," *havdalah* and blessings over food,
demanded special attention.  One of these topics, blessings over
food, is the same subject that elicited the large number of
"Additional Cases."  Moreover, the other one, *havdalah*, elicits
several other traditions attributed to Samuel and it plays a
large role within Mishnah itself.

It is not surprising to find the final category, C,
"Textual Notes," in a commentary.  Judging, however, from the
single entry, such a philological, linguistic, textual scrutiny
did not have a central place in Samuel's efforts.

We conclude, therefore, with our opening observation.
The types of comments indicate that Samuel's direct response to
Mishnah was evidently on a work which is to be applied and used
and which forms the basis for action.  This accords with our
understanding of Mishnah, in general.  The types of comments
thus fall within the range of concerns appropriate to a commentary.  After we examine the forms and tradents we can discuss the
circulation of the traditions.  Which generation knew them and
what mode did they take?  In particular, did one portion take the
form of a Commentary on Mishnah?

[1]In Volume One we employed eight categories which are in part similar and in part different from the present classifications.  See below.
Cp. Gordis, who analyzes different types of "Reasons" and "Definitions."

[2]See also #56a which may represent Samuel's opinion and which supplies the liturgical text.

[3]We have printed the anonymous question and response.  Considering that both appear in both b. and y., it is possible that the response constitutes part of Samuel's tradition or, if not, an early addition to it.

[4]See Volume One, pp. 182, 185-186; above chapter four, text to nn. 38-40; and below, chapters nine and ten.  Other formulations for setting out a decision did exist.  See, for example, S. Friedman, "Critical Study," p. 368, for a discussion of one such pattern.

[5]The text assumes that Samuel defines the "substance of eighteen" as "Give us discernment"--something explicit in #54.

[6]See also items #127, 128-129, which we have classified under "A. Definitions of a Word."

[7]See our analysis in chapter two, "Analysis of Traditions," #135 and 136.

[8]See chapter two, and chapter three, n. 80.

[9]See n. 8, to which add, especially, chapter four, n. 16.

[10]See the discussion in Volume One, pp. 185-186.

[11]See the wording in Volume One, p. 185, which applies perfectly again, and below chapters nine and ten.  Gordis likewise found that Definitions entail more than just the simple rendering of words.

# CHAPTER SIX

## THE LITERARY PHRASING OF THE TRADITIONS

### 1. *Introduction*

The chapter's primary concern is to lay out the ways in which the traditions are phrased and to see if the formulations tell us something about the character of these teachings, particularly their relationship to Mishnah. We focus on the formulations of the individual teachings whether or not they ostensibly constitute part of a dispute. The function of the dispute form, which deserves separate attention, is the topic of chapter seven.

We have already seen, in chapter five, that there are several types of comments, each with a different function. As formulations serve the purpose of a teaching, the formulations likewise vary. But those traditions with a similar function-- i.e., which provide an identical type of information on Mishnah-- may, for the sake of brevity, naturally employ a similar phrasing. When these formulations become stereotyped, when they are no longer a substantive part of the comment itself, and, at times, when they are not to be translated literally, we deal with fixed forms.[1] Accordingly, we focus on the ways in which the comments are phrased and their precise words, terms, or patterned language. We are particularly interested in uncovering any formulary structures or patterns which serve repeatedly to ask a similar series of questions from the text and thereby become part of a sustained effort at commentary.

The present focus on the formulation of Samuel's traditions is based upon certain assumptions. It throws light not only on the traditions' present use and relationship to Mishnah, but also on their function and mode of circulation prior to their incorporation in a developing *sugya* and to the pericope's final redaction. This is so in spite of the traditions' later citation and adaptation, which might tend to obfuscate earlier functions, because their earlier literary phrasings and forms often remained intact, enabling them to preserve their original integrity.[2] The phrasings may therefore reflect a fundamental stage of the traditions and indicate if the traditions now or originally were suitable for a commentary on Mishnah. Hence we ask: Do the traditions require Mishnah for comprehension or are they comprehensible by themselves? Secondly, are they formulated so as to circulate along with an antecedent text?

We classify the formulations thus: one form, the B- form,
Category A; five fixed usages, ᵓPYLW, KL ZMN Š-, ᶜD Š-, KDY Š-,
SRYK L-, Categories B-F; four patterns, HLKH K-, Exegeses and
Proof Texts, Liturgical Texts, and Blessing Delineation Sentences
Categories G-J; four nonstandard Mishnah-commentary formulations,
Questions, Dialogues, Discussions, and First Person Reports,
Categories K-N; and two types which lack a clear cut formulation.
Glosses, and Declarative Sentences, Categories O and P.  For each
category we first present its characteristics, then list the
entries, and close with additional discussion of the items.

### 2.  Standard Commentary Formulations

A.  The B- Form: B- + Noun or Verb Which
    Sets Out the Circumstances

We have only two instances of the B- form, both in y.  In
Volume One, we found many instances of the form and laid out its
characteristics.  It serves to set forth the circumstances of an
aforementioned text and introduces a very brief gloss, which,
therefore, requires a referent for comprehension.  Hence we concluded that such comments are--or were originally--tightly woven
into Mishnah.[3]

1-2.  M. 7:1, 4.
(99)  Samuel says, Here it is in the beginning (KᵓN
BTḤYLH).  And here it is in the end (KᵓN BSWP).            (y.)

3.  M. 9:2.
(134)  R. Yose in the name of R. Judah, and R. Yonah
and R. Judah in the name of Samuel, In the beginning--
sufficient for fructification; and afterward--even any
amount.                                                    (y.)

Both cases of the form have brief glosses after the
prefix.  In #99, a demonstrative "here" fittingly precedes the
form as the present version of the teaching serves to distinguish
between the two texts and therefore must differentiate between
two referents.[4]  In #134, a comment in two parts, the first portions of the two parts employ the B- form to which are attached
two different phrases, both identical to those of #99.  The
second half of each part uses a different set of standard terms
to delineate quantities (of rain).[5]

We cannot know why there are so few instances of this
form.[6]  Certainly, despite the tendency for forms to be preserved, additional instances may have once existed but now are
no longer extant, as the traditions have been transformed in
the course of adaptation and transmission.  Indeed throughout

chapter two we noticed the degree to which the traditions have
been shaped by their later use.  We can, however, examine the
traditions to see if there are items where the B-form would have
been appropriate but which lack it.  To do so we first look at
the list of "Definitions of a Case," Type B, in chapter five,
where #94 and 134 appear.  We find that the other entries are
formulated differently to fit their specific usage, for example,
to delineate a criterion.  Accordingly, it seems that the forms
are not used indiscriminately but only for a particular purpose.
Secondly, this also applies to the "Glosses," Category O below,
which lack any specific patterned language.  We shall see there
that none of the instances properly define the circumstances of
Mishnah and we, therefore, would not have expected any of them
to employ the B- form.

*B.  ꜣPYLW*

The word ꜣPYLW, "even," is a common term to emphasize
the extent to which a statement, case, or law applies.  Where it
is followed by a phrase which does not specify the subject and
which lacks an apodosis, it clearly bridges a gloss onto an antecedent text.  In Volume One we described the term's characteristics and history in Mishnah and Tosefta.[7]

We have one instance of the term, in y.

*1.  M. 9:2.*

(134)   R. Yose in the name of R. Judah, and R. Yonah
and R. Judah in the name of Samuel, In the beginning--
sufficient for fructification; and afterwards--even
(ꜣPYLW) any amount.                                              (y.)

In the analysis of the tradition we found that though the
item appears in dispute with other masters, it probably originated independently of them and as a gloss directly on Mishnah.
The portion of the comment introduced by the "even" makes up
Samuel's distinctive position and, therefore, probably constitutes the fundamental element of his tradition.  Nevertheless,
the tradition may have been shaped to fit its context, specifically to respond to the introductory question ("how much
rain . . .?") and to the other opinions.  The "even" thus may
serve to emphasize that Samuel disagrees with the other masters
and it may be a product of the tradents or redactors.[8]

*C.  KL ZMN Š-*

The phrase KL ZMN Š-, "as long as," constitutes one of
several conjunctive phrases to set forth the duration of time in
which something, here a rule in Mishnah, applies.  It aptly makes

up a gloss to define a criterion.  We find numerous instances of
this phrasing in Mishnah and Tosefta,[9] and it is therefore not
surprising to find it within Samuel's repertoire.

We have two instances, one in b. and one in y.

*1.  M. 3:5.*
    (44)  Said R. Judah said Samuel, So long as they
moisten.                                                         (b.)

*2.  M. 8:7.*
    (121)  R. Ḥiyya in the name of Samuel, As long
as he is thirsty from that meal.                                (y.)

While both items appear in dispute with other masters,
they did not originate as such but directly on Mishnah.  In #44,
one disputant is a later Palestinian and the other is Geniva in
the name of Rav.  In #121, the disputant is a Palestinian and his
comment is not balanced with Samuel's.[10]

The tight relationship with Mishnah is also presupposed
by the phrasing itself.  Both instances introduce brief glosses
that lack a referent and apodosis.  Theoretically the glosses
could autonomously circulate along with questions; logically, in
thought, questions precede the formation of such teachings.  In
fact questions do appear in both *Gemarot*.  But these questions
undoubtedly postdate the traditions.[11]  Moreover, both *mishnayot*
themselves contain analogous questions and criteria which Samuel
may therefore assume and, in effect, further concretize, refine,
and supplement.  In any event, the presence of a question does
not preclude the direct relationship with the text.  Such questions and answers introduced by KL ZMN Š- constitute part of a
standard refrain.  Several of the mishnaic and toseftan examples
include the phrase, along with a question.[12]  KL ZMN Š-, accordingly, makes up a standard means to connect a criterion to an
antecedent text.

*D.  ᶜD Š-*

"Until," ᶜD Š-, is a prepositional phrase used to introduce a comment that specifies the duration of an item or rule.
It thus denotes the end of the present status and, in effect, the
inception of the next.  It frequently is used in Mishnah and
Tosefta.[13]

There are two instances, both in y.[14]

*1.  M. 3:5.*

    (45=46)  Samuel said, Until its top has dried.        (y.)

2.  *M. 7:2.*

(101b)  Said R. Avina, *R. Ḥuna and R. Judah, both of
them in the name of Samuel, dispute* [the matter]: *One said--*
Until (ᶜD Š-) he knows how to say a blessing. *And the other
said--*Until (ᶜD Š-) he knows the character of the
blessing.                                                     (y.)

The two traditions constitute brief glosses which
directly comment on Mishnah.  Though #44 appears among a series
of comments and glosses, it is independent of them.  Since it is
either not balanced with them or has a different referent, it is
out of phase with these other opinions.[15]  Number 101 maintains
its fundamental structure in the Gen. R. recension (#101b), though
even there it appears in two versions.  We closely analyzed how
the two versions along with the introductory question have been
recast to integrate the materials into the Palestinian perspective and how in the processes the prepositional phrase was
changed to KDY Š, "When" (=#101a).  The substance of the comment
preserved its integrity.  But the substitution of the preposition
was necessary, for the tradition's emphasis changed, as reflected
in the revised question.  Consequently, we again notice that the
phrases and terms have specific purposes and are not indiscriminately used.

*E.  KDY Š-*

The phrase KDY Š-, "when," or, more literally, "sufficient (that)" introduces a brief clause that specifies an amount.
When the referent is a criterion, the clause sets out when the
criterion is fulfilled.  Depending upon the subject, at that
juncture, e.g., a rule takes effect or a new status is reached.
Mishnah and Tosefta contain numerous instances of this phrase.[16]

We have two primary instances and one secondary one.
The latter is the phrase with which y., #101a, replaces the term
ᶜD Š-, "until," in its revision of Samuel's tradition preserved
in Gen. R., #101b.

[1.  *M. 7:2.*
(101a)  R. Avina said, *R. Ḥuna and R. Judah, both of
them in the name of Samuel, dispute* (the matter): *One
said,* When (KDY Š-) he knows the character of the blessing. *And the other said,* When (KDY Š-) he knows to whom
he says a blessing.                                           (y.)]

2.  *M. 8:6.*
(120)  R. Judah in the name of Samuel, Sufficient
(KDY Š-) that women spin by its light.                        (y.)

3.  *M. 9:2.*
(134)  R. Yose in the name of R. Judah, and R. Yonah
and R. Judah in the name of Samuel, In the beginning--
sufficient (KDY Š-) for fructification; and afterwards
--even any amount.                                            (y.)

All three instances introduce brief criteria which do not
mention the referent and therefore require an antecedent text--or
question--for comprehension. Undoubtedly a question, in thought,
preceded enunciation of the comments, but only in thought. Even
in similar examples in the *Gemara*, where questions appear and
precede the traditions, they are added later, as argued above.
Moreover, Mishnah and Tosefta contain instances of the phrase
(KDY Š-) with and without an antecedent question. Where a question is lacking, the phrase is tacked onto the referent it modi-
fies.[17] In addition, #120 relates to a criterion in M. Ber. 8:6
and the tradition, therefore, in effect revises it. Hence, all
three instances make up glosses which provide exact criteria for
Mishnah's rules.[18] Thus, we again see the diversity and speci-
ficity of the terms and usage in Samuel's teachings.

F.   *ʾYN/ʾYNW ṢRYK L-*

The phrase ṢRK L-, "[One] has to," is an auxiliary verb
which introduces a second verb and together they lay out a
requirement for something to be done.[19] The inclusion of a
negative, ʾYN or ʾYNW yields ʾYN/ʾYNW ṢRYK L-, "[One] does not
have to . . ." and denotes the negation of such a requirement.
It is thus used as a negation. The latter formulation follows
an opinion which asserts the requirement. The ṢRYK L- language
does not necessarily appear in the first opinion though occasionally it does. We find numerous instances of the various combinations in Mishnah and Tosefta.[20]

We have three entries, all in y.

1.  *M. 2:1*.
        (21)   R. Huna, R. Idi, R. Joseph. R. Judah in the
name of Samuel, [One] has to (ṢRYK L-)take upon oneself
the Kingdom of Heaven--standing.                            (y.)

2.  *M. 4:7*.
        (60)   Samuel said, [One] does not have to (ʾYN ṢRYK
L-) innovate something in it.                               (y.)

3.  *M. 9:1*.
        (125)   And Samuel said, [One] does not have to
(ʾYNW ṢRYK L-) say "Thou." [=L MS; (One) has to (ṢRYK
L-) say "our God" = V and S MSS]                            (y.)

While all three instances make up full sentences, they
lack an explicit subject, and so by themselves are not totally
clear; they therefore function as glosses. In #21, the positive
formulation of the verbal phrase refers only to the concept of
the "Kingdom of Heaven." Its need for the context, moreover, is

reflected in the similar use of SRYK L- in the next tradition.
Following a later explanatory pericope, a *baraita* appears which
opens with the SRYK L- formulation and it would be incomprehen-
sible alone.[21]

Similarly, the other two instances, with the negative
formulation, are enigmatic.  Though they appear in a dispute form
with Rav, with whom they are paired, both masters' opinions need
a context for comprehension.  In #60, moreover, the two opinions
employ the indefinite "in it," which refers back to an antecedent
text, here Mishnah.

This gloss-like formulation apparently serves to add a
supplementary relevant matter.  In contrast, for example, to the
B- form which defines Mishnah's circumstances the SRYK L- does
not merely spell out what supposedly is already in the text.  In
#21, Samuel adds a requirement, and, in #60 and #125, he rejects
added obligations, viz., to employ a certain standardized liturgical pattern and to innovate in *Musaf*.[22]

The wording of SRYK L- is not unique to Samuel nor does
it make up a form.  But clearly it is used for specific purposes
and reflects the diversity and differentiation in Samuel's
terminology.  As the phrase forms part of a regular pattern in
which to cite disputes, in #60 and #125, in particular, we do
not know if it is fundamental to the tradition or if it is
imposed upon it when presented in the dispute form.[23]  The case
of #21, however, indicates that even when not in a dispute,
Samuel's traditions can employ this language.

G.  *The Halakhah (does not) follow* . . . .:
    (*'YN) HLKH K-* + *Name of Master*

The phrase, "The *halakhah* follows . . . ," appears with
and without a negative, "not," *'YN*, and serves to decide in favor
or against a master.  Mishnah and Tosefta contain variations of
this pattern and in Volume One we discussed its general characteristics.[24]

We have three instances, all from b. and all with the
positive formulation, though the third one follows a variant
pattern.

*1.  M. 1:1*.
     (1)  Said R. Judah said Samuel, The *halakhah* follows
(HLKH K-) R. Gamaliel.                                          (b.)

*2.  M. 1:2*.
     (7)  Said R. Judah said Samuel, The *halakhah* follows
(HLKH K-) R. Joshua.                                           (b.)

*3.  M. 4:1.*
    (51)   (For) said R. Judah said Samuel, The evening
*Tefillah*--R. Gamaliel says, [It is] compulsory.  R. Joshua
says, [It is] optional.  And the *halakhah* follows (HLKH K-)
the words of the one who says, "Compulsory."            (b.)

In all three cases the decision is not comprehensible by
itself but requires a referent.  In #1 and 7, Mishnah supplies
it, and in #51, the statement of the dispute, which may constitute an amoraic *baraita*, provides the information both for
Samuel's opinion and that of his disputant Rav.  Indeed in the
reading which we have printed,[25] the decision appears appended
to the first part, the "source."  While we cannot know which
portion of the tradition originally was essential, in its present
context the first part, the statement of the tannaitic positions,
fits the redactional need of identifying the master who believes,
"It is optional."  This is reflected in the readings which place
the word "for" at the beginning of the teaching.  Moreover, this
supports our suggestion that the adjudications are meant to circulate along with or in the context of the text and not as part of
a collection of rulings organized by the name of a master or by
subject.

*H.  Exegeses and Proof Texts*

We find three instances, all from b., of an exegetical
use of a verse.  The tradition is made up of: the comparison or
definition; the terminology, "as it is said"; and the supporting
verse.[26]

*1.  M. 6:1.*
    (70)  Said R. Judah said Samuel, Whoever benefits from
this world without a blessing is as if he benefits from
items dedicated to heaven, as it is said, "The earth is
the Lord's and all that it contains" (Ps. 24:1).       (b.)

*2.  M. 9:2.*
    (132)  Said Samuel, Clouds joining in a circle, as
it is said, "The sound of Thy *reamim* in the whirlwind,
the lightning illuminating the world, the earth trembled
and shook" (Ps. 77:19).                                 (b.)

*3.  M. 9:5A [=9:5].*
    (140)  And Samuel said, It [= the evil inclination]
resembles a grain (HTH), as it is said, "Sin couches at
the door" (Gen. 4:7).                                   (b.)

Samuel's comments form part of a dispute with other
masters as to the proper simile for a certain notion or correct
rendering of a word.  Each one cites a supporting proof text.
In #70, the topic is "blessing over food," the subject of
M. Ch. 6.  As the disputants are later Palestinian Amoraim,
Samuel's teaching clearly originates independent of theirs.  His

tradition is autonomously formulated and can stand alone, though
it appropriately appears in the context of M. 6:1, as indicated
both by its context and by the analogues in Tosefta and both
*Gemarot*.[27]

In #132, the focus is the definition of Mishnah's
enigmatic word *reamim*, usually rendered as "thunder." While
there are several other explanations, Samuel's opinion is balanced only with Rav's. They both open their gloss-like definitions with the word "clouds" and cite biblical proof texts. All
the definitions lack a referent and thus need a context--or
Mishnah--for comprehension. As they no longer function as direct
glosses on Mishnah, the anonymous *Gemara* appropriately supplies
an introductory question after the lemma of Mishnah ("What is
*reamim*?").[28]

In #140, the topic is the "evil inclination," mentioned
in M. 9:5, though not explicitly in Samuel's opinion. As it
appears in Rav's opinion which immediately precedes, that reference ostensibly serves Samuel's comment. This follows the pattern
for a variation of the dispute form; the protasis appears in the
first opinion.[29] The two opinions therefore have been redacted
together though they are not totally balanced, and hence may have
developed independently. In chapter two we argued that the
exegetical *sugya* picks up the reference to "evil inclination"
mentioned in passing in the exposition of Deut. 6:5 included in
Mishnah.[30]

As we do not have exegeses attributed to Samuel on the
surrounding verses of Gen. 4:7, Deut. 6:5, or Ps. 24:1 or 77:19,
his comments do not make up part of a commentary on those passages.[31] While the choice for the focus theoretically may be
motivated only by an interest in these topics, the latter do not
make up primary subjects in Samuel's thought. At most, in the
case of *ma^cal*, which Samuel does mention in another context, there
may be a predilection for the topic, which would then represent
a partial factor. Likewise Samuel's interest in natural science
might account for his attention to *reamim*, as it would for several
other items in M. 9:2. But something had to prompt these
expressions.[32] Accordingly, the teachings probably originated
and serve as responses to Mishnah. Mishnah thus provided the
occasion and elicited Samuel's reaction. But the three traditions exemplify the different ways in which such responses may
relate to Mishnah's overall point. Number 70 deals with a
central issue, as attested by Tosefta's analogous scrutiny, and

#132 with a word basic to Mishnah's law.  Number 140, on the
other hand, takes up a secondary issue, not integral to Mishnah's
theme.[33]

*I.  Liturgical Texts*

        Several comments consist of liturgical texts.  We
include two instances, both from b.

> *1.  M. 4:3.*
>         (54)  And Samuel said, Give us discernment (HBYNNW),
> Lord our God to know Thy ways; and circumscribe our
> hearts to fear Thee, so that we may be forgiven and re-
> deemed, and keep us far from agony, and fatten us in the
> pastures of Your land; and the [alt. "our"] dispersed
> from the four [corners of the earth] gather; and those
> who go astray by [alt. "in" or "from"] Your knowledge
> judge, and against the wicked raise Your hand; and let
> the righteous rejoice, in the building of Your city
> and establishment of Your Temple, and in the growth of
> the horn of David, Your servant, and in the preparation
> of a light for the son of Yishai, Your anointed one.
> Before we call, may You answer.  Praised are You, Lord,
> who hearest prayer.                                        (b.)

> *2.  M. 5:2.*
>         (68)  Said R. Joseph, We know neither this nor that.
> Rav and Samuel already arranged for us a "pearl" in
> Babylonia.  "And you informed us, O Lord, our God, Your
> righteous judgments, and taught us to do Your desired
> statutes, and You caused us to inherit occasions of
> gladness and celebrations of free will offerings, and
> You transmitted to us the holiness of the Sabbath and
> the glory of the festival days and the celebration of
> the festival, You divided between the holiness of the
> Sabbath and that of the holiday, and You sanctified the
> seventh day above the six days of creation, You sepa-
> rated and sanctified Your people Israel with Your holi-
> ness."  "And You have given us" etc.                       (b.)

        The fact that a master is motivated to compose or trans-
mit a text assumes an interpretation of Mishnah, as do the
choices of the specific themes, formulation, and wording.
Whether or not that interpretation is preserved or easily
reconstructed, as in #54 on the basis of the juxtaposition with
Rav's view and the y. parallel, #56a and 56b,[34] the process of
interpretation logically precedes the formulation of a text.
But the citation of a liturgical text alone is sufficient to
represent a comment.  Mishnah and Tosefta provide precedents
for the inclusion of such passages.  Moreover, given the history
of prayer it is understandable that liturgical texts make up
part of Samuel's response to Mishnah.  As Heinemann has shown,
third century masters started to spell out the texts of the
prayers whose themes and formulae earlier masters had begun to
standardize.[35]  Our observations apply in part also to items

#71-89, the Delineation of Blessings over diverse foods, Type J,
the Dialogue, L, and several Glosses and Sentences, O and P, which
mention the names of prayers.[36]

### J.  Blessing Delineation Sentences

A certain pattern is recurrently used to designate the
blessing over a specified food.  In chapter two we traced the
history of this phraseology and its variations and cited
examples of its earlier uses in Tosefta.[37]  The basic pattern
consists of: attribution; name of the food; verb plus prepositional phrase (e.g., BT=MBRKYN $^C$LYW; PT=$^ƆWMR $^C$LYW); and the
specified formula.  There are ten instances of the basic pattern,
two in y. (88, 89), and eight, which make up four different traditions, in b. (71=73=74; 81=82=84; 83; 87).

The variations closely conform to this structure.  They
account for seven items, or five different traditions, and less
two identical instances of a tradition which are classified elsewhere, five items and four traditions.  The variations fall into
two types.  (A) The pattern is adapted to the dispute form.  The
name of the food precedes the attribution and thereby serves as
a protasis for the several disputing opinions.  There are three
items, or two traditions in b. (76=79; 86), and one in y. (78).
(B) The pattern is formulated in Aramaic and includes
the verb in the first person plural and, at times, the prepositional phrase placed at the beginning.  There are three items,
or two traditions, all in b. (75; 77=80).  As we classify #77=80
under "Dialogues," though we include it here, we do not count it
towards the overall total.

In all we have seventeen items and eleven different traditions, and less 77=80, fifteen items and ten different traditions.
We also have one case of b. and y. analogues (76=79 and 78), and
therefore we deal with nine different subjects.  They formally
treat only M. 6:1, though in substance they assume most of the
*mishnayot* in the chapter.[38]

#### 1.  M. 6:1.

(71=73=74)  Said R. Judah said Samuel, and thus said
R. Yiṣḥaq said R. Yoḥanan, Olive oil--over it they say
the blessing, "Who createst the fruit of the tree."       (b.)
(75)   And did not say R. Zera said R. Mattena said
Samuel, *Over raw bottle-gourd and barley-flour--over*
*them we say the blessing,* "By whose word all things
come into existence."                                     (b.)
(76=79)  Palm heart--R. Judah said, . . . Samuel
said, "By whose word all things come into existence."     (b.)

[(77=80)   Said Samuel to R. Judah . . . A radish
which eventually hardens *and over it we say the
blessing*, "Who createst the fruit of the earth."          (b.)]

(78)   Palm heart--R. Yaaqov bar Aḥa in the name
of Samuel, Over it one says, "Who createst the fruit
of the tree.". . .                                          (y.)

(81=82=84)   [81: Said R. Joseph, . . . *for*] *Rav
and Samuel both say*, Whatever contains anything of
the five kinds--over it they say the blessing, "Who
createst various kinds of foods."                           (b.)

(83)   *Rav and Samuel both say*, Whatever of the
five kinds--over it they say the blessing, "Who
createst various kinds of foods."                           (b.)

(86)   *Shatita*--Rav said, . . . Samuel said, "Who
createst various kinds of foods."                           (b.)

(87)   Taught R. Naḥman in the name of our Rabbi--
and who is he?  Samuel--Steamed foods, over them they
say the blessing, "Who createst the fruit of the
earth."                                                     (b.)

(88)   R. Abba said, *Rav and Samuel both say*,
Steamed vegetables--over it one says, "By whose word
all things came into existence."                            (y.)

(89)   R. Ze^cira in the name of Samuel, Turnip
heads that have been steamed--if they are in their
original state, over them one says, "Who createst
the fruit of the earth"; that have been ground, over
them one says, "By whose word all things come into
existence."                                                 (y.)

We consider the phrasing a pattern because it is
repeatedly used for a single purpose.  Even its use within the
dialogue, #77=80, reflects this, for the purpose remains to
delineate the proper blessing.  This contrasts with the loss of
the pattern in #72=85 where the tradition has been reshaped, due
to redactional needs, to define what constitutes MZWN, "food."
The pattern is therefore employed in a disciplined and precise
manner.  Moreover, the formulation itself is very defined and
to the point and therefore makes up an appropriate formulation
for a supplement to Mishnah.  The degree to which explicative
supplements are appropriate to a commentary is the degree to
which the formulation is likewise appropriate.

### 3.   Nonstandard Commentary Formulations

The next group of formulations does not represent what
we would expect to find in a commentary though it does reflect
Samuel's interest in the issues of Mishnah.  Whoever transmitted
the items, whether from Samuel's or another master's circle of
students, perceived Samuel in that role and therefore presented
the traditions in the context of their relevant *mishnayot*.  The
pointed out in Volume One, "there were individuals who preserved
materials for their explanatory value on Mishnah yet who did not
necessarily redact or shape those materials into set patterns

used in commentaries."[39] This underscores the fact that where
materials do employ certain formulations, the formulations are
not necessarily the result of levelling of all the traditions
into patterns.

### K.  Questions

One tradition, from B., is formulated as a question which
Samuel poses.[39a]

*1.  M. 8:8*.
        (122) *Samuel asked Rav*, Should a person respond
"Amen" after school children?  He said to him, . . .          (b.)

As mentioned above, the action, here an inquiry of
Samuel along with Rav's answer, is perceived as a normative
teaching and is therefore transmitted.

### L.  Dialogues

In a Dialogue a master's discussion with another master
reveals his interpretation of Mishnah.  The person who cites the
tradition in conjunction with Mishnah perceives this relevance.
The pattern for the Dialogue includes: the name of the masters;
name of the addressee in the vocative; and the substance of the
comment.  Mishnah and Tosefta contain other usages of the pattern.[40]

*1.  M. 6:1*.
        [(76=79)  Palm heart--R. Judah said, . . . Samuel
said, "By whose word all things come into existence."]
        (77=80)  Said Samuel to R. Judah, *Shinena, Your
opinion makes sense.  For behold*, A radish which eventually hardens and *over it we say the blessing*, "Who
createst the fruit of the earth."
        [. . . And even though Samuel praised R. Judah the
*halakhah* follows Samuel.]                                    (b.)

The single instance of the Dialogue appears in two identical pericopae, 77=80.  In the first portion, Samuel agrees
that his own opinion concerning the palm-heart is incorrect.  In
chapter two we discussed what then would constitute Samuel's
opinion.

The Dialogue derives from a time prior to the presentation in a dispute form of the dispute over the palm-heart (76=79).
But the dispute form becomes necessary once the later generations
claimed that the law follows Samuel and not Judah, as reflected
in the clause, "And even though . . .".  The Dialogue thus provides certain circles with Mishnah-related information, though
when its position is rejected it is not obliterated.  It

accordingly constitutes an additional example of an alternative
to a formalized presentation of Samuel's teaching.

*M.  Discussions*

          These items are variations of the Dialogues and First
Person Reports, Categories L and N.  Samuel ostensibly responds
to another master's challenge.  The pattern involves: a tradition;
the challenge; and Samuel's response.

          *1.  M. 9:2.*
               [(127a-b)  And said Samuel, I am as familiar . . .
          except for . . . though I have learnt that it does not
          pass through the constellation of Orion, . . .]
               And lo, we see that it passes through?
               (127c)  Its brightness passes through and it appears
          as if it passes through.                                      (b.)
               [(128a)  Samuel said, If this *ziqa* passes through
          Orion, it will destroy the world.]
               They challenged Samuel, And we saw it pass through.
               (128b)  He said to them, It is not possible.  It
          either [passed] above it or below it.                         (y.)

          As the opposing masters in the two analogous pericopae
are not associated with an alternative opinion as to the law or
interpretation, we cannot properly classify such items as a
"Debate."  We are also unsure whether these items are actually to
be attributed to Samuel or whether they only constitute a question and answer appended at an early stage to Samuel's comment.
But tannaitic materials do include Dialogues between masters,
with the second party either identified or unidentified.  Hence,
it is possible that amoraic circles employed the pattern to transmit Samuel's teachings, if they did not receive them in that
formulation originally.[41]

          We should note, if the clauses belong to the fundamental
stage of the tradition, one might be justified in including the
comments which elicit the challenge together with the challenge
and Samuel's response as a single unit.[42]  Given the purposes of
this chapter, however, it does not matter.  The materials do not
constitute standard commentary formulations.  Nevertheless, they
do provide us with an additional example of how someone believed
that stories narrating Samuel's response are relevant to Mishnah.

*N.  First Person Reports*

          Samuel's accounts of his own practice or knowledge,
whether or not cited by someone else, provides a guide for action
and illuminates Mishnah.  The person who transmits the account
in the context of Mishnah perceives the connection.  The testimony opens with a statement in the first person, "I."  Mishnah
and Tosefta contain other uses of this pattern.[43]

We have five items, two in b. and three in y.

*1.  M. 4:7.*
      (58)  Said to him R. Ḥiyya bar Abin, You are right,
For said Samuel, During my days I individually in
Nehardea never prayed the *Tefillah* of *Musafim* except
on the day in which the king's force came to the city
and the rabbis became terrified and did not pray, and
I individually prayed.                                        (b.)
      (59)  . . . For said Samuel, I never prayed that
of *Musaf* except once when the son of the exilarch died
and the community did not pray [it] and I prayed it.      (y.)

*2.  M. 7:3.*
      (103)  Samuel said, I do not exclude myself from
the group.                                                    (y.)

*3.  M. 9:2.*
      (127a-b)  And said Samuel, I am as familiar with
the paths of the firmament as with the paths of
Nehardea--except for *kokhba deshevit*, which I do not
know what it is, though I have learnt that it does not
pass through the constellation of Orion, and if it
passes through Orion, it destroys the world. . . .        (b.)
      (129)  Samuel said, I am as familiar with the
alleys of the heavens as with the alleys of Nehardea
my city, except for this *ziqa*, which I do not know
what it is.                                                   (y.)

      The fact that b. and y. include analogues on the same
*mishnayot*, #58 and #59, and #127 and #129, underscores the
Reports' perceived relevance to Mishnah.  Numbers 58 and 59 are
complementary, while #127 and #129 are nearly identical.  Moreover, the latter pair is found in larger pericopae on Mishnah
attached to other Samuel teachings; indeed #127 follows a direct
gloss on Mishnah.[44]  Therefore, at a relatively early date the
narrative of Samuel's comment became associated with Mishnah.
In a different way, the above phenomenon likewise applies to
#102.  BT's analogue, #103, is formulated as an autonomous
teaching, "Let a person not . . . ," which is also cited on
M. 7:3.  Number 103 accordingly represents either an example of
the reworking of the tradition into a comment or an alternative
version of Samuel's supposed statement.[45]  These "Reports" along
with the instances of the "Questions," "Dialogues," and
"Discussions," thus provide examples of alternatives to the
standard Mishnah-commentary formulations.

## 4.  *Without a Fixed Formulation*

      We now turn to items which lack any fixed formulary
traits, though the first one by its very nature has a specific
function.

## O. *Glosses*

There are five Glosses, two in b. and three in y., which
illuminate five *mishnayot*. The teachings do not make up complete
sentences nor do they employ a specific phraseology or wording,
according to which we would otherwise classify them. As glosses,
they must circulate along with their referents so as to be comprehensible.[46]

1. *M. 2:1.*
        (8)  Said R. Judah said Samuel, "With great love."    (b.)

2. *M. 4:3.*
        (56)  And Samuel said, The beginning of each
blessing.                                                     (y.)

3. *M. 5:2.*
        (67)  R. Yaaqov b. Aḥa in the name of Samuel, [He]
says it ["as" or "in"] the Fourth blessing.                  (y.)

4. *M. 8:6.*
        (117)  And Samuel said, *yeoto* (Y$^C$WTW).           (y.)

5. *M. 9:2.*
        (126)  Said Samuel, *kokhba deshevit*.                (b.)

The items exemplify the different ways in which glosses
function. Number 8 identifies which blessing Mishnah has in
mind. Number 56 explains the meaning of a cryptic reference to
a type of prayer ("the substance of eighteen"). Number 67 locates
the interpolation of *havdalah* and employs Mishnah's language of
"says it" and, accordingly, approximates a full sentence. The
use of the indefinite object, however, still requires that it
circulate in conjunction with its referent. Number 117 provides
an orthographic reading for a word in Mishnah. Number 126 defines
a term in Mishnah.[47]

All the cases are concise. Their formulation requires
that they either enter the text to which they relate or else
circulate appended to it. Above we raised the question whether
or not any of the simple Glosses might have employed the B- form
and responded in the negative. None of the five instances set
out the circumstances, the function of the B- form. In particular, the form would be totally inappropriate for the textual
comment, #117, and would not be expected in the others.[48]

## P. *Declarative Sentences*

These complete sentences are made up of: attribution to
Samuel; and a simple statement of the issue, either with a
protasis and apodosis or just in apodictic form.[49] None of the
items employ  a specific opening phraseology or formulary

structure.  Thus those traditions which Delineate Blessings over
food and which make use of a recurrent pattern appear separately,
in Category J, except for #72=85, which have been reshaped to
address a different issue, and hence, appear here.  Likewise,
elsewhere we list the "First Person Reports," and "Debates," even
if they are formulated as a simple sentence.

There are twelve items, eight in b. and four in y.  Since
two b. ones are identical traditions (72=85) and six make up three
sets of b. and y. analogues, whether similar or variant (#65 & 66;
115 & 116; 135 & 136), there actually are eight different and
unrelated traditions dealing with eight different *mishnayot*.

### 1.  M. 4:3.
(55)  Said R. Naḥman said Samuel, Throughout the
year a person prays, "Give us discernment" except on
the outgoing of Sabbath and festivals because [one]
has to say *havdalah* in "Who graciously gives
knowledge."                                                                 (b.)

### 2.  M. 5:2.
(65)  R. Ze^Cira, R. Judah in the name of Samuel,
[If] he said it over a cup, he says it in the *Tefillah*.
[If] he said it in the *Tefillah*, he says it over a cup. (y.)
(66)  And did not say R. Judah said Samuel, And
the one who says *havdalah* in *Tefillah* must say
*havdalah* over a cup?                                                      (y.)

### 3.  M. 6:1.
(72=85) . . . *Rav and Samuel who both say that*,
They say the blessing, "Who createst various kinds of
foods" only over the five kinds [of grains].                               (b.)

### 4.  M. 7:3.
(102)  Said Samuel, Let a person never exclude
himself from the group.                                                     (b.)

### 5.  M. 7:4.
(105) . . . Said R. Abba said Samuel, Three who
sat to eat together and still have not eaten, are
not permitted to separate.  An alternative version:
Said R. Abba said Samuel, Thus it is taught, Three
who sat to eat together, even though each one eats
by himself [alt. "each one eats from his own plate"]
are not permitted to separate.                                             (b.)

### 6.  M. 8:5.
(115a)  Samuel said, Therefore we say a blessing
over the fire on the outgoing of the Sabbath since
it is the beginning of its creation.                                        (y.)
(115b) . . . for Samuel says, Why do they say
the blessing over the lamp at the outgoing of the
Sabbath?  Because it is the beginning of its
creation.                                                        (y. in Gen. R.)
(116)  Said R. Judah said Samuel, They do not
say the blessing over the fire except at the outgoing of the Sabbath since it is the beginning of its
creation.                                                                   (b.)

*7.  M.  9:2.*
      (128[a])   Samuel said, If this *ziqa* passes through
Orion, it will destroy the world.                              (y.)

*8.  M.  9:3.*
      (135)    For said R. Yose b. R. Bun in the name of
Samuel, All *misvot* require a blessing while doing
them, except for blowing [the *shofar*] and immersion
[in a *miqvah*].                                               (y.)
      (136)    (For) said R. Judah said Samuel, All the
*misvot*--one says a blessing over them before one
does them.                                                     (b.)

        The function and specific wording varies in each of the
above traditions.  While each one appropriately fits its context,
it is autonomously formulated and could appear by itself.
Number 55 provides a ruling and an exception to the abridged
*Tefillah*.  Numbers 65 and 66 make up b. and y. analogues.  The
former employs the language of Mishnah, "says it."  Numbers 72=85
are cited and shaped to meet the needs of the discussion defining
the term "food."  Number 102 is an apodictic teaching whose y.
analogue appears as a First Person Report.  It is unclear which
version, if either, if not both, is fundamental and which is a
reformulation.  Number 105 employs Mishnah's language.  The two
versions derive from an originally briefer text, which at one
point may have consisted of a gloss on Mishnah.  Numbers 115a-b
represent two versions or recensions of a teaching.  In (a) the
"therefore" connects it to the preceding pericope though it
actually is independent from it, as exemplified in (b).  This is
reflected, as well, in the b. analogue, #116, which, itself,
however, is shaped by redactional considerations.  Number 128(a)
appears as the first item in a pericope that throws light on
*ziqim*, mentioned in Mishnah.  It is followed by a "Discussion"
(= challenge and answer = 128b) with which it may form part of a
unit.  Numbers 135 and 136 constitute two versions of a general
principle.  Number 136's formulation is close to the one used to
delineate a blessing, Category J.[50]

        These items indicate that not all comments relevant to
Mishnah were preserved with fixed formulations or patterns or
formulated with a specific phraseology or as a gloss.  Information basic to a commentary, e.g., Reasons (115-116), Decisions
(55), Definitions of Circumstances (105), as well as Supplements
(72=85), may be formulated as full sentences.  Therefore, as we
have repeatedly pointed out, alternatives to the use of fixed
formulations and brief constructions did exist.  Indeed, we have
noticed that brief and fixed formulations which approximate what
we would expect to find in a commentary are at times expanded
into declarative sentences or otherwise adapted and reused.[51]

Accordingly, where specific phraseologies, terminologies and constructions are employed, they may go back to an early stage of
the tradition.

## 5.  Conclusions

Chart 11, on the following page, summarizes the sixteen
individual lists.

Our focus on the formulations provides us with information
as to the character of the comments.  The chart indicates that
about 27 percent of the items, or less repeated teachings,
29 percent of the traditions, lack a clear-cut formulation
or phrasing. In turn, 73 percent of the items, or 71 percent
of the traditions employ some type of phrasing.  The phrasings
enable distinctive means to express a wide range of comments
on Mishnah, in particular to offer criteria for its rules or
otherwise to apply and develop its principles.  We therefore
deal with a practical response to Mishnah.  This impression
is increased by consideration of the specific results of our
review.

We can divide the formulations into two groups.
Categories A-J, which represent 57 percent of the items and
55 percent of the traditions, are those which one might normally
expect to find used in a commentary on Mishnah.  On the other
hand, K-N, the remaining 16 percent of the items and 16 percent
of the traditions, are not the standard "commentary" formulations.
They generally are not worded as if intended to circulate along
with a text.  Nevertheless, their transmitters might have believed
them to be appropriate in Mishnah's context, for a master's
followers often consider their master's personal statements
and practices as normative.[52]

The items' number and spread are also interesting.  Nine
of the ten categories of A-J have one to three entries and only
one, J, has a considerably larger number.  These Blessing Delineations are the patterns for many of the Related Rulings, which
likewise have a sizable number.  Considering the role of third-
century rabbis, in the liturgy's history, we can understand this
formulation's large role among Samuel's teachings.  Three categories F, G, and H, have three entries each and may reflect the scope
and purpose of the response to Mishnah.  Categories F and G accord
with the foregoing observation as to the role of third-century
rabbis in standardizing liturgical formulae and texts as well as
with the need to apply Mishnah, which often leaves the law unclear.
Category G decides the law and F supplements it with additional

CHART 11

THE LITERARY PHRASING OF THE TRADITIONS*

| Type | Classification | Items | Percent | b. | y. | Comments |
|---|---|---|---|---|---|---|
| Form | A. B- | 2 | 3.2 (3.6) | | 2 | |
| Fixed Usages | B. ʾPYLW | 1 | 1.6 (1.8) | | 1 | |
| | C. KL ZMN Š- | 2 | 3.2 (3.6) | 1 | 1 | |
| | D. CD Š- | 3 (2) | 4.8 (3.6) | | 3 (2) | #45-46 |
| | E. KDY Š- | 3-1=2 | 3.2 (3.6) | | 3-1=2 | #101a = secondary revision of 101b |
| Patterns | F. (ʾYN/W) SRYK L- | 3 | 4.8 (5.5) | | 3 | |
| | G. HLKH K- | 3 | 4.8 (5.5) | 3 | | |
| | H. Exegeses | 3 | 4.8 (5.5) | 3 | | |
| | I. Liturgical Texts | 2 | 3.2 (3.6) | 2 | | |
| | J. Blessing Delineations | 15 (10) | 23.8 (18.2) | 12 (7) | 3 | #71=73=74; 76=79; 81=82=84; not counting 77=80 |
| Non-"Standard" Mishnah Commentary Formulations | K. Questions | 1 | 1.6 (1.8) | 1 | | |
| | L. Dialogues | 2 (1) | 3.2 (1.8) | 2 (1) | | #77=80 |
| | M. Discussions | 2 | 3.2 (3.6) | 1 | 1 | |
| | N. First-Person Reports | 5 | 7.9 (9.1) | 2 | 3 | Two sets of analogous b. and y. comments |
| Without Specific Formulation | O. Glosses | 5 | 7.9 (9.1) | 2 | 3 | |
| | P. Declarative Sentences | 12 (11) | 19.9 (20) | 8 (7) | 4 | #72=85; three sets of b. and y. analogues |
| Total | | 64-1=63 (56-1=55) | 100.2 (99.9) | 34 (27) | 30-1=29 (29-1=28) | |

*Number in parentheses = less repeated items.  See comments.  As
the following employ several formulations, they are counted more
than once: 101 (a and b); 127 (a-b and b); 128 (a and b); 134
(three phrasings).  As we do not count the secondary version of
101 (= 101a) towards the percentages, we subtract it from the
totals, which thus comes to 63 (55).

necessary material.  Category H, on the other hand, provides the
reasons or meaning to terms and notions in Mishnah which likewise
is a necessity for understanding and applying Mishnah.

　　　　The provenance of the teachings is further revealing.  A
pattern emerges as to the length of the teachings in b. and y.
All the entries of A-F, except for one item, in C, appear in y.
and these are the fixed formulations and phraseologies.  Categories G-J, on the other hand, are mostly found in b.; only three
of the numerous Blessing Delineations, J, are in y.  Moreover, in
contrast to the brevity of the y. items, G-J are longer and more
involved and developed teachings.  Below we return to the implications of this spread.

　　　　Among K-N, the First Person Reports, N, have the most
entries and most forcefully reflect the group's overall image of
Samuel as a source of Torah and authority.  Since four of the
nine traditions of K-N come from y., the image is in Palestine as
well as Babylonia.  All four have b. analogues.  This applies even
to the First Person Reports, for which there are two b. instances
and three y. ones, for the third, #103, does have an analogue in
b. though phrased as a Declarative Sentence, #102.  Therefore,
given the early date of circulation of the traditions, which
would account for their structurally similar placement of
analogues in both *Gemarot*, we must be dealing with a rather early
image of Samuel.

　　　　When we consider the remaining items, O-P, we find that
though they may lack a fixed phraseology, they still may be
formulated with Mishnah in mind.  First, O, the Glosses, by their
very nature are fittingly used to comment on a text.  Glosses in
many cultures and periods have served as a primary element of
commentary.[53]  They account for 7.9 percent of the items and 9.1
percent of the traditions.  Considering the size of our sample
and the generally rather low percentages of entries in the other
categories (except for J), these Glosses play a prominent role
in the presentation of Samuel's teachings.  They complement the
use of the B- form and the brief formulary ways in which to focus
on particular aspects of Mishnah.

　　　　P, the "Declarative Sentences," make up the largest group,
with 19 percent of the items and 20 percent of the traditions.
It is difficult to know how many of the sentences preserve the
original wording, and to what degree they have been rephrased.  In
fact, several sentences most likely resulted from the development
of originally briefer formulations.  The sentences as presently
formulated, while relevant to Mishnah, evidently were not intended

to circulate closely along with it.  On the other hand, a commentary need not include only brief passages.  Moreover, as we suggested in Volume One, Samuel may have authored a variety of responses to Mishnah.[54]  We address this issue in chapter nine, where we discuss the diverse models of possible commentaries and try to relate Samuel's teachings to them.

As to the provenance and spread of the O and P Categories, the y. contains one more Gloss than b. and twice as many Sentences. On close examination of the latter, we notice that the y. ones generally are the simpler ones, while the b. items are longer and more detailed.

The above observations indicate that we have a wide range of formulations and that the Glosses, Blessing Delineation Patterns, and First Person Reports, in addition to the Declarative Sentences, account for a disproportionately large percentage of the teachings.  The particular functions of these outstanding items and the overall variety and spread of all the phrasings fit the different purposes of the response to Mishnah.  Glosses and Blessing Delineations are expected in a commentary on a work like Mishnah.  The former have an integral place in a close scrutiny of a legal text and the latter supplement Mishnah with concrete applications of its rules and principles.  Furthermore, Tosefta provides an excellent precedent for the role of both.[55]  Finally, the First Person Reports concretely present the role of an Amora as a teacher and embodiment of Torah.

The formulations, accordingly, make up the essential elements of a commentary designed to enable a person to apply a text. Certainly, as we indicate above, a significant aspect of this commentary apparently is shaped and skewed by the perspective of the later uses of the teachings and the image which Samuel had within later circles.  Both points deserve a full discussion.  In chapters nine and ten, as part of an examination of the purposes of Samuel's commentary and comments, we focus on the practical nature of Samuel's efforts.  There and in chapter eight we deal with the shaping and transformations of Samuel's teachings.

Finally, the formulations also indicate an item's relationship to Mishnah.  First, A-F, mostly in PT, O, the Glosses, and #132 of the Exegeses, H, are dependent on Mishnah in two ways. They are formulated so as to circulate along with Mishnah and they require that text to be comprehensible.  They account for 30 percent of the items and 33 percent of the traditions.

Secondly, we have the items which may need Mishnah for comprehension though they are not formulated so as to be tightly

knit to that text. This involves two of the three entries of G,
the HLKH K- Decisions. The third one is appended to a *baraita*,
which is also attributed to Samuel, and thus indicates that even
it needs an antecedent text, though in this case the dependence
is in formulation as well as for comprehension, and the referent
is a source which explains Mishnah. Categories I, K, and N are
too ambiguous by themselves to appear outside the context of
Mishnah. Category K, the Inquiry, in effect focuses on the
principle of Mishnah and its point emerges only when the question is seen in the context of Mishnah. The purposes and uses of
the Liturgical Texts are meaningless without some additional
information. Category N ostensibly does not need Mishnah but on
closer examination we note that several comments pick up on an
item mentioned in Mishnah. Moreover, four of the five entries
make up two sets of b. and y. analogues (#58 & 59; 127 & 129), a
point which indicates that these teachings are not randomly placed
on Mishnah. This applies even to the fifth item (#103), for it
has an analogue formulated, though, as a Declarative Sentence,
and it is ambiguous without a proper context. These categories
account for 17.5 percent of the items and 20 percent of the
traditions.

The third grouping includes those items that do not need
Mishnah though they make good sense in the context of Mishnah.
These are J, L, M, and two of the three entries of H, #70 and
#140. Together they represent 33 percent of the items and 27
percent of the traditions. Number 140 of the Exegetical Proof
Texts, H, could function as a standard gloss. Number 70 deals
with a central notion of Mishnah; its relevance is indicated by
its content as well as by its analogues in Tosefta and in the two
*Gemarot*. As already pointed out, considering the choice of
verses that receive attention, Mishnah undoubtedly prompted and
elicited these responses. This applies to the third Exegetical
Proof Text to an even greater degree and therefore we placed it
in the first grouping.

Category L, the Dialogue, like J, the Blessing Delineations, clearly are supplements to Mishnah. But when we consider
the nature of Mishnah, evidence of the toseftan analogues, the
purpose and need to set out and refine the principles of Mishnah,
and the social and religious context of the third century, we
conclude that the formulations appropriately fit their use and
the comments appear in their most natural location, in conjunction with M. Ch. 6.[56] Category M, the Discussions, by themselves

constitute materials totally unconnected to Mishnah, but with
other material they make up part of a unit more tightly knit to
Mishnah.

The fourth and last grouping consists of the Declarative
Sentences. This final category involves 19 percent of the items
and 20 percent of the traditions. Materials presented in this
manner can be tied to Mishnah; such formulations make up an
integral building block of Tosefta.[57] In fact, the specific
relationship of these items varies. First, two items, b. and y.
analogues (which differ) are completely independent of Mishnah
(135, 136). This enables the b. version to be cited in b. Pes.
But the latter's relevance to Berakhot, where the y. version is
found, and the relationship of both to Tosefta's response to
Mishnah, indicate their connection to Mishnah. Secondly, five
items or four traditions (55, 66, 72=85, 115), while independent
of Mishnah, make very good sense in its context. Thirdly, two
items and traditions (65, 128), in effect, need Mishnah. Number
65 employs the indefinite "it" and thereby makes use of Mishnah.
Number 128 speaks of "this *ziqa*," a term used as an Aramaic
rendering of Mishnah's Hebrew *ziqim*. Fourthly, one tradition,
#105, probably is the reworking and expansion of a gloss and,
therefore, it originally needed Mishnah.

Chart 12 summarizes our observations as to the relationship to Mishnah. The overall number of traditions is so phrased
as to fit tightly along with Mishnah, or to require it for comprehension, or at least to appear appropriate in the context of
Mishnah. The diverse uses for the Declarative Sentences indicate
that traditions could have lacked specific formulations and could
have made up autonomously phrased teachings. If anything, the
evidence suggests that simple sentences at times are the results
of the development and application of teachings and not vice
versa. This hypothesis forms the problem of chapters eight and
especially nine. There we refine our analysis of the relationships to Mishnah and at the same time determine if the close
dependence on Mishnah derives from the earliest stage of the
tradition or is the result of later transmission and editorial
reworking and rephrasing. To do so we examine the tradents'
role in citing the traditions.

We have also noticed that the PT has a tendency to preserve the briefer comments and those more fully tied to Mishnah.
We can interpret this in two ways. First, it conforms to the
overall nature of the Yerushalmi in contrast to the Bavli. The
end processes of the BT, generally attributed to the so-called

CHART 12

THE COMMENTS' RELATIONSHIP TO MISHNAH*

| Relationship to Mishnah | Categories | Percentage | Comments |
|---|---|---|---|
| In formulation and for comprehension need M. | A,B,C,D, E,F,O, 1 of H | 30.3 (32.6) | The H item = #132 |
| For comprehension need M. | G,I,K,N | 17.5 (19.9) | G: 2 of 3 items by comprehension; third by formulation connected to a *baraita* on Mishnah. |
| Good sense in context of M. | J,L,M, 2 of H | 33.4 (27.2) | Considering nature of Mishnah, third-century teaching, history of liturgy, toseftan analogues: Mishnah prompts the responses. |
| Mix | P | 19.0 (20) | Declarative Sentences: 2 = unconnected yet make up b. and y. analogues which further develop toseftan Mishnah-response. 5 (4) = independent of Mishnah but make good sense in its context. 2 = need Mishnah. 1 = expanded from gloss |

*Parentheses denote less repeated items.

"Saboraim," entailed a complex process of editing and expanding
the text.   The PT, in contrast, tends to preserve materials in a
more pristine and primitive formulation.[58]   Secondly, this observation may relate to the particular transmission of Samuel's
materials in amoraic Babylonia and Palestine.   In Babylonia
Samuel's teachings may have received greater scrutiny, reworking,
and application by successive generations of masters.   In
Palestine, on the other hand, Samuel's teachings, which were cited
due to their relevance to Mishnah, may not have assumed a fundamental role in the development of the Palestinian *sugya*.   At most
they might have been adapted to fit Palestinian perspectives
(e.g., #101) or have been integrated into the pericope (e.g.,
#115).   Once cited, however, the traditions in the course of
additional application may not have been further revised.   We
return to this hypothesis in chapters nine and ten.   We now turn
to the presentation of the traditions, whether they appear and
originate in disputes or individually.   This problem also casts
light on the role of Samuel's teachings in Palestine and
Babylonia.

[1]For a discussion of "Forms," see Volume One, pp. 187-188, Bokser, "Talmudic Form Criticism," and the literature cited there.

Gordis likewise distinguishes between and catalogues different formulations of teachings, in particular those which open with B-, LʾŠNW ʾLʾ and Š- (e.g., WHWʾ Š- and KGWN Š-) as well as those which offer reasons, e.g., MPNY Š- and ʾMR QRʾ. But he does not evaluate whether or not the phrasings constitute stereotyped forms or formulary structures. Moreover, while he does analyze and correlate various characteristics of the phrasings, he does not inquire if certain ones, by their very nature, have a different history than others. Hence, just because certain formulations might be secondary, that does not necessarily prove the case concerning the others. Accordingly, throughout the present study, we face the question whether a formulation is fundamental or whether it is secondary to the tradition. That is why we construct our argument in the way in which we do and attempt to determine which traits may derive from the tradition's earliest stage. In fact, our isolation of forms provides us with one means to distinguish between primary and secondary elements of a tradition and to determine which parts may have been added to fill out an originally briefer formulation. See above, chapter one, n. 6.

[2]See Volume One, chapter four, pp. 187-206, and Bokser, "Talmudic Form Criticism," and note also the observation of Friedman, "A Critical Study," p. 325.

[3]See Volume One, pp. 188-190, and cp. Gordis' treatment of these traditions.

[4]See chapter two, "Analysis of Traditions," #99, subsection ii, and text to n. 340.

[5]See chapter two, text to nn. 508 and 513.

[6]See also #67 (and 65-66), which may have once been an instance of the B- form but which has been contaminated by Mishnah's language. See chapter two, text after n. 157 and to nn. 158-160.

The form does appear among the non-Mishnah comments. See #12 (a comment on a non-Berakhot Mishnah), and cp. #63, a tradition which has been worked over.

[7]Volume One, pp. 192-193 and nn. there.

[8]See chapter two, nn. 509-513 and text thereto.

Among the non-Mishnah comments, the ʾPYLW appears in #12 (a non-Berakhot Mishnah comment which has been expanded); cp. #40-41 and see chapter three, n. 47.

[9]See *Thes. Mis.*, 2:619c-620b (note some of the entries of BZMN Š-, 2:618c-619b, in MSS read KL ZMN Š-, e.g., M. Ter. 11:5 and R. H. 3:8), and *Thes. Tos.* 3:64a-65a.

[10]See chapter two, n. 441 and text thereto. Note, for #44 we also have an analogue in T. Ber. 2:19 which provides a precedent for a comment to be directly on Mishnah. See chapter two, "Analysis of Traditions, #44, subsection ii.

[11]See chapter two, text to nn. 35-36; and n. 439.

[12]See e.g., M. Shev. 1:1; T. Shev. 1:4, p. 166, ll. 18-19; and T. Zev. 8:17, p. 492, l. 10.

[13]See *Thes. Mis.* 3:1310-1316, and *Thes. Tos.* 5:246-254.

[14]We speak of two instances, for #46 is an exact duplicate of #45 within the same pericope.  On the two traditions see chapter two, text to nn. 35-36, 363, and 366, 368 and the last paragraph, and chapter three, n. 98.

[15]While the first tradition there mentions excrement and urine, and the second only urine, Samuel's comment does not specify a referent.  But he deals with excrement, as indicated by the content of his comment, viz., "top" and "dried."  See chapter two, text to n. 35.

[16]See *Thes. Mis.* 2:490a-491a, and *Thes. Tos.* 2:310a-313a (from which the instances must be gleaned).

[17]See the lists cited in n. 16.

[18]Number 101 indicates when a person has sufficient knowledge and is thus no longer a "minor"; #120 refines Mishnah's criterion and indicates the minimum amount of light; and #134, in the portion with the KDY Š- phrase, states the minimum amount of rain for the blessing to be required.  See chapter two, text to nn. 351-353; text between nn. 432-433; and text to n. 508.

[19]For a different usage of ṢRYK, cp. Lieberman, *TK*, 2:785, n. 35; 3:211, 255, n. 40.

[20]See chapter two, "Analysis of Traditions," #21; and text between nn. 117-119; *Thes. Mis.* 1:127c-128a, 4:1534b-c; *Thes. Tos.* 1:208a-209b, 6:32c-34c.  Note the usages in M. M.S. 4:7, 5:6-7; Hal. 4:8; Eruv. 1:1; esp. B.B. 2:9, 4:2 and 9, and 8:7, where the positive and negative appear, and T. Ter. 3:16, p. 120, ll. 63-64.  Cp. the usage in #66, from b. Shab. 150b.

[21]See chapter two, n. 26.

[22]Cp. the explanation of Finkelstein, "The Prayer," which might supply Samuel with a positive emphasis.  Our observation here might tend to support the reading of the L MS which has ᵓYNW ṢRYK as against that of V and S MSS. See chapter two, "Analysis of Traditions," #125.

[23]As we suggested in chapter two, text between nn. 117-119, the need to stress the negative opinion--like the formulation--arises once the opposite position is expressed.

[24]See Volume One, pp. 196-197, esp. n. 21; and *Thes. Mis.* 2:576, the references to M. Men. 4:3, and M. Nid. 1:3, and *Thes. Tos.* 2:477.

[25]See chapter two, text to n. 44; and chapter three, n. 58.

[26]On Exegesis, see Volume One, pp. 198-199, and Neusner, *Pharisees*, 3:39-43.  For a comprehensive list of Exegesis in Mishnah, see Samuel Rosenblatt, *The Interpretation of the Bible in the Mishnah* (Baltimore, 1935). See also Gordis.

[27]See chapter two, "Analysis of Traditions," #70.

[28]See chapter two, "Analysis of Traditions," #132.

[29]In light of the argument which we develop here and throughout the book, the comment may of course have developed as a gloss and would then refer back directly to the mention of the "evil inclination" in Mishnah and not in Rav's opinion.  Alternatively, the comment originally contained the phrase but it was deleted when presented in the dispute form.  Note, the first half of #132 constitues a gloss.  Undoubtedly it originally directly related to Mishnah. Once it became embedded within a *sugya*, however, the connection needed reinforcement through the addition of a question.

[30]See chapter two, text to nn. 538-540.

[31]See, for example, Kasher, *Torah Shelemah*, 2: loc. cit.; the various
entries in Kanovsky, *Samuel*; Bacher, *Babylonischen Amoräer*, pp. 37-45, esp.
43-44; Neusner, *History*, 2:188-199, and 217-222; and *Yalqut HaMakhiri* to
Ps. 24 and 77. Elsewhere we do have examples of an exegetical program which
responds to a whole section of the Bible. See for example Samuel's and Rav's
treatment of Esther, in b. Meg. 10b-17a, on which see A. Weiss, *Studies*
(1962), pp. 276-294, and Neusner, *History*, 2:60-64, 288-290. See also
A. Weiss, *Studies* (1962), pp. 251-260; above, chapter three, items #61-62,
and especially nn. 71-72; and Neusner, *History*, 2:199-202.

[32]This is in contrast to Rav. See, for example, Kanovsky, *Rav*,
pp. 16-17. Contrast this with Kanovsky's entry to Samuel, p. 14. For additional instances of Samuel's reference to Ps. 24:1 and "sacrilege," see
tradition #114, b. Hul. 139a, and chapter two, n. 182. See also, in responses
to Mishnah, b. Men. 21b; b. Meil. 14a (cited in b. B.M. 57b), and b. Meil.
20a, and cp. b. B.Q. 20a (= a different version of the b. Meil. 20a *sugya*;
each has a different tradition attributed to Samuel). See Weiss, *Studies*
(1966), pp. 272-279, and cp. Bacher, *Babylonischen Amoräer*, pp. 43-44, and
David Hoffmann, *Mar Samuel* (Leipzig, 1873), p. 60.

[33]See the discussion in Volume One, pp. 198-199, that instances of
exegesis may form part of a commentary on Mishnah. The Exegeses and Proof
Texts among the non-Mishnah comments include: #5, 6, 13, 19, 22, 29, 42, 43,
53, 61, 62, 64, 69, 97, 114, 130, 131, 142.

[34]See chapter two, "Analysis of Traditions," #55-56.

[35]Heinemann, *Prayer*. See also Neusner, *History*, 2:159-177, and
Elbogen, pp. 197-199, and cp. Heinemann's comments in Elbogen, pp. 198-199.

[36]The Dialogue is #77=80; the Declarative Sentence, whose point no
longer is just to delineate a blessing, #72=85; and the Glosses which define
a reference as, "With Great Love," #8 and 11.

[37]See chapter two, text to nn. 209, 213; #76-80, n. 234, and esp.
subsection iv; and esp. #81-85, 75, subsections ii, v-vi.

[38]See chapter four, nn. 5 and 16.

[39]See Volume One, p. 202.

[39a]See Melammed, *Introduction*, pp. 429-441, esp. 429, 440-441, for a
survey of such amoraic questions. Mishnah and Tosefta use the verb Š²L for
instances of a master who inquires from another master. See *Thes. Mis.*
4:1686, and *Thes. Tos.* 6:302.

[40]See chapter two, text to n. 223. The "Dialogue" differs from the
"Debate" form. In the latter, the disputants marshall arguments to support
each of their positions. See, e.g., *Pharisees*, 3:16-23, which also refers to
instances in Mishnah and Tosefta. See also #127 and #128, in the "Discussions," Category M.

[41]See, e.g., Neusner, *Pharisees*, 3:16-23, and cp. Charles Primus,
*Aqiva's Contribution to the Law of Zera^cim* (Leiden, 1977), p. 148. See also
*Samuel's Commentary*, Volume One, 201-202; and cp. Weiss Halivni, *ST*, 1:17,
and 686-687, n. 4, and Friedman, "Critical Study," pp. 346-351, esp. 351.

[42]Number 127, in b., follows a First Person Report in #127a-b, and
#128b, in y., follows the analogous Declarative Sentence, #128a. In general,
see chapter two, "Analysis of Traditions," #126-129.

[43]See, e.g., Neusner, *Pharisees*, 3:14-16, 23-25, and *Eliezer*, 2:30; and Primus, *Aqiva's*, p. 154.

[44]See chapter two, text to nn. 108, and 486-487.

[45]See chapter two, text to nn. 386-389.

[46]See Volume One, pp. 202-203, and cp. Neusner, *Eliezer*, 2:39-53, 61. Those glosses which employ fixed terminology or language are classified under their appropriate headings in Categories A, B, C, D, E, and I.

[47]Number 8 is duplicated as #11 on M. Tamid. The tradition's formulation as a gloss may enable it to be associated with more than one text. See chapter two, #8, subsection iii; as well as text to nn. 85-87; #67, text after n. 157, and to nn. 158-160, and subsection iv; and text to n. 431.

[48]Note, some readings include a B- in #67. See chapter two, #67-68.

[49]See Volume One, pp. 204-205; Neusner, *Pharisees*, 3:5-14, 23-25, cp. 101-114, *Purities*, 21:165-166, 196-199.

[50]See chapter two, text to nn. 85-87; text to n. 133; #81-85, 72, subsections iii-iv, vi; #102; text after n. 339 and to n. 340; #115-116, text to n. 408 to end; text to nn. 485-487 and nn. 527-528 and text thereto.

[51]See, e.g., #65 and esp. 105.

[52]See chapter ten.

[53]See below, chapter nine.

[54]See Volume One, esp. pp. 206 and 234-238.

[55]See below, chapters nine and ten.

[56]See chapter ten.

[57]See Neusner, *Purities*, 21:247-297.

[58]See Bosker, "Guide," chapter eleven.

CHAPTER SEVEN

MODES OF PRESENTATION: THE DISPUTE FORM

### 1. Introduction

In addition to the formulation or phrasing that a tradition may employ, as a cognitive unit it may appear in one of
three modes. First, a tradition may dispute and be juxtaposed to
an opinion attributed to another master and with which it
ostensibly makes up one of the variations of the dispute form.
Secondly, a tradition may differ with another opinion even though
it is not juxtaposed to it and is not presented with it in a dispute form. Thirdly, the tradition may appear by itself. Since
it is difficult to clearly differentiate between the first two
modes, we shall discuss them together.[1]

We focus on the modes of presentation in order to trace
the role of the dispute form in the history of Samuel's traditions. Since we argue that a significant portion of Samuel's
teachings on Mishnah originated as a "Commentary" on Mishnah,
they--and the remains thereof--would not have initially taken
shape as part of a dispute with a second master but as individual
responses of Mishnah. Accordingly, to test our hypothesis we
must ascertain whether the dispute form is fundamental or secondary to the comments, and if secondary, how it affects the
integrity of the traditions.

### 2. Traditions Juxtaposed and In Dispute

The first category includes the traditions that appear
juxtaposed to another master's opinion and ostensibly in dispute
with it. Many appear to make up one part of a formal dispute
while others do not. The difficulty involved in an attempt to
classify these items into separate groups reflects the problematic
role of the dispute form. Eighteen items and seventeen traditions
at first glance make up one of the variations of the dispute
form[2] (51, 54, 56, 60, 70, 76=79, 78, 86, 87, 115, 117, 120, 121,
125, 132, 140). An additional four items and three traditions
(8, 44, 45=46) perhaps should belong to this group as well,
though they are only one in a series of differing juxtaposed
traditions ostensibly on the same subject. Eleven items and ten
traditions are comments that differ from an adjoining opinion
though they definitely do not presently make up a dispute form
(55, 58, 59, 65, 67, 77=80, 105, 116, 135). Where the traditions

are separated by intervening material, the dispute form may have
been "broken" by a later interpolation or addition. This would
account for their use of identical structures, as in #65, unless
in such cases one opinion has been patterned after the other one
or both were later shaped together.

In all, there are thirty-three items and thirty different
traditions, which constitute 55.9 percent of all the items and
58.8 percent of all the traditions. Eighteen items and sixteen
traditions appear in b. and fifteen items and fourteen traditions
in y. They deal with fifteen different *mishnayot*. Since twenty-
two *mishnayot* are subject to a direct response, the comments
involve 68.2 percent of texts under the focus. Seven *mishnayot*
elicit comments in both b. and y., four only in b. and four only
in y.

The list is structured according to the following pattern:
Mishnah notation; the subject of the comment (where the dispute
contains a protasis it is included to supply the information);
the tradition's number; where appropriate a "Q" to designate the
presence of an introductory question which the anonymous *Gemara*
supplied; the names of the masters disputing; the abbreviation
"vs." to indicate which parties are in opposition with which;
where appropriate, in parentheses, any patterned phrase or key
word found in the tradition or the name of a Category of the
Literary Phrasings which the tradition employs. Where the last
item is missing, the tradition lacks a clear-cut formulation and
phrasing. Finally, double slanted lines denote a tradition in
dispute or agreement with Samuel's tradition or otherwise relevant
to it but which is neither in dispute form with nor juxtaposed to
it.

*1.  M. 1:4*.
      (8)   Q. Second blessing before *Shema*[c]--
Said R. Judah said Samuel; And thus R. Eleazar taught
R. Padat, his son; [One reading:] vs. Rabbis; It was
taught likewise. [Second reading:] It was taught like-
wise; vs. Rabbis.                                                    (b.)

*2.  M. 3:5*.
      Prohibition of liturgy in presence of urine and
excrement--
      (44)   Q. Said R. Judah said Samuel (KL ZMN Š-);
Thus said Rabbah bar Bar Hanah (KL ZMN Š-) vs. Geniva
in the name of Rav (KL ZMN Š-)                                       (b.)
      (45=46)   R. Abba BŠM RAV (--, KL ZMN Š-) vs.
Geniva (KL ZMN Š-) vs. Samuel said (<sup>C</sup>D Š-); Simeon b.
Ba BŠM R. Yohanan (<sup>C</sup>D Š-) vs. R. Yermiah, R. Ze<sup>C</sup>ira
BŠM Rav (<sup>Ɔ</sup>PYLW)                                           (y.)

3.  *M. 3:1.*
    Evening *Tefillah*--
    (51)  (For) said R. Judah said Samuel (*baraita*;
HLKH K-) vs. Rav (HLKH K-)                                    (b.)

4.  *M. 4:3.*
    Substance of eighteen--
    (54)  Q. Rav (Gloss) vs. Samuel (Liturgical Text)
vs. Abaye cursed.                                             (b.)
    (55)  Said R. Naḥman said Samuel vs. Attacked Rava
bar Ishmael; Attacked Mar Zutra; // Said R. Bibi
b. Abaye.                                                     (b.)
    (56)  Q. Rav (SWP) vs. Samuel (RᴼŠ)                       (y.)

5.  *M. 4:7.*
    *Musaf*--
    (58)  Said R. Huna bar Ḥinena said R. Ḥiyya bar
Rav (HLKH K-); Said to him R. Ḥiyya bar Abin, You are
right.  For said Samuel (First Person Report) vs.
R. Ḥanina Qara [= Bible teacher] before R. Yannai
(HLKH K-) vs. R. Yannai (ᴼYN HLKH K-) vs. [?]
R. Yoḥanan (First Person Report concerning R. Yannai)        (b.)
    (59)  R. Bibi BŠM R. Ḥanina (HLKH K-); For said
Samuel (First Person Report) vs. For said R. Yaaqov
bar Idi BŠM Simeon Ḥasida (B-); For said R. Yoḥanan
(First Person Report concerning R. Yannai)                   (y.)
    (60)  Rav (ṢRYK L-) vs. Samuel (ᴼYN ṢRYK L-)             (y.)

6.  *M. 5:2.*
    *Havdalah* in *Tefillah*--
    (65)  R. Yoḥanan to Simeon b. Ba (Sentence) vs.
R. Yaaqov bar Idi BŠM R. Yishaq the Great (ᴼMRH--
ᴼWMRH) vs. R. Zeᶜira, R. Judah BŠM Samuel (ᴼMRH--
ᴼWMRH; ᴼMRH-- ᴼWMRH)                                         (y.)
    (67)  R. Yoḥanan BŠM Rabbi (MṬYN K-) vs.
R. Yishaq the Great BŠM Rabbi (HLKH K-); R. Yishaq
bar Naḥman BŠM R. Ḥunaniah b. Gamaliel (HLKH K-);
R. Abbahu BŠM R. Eleazar (HLKH K-) vs. R. Yaaqov
b. Aḥa BŠM Samuel (ᴼWMRH)                                    (y.)
    (68)  R. Yishaq bar Avudimi in the mame of
Rabbenu said (HLKH) and some say (MṬYN) vs.
R. Yoḥanan (MWDYM) . . . vs. Said R. Joseph, Rav
and Samuel already arranged for us a pearl in
Babylonia (Liturgical Text)                                   (b.)

7.  *M. 6:1.*
    Blessings over food:  Basis and specific bless-
ings--
    (70)  Said R. Judah said Samuel (Simile + Proof
Text) vs. R. Levi (comparing two verses) vs.
R. Ḥanina bar Papa (Simile + Proof Text)                     (b.)
    (76=79)  Palm-heart--R. Judah vs. Samuel
(Blessing Delineation)                                       (b.)
    (77=80)  Said Samuel to R. Judah, *Shinena*,
*Your opinion makes sense.* (Dialogue)  *For behold*,
a radish . . .                                               (b.)
    (78)  Palm-heart.  R. Yaaqov bar Aḥa BŠM
Samuel vs. Taught R. Ḥalafta b. Saul vs. Taught
R. Hoshia (Blessing Delineation)                             (y.)
    (86)  *Shatita*--Rav vs. Samuel (Blessing
Delineation)                                                 (b.)
    (87)  DRŠ R. Naḥman in the name of our Rabbi--
and who is he?  Samuel--Steamed foods . . . [=vs]
And our friends who come from the land of Israel to

Babylonia--and who are they?  Ulla in the name of
R. Yoḥanan, Steamed foods . . . And I [Naḥman] say,
They were taught in a dispute. // And it is not so
[= not a dispute].  Said R. Ḥiyya bar Abba said R.
Yoḥanan vs. R. Benjamin bar Yefet said R. Yoḥanan
(Blessing Delineation)                                          (b.)
     [Preceding pericope: DRŠ R. Ḥisda in the name
of our Rabbi--and who is he?  Rav--Steamed foods
. . . [vs.] And our rabbis who came from the land
of Israel to Babylonia--and who are they?  Ulla in
the name of R. Yoḥanan . . . I [R. Ḥisda] say . . .
[= harmonization of the two positions]]

*8.  M. 7:1&4*.
     Apparent repetition--
     (105) . . . in accordance with that which said
R. Abba said Samuel; An alternative version: Said
R. Abba said Samuel vs. [?] Alternatively in accord-
ance with R. Huna, for R. Huna said.                           (b.)

*9.  M. 8:5*.
     Fire in *havdalah*--
     (115)(a): Samuel (LPYKK) vs. R. Huna BŠM [Rav],
Rabbi Abbahu BŠM R. Yohanan (ᵓP)                               (y.)
     (b): This follows Samuel for Samuel
says . . .                                          (y. in Gen. R.)
     (116)  Said R. Judah said Samuel (ᵓYN ᵓLᵓ); Said to
him a certain elder and some say Rabba bar bar Hana,
Right, and similarly R. Yoḥanan said, Right; Said R. Abba
to Ulla, Is it true that you said in the name of R.
Yoḥanan (ᵓYN ᵓLᵓ) vs. . . . R. Benjamin bar Yefet said
R. Yoḥanan (BYN--BYN)                                          (b.)
*10.  M. 8:6B*.
     Blessing over the lamp when one enjoys its light--
     (117)  Rav vs. Samuel (Glosses)                           (y.)
     (120)  R. Judah (BŠM) Samuel (KDY Š-) vs.
R. Yoḥanan (KDY Š-) vs. R. Ḥanina (KDY Š-) vs. TNY
R. Hoshiah (ᵓPYLW) // R. Zeᶜira                                (y.)

*11.  M. 8:7*.
     Delayed Grace until--
     (121)  R. Ḥiyya BŠM Samuel (KL ZMN Š-) vs.
R. Yoḥanan (ᶜD˙Š-)                                             (y.)

*12.  M. 9:1*.
     Blessing formula--
     (125)  Rav (ṢRYK L-) vs. Samuel (ᵓYNW ṢRYK L-; Alt.:
ṢRYK L-)                                                       (y.)

*13.  M. 9:2*.
     Blessings over natural phenomena: *reamim* . . .
rain--
     (132)  Q. Samuel (Gloss + Proof Text) vs. Rav
(Gloss + Proof Text) vs. R. Aḥa bar Yaaqov (Gloss/
Answer) vs. R. Ashi (Gloss/Answer)                             (b.)
     (134)  Q. R. Ḥiyya BŠM R. Yoḥanan (KTḤYLH KDY--
WBSWP KDY Š-) vs. R. Yannai bar Ismael BŠM R.
Simeon b. Laqish (KTḤYLH KDY--WLBSWP KDY Š-) vs.
R. Yose  BŠM R. Judah, And R. Yonah and R. Judah
BŠM Samuel (KTḤYLH KDY--WLBSWP KL ŠHWᵓ)                        (y.)

*14.  M. 9:3*.
     Blessings over *miṣvot*--
     (135)  Q. R. Yoḥanan (Gloss/Answer) vs. R. Huna

(Gloss/Answer); For said R. Yose b. R. Bun BŠM
Samuel (Sentence)                                                    (y.)

15.  *M. 9:5A*.
        Evil inclination--
        (140)  Rav vs. Samuel (Similes + Proof Texts)        (b.)

Close examination of the thirty traditions reveals that
in the overwhelming majority of cases, the dispute form clearly
is not fundamental to the traditions.  The ways in which the comments relate to each other indicate that Samuel's teachings could
not have initially been enunciated and formulated to form part of
a dispute.  In six instances only does the dispute form appropriately fit the teachings.  Even there, however, the comments are
phrased as brief glosses which may reflect an original stage as
direct responses to Mishnah.  After we review each item, we synthesize our observations which are summarized in Chart 13.

In #8, Samuel is in agreement with Eleazar, a second
generation Palestinian in conjunction with whom the opposing
opinion more likely emerged.  Number 8's origin as a gloss on
Mishnah is reflected especially in its appearance as a gloss on
an identical referent in M. Tamid (tradition #11), which Judah
cites directly on Mishnah.  Numbers 8 and 11 have different surrounding material from which they both are probably independent.[3]
Number 44, formulated as a gloss, originated independent of an
identical and following item attributed to a third generation
Palestinian,[4] and probably also of the opposing opinion attributed to Rav, his contemporary.  The latter is the subject of a
separate focus which apparently was at one time transmitted as a
separate unit.

Number 45=46, as its b. analogue #44, originated independent of the opposing opinions attributed to Yohanan, a
Palestinian, and to Rav.  The latter appears in different versions,
which were therefore probably separately transmitted and cited or
used by different individuals in different ways.  Moreover, Samuel
employs a different phrasing from the preceding teachings and
assumes a different referent.[5]

Number 51's autonomy from Rav is reflected by the lack of
balance between the two.  Samuel's tradition is made up of a
*baraita*-like presentation of tannaitic views to which a HLKH K-
decision is appended while Rav's only includes the latter.[6]

Number 54 is not balanced with the disputant and they
employ different types of comments.[7]

Number 55 is redacted together with an opposing tradition
attributed to later masters, a factor which may explain why they
do not make up a dispute form.

Number 56 constitutes the first instance of well balanced
glosses, though Samuel's language may have been shaped to respond
to Rav's.  On this basis one could argue either for or against
the originality of the dispute mode.  The dispute is primary and
therefore Samuel's language was originally formulated for the purposes of presentation in a dispute.  Alternatively, the dispute
form was later imposed, for otherwise Samuel would not have
employed imprecise language.  Therefore, later needs to transmit
and contrast the opinions must account for the shaping of the
teachings.  Accordingly, the simple glosses could originally have
functioned as separate and direct responses to Mishnah.[8]

Numbers 58 and 59, b. and y. analogues, are greatly out
of phase with their surrounding traditions and are independent of
them.  The tradition which precedes #58 and with which it is in
agreement is attributed to a second-generation Babylonian and
employs a different formulation.  The opposing traditions are
attributed to Palestinians and likewise employ different formulations, two instances of the HLKH K- pattern and one First Person
Report, narrated by one master concerning a different master.
The tradition which precedes #59 and with which it is in agreement
and those which follow it and with which it is in opposition are
attributed to Palestinians and employ different formulations.
Samuel's tradition is presented as if cited by the pericope's
editor.[9]

Number 60, like #56, is a brief gloss and employs a standard pattern.  As Samuel's language responds to Rav's and his
thought may have been formulated with the opposing position in
mind, the dispute form could be fundamental.

Number 65 and several juxtaposed teachings employ
Mishnah's language but they do not make up a dispute form.  The
disputants are Palestinians and the pericope's editor contrasts
them and explicitly draws out their divergent implications.[10]

Number 67 and the opposing teachings, attributed to
Palestinians, are not balanced and employ a different style.[11]

Number 68 does not actually make up a dispute form with
the opposing views.  The latter are Palestinians and Joseph is
the one who cites Rav's and Samuel's "Pearl."[12]

Number 70 originated separately from the opposing views,
both attributed to later masters.  One, Levi, employs a different
structure for his comment, while the other, Ḥanina, patterns his
language upon Samuel's phrasing and in the process revises and
attests it.[13]

Numbers 76=79 make up a pericope with 77=80. The latter presupposes a stage of the tradition other than and prior to that of the dispute form.[14]

Number 78 originated separate from the disputant, a Palestinian, though their teachings are presented together.[15]

Number 86 ostensibly makes up an instance of an appropriate dispute. Hisda, whose comment glosses the two opinions, however, claims that they do not, but rather refer to different cases. Even if Hisda's harmonization is forced, his comment assumes that the teachings initially circulated independently of each other.[16]

Number 87 does not form a proper dispute form. Nahman in an exposition contrasts Samuel's view with a Palestinian's, Yohanan's. Moreover, there are different versions of Yohanan's opinion, according to one of which he does not differ with Samuel.[17]

Number 105 and the other opinions are presented by the pericope's editor as separate teachings, which assumably differ as to a principle, but they are not redacted into a dispute form.[18]

Number 115 is integrated into the pericope by a later editor of the *sugya*. The reading of the attribution is not firm. The tradition may be assigned to Rav as well as to Yohanan. In the b. analogue, #116, the disputant clearly is Yohanan. There the traditions are shaped to respond to each other, though Yohanan's opinion apparently had a separate transmission since it is the subject of discrete focus and circulated in several versions.

Number 117, the third well balanced opinion in a dispute with a contemporary Babylonian, is a very brief and simple gloss and, as mentioned above in the other analogous cases, could have functioned and originated as a direct response to Mishnah.

Number 120 shares with two of the three disputants a similar gloss formulation to set out criteria, yet they and the third disputant, who uses a different formulation, are Palestinians. Zeira, who appears immediately after the opinions, may be responsible for citing Samuel's opinion.[19]

Number 121 is not balanced with the opposing view attributed to a Palestinian, Yohanan.[20]

Number 125 is balanced with the opposing view and may therefore make up the fourth original dispute. It has two textual versions, both of which employ a similar gloss-like formulation, one in the negative and one in the positive. The

one which assigns Samuel the negative pattern responds to Rav in
wording and in the need to emphasize the point.  On the other
hand, it could supplement Mishnah by applying to it a known
notion.  The positive formulation does not as sharply presuppose
an antecedent position to which it would react.[21]

Number 132 appears in a balanced dispute with Rav's
opinion, the fifth such instance.  Both employ a similar opening
phraseology and structure.  The other two views are attributed
to later Babylonians and use a different pattern.[22]

Number 134 is disputed by Palestinians and the traditions
share a similar overall structure.  The comments consist of two
portions.  But only part of the second portion makes up Samuel's
distinctive thought, and therefore it may have constituted
Samuel's original opinion.  If so, the dispute form may have been
imposed upon his opinion, thereby resulting in the first portion
of his comment.

Number 135 is independent of the other material though it
clearly differs with one of the opinions.  An anonymous authority
relates it to the previous teachings, presented in a dispute form.
Samuel, moreover, employs a different formulation and the author
of the opposing position is attributed to a Palestinian.

Number 140 employs a pattern similar to its opposing
opinion attributed to Rav and thus makes up the sixth instance of
a theoretically possible original dispute.  The comments are
closely but not exactly balanced.  As with the other instances,
however, the tradition could function directly on Mishnah.

Several factors thus repeatedly indicate that most of the
traditions without a doubt did not originate in a dispute.

First, in eighteen distinct instances, one of the other
masters, and often the disputant, is a Palestinian or someone who
lived after Samuel and, therefore, a person whom Samuel could not
have confronted in person (8, 44, 45=46, 55, 58, 59, 65, 67, 68,
70, 78, 87, 115, 116, 120, 121, 134, 135, and cp. 132).  At times
the tradition or its position is attributed to other masters in
addition to Samuel and the opposing opinion may have initially
been juxtaposed to it, if it did not originate in its context.

Second, in eight separate cases the traditions' formulations are out of phase with each other or make up different
types of comments, or in some other way are not at all balanced.
They therefore must have circulated at one time outside of the
dispute form and. accordingly, someone must have contrasted them
and imposed the form upon them (51, 54 [to be compared with
#56, the y. version], 58, 59, 67, 121, 134, 135, and cp. #132).

Third, in twelve distinct instances, the traditions differ and are contrasted but do not appear in a dispute form. Rather the tradition's transmitter, a later master, or the pericope's editor presented the opposing opinion, something easily discernible (55, 58, 59, 65, 68, 76=78 in light of 77=80, 87, 105, 116, 120, 135). Many of these traditions are disputed by individuals whom Samuel could not have personally faced (Category One).[23]

Fourth, in three cases the disputing tradition forms the subject of a separate focus and may even be transmitted in different versions. The latter indicates that that tradition was separately and diversely transmitted by different students of the master (44, 45=46, 116).

Fifth, in one case (86) a later master attests that the comments may have originated separately despite their blatant use of the dispute form.

Sixth, in one case (70) the disputant's language is based upon Samuel's wording and in effect revises it. This attests to Samuel's pattern and explains why the language exactly fits Samuel's thought but not his opponents. The formulation probably does not derive from a later authority who imposed it upon the earlier masters, for he would have employed language appropriate to both.

Seven, in one instance we have two uses of the same gloss as a comment on an identical referent in two different *mishnayot* (#8 on M. Berakhot and #11 on M. Tamid). In the latter case, Judah cites the comment directly on Mishnah and it lacks the opposing opinions found in the version on M. Berakhot. Thus the gloss is associated with the phrase in Mishnah and its circulation is not dependent upon the dispute.

In the above cases, the presentation as a dispute must be secondary to the traditions and have originated in the course of their transmission, citation, and application. The comments, therefore, did not take shape in conjunction with other masters' teachings.

But, on the other hand, we do have six cases in which the comments appropriately fit in a dispute form and are rather well balanced with the disputant who is Samuel's contemporary Babylonian, Rav (56, 60, 117, 125, 132, 140). This would apply to #86, as well, if not for Hisdah's comment. The dispute form theoretically could have provided the original context for these teachings. In all but two cases (117 and 132), however, Samuel's language may depend upon or be shaped to respond to that

of his disputant.  As we pointed out above, therefore, on this
basis one could argue either for or against the primacy of the
dispute form.  Moreover, each instance employs some type of gloss
formulation, with or without a specific usage, and could
appropriately function as a gloss directly on Mishnah.

    In the chapter's conclusion and in chapter ten, we return
to the implications of these observations.  There we point out
that Babylonia may have lacked a social context in which Samuel
could have had a formal exchange with Rav.  Therefore, we are not
even assured of the possibility of the six instances of the dispute form.  In any event, they make up only 18.2 percent of the
items and 20 percent of the traditions which ostensibly dispute
other masters, and 10.2 percent of the total items and 11.8 percent of the total traditions.

    Chart 13 summarizes these conclusions.

### 3.  *Traditions Neither Juxtaposed Nor in Dispute*

    Twenty-six items, or twenty-one distinct traditions
appear alone and not in dispute or juxtaposition with an opposing
(or identical) opinion of another master.

    In the list we specify the subject of the tradition, pro-
vide its attribution, and record any patterned language or key
words of the comment's substance.

1.  *M. 1:1*
    Evening *Shema*^c--
    (1)  Said R. Judah said Samuel (HLKH K-)                    (b.)

2.  *M. 1:2.*
    Morning *Shema*^c--
    (7)  Said R. Judah said Samuel (HLKH K-)                    (b.)

3.  *M. 2:1.*
    Attention in *Shema*^c--
    (21)  R. Huna, R. Idi, R. Joseph, R. Judah in the
name of Samuel (ṢRYK L-)                                         (y.)

4.  *M. 5:2.*
    Location of *havdalah*--
    (66)  And did not say R. Judah said Samuel            (b.)

5.  *M. 6:1.*
    Blessings over specific foods--
    (71=73=74)  (For)  Said R. Judah said Samuel, and
thus said R. Yiṣḥaq said R. Yoḥanan (Blessing
Delineation)                                                     (b.)
    (72=85)  . . . *of Rav and Samuel who both say*
that (ꜾYN . . . ꜾLꜾ)                                            (b.)
    (75)  And did not say R. Zera said R. Mattena
said Samuel (Blessing Delineation)                               (b.)
    (81=82=84)  (Said R. Joseph . . . *for) Rav and
Samuel both say* (Blessing Delineation)                          (b.)

(83)  *Rav and Samuel both say* (Blessing
Delineation)                                              (b.)
(88)  R. Abba said, *Rav and Samuel both say*
(Blessing Delineation)                                    (y.)
(89)  R. Ze^cira in the name of Samuel (Blessing
Delineation)                                              (y.)


*6-7.  M. 7:1 & 4.*
     Apparent repetition--
     (99)  Q. Samuel said (KꟷN BTḤYLH KꟷN BSWP)           (y.)


*8.  M. 7:2.*
     Minor counted for summons to Grace--
     (101) (a)  Q. R. Avina said, *R. Ḥuna and R. Judah,*
*both of them in the name of Samuel, dispute* (KDY Š-)     (y.)
            (b)  Q. Said R. Avina, *R. Ḥuna and R. Judah,*
*both of them in the name of Samuel, dispute*
(^cD Š-)                                             (y. in Gen. R.)


*9.  M. 7:3.*
     Formula for summons to Grace--
     (102)  Said Samuel (Sentence)                          (b.)
     (103)  Samuel said, (First Person Report)              (y.)


*10.  M. 8:8.*
     Responding "Amen"--
     (122)  *Samuel asked Rav* (Question)                   (b.)


*11.  M. 9:2.*
     *Ziqim*--
     (126)  Q. Said Samuel (Gloss)                          (b.)
     (127)  And said Samuel (First Person Report +
Discussion)                                               (b.)
     (128)  Samuel said (Sentence + Discussion)             (y.)
     (129)  Samuel said (First Person Report)               (y.)


*12.  M. 9:3.*
     Blessing over *miṣvot*--
     (136)  (For) said R. Judah said Samuel (Sentence)      (b.)

The twenty-six items, eighteen in b. and eight in y.,
include five repetitions and therefore make up twenty-one distinct traditions, thirteen in b. and eight in y.[24] They account
for 44.1 percent of the total items and 41.2 percent of the total
traditions.  They deal with twelve *mishnayot*[25] and thus with
54.4 percent of the *mishnayot* subject to Samuel's scrutiny.  This
percentage along with that of disputing items, in Category A,
exceeds 100 percent because some *mishnayot* are the subject of
both traditions which appear alone and those juxtaposed to other
opinions.

     Two observations emerge from these figures.  A *prima
facie* impression indicates that a significant portion of Samuel's
teachings are so constructed and presented that they need not and
in fact do not belong to a larger pericope.  This accords with
the  characteristics of our hypothesized "Mishnah Commentary."
Samuel taught on Mishnah or in response to Mishnah and his

## CHART 13

### SAMUEL AND DISPUTING OPINIONS

| Disputant | Apparent Dispute Form | Relate to Each Other | Juxtaposed Opinions | Palestinian or Later Master | Out of Phase: In Balance or Type of Comment | BT | PT | Totals* | Comments |
|---|---|---|---|---|---|---|---|---|---|
| Rav | 51,54,56, 60,86,115?, 117,125, 132,140 | | 44,45=46 | | 45=46; 51,54 | 44,51, 54,86, 132, 140 | 45=46, 56,60, 115, 117, 125 | 13(12) | 86 has Hisda's gloss; 115 lacks a firm attribution. |
| Yohanan | 87?,115, 120,121, 134 | 58,59, 65,68, 87?,116 | 135 | X | 58,59,65, 68,121, 135 | 58,68, 87, 116 | 59,65, 115, 120, 121, 134, 135 | 11 | 87's dispute pattern blatantly is the result of Nahman. |
| Hoshia | | | 78,120 | X | | | 78,120 | 2 | |
| Rabbi | | | 67 | X | 67 | | 67 | 1 | |
| Yannai | | 58 | | X | 58 | 58 | | 1 | |
| Simeon Hasida | | 59 | | X | 59 | | 59 | 1 | |
| Yishaq the Great | | 65 | | X | | | 65 | | |
| Halafta b. Saul | | | 78 | X | | | 78 | 1 | |
| Hanina Qara | | 58 | | X | 58 | 58 | | 1 | |
| Huna | | 105 | | | 105 | 105 | | | |

| | 76=79 | [77=80] | | | 76=79 / 78=80 | | |
|---|---|---|---|---|---|---|---|
| Judah | 70 | | | | | 2 (1) / +2 (1) | 77=80 without dispute form, presuppose a difference. |
| Hanina b. Papa | | | X | | 70 | 1 | Patterned on Samuel. |
| Aha bar Yaaqov | | 132 | X | 132 | 132 | 1 | |
| Resh Laqish | 134 | | X | | 134 | 1 | |
| Levi | | 70 | X | 70 | 70 | 1 | |
| Hanina | 120 | | X | | 120 | 1 | See chapter two, n. 436. |
| Hunaniah b. Gamaliel | | 67 | X | 67 | 67 | 1 | |
| Eleazar | | 67 | X | 67 | 67 | 1 | |
| Rabbis | | 8 | ? | | 8 | 1 | See also chapter seven, n. 22 (on #132) |
| Rabbenu | 68 | | X | 68 | 68 | 1 | |
| Rav bar Ishmael | 55 | | X | 55 | 55 | 1 | |
| Mar Zutra | 55 | | X | 55 | 55 | 1 | |
| Ashi | | 132 | X | 132 | 132 | 1 | |

*The totals add up to more than the number of traditions attributed to Samuel as the list includes each tradition which ostensibly differs with or disputes Samuel.

teachings initially were intended to circulate along with
Mishnah or in conjunction with Mishnah.  Accompanying materials
and amoraic discussions form part of the later, literary history
of the traditions.  The present data reveals, therefore, that
even once many of Samuel's comments had been integrated into the
*Gemara*, their discrete nature remained blatant.[26]
        We further notice the items that appear alone employ
diverse formulations and express a wide range of comments.
Accordingly, this mode of representation is not limited to a
single type of formulation of teaching, but makes up a viable
possibility for the full range of Samuel's activities.  In
chapter nine we focus on the correlations of our various findings.
But at this point, the latter observation deserves attention.
It throws light on the nature of the dispute form, to which we
now turn as part of our conclusion to this chapter.

### 4.  *Conclusions*

        The items in Category B without a doubt circulated as
discrete comments though they are now presented in a larger context.  Upon examination of the entries in Category A, we
conclusively found that most of them share this original
independence from other material.  Despite an appearance otherwise, they are thus not redacted into a single pericope with
another tradition.  Rather a later Amora reacts to the tradition
and attacks it, as in #55, or patterns his own comment after it,
as in #70.[26a]  Alternatively, a transmitter, like Zeira, or an
expounder, like Nahman, or the pericope's editor relates Samuel's
tradition to some other item.  Accordingly, the analysis demonstrates that most of Samuel's traditions at one point circulated
as discrete units unconnected to other amoraic material.  For the
sake of classification and underscoring the anomalous nature of
the dispute form, however, we have retained two separate lists.
        What conclusions can we draw from our findings?  Let us
first restate the problem.  When the traditions were composed
and expressed, in what manner did they take shape?  In chapters
two through four we found that the items classified as Mishnah
commentary items (MC and MES) and many of the other items (RC and
RS) intimately deal with Mishnah and respond to it in different
ways, and therefore belong to some type of format structured in
conjunction with Mishnah.  But did that format consist of only
Samuel's teachings and did it directly deal with Mishnah?
Alternatively, did the comments form part of a format which
Samuel did not compose but which had an integrity of its own,

for example, that of a discussion between various masters?  Each
alternative in its understanding of the extant materials shares
certain assumptions and differs in others.  Both alternatives
accord with the regnant theory that the *Gemara* is a literary
working over of traditions which have gone through both oral and
literary stages.  But according to the latter option, the *Gemara*
preserves a record of the amoraic discussions or provides an
analogue of them.  According to the former, however, Samuel
expressed his teachings in one form to his disciples and they or
someone else subsequent to Samuel then used his teachings.  In
course of time, the comments became subject to the various
transmissional, redactional, and editorial processes through
which *Gemara* itself took shape.  In particular, the *Gemara's*
final literary reworking and enrichment would have greatly
affected the traditions.  This latter alternative assumes that at
least two stages would separate the extant materials from the
original teachings.  The first involves the use to which a later
authority put the tradition when he first cited it.  The second
entails the history of the tradition within the literary work
*Gemara*.

It is in light of the above considerations that we
analyzed the modes of presentation to determine the significance
of the dispute form.  The question therefore becomes: Does the
dispute form give the impression of an actual confrontation
between two masters, and, if so, is that an accurate picture of
its origins?

We found that most items are discrete traditions.
Initially we observed that perhaps eighteen items or seventeen
traditions make up one of the variations of the dispute form and
an additional four items, or three traditions, appear in a series
of closely juxtaposed traditions.  But on closer examination we
observed that only in six instances do the traditions actually
appropriately fit a dispute form.  We further found that eleven
items, or ten traditions may differ but are not presented in a
dispute form.[27]  We observed that several factors indicated that
most items do not represent an actual dispute.  These include:
the location or date of the disputing master; the lack of balance
between the traditions; the role of the pericope's editor in
juxtaposing the opinions; the separate transmission and divergent
versions of the disputing opinion; amoraic attestation that the
disputants do not actually differ but rather refer to different
cases; the patterning of one opinion on Samuel's; and the

tradition's appearance with different adjacent materials as a
gloss in a second location on an identical referent.

    Accordingly, the dispute form does not constitute the
sole standard way in which to present Samuel's materials; this
holds true even where the traditions may actually differ with
another master's opinion.  The evidence in fact suggests the
opposite.  In particular, the eight instances in which traditions
are out of phase with each other, though they differ or ostensibly
make up a dispute form, indicates that the opinions originally
circulated independently of each other and were later juxtaposed
together.

    The lack of balance, moreover, supports the reliability
of the extant formulations.[28]  One reservation we repeatedly face
is how to know that any specific wording or pattern is not secondary to the tradition and imposed upon it sometime after it was
originally formulated.  Our findings concerning the modes of
presentation relate to this problem.  Since we have situations
in which traditions could have been shaped to balance each other
but were not, this structural dissimilarity provides some
attestations to the formulation.  Traditions thus were not
rampantly rephrased.

    The last point receives additional credence from the par-
ticular wording of certain traditions.  Where the formulation of
one tradition responds to the other one, it in effect, attests
it.  Thus in #70 Hanina bar Papa patterns his language on
Samuel's.  Accordingly, the latter's tradition must have already
circulated with its present wording in Hanina's day.[28a]

    What then do we make of the six "appropriate" dispute
forms?  The six instances make up part of a larger number of
items in which Samuel differs with another master.  With the
exception of a series of singletons, practically all the cases
involve Yohanan and Rav.[29]  The role of Yohanan indicates, however, that we do not deal with an actual real-life dispute, for
Samuel could not have confronted this Palestinian master.  This
fact reveals that the dispute form is not intended to imply that
the two masters at a single moment, at the same place addressed
the same issue in the same language.  Rather the form serves to
present divergent opinions on a given matter.  We emphasize this
point because this observation must affect our consideration of
the disputes with Rav.  If Samuel actually did confront another
master, Rav would make up a likely candidate.  But in addition
to the general suspicion as to the meaning of the dispute form,
the instances themselves raise doubts.  Of the thirteen items, or

twelve different traditions in which Samuel is juxtaposed with
Rav, only ten ostensibly employ the dispute form.  In addition,
four of these are problematic.  Numbers 51 and 54 are out of
phase with Rav's teaching; #86 is glossed by Hisda who is able to
claim that the two opinions refer to different circumstances.
Number 115, the fourth item, has a poorly attested attribution
and in its y. analogue, #116, it is disputed by Yohanan only and
the latter's view is transmitted separately, for it appears in
several versions and is the focus of its own analysis.  The six
items, therefore, represent the remains after we have rejected
the other items.  In all, they make up 10.2 percent of the total
Mishnah items and 11.8 percent of the total Mishnah traditions.

In addition to the general reservations as to the fundamental nature of the dispute form, we have particular problems
posed by our sample.  First, the balanced dispute in #56 has an
interesting analogue in b., #54.  There Rav is assigned a Gloss
and Samuel a Liturgical text.  Both are consistent with the
positions assumed in y.  In chapter two we pointed out that the
Liturgical Text could be the fundamental form of the tradition,
though the Gloss, in y., may have formed a logical part of
Samuel's *thought* which even preceded the *enunciation* of his
comment.  The fact that the language of the two Glosses precisely
fits only Rav and not Samuel provided a basis for this speculation.  Secondly, #77=80, a dialogue between Samuel and Judah
presupposes that an immediately preceding tradition presented in
dispute form with Judah was not the only form in which the
traditions circulated.  The dialogue assumes a less formal presentation.  But the dispute form fits the needs of the later masters
and the *sugya*.

The preponderance of the evidence therefore indicates
that a dispute form is in fact a transmissional or literary means
to present traditions.  It is in this light that we must recall
our earlier observations that all the six unproblematic instances
of the dispute form could function as individual responses to
Mishnah.  In each, Samuel could have originally glossed Mishnah.

Finally, we also recall our reference above to the findings of David Goodblatt as to the mode of rabbinic instruction
in Sasanian Iran.  In Volume One we related his conclusions to
our study.[30]  In amoraic Babylonia a master taught a circle of
disciples in a disciple circle and not in academies which
transcended the personality of the individual authority.  This
is not to deny that a master could have contact with another
master as suggested, for example, by the question which Samuel

poses Rav, in #122.  But we do not deal with a context in which
two masters would repeatedly confront each other and shape their
teachings accordingly.

The evidence of the modes of presentation therefore does
not contradict our hypothesis as to the existence of a Mishnah
"Commentary."  Indeed it is consistent with it and conforms to
its characteristics.

Our focus on the modes of presentation has led us to
several conclusions.

1.  It is normal for traditions to appear individually
and if there is an irregular mode it is the use of the dispute
form.

2.  No type of comment or formulation is limited to the
traditions which appear in the dispute form.  All types may be
found in the discretely presented traditions as well.

3.  It is common to find traditions contrasted and
juxtaposed to the teachings of another master.  The processes of
transmitting and using Samuel's teachings, therefore, included
not only shaping them to fit the needs of the context, as in
#72=85, but also contrasting them with the positions associated
with other masters.  The latter could even have involved masters
whom Samuel personally could not have confronted, like Yohanan.[31]

4.  Consequently, the dispute form constitues a means in
which to contrast teachings of different masters.

5.  The picture of the nature of the dispute form conforms
to our present understanding of the ways in which masters actually
taught, viz., to a circle of disciples and not in an academy.  It
also accords with our understanding of the formulations of the
*Gemara* itself.  We return to both of these points in chapters
nine and ten.

6.  Instances in which traditions lack balance or in which
a tradition is patterned after Samuel's comment or responds to it
attest the structure or wording of Samuel's teaching.  Therefore,
formulations and patterns are not solely the result of the later
presentations of traditions but may represent their early stage.

### 5.  *Dispute Form Among the "Related" and "Unrelated" Comments*

The above results concerning the nature of the dispute
form find confirmation from an analysis of the non-Mishnah
comments.  Of the eighty-four items and eighty-one traditions
which are found in the *Gemarot* on Berakhot but which do not
directly comment on Mishnah, thirty-one apparently differ from

an adjacent opinion or another master.  They do so in one of
three basic ways.  First, they may express or assume different
views or principles.  These may be closely juxtaposed to each
other or appear in adjacent pericopae.  We have eight items,
five in b. (2, 62, 96, 111, 112), and three in y. (3, 107, 109).
Secondly, they may share a similar formulation and apparently
form alternative positions.  We have two items, one (90a-b) in
b. and one (23) in y.  These two categories are somewhat similar.
Thirdly, they may constitute part of an actual dispute form.
These account for twenty-one items, sixteen in b. (5, 6, 22, 29, 30,
61, 93, 95, 97, 108, 118, 119, 138, 139, 142, 143) and five in y.
(57, 100, 104, 110, 133).  These thirty-one items make up 36.9
percent of the items and 38.4 percent of the traditions.  We
therefore find that even by the most inclusive calculation,
Samuel's teachings more regularly make up single units than
doublets with opposing opinions.

Moreover, the first two groups, which account for ten
items, exhibit anomalous characteristics.  Some traditions which
actually do differ and are even closely balanced do not make up
an actual dispute form.  Others are more closely juxtaposed yet
appear in some way significantly out of phase with the other
opinion.  If the dispute constitutes the standard mode in which
to present teachings and one which derives from Samuel himself,
then it would be more effectively used.  Rather these traditions
have been contrasted and joined together sometime  after their
initial formation.  Thus, only twenty-one good examples of disputing materials remain and these account for only 25 percent of
the items and 25.9 percent of the traditions.

Focus on the use of the dispute form underscores its
secondary nature.  In all but two of the twenty-one more balanced
disputes (100, 143), Samuel differs with Rav.  The citation of
the opinions of these two masters reflects certain conventions
which undoubtedly emerge from their joint presentation and not
from their original enunciation.  In all but one case (133),
Rav's name appears first.  There are two patterns.  Five items
employ the formula:  "Rav and Samuel, One said, . . . And one
said, . . ."  (4, 5, 29, 30, 139).  Surely this very pattern
attests to the fact that the form is a product of the one who
reports the teachings.  Secondly, we have twelve instances of
the regular dispute pattern, in which the opinions provide different apodoses or else make up alternative positions (22, 57, 61,
93, 95, 97).  Elsewhere, even where we find three or four
opinions on the same matter, Samuel's opinion follows Rav's

(61, 93, 95, 97, 142).   In the single instance in which Samuel's
opinion precedes Rav's (133), the reason is not totally clear.
Perhaps while both masters employ the SRYK L-, "[One] has to,"
formulation, the content of Samuel's requirement in substance is
closer to the preceding two opinions.   The latter, like Samuel,
specify a certain liturgical language whose recitation they
require.   Rav, on the other hand, employs conceptual language,
viz., that one mention the "time," ZMN.   In any event, this single
exception accentuates the otherwise universality and artificiality
of the pattern.   Given what we know concerning these two masters,
it is difficult to believe that in a face to face confrontation
Rav would always lead off.[32]

Attention to the content and characteristics of six of
the contrasting and disputing opinions (23, 63, 100, 104, 110,
119) further reveals that the juxtaposition of the opinions does
not derive from their initial enunciation.   In #119, Samuel differs with Rav as to the orthography of the word *edehen*.   From the
perspective of M. Ber. the tradition makes up an "Unrelated"
comment, though from that of M.A.Z. it constitutes a direct
"Mishnah-Comment."   As we pointed out in chapter two, Lieberman
observes that the interpretations of the opinions found in *Gemara*
reflect different original locations for each opinion.   One
comment is based upon M.A.Z. 1:1 and the other upon 1:2.[33]   If
so, their placement together, as if on the same reference in the
same Mishnah, must derive from the stage of presentation and
transmission.   In a different way this likewise emerges from #100
and #110.   In both, Samuel's opinion precedes an opposing opinion
which is formulated to respond to and differ with Samuel's.   While
the content makes its wording logical, the positions could have
been formulated in some other way.   In any event they were not.
In both cases, we note, the disputants are later Palestinians.
In #100, Yohanan and Resh Laqish, and in #110, Yose.   The
disputants' views, especially in #100, therefore, in effect provide formulary attestation of Samuel's opinion and language.   When
their opinions were presented, Samuel's view had already gained
an integrity of its own and probably had its present wording.
That is, these disputing masters could not have responded to
Samuel in person.   Rather they react to the report of Samuel's
teaching or themselves present Samuel's teaching and respond to
it.   The fourth instance, #104, makes up a very balanced dispute
form.   Samuel differs with Rav and both opinions appear as part
of a *baraita*.   The *baraita* makes up a regular tannaitic formulation but amoraic circles at various times used it to represent

amoraic materials.  By its very nature it is not the record of a
face to face dispute.[34]

The last two cases, #23 and #62, though not part of an
actual dispute are contrasted with juxtaposed traditions which
share a very similar pattern.  But again the differing views are
attributed to people with whom Samuel would not have personally
squared off.  In #23 Samuel's view is followed by one attributed
to R. Bun bar Hiyya, a third-generation Palestinian Amora.[35]
In #62, Samuel's view employs a formulation similar to that of
alternative interpretations of Ex. 32:11, the opening one of which
is attributed to R. Eleazar.  A series of his opinions makes up
the rubric for the larger *sugya*.  While it is possible that
Samuel's formulation might even be secondary and adapted to fit
the context, it is clear that it did not originate with Samuel
himself so as to contrast, in a balanced way, with another
master.[36]  Thus, we again see that the dispute form constitutes
merely a means of presenting two contrasting opinions.  It does
not make up the earliest and most natural way in which a master
would present his own teaching.

The already mentioned instances in which differing opinions are not presented in balanced dispute forms, but could have
been also indicates that while Samuel may have had personal contacts with Rav, the evidence does not suggest that the two
Amoraim squared off.  In #96, 109, 111, and 112, Rav and Samuel
have a discussion or dialogue and each master assumes a different
view to some degree.  In #138, Samuel responds in dialogue to
Rav and then presents an alternative apodosis to the issue at
hand.  Whether or not these formulations are fundamental to the
traditions or only means to explain why Samuel differs with Rav,
those responsible for the pericopae believed the dispute form is
not the only means in which to present teachings.  Finally, we
have a pericope (18-19=52-53) in which a master narrates how he
enabled Samuel to learn of Rav's opinion and then Samuel responded
with an explanation or justification of Rav, which thereby became
associated with it.[37]

The larger sample and control group accordingly throws
light on and confirms five of the chapter's six conclusions,
numbers 1, 3-6.  It is normal for traditions to appear individually (number 1).  It is common to find traditions contrasted and
this was done in order to present teachings together (number 3).
Already Samuel's students compared and related the teachings of
different masters, especially those of Samuel and Rav.  The
masters themselves might have met and expressed different points

of view, but they did not necessarily present them in a dispute
form.   Therefore, that formulation represents a secondary means
of transmission (numbers 3-4).   The specific texts, narrative
actions, and transmissional and literary processes fit our understanding of the history of third-century Judaism and the formation
of *Gemara* (number 5).   Samuel's traditions may have had an
integrity of their own even before they were placed in a dispute
form (number 6).

[1] Cp. the separate classifications in Volume One, pp. 207-210, and our observations below text to n. 2, and subsection 4.

[2] On the dispute form, see Volume One, p. 207, n. 1, and Neusner, *Purities*, 21:164-167.

[3] Cp. also #15. On the individual traditions here reviewed, see their respective entries in chapter two. We footnote only special references.

[4] On Rabbah bar bar Ḥanah, see Hyman, pp. 1076-1078, and Margalioth, cols. 773-775.

[5] See esp. chapter two, text to nn. 35-36.

[6] See chapter two, n. 40.

[7] Cp. the other version, #56. See chapter two, text to nn. 67-71, 82.

[8] See chapter two, text to nn. 77 and 82.

[9] On the other masters see, for Ḥanina Qara: Hyman, pp. 499-500, and Margalioth, cols. 350-351; Yannai: Hyman, pp. 758-764, and Margalioth, cols. 564-565; Bibi: Hyman, pp. 264-265, and Margalioth, cols. 171-172; Yaaqov bar Idi: Hyman, p. 777, and Margalioth, col. 572; Simeon Ḥasida: Hyman, p. 1226, and cp. Margalioth, cols. 865-866. See also chapter two, n. 94, and text to nn. 99-101, 106-108.

[10] See chapter two, text to nn. 128, 137.

[11] See chapter two, text to nn. 157-160.

[12] Ibid., text to nn. 162-165.

[13] See chapter two, text to n. 190, references there, and Tewel and A. Weiss, cited in n. 188. The observation applies whether it is Ḥanina who patterns his language after Samuel's comment or whether it is a later party who places both in the same pattern. Cp. below, text to n. 28a.

[14] See chapter two, text to nn. 223, 238.

[15] Ibid., text to nn. 232-236.

[16] See chapter two, text to nn. 276, 277 to end.

[17] See chapter two, text to nn. 289-290, and 292-294.

[18] See chapter two, #99, 105, subsections iii-iv, esp. text to n. 337.

[19] See chapter two, text to n. 433, and nn. 423 and 436. We assume that Ḥanina is not the first generation Babylonian emigré to Palestine of that name.

[20] See chapter two, text to n. 441.

[21] See chapter two, #132, and chapter six, Category F.

[22] See chapter two, text to n. 498. Note n. 492, re the possibility that "Rabbis" might be the disputant and not "Rav." On the other masters, see Hyman, pp. 128-129, 243-259, and Margalioth, cols. 75, 162-166.

[23]The entries here are not exactly identical to those we list at the beginning of the subsection, where we designated the items that definitely do not belong to a dispute form. We do not include #58 and #59 in the earlier list, as they are not appropriate to it. Likewise we list #67 there but not here as material intervenes between the opinions. On the other hand, while the role of R. Yaaqiv bar Aḥa, the tradent, is not clear, conceivably he may have contributed to the presentation of the materials. See chapter eight, subsection 2.J. We enter #87 here and not there as one might consider that it appears to form a dispute with the opposing opinion, be it within Naḥman's exposition. But Naḥman's role remains blatant.

[24]Regarding #7: y. contains an analogue to the decision along with an opposing view attributed to Rav. See chapter two, n. 5. Regarding #66, 99, and 136: the discrete nature of the traditions is consistent with our analysis of their analogues #65, 105, and 135; to wit, the latter can circulate outside the context of disputing opinions. Number 66 appears in b. Shab. 150b and fits the overview of the *sugya* in b. Ber. 33a. In the latter location an opposing view is cited but even there it is not presented in a dispute form with the other traditions. See chapter two, text to nn. 134-142. On #81-84: see chapter two, #81-85, subsection vi. Regarding #89: cp. chapter two, #87-89, as to the possibility that an opposing tradition, though not in dispute form, may have existed. Number 101's principle is not uncontested but opposing views are not redacted together with Samuel's; see chapter two, #101.

[25]The traditions actually deal with more than twelve *mishnayot*, as the comments on M. 6:1 are informed by other *mishnayot* in that chapter. See above, chapter four, n. 16.

[26]If we had found the reverse situation, that Samuel's traditions consistently appear tightly tied to other materials, as in the dispute form, we would then have to prove that such modes and forms are not the original manner in which the teachings took shape. We face this task in a limited way when we address the items, attributed to Rav and Yohanan, which do appear in a tight dispute form with Samuel's teachings. See below, text to nn. 29-30.

[26a]See above, n. 13.

[27]See above, n. 23.

[28]Compare the argument in Volume One, pp. 213-215.

[28a]Cp. above, n. 13.

[29]See Chart 13. All the other disputants except Hoshia appear only once in juxtaposition with Samuel, and he, an earlier Palestinian, appears only twice.

[30]See Volume One, pp. 213-214, esp. n. 5; Goodblatt, *Rabbinic Instruction*, and "Babylonian Talmud," IV. 2c-d; and Bokser, "Talmudic Form Criticism," and below chapter ten.

[31]See n. 28 and Volume One, p. 214, n. 6.

[32]See chapter ten.

[33]See chapter two, "Analysis of Traditions," #117, especially text to n. 431.

[34]On amoraic *baraitot*, see Goodblatt, "The Babylonian Talmud," *ANRW*, IV, 1.a, esp. pp. 287-288, and Bokser, "Guide," VIII, D, esp. p. 187.

[35]See Hyman, pp. 94-95; Margalioth, col. 31; Albeck, *Introduction*, pp. 218-219; and above, chapter three, n. 19.

[36]See chapter three, n. 72.

[37]See the analogous though somewhat different b. version of the pericope, #13-14, and chapter three, nn. 9-10, 14.  Cp. Zuri, *Rav*, pp. 250-253.

CHAPTER EIGHT

TRADENTS AND ATTRIBUTIVE FORMULAE

## 1.  *Introduction*

Chapters eight and nine take up the chain of names which
introduce Samuel's teachings.  Chapter eight focuses on two problems.  First, is there a difference between those traditions
which are introduced by Samuel's name alone and those which
include also the names of other masters, who ostensibly cited the
comment in Samuel's name?  Secondly, if the name of the tradent
indicates that at least the tradition was known and circulated in
that master's generation, can we trace the stages in the presentation of Samuel's teachings?  Moreover, if we can discern any
patterns, what portions circulated in which generation and what
makes up the "earliest" stage?

The nature of this earliest stage forms the central issue
of this study.  Chapter nine traces which specific masters are
associated with what types, formulations, and percentages of the
traditions, as laid out in chapters four through eight.  With
that data we are able to determine what probably constitutes the
most fundamental portion of the teachings.  Our analysis in chapters eight and nine assumes that if a significant portion of the
teachings are remnants of an actual commentary on Mishnah,
aspects of their transmission and citation might differ from
those of the other traditions.  With this information we may be
able to evaluate the role which tradents played in presenting and
shaping the comments.  Chapter nine concludes the argument with a
discussion on the nature of the Mishnah Commentary.  Where necessary we draw upon the non-Mishnah commentary traditions presented
in chapter three in order to test the accuracy of our hypotheses.
The wider implications of these conclusions are treated in chapter
ten, where we discuss the role of Mishnah commentary as one mode
of response to Mishnah and as a central element in the formation
of *Gemara*.[1]

\* \* \*

Traditions are assigned to Samuel in several ways.  By
definition they include Samuel's name or refer to it with a pronoun, e.g., "He."  Some, but not all, also include the name of a
tradent.  The latter prefaces the tradition with the names of one

or more additional masters who ostensibly cited and handed down
the teaching in Samuel's name.  We find fifteen different names in
numerous combinations of formulae, A-O.  Two or more of these
masters may appear together, a phenomenon we focus upon in P, "Two
Tradents."  Traditions which lack the name of a tradent likewise
make up a significant group, accounting for over 40 percent of
the teachings, and fall into several patterns (iv).

Two additional categories are worthy of special attention.
As Babylonian travelers to Palestine or Palestinians who visited
Babylonia may have played a key role in the transmission of
Samuel's teachings we treat them as a unit, v, A.  Finally, a
sizable number of traditions are attributed to another master in
addition to Samuel.  These "Double Attributions" take several
forms (v, B).

## 2. Tradents

### A.  Judah

Judah, as in the materials presented in Volume One, appears
in the attributions of more traditions than any other master.[2]
The traditions fall into four basic variations:

|  |  |  | Percentage of: | |
| Formulae |  | Totals | Items | Traditions |
| --- | --- | --- | --- | --- |
| Ia. | Said R. Judah said Samuel (b.)<br>1, 7, 8, 44, 51, 70, 116, 136 | 8 | 13.6 | 15.7 |
| Ib. | And did not say R. Judah said<br>Samuel (b.)<br>6 | 1 | 1.7 | 2.0 |
| II. | R. Judah BŠM Samuel (y.)<br>120 | 1 | 1.7 | 2.0 |
| III. | Preceded by or with other masters<br>(several variations):<br>R. _____,<br>R. Judah BŠM Samuel (y.)<br>21, 65, 101, 134 | 4 | 6.8 | 7.8 |
| IVa. | Double Attribution:<br>Said R. Judah said Samuel and thus<br>said R. Yishaq said R. Yohanan<br>71=73 [=74] | 2(1) | 3.4 | 3.9 |
| IVb. | Name + Double Attribution (b.)<br>Said Rava to R. Nahman, Do not<br>dispute R. Judah, for Samuel and R.<br>Yohanan hold like him, for said R.<br>Judah and Samuel and thus said R.<br>Yishaq said R. Yohanan<br>74 [=71=73] | 1(1*) | 1.7 | 2.0 |
| Totals |  | 17<br>(15+1*=15) | 28.8 | 29.4 |

*IVb is counted towards the total of items but not the total of traditions,
as the instance of the latter is considered along with its parallels in IVa.

There are thus seventeen items which make up fifteen
different traditions, five items and traditions in y. and twelve
items and ten traditions in b.  They account for nearly 30 percent
of the teachings.

Seven items differ or are presented as if they differ with
an opinion attributed to another master.  Two, #51 and #134,
appear in what one might consider a dispute form, but even these
comments are not totally balanced with the opposing opinion.

8.  [vs.] Rabbis.

44.  vs. Geniva in the name of Rav--apparently only juxtaposed.

51.  vs. Rav.

65.  [vs.] R. Yohanan [to R. Simeon b. Ba] vs. R. Yaaqov bar
Idi BŠM R. Yiṣḥaq the Great.

70.  [vs.] R. Levi vs. R. Ḥanina bar Papa.

116.  [vs.] R. Benjamin bar Yefet said R. Yohanan.

134.  vs. R. Ḥiyya BŠM R. Yohanan vs. R. Yannai bar Ishmael
BŠM R. Simeon b. Laqish.

B.  *Huna*

Huna, a second-generation Babylonian Amora, studied mainly
with Rav and to a lesser extent with Samuel.[3]

He appears in a single attribution.  A third-generation
master cites in his name and in Judah's name alternative versions
of Samuel's comment that defines the category of "minor" mentioned
in Mishnah.  There are two y. recensions of the *sugya* though the
attribution remains basically constant in both.  The only difference is the sequence of the verb, "said," ꟲMR, and the name of
the first master.  In both recensions, Huna's name is spelled as
Ḥuna, following a common interchange of Ḥ and H.[4]

101.  R. Avina said [or: "Said R. Avina"], *R. Ḥuna and R.
Judah, both of them BŠM Samuel, dispute [the matter]: One
said,  . . . And the other said,  . . . (KDY Š- [originally:
ꟲD Š-]) (y.)*

Yerushalmi contains opinions which substantively differ
with Samuel and which, in fact, cause the revision in the tradition's wording and location within the pericope.  PT thereby makes
the tradition conform to the *sugya*'s overall point of view.  This
may explain why the teaching is not formally contrasted with an
opposing position.

## C.  *Mattena*

Mattena was a second-generation Babylonian, student of
Samuel.  We have one instance of a tradition which he transmits
in Samuel's name.  An anonymous authority cites it in the name of
Zera [= Zeira], who in turn transmits it in the name of Mattena
in the name of Samuel.[5]

> 75.  And did not say R. Zera said R. Mattena said Samuel
> (Blessing Delineation) (b.)

## D.  *Abba*

R. Abba was a second-to-third-generation Babylonian who
emigrated to Palestine, where he tried to present Babylonian
teachings in a good light.  He studied with R. Huna and R. Judah
and possibly had direct access to Samuel, as well.[6]

We have two instances, one each in b. and y.  One has a
double attribution to Rav and Samuel.  Samuel's interest in the
particular problem is attested elsewhere and therefore the attribution to him appears reliable.[7]

> 88.  R. Abba said, *Rav and Samuel both say* (Blessing
> Delineation) (y.)

> 105.  This teaches us in accordance with that which said
> R. Abba said Samuel (Sentence) (b.)

While the traditions are cited as individual items, their
*sugyot* and parallels contain opinions which aver different positions.  Therefore, it may be relevant to mention our earlier
observation as to the possible ways in which the traditions may
have been adapted.  R. Abba, in #88, may follow the common practice of shaping teachings which he cites in Palestine.[8]  Number
105 may be the result of the expansion of a gloss-like comment
originally based upon Mishnah's language.[9]

We also find R. Abba in a key role in a y. *sugya* in which
Samuel's tradition appears, #45=46.  In Volume One we raised the
possibility that in such cases, especially where the traveler
appears in a tradition which disputes or glosses Samuel's opinion,
that the traveler may have likewise cited Samuel's tradition.
Here R. Abba as well as R. Zeira cite different versions of an
opposing Rav opinion.[10]

> 45=46.  R. Abba BŠM Rav . . . vs. Samuel ($^C$D Š-) vs. R.
> Yermiah, R. Zeira BŠM Rav . . .//Said R. Hezkiah, R. Abba is
> more stringent . . . (y.)

*E. Naḥman*

Naḥman was a third-generation Amora who had access to Samuel's traditions, though it is not clear if he did so directly from Samuel.[11] We have two instances in which he cites Samuel's traditions, both from b.[12]

55.   Said R. Naḥman said Samuel (Sentence) (b.)

87.   Taught (DRŠ) R. Naḥman in the name of our Rabbi--and who is he?  Samuel--  (Blessing Delineation) (b.)

In both cases Naḥman's citation in effect makes use of an earlier teaching of Samuel and someone else challenges Naḥman.[13]

In #55, Naḥman attests the association of the "Give us discernment" prayer (HBYNYNW) with Samuel.  The latter makes up Samuel's definition of Mishnah's reference to "the substance of eighteen" (#54).  In y.'s version of the latter tradition, #56, the comment appears as a gloss, "The beginning of each blessing," which a different master, perhaps in Samuel's name, defines as HBYNYNW (#56a).  Rava and Mar Zutra attack the tradition which Naḥman cites.

In #87, Naḥman himself contrasts Samuel's view with a different one attributed to "our friends who come from the Land of Israel--and who are they?  Ulla--in the name of R. Yohanan." Naḥman glosses both and states that the two views dispute, though later in the *sugya* it is claimed that they do not differ.  The exposition apparently follows a pattern for setting out two opinions, for Hisda employs it in an adjacent exposition.  Hisda likewise glosses the juxtaposed opinions, and, perhaps following his general tendency, he harmonizes them.[14]

*F. Zeira*

Zeira was a third-generation Babylonian emigré to Palestine.  Abraham Goldberg in particular has pointed to the ways in which Zeria represents Samuel's and other Babylonians' traditions in Palestine.[15]  We have three instances, one from b. and two from y.

65.   R. Ze^cira, R. Judah BŠM Samuel (Sentence) (y.)

75.   And did not say R. Zera said R. Mattena said Samuel (Blessing Delineation) (b.)

89.   R. Ze^cira BŠM Samuel (Blessing Delineation) (y.)

In two of the cases Zeira cites the tradition through an intermediary master.  In the third, the transmitter is not

specified.  In the latter instance, Samuel's teaching applies a
rule to two different circumstances.  This may reflect part of
Zeira's role in adapting Samuel's traditions, a matter we extensively discussed in chapter two.[16]  In this light we note that the
immediately previous tradition which R. Abba transmits in the name
of Rav and Samuel, #88, and which others transmit in the name of
different masters, is formulated as a general statement of the
rule dealt with in Zeira's cited tradition.  Therefore, the latter
either in part differs with the above or else explains and limits
it.  While #75 in its context is not explicitly contrasted with
another opinion, #65 is.  The latter is in a fairly well balanced
dispute with a tradition attributed to R. Yishaq the Great and in
a less balanced one with a comment attributed to R. Simeon b. Ba.
The pericope's editor either contrasts the three opinions or
glosses them to make their differences explicit.

      R. Zeira figures in the pericopae of three additional y.
traditions, #44=46, 56, and 120, and in each may have transmitted
Samuel's teaching.  In #45=46 we also find R. Abba; they both
cite different versions of Rav's opposing opinion.  The possibility that Zeira or another traveler may have cited Samuel's teaching accords with our hypothesis developed in Volume One and
mentioned above.[17]


*G.  Joseph*

      Joseph was a third-generation Babylonian Amora and disci-
ple of Judah, from whom he may have received Samuel (and Rav)
traditions.[18]  We have three instances, two from b. and one from
y.

      21.  R. Huna, R. Idi, R. Joseph, R. Judah BŠM Samuel
(SRYK L-) (y.)

      68.  Said R. Joseph, We know neither this nor that.  Rav
and Samuel already arranged for us a "pearl" in Babylonia
(Liturgical Text) (b.)

      81.  [Cooked *habis*--R. Judah said, . . . R. Kahana said,
. . .]  Said R. Joseph, Seize that of R. Kahana, *for Rav and
Samuel both say* (Blessing Delineation) (b.)

      While the three are presented as individual items and not
as part of a dispute form, they may actually differ with the
opinions of other masters.[19]  Two, #68 and #81, are instances of
Double Attributions and are jointly attributed to Rav and Samuel.
Moreover, #81 appears in two additional locations, though those

instances lack the reference to Joseph and Kahana, #82=84. We consider these below under the entry for "Items Without a Tradent."

## H.   Ḥiyya bar Abin [or Abba]

R. Ḥiyya bar Abin, or Abba, at times called just "R. Ḥiyya," was a third-generation Babylonian who emigrated to Palestine. His access to Samuel's teachings may have been through R. Huna.[20] We have two instances, one each in b. and y.

58.   Said to him R. Ḥiyya bar Abin [to R. Huna bar Ḥinena], You are right, for said Samuel (First Person Report) (b.)

121.   R. Ḥiyya BŠM Samuel (KL ZMN Š-) (y.)

In both cases, opposing opinions appear in the pericope, though they do not make up balanced dispute forms. In #58, Ḥiyya cites Samuel's teaching to support Huna bar Ḥinena's comment, and in #121, the tradition is juxtaposed but out of balance with Yohanan's view.

## I.   Avina

R. Avina was a third-generation Babylonian emigré to Palestine, who had studied with R. Huna.[21] He appears in one attributive formula and transmits Samuel's comment in the name of R. Huna and R. Judah. The latter two masters apparently had cited two different versions of Samuel's tradition and Avina transmits both. In chapter two we saw that while the substance of the comment became revised to integrate it into its larger context, the attribution basically remained unchanged. The earlier recension, preserved in Gen. R., differs only in placing the verb "said," ᵓMR, before and not after Avina's name.

101.   R. Avina said [or: "Said R. Avina"], *R. Huna and R. Judah both of them in the name of Samuel, dispute* [the matter]: *One said, . . . And the other said, . . .* (KDY Š- [originally: ᶜD Š-]) (y.)

## J.   Yaaqov bar Aha

R. Yaaqov bar Aha was a third-, and possibly fourth-, generation Palestinian Amora.[22] We have two y. instances in which he directly cites Samuel's tradition.

67.   R. Yaaqov bar Aha BŠM Samuel (Gloss) (y.)

78.   R. Yaaqov bar Aha BŠM Samuel (Blessing Delineation) (y.)

In both instances Yaaqov cites the tradition ostensibly without an intermediary, though in fact he may rely upon one. While this is logically, and historically, necessary, considering Yaaqov flourished in Palestine, the larger content of #67 may confirm this hypothesis. In an immediately preceding tradition, Yaaqov comments on the ultimate authority who stands behind two traditions. The second one had been transmitted in the name of a Babylonian emigré to Palestine, Eleazar. Yaaqov thus traces the teaching further back. It is therefore possible that he had access to Samuel's teachings through an intermediary, in a similar manner, but in the cases of #67 and #78, the attributive formulae lack the names of the earlier authority.[23] As he was an associate of various Babylonian emigrés to Palestine, Yaaqov would have had no dearth of sources.

*K. Idi*

R. Idi, a third, and possibly fourth-, generation Babylonian emigré, appears in the attributive formula of one tradition, from y.

21.  R. Huna, R. Idi, R. Joseph, R. Judah BŠM Samuel (SRYK L-) (y.).

Since elsewhere R. Idi is associated with R. Joseph, the mention of both is not problematic. It remains unclear, however, if Huna reports the tradition jointly with Idi or does so in Idi's name. In terms of our overall analysis, though, both alternatives have the same effect.[24]

*L. Yonah*

R. Yonah was a fourth-generation Palestinian Amora.[25] He appears in a single instance of an attributive formula of a y. tradition.

134.  R. Yose BŠM R. Judah, and R. Yonah and R. Judah BŠM Samuel (BTHYLH KDY . . . WLBSWP ᵓPYLW . . .) (y.)

Yonah apparently cites a tradition which Judah had transmitted in Samuel's name. Yose's role in the tradition is not clear. If this master is the second-to-third-generation Babylonian emigré to Palestine by that name, perhaps he cites the tradition in R. Judah's name and R. Yonah's point is that the tradition actually derives from Samuel.[26]

*M.  Huna*

R, Huna, a fourth-to-fifth-generation master of this name,
emigrated from Babylonia to Palestine.  He appears in one y.
attributive formula.

21.  R. Huna, R. Idi, R. Joseph, R. Judah BŠM Samuel
(SRYK L-) (y.)

As pointed out above in conjunction with R. Idi, R. Huna
may cite the tradition either along with Idi or else in Idi's
name.  Elsewhere they are associated together and individually as
students of R. Joseph.[27]

*N.  Rava*

Rava, a fourth-generation Babylonian master, apparently
cites a b. tradition attributed to Samuel.[28]

74.  *Said Rava to R. Nahman, Do not dispute R. Judah, for
Samuel and R. Yohanan hold like him, For said* R. Judah said
Samuel, and thus said R. Yishaq said R. Yohanan (Blessing
Delineation) (b.)

Rava appears in a Dialogue with Nahman and refers to
Samuel's tradition.  A text of the tradition is supplied, introduced by the phrase, "For said."  The substance of the comment
fits Rava's reference and may therefore constitute part of his
statement.  If so, he would attest the tradental role of Judah.
In any event, Rava's reference does attest the presence of a
double attribution to Samuel and Yohanan.

*O.  Yose b. R. Bun*

A Palestinian master by the name of R. Yose b. R. Bun
appears as the tradent of one tradition in the name of Samuel.
Elsewhere in *Gemara* this attributive formula does appear again.[29]
But the references to this master do not decisively indicate his
chronology and several scholars, therefore, have suggested that
two individuals by this name flourished in Palestine.  The first
lived in the third-to-fourth generation and the second, in the
fifth.  The latter one traveled to Babylonia for a time.[30]  In
either case, Yose b. R. Bun would have received Samuel's tradition
through some intermediary source.

135.  For said R. Yose b. R. Bun BŠM Samuel (Sentence)
(y.)

An anonymous authority cites the tradition to demonstrate
that Huna's opinion, which is in dispute with Yohanan's, agrees
with Samuel's.

## P.   Two Tradents

Six traditions, two from b. and four from y., have the
names of more than one tradent in the attributive formula and
account for 10.2 percent of the total items and 11.8 percent of
the total traditions.   Above we catalogued each tradent in his
respective individual entry, though we now focus on the phenomenon
as a whole.

21.   R. Huna, R. Idi, R. Joseph, R. Judah BŠM Samuel
(SRYK L-) (y.)

65.   R. Ze^Cira, R. Judah BŠM Samuel (Sentence) (y.)

74.   *Said Rava to R. Nahman, Do not dispute R. Judah for
Samuel and R. Yohanan hold like him, for said* R. Judah said
Samuel, and thus said R. Yishaq said R. Yohanan (Blessing
Delineation) (b.)

75.   And did not say R. Zera said R. Mattena said Samuel
(Blessing Delineation) (b.)

101.   R. Avina said [or: "Said R. Avina"], *R. Huna and R.
Judah, both of them BŠM Samuel, dispute* [the matter]: *One
said, . . . And the other said, . . .* (KDY Š- [originally
CD Š-]) (y. in PT and Gen. R.)

134.   R. Yose BŠM R. Judah, and R. Yonah and R. Judah BŠM
Samuel (BTHYLH KDY . . . WLBSWP . . .) (y.)

Number 74 differs from the other formulae in that the
second tradent is actually a person who in a discussion cites the
tradition and is thus not part of the actual "chain."

The central question as to traditions with two tradents
is: Why do these items mention more than one transmitter and
thereby delineate several stages in the transmission while other
comments do not?   The lack of a full chain applies even to items
which blatantly assume that some unmentioned person did participate.   This applies, for example, to #99 where Samuel is cited
in a y. pericope merely as "Samuel said," and to #78 where a
later Palestinian constitutes the single tradent, viz., "R.
Yaaqov bar Aha BŠM Samuel."   When we correlate the several variables in the traditions in chapter nine we will determine if a
pattern emerges.   At this point, however, we can make several
observations.

Each item includes the name of a second-generation disciple or student of Samuel. In five, we find Judah's name and in the sixth, Mattena. One includes Huna along with Judah. The disproportionate role which Judah plays accords with the overall large percentage of traditions with which he is involved.

In addition, each item includes the name of a third-generation master, which at times is preceded by the name of a later master. In #21 we have R. Huna and R. Idi, fourth- and fifth-generation Palestinians, respectively, who had been in Babylonia, and Joseph, a third-generation Babylonian. In #65 and #75, we find Zeira, a third-generation Babylonian emigré or traveler to Palestine. In #74 Rava, a fourth-generation Babylonian master, and Nahman, a third-generation Amora, appear. In #101, we have Avina, a third-generation Babylonian emigré to Palestine. In #134, Yose, possibly the third-generation Babylonian by that name, plays a role, as does R. Yonah, a fourth-generation Palestinian. Thus each y. tradition involves a Babylonian emigré, who apparently is the one who cited the tradition in Palestine. In other words, a Babylonian emigré transmits Samuel's student's citation of Samuel's teaching. Evidently, the identity of the one who cited the tradition in Palestine is perceived to be important, something which makes sense since Samuel's teachings are not indigenous to Palestine. We find a somewhat analogous situation within y. itself. While a pericope incorporated in the same *Gemara* in which the material originated--e.g., a Caesarean pericope in y. Neziqin--does not mention a tradent but appears anonymously or only with the name of the author, the same pericope in a *Gemara* from a different locality--e.g., non-Neziqin, from Tiberias--includes the name of a tradent.[31] But a comparable explanation can only provide part of the answer, for as mentioned we have other Samuel traditions in y. which do not specify the one who brought the tradition to Palestine or in some other way do not conform to the pattern of a double tradent.[32]

### 3. *Traditions Without a Tradent*

Attributive formulae which specify only Samuel's name and not that of any tradent fall into two basic variations. These include: (A) Samuel's name + Verb + Comment; and (B) Verb + Samuel's name + Comment. In all, these formulae introduce 49.2 percent of the items and 45.1 percent of the traditions and therefore a significant portion of the overall sample.[33]

*A.   Samuel + Verb + Comment*

This first pattern has twenty-two instances, eleven from
b. and eleven from y., which make up eighteen distinct traditions,
eight from b. and ten from y.  One b. tradition, #82=84, has a
third instance, #81, which is preceded by the name of a master
who cited the tradition.  This category accounts for 37.3 percent
of the total items and slightly less of the total traditions; if
one counts #82=84 towards the traditions, we have 34.6 percent of
the total traditions, and if one does not, 33.3 percent of the
total traditions.[34]

All the entries except for one has as the verb a form of
the word "said," $^\jmath$MR.  The exception, #122, uses the interrogative
"asked," B$^C$Y.

*Samuel + Verb + Comment*

|  | | Provenance | | Sequence in Series/ |
| Item | | b. | y. | Dispute* |
| --- | --- | --- | --- | --- |
| 45=46. | Samuel said ($^C$D Š-) | | x | 3 or 4 |
| 54. | Samuel said (Liturgical Text) | x | | 2 |
| 56. | And Samuel said (Gloss) | | x | 2 |
| 60. | Samuel said ($^\jmath$YN SRYK L-) | | x | 2 |
| 72=85. | *Rav and Samuel who both say* (Sentence) | x | | |
| 76=79. | Samuel said (Blessing Delineation) | x | | 2 |
| 82=84. | *Rav and Samuel both say* (Blessing Delineation) | x | | |
| 83. | *Rav and Samual both say* (Blessing Delineation) | x | | |
| 86. | Samuel said (Blessing Delineation) | x | | 2 |
| 99. | Samuel said (K$^\jmath$N B- . . . . K$^\jmath$N B-) | | x | |
| 103. | And Samuel said (First Person Report) | | x | |
| 115. | Samuel said (LPYKK + Sentence) | | x | 1 |
| 117. | And Samuel said (Gloss) | | x | 2 |
| 122. | *Samuel asked Rav* (Question) | x | | |
| 125. | And Samuel said ($^\jmath$YNW SRYK L-) | | x | 2 |
| 128. | Samuel said (Sentence) | | x | |
| 129. | Samuel said (First Person Report) | | x | |
| 140. | And Samuel said (Simile + Proof text) | x | | 2 |

*Unless otherwise indicated the series of juxtaposed opinions or the
dispute involves two views or positions.

The entries are of several kinds.  Number 122 stands out as
a narrative.  While a tradent's name could have preceded the
attributive formula, it could not be part of the chain itself,
because the latter describes or narrates what Samuel did, viz.,
"asked."  Number 122 thus makes up a special case.  Numbers 82=84,
as mentioned, have a third instance as #81, in which we find the
name of the master who cites the tradition.  Numbers 72=85, 83,
82=84, all from b., are jointly attributed to Rav and Samuel and
deal with blessings over diverse foods.  The other items are
attributed to Samuel alone.  Moreover, all the b. items are comments which are autonomously formulated and can circulate without
being dependent upon Mishnah.  They consist of complete Sentences,
First Person Reports, a Question, or a dispute form which contains
a protasis and apodosis.[35]  In contrast to some of the y. items,
therefore, there are no instances of Glosses directly on Mishnah.

Most of the y. items appear in opposition to another master's opinion.  The ones that are not part of a dispute form have
close b. analogues in comparable places on the same *mishnayot* and
therefore are items that must have circulated in a relatively
early period.  Number 99 is paralleled by #105, which is cited or
known by a second-generation master, #103 by #102, with the formula of, "Said Samuel," #128-129, by #126-127, which has the formula of "[and] said Samuel," and which together make up part of
an early unit or pericope.  Below and in chapter nine we return
to this observation as it may help explain which y. items contain
the name of a tradent and which do not.

The formulation of the items may also be correlated with
the presence and absence of a disputing opinion.  Those without a
contrasting position generally make up complete sentences.  In
particular we have eight unopposed traditions, six Sentences or
First Person Reports (72=85, 82=84, 83, 103, 122, 128, 129), and
one double Gloss (99).  The remaining ten traditions appear juxtaposed to or in dispute with an adjacent tradition and Samuel's
opinion generally is not placed first.  Eight of these are the
second of two items in one of the variations of the dispute form
(54, 56, 76=79, 85, 117, 125, 140).  All eight are brief comments
or just apodoses, and are rather well balanced with the opposite
opinion.  Of the other two traditions, #45=46 appears among a
series of different versions of Rav's opinion and thus in effect
makes up the second in a sequence, first Rav's comment and then
Samuel's.  Number 115 precedes an opinion of Yohanan (which may
also be attributed to Rav), and both are full sentences.  In this

instance it may have been logical to place Samuel's opinion first.
It fits into the pericope and is provided with bridging language
to connect it with the preceding material to which it substantively relates.  Yohanan's opinion, on the other hand, deals with
the topic Samuel mentions and is shaped to respond to his formulation.  While it could be presented alone as a discrete item in
the manner in which it indeed did circulate, as attested by the
b. versions, it would then not appear integrated into its present
context.

B.  *Verb + Samuel + Comment*

We have six distinct instances of the second pattern--one
in y. and six items which represent five traditions in b.

|  | Item | Provenance b. | y. | Comment |
|---|---|---|---|---|
| 59. | For said Samuel (First Person Report) | | x | Cited in dispute; has close b. parallel |
| 77=80. | Said Samuel to R. Judah (Dialogue + Blessing Delineation) | x | | |
| 102. | Said Samuel (Sentence) | x | | Has close y. parallel |
| 126. | Said Samuel (Gloss) | x | | Part of early unit. |
| 127. | And said Samuel (First Person Report + Discussion) | x | | Part of early unit |
| 132. | Said Samuel (Gloss + Proof text) | x | | Precedes Rav in dispute |

As five of the six entries come from b., the pattern is
basically one found in that *Gemara*.  The single y. instance, #59,
is not an actual exception, as it is required by the specific use
of the tradition.  Someone refers to Samuel's teaching and employs
the standard bridging letter D-, which is regularly prefixed to
the verb.  In any case, in Volume One we pointed to Lieberman's
observation that in y. the sequence of the verb, ᵓMR, "said," and
the master's name is not significant.  This is in contrast to the
situation in b.  As Categories A and B indicate, we have instances
in both patterns.  The comments in Category A, in which the name
precedes the verb, are either jointly attributed to Rav and Samuel
or else are the second opinions in a dispute.  In the joint attribution, the pattern requires Rav's name to precede.  Those in

Category B, in which the verb precedes the name, on the other
hand, do not appear in a dispute form. At most they may open a
series of opposing opinions. Accordingly, the standard pattern
requires the verb to precede the master's name, and the variation,
for a disputing second opinion, has the name precede. Alternatively, the latter is the standard and the former makes up the
variation.

The four b. items provide different types of information
but with the possible exception of one, #126, they are all formulated as autonomous complete sentences. Number 126 initiates a
portion of material whose remainder has a close y. analogue. All
the others, except for #132, likewise have close parallels or analogues in the opposite *Gemara* on the same *mishnayot*, which probably indicates that they all circulated at a relatively early
time. We lack comparable supporting evidence to suggest that
#132 also circulated at an early time, though it would accord
with the fact that while it appears in a very well balanced dispute with Rav, it is out of phase with other opinions on the
matter. The mode of presentation indicates that the dispute
made up a unit before the other opinions were juxtaposed to it.

*C. Summary*

The following chart summarizes the data in A and B.

CHART 14

TRADITIONS WITHOUT TRADENTS*

|  | Pattern | Provenance: b. | y. | Total | Percentage |
|---|---|---|---|---|---|
| A. | (Name + Verb) | 11([8]7) | 11(10) | 22([18]17) | 37.3 (34.6 to 33.3) |
| B. | (Verb + Name) | 6(5) | 1 | 7(6) | 11.9 (11.8) |
|  | TOTALS | 17([13]12) | 12(11) | 29([24]23) | 49.2 (46.4 to 45.1) |

*Numbers in parentheses denote traditions less repetitions. The variations in
A and the totals are due to whether or not one considers #82=84 as an independent tradition, for in #81 we find a master who cites the tradition. The mode
of calculating the percentages can also vary. If one adds A and B = 34.6 +
11.8 = 46.4. But 24/52 = 46.2%.

BT contains more items than PT and a respectable number
of both patterns. In terms of pattern A alone, however, the
entries are evenly spready in both *Gemarot*. Moreover, assuming

that the choice of one or the other pattern might be significant,
we observe that pattern A with the name preceding the verb appears
when a tradition disputes a foregoing opposing opinion.

The materials in dispute generally tend to be well balanced and make up one of the variations of the dispute form.  Most
of the complete sentences have close analogues in structurally
similar places in the opposing *Gemara* which therefore may indicate
that these traditions circulated at a rather early time.  This
correlation gains significance when we try to account for the
presence or lack of the name of a tradent in the attributive
formulae of y. traditions.  Where a tradent appears it is generally a traveler from Babylonia.  His name often stands before the
name of one of Samuel's students.  Accordingly, these traditions
perhaps are those which a third-to-fourth-generation traveler from
Babylonia received in Babylonia from one of Samuel's students and
later cited in Palestine.  On the other hand, the other traditions
without the name of a tradent, circulated in an earlier period,
perhaps in conjunction with Mishnah or as a formalized tradition.
They may have gained an integrity of their own, for example, when
they were cast into a dispute form in Palestine.

### 4.   Additional Patterns

A.   Travelers: Specified
     and Reconstructed

Above we referred to the possible role that travelers may
have taken in the transmission of Samuel's teachings.[36]  In order
to receive an overview of this phenomenon we integrate the separate entries.  Where a traveler's name appears in the chain it
makes sense that he is the one who brought the tradition to Palestine.  But this may likewise apply to the instances in which a
traveler's name appears not in the attributive formula of Samuel's
opinion, but in that of an adjoining tradition, especially where
it disputes or glosses Samuel's tradition.

We have identified six travelers.[37]  Two travelers are
jointly associated explicitly in the chain of one tradition, #21.
Two appear in traditions adjacent to #45=46, in different versions
of an opposing Rav opinion.  Others appear singly.  In all, the
travelers are found in the chains of nine traditions, two in b.
and seven in y., and their role may be reconstructed in the transmission of four additional y. traditions.  They thus probably
played a role in the presentation of eleven traditions, which make
up 18.6 percent of the total items and 21.6 percent of the total

traditions.  We also take note of the role of one Palestinian,
Yaaqov bar Aha, who apparently scrutinized traditions which travelers cited.

1.  Abba

88.  R. Abba said, *Rav and Samuel both say* (Blessing
Delineation) [Steamed vegetables] (y.)

105.  This teaches us in accordance with that which said
R. Abba said Samuel (Sentence) [M. 7:1 vs. 7:4] (y.)

[45=46.  R. Abba BŠM Rav . . . vs. Samuel (<sup>C</sup>D Š-) vs.
. . . R. Yermiah, R. Ze<sup>C</sup>ira BŠM Rav [Duration of prohibited
prayer near excrement and urine] (y.)]

2.  Zeira

65.  R. Ze<sup>C</sup>ira, R. Judah BŠM Samuel (Sentence) [*Havdalah*
over a cup and in *Tefillah*] (y.)

75.  And did not say R. Zera said R. Mattena said Samuel
(Blessing Delineation) [Raw bottle-gourd and barley-flour]
(b.)

89.  R. Ze<sup>C</sup>ira BŠM Samuel (Blessing Delineation) [Ground
and unground steamed turnip heads] (y.)

[45=46.  R. Abba BŠM Rav . . . vs. Samuel (<sup>C</sup>D Š-) . . .
R. Yermiah, R. Ze<sup>C</sup>ira BŠM Rav [Duration of prohibited prayer
near excrement (and urine))] (y.)]

[56.  And Samuel said (Gloss) [Definition of "substance
of eighteen," the abridged *Tefillah*] // R. Ze<sup>C</sup>ira sent to R.
Nahum via R. Yanai b. R. Ishmael, What is the "Seven the
substance of eighteen" of Samuel? (y.)]

120.  R. Judah BŠM Samuel (KDY Š-) [Criterion of "enjoy-
ing" light to say blessing over it] // R. Ze<sup>C</sup>ira (y.)]

3.  Hiyya bar Abain (or Abba)

58.  Said to him R. Hiyya bar Abin [to R. Huna bar
Hinena], You are right, for said Samuel (First Person Report)
[*Musaf* individually] (b.)

121.  R. Hiyya BŠM Samuel (KL ZMN Š-) [Criterion for duration of Grace's requirement] (y.)

4.  R. Avina

101.  R. Avina said [or: "Said R. Avina"] *R. Huna and R.
Judah, both of them in the name of Samuel, dispute* [the mat-
ter]: *One said, . . . And the other said* (KDY Š- [originally
<sup>C</sup>D Š-]) [Definition of the category "minor"] (y. in PT and
Gen. R.)

5-6.   Idi and Huna [the fourth-to-fifth-generation Huna]

21.   R. Huna, R. Idi, R. Joseph, R. Judah BŠM Samuel
(SRYK L-) [*Shema<sup>c</sup>* standing] (y).

7.   Palestinian scrutinizer and associate of travelers: Yaaqov
bar Aha

67.   R. Yaaqov bar Aha BŠM Samuel (Gloss) [Location of
*havdalah*] (y.)

78.   R. Yaaqov bar Aha BŠM Samuel (Blessing Delineation)
[Palm-heart] (y.)

B.   *Double Attributions*

Eleven items, which make up six different traditions, are
jointly attributed to a second master in addition to Samuel.[38]
They thus account for 18.6 percent of the total items and 11.8
percent of the total traditions.   The double attributions have
two basic patterns, with variations.

1.   The double attribution appears within a single formula.

68.   Said R. Joseph, We know neither this nor that.
Rav and Samuel already arranged for us a "pearl" in Babylonia (Liturgical Text) (b.)

72=85.   *Let us say that it constitutes a refutation of
Rav and Samuel who both say* (ᵓYN . . . ᵓLᵓ Sentence) (b.)

81=82=84.   [81: Said R. Joseph, Seize that of R.
Kahana, *for*] *Rav and Samuel both say* (Blessing Delineation) (b.)

83.   *Rav and Samuel both say* (Blessing Delineation)
(b.)

88.   R. Abba said, *Rav and Samuel both say* (Blessing
Delineation) (y.)

In #81, R. Joseph is represented as citing the formula
along with the tradition.   He does so in an ostensible discussion
to support the position of R. Kahana.   Joseph, in #68, likewise
refers to the joint liturgical activity of Rav and Samuel.   In
#88 it is R. Abba who cites Rav and Samuel.   These three tradi-
tions accordingly are entered into their respective places above,
under the name of the tradent.   The others, 72=85, 82=84, and 83,
lack the name of a tradent and appear in the category for such
items, above.

2.   Two attributive formulae are juxtaposed before the substance of the tradition.

71=73=74.   [74: *Said Rava to R. Nahman, Do not dispute
R. Judah, for Samuel and R. Yohanan hold like him, for*]

said R. Judah said Samuel and thus said R. Yishaq said R.
Yohanan (Blessing Delineation) (b.)

In #74, Rava cites and attests the double assignment to
Yohanan and Samuel. As the three instances include the name of a
tradent, they appear in their respective entries above.

The instances of both patterns introduce traditions concerning liturgical matters. Number 88 presents a special abridged
*Tefillah* while the remaining comments involve Blessing Delineations. The focus in #72=85, a reworking of #81=82=84, has been
altered to respond to a different problem. Actually, though,
#81=82=84 and #83 themselves all derive from a single tradition.

At present we still do not fully understand the origin of
the double attribution.[39] At least four possibilities exist, as
we point out above and in Volume One. The two masters jointly
said the tradition. The two masters separately enunciated the
tradition and fortuitously used the same language. The two masters
separately enunciated the tradition and the language of one of them
has been dropped and the other one's employed. The two masters
separately enunciated the tradition and the extant tradition incorporates a compromise between their two formulations or employs a
third formulation and, therefore, is not identical with either of
their wordings.

The first possibility assumes that the attributive formula
reflects the social context out of which the tradition emerges,
viz., that two masters squared away, while the others do not. The
latter assume that the two traditions--and attributions--have been
combined by a third party, a process that we found applies to the
dispute form. That is, the one who sets out the material is
responsible for the attribution as well as the placement of the
tradition in the dispute form. Since this more likely conforms
to reality, we prefer one of the latter possibilities. Moreover,
to some degree the specific traditions upon which we focus may
support this hypothesis. In #81 and #84 we discern the role of
Joseph and Rava respectively and they may be the authorities who
join the two attributions.[40] In addition, #72=85, the reformulated tradition, preserves its earlier attributive formula. This
proves that we should not automatically conclude on the basis of
the formula that the assigned masters together said the exact
words jointly attributed to them. In any event, while we remain
unsure to what degree the language of the traditions and attributions derive from Samuel's circle, the other traditions, including
the related items (RC and RS) attest Samuel's interest in these
topics. They therefore properly belong in our study.

### 5. Conclusions

Charts 15 and 16 summarize and synthesize the above material.

1.   Charts 15 and 16 indicate that the largest *single* group consists of the comments without tradents.  They account for 49.2 percent of the items and 45.1 percent of the traditions. Thus the use of tradents is not the overwhelming standard pattern. On the basis of our initial observation, it appears that those materials without a tradent either are briefly formulated in balanced dispute forms or else make up complete sentences and have close analogues in structurally similar locations in the opposite *Gemara*.  The dispute form may have required only the name of the comment's author.  Alternatively, once the tradition became cast in the dispute form it made up a unit of its own.  In either case the tradition was cited in that formulation without a tradent and perhaps in a relatively early period.  Earlier we reviewed the several modes of presentation and concluded that the dispute form is not fundamental to the tradition yet it probably originates at a relatively early time as a means to transmit Samuel's teachings along with those of another master.  Those comments that are formulated as a gloss, in particular, may have originated with that formulation directly on Mishnah.  The remaining items without a tradent, the complete sentences with analogues in the other *Gemara*, clearly circulated at a relatively early period. In chapter nine we fully correlate the characteristics of the traditions and there we shall be able to refine this observation. If correct, it implies that half of Samuel's comments on Mishnah already circulated at a relatively early period.

2.   As to the items with a tradent, Judah is the only master who stands out and he does so prominently.  He is involved in about 29 percent of the items and traditions and accordingly must be considered Samuel's main disciple.  As other students or associates we find only Huna, Mattena, and possibly Abba, and they contribute only an additional 5.1 percent of the items and 5.9 percent of the traditions.  If we consider Abba among the travelers we are left with only 1.7 percent of the items and 2.0 percent of the traditions.  Even if we would individually consider Huna's and Judah's alternative versions in #101 as two traditions, we would only have an additional 2 percent.[41]  Samuel must therefore have had only a limited number of students and Judah predominated among them.

The next stage in the presentation of Samuel's teachings
involves the third generation masters and travelers, Nahman,
Zeira, Joseph, Hiyya bar Abin, Avina, and possibly Abba.  They
had access to Samuel's ideas and comments either directly from
the master or else through one of his students, chiefly Judah.
Less Abba, they account for 11.9 percent of the items and 13.7
percent of the traditions.  Since Abba not only studied with
Samuel but also traveled to Palestine, he may be joined to this
group and if so he would provide an additional 3.4 percent of the
items and 3.9 percent of the traditions.  We may also be able to
trace the role of the tradents in the transmission of an additional four items (45=46; 56; 120, which mentions Judah as a
tradent), 6.8 percent of the total, which make up three distinct
traditions, 5.9 percent of the total.  These travelers also
appear as secondary tradents in four items (65, 75, 101, 21);
therefore they are actually involved in the transmission of an
additional 6.8 percent of the items and 7.8 percent of the traditions.  In all, we can discern the efforts of these masters in
the presentation of 28.9 percent of the items and 31.4 percent
of the traditions.[42]

Moreover, these travelers apparently played a key role in
the transmission of Samuel's traditions in Palestine in the third
generation.  Above we tentatively suggested that, in the y. traditions, the naming of a tradent indicates that the comment was
cited in the locality of the pericope's origin, i.e., Palestine,
in the generation of that master, while those teachings without
the tradent may have been from an earlier period.  In chapter
nine we shall focus on this question in greater detail.

The final stage in the history of Samuel's teachings consists of the circulation and use of the comments in the late
third to fifth amoraic generations.  With the single exception of
Rava all such items come from y. and involve Palestinians.  Therefore, if the traditions whose chains name a tradent first arrived
in Palestine in the tradent's generation, then that generation
represents those traditions' "first Palestinian generation."
Moreover, the late third to fourth generation of masters in turn
becomes the "second" generation of the use, scrutiny, and application of those comments.  By this time in Babylonia, on the other
hand, Samuel's teachings would have become well known and already
subject to evaluation.  They could accordingly circulate in their
own terms and need not be specifically cited.  At most one could
apply them to new situations or use them in the discussion of some

CHART 15

TRADENTS AND ATTRIBUTIVE FORMULAE

| Tradent and Generation | Total Entries* | Secondary Tradent** | | | | Percentage of | | + As Reconstructed | Comment |
|---|---|---|---|---|---|---|---|---|---|
| | | b. | y. | + | = | Items*** | Traditions*** | | |
| II. Judah | 17(15) | 12(10) | 5 | 4 | | 28.8 | 29.4 | | 3 instances of double attribution of one tradition; 1 item has alternative version transmitted by Huna. |
| Huna | 1*** | | 1*** | 1 | | [1.7] | [2.0] | | Has an alternative version transmitted by Judah. |
| Mattena | 1 | 1 | | 1 | | 1.7 | 2.0 | | |
| II-III Abba | 2 | 1 | 1 | | | 3.4 | 3.9 | 2(1) | 1 has double attribution; #45-46 reconstructed with Abba or Zeira. |
| III Nahman | 2 | 2 | | | | 3.4 | 3.9 | | Adapting traditions. |
| Zeira | 3 | 1 | 2 | 2 | | 1.7[5.1] | 2.0[5.9] | 4(3) | Only #89 directly cites Samuel. |
| Joseph | 3 | 2 | 1 | 1 | 1 | 3.4[5.1] | 3.9[5.9] | | In #21 as secondary tradent cited by Huna and Idi. #81 with double attribution; #68 directly cites Samuel. |
| Hiyya | 2 | 1 | 1 | | | 3.4 | 3.9 | | Cites Huna and Judah. |
| Avina | 1 | | 1 | | 1 | [1.7] | [2.0] | | |
| III-IV? Yaaqov b. Aha | 2 | 2 | | | | 3.4 | 3.9 | | Scrutinizer and associate of travelers. |
| Idi | 1 | 1 | | | 1 | [1.7] | [2.0] | | |
| IV- Yonah | 1 | | 1 | | 1 | [1.7] | [2.0] | | With (late) Huna, cites Joseph. |

| | | | | | | Comments |
|---|---|---|---|---|---|---|
| Huna | 1 | | 1 | 1 | [1.7] | [2.0] | With Idi, cites Joseph. |
| Rava | 1 | 1 | | 1 | [1.7] | [2.0] | In dialogue; cites double attribution. |
| ?III-IV or V / Yose b. R. Bun | 1 | | 1 | | 1.7 | 2.0 | |
| 2 Tradents | 6 | 2 | 4 | | [10.2] | [11.8] | #21 has several tradents. |
| Without Tradents | 29(33) | 17(12) | 12(11) | | 49.2 | 45.1 | Reconstruction: 45=46;56;120. #82=84 has tradent in #81, where counted as tradition; here only as "items." |
| Double | 11(6) | 10(5) | 1 | 4(3) | [18.6] | [11.8] | |

*The number in parentheses denotes items less repeated instances and thus the total of distinct traditions.

**Secondary tradents. The "+" lists additional entries in which the master appears as a secondary tradent. The "=" lists the number of entries in the first columns in which the master appears as a secondary tradent. To determine the instances of a primary role, subtract this number from the total in column one. See "Comments" and Chart 16.

***Totals for percentages are calculated on the basis of 59 items and 51 traditions. Only the name of the authority closest to Samuel is considered and not secondary tradents. Number 101 is counted under the version with Judah and not Huna. Numbers 82=84 are counted as two instances of items but not as a separate tradition, as its third instance, #81, appears under the name of the tradent Joseph. The percentages in brackets denote the respective figure's percentage within the sample of 51 and 59, though the entries are counted in another category; accordingly these totals are not considered towards the final total of 100%.

CHART 16

PRIMARY ROLE OF TRADENTS AND TRADENTLESS TRADITIONS

| Generation | Tradent | Entries | BT | PT | Percentage | |
|---|---|---|---|---|---|---|
| II | Judah | 17 (15) | 12 (10) | 5 | 28.8 | (29.4) |
| | Mattena | 1 | 1 | | 1.7 | (2.0) |
| II-III | Abba | 2 | 1 | 1 | 3.4 | (3.9) |
| III | Nahman | 2 | 2 | | 3.4 | (3.9) |
| | Zeira | 1 | | 1 | 1.7 | (2.0) |
| | Joseph | 2 | 2 | | 3.4 | (3.9) |
| | Hiyya | 2 | 1 | 1 | 3.4 | (3.9) |
| III-IV | Yaaqov bar Aha | 2 | | 2 | 3.4 | (3.9) |
| III-IV or V | Yose b. R. Bun | 1 | | 1 | 1.7 | (2.0) |
| A. Total with Tradents | | 30 (28) | 19 (17) | 11 | 50.8 | (54.9) |
| B. Without Tradents | | 29 (23) | 17 (12) | 12 (11) | 49.2 | (45.1) |
| A + B | | 59 (51) | 36 (29) | 23 (22) | 100.0 | (100.0) |

other topic.[43] Thus the numerous instances of the Blessing
Delineations and in particular the late adaption of one into a
sentence addressing the definition of "food," #72=85, may indicate
that the traditions might be reapplied, anonymously cited, and
further analyzed.  But the initial task of presentation had been
completed.[44]

Chart 17, on the following page, broadly outlines these
stages in the history of Samuel's comments on Mishnah.  The right
side of the chart indicates where we might add or subtract
entries.

### 6.  Comparison with Non-Mishnah Comments

#### i.  Introduction

The focus on the presence or lack of tradents in the
attributive formulae of Samuel's "Related" and "Unrelated" Comments throws light on the above conclusions.  First, it tends to
confirm certain of the observations.  Secondly, though, it raises
questions as to what may be deemed unique characteristics of the
"Mishnah-Comments."  If we argue that certain traits are characteristic of an actual Mishnah Commentary or reflect the remnants
thereof, then ostensibly we should not find those elements among
the non-Mishnah commentary items as well.  The question then
becomes how these non-Mishnah comments may have circulated and the
degree to which that mode is analogous to that of the Mishnah-
comments.  That there be some similarity is not surprising for,
as we already observed in chapter four, the Mishnah played a
formative role even for most of the "Related" and "Unrelated"
items.  The resulting necessity to refine our argument and thesis
provides a natural transition to chapters nine and ten where we
examine the nature of Samuel's Mishnah Commentary and trace how
Mishnah commentary provided a transition to independent teaching.

#### ii.  Items Without a Tradent

Of the eighty-four items and eighty-one traditions we find
forty-nine which appear without a tradent.  We divide these into
several types.

#### A.  Verb + Samuel's Name

We have twelve instances in which the verb precedes
Samuel's name in the attributive formula.  Ten are in b. (4, 13,
14, 39, 42, 63, 69, 90, 138, 141) and two in y. (2, 3).  While one
of these (90) should be deleted, as it may actually have a tradent,

CHART 17

STAGES IN THE PRESENTATION OF SAMUEL'S TEACHINGS*

| Stage | Percentage of | | Variations | Percentage of | |
|---|---|---|---|---|---|
|  | Items | Traditions |  | Items | Traditions |
| A. Immediate disciples | 33.9 | 35.3 | Less Abba | 30.5 | 31.4 |
| B. Second-third Generations | 11.9 | 13.7 | With Abba and reconstructed [+ secondary roles] | 22.1<br>28.9 | 23.5<br>31.3] |
| C. Late third to fifth | 5.1 | 5.9 | ............ [+ secondary roles] | 5.1<br>11.9 | 5.9<br>13.7] |
| Without tradent: possibly early(?) | 49.2 | 45.1 | Less reconstructed 4(3) | 42.4 | 39.2 |
| Totals | 100.2 | 100.0 |  | 100.1 | 100.0 |

*The percentages are calculated on the basis of the total number of items and traditions within a category and not on the addition of rounded-off individual entries or group of entries. The latter figure may slightly exceed the former one and this accounts for the slight discrepancies between the percentages in Chart 16, above, and those here in Chart 17, in the "variations."

another (96) perhaps should be added to the list.  It forms part
of a Dialogue which requires the statement to open with, "Said to
him Samuel, . . ."  The two y. items are both *baraitot*, which
probably determines the sequence.  All Samuel-*baraitot* in y.
place TNY, "teaches," before Samuel's name.[45]  The pattern accordingly constitutes a regular sequence for teachings only for b.

*B.  Samuel's Name + Verb*

        There are thirty-six items and thirty-five traditions in
which the reference to Samuel precedes the verb.  We can subdivide
the category into four groups.

1.  "Samuel" + Verb

        In twenty-six items and twenty-five traditions Samuel's
name (and not a pronoun or another means of reference) precedes
the verb.  Twelve come from b. (22, 61, 62, 95, 97, 106, 108, 123,
130a-b, 131, 142, and 93, whose reading is suspect), and fourteen
items and thirteen traditions come from y. (17, 19=53, 23, 24, 26,
27, 43, 57, 100, 104, 118, 119, 133).  We further divide this
category into three groups:

   a)  "Samuel" + the verb "said" plus an additional verb.  There
       are two instances, one in b. (123) and one in y. (24).

   b)  "Samuel" + a verb other than "said."  There is one
       instance, from b. (130).

   c)  "Samuel" + the verb "said."  This group consists of the
       remaining twenty-three items and twenty-two traditions.
       Though the formula itself in 19=53 includes only Samuel's
       name, we should properly subtract these two items, as the
       preceding portion of the pericope identifies the tradent.

2.  "He" + Verb (= "Said")

        We have four instances in which the pronoun "He," which
refers to a previous mention of Samuel, precedes the verb.  Two
are from b. (111, 124) and two from y. (25, 109).

3.  Dispute Pattern

        We have five instances in which Samuel's name appears in
an attributive formula tailored to a dispute form.  All are from
b. (5, 6, 29, 30, 139).

   a)  "Rav and Samuel, One said, . . . And one said, . . ."
       There are three instances (5, 6, 139), each used to set out

an exegetical dispute.  A verse serves as the protasis
and the opinions as alternative apodoses.[46]

b) Pattern (a) along with an alternative attribution: "Rav
and Samuel, and some say R. Yohanan and R. Eleazar.  One
said, . . . And one said, . . .:"  There are two items
(29, 30).

## 4.  Double and Alternative Attribution

The pattern consists of "And Rav and Samuel both say, and
some say it [in the name of] R. Yohanan and R. Eleazar (alt.,
"Resh Laqish"].  We have one instance (64) from b.[47]

## C.  *References to Samuel*

We have three pericopae which do not make up statements
attributed to Samuel but rather contain references to the master.
Two come from b. (31, 32); the second one places the reference in
the mouth of R. Papa.  One instance comes from y. (28).  The
latter uses the full form of Samuel's name, "Samuel bar Abba," an
appellation occasionally found in y.[48]

## D.  *Conclusions*

Chart 18 summarizes the several patterns.

The category of materials Without a Tradent, as among the
direct Mishnah-comments, accounts for the largest single group of
traditions.  We have forty-nine of eighty-four items and forty-
nine of eighty-one traditions which represents 58.3 percent of
the items and 60.5 percent of the traditions.

The category employs several formulae but each one (A, B,
C) is not equally used.  The sequence of the verb + Samuel's name
primarily appears in b.  The y. instances are apparently due only
to the specific usage.  The second major sequence, "Samuel" or
"He" + verb, on the other hand, has a significant number of
entries in both b. and y.

BT follows an apparent pattern in its use of the two
formulae.  Generally where Samuel disputes a contemporary, especially Rav, we find sequence B, with Samuel's name preceding the
verb.  Moreover, his name and/or his opinion follows that of the
other master.  PT generally places the name first, though here,
as Lieberman suggests, the sequence of name and verb may be incon-
sequential.  These observations accord with those made on the
basis of the more direct "Mishnah-comments."

CHART 18

"RELATED" AND "UNRELATED" TRADITIONS WITHOUT TRADENTS

| Type | Totals | b. | y. | Problems |
|---|---|---|---|---|
| A. Verb + Samuel's Name | 12 | 10 | 2 | - #90; + #96 |
| B. Samuel's Name + Verb | | | | |
| 1. | 26 (25) | 12 | 14 (13) | - (#19=53 of y.) = 12; #93 = reading suspect |
| 2. | 4 | 2 | 2 | |
| 3. | 5 | 5 | 0 | |
| 4. | 1 | 1 | 0 | |
| C. References to Samuel | 3 | 2 | 1 | |
| Subtotals (A + B + C) | 51 (50) | 32 | 19 (18) | - 90; + 96; - (19=53) = - 2 (1) y. |
| Total | = 49 | 32 | 17 | |

A close examination of the locations of the "Related" and
"Unrelated" tradentless traditions indicates that while b. contains representatives of each, y., in effect, does not.  As we
concluded in chapter four, all the y. instances of "Unrelated"
traditions initially did pertain to Mishnah.  They refer to a non-
Berakhot passage or to a *baraita* that supplements M. Berakhot
or belong to a larger pericope relating to Mishnah.  Only from the
perspective of the single tradition and from its later use within
the *Gemarot* on M. Berakhot does it appear unrelated to M. Berakhot.
This observation applies to the items with tradents, as well, to
which we now turn.

### iii.  Items With Tradents

The non-Mishnah teachings include the name of a tradent
in the attributive formulae of thirty-five items which make up
thirty-two distinct traditions.  Some formulae also contain the
name of a second master who ostensibly cited the tradition along
with the earlier tradent.  The following lists lay out by generation the role of the various tradents.

| Generation | | Name; Items; Observations | Role as Primary Tradent |
|---|---|---|---|
| II. | 1. | Judah.  17 items, all in b. Standard pattern: 9, 10, 12, 20, 33, 34, 36, 37, 38, 47, 48, 49 [Naḥman = alternative reading]. Narrative describing: 11, 40-41. Decision within narrative: 90b [90a also?].  Blessing Delineation within narrative: 91.  Judah's fellows: 90a?  Secondary tradent in 91. | 17 [#49?] |
| | 2. | Huna.  1 from y. (113).  Embedded within narrative which Zeira apparently presents.  Cp. reading of #110. | 1 |
| | 3. | Mattena.  3(2) instances.  #11 in b. and 15=16 in y.  #11: back-ground for Judah.  15=16 directly cites, though Abba glosses and perhaps presents it. | 2(1) |
| | 4. | Taḥlifa bar Avdimi.[49]  2 in b. (50, 112), both with analogues. | 2 |
| | 5. | Ḥannan bar Ba.[50]  Definitely describes Samuel's action (18=52) and probably cites his comment (19=53), all in y. with b. analogue.  R. Ami glosses. | 4(2) |

| Generation | Name; Items; Observations | Role as Primary Tradent |
|---|---|---|

|  | 6. Kahana. 1 from y. (110) as immediate tradent. Persented perhaps by Yose, the disputant, or by Zeira. | 1 |
|  | 7. Menashia bar Yermiah. 1 from b. (137). With Samuel as one of several alternative attributions. | 1 |
|  | 8. Ami (or Ṭabi) bar Mattenah.[51] 1 from b. (143). | 1 |
|  | [Eleazar with reconstructed role in #27?] | |
| II-III. | 9. Abba. Tertiary role of #11 of b. Reconstructed role in 15-16, 17. | |
|  | 10. (R)Abbbah bar R. Huna. Part of chain in #11 of y. | |
|  | 11. Amram. Secondary tradent in #98 of b. | |
| III. | 12. Naḥman. Primary role in longer chain in #98 of b. Variant to Judah in 49. | 1   +1(#49)? |
|  | 13. Yosi bar Abba. Inquires; in effect background of #11 of b. Unclear reading in #110.[52] | |
|  | [Zeira. Reconstructed role in: 109, 111, 113, 114?, 118-119?][53] | |
|  | [Asi. Reconstructed role in: 24-26, and possibly 27, which Eleazer, though, more likely transmits.] | |
|  | [Ami. Reconstructed role in 19 and possibly 18.] | |
| III/IV?-IV. | 14. Yaaqov bar Aḥa. Scrutinizer. 2 items from y. (92, 94). | 2 |
|  | 15. Idi bar Abin.[54] Tertiary role in 98 of b. | |
|  | [Avun=Avin=Rabin.[55] Possible reconstructed role in 90.] | |
| IV. | 16. Yosi. Apparently begins long chain, 110 of y.[56] | |
|  | 17. Aḥa. In y., definitely in 114 and probably correct reading in 107.[57] | 2 |
|  | 18. Papa. Reference to Samuel in 35 of b. | 1 |
| Total |  | 35(32): 23b.&12(9)y. |

Six different travelers between Babylonia and Palestine apparently played a role in the transmission of Samuel's traditions.

1. Eleazar. Reconstructed role in 27.                    = 1

2. Abba. Reconstructed role in 15=16;                    = 3(2)
   definite role in 17.

3. Zeira. Definite role in 109. Cp. b.                   = 2+4
   parallel, 111. Definite role in 113,
   and possibly in 114. Reconstructed
   role in 107 and 118-119 on the basis of
   earlier role in *sugya* = 2 definites; 4
   possibles.

4. Asi. Reconstructed role in 24-26 and                  = 3
   possibly 27, which Eleazar, though, more
   likely transmits.

5. Ami. Reconstructed role in 19, a tradi-               = 1+1?
   tion which he glosses, and possibly 18.

6. Avun. Reconstructed role in 90, a y.                  = 1
   tradition transferred from y. Suk. He
   glosses it and another b. tradition.
                                                         _____

TOTAL                                                    11 (10) + 5?

The list of tradents decisively indicates that we again find that Judah is involved in the largest number of traditions and he is the only master who stands out. He transmits seventeen traditions; if #49, however, is assigned to Nahman we actually have sixteen traditions. Of the materials with tradents he is responsible for 48.6 percent of the items and 53.1 percent of the traditions. Of the total "Related" and "Unrelated" materials this represents 20.2 percent of the items and 21.0 percent of the traditions.

In addition to Judah we find seven other second-generation masters but they account for only twelve items and nine traditions, eight items and five traditions in y. and four of each in b. Two of the masters, Huna and Mattena, also appear in the attributions of the direct Mishnah comments. Among the latter masters only Nahman, who cites one tradition, could possibly have reported the teaching directly from Samuel. The remaining five items, presented by Yaaqov bar Aha and Yosi, in addition to Papa's reference must ultimately have derived from an intermediary authority who is not mentioned. We can discern one such secondary role in the work of the travelers. These six individuals definitely function in eleven items and ten traditions and possibly in five additional traditions. This represents 13.1 percent of the items and 12.3

percent of the traditions up to a maximum of 19 percent of the
items and 18.5 percent of the traditions.

## iv.  Conclusions

1.  Chart 19 summarizes the spread of the "Related" and
"Unrelated" materials.

We can compare these totals with those of the direct
"Mishnah-Comments."  (See Chart 20.)

PT apparently contains a lower percentage of "Related"
and "Unrelated" items and traditions than "Mishnah-Comments."
This may be the result of the nature of our categories.  As we
laid out in chapter four, all the y. items initially formed part
of a Mishnah focus.  They either relate directly to a mishnah or
to a *baraita* that supplements Mishnah or else belong to a unit of
materials, the rest of which treats a mishnah.  As several of the
items take up *mishnayot* not in Berakhot, from the perspective of
Berakhot they were classified as "Unrelated," i.e., unrelated to
M. Berakhot.  Accordingly, all the true "unrelated" materials that
address matters totally unconnected to Mishnah are found in b.[58]
BT, therefore, has to make room for a greater range of the overall
corpus of Samuel teachings.

Our observation that y. apparently contains Samuel-
traditions that originally dealt with Mishnah, even though they
may now be reused by a later Palestinian authority for some other
purpose, would suggest that these materials represent an early
stage of Samuel's heritage.  They probably therefore do not
derive from later masters who "discovered" and reported the teachings in Samuel's name.  Likewise, the y. stories concerning Samuel
would be those that travelers, especially those of the third
generation, told about him.  They, accordingly, do not represent
merely late narratives concerning the early master Samuel.  We
can confirm our deduction as to the early date y. materials
reached Palestine from the place of the tradents in the attributive formulae and from other factors, to which we now turn.

2.  A close examination of the place or absence of
tradents in the formulae of the y. materials reveals a consistent
image.  There are twelve items and nine distinct traditions which
include the name of a tradent in the transmissional chain (15=16;
18-19=52-53; 92; 94; 107; 110; 113; 114).  In each case, except
ostensibly one, the role of the traveler is explicit or recon-
structable.  We can thus trace a traveler's role in the following
items:

## CHART 19

### "RELATED" AND "UNRELATED" TRADITIONS: TOTALS

| Type | Amounts | b. | y. | Totals | b. | y. | Percentage |
|---|---|---|---|---|---|---|---|
| 1. With Tradents: Generation | | | | | | | |
| II | 29 (26) | 21 | 8 (5) | | | | |
| III | 1 | 1 | | | | | |
| Late III+ | 5 | 1 | 4 | | | | |
| Subtotal | | | | 35 (22) | 23 | 12 (9) | 41.7 (39.5) |
| 2. Without Tradents | | | | 49 | 32 | 17 | 58.3 (60.5) |
| Total | | | | 84 (81) | 55 | 29 (26) | |

## CHART 20

### SPREAD OF ALL THE TRADITIONS

| Type | Totals | b. | y. | Percentage Per Type | |
|---|---|---|---|---|---|
| | | | | b. | y. |
| MC | 59 (51) | 36 (29) | 23 (22) | 61.0 (56.9) | 39.0 (43.1) |
| R & UR | 84 (81) | 55 | 29 (26) | 65.5 (67.9) | 34.5 (32.1) |
| | 143 (132) | 91 (84) | 52 (48) | | |

15=16.  Mattena + Abba.  As the tradition is a gloss on an antecedent text the attributive formula along with the tradition probably made up a unit that could not be broken by the addition of the tradent.

18-19=52-53.  Ḥannan bar Ba + Ami.  Ami's role appears definite in #19 and probable in #18.

94.  Yaaqov bar Aḥa + Avun.  Yaaqov bar Aḥa himself is known as a scrutinizer of traditions.  See below.

107.  Aḥa + Zeira.  The editor of the pericope relates the tradition to the context or makes the relationship explicit.

110.  Kahana + Zeira.

113.  Huna + Zeira.

114.  Aḥa + Zeira.  The tradition forms part of material which relates to a narrative which Zeira explicitly transmits.

The single exception is #92.  But this is attributed to Yaaqov bar Aḥa whom we have seen elsewhere as a Palestinian who associated with Babylonian emigrés and travelers and who scrutinized traditions as to their original authors.  It is thus likely that he had access to #92 through a traveler, whose name though does not appear within the pericope.  Of note, the tradition constitutes a decision as to the law in a *baraita*.  As we have seen elsewhere such teachings generally include the name of a tradent.  We suggested that the tradent's name in effect contributes to the impact of the teaching, for the tradent is supporting the adjudication which he cites.  This might account for the presence of Yaaqov bar Aḥa's name in the formula, as he may be lending his weight to Samuel's decision.  We thus see that each instance of a tradition with a tradent conforms to the pattern of a Tradent + Traveler.  Since we can safely assume that a teaching with which a traveler is associated was known and circulated in Palestine at least in the generation of that traveler, all of these materials were known basically in the third generation.[59]

The y. items without a tradent and whose formulae only include, or refer to, the name of Samuel also appear to have circulated at a relatively early period.  We have seventeen items which make up seventeen distinct traditions (2; 3; 17; 23; 24-25, 26-27; 28; 43; 57; 100; 104; 109; 118-119; 133).

One or more of several factors invariably indicate that the traditions in effect did circulate early.  We can reconstruct the roles of eight travelers; point to b. analogues to five of

the y. traditions; and twice observe the use of a form which is
used in early amoraic times.  Often we can discern some factor
which further explains why the teaching lacks a tradent or why
the absence of a tradent poses no problem.  We thus find four,
and actually six, traditions which appear as part of a narrative;
two which are formulated as a *baraita:* and six which belong to
fairly well balanced dispute forms, five of which are with Rav
and one with Yohanan and Simeon b. Levi, who therefore provide
formulary attestation for Samuel's teaching.  The following list
lays out the tradentless materials.

2.  *Baraita.*

3.  *Baraita.*

17.  Reconstructed role of Abba; with b. analogue, #9,
which has a tradent.

23.  Brief statement whose patterned language appears in
an adjacent tradition of a third-generation Palestinian who
may thereby provide attestation of Samuel's teaching.

24-25.  Reconstructed role of Asi; narrative of Samuel's
action and statement.

26.  Reconstructed role of Asi; clearly relates to M.
Niddah.  Part of unit 24-27.

27.  Reconstructed role of Asi or more likely Eleazar;
part of unit 24-27.

28.  Transfered from elsewhere; reference re Samuel.

43.  Brief statement with later added verse; with b.
analogue #42.

57.  Dispute form with Rav; with variant version in b.,
#37. [60]

100.  Dispute form with Yohanan and Simeon b. Levi, who
provide formulary attestation; on M. San.

104.  Part of *baraita* dispute form with Rav; with alternative version in b. #98. [61]

109.  Reconstructed role of Zeira; part of narrative;
with b. analogue, #111.

118-119.  Reconstructed role of Zeira; dispute form with
Rav, originally on M. Eruv. and M.A.Z.; with b. analogues. [62]

133.  Juxtaposed ostensible dispute with Rav, both using
SRYK L-, "[one] has to," pattern to set out gloss-like additions on a *baraita* attested subject.

* * *

Our analysis of the y. materials with and without a
tradent thus reveals that in every case we have sufficient ground
to conclude that the teachings circulated in Palestine by about
the third generation, or at times the early fourth generation.
This observation accords with our conclusion in chapter four that
all the y. materials originally pertained to Mishnah. They either
referred to a passage not in M. Berakhot or to a *baraita* that
supplements Mishnah, or else they formed part of a pericope, the
rest of which integrally is connected to Mishnah. We classify
these teachings as "Unrelated" items due to the way in which the
later Palestinian authorities employed them within y. Berakhot.

Accordingly, this selection means that y. does not incorporate the full Samuel "heritage." While we discuss the implications of this in chapter ten, we may make the following observations at this juncture. Early Amoraim naturally responded to
Mishnah and its topics as well as to pressing contemporary needs,
even if not mentioned in Mishnah. Later Amoraim concerned themselves with both of these areas as well as with the teachings of
their amoraic predecessors. They treated the latter as subjects
in their own right. PT does not tramsmit Babylonian teachings
from all of these areas. In particular, it lacks the extra-
mishnaic materials. BT, on the other hand, includes them,
undoubtedly, because they formed an integral part of the
Babylonian heritage. Samuel's students and students' students
naturally preserved and presented the full range of their master's
teachings. But in Palestine the authorities had their own earlier
Palestinian masters and their natural interest centered in transmitting their own indigenous heritage. Their interest apparently
extended to non-Palestinian teachings when they related to something already of interest to them, primarily Mishnah and its
themes, which indeed makes up the major common denominator between
Babylonian and Palestinian masters. Accordingly, Palestinians
represented in y. originally exhibited an interest in Samuel's
teachings when they appeared relevant to Mishnah.[63] This hypothesis is based upon our interpretation of the present sample of
Samuel's teachings in y. Future research must test it on the
basis of additional materials and masters. Likewise it must
inquire if the reverse is true as well. For example, is there a
pattern as to which Palestinian materials are included in BT?

3. In our analysis of the "Related" and "Unrelated"
materials with and without a tradent, we have observed various
phenomena. When we discerned comparable features among the

Mishnah-Comments, we employed some of them to support our argument
that an actual Mishnah Commentary existed.  For example, we concluded that the lack of a tradent may be due to the use of the
teaching or the form in which it is presented or else it may
reflect the fact that the tradition circulated in an early period
when it sufficed to include Samuel's name alone.  In addition,
such materials may have circulated prior to those items which
include the name of a tradent and a traveler and which we posited
reached Palestine in the third generation.  The above factors
would apply to brief glosses that were meant to circulate along
with Mishnah, items which would make up a central element of a
Mishnah commentary.  We must, accordingly, more closely correlate
the characteristics of the "Related" and "Unrelated" items to
determine if comparable phenomena vitiate our conclusion as to
the original function of such brief "Mishnah-Comemnts."  Therefore, we now review and synthesize our earlier observations as
to the nature of the b. and y. tradentless "Related" and "Unrelated" materials.

First, eighteen traditions have analogues in the opposite
*Gemara* and therefore undoubtedly represent material that circulated in Samuel's name at a relatively early time.  These include:
#13-14 of b., analogous to y. #19=53, which has a second genera-
tion tradent, whose identity emerges in light of #18=52; #17 of
y., analogous to b. #9, which mentions the name of a tradent,
Judah; #24-27 of y. whose b. analogues appear outside of
Berakhot;[64] #57 of y., whose b. analogue #37 has a tradent; #42
of b., analogous to y. #43; #104 of y., whose b. analogue, #98,
has a tradent; #108, whose partial b. analogue, #107, has a
tradent; #109, of y., analogous to b. #111; and #118-119, analogous to traditions in b. Eruv and b. A.Z.  We also have two
adjacent traditions which form part of a larger unit, the rest of
which has an analogue in the other *Gemara* and therefore probably
also represents an early unit of material.  This entails #130-131,
which forms part of a larger pericope with b. "Mishnah-Comments"
#126-127, whose y. analogues are #128-129.

Secondly, twelve items belong to some type of a narrative
which describes what Samuel did or purports to record what Samuel
said (24-26, 28, 31, 32, 35, 96, 109, 111, 123, 124).  The name
of a tradent would be inappropriate before such a citation or
reference.  Earlier we discussed the suitability of such biograph-
ical descriptions of Samuel within a Mishnah commentary.  As a
result of our conclusion that all the y. materials originally

in effect related to Mishnah or formed part of a unit which
relates to that text, we can understand why such stories would
be presented and preserved in Palestine.[65] Those narratives
unconnected to Mishnah, which in effect means the b. ones, pose
a different problem. Naturally the problematic ones are those
brief statements attributed to Samuel which did not originally
circulate with the story in which they are presently embedded.
The narrative context could not throw light on the earlier history
of the tradition nor explain its possible lack of a tradent.
Below we return to this problem.

Thirdly, sixteen items directly relate to a source other
than M. Berakhot. If their formulation to whatever degree
represents a fundamental stage of the teaching, this characteristic would be similar to many Mishnah-comments which we claim
originally circulated along with Mishnah. These items would
have been intended--at one point--to circulate along with some
work. These include four traditions that gloss *mishnayot* other
than Berakhot (33, 100, 118, 119)[66] but which are cited in the
*Gemarot* of Berakhot for various reasons. Two teachings go along
with a *baraita* (39, 63).[67] Eleven items respond to a verse and
could form part of a midrashic unit structured around biblical
verses in general or selected verses or themes (5, 6, 29, 30, 61,
62, 130-131, 142, 143). The relationship to these three different
types of texts suggests that a person might know or search out
*mishnayot, baraitot,* and verses or groups of verses and respond
to them. We consider this possibility immediately below and in
chapter ten.

Fourthly, nine tradentless items are in fact briefly
formulated. While one is a single item on a verse without a
juxtaposed opposing opinion, most make up a dispute and often an
exegetical dispute form (57, 93, 95, 104, 108, 133, 138 [in
part], 139 and 131, the one on a verse by itself).

There are two additional items which do not fit into one
of the above categories. Both are autonomously formulated
teachings. One, #23, is a brief statement and depends upon its
context for comprehension. Since it employs a phraseology found
also in the immediately following teaching attributed to a
third-generation Palestinian, that master in effect provides a
third-generation date of attestation. Considering that it is a
First Person Report in which Samuel describes his practice concerning a Mishnah related matter we can understand why someone
transmitted and presented it. The remaining item, b. #141, is a

somewhat longer phrased tradition which can be considered as a
"wisdom teaching." We can understand why someone might remember
Samuel's "Torah" on such a matter.

What do we make of the above observations? Where we
found briefly formulated teachings among the Mishnah-comments
we suggested that they originally glossed Mishnah itself. We
claimed that those that appear within a dispute form likewise
originally individually glossed Mishnah and only later were cast
into a different mold. Would this apply to the brief "Related"
and "Unrelated" items? Does not our classification of traditions
as "Related" or as "Unrelated" teachings by definition preclude
the possibility that they circulated along with Mishnah?

There are several alternatives. Brief items that relate
to a verse do not pose a problem. It is reasonable to assume
that Samuel responded to selected or successive biblical texts
and that such comments would be remembered along with the
verses.[68] But what do we do with the other teachings? Could he
have addressed and glossed independent statements or themes?
Alternatively, did disputes on such matters originally make up
two separate autonomously formulated full statements? In light
of the history of rabbinic literature, the latter is a theoretical
possibility, as tannaitic collections including Mishnah provide
examples of how single items become joined into a dispute.[69]
Hence, did these teachings initially circulate as brief comments
or did they originally make up longer traditions which someone
cited and reformulated? If the former hypothesis is true, however, how did such brief items circulate, for they could not have
glossed Mishnah?

As mentioned above and as we discuss in chapters nine
and ten, in addition to focusing on Mishnah Samuel must have
addressed independent issues as well. He found many of these
topics mentioned in Mishnah, if only in passing. A student or
later authority could collect groups of these traditions. The
several tannaitic works, especially Mishnah, provide examples of
such collections. While Mishnah constitutes a highly redacted
corpus, its style and composition indicate that it incorporates
materials drawn from diverse collections of teachings of individual masters or teachings organized by a formal trait or subject.[70]
Consequently, it is reasonable to assume that Samuel's disciples
or some other post-Samuel circle likewise would have collected,
transmitted, and repeated the teachings of Samuel.[71] Moreover,
teachings on topics and texts other than Mishnah itself must have

existed. Amoraim knew of *baraitot*. Various Samuel "Mishnah" and
"Related" comments assume a development of Mishnah's law, often
the very stage which is found in a *baraita* or toseftan passage
and which Samuel, in turn, further develops. Indeed, in chapter
four, we traced how Mishnah played a formative role even among
the "Related" items.[72] Masters atomized the text of Mishnah and
they treated each element as a subject in its own right and not
just in terms of the overall themes and perspectives of Mishnah.
In chapters nine and ten we attempt to trace the processes
through which Mishnah-comments in fact lead into independent
teachings.

  We therefore can conclude that sources in addition to
Mishnah existed and could have elicited Samuel's response. But
such teachings on a verse or theme or even on a *baraita* could not
provide the framework which determined the structure of *Gemara*.
The crux of this discussion therefore hinges upon the manner in
which *Gemara* emerged. We can undoubtedly find similarities
between Mishnah comments and non-Mishnah comments which respond
to and clarify a non-Mishnah Berakhot text or theme. Moreover,
both of these types of comments share characteristics with
traits of tannaitic works, including Mishnah and Tosefta. In
chapter nine, for example, we observe that Mishnah and Tosefta
both contain precedents for glosses. But *Gemara* differs qual-
itatively from Mishnah and from Tosefta. *Gemara* does not consist
merely of a collection of glosses on *baraitot* or biblical
verses.[73] Though we presently know the *Gemara's* final literary
enrichment greatly affected the amoraic materials and contributed
much to the so-called "talmudic arguments," *Gemara's* distinctive
traits began to emerge in its early stages.[74]

  Accordingly, we are interested in the early elements that
set the processes in motion and the preliterary history of the
elements. In other words, we are trying to isolate the central
structure around which teachings emerged and the sources which
set the paradigm for the literary work of *Gemara*. Our hypothesis
is that Samuel, and presumably others, including Rav, taught a
commentary directly on Mishnah and later masters taught and
learned Mishnah with Samuel's comments. Samuel's specific purposes which guided his comments and motivated him to form a
Commentary affected and characterized the work's very nature and
distinguishes it from Tosefta and other possible models of a
Mishnah commentary. The existence of such a Mishnah Commentary,

however, does not preclude the possibility that other teachings
circulated and that they were incorporated into the emerging
*Gemara.*

　　　We have just anticipated several points in our discussion
in chapters nine and ten as to the nature of Samuel's mishnaic
commentary and as to the context in which such a commentary may
have emerged.  The central point which relates to the issue of
the present chapter is therefore worth restating.  "Related" and
"unrelated" items that lack a tradent, especially those briefly
formulated, may have circulated in an "early" time.  Some were
connected to a text or source; some directly addressed independent
themes, many of which are developed from Mishnah itself; some
originally constituted longer autonomous teachings.  But the fact
that some comments may have been briefly formulated and circulated
at an early time does not undermine our use of such brevity among
the "Mishnah-Comments" to argue that a Mishnah Commentary existed.
Hence, we can still consider "brevity" and gloss-like formulation
central traits of a Mishnah commentary and correlate these characteristics with the teachings' degree of dependence upon Mishnah
and their lack of a tradent in the attributive formulae.

[1] Cp. our introduction to chapter six, in Volume One, p. 216.

[2] See Volume One, pp. 216-217. Gordis likewise observed this phenomenon.

[3] See Volume One, p. 217, and n. 1.

[4] See chapter two, n. 351.

[5] For other instances, see *Thes. Nom.* 3: 1062a-1064a, esp. 1063b. See also chapter two, n. 204, and text thereto, and chapter three, #11.

[6] See Frankel, p. 65b; Hyman, pp. 3-8, who claims that Abba originated in Palestine, went to Babylonia, and then returned to Palestine; Margalioth, cols. 1-3; Albeck, *Introduction*, p. 210; *Thes. Nom.*, 1: 2-10, esp. 9c; Neusner, *History*, 3: 218-220; Goldberg, "R. Ze$^c$ira," *Tarbiz* 36 (1967): esp. 332-333, and 337; and above, chapter two, n. 321.

[7] See chapter two, #88, and cp. Goldberg, *Tarbiz* 36 (1967): 333, n. 20.

[8] See chapter two, text to n. 297.

[9] See chapter two, text preceding n. 337.

[10] See below, esp. 2. P, and n. 17.

[11] See Volume One, p. 218 and nn. 4-5, to which add *Thes. Nom.*, 3: 100b-101b.

[12] In #87 we follow the identification of "our Rabbi" with Samuel. It is unclear, however, whether this is part of the exposition or whether it is an anonymous interpolation. Note an analogous identification in the analogous structure attributed to Hisda, cited below. See *Thes. Tal.*, 23: 159c-161a for numerous instances of such anonymous identifications of masters.

[13] On the role of Nahman, see also Volume One, pp. 21-26, esp. 23 and 26, which present other cases in which Nahman uses Samuel's teachings; Neusner, *History*, 3: 65, 165-166, 171-172, 292; and the pericope in which #74 appears, presented in chapter two.

[14] See *Thes. Tal.*, 9: 443b. Cp. Florsheim, "R. Hisda," *Tarbiz* 41 (1971): 26-29.

[15] Goldberg, "R. Ze$^c$ira," *Tarbiz* 36 (1967).

[16] See chapter two, nn. 295-306, 315, and text thereto. See also chapter two, nn. 136-137 and text thereto.

[17] See Volume One, pp. 224-225, 235; above (chapter eight), text to n. 10; and below 2. P.

[18] See Volume One, pp. 218-219, to which add Albeck, *Introduction*, pp. 291-293, and *Thes. Nom.* 3:847.

[19] See chapter two, esp. n. 154.

[20] See the references in chapter two, n. 438, to which add *Thes. Nom.*, 2: 480-482, esp. 481c.

[21]See chapter two, text to n. 351 and the references in n. 351, to which add *Thes. Nom.*, 1: 96-97.

[22]See the references in chapter two, n. 234, to which add Hyman, pp. 774-776; *Thes. Nom.*, 3: 896; and cp. Frankel, pp. 104b-105a.

[23]See chapter two, text to n. 157, and, above, n. 22. Intermediaries would apparently play a role in #92 and #94, as well. See chapter three.

[24]See Margalioth, cols. 85-86; Albeck, *Introduction*, pp. 318-319; and esp. Hyman, p. 140.

[25]See Volume One, p. 220.

[26]One Yose, see Volume One, pp. 219 and 224.

[27]The span of the career of this Huna is not totally clear. See Frankel, p. 73b; Margalioth, cols. 233-236; Albeck, *Introduction*, p. 387, and cp. 232; and esp. Hyman, p. 345, Lieberman, *Caesarea*, p. 90, and n. 32, and Bacher, *Tradition*, pp. 316 and 498.

[28]See Neusner, *History*, Volume 4, passim, and Dor, *The Teachings*, pp. 11-78. As to the latter's pp. 13-14, cp. the observations in chapter two, #74.
See also #84, which likewise is a Blessing Delineation with a double attribution to Rav and Samuel. The textual reading, however, is unclear and an anonymous authority and not Rava may be the one who cites this tradition.

[29]See Bacher, *Tradition*, p. 488.

[30]See Lieberman, *Caesarea*, p. 99, n. 72; Rabinovitz, *STEI*, pp. 16-17; Albeck, *Introduction*, pp. 336-337, 395-396. See also Hyman, pp. 717-719; Weiss Halivni, *ST*, 2: 505, n. 1; and cp. Frankel, p. 102a, and Margalioth, cols. 529-530.

[31]See Lieberman, *Caesarea*, pp. 11-12, and *SZ*, pp. 126-132, esp. 130-131.

[32]See our discussion below. Note the following items: 59, 60, 99, 103, 115, 117, 125, 128; in addition to 45=46, 56, and 120, for which we may be able to reconstruct Zeira's role; and 67 and 78, concerning which, however, see Category J, as to the role of Yaaqov bar Aha.

[33]Cp. Volume One, where we found that traditions without a tradent account for 51 percent of the sample there. Gordis' findings again are likewise in agreement in this matter.

[34]The calculation is as follows: #82=84 as an additional "Tradition" yields 52 separate traditions and thus 18/52 = 34.6 percent. Without the additional "Tradition" we have 17/51 = 33.3 percent.

[35]These make up the Mishnah Explicative Supplements and while they are not dependent upon Mishnah they do make sense in its context. See chapter four.

[36]See above, chapter eight, nn. 10 and 17, and text thereto; and Bokser, "Guide," chapter eleven, pp. 187-191, esp. the references to Frankel, Steinsaltz, and M. Beer.

[37]See also item #134, esp. above chapter eight, text to n. 26. In this attributive formula, the master Yose may be the traveler by that name and he may be the one who initially transmitted the tradition.

[38]In the present category, we do not include the presentation of two discrete and identical traditions which are separately attributed to different masters.  See Gordis, esp. to texts #213, 214, 216, for a discussion of several instances of the double attribution to Rav and Samuel.

[39]See chapter two, to the instances, e.g., #81=82=84, and Volume One, pp. 220-221.

[40]Cp. Goldberg, "R. Ze$^c$ira," *Tarbiz* 36 (1967): 333, n. 20, and Dor, *The Teachings*, pp. 13-14, to which cp. our analysis in chapter two.

[41]If we considered #101 as two separate comments and therefore calculated on the basis of totals of 60 and 52, and not 59 and 51, the difference would be miniscule: 1.66 percent instead of 1.69 percent of the items and 1.92 percent instead of 1.96 percent of the traditions.

[42]See also chapter two, #134, as to the possible role of Yose in that tradition, and above chapter eight, n. 26, and chapter seven, text immediately after n. 22.

[43]See, e.g., #11, 26, 35, 40-41, 52, 58, 74, 77=80, 81, 87, 94, 96, 109-112, and below subsection 6, and chapter ten.

[44]Cp. our observations here with those in Volume One, pp. 225-226, and our review of the non-Mishnah comments below, in subsection 6.

[45]See Higger, 1: 153-157.

[46]On #139 see chapter three, n. 152.

[47]See chapter three, n. 74.

[48]See Volume One, pp. 98-99, n. 275.

[49]On Taḥlifa's chronology, see Margalioth, col. 882, and Albeck, *Introduction*, p. 210.

[50]On Hannan's chronology, see chapter three, n. 4.

[51]On the problem of the correct reading in the attributive formula, see chapter three, nn. 162-163.

[52]Cp. the formula in #110, whose reading, however, is problematic and on which see chapter three, n. 112.

[53]See chapter two, nn. 425, 426, 432, and texts thereto.

[54]On Idi see Hyman, pp. 140-141; Margalioth, cols. 86-87; and Albeck, *Introduction*, p. 257.

[55]See chapter three, n. 90.

[56]On the problems of the reading see chapter three, n. 112.

[57]See chapter three, n. 104.

[58]See chapter four, text to nn. 38-40.

[59]On the place of a tradent in the formulae of decisions, HLKH K-, see Volume One, pp. 196-197, 227, and especially 237; and above chapter six, Category G, and below chapters nine and ten.

We further note, the content and use of the traditions in several instances make the absence of the name of a tradent understandable. For example, 18=52 is part of a narrative and 19=53 presents a tradition without a tradent's name, but there is very little doubt that the narrator in 18=52 also cites Samuel's tradition in 19=53.

[60] See chapter three, n. 67.

[61] See chapter three, n. 100.

[62] See the references in chapter eight, n. 53, to which add chapter two, text to n. 428.

[63] See, for example, Epstein, *ITM*, pp. 166-404, and Baruch M. Bokser, "Jacob N. Epstein's *Introduction to the Text of the Mishnah*," in *The Modern Study of the Mishnah*, ed. Jacob Neusner (Leiden, 1973), pp. 22-24, and esp. 32-33; and chapter ten, below. Cp. Lieberman, *Caesarea*, pp. 22-23, who briefly discusses factors which may have influenced which Babylonian materials would be preserved in y. See also Bokser, "Minor For Zimmun."

[64] See chapter three, n. 21.

[65] See chapter six, subsection 3, and chapter four, text to nn. 38-40.

[66] Cp. #11 and 15.

[67] Cp. #90.

[68] See chapter six, Category H, and the literature cited in nn. 29-31 there.

[69] See, e.g., Neusner, *Purities*, 21: 166-190, and above, chapter seven.

[70] See, e.g., Neusner, *Purities*, 21: 17-18; 29-112, esp. 37-75, 104, 107, 112; 113-126, esp. 125, n. 1; 263-264; and esp. 300-301 and n. 1.

[71] See Goodblatt, "The Babylonian Talmud," *ANRW*, Ch. IV, 1-2, pp. 285-304, especially 303.

[72] See chapter four, subsection 3, B. iii, and Charts 8-9.

[73] Collections of *Baraitot* and midrashic exegeses might resemble the materials collected in Higger and in E. Z. Melamed, *Halachic Midrashim of the Talmud I. Halachic Midrashim in the Talmud Babli* (Jerusalem, 1943), respectively.

[74] See the materials discussed in Goodblatt, cited in n. 71. Yerushalmi which did not undergo the saboraic, late literary enrichment demonstrates that the structure of *Gemara* and the nature of the *sugya* does not depend upon just the final expansive editing processes.

CHAPTER NINE

CORRELATIONS AND CONCLUSIONS: THE NATURE
OF SAMUEL'S COMMENTARY

*1.  Introduction*

In the previous chapters we focused upon different aspects
of Samuel's comments which directly relate to Mishnah as well as
those which are less intimately, if at all, attached to it.  We
asked what might constitute the characteristics of a commentary
on Mishnah and examined the traditions for traits that we would
expect to find and for those we would not expect to find.  We
analyzed the teachings' spread, the type of information which
they convey, and their formulations and mode of presentation.  We
demonstrated both a *prima facie* case and an actual probability
that a Commentary existed.

Presently, we correlate the diverse phenomena which we
laid out as the final stage in our argument and then attempt to
describe the contours of the Commentary.  With that information
we are able to discuss how this reconstructed Commentary and its
characteristics relate to diverse models of a possible commentary.
Since people undertake the task of commentary with diverse assumptions, needs, and goals, naturally they likewise end up with
different results.  Consequently, by comparing Samuel's activity
with those of others we can better appreciate his efforts.  Moreover, we can place Samuel's endeavors within their historical
context and, in particular, trace their impact on subsequent
generations.  We do so in chapter ten, where we relate our picture
of Samuel to the wider framework of third-century Judaism and
the beginnings of the Talmud.

Section One: Correlations

*2.  Correlations of Tradents
and Types of Comments*

Charts 21 and 22 correlate the tradents and the types of
comments.  The charts make clear the significant role that Judah
plays in the transmission of Samuel's teachings.  He cites a
cross section of the diverse types of comments though he does not
treat each category equally.  While he accounts for 28.8 percent
of the items and 29.4 percent of the traditions, he disproportionately focuses on several types.  These include the Case Definitions (44.4 percent of the items and 50 percent of the traditions);

## CHART 21

### TRADENTS AND TYPES OF COMMENTS

| Type | Judah b. | Judah y. | Huna | Mattena | Abba | Naḥman | Zeira | Joseph | Ḥiyya | Yaaqov b. Aḥa | Yose b. R. Bun | Tradentless b. | Tradentless y. |
|---|---|---|---|---|---|---|---|---|---|---|---|---|---|
| Word Definitions | 8 | | | | | | | | | | | 54,126-127,132,140 | 56, 128-129 |
| Case Definitions | 44,120 | 101*, 134* | [101*] | | 105 | | | | 121 | | | | 45=46, 99 |
| Textual Notes | | | | | | | | | | | | 117 | |
| Reasons | 70,116 | | | | | | | | | | | | 115 |
| Decisions | 1,7,51 | | | | | 55 | | 68 | 58 | 67 | | 102 | 59,103 |
| Related Rulings | 66,136 | 21, 65 | | | | | | | | | 135 | 122 | 60,125 |
| Additional Cases and Applications | 71=73=74 | | | 75 | 88 | 87 | 89 | 81** | | 78 | | 72=85 76=79 77=80 82=84** 83,86 | |

*#101 is to be assigned to Judah or Huna (or both). #134 may also be cited by Yonah.

**#82=84 are counted as separate items but do not make up an instance of a "Tradition" as it is included under Joseph who cites it as #81.

CHART 21--Continued

| Type | Reconstructed Tradent | + Second Tradent | Double Attribution + Rav | Travelers: Primary and Secondary*** |
|---|---|---|---|---|
| Word Definition | 56 (Zeira) | | | [56] |
| Case Definition | 45=46 (Abba or Zeira) | 101 (+ Avina)<br>134 (+ Yose, Yonah) | | [45=46],101,105,<br>120,121 |
| Textual Notes | | | | |
| Reasons | | | | |
| Decisions | | | 68 (tradent = Joseph) | 58,67 |
| Related Rulings | | 21 (+ Huna, Idi, Joseph)<br>65 (+ Zeira) | | 21,65 |
| Additional Cases and Applications | | 74 (+ Rava)<br>75 (+ Zeira) | 72=85 (tradentless);<br>81=82=84 (81: tradent =<br>Joseph; 82=84 tradentless);<br>83 (tradentless);<br>88 (tradentless) | 75,78,88,89 |

***Instances of reconstructed roles of a traveler are bracketed. We include instances of Yaaqov bar Aha, the scrutinizer of traditions.

CHART 22

TRADENTS AND TYPES OF COMMENTS: TOTALS

| Type | Judah | Huna Mattena | Abba, Nahman, Zeira, Joseph, Hiyya | Yaaqov b. Aha, Yose b. R. Bun | Tradentless | Reconstructed |
|---|---|---|---|---|---|---|
| Entries=% | 17(15)=28.8 (29.4) | 1*=1.7(2.0) | 9=15.3(17.6) | 3=5.1(5.9) | 29(23)=49.2 (45.1) | |
| Word Definition 9=15.3(17.6) | 1 | | | | 8 | 1 |
| Case Definition 9(8)=15.3(15.7) | 4* | [+1*] | 2 | | 3(2) | 2(1) |
| Textual Notes 1=1.7(2.0) | | | | | 1 | |
| Reasons 3=5.1(5.9) | 2 | | | | 1 | |
| Decisions 10=16.9(19.6) | 3 | | 3 | 1 | 3 | |
| Related Rulings 8=13.6(15.7) | 4 | | | 1 | 3 | |
| Additional Cases and Applications 19(12)=32.2(23.5) | 3(1) | 1 | 4** | 1 | 10(5)** | |

*One item may be assigned to Judah or Huna, or both, as they cite different versions of the tradition.

**One teaching which appears three times, in one instance is cited by a master, Joseph, under whom it is catalogued as a "Tradition."

the Reasons (66.7 percent), though in this case the sample is
somewhat small; and the Related Rulings (50 percent).  His focus
on the Decisions constitutes approximately what we would expect,
though as we shall see below, all the instances employ a certain
formulation.  On the other hand, he has a disproportionately low
involvement in the Word Definitions and Additional Cases and
Applications and none in the Textual Notes, though the latter
sample includes only one instance.

The other tradents are involved in single instances of
various types of comments.  None of the five masters with whom
we have more than one comment cites more than one instance of a
given type of comment.  The tradents other than Judah, as a group,
are associated with Decisions (40 percent), which below we shall
see are of a certain formulation; Additional Cases and Applications (31.6 percent of the items and 50 percent of the traditions);
Case Definitions (22.2 percent of the items and 25 percent of the
traditions); and Related Rulings (12.5).

On the other hand, while the tradentless items appear in
each category they are disproportionately found among Word Definitions (88.9 percent) and among Textual Notes (100 percent, but
the sample of one instance--by itself--is too small to be significant).  The tradentless teachings represent an expected percentage of the Additional Cases and Applications (52.6 percent of the
items and 41.7 percent of the traditions) and a somewhat less
than expected number of Related Rulings (37.5 percent).  The percentages are even less for the Reasons (33.3 percent), Case Definitions (33.3 percent of the items and 25 percent of the traditions), and of the Decisions (30 percent).

If there is a logical connection between the identity of
a tradent or the presence or absence of a tradent and the type
of comment, we can draw several conclusions.  Most Decisions,
Reasons, Related Rulings, and Case Definitions mention a tradent
in their chain.  The tradents also play a significant role in the
Additional Cases and Applications, especially in terms of the
number of the traditions less repeated items.  These several categories of comments provide information necessary for the application of a legal text like Mishnah.  While Judah plays a very
prominent role in these efforts, we also find other tradents.  The
latter's role is greater than Judah's among the Decisions and
Additional Cases and Applications.  As we shall see below, however,
Judah and the other masters cite different types of decisions.
The latter are formulated somewhat like Additional Cases and

Applications while Judah's are the standard HLKH K- pattern.  This
suggests that later generations perceive Samuel in the role of the
one who expands Mishnah's law, a point to which we return below.

The tradentless items also appear to make up a pattern.
The areas in which they are prominent, the Word Definitions and
the Textual Notes, are those that convey the type of information
essential for a simple reading of a text.  The tradentless comments provide a balanced portion of the Reasons, Related Rulings,
Additional Cases and Applications and somewhat less so of the
Case Definitions and Decisions.  These two overall patterns gain
even greater significance when we recall our argument above that
the tradentless items may in fact have circulated prior to the
third century and make up an early core of Samuel's teaching.
Consideration of the type of information therefore coincides in
indicating that what is essential and thus integral to a commentary circulated early.  When below we take account of the formulation of the teachings, in particular the tradentless Reasons,
Decisions, and Related Rulings, we shall have evidence that
they circulated in any early time and that the Additional
Cases and Applications make up the special cases of Blessing
Delineations.

Moreover, when we take account of the reconstructed
tradents, the resulting slight realignment does not change the
pattern; indeed, it in effect strengthens it.  First, the assignment of one of the Word Definitions to Zeira has little impact.
We have six instead of seven--of nine--traditions without a
tradent.  Moreover, as we shall see, Zeira apparently cites or
employs a gloss which may make up a self-contained unit with its
own integrity and which therefore does not include his name in
the chain.  Secondly, however, when we decrease the number of
Case Definitions from three items and two traditions to one--of
nine--we further see the central role of tradents in citing the
Case Definitions.

We, therefore, find that those things which we would
expect to find as primary in a Commentary, i.e., those which are
required for the simple meaning of the text, are primary in circulation; and those which are required for the secondary meaning
of the text are secondary in circulation.  Of note, while our
tentative conclusion to this point generally conforms to the
results found in Volume One, there is one variation.  There we
found that most (five of eight) of the Word Definitions are
tradentless as are most of the Case Definitions (thirteen to

eleven of twenty). We also noticed, though, that the latter are tightly formulated and require a referent for comprehension and therefore constitute glosses. Once we correlate the present sample's formulations with the type of comments and tradents we will be better able to refine our results.

On the basis of our correlations we can make three additional sets of observations. First, the travelers play an explicit role in the transmission of twelve items. These include Case Definitions, Decisions, Related Rulings, and Additional Cases and Applications of Mishnah. As we shall see below, the two instances of Decisions are phrased as autonomously formulated teachings on a specific theme. All of these items involve the application of Mishnah. The three reconstructed items (one Word Definition and two Case Definitions), which we hypothesized were transmitted in Palestine by travelers, do not substantively affect the picture. The integrity of the text of the Case Definitions may have prevented interpolation of the tradent's name. In any event the traveler's connection to Samuel's heritage apparently is tied to his use of the teachings, especially to apply Mishnah and its themes or principles in precise terms to new cases.

Secondly, the six instances of the traditions with two or more tradents all mention one of Samuel's direct disciples. In five instances it is Judah and in one Mattena. Moreover, the comments address the application of Mishnah in its own terms, by defining its cases, or in new terms, in relating Mishnah to related or additional cases. Each of these areas has numerous instances of entries with tradents. That is, none forms an entire category by itself.

Thirdly, five of the Double Attributions introduce comments that provide additional Cases and Applications of Mishnah's law and the sixth instance introduces a Decision. The Decision has a tradent, Joseph, but only one of the Additional Cases does. The exception among the latter, however, makes sense. Those without tradents are in b. and employ a patterned formula to delineate blessings or revise it to make the teachings address the definition of "food." As the attributive formula in the latter case was not revised, clearly it had an integrity of its own and it would have been inappropriate to add names of tradents. The exceptional instance with a tradent comes from y. and it is reasonable that in Palestine someone had to cite the tradition. The tradent fittingly is Abba, the early traveler who in fact may have had direct access to Samuel himself. We further note that

both categories of Decisions and Additional Cases have entries
with tradents other than Judah.  These categories are thus not
quintessentially Judah--transmitted materials.  Indeed Judah and
Mattena, the other second-generation master, are not disproportionately found here.  Rather later masters are the ones interested in these kinds of teachings.  This makes sense as they are
extensions and further applications of Mishnah's principles,
activities of interest especially to later Amoraim, as we discuss
below.  Our assumption as to the stage of the tradition also
accords with the fact that while the formula may have gained an
integrity of its own, it is not fundamental to the tradition.
Someone must have combined the teachings of Samuel and Rav.  When
we discussed the dispute form we pointed to evidence as to this
fact.[1]

        The question remains, Why was it necessary to present a
Double Attribution?  While we may never definitely know the
motivating factors we can observe the impression that such a
formula makes.  It serves to strengthen the authority of the
specified opinion.  This, in turn, suits the fact that these
particular teachings present not first order information of a
commentary but rather material which expands and uses Mishnah's
principles.  This, in effect, also holds true for #68.  The substance of this tradition is not formulated as a standard HLKH K-,
"the *halakhah* follows," Decision but as a Liturgical Text.  But
by its use it functions as a decision and at the same time applies
that Decision.  It thus lays out how one may act upon a certain
adjudication.  After we correlate the literary formulations we
can further refine this last point.

                    *3.  Correlations of Tradents*
                      *and Literary Formulations*

        Charts 23 and 24 correlate the literary phrasing of the
traditions with the identity of their tradents, or the fact of
the absence of a tradent.  As we found in chapter six, several
traditions employ more than one fixed usage and therefore when
we calculate the percentages of entries we must do so on the
basis of sixty-three items and fifty-five traditions.

        The correlations of the literary phrasings of the teach-
ings with the method in which they are cited, whether by a specific tradent or whether by no tradent at all, reflects several
patterns.  The patterns are quite revealing as to the history of

the presentation of Samuel's traditions and accord with basic
aspects of our hypothesis developed in Volume One and throughout
this volume.  As we shall see, the literary formulations, like
the types of the comments, indicate that Samuel's commentary provided primary, secondary, and tertiary information--that which is
necessary for understanding, applying, and extending Mishnah,
respectively--and the more essential elements circulated earlier
than the less essential ones.

      Judah is associated with a cross section of formulations.
This includes both precise phrasings and usages made up of brief
gloss-like elements which define Mishnah's case and set out its
criteria and which generally come from y., as well as long patterns, found in b.  He does not, however, transmit any of the
"non-standard" Mishnah commentary formulations, i.e., the Questions, Dialogues, Discussions, and First Person Reports.[2]  A
close examination of the ostensible exceptions to this breakdown
indicates that they do not vitiate these generalizations.  First,
#44, a briefly formulated instance of the KL ZMN Š- pattern, is
found in b.  But in this case the name of the tradent, Judah, may
be needed due to its context.  An essential aspect of the pericope
centers on the identity of the master who cites a tradition in
the name of Rav.  Therefore, for the sake of balance someone may
have included the name of Samuel's tradent.  Secondly, #8, a
brief gloss, makes up the opening phrase of a liturgical text.
As other identifications of the referent in Mishnah circulated,
the teaching has direct adjudicatory overtones.  Moreover, we
have a second instance of this teaching, in which it is applied
to M. Tamid, #11.  There we see how several masters search out
the proper meaning of Mishnah and when Judah is approached he
cites Samuel's comment.  If that narrative circulated and made
up the source for Samuel's tradition, we could understand why
someone might later just cite the tradition in Judah's name and
apply it to M. Berakhot.  Moreover, the y. version of the second
location, on M. Tamid, presents the teaching in a more generic
formulation, viz., "This is the blessing over the Torah" (#15-16).
Interestingly, the tradition is transmitted by Mattena, another
second-generation student of Samuel.  If this formulation represents a more fundamental stage of the teaching, Judah himself may
have played a role in the version which he cites; he may have
further defined and interpreted it.  Third, the single exception
among the y. items, #65, is noteworthy.  It employs the language
of Mishnah, "say it," and is gloss-like in formulation.  Its

## CHART 23

### TRADENTS AND THE LITERARY PHRASING OF THE TRADITIONS*

| Phrasing | Judah b. | Judah y. | Huna | Mattena | Abbā | Naḥman | Zeira | Joseph | Ḥiyya | Yaaqov b. Aḥa | Yose b. R. Bun | Tradentless**** b. | Tradentless**** y. |
|---|---|---|---|---|---|---|---|---|---|---|---|---|---|
| B- | | 134* | | | | | | | | | | | 99 |
| ʾPYLW | | 134* | | | | | | | | | | | |
| KL ZMN Š- | 44 | | | | | | | | 121 | | | | |
| ᶜD Š- | | 101b* | [101b*] | | | | | | | | | | 45=46 |
| KDY Š- | | 101a*, 120, 134* | [101a*] | | | | | | | | | | |
| (ʾYN) SRYK L- | | 21 | | | | | | | | | | | 60,125 |
| HLKH K- | 1,7, 51 | | | | | | | | | | | | |
| Exegesis | 70 | | | | | | | | | | | 132,140 | |
| Liturgical Text | | | | | | | | 68 | | | | 54 | |
| Blessing Delineation | 71= 73= 74 | | | 75 | 88 | 87 | 89 | 81 | | 78 | | 76=79,[77= 80***], 82=84**, 83,86 | |
| Questions | | | | | | | | | | | | 122 | |

| | Declarative Sentences | Glosses | First Person Reports | Discussions | Dialogues |
|---|---|---|---|---|---|
| Dialogues | | | | | [76=79***] 77=80 |
| Discussions | | | | [127a-b] 127c [128a] 128b | |
| First Person Reports | | | 58 | 127a-b | 59,103 |
| Glosses | 8 | 105 | 67 | 126 | 129 |
| Declarative Sentences | 66, 65, 116, 136 | 55 | 135 | 72=85, 102 | 56,127 |

*Three traditions have several parts and formulations: 127a-b-c (tradentless); 128a-b (tradentless); 134 (cited by Judah, with three phrasings). The total entries of phrasings, therefore, add up to 63(55). In 101 Judah and Huna cite different versions of Samuel's teaching. The tradition, moreover, appears in two recensions, 101a, the secondary one, and 101b, the primary one, which is the one catalogued. 134, with three phrasings, is also cited by Yonah.

**82=84=81, though the third one has a tradent, Joseph, under whom the comment is counted as a "Tradition."

***76=79 counted under Blessing Delineations and 77=80 under Dialogues.

****Instances of reconstructed roles of a traveler are bracketed. We include instances of Yaaqov bar Aha, the scrutinizer of traditions.

CHART 23--Continued

| Phrasing | Reconstructed Tradent | + Second Tradent | Double Attribution + Rav | Travelers: Primary and Secondary ** |
|---|---|---|---|---|
| B- | | 134 (Yose, Yonah) | | |
| ᵓPYLW | | 134 (Yose, Yonah) | | |
| KL ZMN Š- | | | | 121 |
| ᶜD Š- | 45=46 (Abba or Zeira) | 101* (+ Avina; also Huna) | | [45=46],101 |
| KDY Š- | | 101* (+ Avina; also Huna); 134* (Yose, Yonah) | | 101*,120 |
| (ᵓYN) SRYK L- | | 21 (+ Huna, Idi, Joseph) | | 21 |
| HLKH K- | | | | |
| Exegeses | | | | |
| Liturgical Texts | | | 68 (tradent = Joseph) | |
| Blessing | | 74 (+ Rava) 75 (+ Zeira) | 81=82=84 (81: tradent = Joseph) 82=84 (tradentless), 83 (tradentless), 88 (tradentless) | 75,78,88,89 |
| Questions | | | | |
| Dialogues | | | | |

| | | | |
|---|---|---|---|
| Discussions | | | |
| First Person Reports | | | 58 |
| Glosses | 56 (Zeira) | | [56],67 |
| Declarative Sentences | 65 (+ Zeira) | 72=85 (tradentless) | 65,105 |

*In 101 Judah and Huna cite different versions of Samuel's teaching. The tradition, moreover, appears in two recensions, 101a, the secondary one, and 101b, the primary one, which is the one catalogued. 134, with three phrasings, is also cited by Yonah.

**Instances of reconstructed roles of a traveler are bracketed. We include instances of Yaaqov bar Aha, the scrutinizer of traditions.

## CHART 24

### TRADENTS AND LITERARY PHRASINGS: TOTALS*

| Phrasing | Judah | Huna Mattena | Abba, Nahman, Zeira, Joseph, Hiyya | Yaaqov b. Aha Yose b. R. Bun | Tradentless | Reconstructed |
|---|---|---|---|---|---|---|
| Entries*=% | 19(17)=30.2 (30.9) | 1*=1.6 (1.8) | 9=14.3(16.4) | 3=4.8(5.5) | 31(25)=49.2(45.5) | |
| B- 2=3.2(3.6) | 1* | | | | 1 | |
| ꜥPYLW 1=1.6(1.8) | 1* | | | | | |
| KL ZMN Š- 2=3.2(3.6) | 1 | | 1 | | 2(1) | |
| ᶜD Š- 3(2)=4.8(3.6) | 1* | [+1*] | | | | 2(1) |
| KYD Š- 3-1=2=3.2(3.6) | 3-1=2* | | | | | |
| (ꜥYN) SRYK L- 3=4.8(5.5) | 1 | | | | 2 | |
| HLKH K- 3=4.8(5.5) | 3 | | | | | |
| Exegeses 3=4.8(5.5) | 1 | | | | 2 [gloss-like] | |
| Liturgical Texts 2=3.2(3.6) | | | 1 | | 1 | |

| | | | | |
|---|---|---|---|---|
| Blessing Delineation 15(10)=23.8 (18.2) | 3(1) | 1 | 4 | 1 | 6(3**) |
| Questions 1=1.6(1.8) | | | | | 1 |
| Dialogues 2(1)=3.2(1.8) | | | | | 2(1) |
| Discussions 2=3.2(3.6) | | | | | 2 |
| First Person Reports 5=7.9(9.1) | | | 1 | | 4 |
| Glosses 5=7.9(9.1) | 1 | | | 1 | 3 |
| Declarative Sentences 12(11)=19.0(20) | 4 | | 2 | 1 | 5(4) |

64-1=63(56-1=55)

*Three traditions have several parts and formulations: 127a-b-c; 128a-b; and 134 (with three phrasings). We include these four, and not the phrasing in the secondary version of 101 (i.e., 101a), in the totals and percentages of the various phrasings and entries under each tradent. In the latter we have an additional two each under Judah and under "Tradentless." If we count 101 under Huna and not, or along with, Judah we would have an additional item under Huna. The two masters cite different versions of Samuel's teaching.

**82=84 are counted as "items" but not as an instance of a "Tradition." The latter is catalogued under Joseph, the tradent in the third instance, 81.

brevity especially stands out in contrast to its b. analogue, #66,
which is an autonomous statement. The fact that we have a parallel would also indicate that the teaching circulated at a rather
early time, which might explain why it is cited by Judah and not
a later tradent.

Consideration of the exact percentages refines the above
breakdowns. Judah is responsible for all instances of ᵓPYLW,
KDY Š-, and HLKH K- pattern. They facilitate the simple application of Mishnah and thereby fulfill needs intermediary between
the simple reading of a text and its more expansive extension
and application. Judah takes a disproportionately large role
in transmission of traditions with the B- form and KL ZMN Š-
phrase (both 50 percent) and an expected role in the citation of
comments with ᶜD Š- (33.3 percent of the items and 50 percent of
the traditions), SRYK L- (33.3 percent), Exegesis (33.3 percent),
and Declarative Sentences (33.3 percent of the items and 36.4
percent of the traditions). On the other hand, he takes a minor
role in citing Blessing Delineations (20 percent of the items and
10 percent of the traditions) and no role in Liturgical Texts,[3]
Questions, Dialogues, Discussions, and First Person Reports.

In all, *Judah plays a role in the transmission of the
types of materials required by a person who wants to use Mishnah
and put it into effect.* The y. generally includes the briefer
teachings which set out criteria and such. This conforms to our
general observation that y.'s materials are generally briefer
than those of b. This may be due to the fact that the y. teachings underwent less scrutiny and fewer revisions in Palestine
and therefore were preserved in a more pristine formulation.[4]

By their very nature, materials required for the simple
understanding of Mishnah are needed before those required for its
application. Hence, it is reasonable that the former are presented prior to the latter. The mention of Judah's name thus
may accord with the history of the circulation of Samuel's teachings. *Judah would be associated with a second stage in the
presentation of Samuel's heritage.*

The last correlation in a different way may apply to the
"longer" comments. Where we find instances of entries in a
category other than those which Judah cites, they are briefer and
more gloss-like than Judah's. For example, the tradentless
Exegeses in effect gloss Mishnah while Judah's instance of an
Exegesis is an autonomous statement. The latter's longer formulation does not preclude its direct relevance to Mishnah,[5] but since

it is not formulated so tightly as to go along with the text of
Mishnah, it may require the mention of the tradent's name.  Moreover, several of Judah's longer items are made up of individual
parts which separately may have once functioned as simple brief
glosses but which presently are combined into a single unit.
This includes #101 and #134.[6]  Similarly, #120, like #121, is
tightly knit to Mishnah though it is not very brief in formulation.  Consequently, we are left with the impression that *in
their present wording these longer comments are directly relevant
and connected to Mishnah but may reflect the role of a tradent
who expands, combines, or otherwise shapes more briefly formulated materials.  This accounts for the inclusion of the tradent's
name.*  Naturally some teachings themselves may not have originated
as simple glosses or due to their context may have required the
mention of a tradent.  The three instances (100 percent of the
entries) of the HLKH K- pattern exemplify such a phenomenon.
Here as we have already pointed out, the specification of the
tradent may contribute to the force of the decision.

      The remaining items which specify a tradent, either one
of Samuel's direct disciples or a third-generation master (especially those who traveled to Palestine), or one of the several
later authorities, may vary slightly from the above patterns.
In effect, however, they conform to the emerging larger picture.

      First, #121, the KL ZMN Š- teaching, is not a very brief
gloss that might have easily entered the text of Mishnah itself.
As it appears in y., the name of a traveler (Hiyya) is not inap-
propriate--if it reached that land in that master's generation.
Moreover, since the comment is juxtaposed to a disputing opinion
attributed to a Palestinian, its full source may have been relevant to trace.  In #68, Joseph responds to a discussion and
employs Samuel's Liturgical Text to decide and concretize the
law.  In #58, Hiyya employs a First Person Report for a similar
purpose.  The Gloss (#67) and Declarative Sentences likewise
have direct bearing and implications as to the law.

      Number 55 builds upon an earlier teaching, a Decision.
As we pointed out above, such developments of earlier teachings
may be characteristic of Nahman.  Number 105 apparently is an
expansion of a gloss.  The third Declarative Sentence appears in
y.  It includes an exception which is disputed by other authorities.  Moreover, the teaching itself is used to bolster the view
of another Babylonian who disputes a Palestinian.  It would

therefore be appropriate to mention the name of the authority who
made the teaching known as he presumably also supports this
position.

The two areas in which we have multiple instances of
tradents other than Judah are the Declarative Sentences and
Blessing Delineations.  Above we discussed why the former reasonably include the tradent's name.  This applies as well to the
latter, which in fact makes up the single category in which the
entries add up to a significant number.  Without Yaaqov bar Aha's
cited tradition, they are associated with 33.3 percent of the
items and 50 percent of the traditions, and along with it 40
percent of the items and 60 percent of the traditions.  The
tradents generally are later masters.  Only one, #75, is transmitted by a direct disciple of Samuel, Mattena.  Even when we
include Judah we have only one additional tradition, #71=73=74.
Moreover there are tradentless instances of these teachings.
*The inclusion of the tradent therefore apparently reflects that
master's role in the comment's presentation.*  They are those which
a master cites to bolster another argument or position (#81),
part of an exposition (#87), or else are cited in y. (78, 88-89),
which has a predilection to include the name of a traveler.
These various *Blessing Delineations as a group employ Mishnah's
principles drawn from one case, apply it to another one, and
hence supplement and expand Mishnah itself.*  As we earlier saw,
Tosefta, both in formulation and content, provides a paradigm
for such teachings.

Finally, in contrast to Judah's materials, the other
tradents employ earlier teachings or present teachings in a way
that they make a ruling with obvious *halakhic* implications.  But
in contrast to Judah's materials, the *perspective apparently is
no longer just the simple application of Mishnah's law in terms
of how Mishnah itself defines the issues.*  What we have found,
in effect, merely paraphrases our observation that many of the
items are transmitted by travelers or are cited within a pericope
to serve a function in that context.  These purposes by their
very nature may have required the name of a tradent; moreover,
by definition they involve the use of Mishnah's law and are not
just its simple rendering and application.  But the need to supplement Mishnah originates as soon as one wants to put Mishnah
into effect and to develop its principles.  In chapter ten we
trace this wider context implicit in the response to Mishnah.

The tradentless items account for a large percentage of Samuel's traditions. Above in chapter eight we argued that they may have circulated at a relatively early period. We based this observation on the presence of analogous traditions in comparable locations in the opposite *Gemara* and on the ways in which they are used in disputes with other masters. Charts 23 and 24 further reveal that they make up a sizeable portion of the briefly formulated precise patterns which appear in y. These include the following phrasings: the second instance of the B- form (#99) and of the $^{C}$D Š- phrase (45=46); the second and third instances of both the SRYK L- pattern (#60, 125), which are the brief ones, and the Exegeses (#132, 140), which likewise are the gloss-like entries; and two simple Glosses (#56, 117).

The tradentless traditions also account for some of the more involved patterns, most of which appear in b. They account for 40 percent of the Blessing Delineation items and 30 percent of their traditions; 100 percent of the Questions, though the single entry amounts to a too insignificant sample by itself; and the single Question and all the Dialogues and Discussions. These last three by their very nature in purporting to describe what Samuel said and its context would naturally not present Samuel's comment along with a chain of transmission. Moreover, they account for 80 percent of the First Person Reports. The other 20 percent, the fifth item, has a tradent, as he is the authority who cites the tradition to bolster a certain position. As all the First Person Reports make up b. and y. analogues, they must have circulated in a relatively early period.

Thus the *tradentless teachings are of two sorts. They make up a small portion of the precise comments though they are the briefer ones and presumably early. Alternatively they are longer patterns which also may be early and which by their very nature may preclude mention of a tradent.* When we take account of the three instances of reconstructed tradents this observation is further confirmed. We can identify the one who transmitted #45=46 and, therefore, are left with no tradentless entries of the $^{C}$D Š- phrasing. Even if our identification is correct, we note that the mention of the transmitter has not entered the attributive formula. The comment has thus maintained an integrity of its own. This would accord with the fact that the teaching is basically a gloss that could circulate along with the text of Mishnah itself. We find a similar phenomenon in #56, a gloss whose transmitter likewise can be reconstructed on the basis of

material elsewhere in the pericope.  But the tradition itself
remains as a gloss.

The correlations of the materials with more than one
tradent likewise poses no problems.  Later masters cite Samuel's
definitions of Mishnah's case.  Alternatively, they imply what
constitutes the correct opinion in Mishnah when they present
Samuel's view in Palestine or cite and use his tradition in some
specific context.  The traditions with a double attribution are
cited and used with similar implications.  In #68, Joseph cites
the Liturgical Text in the midst of a discussion about the law.
In referring to Samuel and Rav he in effect makes a more impres-
sive statement.  This applies to the Blessing Delineations as
well.  But once the tradition has an attributive formula apparently it, too, becomes part of the teaching.  Thus, #72=85 preserves the attributive formula found in the tradition from which
it was reworked.  Even in its new form, the double attribution
ostensibly implies that the opinion has great authority behind it.

* * *

Consideration of the correlations between the literary
phrasings and the tradents contributes to our argument that
Samuel actually composed a Commentary on Mishnah.  Brief materials
that depend upon and gloss Mishnah often lack a tradent.  Apparently at an early stage of the transmission of Samuel's teachings,
Samuel's name alone sufficed.  Indeed, requirements for such a
circulation precluded the name of a tradent and any other unnecessary language.  Later when someone cited the tradition either
for legal implications or to expand the law the name of the citer
was mentioned.  But Samuel as well responded to Mishnah in ways
other than simply glossing the text.  Independently formulated
materials, though dependent upon Mishnah for comprehension,
served to supplement Mishnah and even to explain the text (#127,
128).  The existence of the b. and y. analogues indicates that
these longer formulated materials must have circulated at an early
period.

The fact that we can reconstruct the identity of several
tradents, though the names do not enter the chain of the tradition, further reflects the integral nature of the traditions.
The fact that such glosses could serve as comments on two identical instances of the same referent in two different texts
(#8 and 11) has implications as well.  It reflects the fact that

such comments did not necessarily make up fully autonomously
formulated teachings which would include the referent and context
as part of the tradition.  In turn we see that we should not
automatically assume that a tradent is the one who reworks a
tradition into a gloss.  These observations support our earlier
argument based upon formulary attestation.  We found instances
in which Samuel's teaching is juxtaposed with a disputing tradition, attributed to Yoḥanan, for example, which responds to, and
thereby attests, Samuel's formulation.[7]  Samuel's tradition,
therefore, must have had its present phrasing by the date of the
attestor.

The present sample of Samuel's teachings provides a richer
picture of the history of Samuel's teachings than that of the
sample in Volume One.  The former differ from the latter in terms
of the amount of post-Samuel amoraic and saboraic focus and
scrutiny.  In contrast to Zera$^c$im's agricultural topics, Berakhot's
liturgical subjects remained an important topic and gained in
significance.[8]  As Heinemann and others have observed, the Amoraim
played an important role in standardizing many of the patterns
and themes and providing specific guidelines how to do the things
which Mishnah mentions.[9]  This may account for the greater degree
of later reuse of Samuel's teachings which we find in Berakhot.
The traditions which Judah transmits generally do not reflect
this reemployment.  Rather they represent Samuel as an authority
who enables people to know how to practice what Mishnah lays out,
viz., whose opinion in Mishnah to follow and how to concretize
its criteria and principles.  The materials, on the other hand,
with which third-generation masters generally are associated,
in effect present Samuel as one who extends Mishnah's principle
to new areas and who builds upon the decided law.

To reemphasize, such supplementary teachings can be just
as fundamental to Samuel as the glosses.  Tosefta provides examples of both.  But each may have circulated differently and may
have taken different roles within Samuel's Commentary.  One aspect
of the Commentary apparently was tightly tied to the text of
Mishnah and explained it.  A second portion while also tightly
related to Mishnah had longer formulations and would not, indeed
could not, enter Mishnah's text.  But a person could still remember such teachings along with Mishnah.  A third type of Mishnah-
teaching supplements Mishnah with completely autonomous traditions.  While these likewise would be remembered in the context
of Mishnah, they develop Mishnah's principles, at times assume a

previous development extant, for example, in Tosefta, and belong
to the expansive role of using Mishnah as a bssis for additional
teachings and for organizing one's own teachings.

Mishnah thus constitutes not a final and full guide but
an encompassing source of topics.  Later generations would naturally focus on this last dimension, for it is the one that provided a paradigm for their own activities and needs.  This is not
to say that the later generations did not attribute authority to
Mishnah; they did.  As J. N. Epstein has shown, they, in particular, tried to harmonize early amoraic teachings with the text of
Mishnah.[10]  But that need to harmonize reflects the coincidence
of several needs and attitudes.  Mishnah had authority and it
also was assumed to provide information and guidance for teachings
not explicitly contained in it.  In an earlier generation, some
of these teachings may have been based not on Mishnah but on
other tannaitic sources or on the authority of the master himself.
Now, however, it was automatically assumed that Mishnah spoke to
these issues as well.

We must, therefore, conclude that Samuel apparently did
compose a Commentary on Mishnah whose contents are no longer in
their original guise but in a form shaped by their later conception and use.  But in spite of these changes, the patterns and
formulations of the teachings have enabled us to trace fundamental
features of the Commentary and of the traditions themselves.

### 4.  The Argument for a Commentary: A Review

We have proved that Samuel composed a Commentary on
Mishnah.  We have laid out a *prima facie* case and have demonstrated that it is an actual reality.  We now review the building
blocks of our argument so that we can appreciate the role each
one plays in the overall thesis.

### i.  Chapter Four.  "The Prima Facie Case for Mishnah-Commentary"

Samuel's direct comments on Mishnah do not represent a
selected cluster of comments on a selected group of Mishnah passages in M. Berakhot.  The spread of the comments and *mishnayot*
indicates that the teachings responded to Mishnah in general and
were not intended to circulate as a single collection of teachings by themselves.

In particular, we found fifty-nine Mishnah comments,
twenty-three in y. and thirty-six in b., which represent

fifty-one distinct traditions.  The comments deal with twenty-two
different Mishnah passages.  While this accounts for only 39
percent of the tractate, the focus entails every chapter, every
theme, and all the major topics within each section.  The existence of b. and y. analogues in structurally similar places in the
two *Gemarot*, for example, indicates that the traditions are not
a collection of Samuel's teachings organized and preserved as a
group on the basis of their content, literary formulations, or
some other internal characteristic.  The relationship of Mishnah
to the "Related" and "Unrelated" comments indicates that the
sample of "Mishnah-Comments" is not self-serving.  Rather Mishnah
had a significant impact upon the full range of Samuel's teachings.  The "Related" comments enrich, extend, and supplement
Samuel's focus on mishnaic topics.  Moreover, the y. "Unrelated"
items initially represented mishnaic-related materials.  Only in
terms of their later history as single items do they appear
unrelated to M. Berakhot.

ii.   Chapter Five.  "The Types of Comments"

The comments reflect a spectrum of interests and supply
information which are appropriate in a response to a legal work
like Mishnah.  They provide for a simple understanding of the
text, the practical and concrete use of its rules, and the refinement and hence application of its principles to other related
cases.  Mishnah, in turn, forms a guidebook for practice and
action and a point of departure for further legal teaching.  One
topic, that of blessings over diverse foods, elicits greater
attention than others.  This concern, however, exemplifies the
practical nature of Samuel's response.

The specific types of comments include: the definition of
words and references; the specification of circumstances, situations, and criteria; the fixing of an orthographic reading; the
setting out of reasons for views or institutions; the ruling as
to which of several opinions constitute the authoritative position; the taking up of Mishnah's themes and their supplement with
rulings on related matters; and the addition and further exempli-
fication of cases contained within Mishnah, resulting in the
refinement of its principles.  While we do not have such comments
on every single passage of Mishnah and while the Commentary may
have once included more teachings than are presently extant, the
spread and diversity of the sample indicates they belong to a
response to Mishnah as a whole.

iii.   Chapter Six.   "The Literary Phrasing
of the Traditions"

The traditions employ distinctive means to express a wide
range of comments, offer criteria, apply and develop Mishnah, and
in other ways provide a practical response to it.  They repeatedly
and precisely use specific phrasings, patterns, and formulations
to ask a series of questions from the text of Mishnah and therefore reflect a sustained and refined effort to explain Mishnah.
Seventy-three to seventy-one percent of the teachings employ a
clear cut phraseology and significant portions of the others are
Glosses, which by their very nature set forth certain kinds of
comments.  We found that the phrasings are not used indiscriminately.  Where, for example, #101 is revised to address a different problem, the phrasing is also altered.  We found that the
present instances of the B- form are the only ones appropriate
for the form and it could not have appropriately been used for
any of the other Definitions and Glosses.  Moreover, alternatives
existed to fixed formulations, as exemplified in the Declarative
Sentences; traditions therefore were not automatically and secondarily cast into a fixed formulation.  Evidence, in fact, exists
that the use of Declarative Sentences at times is the result of
the development and further application of a tradition with a
fixed formulation and not vice versa.  The phrasings are thus
those appropriate to a commentary on Mishnah and they should not
automatically be classified as secondary improvements.

The formulations often preserve the integrity of the
tradition and indicate how it may have related to Mishnah in the
teaching's fundamental stage.  As we graphically laid out in
Chart 12, many comments need Mishnah for comprehension and are so
formulated as to circulate along with Mishnah as well.  Others,
though formulated in a fashion less tightly knit to Mishnah, need
Mishnah for comprehension.  And others, while ostensibly fully
autonomous, make very good sense in Mishnah's context--indeed, in
effect, they make very little sense outside of Mishnah's context.
A portion of the teachings which do not appear as "standard commentary" formulations, the Questions, Dialogues, Discussions, and
First Person Reports, nevertheless throw light upon Mishnah and
were associated with Mishnah.  Their presence in structurally
similar locations in both *Gemarot* indicates that at a relatively
early period they must have circulated along or in conjunction
with Mishnah.  This close relationship with Mishnah indicates
that the teachings are intended to be structured around--or

within--Mishnah.  Those very tightly tied to it evidently were
to circulate with the text of Mishnah.  Moreover, the close
dependence on Mishnah derives from the earliest stage of the
traditions and is not from later transmissional and editorial
reworking and rephrasing.

iv.   Chapter Seven.   "Modes of Presentation:
The Dispute Form"

As fitting for a commentary on Mishnah, Samuel's teachings
originated individually in response to Mishnah.  The dispute form
is imposed upon the teachings.  A large portion is not even presented in a dispute form and only a very small percentage of the
comments theoretically exhibit the characteristics necessary for
an actual confrontation between two masters.  The evidence indicates that the dispute form is a transmissional and literary means
in which to present two teachings on a related or identical issue.
Often the discrete nature of the teachings remains blatant.  The
fact that traditions that actually differ are not put into a
dispute form, that traditions appear out of phase with each other
despite their juxtaposition into a dispute pattern, and that they
have not been totally balanced even where they could have been,
supports the notion that the formulations as single units may be
preserved.  The traditions, therefore, have not been thoroughly
rephrased.  Likewise, the origin of all the traditions as single
units and not parts of disputes explains why no type of comment
or formulation or language is limited to the traditions which
appear in the dispute form.  All these types and formulations are
attested in those comments which appear individually, without
juxtaposed opposing opinions.  Moreover, the discrete nature conforms to the present understanding of the social context in which
early masters flourished.  Samuel lacked a context in which he
could regularly square off with another master.  Rather he taught
a circle of disciples.

v.   Chapter Eight.   "Tradents and
Attributive Formulae"

Those traditions which appear to make up commentary material by requiring Mishnah for comprehension and circulation do so
fundamentally and not as a result of secondary developments.  A
large portion of these are tradentless and circulated in an early
period.  Many make up simple glosses.  Others are longer statements that have analogues in structurally similar places in the

other *Gemara*.  The lack of a tradent makes sense and indeed it
would have been inappropriate to mention one in a compact commentary on Mishnah.  Undoubtedly, in an early period Samuel's name
alone would and could suffice.  Chained materials, on the other
hand, indicate when a teaching was used.  This applies especially
to the y. items which include the name of a traveler.  Thus,
first, the mention of a tradent does not constitute the standard
pattern and, secondly, tradentless comments are early.

     In particular, we can trace the several stages in the
transmission and circulation of the teachings.  Judah cites 29
percent of the comments and thus plays a key role.  Other second-
generation masters are responsible for only a few more and
together with Judah account for 33-35 percent of the comments.
The next stage includes the late second- to third-generation
masters, who accont for about 11-13 percent of the teachings.
When we consider all the comments with which the travelers are
associated, whatever be their role, we find them involved in
about 30 percent of the teachings.  The last stage includes the
late third- to fifth-generation masters, mainly from Palestine.
As most of the teachings with which they deal reached Palestine
in the third generation, their activity represents, for Palestine, a second-stage, that is, one in which teachings are applied
and used.

### vi.   Chapter Nine.  "Correlations and Conclusions"

     The teachings make up several different types of commen-
taries on Mishnah.  Those that are formulated most appropriately
for a commentary tightly knit to Mishnah are those that in fact
convey information necessary for a simple reading of a legal text
like Mishnah.  These constitute the primary "Mishnah Commentary."
Judah transmits a second-stage of commentary.  He is associated
with teachings required for the simple application of a legal
text.  Other tradents, likewise, concretely apply Mishnah, though
more extensively.  Especially the later Amoraim, in particular the
travelers, offer additional cases and applications and thereby
supplement and extend Mishnah.  *All three elements make up component parts of a comprehensive commentary yet each serves a
different function and initially may have circulated in a different format.*

     While different elements of the Commentary may have been
reused, applied, and combined into longer comments, especially by

later travelers, the component parts still maintain a certain
integrity of their own.  Some traditions include the pattern of
Traveler + Tradent in the chain and we can readily trace the uses
and extensions in Palestine.  On the other hand, the tradent's or
traveler's name often does not enter the attributive formula,
though we can reconstruct the traveler's role and at times even
the presence of the later use of an early element, e.g., a gloss-
like comment.[11]  The chain along with the comment, evidently
from an early time, made up a single unit.  The nonstandard commentary formulations, e.g., the First Person Reports and Dialogues
embedded within stories about Samuel which have implications
concerning the meaning of Mishnah, do not belong to the early,
primary "commentary" core.  Disciple circles, though, deemed
whatever Samuel did or said relevant to Mishnah as important and
therefore transmitted it as part of their master's "Torah."  Such
materials could and did circulate at an early time, as evidenced
by the analogues in structurally similar places in both *Gemarot*
though clearly they would not circulate tightly knit to Mishnah
itself.  We thus have a double process.  Traditions maintained
a degree of integrity and remained dependent upon Mishnah and,
accordingly, continued to exhibit characteristics of their early
function in response to Mishnah.  At the same time, they took on
characteristics of their later use.  A tradent incorporates into
Samuel's teachings elements to balance with Palestinian interpretations of Mishnah or he builds upon Samuel's decision and applies
the ruling to a special case.  Someone with access to Samuel's
teachings and those of another master relates them together with
a double attribution ("Rav and Samuel both say") so as to lend
weight to practical rulings.  This provides a teaching with the
impression of double authority and greater force.  Finally, the
later authorities naturally focused upon the kinds of teachings
both in content and character which they found important in their
own day.  For Berakhot this great degree of continued scrutiny
and interest undoubtedly derives from the nature of the materials.
Liturgical matters and teachings constitute a central theme in
early Rabbinic Judaism as part of its program to demonstrate
that there are effective and meaningful replacements for the
Temple cult and ones in which every individual could participate.
Samuel in the first post-mishnaic generation naturally played a
key role in teaching and applying this thesis in Babylonia.  His
efforts, therefore, reflect his pivotal position among late
antique Amoraim in the process of formalizing and standardizing

the themes, formulae, wording, and rules of prayers and blessings.

> Section Two: The Nature of Samuel's Commentary
> and Its Distinctive Place Among
> Ancient Commentaries

> *5.  The Nature of Samuel's Commentary:*
> *A Restatement*

We can now provide a synthetic picture of Samuel's commentary activity.

1.  Samuel's comments make up a "Commentary" on Mishnah.
The teachings convey different sorts of information and are
intended to do different things.  They also employ a diverse set
of precise phraseologies specifically used in a disciplined way
for the several different purposes.  But the presence of these
heterogeneous characteristics is not problematic, as commentaries
in general may have different purposes and elements and include
teachings of various sorts.[12]  Some of Samuel's comments closely
gloss the text of Mishnah and depend upon it for comprehension
and in formulation.  These include: the B- form; the ᵓPYLW, KL
ZMN Š-, KDY Š-, and (ᵓYN) SRYK L- phrasings; and the Glosses.
Others complement and supplement Mishnah though are still dependent upon it for coherence.  These use the HLKH K-, gloss-like
Exegeses, Liturgical Texts, Questions, and First Person Reports
patterns.  These can be remembered along with Mishnah though they
would not enter the text of Mishnah.  The first group makes up
primary elements of Samuel's Mishnah Commentary and the second
one a second-order Commentary.  The former enables Samuel's students to understand the text of Mishnah and concretize its rules.
The latter provides them with the means to apply it fully.  Other
related, completely autonomous comments which supplement Mishnah
but which are not dependent upon it in formulation remain most
coherent in the context of Mishnah.  These include the Blessing
Delineations, Dialogues, Discussions, some Exegeses, and some
Declarative Sentences.  These therefore assume that someone would
study Mishnah and at the appropriate point recall Samuel's comments on the text.  *In a sense, these least tightly formulated*
*teachings most profoundly reflect the fact that Mishnah became*
*the structure around which Amoraim taught and studied.*[13]  Otherwise the comments would be fully autonomous and totally coherent
independent of Mishnah.

All three of these elements may derive from the first
generation and from Samuel himself or from the circles which provide the most fundamental images of Samuel.  All three may have
circulated at an early period.  But each portion fulfilled
different needs.  The first responded to the most immediate need
to understand the text and the rules of Mishnah.  The second
responded to the vital need to apply Mishnah.  The third builds
upon the other two and enables a person to appreciate the full
ramifications of Mishnah and to develop its principles and further
apply and supplement them.  Mishnah thus functions as an authoritative point of departure for further teaching.  The perspective
of the comments and of the Commentary as a whole, moreover, is
not that of an intellectual, theoretical exercise.  Rather it is
shaped and directed by a practical dimension which is reflected
in the choice and spread of Samuel's focus, in the types of comments which he offers, and in the literary phrasings which he
employs.[14]

2.  The Commentary is not a rearrangement of materials
composed originally for some other purposes.  Rather Samuel
responded to Mishnah and one portion of his response constitutes
the "Commentary."  While some elements of the Commentary are more
integral to Mishnah than others, Mishnah prompts all of them.
This is reflected in the spread of the comments, as demonstrated
in chapter four, as well as in the choice and locations of various
specific groups of traditions.  The latter notably include: first,
the several Exegeses, which we demonstrated cannot be considered
as transferred or reused comments which had originated elsewhere
as part of a systematic study of the Bible; secondly, the Liturgical Texts which assume an interpretation of Mishnah; thirdly
the instances of b. and y. analogues in structurally similar
places in both *Gemarot*; and fourthly, substantive analogues
between Tosefta's treatment of Mishnah and its type of comments
and those of Samuel.[15]  The role of Mishnah likewise accords with
our conclusion that those comments presently found in a dispute
form originated as individual responses to Mishnah.

We also have numerous "Related" comments, laid out and
discussed in chapters three and four and elsewhere above.  These
further extend and enrich the treatment of Mishnah.  But these
respond to Mishnah less directly and intimately than the "Mishnah
Comments."  Their perspective is no longer shaped merely by the
text of Mishnah, by its points, and by the ways in which it

defines its themes.  On the other hand, even here Mishnah provides
the occasion and prompts the extended developments and discussion.

3.  Samuel's treatment of Mishnah laid the foundation for
further teaching which led into *Gemara*.  Disciples cite his
teachings along with Mishnah and in association with Mishnah.
Later masters continued to apply the teachings, to reuse them,
and to shape them in light of pressing contemporary issues and
the natural developments of the law.  Practically every *sugya*
exemplifies these developments, though several stand out.

First we saw how the y. "Unrelated" items originally did
directly pertain to Mishnah or belong to a pericope relating to
Mishnah, but were later reworked into Berakhot.  Secondly, #101
provided a graphic example of a pericope with two recensions.
In its more fundamental version, as perserved in Gen. R., it
defines the term "minor" in M. Ber. 7:1.  PT's version revises
Samuel's tradition to respond to a different Palestinian issue.
In #63 a b. tradition is transferred from elsewhere in *Gemara*
and slightly revised.[16]  Similarly these later circles may have
developed Declarative Sentences out of briefer or more formulized
comments.  Thus 72=85 is developed out of the Blessing Delineation in #81=82=84 so as to respond to the issue of the definition
of "Food."  The later masters in a sense use Samuel as a paradigm
for extending Mishnah to new areas.  The traditions which Naḥman
cites, #55, 87, apparently exemplify this process.[17]  Samuel's
traditions thereby provided a foundation for the later independent
teachings.  Certain authorities related Samuel's comments to
those of other early masters and at times even combined them into
ostensible dispute forms.  In chapter seven, we extensively
traced these transformations.[18]

Even the attributive formulae at times may reflect the
reuse of Samuel's teachings.  We found that the pattern of
TRAVELER + TRADENT generally consists of a third-generation
traveler who cites Samuel's tradition, which he hears in Babylonia
from one of Samuel's disciples and which he transmits and cites
in Palestine.  We can often discern from the pericope how the
traveler--or some later source--employed and even reshaped and
adapted the tradition to fit the y. context.  Accordingly, concern
soon enough focused as much on the content of the law and its
development as on preserving Samuel's Torah.

4.  Samuel's teaching thus initially responded to Mishnah
and functioned as a commentary to that text.  But in later

generations, the comments on Mishnah also took on the characteristics of a first stage in the developing "Post-Mishnahic teaching." His comments thereby became subject to interpretation and
development. Eventually in that stage the teachings were collected and transmitted as part of larger units and subsequently
went through processes of literary enrichment. Moreover, the
comments originated as a part of a Commentary. But that Commentary became subsumed in the emerging and developing *Gemara*. While
they gained characteristics of the latter, they did not totally
lose those of the former. As Mishnah continued to play an important role among the Amoraim and as Samuel's Mishnah Commentary-
teachings became part of the developing *Gemara*, Samuel's traditions became one of the central frameworks around which the
*Gemara* itself was organized and structured.[19]

### 6. Antecedents for Samuel's Commentary: A Comparison and Search for Models

#### i. Approaches, Categories, and Formats of Commentaries

Our reconstructed picture of Samuel's Commentary exhibits
heterogeneous characteristics. We have suggested that the disparate nature and purposes of Mishnah and of Samuel's commentary
activity account for the diverse elements of his work. To
demonstrate this thesis we now turn to "commentary" as a genre
in its own right. As we shall see, while Samuel's Commentary
does develop earlier literary types and forms, its basic structure
and features differ from earlier extant literary works. Hence
Samuel's Commentary is not the result of a linear development of
an earlier type of activity within Judaism and antiquity. In
order fully to understand the phenomenon of "commentary" we
draw upon examples and modern scholarly discussion of ancient,
medieval, and modern commentaries.

A commentary may reflect different objectives which influence its final form. The background of every exegete may con-
sciously or unconsciously affect his efforts. Where the work
involves religious and legal matters, naturally the exegete's
social, cultural, and religious predilections will have an impact.
While modern writers are quite conscious of their motivations,
ancient and medieval ones often were equally aware and even
included statements of their motives in the introductions to
their works. Contemporary scholars have traced the impact of
these orientations in particular on the study of the Bible.[20]

For example, Medieval Jews and Christians were aware of the
multiplicity of approaches and divided them into four major types,
commonly called *pardes* (PRDS), which stands for the literal,
allegorical, hermeneutical or homiletical, and mystical methods.
Modern interests have refined and increased the number of areas
to include, among others, textual, philological, literal, homiletical (midrashic), mystical and allegorical, as well as philo-
sophical, halakhic-legal, and literary, tradition-, source-, and
redaction-criticism.  Moreover exegetes may include more than one
of these approaches in their work as well as a history of interpretations and explanations.[21]

     Salo Baron and others have reviewed the medieval Jewish
biblical studies and have characterized the various works in
terms of their genres.[22]  Gershom Scholem, in particular, has
vividly analyzed the role of religious motives behind the allegorical and mystical interpretations of the Bible and demonstrated how similarities in purposes may account for similarities
in results.[23]  Such factors affect modern works as well.  Brevard
S. Childs, for example, has reviewed the characteristics of the
major modern Bible commentary series and presents in his commentary on Exodus a clear statement of purpose.[24]  He lays out how
his "theological" interests determine and shape his focus and the
choice of questions which he addresses as well as his format.[25]

     Hence the proposition that purposes and traits of commen-
taries may vary in general appears cogent.  To apply it to Samuel
we must examine his commentary's distinctive qualities.  To
appreciate those elements, though, we must consider the various
possibilities which theoretically lay before Samuel and place his
efforts within a wider context.  Accordingly, we first review the
specific purposes and types of commentaries in antiquity.

                              *  *  *


     People are motivated to employ commentaries for several
reasons.  When a society or an individual believes that a certain
work contains or expresses the "truth" on a certain matter, as
time passes and conditions change they need a means to understand
the work in contemporary idiom and in the light of the new conditions and values.  Moreover, when the work developed or originated with one purpose but later assumed a different role, the
need to bridge the gap between the work and contemporary realities
is compounded.  Often, as well, the original composition may lack

sufficient clarity and require clarification.  In addition, where
multiple understandings are theoretically possible, one may need
to make explicit what is implicit in the text.[26]  One of the means
which later individuals employ to respond to this problem constitutes interpretation and commentary.  Finally, according to
Jonathan Z. Smith, the very nature and thought of the scribal
craft involves using and reworking earlier paradigms and literature.  As part of his argument Smith traces successive reworkings
of ancient and Hellenistic Mesopotamian, Egyptian, and Jewish
literature and suggests how the task led to the creation of various exegetical techniques.[27]

       A person may tacitly interpret a text when he or she makes
use of one of its references or themes and employs it in a new
context.  Alternatively, one may make a more explicit response to
a text.  It is with the latter that we are concerned.  These
formal responses may occur in one of at least three major ways.

       First, they may add information to the text.  The former
becomes subsumed in the latter and together both appear to make
up a single work.  Examples include glosses or whole pericopae
interpolated into a text.  Instances are found in ancient Jewish
(Israelite) and non-Jewish literature.[28]  J. Weingreen, G. R.
Driver, and others have discussed the purposes and characteristics
of glosses.  Weingreen notes that the glosses are succinct single
words or terse phrases that comment on a word or phrase to
clarify it or to draw attention to some item of information
assumed relevant to the text, and that originally the glosses
were external to the text but later entered it.  He distinguishes
the glosses from editorial notes which, he believes, were intended
to enter the text, refer to the subject of the passage, supply
additional information, and extend the range of the text's
application.  Though these notes can be longer than glosses, they
do not break the flow of the text since they are placed after the
statement of importance.[29]  In various literatures glosses constitute an early stage of commentary.[30]

       Secondly, the later individual may require the text to
conform to the new values and to incorporate new sources or a new
point of view.  In this case we naturally deal with the composition of a unitary work, a new one which has replaced the old one.
Ancient Judaic examples include the Books of Chronicles, which
reworks the Books of Samuel and Kings, Jubilees, Genesis Apocry-
phon, Pseudo-Philo [= *Liber Antiquitatum Biblicarum*], and
Josephus' *Antiquities of the Jews*.  These paraphrase and rework

different portions of the Bible.  In addition, any translation of
an earlier work which is read by itself makes up a further
example of a "rewriting" kind of interpretation.  Examples
include the Greek and Aramaic translations of the Bible.[31]

Thirdly, the individual may produce a separate work which
is to be associated with the first one and which contains the
requisite information.  The new work may take the form of glosses
on the margin of a text.  If in the course of time these glosses
enter the text itself, they become examples of Category One,
"information subsumed in the original work."[32]  But when the distinction is preserved the materials appear as two separate com-
positions.  In the latter case the two may nevertheless still
be associated and circulate as part of a larger whole.[33]

Samuel's comments and his Commentary as a whole generally
do not exhibit the characteristic of the Second Category, the
"rewritten text."  The only exceptions may lie in the Instructions to a *Tanna*, which we found in Volume One.  While Epstein,
for one, argues that these comments were in Samuel's own arrangement of teachings and not in the Mishnah itself, some individuals
may have understood these alternative formulations as replacements and emendations of Mishnah itself.  Accordingly, most of
Samuel's teachings ostensibly belong to Category Three and some
to Category One.[34]

The commentaries may also vary in focus and format.
Those in ancient Babylonian sources fall into three basic patterns.  One, the *satu* commentary, written on a tablet by itself,
e.g., in four columns, contains excerpts of single words from a
text and comments on it, and thus consists of a glossary word
list.  Such lists occasionally were expanded with new items and/
or further explanations or both to make up a larger recension.
Secondly, the *mukallimtu* commentary contains excerpts of whole
lines from a text and comments on one word thereof.  As the
lemmata were full phrases the composition constituted an independent work.  The third format, structured as a totally independent
work, is a combination of the first two patterns, with comments
on single words and whole phrases.[35]

The models of commentaries in Hellenistic Greek sources
exhibit similarities and differences from the Babylonian ones.
Rudolf Pfeiffer, in the *History of Classical Scholarship*,
describes several types of interpretive genres.  In addition to
individual exegeses of passages there are two types of commentaries which make up works in their own right.  The first

consists of continuous, running commentary to a text (*upomnemata*),
and appears in two forms.  One is made up of marginal and inter-
linear notes or scholia, perhaps associated with the presentation
of the text.  The other is a composite work that includes lemmata
from the text, textual critical notes, and an exegetical part.
The second type of commentaries is actually monographs (*suggram-*
*mata*), that is, *peri* literature on selected aspects and problems
of a text, its language and subject.[36]

     An additional and somewhat different type of commentary is
known from Iran and is significant to our study.  While scholars
believe oral commentaries may have existed in various cultures,
they have firm evidence for Iran, in particular, on the Avesta.
The Avesta in Avestan language circulated orally, memorized by a
reciter probably along with an ancient commentary, called Zand,
also in Avestan language.  Subsequently, in Sasanian times the
Avesta was translated into Middle Persian and it, too, circulated
orally along with a Middle Persian Zand or Commentary.  The commentary produced by different priestly scholars explained words
and phrases.  When written down, in later Sasanian times, the
redactor who cited conflicting opinions often produced lengthy
exegetical passages.  Thus the earliest commentary consisted of
oral glosses, often incorporated into the Avestan text and, in
the Middle Persian recension, both glosses and exposition.  The
problems of unraveling the earliest stages of the Zand and the
relationship of its oral to its later written, compiled format
provides a striking parallel to the problem of the pre-literary
stage of Samuel's teachings and their later role in *Gemara*.[37]

     In chapter ten we further discuss this last type of com-
mentary.  Additional types and formats also existed in antiquity.
Our brief survey, however, already makes clear that commentaries
appeared in different formats, some brief and others more extensive, that a work may include several different types of comments,
and that a composition might undergo expansion.

        ii.  Comparisons and Search for Models:
               Pre-Rabbinic

     We now turn to biblical and Second Temple Jewish and
Hellenistic literature and search for parallels to the types and
forms of Samuel's Mishnah comments which make up his Commentary
on Mishnah.  We shall see that the literary phrasings are not
the result of a linear development of genres extant from ancient
Israelite literature and teaching.  Rather they are tied to the

changed social function of a teacher in Greco-Roman and late-
antique Judaism.  The particular traits of the Commentary as a
whole emerge from the rabbinic context in a distinctive way.
While we find parallels and analogues for various smaller units,
as laid out in chapters five and six, these forms in and of themselves do not make the materials into a commentary.  Rather the
ways in which Samuel employed these phrasings and patterns and
the ways in which his students transmitted them,[38] made them
suitable commentary material.  What provides the comments with
the characteristics of a commentary is their specific relationship to a text.[39]  Thus, for example, among the earlier examples
of glosses none relate to a text in the manner in which Samuel's
glosses relate to Mishnah.  Certainly, some scholars have suggested that Midrash and midrashic exegesis, which relate to the
biblical text, have ancient roots and precede the type of teaching which characterizes Mishnah.[40]  But while midrashic exposition is assumed in much of Second Temple literature and in the
Bible itself and is literarily expressed in the "rewritten Bible"
genre (as in the Septuagint and Jubilees), there are no extant
examples of exegetical midrashic *works* until the rabbinic Midrashim of the second-third centuries C.E.  The only exceptions,
discussed below, are allegorical interpretations of the Bible,
best exemplified by Philo, and Qumram *pesharim*.[41]

I.  The Hebrew Bible.

Otto Eissfeldt, in *The Old Testament*, reviews the literary
types of smaller units of biblical materials.[42]  Only several of
the types which he assembles are similar to those found in the
Mishnah comments.  But while they are similar in formulation, they
differ in purpose and use.  By definition none are intended to
form or are preserved as a commentary related to but different
from another text.  We may mention, of his categories, the following:

A.  *Prose Types*

a.  Speeches and Sermons are lacking in our sample but
found elsewhere in talmudic literature; those in Dialogue formulation are found in our sample among the "nonstandard" commentary
phrasings; and Prayers are found in our sample as Liturgical
Texts.[43]  Our instances of Prayers, however, serve a different
function and exhibit greater patternization and formalization.
Notably, the Bible lacks instances of Blessing Delineations, an
important liturgical pattern in our sample.

      b.  Materials which purport to represent "records": Con-
tracts, Letters, and Lists are lacking in our sample though found
elsewhere in talmudic literature and even among Samuel's other
teachings;[44] Laws and Cultic Ordinances make up special subgroups
of this category because they provide a potentially rich source
of parallels to Samuel's comments.

      Eissfeldt's introductory observations concerning the
"Laws" describe one of the central problems which our study
addresses.

> Before these [legal precepts] were incorporated in law
> books which have been preserved in the Old Testament . . . or
> rather before they were incorporated in the smaller bodies of
> law which underlay these, they must have existed singly or
> combined into merely quite small groups.  A considerable
> proportion of the relevant material is not preserved in prose,
> but in the form of songs or more often of sayings, and this
> will be discussed below.[45]

Eissfeldt classified the Laws and Cultic Ordinances into various
kinds, in particular casuistic and apodictic.  But Samuel's teachings, whether those with a protasis and apodosis or glosses, or
whether with the SRYK L- formulation or some other phrasing which
sets out a condition, differ in style and in formulation from
the biblical modes.  They are distinct in a greater use of the
participle construction and less explicit use of the word, "if,"
$^C$M, to open the condition.  Likewise they are more formulaic and
at the same time more detailed and specific.[46]  These differences
in part reflect the changes and developments in Mishnaic Hebrew.[47]
Moreover, in our sample, most of the parallel legal teachings fit
into the category of "Sayings," which belong to a separate area.


      c.  Narratives: Poetic (Introductory: Myths; Fairy-tale,
Fable, Tale; Saga; and Legends) and Historical (Reports; Popular
History; Autobiography; Accounts of Dreams and Visions; Prophetic
Autobiography).  Among Samuel's "nonstandard" commentary formulations there are parallels to several subtypes of biblical Narratives, including Narratives to make or reflect a legal point,
Prophetic Legends, Reports and Autobiographical Accounts and
Prophet's First Person Narratives.[48]  Additional instances may be
found among Samuel's "Related" and "Unrelated" comments.  The
biblical materials like those of Samuel's have a didactic role and
serve to exemplify or make a point.  Even in the Bible this may be
a legal issue.  In our sample, the narratives are preserved due to
their perceived relevance to Mishnah and its law and may include

within it a discussion which involves Samuel or a statement
attributed to him.

*B.  Sayings*[49]

     a.  Sayings from the life of the individual and from the
life of the community are lacking in our sample.

     b-c.  Legal and Cultic Sayings provide a natural parallel
to rabbinic teachings, including those of Samuel, especially
among his "Related" and "Unrelated" comments.[50]  But, as with the
prose laws, the two groups differ in style.  On the other hand,
both purport to present teachings or statements of an individual.
Eissfeldt's observation as to the probably pre-literary state and
earliest stage of the apodictic Sayings throws light on the problem of the fundamental stage of Samuel's teachings.

> Originally sayings in the form of an address . . . , or
> beginning with a participle . . . , or with a relative
> clause . . . , or introduced by a curse . . . may well have
> existed independently.  But very soon, no doubt already at
> the oral stage, they were gathered into groups, especially in
> tens and twelves, consisting of sayings which deal with cases
> of a similar kind.  These groups have in several cases been
> preserved as such in the Old Testament.[51]

Whether or not Eissfeldt accurately describes the history of
these biblical laws, his differentiation between an original oral,
fundamental state and the later use applies to Samuel's teachings
as well.  Many amoraic teachings are presented and probably preserved in groups, as argued by Abraham Weiss, though this does
not apply to Samuel's Mishnah comments.  By their very nature they
were intended to circulate in association or along with Mishnah.
This seems to apply, as mentioned above, even to the autonomously
formulated teachings which make good sense only in the context of
Mishnah.[52]

     d.  Prophetic and Lay Sayings, Blessings, and Curses lack
parallels in our sample though they are found elsewhere in rabbinic literature.

     e.  Proverbs and Riddles lack parallels in our sample;
and Wisdom Sayings and Parables while not found among the Mishnah
comments do appear among the "Related" and "Unrelated" teachings.[53]

C.  *Songs*[54]

     a.  Work Songs; Wedding Songs; the Watchman's Songs.

     b.  Mocking Songs; Funeral Dirges.

     c.  Royal Songs; Victory Songs.

     d.  Cultic Songs: Royal Cult Songs, "Spirutual Songs," Hymns, Accession Songs, the "Sentence of Judgment," National Laments, Collective Songs of Trust, the Individual Laments, Individual Songs of Trust, Collective Songs of Thanksgiving, Individual Song of Thanksgiving.

     e.  Wisdom Poems.

We have grouped together the numerous types and subgroups of Songs as they all lack parallels among Samuel's Mishnah comments. On the other hand, the Funerary Dirges, Lamentations, Hymns, and Thanksgiving Songs are found among other amoraic materials.

     II.   The Apocrypha, Pseudepigrapha, and other Second
           Temple Literature.

The Second Temple works further develop the biblical literary genres and employ additional ones as well. Thus, for example we find the Apocalyptic, as in Daniel and Enoch, as an independent work, and additional instances of Wisdom Sayings, as in the Wisdom of Ben Sira. The developments in the types, moreover, are not insignificant, for some types now have greater affinities with their later rabbinic versions. These characteristics include, for example, the literary devices of stories and narratives and the more idealized portraits of exemplary Jewish individuals.[55] But what is relevant to our problem is that we find for the first time an overall composition constructed like Samuel's teachings. These are the Qumran *midrashim* and *pesharim* and the allegorical interpretive works.

The desired literary model is a commentary where the material relates to or revolves around another text. The first extant example comes from the Dead Sea Scrolls and the portion thereof preserved in the Zadokite fragments. They contain numerous instances of biblical exegeses. Verses are cited and explained through several means. Schiffman divides them into two categories, that of *perush* and *midrash* for legal texts, and

*pesher* for aggadic commentaries.  In both kinds, the comments
are on a text yet remain distinct from the verses.  We also have
examples of commentaries written as separate books, e.g., the
Habbakuk Pesher, in addition to individual pericopae of citations
or references to a verse and their exegesis.[56]  The former therefore constitutes a precedent for pursuing a commentary activity
in its own right.  The latter attest the process and provide
examples and uses of the Exegetical type of comment, catalogued
in chapter five.

Certain dynamics of the exegesis may be analogous to
Samuel's teaching.  According to Schiffman, *perush* and *midrash*
exegesis (the former lacks citation of corroborative biblical
material and the latter includes it), "performed on a written
text took place in regular sessions presided over by *ish ha-doresh*"
and could be done orally.  But "the laws were then arranged in
written lists called *serakhim*.  Written, not oral, transmission
was the norm at Qumran."[57]  While these topical lists may more
closely parallel Mishnah itself, Schiffman's reconstruction provides one model for the transition from an oral origin to a
written stage for transmission.

The techniques and types of Qumran exegesis have been
studied and the specifics need not detain us.  But we see that
commentary flourishes in a social context in which people try to
make a text fit their particular situation.[58]

Philo provides us with the second clearly attested and
extant instance of a commentary as a separate literary genre.
There are earlier individual instances of allegorical interpretations in other books, for example the Book of Wisdom of Solomon
and sections within the Letter of Aristeas and especially the
fragments of Aristobulus, of the first half of the second century,
B.C.E.  In Aristobulus, the interpretations are presented in an
expository and apologetic essay addressed by the author to King
Ptolemy Philometer and mainly devoted to answering common questions about the Pentateuch, as reflected in its title, "An Explanation of the Mosaic Law."[59]

Accordingly, while Aristobulus may actually constitute an
earlier model, Philo fully develops this genre and from him we
have the first extant complete works of this sort.  His writings
are composed in the form of a running commentary to the Pentateuch,
as the *Questions and Answers to Genesis and Exodus*, or in that of
discourses on specific topics from the Bible, as *On the Special
Laws*, or on particular problems.  These works thus fall within the

different formats of Hellenistic commentaries, as laid out by
Rudolf Pfeiffer.  They extensively employ the allegorical method
of biblical interpretation and their contents are greatly shaped
by the function and role of Scripture.[60]

> III.   The early Christian literature, especially the
>        portions that derive from Jewish or Jewish-Christian
>        circles.

The earliest Christian works, first, provide examples of
the allegorical and midrashic use of Scripture but, so far as
the New Testament goes, no actual commentaries.[61]  Secondly, they
contain additional instances of already attested parallel types
and forms of small literary units as well as previously unattested
ones.  But as we noticed before, wherever these types and forms
are found among the Mishnah-Commentary teachings, they are used
differently.  We especially note the apopthegms or sayings of
Jesus.  Like the teachings of Samuel, they originated in one
mode, oral, and later went through a transmission and literary
process and we presently find them as part of a context quite
different from that in which they originated.  Morton Smith
reminds us, however, that the sayings of Jesus and of the rabbis
nevertheless do differ.  The New Testament sayings are used to
set out the teachings of Jesus, the rabbinic sayings, to set out
the oral law, "of which the rabbis are thought to be interpreters,
not originators."[62]

*   *   *

In reviewing our conclusions to this point it is worth-
while to underscore how they relate to our search for models for
Samuel's Commentary.  We suggested that the nature of Mishnah and
of Samuel's efforts shaped Samuel's activities.  In order to
appreciate Samuel's distinctive traits we sought to compare his
efforts with other possible ways in which he could have cast and
organized his teachings.  We traced types and forms of small
literary units and found that the few parallels in earlier literature serve a different function when in Samuel's Mishnah comments, since in the latter they are used to relate to a separate
text.  It is for this reason we described the nature and role of
the genre of commentaries.

We discussed how the process of commentary constitutes
one means to interpret a text.  It enables a person to clarify
it and to bridge the gap of understanding and reality that

separates it from the reader.  The individual may be explaining
and presenting the classics, e.g., Greek poetry, or may be pursuing wisdom and guidance.  They and those involved in the transmission of a text naturally will develop techniques for exegesis.

　　　　We found that commentary is an ancient genre, attested
in Mesopotamian, Egyptian, Greek, and Roman cultures, in particular in ancient dream and omen texts, in studies of the Greek
classics and in the allegorical interpretations of Hesiod and
Homer, and in the works of the Alexandrian grammarians and Roman
rhetoricians and legal scholars.[63]  In Israelite-Judaic literature, Glosses, the earliest and most fundamental mode of commentary, are apparently found in ancient times, in the Bible.  But
the first extant version of the more extensive types of commentaries, whether as epexegetical additions or as a full literary
work on its own, is not discernible until the Hellenistic period,
possibly in Aristobulus, and definitely in Philo and the Qumran
Scrolls.

　　　　Hence the question now arises: Why in the Hellenistic
period do Jews resort to commentaries as an additional means to
respond to Scriptures?  While previously commentaries may have
been composed, apparently they were not deemed important enough
to be preserved.  This would support the historical interpretation that commentaries in that earlier period did not play a
central role in society.  It is possible that the change took
place because of the increased importance of the study of the
Bible.  Tied to certain social and political developments we find
"applied" exegesis and midrash through which a group employs
Scripture to justify its practices and ideas.  Moreover, the
Bible is perceived as a source for truth in a new way: it is a
means for people to relate to and experience the divine and
directly to gain its guidance.  In Ben Sira, this notion becomes
noticeable and among the rabbis it reaches maturity as a responsibility for every individual Jew.  The religious leader as a
result becomes the "wise man."[64]  Those who earlier and contempo-
raneously did not adopt this orientation certainly held the
biblical heritage in great esteem.  But they either did not con-
sciously try to bridge the gap that separated them from biblical
and "traditional" institutions, as with the Samaritans, or else
tried to respond but in a different manner.  The latter forth-
rightly adapted and revised the biblical record through a new
comparable revelation, as in the form of a "rewritten Bible."
Thus one  prophet  creatively adapted another prophet's words, or

Chronicles reworked the Books of Samuel and Kings, or the authors
of Daniel employed earlier biblical motifs in a newly composed
work.

Accordingly, the changed role in the study and use of the
Bible may integrally relate to the rise of commentaries.  What
makes this mode of interpreting the Bible distinctive is the
belief that one could no longer continue in the biblical process
and compose new prophecies.  It is not surprising, therefore,
that Philo and Qumran provide the models, be it different, for
the rabbis.  As various scholars have observed, all three share
a similar social and religious situation.  They deal with a discontinuity that separates them from the traditionally defined
institutions of the biblical world and they try to provide a new
basis for their systems.[65]

iii.  Comparisons and Search for Models: Rabbinic

The rabbinic literature presents us with materials from
the same religious and cultural world as Samuel's Mishnah teachings.  We would therefore expect to find that the rabbinic works
would provide us with models fairly close to Samuel's response to
Mishnah.  But in fact these works exhibit similarities and differences.  Accordingly, to the degree that these variations
reflect the realities of those who composed and transmitted the
teachings, we may have evidence as to differences within the
larger rabbinic world.  Hence our continued pursuit of models
may throw light on Samuel's role and on third-century Judaism in
general.

A.  *Midrash*

Samuel's Mishnah comments find structural affinities with
the exegetical or halakhic Midrashim to the Pentateuch.  These
works contain teachings attributed to the Tannaim though they are
not edited, at the earliest, until apparently the third century.
In each, most pericopae are exegetical and some are nonexegetical.
The former, as the works as a whole, are structured around Scripture and present numerous comments and series of comments on
successive verses of most sections in Ex., Lev., Num., and Deut.
Their literary, linguistic, and formal characteristics and origin
of each work and even of sections within a work differ.  But the
Bible shapes their focus and basically defines the themes which
are discussed.  One receives the impression that most of the
comments originated in response to these verses.  As Morton Smith

observed in regard to a section of Mekilta, "The essential connection of the material was effected . . . by its relation to the
text expounded."[66] We have precise data to understand one huge
block of Sifra.  Jacob Neusner's careful analysis indicates that
it consists mostly of exegetical pericopae of two sorts.  First,
an earlier core of simple exegesis on selected contiguous verses
and, secondly, a larger, more dialetical exegesis which is later,
which probably represents the views of the editors, and which in
effect argues that the law cannot have been derived by reason and
logic; rather revelation was necessary.  The nonexegetical materials which constitute s small proportion of the whole, are
basically shared by Mishnah-Tosefta.  Both probably drew upon a
common source.[67]

On the basis of these observations we can conclude that,
first, in form the Midrashim are structurally similar to Samuel's
comments on Mishnah.  Both relate to a text.  But when we compare
the two we compare unequal things.  Samuel's teachings are
authored by a single individual while the Midrashim include
teachings of numerous named and anonymous people.  Accordingly,
the Midrashim are far more systematic in their detailed focus on
the text.  As a result, the Midrashim more closely parallel the
finished product of *Gemara*, which contains interpretations of
many individuals.[67a]

Second, both the Midrashim and Samuel's Mishnah-comments
employ precise phraseologies.  The Midrashim use numerous technical terminologies, wordings, and patterns to lay out the comments.  These generally are presented anonymously as if from the
anonymous editors.  Moreover, the individual comments employ
various formulaic and fixed usages and patterns.  Wilhelm Bacher
and others have systematically studied these formulations.[68]

Third, the differences between the Midrashim and Samuel's
Mishnah comments may reflect disparate formations.  Shalom
Spiegel has aptly suggested the form of the exegetical Midrashim
reflects an academic setting.  In the following quotation he
refers to Genesis Rabba, which in the respects that concern us
exhibits characteristics similar to those of the halakhic
Midrashim.

> The form in which the legends were grouped around Scrip-
> ture usually followed from their function.  Collections of
> legends which adhered to the order of the biblical text were
> the product of instruction and answered the needs of the
> *school*.  An early example of such a work is founded on the
> book of Genesis and was compiled in the fifth century.[69]

We can directly relate Spiegel's suggestion to our present discussion.  The systematic focus on successive verses and especially
the inclusion of numerous comments on a single verse reflects
painstaking instruction and a literary working over of various
exegetical comments.  This certainly applies to the more dialec-
tical portion of the Midrashim, as in Sifra, and to an earlier
core, whether anonymous or attributed, when its focus is also
exhaustively systematic on numerous verses.  The projected academic setting of a master teaching students would fit both a
formal academy as well as an informal circle.  In any event, it
precludes a more public and popular context, as Spiegal himself
makes clear in the rest of the passage.  He contrasts those
materials structured around the biblical text with those which
are "the outgrowth of preaching" and were designed for "worship."
The latter would yield a more selective and refined body of
material.

        At this point, we remain unsure how the earliest core of
the teachings attributed to a single master would have originated.
They could have been part of instructional exercises carefully
analyzing a text or part of a teaching giving a student guidance,
or a combination of both.  Logically we assume the second mode
would be somewhat more selective.  Similarly we do not know what
may have constituted the purpose motivating the master's explanation of the Bible.  Would it involve more than the longstanding
pattern of mediating the written Scriptures--now done in terms of
the rabbinic perspective on religious leadership and institutions?

        Nevertheless, it is clear that the Midrashim as a whole
constitute highly worked over literary corpora.  Hence in terms
of the present perspective, Samuel's more selective and pragmatic,
though comprehensive, focus reflects a less structured and technical academic effort.  In addition, on the one hand, the scrutiny and exegesis of the Scriptures, the Written Torah, parallels
Samuel's scrutiny and exegesis of Mishnah, the Oral Torah.  But
on the other hand, the Scriptures by definition are a written
text and the Midrashim, by their very nature, were intended to
circulate in written form, while Mishnah, in terms of its use,
was an oral work and the fundamental core of Samuel's Mishnah
comments were designed to circulate orally.[70]

B.  *Mishnah, Tosefta, and Baraitot*

        Mishnah is not a commentary to another work though it
does provide examples of various types and forms of small

literary materials which are found in the teachings of Samuel and
other Amoraim.[71]   Earlier we noted the instances of the types
and phraseologies of comments that are paralleled in Mishnah as
well as Tosefta.   Indeed we can point to an analogue or a different use or variation of every pattern listed in chapters five
through seven.[72]   Many appear in materials which function in a
way analogous to Samuel's teachings.   Mishnah contains phrases
and pericopae which gloss, explain, limit, or extend another
phrase or pericope.[73]   For example, as graphically laid out in
our analysis of tradition #101 and in our longer study, "Minor
For Zimmun," Mishnah itself often defines the category of a
"minor" in a way quite close to that of Samuel's comment on M.
Ber. 7:1.   In this sense, such materials constitute a parallel
to Samuel's efforts.   Abraham Goldberg has focused on this aspect
of Mishnah and has compared it to Tosefta's response to Mishnah.
Each layer of Mishnah stands in relation to another, ostensibly
earlier, layer as Tosefta stands in relation to Mishnah's last
layer.[74]   Whether or not Goldberg correctly classified the strata
in Mishnah and Tosefta, his observations aptly serve to focus on
the literary phenomenon.[75]

        Various scholars have naturally noticed how Tosefta con-
tains teachings which gloss, explain, and otherwise relate to
Mishnah.   Albeck, Epstein, Melammed, and others have tried to
delineate and differentiate the ways in which this occurs.[76]
Goldberg, as mentioned, emphasizes the close connection Tosefta
has with Mishnah and whatever the merits of his wider thesis as
to the history of Mishnah, his argument certainly demonstrates
this relationship.   Lieberman throughout his commentary on
Tosefta, *Tosefta Ki-fshutah*, shows how Tosefta contains lemmata
of Mishnah which are then glossed, as well as clauses which
directly refer to and depend upon the text of Mishnah.[77]   Jacob
Neusner, in his *History of the Mishnaic Law of Purities*, systematically lays out the relationship between the two documents.[78]
He proves that Tosefta's materials are structured on the basis
of their relationship to Mishnah.   There are three sorts of
materials.   First, glosses which depend in formulation and for
comprehension on Mishnah; complementary pericopae which for
comprehension need Mishnah; and supplementary materials which do
not depend upon Mishnah but which supply Mishnah with additional
materials on Mishnah's topics or on something mentioned in
Mishnah.   Tosefta for each section of Mishnah separately presents
each of these groups as connected teachings.   In Neusner's
words:[79]

Tosefta redactionally correlates with Mishnah.  Its
intermediate divisions are determined not principally by
shifts in theme and in form, but by three fixed relationships
*to* Mishnah itself:  (1) Tosefta may explicitly cite and gloss
Mishnah.   (2) It may complement Mishnah, without clearly
citing its exact language or glossing it.   (3) Tosefta may
supply a supplement, autonomous, or, and merely relevant in
a general way to, Mishnah.

While other scholars including Goldberg suggest that
Tosefta provides an early *Gemara* to Mishnah, Neusner's analysis
enables us to demonstrate this.[80]   Our classification of Samuel's
Mishnah-teachings into three broad categories, as laid out in
chapters eight and nine, closely correlates with Neusner's three
classifications.[81]

Tosefta thus provides an example of a commentary.   In
addition, like Mishnah, it contains analogues to the literary
formulations of Samuel's individual comments.[82]   Moreover, Tosefta
is a model that Samuel may have known.   In chapter four we showed
how the substance of numerous comments find analogues in Tosefta.
In addition, not infrequently the comments assume a development
of Mishnah's law to the next logical stage which Samuel then
further develops.   We suggested that this fact supports our argument as to Samuel's connection with Mishnah.   Therefore, whether
or not Tosefta as we presently know it circulated in the third
century, Samuel must have known the various *baraitot* that are
found in Tosefta.[83]

The final analogue to Samuel's teaching consists of the
diverse *baraitot* which are cited in *Gemara*, which briefly or more
extensively gloss, complement, and supplement Mishnah, and many
of which are clearly so formulated to depend upon and circulate
along with Mishnah.[84]   Even Albeck who denies that Tosefta
existed in the third century agrees that these *baraitot* circulated
immediately after the time of the formation of Mishnah.   One of
the types of *baraitot* consists of those attributed to early
Amoraim, including Samuel.   These Samuel *baraitot* attest to
Samuel's teaching on Mishnah.[85]   Tradition #51 may constitute an
instance to which is appended a decision.   In Volume One we
analyzed several of the additional instances.[86]

Considering that Tosefta and the *baraitot* constitute
commentaries to Mishnah, did they in fact provide Samuel with a
model for his activity?   Moreover, what light do these parallels
throw on the nature of Samuel's first teaching?

First, these two analogous genres certainly are relevant.
Goldberg and Neusner, though they differ in the interpretation

of their observation, agree that Mishnah and Tosefta are integrally related.[87]  Hence, Tosefta and the talmudic *baraitot*
indicate that it is natural for someone to comment directly on
Mishnah and they may do so in diverse ways, some more tightly
tied to the text than others.  Some comments could circulate even
along with Mishnah itself, appended to the text, and not just
associated with it.[88]  This accords with the very nature of
Mishnah which is so constructed that it elicits exegesis.  Its
style and grammatical, formal structure as well as what it
includes and what it does *not* include assume that whoever learns
the text will relate one part of it to another, clarify and
amplify unclear portions, and develop its laws.[89]

Secondly, we have literary parallels.  The analogous
terms, phraseologies, and usages are relevant as sources which
Samuel may have adopted and developed.  Tosefta and occasionally
Mishnah even include stories relevant to Mishnah's law or theme
for the sake of the light they throw on the subject or to support,
clarify, or limit a ruling or opinion.  As we indicated above,
Scripture itself may use narrative materials for this purpose.
But the use of these stories as Mishnah comments underscores the
differences between Tosefta and Samuel's teachings.  We found
that such stories would not have originated as a fundamental part
of what Samuel intended to be commentary on Mishnah.  Rather his
disciples included and circulated them because of their relevance
to Mishnah.  They thus do not make up "primary" Mishnah-commentary
material.  On the other hand, they integrally fit into Tosefta.
Tosefta is a composite of various teachings by different people
and editors and it is exhaustively systematic as well as comprehensive.  The overwhelming number of clauses and laws in Mishnah
elicit attention.  Editors designed Tosefta to include everything
they deemed relevant to Mishnah.  This kind of close scrutiny
derives from a setting in which one can painstakingly pursue
textual and exegetical exercises, in part reminiscent of the
scribal practices described by Jonathan Z. Smith.  Tosefta's
degree of complexity and anthologizing led Neusner aptly to point
out that Tosefta was not formulated to circulate orally.[90]

Therefore, we find that Samuel's teachings, in contrast
to Tosefta, are comprehensive and deliberate but not exhaustively
systematic.[91]  This applies even more so to the instances of
Samuel's *baraitot* and his instructions to a *tanna*, which are
fewer in number than the direct Mishnah comments.  Samuel's
response to Mishnah thus covers much of the text but not every
Mishnah passage.

Accordingly, we must differentiate between Samuel's teachings and Tosefta's treatment of Mishnah as we earlier differen-
tiated between Samuel's teachings and the halakhic Midrashim's
treatment of the Bible.  This accords with our observation of
Samuel's pragmatic motives reflected in his activity.  Samuel as
a first generation post-Mishnaic master taught Mishnah, instructed
a *tanna* and students.  He dealt with all the major topics of
Mishnah and offered diverse kinds of comments on Mishnah to
respond to different needs that one would have in reading, understanding, and applying Mishnah and in developing its laws.  The
examples from Berakhot indicate how such a commentary can contribute a great deal to the development of liturgical practices and
prayers.  They add up to a substantive body of teachings, as we
demonstrated in chapter four.  Samuel's disciples consider his
sayings and actions as Torah and therefore transmitted in conjunction, or along with Mishnah, anything he said that appeared
relevant to Mishnah.

## 7.  Conclusions

1.  Samuel composed a Commentary to Mishnah which, like
other commentaries in antiquity, was made up of heterogeneous
elements.  His activity, though, was greatly shaped by the nature
of the work he commented upon--a legal guide--and by his pragmatic motive to make Mishnah applicable.  Different generations
of masters concentrated upon different parts of the Commentary
and transmitted, applied, and used the teachings.[92]  The Commentary preserved the characteristics of its fundamental function
at the same time as it took on the new characteristics of its
later use and its transformation into one of the basic building
blocks of the developing *Gemara*.

2.  Commentary constitutes one distinct way of dealing
with revered texts which appears in the latter centuries of the
pre-Christian Common Era.  Within Rabbinic Judaism it gains a
prominent role due to the way in which Torah and its study
developed into a center of piety and a basis for practical guidance as well as a part of the national heritage.  The ideology
of the Oral Torah espoused by the rabbis provided them with a
model which shaped their imaginations and the method and content
of their teaching and interpretation of earlier teachings.  Their
teachings, moreover, had an actual social outlet.  Rabbis not
only had personal prestige and influence but also due to their

connection with the Exilarch in Babylonia or the Patriarch in
Palestine, they wielded limited but real authority in several
areas of life.  Accordingly, commentary provided rabbis with a
means and a resource which they could draw upon in these
spheres.[93]

In a sense, the misrashic, pseudepigraphic genre of
rewritten Bible which sought to duplicate and revise as well as to
interpret earlier biblical passages finds a parallel in the commentary activity of the rabbis.  They act out their claims that
their study actually continues the process of revealing the Torah,
though now the Oral Torah.  Therefore, contemporaneous with the
cessation of imitating, replicating, and continuing the revelation of the Written Bible, rabbis sought to imitate, replicate,
and continue revelation of the Oral Torah.  This sense of continuity and relationship of the Oral and Written Torah is reflected
in the chain of tradition in M. Avot 1:1 and the ensuing pericopae
which trace the chain from Moses to the rabbis, including the
Mishnah's editor.[94]  Moreover, Samuel himself is associated with
this notion.  A tradition attributed to him explicitly compares
the proper method and rewards of the study of the Written Torah
and Oral Torah.  One must distinctly pronounce the words when one
reads the Scriptures and when one orally repeats Mishnah.  In
return one receives good health.[95]

> Said Samuel to R. Judah, *Shinena*, "Open your mouth and
> read (QRY) [the Scriptures], open your mouth and repeat (TNY)
> [Mishnah] so that it may remain with you and your life be
> lengthened,
>     as it is said, "For they are like unto those that find
> them and a healing to all their flesh" (Prov. 4:22).  Read
> not "to those that find them" but "to him that causes them to
> come out of their mouth."
>                          (b. Eruv. 54a)

A different tradition, also attributed to Samuel, evidently assumes a hierarchy in the subjects of study.  Explication
of one's learning, *talmud*, gives one peace of mind and therefore
is more important than just learning, i.e., repeating and memoriz-
ing, Mishnah itself.  Samuel's view is juxtaposed with those of
Rav and Yohanan.

> Said Rav, As soon as a person leaves a matter of
> *halakhah*,[96] he no longer has peace.
>     And Samuel said, This refers to one who leaves *talmud*
> for Mishnah.
>     And R. Yohanan says, Even from [one section of] *talmud* to
> [another section of] *talmud*.
>                          (b. Hag. 10a)

Since study continued the process of revelation and made
up a central act of piety, it is not surprising that rabbis,
including Samuel, picture biblical figures and even God teaching
and studying.  They follow the same methods and practices that
rabbinic masters and disciples follow.[97]  These rabbis thereby
projected back their own notions as to how a person may experience
the Divine and receive revelation.  In a similar manner they
borrow motifs from the biblical account of the Sinai theophany to
describe what occurs when a person studies Torah.  God's presence
is with them.[98]  Accordingly, it is understandable that Samuel
requires a blessing be said before one studies Torah.  It is a
central means of divine worship.[99]  Hence, Samuel's work as a
commentator reflects and acts out rabbinic notions of Torah.

3.  Samuel's Commentary is not a linear development of
earlier types of activity within Judaism and antiquity although
it shares characteristics of other commentaries on a text and its
small literary units have analogues in earlier Jewish works.
These earlier instances generally do not make up part of a commentary.  But even where they belong to a commentary-type work,
as in the halakhic Midrashim or portions of Mishnah and Tosefta
and we can trace developments in the types and forms, the present
character of these works differs from Samuel's activity.  The
former are composite, highly worked over literary corpora.  Certainly it is possible that these works made use of earlier, less
systematic efforts at commentary which had been associated with
individual masters.  We have numerous instances of prescriptions
and descriptions of how a master should and did teach or learn
as well as interpret individual blocks of traditions.[100]  But the
present state of the analysis of the extant available evidence
does not enable us to evaluate the true character of such activity
nor to trace its stages.  Once we have more historical and
critical studies of the Midrashim, though, we may be able more
directly to address this problem.  What remains clear, however,
is that Samuel's teachings are wide ranging, comprehensive, and
deliberate, and in that sense systematic, but not exhaustively
so.  Moreover, his efforts accord with our present image of
Babylonian masters who, with pragmatic concerns to spread rabbinic
Judaism and their interpretation of Torah, taught a group of
disciples and made use of reciters.  It accords less with a picture of theoretical, academic exercises in a school.  As we saw,
Samuel also used Mishnah as a point of departure and thus as a

comprehensive statement of topics which he treated in their own
terms.   Indeed in chapter four we demonstrated how Mishnah
affected even these comments which did not directly respond to
Mishnah.

In the next chapter we turn to the implications of our
conclusions, especially in terms of the beginnings of *Gemara* and
the picture of third-century Judaism.

[1] See Volume One, pp. 207-209, and above, chapter seven.

[2] See below and chapter ten, especially our reference to Philip Rousseau, *Ascetics, Authority, and the Church In the Age of Jerome and Cassian* (Oxford, 1978).

[3] Cp., however, #8, on which see immediately above.

[4] See Volume One, p. 236, and above, chapter six, text to n. 58; and especially Bokser, "Guide," Ch. XI.

[5] See above, chapter six, and below.
Gordis, p. 313, n. 6, mentions our observation that tradentless items tend to be the brief ones that may have been designed to be tightly tied to Mishnah. He points out, however, that this pattern does not fit the traditions which open with MNHNY MYLY, which is used to lay out the basis or origin of an earlier teaching. But this need not vitiate our hypothesis. One must consider the nature of this type of comment and its possible place within the history of the presentation of Samuel's comments and whether this formulation frequently may have been expanded or filled out. See also above, chapter one, n. 6.

[6] See, e.g., above, chapter six, text to n. 8, and n. 54 and text thereto.

[7] See above, chapter seven, text to n. 28.

[8] See e.g., Volume One, p. 4 and the reference to Sussmann.

[9] Heinemann, *Prayer*. See also Neusner, *History*, 2: 170-180; and below, chapter ten.

[10] J. N. Epstein, *ITM*, pp. 166-438. See Bokser, "Epstein's *Introduction*," pp. 22-25, and especially 32-33.

[11] Cp. in general the role of Zeira and the other travelers, on which see chapter eight, subsection 4.A, and Goldberg, "R. Ze^cira," *Tarbiz* 36 (1967).

[12] See below, subsection 6, under the "Models of Commentaries," for a discussion of diverse kinds, purposes, and elements of commentaries.

[13] See chapter six and its respective categories, especially Charts 11 and 12 and the conclusions. Above, in this chapter, we differentiate between a "First" and "Second" stage within the "primary" commentary component. On what we here call the "third" element, see chapter six, text to nn. 39, 52.

[14] On the practical characteristics see above and throughout chapters four, five, and six. Note in particular:
First, chapter four, subsection 2, in particular our observations on: (a), M. Ber. 1:3. There we suggest that a certain Houses' dispute lacks a comment attributed to Samuel as the issue had been decided and clarified already within the mishnaic period, as reflected elsewhere in M. Ber. chapter one. (b) M. Ber. chapter six, which elicits a disproportionate number of comments. This may undoubtedly reflect a special interest in the principles for appropriate blessings for diverse foods. Tosefta to this chapter likewise presents an extended focus. (c) The Houses' disputes in chapter eight. Samuel's most extensive treatment is on the issue of *havdalah*, the topic to which Mishnah itself devotes the greatest attention. (d) M. Ber. 6:6 and chapter eight. There we suggest that certain passages in Mishnah elicit less or no comments as the social conditions and institutions which they assume may

have fallen into desuetude. See especially chapter four, text to n. 18. While
this factor provides a cogent reason, we must carefully apply it. Theoretically it would apply to much of M. Zera$^C$im, which, however, does elicit a considerable number of comments, which we concluded in Volume One represent  the
remains of a Commentary. See Volume One, especially pp. 9-10.

    Secondly, chapter five, especially subsection 3. The choice and
spread of the types of comments indicate the practical concerns. The two
largest categories, the Additional Cases and Applications and the Decisions,
explicitly deal with the practical application of Mishnah and they account for
49 percent of the items and 43.1 percent of the traditions. This is also
reflected in the other comments. For example, the second largest group of
categories, the Definitions of Words and Cases, necessary for concretizing
criteria or rules, account for 30.6 percent of the items and 33.3 percent of
the traditions. Even where we have few entries of a category, the choice may
be significant. Thus the reasons explain aspects of *havdalah* and blessings
over food, items of special, practical interest, as we noted above in conjunction with our observations in chapter four.

    Thirdly, chapter six, especially subsection 5 and Charts 11-12. As
mentioned above, text to n. 13, the choice of the phrasings and formulation
reflects the concrete interest in applying Mishnah. The exegetical and chronological stage in which each type of information logically would be needed
coincides with those of the history of the presentation and use of Samuel's
comments, as we lay out above in chapter nine.

[15]See chapter six and Bokser, "Minor For Zimmun."

[16]On #63, see chapter six, text to n. 8. See also #134.

[17]See chapter eight, subsection 2.E.

[18]See esp. chapter seven, text to n. 26, and subsection 4.

[19]Cp. Neusner, *Pharisees*, 3: 282-286. See n. 18, and on our conclusion
cp. the formulation in Volume One, pp. 237-238.

[20]See the following articles along with their bibliographies: esp.
*IDBSup*, pp. 296-303, s.v. "Exegesis," by L. E. Keck and G. M. Tucker; *EJ*,
4: 890-899, s.v. "Bible. Exegesis and Study, Medieval," by Avraham Grossman,
et al.; Nahum Sarna, "Hebrew and Bible Studies in Medieval Spain," in *The
Sephardic Heritage*, ed. R. D. Barnett (London, 1971), pp. 323-366; and the
lucid study by Frank Talmadge, *David Kimhi, The Man and the Commentary* (Cambridge, 1975). See also the additional works cited in nn. 21-25.

[21]See Gershom G. Scholem, *On the Kabbalah and Its Symbolism* (New York,
1965, 1969), pp. 32-86, esp. 50-65; Beryl Smalley, *The Study of the Bible in
the Middle Ages* (New York, 1952); Harry Austryn Wolfson, *Philo*, 2 vols. (Cambridge, 1947, 1968), 1: 115; and Salo Baron, *A Social and Religious History
of the Jews*, Vol. 6 (New York, 1958), pp. 235-313.

[22]See Baron.

[23]Scholem, esp. pp. 32-35, and n.b. p. 34.

[24]Brevard S. Childs, "Interpreting in Faith: The Theological Responsibility of an Old Testament Commentary," *Interpretation* 18 (1964): 43-49.

[25]Brevard S. Childs. *The Book of Exodus* [=*The Old Testament Library*]
(Philadelphia, 1974), pp. ix-xvi. See also Jacob Neusner, *A History of the
Mishnaic Law of Holy Things*, 1: Zebahim (Leiden, 1978), pp. ix-xii, in which
he makes clear how his purpose shapes his exegesis and discussion; and Baron,
pp. 27-62.

[26]See, e.g., Jacob Weingreen, *From Bible to Mishnah* (Manchester, 1976),
pp. 35, 36; Renee Bloch, "Midrash," in *Approaches to Ancient Judaism: Theory*

*and Practice* [=*Brown Judaic Studies*. 1] (Missoula, 1978), pp. 29-50; and esp.
Geza Vermes, "Bible and Midrash: Early Old Testament Exegesis," in *The Cambridge History of the Bible*, vol. 1, ed. R. R. Ackroyd and C. F. Evans (Cambridge, 1970, 1975), pp. 199-231. Though Bloch and Vermes address the characteristics of Midrash, their comments apply to commentaries in general. See
also Judah Goldin, "Of Change and Adaption in Judaism," *History of Religions*
4 (1965): 269-294.

[27]Jonathan Z. Smith, "Wisdom and Apocalyptic," in *Religious Syncretism
in Antiquity* (Missoula, 1975), pp. 131-156, esp. pp. 135-144, and 154. See
also William S. Green, "Reading, Writing, and Rabbinism: Towards a Description
of the Rabbinic Intellect," lecture delivered at American Academy of Religion
Annual Meeting, New York, 18 November 1979.

[28]See, e.g., A Leo Oppenheim, *Ancient Mesopotamia* (Chicago, 1964, 1968),
p. 249; *IDBSup*, pp. 3-5, s.v. "Abbreviations, Hebrew Texts," by Michael
Fishbane, and pp. 436-438, s.v. "Interpretation, History of," by Jacob
Weingreen, esp. sections A, 1. b and c; Weingreen, *From Bible*, esp. pp. 32-54,
and 55-57; and the additional literature cited in nn. 29-30.

[29]Weingreen, *From Bible*, and "Interpretation"; G. R. Driver, "Glosses
in the Hebrew Text of the Old Testament," in *L'Ancien Testament et L'Orient*
[=*Journees Bibliques de Louvain* 6] (Louvain, 1957), pp. 123-162; and the materials in n. 30, and text to n. 37. For sure, Weingreen's distinction between
glosses and editorial notes may be somewhat arbitrary.

[30]See Oppenheim, p. 249; Weingreen, *From Bible*, pp. 49-50; G. R. Driver,
*Semitic Writing*, newly rev. ed. (London, 1976), p. 67; Erle Leichty, *The Omen
Series Summa Izbu* (New York, 1970), pp. 23-24, 211-233; and *CAD*, vol. "Ṣ,"
(=vol. 16), s.v. "ṣatu," pp. 116, 119. Leichty points out that ṣatu brief
glosses were often later expanded. See text to nn. 35 and 37. Rudolf Pfeiffer,
*History of Classical Scholarship* (Oxford, 1968), esp. pp. 29, 213-214; Simha
Assaf, *Tequfat HaGeonim Vesifrutha* (Jerusalem, 1955), pp. 137-146; Baron,
p. 28; E. E. Urbach. *The Tosafists* (Jerusalem, 1955), pp. 27-29, 523-538.

[31]See Bloch; Vermes, "Bible and Midrash" and *Scripture*, pp. 67-126;
Oppenheim, p. 231, concerning ancient law collections; D. J. Wiseman, "Books
in the Ancient World," in *Cambridge History of the Bible*, vol. 1 (Cambridge,
1970, 1975), p. 45; Sara Japhet, *The Ideology of the Book of Chronicles and
Its Place in Biblical Thought* (Jerusalem, 1977); Harold W. Attridge, *The
Interpretation of Biblical History in the Antiquitates Judaicae of Flavious
Josephus* (Missoula, 1976); esp. Gary Porton, "Midrash," in *ANRW*. II.19,2: 103-
138, esp. 122-125; and E. J. Bickerman's various studies on the Septuagint,
esp. "The Septuagint as a Translation," *PAAJR* (1959): 1-39, and "Notes On the
Greek Book of Esther," *PAAJR* 20 (1951): 101-133.

[32]See Oppenheim, pp. 249, 255; Driver, "Glosses;" Weingreen, *From Bible*;
and text to n. 37.

[33]See Rudolf Pfeiffer, e.g., pp. 212-222 and the references in nn. 32
and 35.

[34]See below n. 85 and text thereto.
    The "rewritten text" does make up one of the standard talmudic modes
of commentary. David Goodblatt, 28 January 1980, personal communication,
observes: "One thing that struck me as I read the material was the degree to
which rabbinic literature 'comments' by rephrasing and reformulating the
original. I am thinking especially of Bavli and the way it treats *baraitot*
and Palestinian Amoraic sources. Rather than citing exactly and then commenting, Bavli--it seems to me--reworks the sources so that as now cited it
already includes the Babylonian interpretation. Of course, this is what
Epstein showed with regard to the Mishnah, but it extends to other sources as
well." Moreover, this phenomenon is what Weiss Halivni, *ST*, tries to trace.

See his theoretically remarks in "Contemporary Methods of the Study of Talmud," *JJS*, 30 (1979): 192-201.

[35]See Leichty, pp. 23-24, 211-233, and Driver, *Semitic Writing*, pp. 67 and 236, for a slightly different definition of these works and for additional bibliography. See also *CAD*, vol. "Ṣ," (=vol. 16), "s.v. "ṣatu," pp. 116, 119, and vol. "M," Part 2 (=vol. 10), s.v. "mukallimtu," pp. 181-182.

[36]Rudolf Pfeiffer, esp. pp. 210-234, 274-279, and n.b. 213, 215, 222-223, and esp. his observation, p. 212, as to the possible initial oral stage of certain comments.

[37]See H. W. Bailey, *Zoroastrian Problems in the Ninth-Century Books* (Oxford, 1943), pp. 149-176, esp. 158-163; Geo Widengren, "Holy Book and Holy Tradition in Iran: The Problem of the Sassanid Avesta," in *Holy Book and Holy Tradition*, ed. F. F. Bruce and E. G. Rupp (Manchester, 1968), pp. 36-53, esp. 51-52; esp. Mary Boyce, "Middle Persian Literature," in *Handbuch der Orientalistik. I.4. Iranistik. 2. Literatur* (Leiden, 1968), pp. 33-38. See also Jonas Greenfield, "Ratin Magusha," in *Exploring the Talmud. 1: Education*, ed. Haim Z. Dimitrovsky (New York, 1976), pp. 270-276.

[38]The role of the transmitters and disciples especially affects the "nonstandard" commentary formulations, e.g., the First Person Reports.

[39]See Morton Smith, *Tannaitic Parallels to the Gospels* [*JBL Monograph Series*, 6] (Philadelphia, 1951, 1968), p. 118.

[40]See e.g., Jacob Lauterbach, "Midrash and Mishnah," in *Rabbinic Essays* (Cincinnati, 1951), pp. 163-256; and E. E. Urbach, "The Derasha as a Basis of the Halakha and the Problem of the Soferim," *Tarbiẓ* 27 (1958): 166-182, and vi-viii.

[41]See e.g., Porton, "Midrash"; Robert Le Deaut, "Apropos a Definition of Midrash," *Interpretation* 25 (1971): 259-282; and Neusner's observations in *Purities*, 7: ix-xi and 3, and 22: 40-41, 48-49, 51-109, 133-136. Some scholars try to argue that one or many pericopae in a rabbinic Midrash actually derives from an earlier period. See e.g., Louis Finkelstein, *New Light from the Prophets* (New York, 1969). But such claims are frought with speculation and impossible to prove. See below n. 67 and the references there to Neusner and Wacholder.

[42]Otto Eissfeldt, *The Old Testament* (New York, 1965), pp. 12-128. See Neusner, *Pharisees*, 3: 68-69, for his search for analogues to forms and types of the traditions which rabbinic sources attribute to the Pharisees. Our analysis has been greatly shaped by his comments.

[43]Eissfeldt, pp. 12-18.

[44]Eissfeldt, pp. 18-26.

[45]Eissfeldt, pp. 26-27.

[46]Eissfeldt, pp. 26-29. Cp. Neusner, *Pharisees*, 3: 72-73, and esp. Lawrence H. Schiffman, *The Halakhah at Qumran* (Leiden, 1975), pp. 80-83, which refers to additional literature on the formulations of legal traditions, to which add F. C. Fensham, "Aspects of Family Law in the Covenant Code in Light of Ancient Near Eastern Parallels," *Dine Israel* 1 (1969): v-xix, esp. vi-vii.

[47]See, e.g., Abba Bendavid, *Biblical Hebrew and Mishnaic Hebrew Compared*, 1- (Tel Aviv, 1967-), vol. 2, passim, esp. pp. 567-603, 856-879, 886-891, 901-924; Schiffman, pp. 80-83; and Neusner, *Pharisees*, 3: 72-73.

[48]Eissfeldt, pp. 31-56, esp. 31-32, 45-47, 48-52, 55. See also David Daube, *Studies in Biblical Law* (Cambridge, 1947, reprinted, New York, 1969),

pp. 1-73, John Hayes, *Old Testament Form Criticism* (San Antonio, 1974), pp. 137-139; Goodblatt, "The Babylonian Talmud," *ANRW*, p. 302 and n. 51a; and Baruch M. Bokser, "Redaction Criticism of the Talmud: The Case of Hanina Ben Dosa" (forthcoming).

[49]Eissfeldt, pp. 57-88.

[50]Eissfeldt, pp. 69-70, 73-75.

[51]Eissfeldt, pp. 69-70.

[52]Abraham Weiss, *Studies* (1962); David Goodblatt, "Abraham Weiss: The Search for Literary Forms," in *The Formation of the Babylonian Talmud*, ed. Jacob Neusner (Leiden, 1970), pp. 95-103, esp. 100-103; Friedman, "A Critical Study"; and see below our observations concerning Midrash and Morton Smith's incisive remarks quoted from *Tannaitic Parallels*, p. 118.

[53]Eissfeldt, pp. 81-87, esp. 86-87, above, and chapter three, e.g., traditions #107 and 141.

[54]Eissfeldt, pp. 87-127.

[55]See Robert H. Pfeiffer, *History of New Testament Times* (New York, 1949), pp. 101-110, 197-230; Moses Hadas, *Hellenistic Culture* (New York, 1959, 1972); Neusner, *Pharisees*, 3: 73-74; and the numerous studies by Henry A. Fischel, esp. "Story and History: Observations on Greco-Roman Rhetoric and Pharisaism," [originally published in 1969] in Henry A. Fischel, *Essays in Greco-Roman and Related Talmudic Literature* (New York, 1977), pp. 443-472. The "Additions" in the Bible versions to various canonical books do not con-stitute actual separate additions but rather form an integral part of the paraphrase of the original biblical book; these sections merely lack analogues in the original.  See Bickerman's various studies, e.g., "Notes to the Greek Book of Esther."

[56]Schiffman, pp. 41, 54-60, 75.  See Joseph A. Fitzmyer, "The Use of Explicit Old Testament Quotations in Qumran Literature and the New Testament," in *Essays on the Semitic Background of the New Testament* (Missoula, 1974), pp. 3-58, esp. 5-7, which reviews the various sources.  Maurya P. Horgan, *Pesharim: Qumran Interpretations of Biblical Books*, Catholic Biblical Quarterly Monograph Series, no. 8 (Washington, DC, 1979), presents a corpus of the texts; see esp. pp. 1-6, 249-159.

[57]Schiffman, p. 76.

[58]We have found the following additional literature on the Dead Sea Scrolls particularly helpful: A. M. Habermann, *Edah We^ceduth* (Jerusalem, 1952), pp. 39-56; F. F. Bruce, *Biblical Exegesis in the Qumran Texts* (London, 1959, 1960); Fitzmyer, esp. "Old Testament Quotations," and "'4QTestimonia' and the New Testament," in *Essays*, pp. 59-89; Lou H. Silberman, "Unriddling the Riddle.  A Study in the Structure and Language of the Habakkuk Pesher," *Revue de Qumran* 3, part 11 (1961): 323-364, esp. 324; Geza Vermes, "The Qumran Interpretation of Scripture in its Historical Setting," [originally published in 1969], in Geza Vermes, *Post Biblical Studies* (Leiden, 1975), pp. 37-49, esp. 38: Neusner, *Pharisees*, 3: 74-78; Schiffman, esp. pp. 32-41, 54-60, 75-76, and 80-83 and the literature cited there.  For a list of the biblical exegetical texts, especially the numerous ones from Cave 4, see Joseph A. Fitzmyer, *The Dead Sea Scrolls: Major Publications and Tools for Study* (Missoula, 1975), esp. pp. 33-34, 110-111; and Horgan.

[59]See Robert Pfeiffer, pp. 212-225; Martin Hengel, *Judaism and Hellen-ism*, English, 2d rev. and enl. ed., 2 vols. (Philadelphia, 1974), 1: 163-169, and 2: 106-107, nn. 378, 382; and David Winston, *The Wisdom of Solomon* [=The Anchor Bible] (Garden City, 1979).  I thank Professor Morton Smith for the wording used to describe the contents  of Aristobulus.

[60]See Wolfson, 1: 87-163, esp. 87-88, 94-98; 115-117, 122, 126-134; and
V. Nikiprowetzky, *Le Commentaire De L'Écriture Chez Philon D'Alexandrie*
(Leiden, 1977), esp. 170-235.

[61]See Fitzmyer, "Old Testament Quotations."

[62]See Rudolf Bultmann, *History of the Synoptic Tradition*, Revised ed.
(New York, 1963, 1976), pp. 11-205; and esp. Neusner, *Pharisees*, 3: 78-89, and
Morton Smith, "A Comparison of Early Christian and Early Rabbinic Tradition,"
*JBL* 82 (1963): 169-176. See also *IDBSup*, pp. 787-789, s.v. "Sayings of
Jesus," by D. Lührmann, and pp. 641-642, s.v. "Parable," by C. E. Carlson, and
below, chapter ten. The clause in quotations is added from Morton Smith,
21 June 1980, personal communication.

[63]See David Daube, "Rabbinic Methods of Interpretation and Hellenistic
Rhetoric," *HUCA* 22 (1949): 239-264, "Alexandrian Methods of Interpretation
and the Rabbis," [originally published in 1953] reprinted in Fischel, *Essays*,
pp. 165-182, and "Text and Interpretation in Roman and Jewish Law," [originally
published in 1961], reprinted in Fischel, *Essays*, pp. 240-265; Lieberman, *HJP*,
pp. 26-27, 28-99, esp. 48-49, 58, 70-71, 75-79. See also Wolfson, *Philo*, 1:
131-135; Robert Pfeiffer, pp. 114-116, 137-213; J. Z. Smith, "Wisdom"; the
other, noncited essays printed in Fischel, *Essays*, esp. that of I. I. Halevy;
and the items in nn. 35-36, above.

[64]See Hengel, 1: 135-136, 173-175, 227, 240, 246, esp. 206; Neusner,
*Eliezer*, 2: 302-304; Joseph Blenkinsoff, "Prophecy and Priesthood in Josephus,"
*JJS* 25 (1974): 239-262; Ellis Rivkin, "Ben Sira--The Bridge Between the
Aaronide and Pharisaic Revolutions," *EI* 12 (1975): 95-104.

[65]Various scholars have observed this transition, though they use this
fact in different ways. See, e.g., Daube, "Text and Interpretation"; Urbach,
*"Derasha"* and *"Mavo LaMishnah* [of H. Albeck] and One Hundred Years of
Mishnaic Research," *Molad* 17 (1959): 427; Vermes, "Qumran Interpretation,"
p. 38; Hengel, 1: 136-137; Jacob Neusner, "The Formation of Rabbinic Judaism,"
in *ANRW*. II.19,2: 3-42, *Purities*, vol. 22, "From Scripture to Mishnah: The
Origins of Tractate Niddah," *JJS* 29 (1978): 135-148, esp. 147-148, and esp.
"Comparing Judaisms," *History of Religions* 18 (1978): 184, n. 8, and "From
Scripture to Mishnah: The Origins of Mishnah's Fifth Division," *JBL* 98 (1979):
269-283, and the additional references in n. 64. Cp. D. S. Russel, *The Method
and Message of Jewish Apocalyptic* (Philadelphia, 1964), pp. 178-202.

For examples of works which try to correlate the different social and
religious contexts of Qumran, Philo, and Early Rabbinic Judaism, see for
example, Shemaryahu Talmon, "The 'Manual of Benedictions' of the Sect of the
Judean Desert," in *Revue de Qumran* 2, part 8 (1960): 475-500, and "The Emergence of Institutionalized Prayer in Israel in the Light of Qumran Literature,"
in *Qumran, Sa piété, sa théologie et son milieu*, ed. M. Delco [=*Bibliotheca
Ephemeridum Theologicarum Lovaniensium* 46 (1978)], (Louvain, 1978): 264-284;
Jacob Neusner, *The Idea of Purity* (Leiden, 1973), and *Purities*, vol. 22;
Baruch M. Bokser, *Philo's Description of Jewish Practices*, Center for Hermen-
eutical Studies in Hellenistic and Modern Culture. *Protocol of the Thirtieth
Colloquy*, ed. Wilhelm Wuellner (Berkeley, 1977), and *Passover Eve Celebration
and Early Rabbinic Judaism* (Chico, in press).

[66]Smith, *Tannaitic Parallels*, p. 118. On this literature, see Neusner,
*Purities*, 7: 187-231, 10: 104-117, 13: 220-223; the references below in nn. 67-
69, to which add Ezekiel Kutscher, "Geniza (G) Fragments of the Mekilta of
Rabbi Yišmae$^c$el," *Lešonenu* 32 (1967-68): 103-116, which provides important
linguistic evidence that Mekilta cannot have been edited at a late date. Cp.
A. Weiss, *Studies* (1962), who compares the structure of amoraic interpretation
of Mishnah and its arrangement in *Gemara* with that of the halakhic Midrashim.

[67]Neusner, *Purities*, 7: 187-231. See also vol. 10: 104-117, 13: 220-
223, 15: 152-162, 17: 116-123, and 18: 95-115. From a different perspective

B. Z. Wacholder has come to a similar conclusion; B. Z. Wacholder, "On the Origins of Midrash," lecture delivered at the Seventh Annual Association for Jewish Studies Conference, Boston, Massachusetts, 23 December 1975.

[67a]See now David Weiss Halivni, "Whoever Studies Laws . . . ," *Proceedings of the Rabbinical Assembly* 41 (1979): 303, n. 11.

[68]Wilhelm Bacher, *Die Exegetische Terminologie der Jüdischen Traditionasliteratur*, 2 vols. in 1 (Leipzig, 1899 and 1905, reprint ed. Darmstadt, 1965), and in Hebrew trans.: *Erche Midrash*, 2 vols. (Tel Aviv, 1923, reprint ed. Jerusalem, 1970). See also Isaac Heinemann, "Hitpaṭḥut HaMunaḥim HaMiqso-Ciyim Leferush Hamiqra," *Lešonenu* 14 (1945-46): 182-189, vol. 15 (1946-47): 108-115, vol. 16 (1947-48): 20-28; Lieberman, *HJP*, pp. 20-82, and note the careful formulation of his argument, pp. 26-27, 31, 37, 46, 47-82, and esp. 77-79, and *SZ*, on the distinctive terminology in Sifre Zutta; Melammed, *Introduction*, 170-222; and Moshe Greenberg, *Encyclopedia Miqrait, Supplement Volume* (forthcoming), "Biblical Exegesis, Rabbinic." See also Porton, *Ishmael*, 2: 3-7, and vol. 4.

[69]Shalom Spiegel, "Introduction (to *Legends of the Bible* by Louis Ginzberg [New York, 1956])" in *The Jewish Expression*, ed. Judah Goldin (New York, 1970), pp. 134-162, quotation from p. 136. See also Vermes, "Bible and Midrash."

[70]On the Midrashim, in addition to the above references, see Epstein, *ITL*, pp. 495-746, esp. 549; Albeck, *Introduction*, pp. 79-143, esp. 84-102; Melammed, *Introduction*, pp. 161-317, esp. 167, 169, 178-180, 184-185, 210; *EJ*, 11: 1507-1514, s.v. "Midrash," by M. D. Herr, and 11:1521-1523, s.v. "Midreshei Halakhah," by M. D. Herr. See also Silberman; Lieberman, *HJP*, pp. 28-37, 26-27, 47; Yehezkel Kaufmann, *History of the Religion of Israel*, vol. 4, English trans. C. W. Efroymson (New York, 1977), pp. 563-568; *EJ*, 15: 79-81, s.v. "Soferim," by Y. D. Gilat; and Porton, *Ishmael*, 2: 2-7.

[71]While Mishnah, like Tosefta, does contain midrashic exegetical pericopae, these make up a small percentage of the contents and the verses do not set the structure for the text. The few exceptional series of pericopae, as in Tosefta Ber. Ch. 1, are exceptions that prove the rule. For a list of biblical verses in Mishnah, see Samuel Rosenblatt, *The Interpretation of the Bible in the Mishnah* (Baltimore, 1935), and cp. Melammed, *Introduction*, pp. 223-233.

[72]See chapters five and seven. For instances of Reasons, see, e.g., M. Ber. 1:3 and 8, and for Decisions, M. Ber. 1:3 and Epstein, *ITL*, pp. 205-211.

[73]See, e.g., Epstein, *ITL*, pp. 25, esp. 30, 36, 72, 79, 96-159; and in *Modern Study of the Mishnah*, ed. Neusner, the references to Epstein, pp. 38, 40, 41, 42, 49, 54, to Frankel, pp. 66, 73, to Brüll, p. 83, to Y. I. Halevy, pp. 136, 138, esp. 141-142, 145-147, 149, and cp. 153-154, to Zuri, p. 174, and to DeVries, p. 245. See also Neusner, *Pharisees*, 3: 199-223, 282-286, and the additional literature in nn. 74-79.

[74]Abraham Goldberg, "Tosefta to Tractate Tamid," in *Benjamin DeVries Memorial Volume* (Jerusalem, 1968), pp. 18-42, esp. 19, 22, 30, 32, 40, 42; and *Mavo LaMishnah UTosefta*, ed. Michael Asolin (Jerusalem, 1973), pp. 102-104; "Review" [of Albeck, *Introduction*] in *KS* 47 (1972): 9-19, esp. 3-14; and *Commentary to the Mishna. Shabbat* (Jerusalem, 1976), pp. 21-33.

[75]See William S. Green, "Abraham Goldberg," in *Modern Study*, ed. Neusner, pp. 226-232, and note Joel Gereboff's observation, in *Modern Study*, p. 66. On the enormous literature to the Mishnah, see the following: Albeck, *Mavo LaMishnah* (Jerusalem, 1959, 1967); Epstein, *ITM* and *ITL*; Urbach, "Mavo LaMishnah [of Albeck] and One Hundred Years of Mishnaic Research," and "Mishnah," s.v. in *EJ*, 12: 93-109; Goldberg, *Mavo Lamishnah*; Melammed, *Introduction*,

pp. 13-147; Neusner, ed. *Modern Study*; and Neusner, *Purities*. Urbach's review, Goldberg, Albeck, *Mavo*, and Neusner, *Modern Study*, contain critical surveys of modern scholarship and comprehensive bibliographical references.

[76]See, e.g., Albeck, *Studies*, pp. 60-184, esp. 139-184, and *Introduction*, pp. 73-85; Epstein, *ITL*, pp. 241-262; Melammed, *Introduction*, pp. 148-153. See also Goldberg, *Mavo*, esp. pp. 121-133; Benjamin DeVries, *Studies in Talmudic Literature* (Jerusalem, 1968), pp. 96-129; Boaz Cohen, *Mishnah and Tosefta* (New York, 1935); Richard S. Sarason, *A History of the Mishnaic Law of Agriculture. Demai* (Leiden, 1979); and the literature in nn. 77-79.

[77]Lieberman, *TK*, 1-. Cp. Eliezer Shimshon Rosenthal, "HaMoreh," *PAAJR* 31 (1963), Hebrew Section: 1-71, esp. 52-56.

[78]Neusner, *Purities*, vols. 1-21, esp. 21: 15-16, 247-297.

[79]*Purities*, 21: 15.

[80]Goldberg, *Mavo*, p. 147, "Review," p. 13, and cp. *Commentary Shabbat*, p. 24. Neusner, *Purities*, 21: 270 likewise explicitly makes the comparison.

[81]When we classified and analyzed Samuel's traditions on Berakhot we were mindful of Neusner's general classification and division of Tosefta into two large blocks, as laid out in *Purities*, vols. 1-20. We came to appreciate the significance of the diverse relationships to Mishnah in terms of Samuel's teachings at the same time that Neusner, in vol. 21, focused on the third division and drew the wider implications. See above chapter four and below, chapter ten. See now Zahavy, who finds a similar relationship between Tosefta and Mishnah Berakhot.

[82]See, in particular, n. 72, above. On amoraic focus on the Mishnah, see: Epstein, *ITM*, pp. 166-672; Melammed, *Introduction*, pp. 330-441 (despite the fact that occasionally one may have to revise his analysis of individual passages, he graphically lays out the spectrum of teaching); Goodblatt, "Babylonian Talmud," p. 285, n. 36 and text thereto, and the references to J. Florsheim, J. Frankel, S. K. Mirsky, J. J. Weinberg, M. Zucker, to which add: Jechiel J. Weinberg, "Talmudic Exegesis of Mishnah," *Isaiah Wolfsberg Jubilee Volume* ed. Yosef Tirosh (Tel Aviv, 1955), pp. 86-105.

[83]On the date of Tosefta's composition, see n. 87. See also Gordis, who discusses Samuel's reliance on *baraitot*.

[84]See Albeck, *Studies*, esp. pp. 12-15, 59, and *Introduction*, pp. 41-50; Epstein, *ITL*, p. 253, and *ITM*, esp. 1-352; Goldberg, *Mavo*; and Higger, which systematically lists all the *baraitot* found in both *Gemarot*.

[85]See Goodblatt, *Rabbinic Instruction*, pp. 132-135, for a full discussion and literature on Samuel's *baraitot*, and "Babylonian Talmud," pp. 286-288, esp. 288; and above, chapter two, n. 44.

[86]See Volume One, pp. 184, 199-201.

[87]At this point it is worth synthesizing our observations that may have implications as to the date of Tosefta. Literary and logical factors support the notion that Tosefta or a version of it, even if not exactly identical to the extant corpus of that name, existed in the third century. (1) Tosefta integrally relates to Mishnah. Certainly theoretically at any time after Mishnah's composition someone could have tried to arrange a work like Tosefta. But it is problematic to assume that someone would have had access to the necessary sources. Secondly, why should a person want so systematically to gloss, complement, and supplement Mishnah except soon after Mishnah appeared as a way to provide for the maximum use of Mishnah and the full range of tannaitic teachings. Mishnah itself is so constructed that it elicits exegesis.

See text to n. 89, and Goldberg, "Review," p. 16. Moreover, the wide ranging
response to Mishnah accords with the fact that despite Rabbi's apparent desire
to present an authoritative arrangement of Early Rabbinic teachings, many
contemporary and later masters rejected Rabbi's claim and asserted their freedom individually to evaluate the merits of the diverse tannaitic teachings.
See Lieberman, *SZ;* Bokser, "J. N. Epstein on the Formation of the Mishnah,"
in *Modern Study,* ed. Jacob Neusner, p. 53; and David Weiss Halivni, "The
Reception Accorded to Rabbi Judah's Mishnah," Paper read at the conference on
"Judaism and Christianity in the First Two Centuries: Problems of Self Definition." McMaster University, Hamilton, Ontario, June, 1979.  (2) Our observation as to the ways in which Samuel's comments substantively attest numerous
toseftan passages provides a strong argument that such *baraitot* circulated.
P. R. Weiss, "The Controversies of Rab and Samuel and the Tosefta," *Journal
of Semitic Studies* 3 (1958): 288-297, makes a similar argument, however, based
upon the teachings of Rav.  Weiss believes that Samuel's teachings are based
directly on Mishnah.  Whether or not he is correct in the interpretations of
the individual passages in his sample from M. Ketubot, his study provides an
analogous argument.  Cp. also Abraham Goldberg, "The Use of Tosefta and the
Baraitha of the School of Samuel by the Babylonian Amora Rava for the Interpretation of the Mishnah," *Tarbiz* 40 (1971): 144-157.  The studies by P. R.
Weiss and Abraham Goldberg also throw light on the background in which Samuel
taught and in which Tosefta emerged.  That is, third-century masters exhibit
great interest in explaining Mishnah.  See also our reference to Gordis in
n. 83.  (3) The contrary objections are not cogent: (a) Why does an Amora not
cite Tosefta when he offers a similar interpretation of Mishnah?  We pointed
out in Volume One, p. 7, that the function of the amoraic teaching as a suc-
cint comment on Mishnah may have precluded citation of sources.  (b) Why does
*Gemara* totally ignore relevant sources in Tosefta, or else present citations
of *baraitot* analogous to those in Tosefta frequently at the end of a *sugya*
and not draw upon them earlier in the midst of the discussion?  Does this not
indicate that the earlier masters did not know these sources?  This argument
insufficiently takes account of the literary composition of the *Gemara* and the
role that the anonymous late editors took in arranging the material.  See
Goldberg, "Review," pp. 12, 13-17, esp. 12, 15; Judy Hauptman, "The TNYꝰ NMY
HKY *Baraitot* in the Babylonian Talmud," (Ph.D. Dissertation, Jewish Theological Seminary of America, 1979).  See also Friedman, "Critical Study";
Goodblatt, "Babylonian Talmud," pp. 286-287; and Bokser, "Guide," pp. 173-178.

[88]See also Lieberman, *HJP,* pp. 97-99.  Cp. Albeck, *Introduction,* pp.
34-35, 46-50, and *Studies,* pp. 15-43; Epstein, *ITL,* pp. 246, 248-252; and
Goldberg, *Mavo,* p. 31.

[89]See Neusner, *Purities,* 21: 308, 317, n. 1, 318, and vol. 22; and
W. S. Green, "Reading."

[90]Neusner, *Purities,* 21: 300.  According to Zahavy's calculation
toseftan materials relate to all but seven Mishnah units, M. 3:6; 4:7; 5:3-5;
7:5; and 8:7.  His chart, though, apparently indicates that this also applies
to M. 2:2 and 3:3.

[91]We thank Professor William S. Green for the suggestion of the present
choice of words to differentiate between the different types of responses.

[92]This is reflected in particular in the location of the "nonstandard"
commentary formulations, e.g., the First Person Reports, which appear in
structurally similar places in both *Gemarot.*  See Weinberg, pp. 89-90, 94-95,
who despite his overly monolithic and hagiographic perspective, recognizes
the impact of the type of work commented upon and of the role and practical
needs of the rabbis.

[93]See Neusner, *History,* vols. 1-5, esp. 1: 163-164, 169, 174-177; and
"Rabbis and Community in Third-Century Babylonia," in *Religions in Antiquity,
Essays in Memory of E. R. Goodenough,* ed. Jacob Neusner (Leiden, 1968, 1970),

pp. 438-459: Lee L. Levine, *Caesarea Under Roman Rule* (Leiden, 1975), esp.
pp. 95-97 and nn. and "The Jewish Patriarch (Nasi) in Third Century Palestine,"
in *ANRW*. II.19,2: 649-688.  See also Goodblatt, *Rabbinic Instruction*, pp.
272-280, and 282-283.  Cp. Weinberg, pp. 90, 94-95.

[94]See, e.g., Albeck, 4: 347; and Neusner, *Pharisees*, 1: 15-23.  On the
rabbis acting out their picture of the transmission of the Oral Torah, see
Jacob Neusner, "The Rabbinic Traditions About the Pharisees Before A.D. 70:
The Problem of Oral Transmission," *JJS* 22 (1971): 1-18, esp. 17, and "The
Written Tradition in the Pre-Rabbinic Period," *JSJ* 4 (1973): 56-65.

[95]Rashi's rendering of the result clauses receives support from the
reading in *Aggadot HaTalmud*, which reverses the order of the two clauses.  See
also *Yalqut Shimoni* to Prov. 4: 22, #937, in the first ed., Salonika, 1521,
p. 144c.  On the present notion see also the additional expositions in b. Eruv.
34a-b and b. Pes. 68b; Neusner, *History*, 2: 227, 3: 125, 132, 135; Urbach,
*Sages*, pp. 254-278, 539-557, esp. 270; and Birger Gerhardsson, *Memory and
Manuscript* (Uppsala, 1961), pp. 163-168.

[96]The printed editions of BT add here "for a Scriptural matter" and
thus incorporate an explanatory gloss into the text of *Gemara*.  See *DS* 27:1;
*Aggadot HaTalmud*; Vatican MS 134.  Makor ed. Series A, 2: 242.  On the terminology of the passage, see Albeck, *Introduction*, pp. 3-4; and Goodblatt,
"Babylonian Talmud," p. 261, n. 3.  See also Gehardsson, pp. 115-116; and
David Weiss Halivni, "The Apodictic and Argumentational in the Talmud," paper
delivered at the Society of Biblical Literature Annual Meeting, New York,
15 November 1979, and in its earlier version, "Whoever Studies."

[97]See, e.g., b. Temurah 15b (Samuel re Moses); b. Yoma 28b (Rav); b.A.Z.
3b (Rav re God).  See also Neusner, *History*, 2: 151-152, 189, 202, 222-229;
and Nahum N. Glatzer, "A Study of the Talmudic-Midrashic Interpretation of
Prophecy," *Review of Religion*, 1946, reprinted in *Essays in Jewish Thought*
(University, Alabama, 1978), pp. 16-35.  On Moses pictured as a rabbi, see
also Gerhardsson, pp. 120-121; and Neusner, "Oral Transmission," pp. 4 and 16.

[98]See M. Avot 3:2; b. Shab. 119b, where a tradition attributed to Rav
claims that disciples of a master are like prophets.  See Neusner, *History*,
3: 135, 150, 4: 290-295, 309-315, esp. 309, n. 2; E. E. Urbach, "HaMasoret
[C]al Torat HaSod biTequfat HaTannaim," in *Studies in Mysticism and Religion*.
Festschrift Gershom Scholem, ed. E. E. Urbach, et al. (Jerusalem, 1967), pp.
1-28; E. P. Sanders, *Paul and Palestinian Judaism* (Philadelphia, 1977), pp.
220-223; and David Joel Halperin, "Merkabah and Ma[C]aseh Merkabah According to
Rabbinic Sources" (Ph.D. dissertation, University of California, at Berkeley,
1977), pp. 194-240, esp. 221-228 [rev. ed., in press, *American Oriental
Series*].  Urbach and Sanders must be read in light of Halperin's fully comprehensive review of the use of the imagery of the Sinaitic revelation in the
story of R. Yohanan b. Zakkai.

[99]See traditions #9, 10, 15=16, and 17; Ginzberg, *Commentary*, 1: 170;
and Lieberman, *TK*, 1:102 and n. 10.

[100]See, e.g., materials in Goodblatt, *Rabbinic Instruction*, pp. 108-259;
and in Gerhardsson, pp. 93-170.

CHAPTER TEN

THIRD-CENTURY JUDAISM AND THE BEGINNINGS OF *GEMARA*

Our study of Samuel's Commentary and of his teachings in
b. and y. Berakhot throws light on the nature of third-century
Judaism and the beginnings of *Gemara*. In the present chapter we
point to specific implications, discuss their effect on the current state of scholarship in these areas, and suggest how one may
further pursue these matters. We conclude with a final note as
to the impact of our sample on our overall results.

### 1. *Third-Century Babylonian Rabbinic Activity*

The nature of Samuel's teaching enables us more fully to
define the role of Babylonian rabbis in the first post Mishnaic
generation. Traditional and modern scholars at least since the
time of the authors of *Seder Tannaim Ve'amoraim*, ninth century,
and of the "Preface" to the *Account of R. Natan Habbavli*, eleventh
century, have recognized that the generation of Samuel and Rav
make up a transition period in the history of Judaism.[1] Certainly,
Babylonian Jewry since the Babylonian exile in the sixth century
B.C.E. had evolved indigenous institutions and traditions. But
Early Rabbinic Judaism had crystallized and further developed
various trends that had emerged in the years preceding the
destruction of the Second Temple, in 70 C.E. Accordingly its new
arrangement and adaptation of ideas, institutions, and practices
represented a departure from what had preceded. Babylonian Jewry,
and even, indeed, much of Palestinian Jewry until the second and
third centuries, would have been unfamiliar with many of these
developments and surely with their details. While Babylonian
Jewry may have maintained contacts with Palestinians and learned
of events and changes in that country, even the inroads of second-
century Palestinian rabbis and individuals, who fled the holy
land during the Bar Kokhba upheavals, could not have made a significant impact upon the masses of Jews.[2]

Samuel therefore flourished in a key period and at the time
of the first organized attempt to rabbinize a diaspora community.
Jacob Neusner has suggested that the rabbinic movement succeeded
in Babylonia due to the overlapping interests of the exilarch and
the rabbis. The exilarch needed well-trained individuals to staff
his courts and bureaucracy and the rabbis provided an apparent

malleable and potentially effective group.  They were enthusiastic
propounders of the prestigious new Mishnah edited by Rabbi Judah
the Patriarch, in Palestine.  Moreover, perhaps because of their
shared experience in becoming a rabbi and of their commitment to
Mishnaic laws and rabbinic discipline, they appeared to have
fewer vested interests within Iranian Jewish economic and social
life than other groups.  As a result people could more reliably
turn to them for assistance and trust their judgment.  Likewise,
Jews respected them for their devotion to Torah, something that
the rabbis evidently cultivated.  They set out to be holy men.
People came to expect them to be able to do the things that other
ethnic and religious communities said their own holy men could do.

     Hence, rabbis taught their Torah and their interpretation
of Judaism both by example and through their word.  They had most
success with their disciples, who, in particular, tried to imitate
their masters.  Naturally they had less impact on the other groups
of Jews.  While the rabbis in their teaching addressed all aspects
of life they had actual authority to enforce their views only in
certain spheres.  But their power was real in these latter areas,
including the markets and the courts, which had jurisdiction over
personal and civil disputes.  Since documents were filed in the
courts, the rabbis also could regulate anything involving documents, their use and formulae.[3]

     *Seder Tannaim Ve'amoraim* and the "Preface" to the *Account
of Natan Habbavli* and some modern writers who claim that academies, or *yeshivot*, existed in Babylonia, agree they did not arise
until after the generation of Rav and thus also of Samuel.[4]  Such
formal educational institutions transcend the personalities and
lives of the individual masters.  More recently, David Goodblatt
has argued that such institutions did not exist in Sasanian Iran
but are products of the Islamic or Geonic period.  The primary
means of instruction in Amoraic Babylonia consisted of a master
teaching a small circle of disciples.  By the end of the third
century and during the fourth, developments may have occurred in
these modes of instruction.  Occasionally gatherings of large
sessions at a *pirqa* took place.  They were irregularly supplemented by a more public gathering at a *kallah*.  But all of these
institutions centered around an individual master, perhaps at most
aided by assistants.[5]  Due to the rabbis' connection with the
exilarch and service in his bureaucracy they were able to effec-
tuate some of their teachings in actual life.  Hence, Goodblatt
suggests, the disciples also took on the role of lawyer-

apprentices. They trained under their master, observed him in his court, and questioned him concerning practical matters.[6]

The central work around which rabbis taught their disciples and Jewry at large was the Mishnah. It presented the basics of their interpretation of Judaism and it thus amounted to their "holy book."[7] We can assume that Jews knew the Bible. The murals of Dura Europos, a Jewish but not necessarily "rabbinic" synagogue, reflect the widespread use and adaption of biblical themes.[8] But the rabbis claimed this Written Torah had a companion also revealed at Sinai but orally transmitted. If Jews followed this Oral Torah they would live a meaningful and healthy life.

The contents and methods of Samuel's teaching on Berakhot accord with this picture of Babylonian Jewry. Some of his comments, directly on Mishnah as well as others, reflect the upheavals attending the rise of the Sasanian empire and the transition in the history of Judaism. Samuel is represented as insisting with biblical proof texts that a priest, i.e., by extension a rabbi, be respected (#113-114). A teaching is associated either with military inroads into the community or the death of the exilarch's son (#58-59). The latter version reflects Samuel's respect for the exilarch. Samuel is pictured as a sage before Shapur, like Joseph before Pharoah (#123-124). He is an expert in dreams, astronomy, calendar, and natural science (#2, 3, 4, 123, 124, 126-131, 132, 134, 141). He offers a practical, politically realistic definition of Messianism. The messianic age will not miraculously transform the world; rather it will entail the end of political subjugation (69). Samuel's belief, though, is a real one and he channels hopes for God's intervention into the liturgical texts he develops or shapes (#54, 56a, 68).

The above correlation of Samuel's teaching with third-century events is not new. Earlier studies recognize the relevance of most of the passages.[9] But our analysis of the scope, nature, and methods of Samuel's teaching provides additional information. We found that he comprehensively deals with all the major issues and themes in M. Ber. but not every single passage. Therefore his Commentary is not totally systematic. We suggested that this reflects Samuel's pragmatic and practical goals. He focused upon everything necessary. His choice and types of comments enable a person to understand Mishnah, define its rules, decide between opposing positions, or draw upon positions not found in Mishnah. He complemented and supplemented Mishnah with additional rules. Accordingly, he provided details and procedures for numerous mishnaic rules.[10] We noted that issues that

assume a situation or reality no longer operative in third-century
Iran are not given sustained attention.  Certain Houses' disputes
which assume the context of a meal fall into this category.[11]
Other matters received considerable attention.  This includes the
delineation of the proper blessings over foods that appear in the
*Gemara* to M. Ber. 6:1.  Since the rabbis, including Samuel, wanted
other Jews to follow their practices Samuel provides reasons for
certain key notions.  Samuel designed these to reach wider circles
either directly or through his disciples who would teach them to
others.  In tradition #70 he defines cultic language earlier used
to draw upon the people's respect for the Temple and he cites a
verse which emphasizes God's role throughout the world, assumably
even in Babylonia.  A person should say a blessing over food
because the blessing frees the food from the status of something
dedicated and belonging to God.  In our analysis of the tradition
we traced Samuel's distinctive contribution in bolstering the
notion.  In #115 and 116 he explains the role of fire in the
*havdalah* ceremony by reference to a supposed etiology of fire.  He
associates the use of fire with a legend that God first provided
Adam with fire on the outgoing of the Sabbath.  In #107 Samuel is
associated with a parable which explains the sequence of items in
a special case of *havdalah*.

Samuel's attempt to present and explain key rabbinic
notions is likewise reflected in his specific use of the ideology
of the Oral Torah.  He requires a person to say a blessing over
the study of Torah and delineates the blessing's theme, formula,
or text.  While Mishnah's concern was that a blessing be said at
a certain juncture in the liturgy, Samuel made the blessing a
subject in its own right.  In one version of the teaching, Samuel
projects this blessing into the priestly Temple liturgy, which in
effect lends it greater weight and a strong precedent.[12]

Samuel also gives much attention to Mishnah's concern for
proper intent in prayer.  By teaching on proper intent the rabbis,
particularly those who lived in the aftermath of the Temple's
destruction, were able to provide Jews with a sense of personal
autonomy and power to change their own lives.  They thereby
rejected the notion that the world has its own "reality" and fate
unaffected by human actions.  This message became glaringly evident on the fall of one world empire, the Parthian, and the rise
of a new one, the Sasanian.  During this crisis Samuel gave much
specific advice on how a person could attain and maintain the
proper composure, frame of mind, and attention in prayer.[13]

Samuel's disproportionate attention to blessings might reflect his belief not only in the importance of this subject but also in the effectiveness of his teaching in this area. The notion that one recites a blessing before eating is common, fits within biblical conceptions, and finds a formal application in the Dead Sea Scrolls. It is likewise a plausible extension of the Pharisaic and rabbinic ideas that the physical Temple is not the only place to experience the divine presence. Moreover, Zoroastrains also had an elaborate system of blessings before eating food and hence such practices and requirements would not have seemed strange to Babylonian Jews.[14]

In addition, the overall themes of blessings, prayer, and liturgy may reflect the disciple context of Samuel's teaching. Samuel would not have had direct actual authority to enforce such matters over the masses. It is not surprising therefore that in several pericopae Samuel's students are represented as citing Samuel's teaching and employing it to solve problems as to the proper blessing over food or in the liturgy or as to the correct place to bow. Thus we see the role of the individual student in the preservation and citation of Samuel's comments.[15]

Finally, this historical reconstruction also receives support from the very fact that Samuel composed an actual Mishnah Commentary. While the notion of a master-disciple circle provides a reasonable *sitz-im-leben* for a Mishnah Commentary that makes up a fundamental building block of the Talmud, our proof for the existence of the Commentary did not depend upon that historical picture. We proved it on the basis of the spread, types, and formulations of the traditions and the place or lack of tradents in their attributive formulae. Therefore, we may consider our results corroborative evidence for Goodblatt's conclusions. A Mishnah Commentary appropriately fits in the context of a master teaching a circle of disciples. The disciples are to learn Mishnah and to remember along with it Samuel's response to the text. A more formal institutionalized structure might include a more involved and complex collection of materials.[16]

This last point likewise relates to the nature of the dispute form. We found that most traditions do not appear even in ostensible dispute forms with opinions of other masters and that the form actually represents a literary device to transmit two opinions on a single theme. Hence its use is secondary to the tradition. In the formulation of the dispute form, though, we find support for the notion of disciple circles. As masters basically taught individually they did not have a context in

which to square off with another master.  Rather disciples of
Samuel and another master, e.g., Rav, transmit their masters'
teachings.  Someone learns of both teachings and for the sake of
convenience combines the two together.[17]

The above implications enable us to throw light on several
additional problems.  The way in which Samuel uses Mishnah both in
glossing it and in offering more expansive comments reflects the
central role of Mishnah.  Likewise the ways in which his students
remembered and transmitted those comments formulated not in "standard commentary" ways but, for example, as a part of a story or a
First-Person Report, reflect the fact that teaching was structured
around Mishnah.  The presence of analogues in structurally similar
places in the opposite *Gemara* makes such an argument quite strong.
This further accords with the observation of several scholars that
Babylonian rabbinic circles may have accepted the authority of
Mishnah more fully than did the Palestinians.[18]  These scholars
themselves admit, paradoxically, that early masters nevertheless
felt free to disagree with Mishnah.  Elsewhere we presented the
latter position.

> Rabbi intended the Mishnah to be authoritative, and there-
> fore taught some views anonymously.  But early Amoraim rejected
> Rabbi's purpose.  They asserted their autonomy to rely on any
> Tannaitic source or tradition, even those contradicting Mish-
> nah.  They therefore tried to identify the anonymous parts of
> Mishnah, to see if they represent individual or collective
> views.[19]

To resolve the apparent paradox in the attitudes of the
early Amoraim we must refine our observations.  The issue is not
just that of accepting and rejecting Mishnah.  Rather Samuel's
teaching of Mishnah enabled one to understand and to apply Mishnah
in legal questions; this itself gave it greather authority.  He
also used Mishnah as a point of departure and as a means to organize further teaching.  Accordingly, in the process Mishnah set,
but did not limit, Samuel's agendum for study and teaching.[20]

Further research must compare the above correlations with
the modes of teaching and the social role of third-century Palestinian masters.  These latter masters lived in a different social
and religious context from their bretheren in Babylonia.  For
example, first, they had established academic institutions and
traditions of teaching and learning.  Second, rabbis had already
gone through several stages in their relationship with the Patriarch.  Since the Patriarchate and Exilarchate had different origins and needs, the rabbinic-patriarchal connection assumably
would differ from that of the rabbinic-exilarchic connection.

Third, the rabbinic movement expanded in Palestine before it did
in Babylonia.  Already in second-century Palestine it had made
significant strides.  Fourth, Palestinian Jews lived in the "holy
land" under Rome and not in a diaspora under Iran.  Fifth, Palestine went through significant agrarian and economic transformations
which produced special social problems and needs which rabbis had
to address.  In light of the above variables one must inquire to
what degree the social role of the rabbis and their context
affected the mode, form, and content of their teaching.[21]

## 2.  *Creative Transmission of Teachings*

The formation and history of Samuel's comments provide a
second area of implications.  First, Samuel's pragmatic interests
greatly affected his response to Mishnah.  He did not evidently
believe himself bound by Mishnah's own overall point or reason for
which it cited rules or themes.  This enabled him to focus upon
items mentioned only in passing, as the nature of the "evil inclination," in M. Ber. 9:3.  The reference appears only as part of a
larger unit which contains a portion relevant to the point of Mishnah.  Samuel's freedom from, but close response to, Mishnah
accords with his acceptance of Mishnah as an authoritative, but
not totally binding, work and statement of topics.  As Isadore
Twersky has observed in conjunction with medieval Jewish codes,
the very process of scrutiny and understanding of a code makes
possible and entails the reevaluation of its opinions and decisions.[22]  Thus Samuel wanted to make Mishnah functional in real-
life situations.  In order words, comments that define the circumstances of Mishnah's rules or cases indicate that he did not
intend merely to facilitate people's memorization of Mishnah.  This
accords with the tradition cited earlier in which Samuel insists
that a person should try to understand Mishnah.[23]  Moreover, the
very fact that Samuel presented his teachings as part of a commentary to Mishnah, to circulate attached to or in association with
that work, indicates that the understanding of Mishnah has become
as important as knowing its wording.[24]

Later authorities follow Samuel's example and let personal
interests affect their relationship to Samuel's teachings.  We see
this in two ways.  First, different generations of masters exhibit
greater interest in different parts of the Commentary.  We isolated
three essential and fundamental, though different, components.
Those comments necessary for a simple understanding of the text and
its rules circulated immediately along with Mishnah.  Those traditions which provide rulings or which are necessary to enable one

to apply Mishnah are associated with the second-generation masters.
Those teachings which more extensively apply and use Mishnah are
of special interest to later masters.

Second, some of the later masters who present Samuel's
application and extension of rules, like Nahman, may actually
build upon Samuel's comment and further apply his ruling or teaching.[25] Moreover, Babylonian emigrés or travelers to Palestine, in
addition to later Palestinian masters, in the process of presenting
Samuel's teachings often shape them to address Palestinian definitions of the issues.

This creative transmission of Samuel's comments actually
exemplifies the nature of the Oral Torah.  Torah was not a static
thing.  Rabbis were not antiquarians retelling what previous teachers had said.  Rather they transmitted legal and narrative materials for didactic purposes, to address live issues and to respond
to the needs of real people.[26]  This observation relates to different points emphasized by Morton Smith and Jacob Neusner.

Smith points out, as cited above, that rabbinic teachings
even where they may share similarities in form, type, and substance with those of the Gospels nevertheless sharply differ due
to their purposes.  Materials are included in the Gospels to fill
in the life of Jesus and make clear the meaning of his death.
Materials are included in rabbinic works to address issues of law
(and rabbinic values or notions) and to enable a person effectively to follow the Torah and gain satisfaction from it.[27]

Jacob Neusner points out that talmudic literary and historical critics do not yet know what, if any, factors affect tradents
in their transmission of amoraic teachings.[28]  We can phrase this
somewhat differently.  Do all the variations that traditions
undergo arise only from the particular forms of teachings that a
master chances to know?

Our results relate to both points.  They enable us, if
only tentatively, to formulate a theory or the basis for a theory.
In chapter eight we argued that items without a tradent introduce
materials which are appropriate to the most fundamental elements
of a commentary.  These items circulated along with Mishnah.  Even
where we can reconstruct the name of a tradent who cited one of
these brief comments, the lack of identification is not surprising.
It would have been inappropriate to include that tradent's name in
the chain, for the tradition already had an integrity of its own.

On the other hand, the tradents appear in the attributive
formulae of traditions which they cite and relate to a specific
context.  We observed this phenomenon in particular in terms of

Samuel's teachings in Palestine.  Generally, third-generation travelers cite Samuel's comment through the intermediary role of a
second-generation disciple and often adapted them to address a
Palestinian issue.  Abraham Goldberg pointed to these factors and
we found additional instances of them.[29]

We likewise found that y. narratives concerning Samuel
relate to Mishnah.  These have b. analogues in structurally similar
locations and therefore at an early time must have circulated in
conjunction with Mishnah or have been associated with it.  Moreover,
all of Samuel's y. traditions initially related to Mishnah, either
directly or through a *baraita* that complements Mishnah or as part
of a larger pericope that deals with a mishnaic topic.  BT, on the
other hand, includes teachings actually totally unrelated to Mishnah.  Babylonians apparently believed that whatever Samuel said or
whatever was told about Samuel constituted "Torah" and of potential
value.  Babylonians wanted to preserve the heritage of their masters.  But those responsible for the y. evidently were interested
in Samuel's teachings only when the latter appeared relevant to an
issue of concern to them.  Since Mishnah made up the primary common
denominator between Babylonians and Palestinians, naturally Mishnah
became the criterion of selection or preservation.[30]  This hypothesis accords with Lieberman's suggestion that Palestinian editors of
y. evaluated Babylonian traditions in terms of their relevance and
integration into Palestinian interpretations of Mishnah.[31]

Thus the legal and narrative, or aggadic, teachings in
diverse ways may reflect different images of Samuel.  Samuel's
Torah remained important yet had a different history in different
groups and generations of rabbis.  These observations can form the
basis for further research and we can test our interpretive suggestions with more extensive studies.  We should focus on three
points: First, how does the wider context of a *sugya* affect the
selection and presentation of the individual component parts,
including the narrative portions?  In Volume One we presented the
hypothesis that the wider context does have such an effect and in
our present sample we have found more support for it.  Elsewhere
in "Redaction Criticism of the Talmud: The Case of Ḥanina Ben
Dosa," we addressed this problem in its own terms.[32]  Systematic
analysis on large blocks of *Gemara* must now be undertaken.

Secondly, various modern writers have analyzed the images
of ancient masters and teachers and have demonstrated how the
descriptions of these masters often inform us of the beliefs,
imaginations, and needs of the storytellers and transmitters and
of their projected audiences.  Peter Brown and Ramsey MacMullen

have discussed various types of virtuosos from different cultures
and social groups.[33]   Henry Fischel has analyzed the specific
"Hellenistic" traits with which rabbis are depicted.[34]   Jacob
Neusner and others have traced the images of Pharisees and various
Yavnean masters in rabbinic sources.[35]   Neusner has also pointed
out that Babylonian Amoraim are depicted as "holy men."[35a]   Our
present investigation indicates that further study of the Amoraim
may provide profitable results.  We can trace the changes in the
depiction of individual masters and also try to integrate the
master's image as a halakhic figure with the image that emerges
from narrative descriptions of his actions.

We can also examine if the very change from oral transmission of traditions of or about a master to a written presentation
forming part of the developing *Gemara*, which prominently included
"stories" in addition to "sayings," tells us something about the
role of the master and his later image.  Philip Rousseau is one
writer who has done this for Christian ascetics.  He tries to
differentiate between more and less fundamental and reliable pictures of the ascetics on the basis of *apopthegmata* literature.  He
discusses the impact of the transition from an oral account to a
written form and traces how later needs often affected the depiction of earlier masters.  Thus once the ascetic movement grew and
time and distance separated the master from the later disciples,
people required reassurance as to the master's authority and spir-
itual power.[36]   The observations in the following quotations could
be the basis for further study in the rabbinic materials.

> The *Apopthegmata Patrum*, the *Lives* and *Rule* of Pachomius,
> helped to create the world they revealed; and the authors
> regarded not only their interpretation of events but also the
> literary forms in which it was expressed as the natural culmin-
> ation of ascetic history.  Once again, the pace and pattern of
> change had encouraged, indeed compelled, those in authority to
> exercise power and protect the leadership in new ways--in this
> case by writing. . . .
>     Decline in charismatic power, growth in numbers, and an
> increasing emphasis on example brought about important changes
> in the relationship of ascetics one with another. . . . The
> impact of monk upon monk, now beyond the immediate reach of
> ascetic masters, had still to be regulated by a lasting and
> universal sanction; and written texts met such a need.  The
> preservation of authority itself was at stake. . . .
>     As with the *Rule* of Pachomius, therefore, so with other
> sources: the written word was seized on as a more accessible
> alternative to the charismatic authority of the holy man.
> . . . By presenting as examples the lives of holy men, he [=
> the compiler of the *Apopthegmata Patrum*] hoped that his readers
> would become examples in their turn. . . .
>     The move from an oral to a written culture was made easier
> by the sense among ascetics that their true masters were not
> dead.  By the end of the century, leadership had passed to a

new generation of man, who always thought of themselves as
disciples, dependent for their teaching on the insights of the
past. They therefore appealed to the words, counsel, or example of their predecessors, "memory of whom must remain forever
flesh."[37]

The third area involves a comparison and control within
rabbinic sources. To contrast and test our analysis of the history of Samuel's image we can pursue several questions. Do the
images of other Babylonians in BT exhibit similarities or differences from that of Samuel? Secondly, how do the Palestinians fare
in the BT? Third, how do these seveal pictures contrast with the
images for each in the PT?[38]

The answers to the above questions will also throw light
on a long-standing problem. Scholars have discussed the attitudes
Babylonians and Palestinians had towards each other and the impact
of these on their relationship. Overly romanticized views assume
everything remained harmonious between the two communities and
their leaders and that throughout Jewish history Jews consistently
deferred to the holy land and its authorities. But this is a false
picture. Abraham Goldberg has pointed to the ways in which some
Babylonians in Palestine tried to glorify their (former) Babylonian masters.[39] Literary critics like Epstein had already noted
the obvious instances in which one *Gemara* cites rabbis from "there,"
a clear indication of that *Gemara*'s perception of different social
groups.[40] Steinsaltz, Neusner, M. Beer, Lieberman, and Kimelman
have addressed this problem and have offered diverse cultural and
historical suggestions.[41] But a definitive evaluation of the
relationship cannot rely just on statements which refer to masters
from one or the other country. Rather we must examine how people
in each land actually treated the laws and stories concerning
masters from the other land.[42] Our own conclusions based upon our
sample make up only a working hypothesis based upon certain solid
observations. With further data we can determine whether or not
they are representative of a wider phenomenon.

### 3. From Mishnah to Gemara

Our conclusions throw light on the processes that led to
the creation of the early building blocks of Talmud. In discussing this problem, we first focus on why this is a problem and
then on how our results contribute toward its resolution.

The origins of the *Gemara* have generally been treated as
a literary problem. People have asked about the stages in the
processes through which the *Gemara* was edited, redacted, worked

over, and given its final touches.  For example, when does the
stage of redaction end and that of textual history start?  Some
scholars suggest that the contents of *Gemara* went through constant
accretions.  Some posit accretions and several stages of mini-
editing, the earliest, according to certain writers, in the late
third century. [43]

     These theories, however, do not make clear what the first
stages of *Gemara* resembled nor how they took shape.  Scholars
naturally assume that Mishnah provided "the external framework and
the internal continuity" of the text and that early Amoraim
explained Mishnah. [44]  These amoraic explanations in some unspecified
way became the *Gemara*'s first stratum.  Recent form and source
critics of the Talmud, including Hyman Klein, Abraham Weiss, David
Weiss Halivni, and Shamma Friedman, have tried to distinguish
between early and late elements of the Talmud.  They speak in particular of "brief" and "discursive" materials and generally assign
one, usually the brief, to the early stage of the amoraic analysis
and application of Mishnah.  Accordingly, out of these brief or
less involved teachings the *Gemara* somehow grew. [45]

     One of the reasons that scholars generally did not make
explicit how the initial stage took shape is because they did not
try to relate their results to the nature of the social context in
which the rabbis worked.  Most scholars assumed that early masters
explained or discussed Mishnah within a permanent academic institution, that is, a *yeshiva* or academy.  *Gemara* would then consti-
tue a record of the *yeshiva*'s debates.  But modern literary analysis of the Talmud demonstrates that much of *Gemara*'s image of
complex discussions and arguments are literary devices supplied by
later authorities who added the framework and bridging language.
Today we better appreciate the processes of individual transmission
of teachings, of constant presentation, juxtaposition with other
opinions, interpretation, and revision.  David Weiss Halivni in
particular has shown how transmission has affected the history of
amoraic materials. [46]  Moreover, as we discussed above, the extant
evidence from amoraic Iran does not support the notion that perma-
net academic institutions existed.  Our own results support the
contention that rabbinic instruction took place within the context
of a master and a circle of disciples.

     Several scholars do address peripheral aspects of the
problem.  For example, Abraham Weiss points to groups of collections of teachings which students may have gathered after their
master's death or those of an important master which another

master collected.  Later masters remembered these teachings as a unit and then incorporated them into the *Gemara*.  Shamma Friedmann, who offers a complementary or alternative theory as to the presence of tripartite series of teachings, recognizes that the extant teachings are reworkings of original oral materials.[47] Therefore, the question remains how the earliest teachings originated and how the *Gemara*'s first stratum emerged from these teachings.  Were the teachings taught by a master to disciples who collected them and then later, when these teachings were transmitted, were they worked over into units and subsequently, even later, were they further adapted to fit their use within the layout of *Gemara*?  Certainly, we could accept the possibility that a social context existed in which disciples remembered a group of teachings as a unit.  But such materials would account for a small portion of the Talmud.  In addition, as pointed out in chapter eight, the character of *Gemara* is not set by these teachings.  *Gemara* follows the structure of Mishnah, as most scholars naturally observe.[48]

Accordingly we face the problem of penetrating to a pre-literary state of the teachings.  Scholars in their analysis of other literatures have addressed the identical problem.  Teachings presently found in one context and form may have originated in a different one and in the process of transition may have undergone changes.  Actually, the material may go through several stages. These include, first, oral or written composition, second, oral or written initial transmission, third, oral or written integration into the state in which it is presently found, and, fourth, final writing down and editing of the materials in stage three.

The biblical prophetic books pose analogous problems.  How can we determine the original context of an oracle?  Did it originate as a single unit or as part of a larger collection comparable to the extant chapters?  Did these materials circulate orally or in written form?  When they did receive written form, what impact did that transformation have on the style, organization, and content?  These questions may likewise apply to other portions of the Bible.  In chapter nine, we quoted Eissfeldt's observations on this subject in terms of biblical laws.  As he points out, some scholars believe that series of biblical laws originated as individual items.[49]

This issue lies behind the problem of the New Testament *apophthegms* of Jesus.  Whether or not many of these sayings derive from Jesus, their present context is secondary.  Often when one compares the three synoptics one can find more than one context for the same saying.  Frequently the point of the saying does not

exactly fit its location.  In the latter cases, either the context
has been added to supply a background for the teaching or the saying has been used to highlight a certain stage in Jesus' career.[50]

A different instance of the *apopthegm* is that of the
Christian monks.  Their sayings presently circulate in several
written collections.  But they originated as individual sayings
and therefore have been collected, adapted, and presented in
larger units.  Several scholars have shown how variations exist
between the several versions of a saying.  Philip Rousseau, cited
above, has tried in particular to trace the impact of the transition from the oral account to the written records.[51]

Accordingly, the problem of the early amoraic teachings
and their pre-literary stage is not unique.  Our problem, however,
has an added dimension.  How did these individual teachings eventually become the basic structural elements of *Gemara*?

Thus our present study takes account of the character of
*Gemara*, set by Mishnah, and the need to transcend the gulf between
the literary and pre-literary stages of the teachings.  Hence we
had to build upon earlier scholarship.  For example, several
scholars including J. N. Epstein had recognized that Samuel and
other early masters taught *baraitot* which parallel Mishnah and that
many of Samuel's traditions deal with Mishnah.[52]  Abraham Weiss
further observed that teachings of Rav and Samuel apparently make
up a framework around which much of *Gemara* is structured.[53]
Indeed early Babylonian Amoraim commented upon Mishnah and even
their wide-ranging response to the text was set within the structure of Mishnah along with which it was studied by later authorities.  The later study of Mishnah and expansion of the extra-
Mishnah material developed into the *Gemara*.[53a]  Moreover, Abraham
Weiss and other talmudic critics speak of individual *memrot*, statements, as the primary element of *Gemara*.[54]  While such theories do
account for the structure based upon Mishnah, they do not sufficiently, if at all, address the pre-literary stage.[55]  Consequently
we argued that Samuel originally taught his disciples a commentary
on Mishnah and designed a fundamental part of it to circulate along
with Mishnah.  This accords with the rabbis' self-image and notion
of Oral Torah.  Teaching Mishnah enables one to participate in
revelation.[56]

In chapter six, we showed how the comments related to
Mishnah.  About 30 percent of the items and 33 percent of the
traditions require Mishnah for comprehension and depend upon it in
formulation.  About 18 percent need Mishnah for comprehension
though they are somewhat autonomously formulated.  About 33

percent supplement Mishnah and while they could technically circulate independently they make best sense in their present locations,
on *mishnayot* in Berakhot. A fourth group of Declarative Sentences
makes up 19 percent and while they likewise are independently
formulated, their close relationship to Mishnah is obvious. Two
blatantly need Mishnah. One is the expansion of a simple gloss.
Two have close analogues in the opposite *Gemara* and further develop
a response to Mishnah initiated in Tosefta. Five make good sense
in the context of Mishnah.[57] Earlier we pointed out that the
presence of analogues in structurally similar locations and, in
general, the close association to Mishnah of materials which are
autonomously formulated most profoundly reflects the importance of
Mishnah as the text around which teachings are organized.

The model we propose in theory poses no problem. It is
well attested that Mishnah itself circulated orally. Reciters
memorized the whole corpus. Students, moreover, were expected to
learn part of Mishnah along with explanations.[58] Notably, the
Sasanian Avesta provides an Iranian analogue to our picture.
People recited portions of the Avesta along with its commentary,
the *Zand*, which a student then studied, section by section.[59]

When a master cited or reused an earlier teaching he may
have slightly expanded or revised it and at times shaped it to
address or emphasize the issue for which it is presented. The
dispute form provides us with an example of the transition from a
Mishnah Commentary to a "teaching." The original context and
function has become subservient to the need and desire to present
two opinions on a matter and to elucidate and preserve the law.
Apparently, once people remembered the teachings in these wider
formats and according to their later use, we have what became the
first stratum of *Gemara*,

Our theory that Mishnah played the key role in the preservation and use of teachings also accounts for the existence of
numerous narrative materials. We demonstrated this in absolute
terms for the y. materials. We found that all y. "unrelated"
items initially did relate to Mishnah. We also found that Samuel's
Babylonian disciples apparently preserved accounts of whatever
Samuel did. In contrast to y. authorities, who were interested
only in Samuel's comments which by themselves or as part of a
pericope were related to Mishnah, the Babylonians perceived all
of his teachings and actions as Torah and transmitted them. In
Berakhot these "unrelated" materials make up 26 of 143 comments
or 18.2 percent of the traditions.[60] While we cannot fully
understand how these teachings, which do not at all respond to

Mishnah, become part of *Gemara*, a review of all of Samuel's teachings in light of our hypothesis may provide a partial answer.

There are 143 items which make up 132 distinct traditions.
We broke these down as follows.  First, 59 items, or 51 traditions,
which represent 41.3 percent of the items and 38.6 percent of the
traditions, properly belong to a direct Mishnah Commentary.  We
also subdivided these materials into three subgroups in terms of
their specific relationship to Mishnah, as mentioned above.
Secondly, 46 items, or 45 traditions, which account for 32.2
percent of the items and 34.1 percent of the traditions, respond
to Mishnah by complementing or supplementing it and extending its
subjects independently of Mishnah's overall concerns and framework.
It is not surprising that Samuel's disciples remembered these
teachings and where appropriate cited them as part of an extended
discussion and study of Mishnah.  But such items are not designed
to make up part of a "Commentary."  Thirdly, 38 items, or 36
traditions, which represent 26.6 percent of the items and 27.3
percent of the traditions, fail to relate to Mishnah.  Of this
last group, though, 12 items or 10 traditions are found in y. and
are classified as "unrelated" only due to their present use in y.
Berakhot.  But initially they did relate to Mishnah.  Mishnah
played a formative role in the first two of these broad categories,
i.e., for 105 items and 96 traditions, 73.4 percent of the items
and 72.3 percent of the traditions.  With the additional 12 items
and 10 traditions from y. this represents 81.8 percent of the items
and 80.3 percent of the traditions.

Mishnah thus clearly made up the point of departure and
the structure for the overwhelming number of teachings.  Those
which circulated along with Mishnah eventually provided the main
framework for *Gemara*.  Moreover, they frequently were combined or
juxtaposed with Mishnah teachings of other early masters.  The
complementary traditions found a natural place alongside of the
Mishnah comments.[61]  Later authorities cited, in Berakhot, traditions which originated on *mishnayot* elsewhere and had them address
issues in their new context.  This applies in particular to the y.
"unrelated" items and traditions.  The remaining "unrelated" items,
19 percent of the total sample, were taught by Samuel and remembered by his disciples.  Apparently once a discussion turned to
certain topics, the disciples repeated Samuel's comments on these
matters.  Alternatively a later authority knew of Samuel's teachings from another context or structured on some other basis, e.g.,
verses of the Bible, and incorporated them into the structure of
Mishnah.  Our notes to these items in chapter three show how they

are connected to their *sugyot*.  But further research will throw
additional light on these later processes through which traditions
were integrated into larger contexts.

        Thus our argument for a commentary directly on Mishnah
fulfills our initial two requirements.  First, the earliest
stratum of *Gemara* is a reworking of an apparently oral commentary
on Mishnah.  Second, the spread and number of traditions reflects
the central role that Mishnah took in the initial formation of the
teachings.  The question remains, however, *why such an expansive
scrutiny initally emerged*.  In chapter nine's discussion of the
nature of Samuel's commentary and above in our discussion of the
third-century academic and social roles of the rabbis we mentioned
several key factors.  We must now more fully address the problem.

        First, we must consider the function, purposes, and style
of Mishnah, on the one hand, and the literary forms, functions,
and purposes of the teachings of the early Amoraim, on the other.

        The editors of Mishnah presented Mishnah as their inter-
pretation of a Judaism without a Temple and as detailed proof that
Judaism can continue and efficaciously and meaningfully deal with
the religious needs and sensitivities of people.  The editors also
drew upon the intellectual heritage of several groups, especially
those from pre-70 C.E.[62] and in the process of employing and
adapting those teachings they present an image of a unified or
consensus Judaism.  Accordingly, Mishnah-tractates consist of
individual laws redacted into a wider whole which, in effect, make
up an essay on a given theme.  In turn, the overall problematic or
concern affects the selection and arrangement of the materials.
For example, M. Tehorot in various ways "assume(s) the conviction
that common unconsecrated produce is to be eaten outside of the
cult in conditions of cultic purity, that the table of the Israelite in one's home is like the table of God in the Temple, and that
the non-priests are to behave as if they were priests."[63]  In a
like manner an overall concern shapes M. Berakhot.  It reflects the
rabbinic standardization of prayer as a mandated and totally efficacious means of expressing one's petitions and thanksgiving to
God.  This system of prayer, now a requirement of the community
and the individual, is no longer merely an optional means of
religious expression left up to the discretion of the pious individual and a mere complement to the sacrificial system.[64]

        The later rabbis would find the above notions interesting
but hardly the major issues which posed serious religious problems.
They no longer faced the religious crisis of a Judaism bereft of
the central symbol and institution of the Temple.  They accepted

the idea that prayers are effective means to express one's religious feelings.  Moreover, they were in a position to carry forward
the earlier notions and in their own way to elaborate upon the
ideal cult and society which Mishnah portrayed.  Indeed, the needs
of third-century Iran and the spread of rabbinic Judaism there
resulted in a social setting quite different from that of first-
and second-century Palestine.[65]

Early Amoraim, therefore, employed Mishnah for a comprehensive statement of the important topics, themes, and laws.  As
stated, they did not need to reassure Jews that Judaism can continue without a Temple.[66]  In addition, they had to apply, make
concrete, and spell out the rituals and practices which Mishnah
prescribes and do it in a way that people could actually perform
them, even where two different religious requirements might coincide or where the mishnaic projected conditions might not be identical to those of their life situation.  Accordingly, the early
masters, including Samuel, atomize the text of Mishnah and focus
on its individual parts irrespective of their primary or secondary
role within the work.  In addition, they develop the law and
relate one passage to a principle or concern found elsewhere in
Mishnah.

Secondly, in addition to the differing social settings of
the mishnaic editors and of third-century masters, the very nature
of the type of commentary that these masters undertake involved a
far-ranging response to Mishnah.  As Neusner explains, the grammar,
style, and contents of Mishnah elicit commentary.  But the early
Amoraim did not undertake a mere explication or a commentary as a
literary exercise.  In a literary exercise or explication, a writer
examines a text and systematically explains each word in it, and
sets out the redactional or overall theory or purpose of the work
and its contents.  The concerns of the primary work largely determine the commentator's topics.  Such a commentator generally does
not independently develop the themes of the primary work, here
Mishnah.  But in our case, Samuel and other early Amoraim who
teach a group of disciples, teach Mishnah as a special book.
Mishnah provides the basis of the rabbinic interpretation of
Judaism which these masters are trying to spread.  These early
masters, therefore, comment on Mishnah with definitions and
explanations, decide Mishnah's laws, complement and supplement
Mishnah with additional information, expand the themes and reason-
ing of Mishnah, and apply Mishnah to new situations.  Hence, due
*to the very nature of this activity, these masters disregard*

*Mishnah's overall framework and redactional point and atomize*
*Mishnah's contents and use Mishnah as a point of departure or*
*reference.* [67]

The following five examples exemplify these dynamics.  We
could complement them with numerous additional instances from
chapter three. [68]

First, in #8, Samuel identifies an unspecified reference
in M. Ber. 1:4.  Mishnah emphasizes that the *Shema$^c$*, now no longer
a prayer said daily only by pious individuals, constitutes an
integral part of the prayer service surrounded by blessings.
Therefore, Mishnah states that blessings precede and follow the
*Shema$^c$*.  Samuel identifies one of the former with the phrase,
"With Great Love."  Thus Samuel's comment supplies information
integral to a text like Mishnah.

Second, in #9, Samuel deals with something mentioned in M.
Ber. 1:4 but not in terms of the purposes for which Mishnah presented it.  As mentioned, Mishnah is concerned that a blessing
precede the *Shema$^c$*.  Samuel develops the implication of the particular blessing in terms of its possible use as a blessing over study
of Torah.  Accordingly, Samuel atomizes and develops Mishnah
according to his own interests.

Third, in #140, Samuel and Rav offer similes for the "evil
inclination," an item mentioned in the exegesis of Deut. 6:5, a
midrashic text cited in M. Ber. 9:5.  Mishnah, however, makes this
reference only in passing.  Mishnah rules that a person must accept
whatever God metes out and be thankful for it, whether perceived
as good or evil.  One or two parts of the midrashic text provide
biblical support for this notion.  The reference to "evil inclination" forms a unit with the relevant portion and, accordingly, is
cited along with it.  Thus we see that the early Amoraim may
respond to Mishnah but not only in terms of the main themes and
overall purposes of Mishnah.  What makes up a secondary element,
here the reference to "evil inclination," may become subject of an
extensive analysis and scrutiny.

The fourth and fifth examples demonstrate Samuel's development of Mishnah's rules.  We pointed out that his comments may
assume earlier developments of Mishnah, often found in a toseftan
*baraita*, and he extends them further.  Thus in our fourth example,
#13-14 and 18-19, b. and y. analogues, Rav and Samuel deal with
bowing.  Rav stipulates when one bows and rises in the *Tefillah*
and Samuel cites a verse to explain the reason.  M. Ber. 1:4
speaks of the types of blessings which precede and follow the
*Shema$^c$*.  T. Ber. 1:5-9 focus on the subject in terms of a general

principle and supplement it with additional principles concerning
the several types of blessings and the procedures followed when
saying them.  One rule (T. 1:8) deals with bowing at the "appropriate" locations in the liturgy.  Clearly then, Rav and Samuel's
comments in effect concretely apply a version of this principle.

Fifth, in #98 we have a graphic example of the transition
from mishnaic supplement into independent tradition and discussion.
M. Ber. 7:1 assumes that Grace is said and defines when a group of
three people are required to say Grace communally.  Samuel's tradition appears in the *Gemara* on this Mishnah.  It deals with making
special reference to the New Moon in the Grace and in the *Tefillah*,
and focuses on the procedure when one errs and fails to make the
reference.  How does Mishnah yield such a comment?  Elsewhere
Mishnah exhibits an interest in special interpolations in the
liturgy.  M. Ber. 5:2 deals with them in reference to the *Tefillah*
and M. Ber. chapter eight does so in reference to ushering in and
escorting out the Sabbath.  T. Ber. 3:8 provides a general principle to mention the "special day" as an *interpolation in Grace*.
The next passage, T. Ber. 3:9, raises the issue of "forgetting,"
but does so only in terms of the special interpolations in the
*Tefillah*, for example, for rain.  Thus, it adds to M. Ber. 5:2's
mention of interpolation in *Tefillah*, but does not mention Grace
After Meals.  Samuel's comment, however, makes the later connection and further extends the law.  He and the other early masters
may have responded to a source substantively identical to the
toseftan *baraita* and discussed to what degree one applies the
logic of repeating, found in *Tefillah*, to the case of Grace.[69]

In chapter nine, we pointed out that the contents and
logical development of a law or notion as well as the types and
forms of Mishnah comments of early Amoraim find analogues and at
times parallels in several other works composed in the second to
third centuries.  First, one clause of Mishnah may explain or
expand an antecedent and ostensibly earlier clause.  Second,
pericopae in the halakhic Midrashim comment on and respond to the
Bible.  Third, Tosefta responds to Mishnah by glossing, complementing, and supplementing it, and the three types of relationships determine the manner in which the pericopae are grouped and
structured in Tosefta itself.  The three modes of dependence upon
Mishnah in the Toseftan materials and in the three basic components of Samuel's Mishnah Commentary make up striking parallels.

On the other hand, we also distinguished between the commentary activities of Samuel and of these three other works,
including Tosefta.  First, Tosefta's response remains basically

an explicative, supplementary scrutiny of Mishnah structured around Mishnah. It develops Mishnah's law or notion at most to the next logical step and at times may offer a general principle behind Mishnah's teaching. Furthermore, Tosefta does this in a very systematic way. It includes something, if not several pericopae, on practically every clause of Mishnah. But the early Amoraim, in developing Mishnah's subjects, may even extend them through several stages. Samuel and the other masters apply Mishnah's laws and provide them with concrete details, relate them to specific situations, and frequently offer decisions as to what constitutes the normative position. The last of the above five examples exemplifies these different qualities. Moreover, while Samuel's response may be comprehensive and not episodic, in that it treats practically every theme of every chapter, it still is not exhaustively systematic. He does not treat every clause nor every single Mishnah passage.

Secondly, the works reflect different literary histories. Tosefta is composed as a literary work structured around Mishnah. On the other hand, *Gemara* is the result of a complex process of collection and redaction of what definitely were individual units of teaching, many of which applied Mishnah and which circulated individually. This arrangement of generations of teachings is set into a literary framework with language to bridge the individual statements, pericopae, and *sugyot*. Our focus on the teachings of an individual master, Samuel, enabled us to isolate his comments and to appreciate his distinctive response to Mishnah. Hence, we were able to differentiate it from the more comprehensive and systematic scrutiny provided by *Gemara* as a whole. Accordingly, only from the later perspective of the final product and its juxtaposition of the teachings of the various Amoraim along with the anonymous late analysis of Mishnah does *Gemara* at all resemble the full-fledged response to Tosefta.

Thirdly, however the individual pericopae in Tosefta originated, Tosefta as a work in its own right did not originate as part of an effort to mediate and apply Mishnah to a new social setting in which rabbinic Judaism was expanding. Rather Tosefta apparently is designed to provide a resource for a full range of tannaitic teachings and to explicate Mishnah in the process.[70]

Due to the above different scopes, literary histories and arrangements, and purposes, Tosefta's and Samuel's responses to Mishnah involve very different types of commentary. Certainly Samuel's teachings took on a new role in their later history and we have indicated how they make up the rubric of the literary

work *Gemara*.  But with the aid of form criticism and with a sensitivity to the dynamics of transmission and redaction of Samuel's
traditions we have discerned those traits that derive from the
comments' fundamental function as part of a Mishnah Commentary.

### 4.  *Further Research: The Impact of the Sample*

        We have refined our understanding of Samuel's Mishnah
Commentary and in the process have dealt with various literary
and historical problems.  Our observations and conclusions, though,
have led us into numerous areas for further research.  But additional study of the amoraic Mishnah Commentary itself remains.

        First, we must see if other Babylonian masters, chiefly
Rav, also composed a Mishnah Commentary.  We should consider the
relationship of his Mishnah comments to his remaining teachings in
a given tractate so as to consider the overall impact of Mishnah
and the ways in which his Mishnah response may have developed into
more autonomous and independent teaching.[70a]  We should likewise
analyze the teachings of the Palestinian masters, chiefly Yohanan,
and examine their response to Mishnah.  How were their comments
designed to function and what role did they take in the formation
of PT?  Considering the social, political, and religious differences between Babylonia and Palestine and the variations between
b. and y., the comparison of the data may prove very informative.

        Secondly, we should continue to analyze Samuel's teachings
on Mishnah.  This will further test and help us to refine our
hypothesis.  But the different tractates which we examine will
also throw light on various additional problems.  We have already
seen this in the variations between our present sample and that in
Volume One.  Post mishnaic masters, in particular after the first
amoraic generation, and medieval authorities focused less direct
attention on M. Zera$^C$im than on other tractates, especially
Berakhot.  The latter in particular was the object of much study
due to its immediately practical implications on daily liturgy
and synagogue practices.[71]  Does this fact have an impact upon the
history of the amoraic materials?  In Volume One we suggested that
Samuel's teachings on Zera$^C$im would have less likely been revised
if they were less used.[72]  This hypothesis accords with our observation here.  We more frequently noticed that Samuel's teachings
in Berakhot were adapted and revised than we did in Zera$^C$im.
Masters found Samuel's teachings on Berakhot of continued relevance and tried to employ them to respond to their contemporary
liturgical and blessing needs.[73]  Nevertheless, even here we

discerned the traits of the original function as part of a Mishnah Commentary.

Similarly the following three sets of tractates will have special implications. First, we can examine the role of Samuel's teachings in the five and one-half tractates which had a different redactional history than the rest of b. These are Nedarim, Nazir, Me$^c$illah, Keritot, and Tamid and the pericopae introduced by the phrase *lishna aharina* in Temurah.[74] These may have been redacted earlier than the remaining tractates and received less or none of the text's "late" anonymous literary enrichment. This focus would enable us further to clarify the nature of these "five and one-half" tractates and more carefully identify the stages in the history of Samuel's teachings.

Secondly, we can analyze the nature of Samuel's teachings on the several Mishnah tractates or portions thereof which some scholars claim reached Babylonia earlier than other tractates. These include parts of Yoma, Sukkah, and Sheqalim.[75] We can test this hypothesis and, if found true, see what it implies concerning the nature of Samuel's Commentary. For example, would other masters have preceded Samuel in an initial response to Mishnah? Would his Commentary have played a less significant role?

Third, we can analyze Samuel's comments in areas in which he presumably would have had actual authority. The overall subjects of certain tractates, e.g., Gittin and those of Neziqin, would represent prime instances of such topics. Our results would directly relate to the impact of Samuel's pragmatic goals and how they affected his scrutiny in these areas.

\* \* \*

Many scholars have focused upon the editing and redaction of *Gemara* and have hoped in that way more fully to understand the nature of *Gemara* as a whole as well as its individual teachings. Our research has started at the opposite end of the spectrum and has focused upon the building blocks from which *Gemara* emerged. Research in both areas and from both perspectives must continue. As we found it necessary always to keep in mind the dynamics involved in *Gemara*'s redaction, so further work on the *Gemara*'s composition must never lose sight of the question of how the individual teachings were designed to function and to circulate. Once we are able to recognize the degree to which teachings may still reflect those early stages, we can better understand their

original import and use as well as better appreciate the ways in
which they have been subsequently shaped, interpreted, and applied.

[1] See Goodblatt, *Rabbinic Instruction*, pp. 16-43; and e.g., Heinrich Graetz, *History of the Jews*, vol. 2, English ed. (Reprint ed. Philadelphia, 1892), pp. 503-530 [in the Hebrew ed. *Divre Yime Yisrael*, with additional notes, S. P. Rabinowitz, vol. 2 (Reprint, Warsaw, 1907), pp. 340-370]; and I. H. Weiss, *Dor Dor VeDorshov*, vol. 3 (Reprint ed. New York, 1924), pp. 145-176.

[2] See Neusner, *History*, vol. 1; *Purities*, vol. 22; *Politics to Piety*; "The Formation of Rabbinic Judaism: Yavneh (Jamnia) from A.D. 70 to 100," in *ANRW*. II.19,2: 3-42; and "Studies on the Problem of Tannaim in Babylonia," *PAAJR* 30 (1962): 79-127.

[3] See Neusner, *History*, vols. 1-5, passim.

[4] See David Goodblatt, *Rabbinic Instruction*, pp. 16-43. Even Isaiah Gafni, *Babylonian Jewry and Its Institutions in the Period of the Talmud* (Jerusalem, 1975), and "Yeshiva and Metivta," in *Zion* 43 (1978): I-II, 12-37, who claims that actual permanent academic institutions did exist in Babylonia and who explicitly differs with Goodblatt, agrees that such institutions did not arise till the second amoraic generation. See n. 5. Likewise, Jacob Sussmann's analysis, in *Babylonian Sugyot*, of Babylonian *sugyot* on Zera^c^im and Tehorot indicates a difference between the first and later Babylonian amoraic generations. He found that the first-generation masters directly studied these portions of Mishnah while the later ones did so indirectly, only when they were mentioned or cited as part of another context. The mode or character of study thus differed. See also A. Weiss, *Studies* (1962), pp. 10-23.

[5] See Goodblatt, *Rabbinic Instruction*. As mentioned in n. 4, Gafni rejects Goodblatt's thesis. But Gafni fails to distinguish between academic institutions and *permanent* academic institutions. Goodblatt does not claim that a master might not be associated with a specific place but that whatever occurred at a specific "place of Torah" depended upon the individual master and ceased when that master died. Accordingly, Gafni's proofs do not respond to the real issue. See Goodblatt's response to Gafni, in *Zion* 45 (1980).

[6] Goodblatt, *Rabbinic Instruction*, esp. pp. 272-280. See also Neusner, *History*, 2: 101, 111-119, 136, where Neusner discusses the passages which indicate that some Jews functioned as judges even before Samuel and Rav. Hence, rabbis apparently took over these functions.

[7] See Neusner, *History*, 1: 163-164, 169, 174, 176-177; 2: 92-125, 284-287; 3: 134-135. See also Weinberg, pp. 90, 94-95; and Epstein, *ITM*, esp. pp. 211-234, on Rav's and Samuel's response to Mishnah; and the various studies in F. F. Bruce and E. G. Rupp, *Holy Book*.

[8] See Neusner, *History*, 1: 101-103, 161-164 (on the Grace After Meals fragment, see above, chapter two, #125, esp. nn. 457 and 465); Dalia Tawil, "The Purim Panel in Dura in the Light of Parthian and Sasanian Art, *Journal of Near Eastern Studies* 38(1979): 93-109; and the several studies in Joseph Gutmann, *The Dura-Europos Synagogue: A Re-evaluation* (Missoula, 1973), esp. Bernard Goldman, "The Dura Synagogue Costumes and Parthian Art," pp. 53-77, and cp. Joseph Gutmann, "Programmatic Painting in the Dura Synagogue," pp. 137-154.

[9] See, for example, David Hoffman, *Mar Samuel* (Leipzig, 1873), esp. pp. 37-61, and Neusner, *History*, vols. 2-3.

[10] See chapter four and chapter nine, n. 14, and cp. Weinberg, pp. 89-90, 94-95.

[11]See chapter nine, n. 14.

[12]See chapter two, #8, and the other versions, #11 and 15, analyzed there. See also #29, 30, and 143, and chapter one, n. 5. Zahavy demonstrates that intent in prayer becomes a central concern of the Ushans.

[13]See, e.g., #20, 21, 22, 23, 39-47, 57, 60, esp. 94. See also #38 and chapter three, n. 42a, and #54 and 121.

[14]See Talmon, "Manual of Benedictions;" Mary Boyce and Firoze Kotwal, "Zoroastrian bāj and drōn-II," *Bulletin of the School of Oriental and African Studies* 34 (1971): 298-313, esp. 299-305, 313; and Greenfield, p. 273.

[15]See #74, 77=80, 81, as well as #11, 14, 18-19, 52-53, 90-91, and 98. See also Neusner, *History*, 2: 117-118.

[16]See below text to n. 43, concerning *Gemara* not being a "record of debates," and cp. A. Weiss, *Literary Unit*, pp. 2-3, and *Studies* (1962), pp. 10-23.

[17]See chapter seven, and the references in nn. 29-31; Goodblatt, *Rabbinic Instruction*, p. 125; Friedman, "A Critical Study," pp. 349 and 369, n. 48; and S. M. Rubinstein, *Leheqer Siddur Hatalmud* (Kovno, 1932, reprint ed. Jerusalem, 1971), pp. 48 and 63 and his reference to Frankel; and esp. A. Weiss, *Studies* (1962), pp. 2-3, 10. Cp. the comments of Zuri, *Rav*, pp. 250-253, as to how Samuel learnt of Rav's teachings and thus of the formation of disputes.

[18]See Neusner, *History*, 1: 163-164, 176-177, and 2: 110; Epstein, *ITM*, pp. 171-177; Lieberman, *SZ*; Goldberg, "The Use of the Tosefta," pp. 147-150, esp. n. 11; David Weiss Halivni, "Talmudic Criticism: A Historical Review," paper delivered at the Association for Jewish Studies, Fifth Annual Conference. Harvard University, Cambridge, Massachusetts, 21 October 1973, and "The Reception"; and Bokser, "Talmudic Form Criticism," n. 36 and text thereto.

[19]Bokser, "Jacob N. Epstein on the Formation of the Mishnah," in Neusner, *Modern Study*, p. 53. See also, e.g., Epstein, *ITM*, pp. 175-181, 187, 214-234; and Goldberg, "On the Use of the Tosefta"; and Weiss Halivni, "The Reception."

[20]Cp. our formulation in Volume One, pp. 237-238, and below. See also Weinberg, pp. 90-94, and A. Weiss, *Studies* (1962), pp. 116, 119.

[21]See, e.g., Saul Lieberman, "Palestine in the Third and Fourth Centuries," [originally published in 1946] in *Text and Studies* (New York, 1974), pp. 112-177; Michael Avi-Yonah, *The Jews of Palestine* (Oxford, 1976); Daniel Sperber, *Roman Palestine 200-400: Money and Prices* (Ramat Gan, 1974), and *Roman Palestine: 200-400. The Land* (Ramat Gan, 1978); Lee Levine, *Caesarea*, and "The Jewish Patriarch"; and Kimelman, "R. Yohanan." David Goodblatt, in *Rabbinic Instruction*, while dealing with Babylonian academic institutions often points to the contrasting institutions in Palestine. Cp. A. Weiss, *Studies* (1962), pp. 10-23, which attempts to correlate modes of teaching with differing Palestinian and Babylonian realities. Certainly, differences may also exist within a single land. See, e.g., Weiss Halivni, *ST*, passim; our comments concerning Zuri, in n. 38, below; and above, chapter two, n. 11.

[22]Isadore Twersky, "The *Shulhan Aruk*: Enduring Code of Jewish Law," [originally published in 1967], in *The Jewish Expression*, ed. Judah Goldin (New York, 1970), pp. 322-343. See also *The Jewish Law Annual* 2 (1979), which contains several articles on the nature of codification. Cp. Weinberg, p. 90.

[23]Chapter nine, text to n. 96.

[24] See chapter nine, nn. 88 and 100 and texts thereto, to which add Jacob Neusner, *There We Sat Down* (Nashville, 1972), p. 87; Neusner, *History*, 3: 192-193; and Greenfield. Neusner's revised comparison and contrast of the rabbi and magus receives support from Greenfield.

[25] See, e.g., Neusner, *History*, 3: 158-179, esp. 172 and 218, and above, chapter nine, n. 18 and text thereto.

[26] See, e.g., Weiss Halivni, *ST*, vols. 1-2, passim; Goldberg, "R. Ze$^C$ira." The need creatively to adapt a religious tradition and legal system is present whenever they are to continue and not become petrified. See, e.g., chapter nine, n. 26; Gershom Scholem, "Revelation and Tradition as Religious Categories in Judaism," [originally published in 1962], in *The Messianic Idea in Judaism* (New York, 1971, 1972), pp. 282-303; and Ignaz Goldziher, *Muslim Studies*, ed. S. M. Stern, 2 vols. (Aldine, 1971), 2: 15-251, on the analogous phenomenon in the transmission of Islamic Hadith.

[27] See chapter nine, n. 62, and text thereto, and Smith, *Tannaitic Parallels*.

[28] Neusner, *History*, 3: xiii.

[29] See, e.g., chapter two, #101, and chapter nine, subsection 3; Bokser, "Minor For Zimmun"; and Goldberg, "R. Ze$^C$ira." Friedman, "A Critical Study," p. 350 and n. 34 likewise observes that a comment could circulate along with a text. Cp. A. Weiss, *Literary Unit*, pp. 2-3, and *Studies* (1962), p. 119.

[30] See chapter four, subsection 3.

[31] See Lieberman, *Caesarea*, pp. 20-25, esp. 22-23, and above, chapter two, #101, esp. n. 363.

[32] Volume One, p. 152, n. 467, and p. 156, nn. 475-476; and above, chapter two, #101, esp. n. 372; and "Redaction Criticism of the Talmud: The Case of Hanina Ben Dosa," paper delivered at the Third Max Richter Conversation on the History of Judaism, Brown University, Providence, R.I., 28 June 1977 (forthcoming).

[33] See, e.g., Peter Brown, *The Making of Late Antiquity* (Cambridge, 1978), and "The Rise and Function of the Holy Man in Late Antiquity," *Journal of Roman Studies* 61 (1972): 80-101; and Ramsay MacMullen, *Enemies of the Roman Order* (Oxford, 1967).

[34] See, e.g., Henry Fischel, "Story and History: Observations on Greco-Roman Rhetoric and Pharisaism," [originally published in 1972] in idem, *Essays*, pp. 443-472.

[35] See, e.g., Neusner, *Pharisees*, and *Eliezer*; Porton, *Ishmael*; Joel Gereboff, *Rabbi Tarfon* (Missoula, 1979); William S. Green, *Rabbi Joshua* (Leiden, 1979-1980), and esp. "Palestinian Holy Men: Charismatic Leadership and Rabbinic Tradition," in *ANRW*. II.19,2: 619-647; and Shammai Kanter, *Rabban Gamaliel* (Chico, 1980).

[35a] Neusner, *History*. See above, n. 24.

[36] Rousseau, pp. 19-32, 68-76, 92-95, 221-226, esp. p. 13, n. 10, and pp. 28-29, 68-76, 224.

[37] Rousseau, pp. 68-71.

[38] Cp., e.g., Dor, *The Teaching of Eretz Israel in Babylon*; Ophra Meir, "The Acting Characters in the Stories of the Talmud and the Midrash (A Sample)," (Ph.D. dissertation, Hebrew University, 1977), which compares the

stories in b. and y. Berakhot and in two Palestinian Midrashim to Genesis; and
Kimelman, "Rabbi Yohanan," Ch. 4. E, and the additional literature cited there.

Zuri for one does analyze the traditions of Rav and does compare them
with those of Samuel and other masters.  He tries to demonstrate how Rav and
Samuel had different trainings, interests, and approaches which affected the
content and form of their teachings.  See J. S. Zuri, *Toldot Darkhe HaLimmud
Bishivot Darom, Galil, Sura, VeNeharde^Ca* (Jerusalem, 1914), and esp. *Rav*, pp.
170-177, 211-233.  While Zuri frequently points to the wider implications of
the teachings and the interrelationship of diverse comments, his overly monolithic theories cause him to disregard exceptions and to level divergences.
See, e.g., Shamai Kanter, "I. H. Weiss and J. S. Zuri," in Neusner ed., *Formation*, pp. 11-25, and Neusner, *History*, 2: 183, 232-236.  Neusner evaluates
Zuri's theory as well as offers a somewhat different interpretation.  Gordis
reviews the theories of Zuri and others concerning Rav and Samuel and analyzes
numerous--but not all the--traditions attributed to these two masters to determine the degree to which they reflect two distinct approaches and methods.

[39]Abraham Goldberg, "Palestinian Law in Babylonian Tradition, as
Revealed in a Study of Pereq ^CArvei Pesahim," *Tarbiz* 33 (1962-1964): I-II,
337-348; and "R. Ze^Cira."

[40]Epstein, *IAL*, pp. 292-322.  See Bokser, "Guide," in *ANRW*, Ch. 11, pp.
187-191.

[41]See Adin Steinsaltz, "Links Between Babylonia and the Land of Israel,"
*Talpioth* 9 (1964): 294-306; Neusner, *History*, 3: 217-220; Moshe Beer, "Nehutei,"
in *EJ*, s.v. vol. 12: 942-943, and *The Babylonian Amoraim* (Ramat Gan, 1974),
pp. 158-159, 180-191; Saul Lieberman, "Eres Yisrael VeYahadut HaOlam BeTequfat
HaMishnah VeHaTalmud," *Erev Iyun LeZeker Moshe Habib* (Tel Aviv, n.d. [1976?]),
pp. 28-37; and esp. Kimelman, "Rabbi Yohanan," Ch. 4.D, who provides the best
study to date, in terms of the teachings of R. Yohanan.

[42]Cp. Shmuel Shiloh, "The Attitude of R. Yosef Migash to the Gaonim,"
(Hebrew) *Sinai* 66 (1970): 263-267, for a very suggestive study.  The author
tries to define Ibn Migash's attitude to Gaonim not by his self-proclaimed
attitude but by the way in which he treats their halakhic opinions.

[43]See Goodblatt, "Babylonian Talmud," pp. 273, 291, 293, 305, 307, 315.
Since Goodblatt systematically reviews the literature on the formation and
editing of the BT, we refer to his study and cite only specific examples of
works which exemplify our observations in the text.

[44]We borrow the phrase in quotes from Goodblatt, "Babylonian Talmud,"
p. 259.  Graetz, 2: 515, 519-520, 607-608, and I. H. Weiss, 3: 153, 167-168,
provide two examples of descriptions of Rav's and Samuel's Mishnah efforts.
Both emphasize Rav's Mishnah study more than Samuel's but their particular
descriptions of Rav's scrutiny would just as aptly fit Samuel, as we saw in
Volume One and the present Volume.  Cp. Zuri, *Rav*, e.g, pp. 226-227.  See
below, nn. 46 and 52 and text thereto.

[45]We have drawn upon many of the works of these scholars.  See our
bibliography, and Bokser, "Minor For Zimmun," n. 1, and "Talmudic Form Criticism," n. 1; Friedman, "Critical Study" and Goodblatt, "Babylonian Talmud,"
for critical reviews of these works.  In particular note A. Weiss, *Studies*
(1962), pp. 116-117, 136-152.

[46]Weiss Halivni, *ST*, vols. 1-2, and David Weiss Halivni, "Contemporary
Methods of the Study of Talmud," *JJS* 30 (1979): 192-201.  Our presentation
of the history of the formation of *Gemara* is highly schematic and does not
fully convey the subtlety and variety of the different approaches.  For example, first, Graetz, 2: 607-608, assumes R. Ashi "began the gigantic task of
collecting and arranging the explanations, deductions, and amplifications of
the Mishnah, which were included under the name 'Talmud.'"  He worked on this

for more than fifty years.  Each year with the assembled disciples and pupils in the Kalla he reviewed the tractates of Mishnah, "together with the Talmudical explanations and corollaries."  Thus teachings and explanations were remembered and transmitted.  But R. Ashi and the discussions with his students and colleagues provided the structure for the "Talmud."  Second, I. H. Weiss, 3: 153-154, concerning Rav's study of Mishnah, emphasizes that teaching was done orally and that Rav would teach DRK QSRH, that is, succinctly and briefly, so that the students could remember the teachings.  Weiss even provides a fair description of the types of amoraic interpretations of Mishnah.  But Weiss does not explain how this yielded the *Gemara* or the processes of transformation.  Cp. pp. 1-10, 208-216.  Third, Goldberg, in "Review [of Albeck, *Introduction*]," pp. 10-11, believes Albeck assumes that the variations in amoraic teachings reflect the forms of study in the different schools. Goldberg contrasts this with the literary factors involved in the *Gemara's* editing which actually is responsible for many of the Talmud's characteristics and its layout.  But while Albeck and Goldberg have significantly contributed to the understanding of the text of the *Gemara* and its contents they, in effect, focus on the later stages in its formation.  Cp. Kimelman's use of Albeck, in "Rabbi Yohanan," Ch. 4. D.  The questions remain, as we emphasize in the text: How did the initial teaching set the structure for the developing *Gemara* and how did it circulate?  See below, n. 48 and text thereto.

[47]Abraham Weiss, *Studies* (1962), pp. 221-225; and Friedman, "Critical Study," esp. p. 309.  Cp. also the references to A. Weiss, below in nn. 52-54 and text thereto.

[48]See chapter eight, subsection 6. iv, esp. text to nn. 68-74.  Cp. the remarks of M. Smith and S. Spiegel, cited in chapter nine, nn. 66 and 68 and text thereto, that the structure of the biblical text affected the midrashic teachings.  See Lieberman's analogous observations in *HJP*, p. 118.

[49]See chapter 9, nn. 45 and 51 and text thereto.  See also W. R. Watters, *Formula Criticism and the Poetry of the Old Testament* (New York, 1976), esp. pp. 12-19, 48-80, which discusses the use of formulae in oral and literarily composed poetry and the effect of transmission and editing on originally orally composed material.

[50]See chapter nine, n. 62.

[51]See above (chapter ten), nn. 36 and 37 and text thereto.  Earlier research includes Wilhelm Bousset, *Apophthegmata* (Tübingen, 1923, reprint ed. 1969), and Jean-Claude Guy, *Recherches sur la Tradition Grecque des Apophtegmata Patrum* (Brussels, 1962).

[52]Epstein, *ITM*, pp. 212-214.  See chapter nine, nn. 84-85 and the literature cited there; Hoffmann, pp. 29-34; above (chapter ten), n. 44; and Volume One, p. 2.

[53]Abraham Weiss, *Literary Unit* (1943), pp. 1-44, esp. 6-14.  See Volume One, pp. 2-3, esp. n. 6.

[53a]A. Weiss, *Studies* (1962), pp. 116-117.

[54]See above (chapter ten), n. 45, for references.  Goodblatt, in particular, systematically correlates the different theories.  See also Weiss Halivni, "The Apodictic," and "Whoever Studies."

[55]Cp. Haim Z. Dimitrovsky, *Exploring the Talmud* (New York, 1976), p. xvi, who criticizes J. N. Epstein's disproportionate, if not total, emphasis on the literary character of talmudic materials.

[56]See chapter nine, nn. 94-99 and text thereto.  Note Anthony J. Saldarini, "Review [of E. P. Sanders, *Paul and Palestinian Judaism* (Philadelphia, 1977)]," *JBL* 98 (1979): 299-303, esp. p. 300, where he formulates the

idea thus: "Torah (meaning written and oral law) was God's revelation, gift, guidance, and presence--the center of their consciousness, piety, and behavior."

[57] See chapter six, chart 12, and text thereto.

[58] See chapter nine, nn. 88, 96, 100, and chapter ten, n. 24, and the texts to each.

[59] See chapter nine, n. 37.

[60] See above (chapter ten), n. 17, and chapter four, subsection 3.A,iii.

[61] See chapter four; chapter nine, n. 10; and chapter ten, nn. 7 and 10, and text thereto.

[62] See, e.g., Urbach, "'*Mavo LaMishnah*' [of H. Albeck]," p. 439, and "Mishnah," in *EJ*, s.v., vol. 12: 104; Goldberg, *Commentary Shabbat*, pp. xiv-xviii, and 3; and Neusner, *Purities*, vol. 22.

[63] See, e.g., Neusner, *Purities*, vol. 22, and Richard Sarason, in "Mishnah and Scripture: Preliminary Observations on the Law of Tithing in Seder Zera$^c$im," paper delivered at the Fourth Max Richter Conversation on the History of Judaism, Brown University, Providence, R.I., 27 June 1978, from whom I draw the cited quotation. See also, e.g., Sarason, on M. Zera$^c$im; Goldberg, *Commentary Shabbat*, pp. xiii-xiv, on M. Shabbat; Baruch M. Bokser, *Passover Eve Celebration and Early Rabbinic Judaism* (Chico, in press) on M. Pesahim Ch. 10; and Neusner, "From Scripture to Mishnah: The Origins of Mishnah's Fifth Division," on M. Qodshim.

[64] See Albeck, 1: 7-12; Heinemann, *Prayer*; above chapter nine, n. 9 and text thereto, and our layout of the tractate in chapter four, subsections 2 and 3.B; Zahavy; and Talmon, "Emergence."

[65] See above (chapter ten), nn. 1-21 and text thereto. The one similarity between the first-second and third centuries that we mention above is the continued need to emphasize the potency of personal "intent."

[66] See Baruch M. Bokser, "Response to Catastrophe: From Continuity to Discontinuity" (forthcoming).

[67] See chapter nine, subsection 6, esp. text to nn. 87-93, in particular the reference to Neusner, *Holy Things*, 1: x-xi; and Weinberg, pp. 90-95. Cp. Quintin Johnstone and Dan Hopson, Jr., *Lawyers and Their Work* (Indianapolis, 1967), esp. pp. 77-130. See our discussion above (chapter ten), nn. 18-20 and text thereto, where we indicate in what way Mishnah represents an authoritative corpus and not just an anthology for study.

[68] For a discussion of these passages, see our respective analyses in chapter two and nn. of chapter three.

[69] As we point out in chapter two, b. and y. present and rework the toseftan *baraita* so that it applies to Grace After Meals on the New Moon. See our discussion there and the reference to Ginzberg, *Commentary*.

[70] On Tosefta, see chapter nine, subsection 6.iii,B, esp. n. 87.

[70a] While Zuri, *Rav*, and Gordis discuss the various aspects of Rav's teaching, they do not raise the possibility that that master composed a formal "Mishnah Commentary." See n. 38, above.

[71] See chapter nine, nn. 8-9 and 14, and chapter ten, n. 4 and texts thereto; Saul Lieberman, *HY*, p. 7, and esp. *TK*, 1: 33; S. D. Goitein, *Sidre*

*Ḥinukh Bime Hagge<sup>ɔ</sup>onim* (Jerusalem, 1962), p. 158; and Sussmann, *Babylonian Šugyot*, esp. pp. 242, 273-277, 287, n. 176.

[72] See Volume One, p. 4, esp. nn. 9-10.

[73] See above (chapter ten), n. 25; chapter eight; and cp. Kimelman, "Rabbi Yohanan," Ch. 4.E.

[74] See, e.g., Epstein, *IAL*, pp. 55-56, and *GBA*, p. 15, and esp. Goodblatt, "Babylonian Talmud," pp. 304-307, 318, and n. 54a, for his discussion and analysis of earlier literature, including a cogent critique of Epstein.

[75] See, e.g., Epstein, *ITM*, 21-164, 171-177, esp. 171, and *ITL*, pp. 25-27 (cp. Lieberman, *TK*, 4: 695), 36-40; Neusner, "Tannaim in Babylonia," and *History*, 1: 162-163, esp. n. 1; Goldberg, note in Neusner, "Tannaim in Babylonia," p. 127, n. 38, and "The Use of the Tosefta"; and Goodblatt, "Babylonian Talmud," pp. 285-288.

BIBLIOGRAPHY

I.  TEXTS AND COMMENTARIES

The Bibliography contains only works that have been cited in the text and footnotes and generally only the relevant volumes.  Hence it does not list other works which may have been consulted but to which there is no direct reference.  Comprehensive listings may be found in: Menahem M. Kasher and Jacob B. Mandelbaum, *Sarei Ha-Elef* (New York, 1959), and its "Supplement," published in Haim Liphshitz, ed., *Sefer Adam Noah* (Jerusalem, 1970); for items written after 1500, P. Jacob Kohn, *Thesaurus of Hebrew Halachic Literature* (London, 1952); David Goodblatt, "The Babylonian Talmud," *ANRW*, II.19, 2: 257-336; and Baruch M. Bokser, "An Annotated Bibliographical Guide to the Study of the Palestinian Talmud," *ANRW*, II.19, 2:139-256.

*i.  Classical Rabbinic Texts and MSS*

A.  Mishnah

*Shisha Sidre Mishnah*.  12 vols.  Jerusalem: El Hamekorot, 1954-1955, 1957-1958. Based on Vilna ed. with additional commentaries.

*Shisha Sidre Mishnah*.  Ed. Chanoch Albeck, 6 vols.  Jerusalem, 1954-59.

*Ginze Mishna*.  Ed. Abraham I. Katsh.  Jerusalem, 1970.

*Mishnacodex Kaufmann A 50*.  Jerusalem, 1968.

*Mishna Codex Paris: Paris 328-329*.  Jerusalem, 1973.

*Mishna Codex Parma 138*.  Jerusalem, 1970.

*The Mishnah on which the Palestinian Talmud Rests*.  Ed. W. H. Lowe.  Cambridge, 1883.  Reprint.  Jerusalem, 1967.

*Mishnah Naples*.  p.e., 1492.  Reprint.  Jerusalem, 1970.

*Mishna Sedarim Zeraim, Moed, Nashim: Unknown Edition*.  Jerusalem, 1970.

*Mishnah Zera^cim: I*.  Ed. Nisan Zachs.  Jerusalem: Makhon-HaTalmud, 1972.

B.  Tosefta

*The Tosefta*.  Ed. with a Brief Commentary by Saul Lieberman.  Vols. I-  , New York, 1955-   .

*Tosephta*.  Ed. M. S. Zuckermandel.  Reprint.  Jerusalem, 1963.

C.  Babylonian Talmud

Babylonian Talmud.  20 vols.  New York: Otzar Hasefarim, 1965.  [Reprint of Vilna: Romm, 1895, edition with additional commentaries.]

Babylonian Talmud.  *Codex Florence*.  Florence National Library II I 7-9. 3 vols.  Jerusalem, 1972.

Babylonian Talmud.  *Codex Munich 95*.  3 vols.  Jerusalem, 1971.

Babylonian Talmud.  Columbia MS X 893-T14 to Tractates Beṣah, Megillah, and Pesahim.  Microfilm provided by Columbia University Library.

493

Babylonian Talmud. *Seder Nezikin: Codex Hambourg*. Facsimile of the Original
MS and a Reprint of the Goldschmidt Edition of Berlin, 1914. Jerusalem,
1969.

Babylonian Talmud. *Tractate Abodah Zarah*. MS. Jewish Theological Seminary
of America. Ed. Shraga Abramson. New York, 1957.

Babylonian Talmud. *Tractate Hullin: Codex Hamburg 169*. Jerusalem, 1972.

Babylonian Talmud. *Tractate Ketubot*: I. Ed. Moshe Hershler. Jerusalem:
Makhon HaTalmud, 1972.

Babylonian Talmud. Venice p.e. 1520-23. Reprint. Jerusalem, 1970-72.

*Manuscripts of the Babylonian Talmud in the Collection of the Vatican Library*:
Series A. 3 vols. Jerusalem, 1972. Series B. 3 vols. Jerusalem, 1974.

"Meginzeh Yehudah. A MS Page of Gemara." Ed. I. I. Ḥasida. *Sinai* 37 (73)
(1973): 224-229.

        See also Coronel, Hershler, Malter, Naeh, Rabinovicz, and Sacks,
in II, below.

### D. Palestinian Talmud

"Geniza Fragments to Palestinian Talmud. 3, 4-6." Ed. J. N. Epstein.
*Tarbiz* 3 (1932):121-136; 237-248.

Ginzberg, Louis. *Yerushalmi Fragments from the Geniza*. New York, 1909.
Reprint. Jerusalem, 1969.

"New Fragments of y. Pes. Chs. 5-7." Ed. D. Levinger. *Alexander Marx Jubilee
Volume*. New York, 1950. Hebrew Section. Pp. 237-83.

Palestinian Talmud. *Codex Vatican 133*. Jerusalem, 1971.

*Palestinian Talmud: Leiden MS Cod. Scal 3*. Jerusalem, 1971.

*Palestinian Talmud*. Venice, p.e., 1522-23. Reprint. N.p., n.d.

*Talmud Yerushalmi*. 7 vols. New York: Talmud Yerushalmi, 1959. [Reprint of
Vilna, 1922, edition with additional commentaries.]

        See also Luncz, in II, below.

### E. Other

*Bereschit Rabba*. Ed. J. Theodor and Ch. Albeck. 2d ed. 3 vols. Jerusalem,
1965.

*Massekhet Soferim*. Ed. Michael Higger. New York, 1937. Reprint. Jerusalem,
1970.

*Mechilta D'Rabbi Ismael*. Ed. H. S. Horovitz and I. A. Rabin. 2d ed.
Jerusalem, 1955.

*Mechilta D'Rabbi Ishmael* . Venice, p.e., 1515. Reprint. Jerusalem, 1971.

*Mekhilta D'Rabbi Sim^con b. Jochai*. Ed. J. N. Epstein and E. Z. Melamed.
Jerusalem, 1955.

*Mekilta de-Rabbi Ishmael*. Ed. J. Z. Lauterbach. 3 vols. Philadelphia, 1933,
reprint 1976.

*Midrasch Pesikta Rabbati*. Ed. M. Friedmann. Vienna, 1880. Reprint.
  Tel Aviv, 1963.

*Midrash Bereshit Rabba Codex Vatican 30*. With an Introduction and Index by
  M. Sokoloff. Jerusalem, 1971.

*Midrash Bereshit Rabba*. *Codex Vatican 60*. A Page Index by A. P. Sherry.
  Jerusalem, 1972.

*Midrash Debarim Rabbah*. Ed. Saul Lieberman. 2d ed. Jerusalem, 1964.

*Midrash Rabbah*. With commentaries. Reprint of Vilna edition. Jerusalem,
  1961.

*Midrash Rabbah*. Ed. E. E. Halevi. Tel Aviv, 1956.

*Midrash Tanhuma*. Constantinople, 1520-1522. Reprint. Jerusalem, 1971;
  Mantua, 1563. Reprint. Jerusalem, 1971; with commentaries.
  Tel Aviv, n.d.

*Midrash Tanhuma*. *HaQadum Vehayashan*. Ed. Salomon Buber. Reprint.
  Jerusalem, 1964.

*Midrash Tanna'im*. Ed. David Hoffmann. Berlin, 1909. Reprint in 2 vols.
  Tel Aviv, n.d.

*Midrash Tehillim*. Ed. Salomon Buber. Vilna. 1891.

*Sifra Codex Vatican 31*. Jerusalem, 1972.

*Sifra D'Be Rav*. With commentaries of Rabad, Sens et al. Jerusalem, 1959.

*Sifra D'Be Rav*. Ed. I. H. Weiss. Vienna, 1862. Reprint. New York, 1946.

*Sifra or Torat Kohanim According to Codex Assemani LXVI*. New York, 1966.

*Sifra*. Venice, p.e., 1545. Reprint. Jerusalem, 1971.

*Sifre on Deuteronomy*. Ed. Louis Finklestein. New York, 1969.

*Sifre Numbers-Deuteronomy Codex Vatican 32*. Jerusalem, 1972.

*Sifrei*. *Numbers-Deuteronomy*. Venice, p.e., 1546. Reprint. Jerusalem, 1971.

*Siphre D'Be Rab*. *Siphre ad Numeros adjecto Siphre zutta*. Ed. H. S. Horovitz.
  2d printo. Jerusalem, 1966.

　　　　For *Yalqut HaMakhiri*, *Midrash HaGgadol*, and *Yalqut Shimoni*, see I. ii,
Machir ben Abba Mari; David Ben R. Amram of Eden Adenai; and Shimeon HaDarshon.

### ii.  *Commentaries and Rabbinic Works:*
### *Medieval and Early Modern*

Aaron b. R. Yosef Halevi of Barcelona. *Commentary on Alfasi Tractate
  Berachoth*. 1874. See R. Jonathan of Lunel.

Aaron haKohen of Lunel. *Orḥot Ḥayyim*. Part 1. Reprint. Jerusalem, 1956.

Abarbanel. *Commentary on the Former Prophets*. Jerusalem, 1955.

Abraham b. R. Azriel, R. *Sefer Arugat Habosem*. Edited by E. Urbach. 4 vols.
  Jerusalem, 1939-63.

Abraham ben David. *Temim De*ᵓ*im*. Warsaw, 1897.

Abraham b. R. Isaac of Narabone. *Sefer HaEshkol*. Edited by Shalom Albeck.
   2 vols. Jerusalem, 1934-1938; edited by Abraham Ehrenrich. Reprint.
   Tel Aviv and New York, 1962.

Abraham of Montpellier. *Commentary on Nedarim and Nazir*. Edited by M. Y.
   Blau. New York, 1962.

Abraham Baer Dobsevage. *Sefer HaMeṣaref*. Odessa, 1871. Reprint. Jerusalem,
   1970.

Abulafia, Meir Todros HaLevi ["HaRamah"]. [= Commentary] To Tractate
   Sanhedrin. Warsaw, 1895.

Adler, Nathan. *Mischnat Rabbi Nathan*. Frankfurt, 1892.

Adenai, R. David b. R. Amram of Eden. *Midrash HaGgadol on the Pentateuch*.
   To Genesis. Edited by M. Margulies. Jerusalem, 1947, 1967. To Exodus.
   Edited by M. Margulies. Jerusalem, 1947, 1967. To Leviticus. Edited by
   E. N. Rabinowitz. New York, 1932. To Numbers. Edited by Z. M.
   Rabinowitz. Jerusalem, 1967. To Deuteronomy. Edited by Solom Fisch.
   Jerusalem, 1972.

Adret, R. Solomon Ben. *Novellae*. 3 vols. 1-2. Uzapaph, 1874. 3. Reprint.
   Jerusalem, 1962.

_____. *Novellae to Tractate Rosh HaShanah*. Edited by H. Z. Dimitrovsky.
   New York, 1961.

Agamati, Zekharya b. Yehudah. *Sefer HaNner to Tractate Berakhot*. Edited by
   M. D. Ben-Shem. Jerusalem, 1958.

Alfasi, Isaac. *Halakhot Rabbati of R. Isaac Alfasi. MS Jewish Theological
   Seminary of America Rab. 692*. Reproduced in Facsimile with an Introduction
   by Shamma Friedman. 2 vols. Jerusalem, 1974.

_____. "Hilkhot HaRif." In standard editions of BT and *Hilkhot HaRif*.
   Constantinople, 1509. Reprint. Jerusalem, 1973.

Amram b. Sheshna Gaon, R. *Seder*. Edited by Daniel Goldschmidt. Jerusalem,
   1971.

Anav, Judah ben Benjamin Ha-Rofe. "Perushe Ribban." In *Ginze Rishonim*.
   *Berakhot*. Edited by Moshe Hershler.

Anav, Zedekiah b. Abraham. *Shibbolei HaLeqet*. Edited by S. Buber. Reprint.
   New York, 1959. Edited by S. K. Mirsky. Vol. 1. 1966.

Ashbili, [or al-Ishbili = of Seville] R. Yom-Tov b. Abraham. [= Ritba]
   *Novellae*. 3 vols. Reprint. New York, 1964. New critical edition:
   *Ḥidushe HaRitba al HaShas*. To Masekhet Sukah. Edited by Eliyahu
   Lichtenstein. Jerusalem, 1975. See also Ashbili, Abraham.

_____. *The New Hiddushey Ritba to Baba Metzia*. Edited by S. A. Halpern.
   London, 1962.

_____. *Commentary of the Ritva on Baba Bathra*. 2 vols. Edited by M. Y.
   Blau. New York, 1953-54.

Ashbili, [or al-Ishbili = of Seville] Abraham. *Shitah LeHar"a Alshbili*.
   Edited by Moshe Hershler. In *Ginze Rishonim*. *Berakhot*. Jerusalem:
   Makhon HaTalmud, 1967. [Author may actually be Yom-Tov Ashbili.]

Asher b. Yeḥiel. "Piskei HaRosh" [= Hilkhot HaRosh"]. In standard editions
   of BT and Ven. p.e.

_____. *Tosefe HaRosh to Tractate Qidushin*. Edited by Moshe Shmuel Shapira.
   Tel Aviv, 1969.

_____. *Tosfot HaRosh*. *Bava Meṣiᶜa*. Edited by Moshe Hershler and Joshua
   Dov Gorodeziṣqi. Jerusalem, 1959.

Ashkenazi, Bezalel. Shiṭah Mequbeṣet. 4 vols. Reprint. New York, 1966.
   On Berakhot see *Berakhah Meshuleshet*.

Ashkenazi, Mordekhai b. R. Hillel. "Mordekhai." In back of standard edition
   of BT and in Constantinople, 1509 edition of *Hilkhot HaRif*.

Ashkenazi, Samuel Jaffe b. Isaac. Yefe Mareh to Aggadot HaYerushalmi.
   Venice, 1590. To Berakhot. Reprint in *Yerushalmi Zeraᶜim*.

_____. Yefe Toᵓar. Commentary to Midrash Rabba. Venice, 1600. Digested
   in *Midrash Rabba*. Vilna, 1878. Reprint in *Midrash Rabbah with
   Commentaries*. Jerusalem, 1961.

Azikri, Eleazar. "Sefer Haredim." Commentary on PT. In Vilna editions of PT.

Azulai, Ḥayyim Joseph David. *Petaḥ Enayim*. 2 vols. Jerusalem, 1959.

Benvenisti, Joshua. *Śedeh Yehoshua*. Reprint in *Yerushalmi Zeraᶜim*.
   Jerusalem, 1972.

*Berakhah Meshuleshet ᶜal Masekhet Berakhot*. Includes: 1. Tosefot R. Yehudah
   HeHasid [actually: R. Judah ben Isaac, Sir Leon]. 2. Tosefot HaRosh.
   3. Shiṭah Mequbeṣet of Bezalel Ashkenazi [incorrect attribution; probably
   of Yom Tov--or Abraham--Ashbili]. Warsaw, 1863. Reprint. New York, 1947.

Bertinoro, Obadiah ben Abraham of. Commentary on the Mishnah. In standard
   editions of Mishnah.

Corcos, R. Joseph. "Commentary on Maimonides' *Mishneh Torah*." Selected
   sections. In back of y. Dinglas ed. with Sirillo.

David b. Levi of Narbonne. "Sefer HaMiktam" on Berakhot. In *Ginze Rishonim.
   Berakhot*. Edited by Moshe Hershler. Jerusalem, 1967.

Dinglas, Ḥaim Yosef. "Emunat Yosef." See Sirillo.

Einhorn, Zeᵓev Wolf. "Meharzu." Commentary on Midrash Rabbah. In Vilna
   edition.

Eisenstein, Israel. "Amude Yerushalayim." In standard Vilna editions of PT.

Eleazar ben Judah of Worms. *HaRokeah ha-Gadol*. Edited by Baruch Schnerson.
   Jerusalem, 1967.

Eliezer b. R. Joel HaLevi. *Sefer Rabiah*. Edited by V. Aptowitzer. Revised
   in 4 vols. by Elijah Prisman. Jerusalem, 1964-65.

Eliezer b. Nathan. *Sefer Raaban*. Reprint. Jerusalem, 1975.

Elijah b. Loeb of Fulda. "Commentary on Yerushalmi." Reprint in *Yerushalmi
   Zeraᶜim*. Jerusalem, 1971.

Elijah of London, R. *The Writings of*. Edited by M. Y. L. Sacks. Jerusalem,
   1956.

Elijah of Vilna, Gaon.  "Commentary on y. Zera^Cim."  In back of modern editions
    of y. with commentaries.

_____.  "Haggahot and Notes" to *Shulḥan Arukh*.  See Joseph Cairo.

_____.  *Sefer Ḥiddushe Ubeure HaGRA ^Cal Masekhot Berakhot*.  Compiled by
    Abraham Droshkavitz.  Jerusalem, 1973.

_____.  "Shenot Eliyahu."  In modern standard editions of Mishnah.

Emden, Jacob.  "Novellae."  In back of standard editions of BT.

Engel, Joseph.  *Giljonei Haschass*.  Vienna, 1924.  Reprint in 2 vols. n.p.,
    n.d. [= Jerusalem, 197?].

Falk, Jacob Joshua b. Zevi Hirsch.  *Penei Yehoshua*.  Vols. 1-2.  Reprint.
    Jerusalem, 1970.

Fraenkel, David of Berlin.  "Qorban HaEdah" and "Shire Qorban."  In standard
    editions of y. with commentaries.

Gershom, Rabbenu.  Commentary to Bavli.  On margin of the page in standard
    editions of BT.

*Ginze Rishonim.  Berakhot*.  Edited by Moshe Hershler.  Jerusalem, 1967.

Gutmackhar, Eliyahu.  Notes to BT.  In back of standard editions of BT.

Hachmei Anglia.  *Tosfoth Hachmei Anglia on Tractates Betzah, Megilah, Kidushin*.
    Edited by Abraham Schreiber.  Jerusalem, 1970.

Haedani, Solomon.  "Melekhet Shelomo."  In standard editions of Mishnah.

*Haggadoth HaTalmud*.  [Aucture Anonymo Hispaniens].  Constantinople, 1511.
    Reprint.  Jerusalem, 1961.

"Haggahot Maimuniyyot."  Identified author as Meir HaKohen of Rothenberg.

Hakohen, Malakhai Jacob.  *Yad Malakhai*.  Berlin, 1857.  Reprint.  Israel, 1964.

*Halakhot Gedolot ["I"]*.  Edited with comments by S. A. Traub.  Warsaw, 1874
    [= based upon Venice, 1548 ed.].

*Halakhot Gedolot ["II"]*.  *Halachoth Gedoloth nach dem Texte der Handschrift
    der Vatican*.  Edited by J. Hildesheimer.  Berlin, 1888.

*Halakhot Gedolot ["III"]*.  *Sefer Halakhot Gedolot* based upon MSS with notes
    and introduction.  Edited by Ezriel Hildesheimer.  Vol. 1.  Jerusalem,
    1971.

Ḥalavah, Moshe.  *Commentary on Tractate Pesaḥim*.  Jerusalem, 1873.  Reprint.
    Jerusalem, 1972.

Hananel, Rabbenu of Qayrawan.  [Commentary on Bavli].  On side of page in
    standard editions of BT and in *Ozar HaGaonim*.

*Haslamah LiYerushalmi*.  Vilna, 1928.  Reprint.  Jerusalem, 1971.

Heller, R. Yom Tov Lippman.  "Divre Ḥamudot."  Notes on Rosh, in standard
    editions of BT.

_____.  "Tosefot Yom Tov."  In standard editions of Mishnah.

Hillman, Shmuel Isaac.  *Sefer Or HaYashar ^Cal Yerushalmi*.  Jerusalem, 1947.

Horowitz. Eleazar Moshe HaLevi. "Haggahot VeḤiddushim." In standard editions
of BT.

Ibn Ezra. Abraham. Commentary on the Pentateuch. In Rabbinic Bibles.
Edited with commentary *Meḥoqeqe Yehudah* by Yehudah Leib Krinsky. 5 vols.
Vilna, 1928. Reprint. Tel Aviv, 1961.

Ibn Gayyat, Isaac b. Judah. *Lekutay to Tractate Berachot*. Edited by C. Z.
Taubes. Zurick, 1952.

_____. *Sha^care Śimḥah*. Edited by I. Bamberger. Pirtah, 1860. Reprint.
Israel, n.d.

Isaac, Ephraim of Premishla. "Mishnah Rishonah." In standard editions of
Mishnah.

Isaac b. Moshe. *Or Zarua*. 4 vols. Reprint in 2 vols. New York, n.d.

_____. *Responsa*. Lipsia, Poland, 1860.

Isaiah the Elder of Terrani. *Piskei Harid and Piskei Hariaz*. Vol. 1:
*Tractate Berakhot and Shabbat*. Edited by Abraham Yosef Wortheimer, et al.
Jerusalem, 1964.

_____. *Tosefot*. Reprint. New York, 1955. For selected portions, on the
margins of the page in standard editions of BT.

Isaiah the Younger of Terrani. *The Rulings of* [= Piskei Hariaz]. See Isaiah
the Elder of Terrani.

Issachar Berman b. Naphtali HaKohen. "Mattenot Kehunah." Commentary on
Midrash Rabbah. In Vilna editions.

Jacob b. Asher. *Arba^cah Turim* [= *Tur Shulḥan Arukh*]. Four parts in 7 vols.
Reprint. New York, n.d.

Jaskobovitz, Zeb. "Ambuha DeSifre," in *Sifre Zutta*. Ludz, Poland, n.d.

Jehudai Gaon. *Sefer Halachot Pesuqot*. Edited by S. Sasoon. Jerusalem, 1950.

Jonah b. Abraham Gerondi. "Perush." On Alfasi. "Hilkhot HaRif." In standard
editions of BT and in Constantinople, 1509 1st ed. Reprint. Jerusalem,
1973.

Jonathan of Lunel, R. Commentary on Alfasi Tractate Berakhot. In M. Blau,
editor, *Commentaries on Alfasi Tractate Berakhot By R. Jonathan of Lunel
and R. Aaron of Barcelona*. New York, 1957.

_____. *The Commentary of R. Jonathan HaKohen of Lunel*. *Bava Kamma*.
Edited by Shamma Friedman. New York, 1969.

Joseph Bekhor Shor. *Perush ^cal HaTorah*. 3 vols. Jerusalem, 1957-59, and
London, 1960.

Joseph Cairo. *Shulḥan Arukh*. With the complete Rabbi Aqiva Eger. 4 parts in
8 vols. Tel Aviv, 1977.

_____. "Beit Yosef." Commentary on *Tur Shulḥan Arukh*. See Jacob b. Asher.

Judah b. Benjamin R. "Perushe." In *Ginze Rishonim. Berakhot*.

Judah ben Isaac Sir Leon, R. *Tosefot*. Edited by Nisan Sacks. 2 vols.
Jerusalem, 1969-1972.

Judah b. Qalonymous. *Yehuse Tanna^Cim VeAmora^Cim*. Edited by Judah Leib Maimon.
    Jerusalem, 1963.

Lehmann, Meir HaLevi. "Meir Netiv." Notes on Sirillo. Mainz, 1875. Reprint
    in Vilna edition of PT.

Lipschutz, Israel. "Tiferet Yisrael." In standard editions of the Mishnah.

Lublin, Meir b. Gedaliah. "Me^ɔir Einei Hakhamim." In back of standard
    editions of BT.

Luria, Solomon. *Hochmat Shelomo Hashalem*. Cracow, 1541 or 1547. Reprint.
    Jerusalem, 1972.

"Ma^Carekhet HaArukh." Anthology from *Aruch* with notes of Benjamin Musafiah.
    "Musaf HaArukh." In PT. Reprint in *Talmud Yerushalmi*.

Maari, Isaac b. Abba. *Sefer HaItur*. Reprint. Jerusalem, 1970.

Machir ben Abba Mari, R. *Jalkut Machiri*: To Psalms. Edited by Salomon Buber.
    Berdyczew, 1899. Reprint. Jerusalem, 1964. To Isaiah. Edited by Judah
    Z. K. Spira. Berlin, 1894. Reprint. Jerusalem, 1964.

Maimonides. *Hilkhoth HaYerushalmi of Rabbi Moses Ben Maimon*. Edited by
    Saul Lieberman. New York, 1947.

_____. *Mishnah Im Perush Rabenu Moshe Ben Maimon*. 7 vols. Edited by
    David Qapiah. Jerusalem, 1963-69.

_____. *Mishneh Torah*. Constantinople, 1509. Reprint. Jerusalem, 1973.
    With additional commentaries. New York, 1963.

_____. *Sefer Ha-Miṣvot*. Edited by Ch. Heller. Jerusalem, 1946.

Margaliot, Moses. "Pene Moshe" and "Mareh HaPanim." In standard editions of
    y. with commentaries.

Marim, Meir. *Sefer Nir*. *Zera^Cim*. Reprint in *Yerushalmi Zera^Cim*. 2 vols.
    Jerusalem, 1971. *Mo^Ced*. Vilna, 1890.

Masnuth, Samuel ben Nissim. *Majan-Gannim*. Commentary to Job. Edited by
    Salomon Buber. Berlin, 1889.

Meir of Narbonne. *Sefer Ham'oroth* and Rabenu Meshulam of Beziers. *Sefer
    Hahashlamah on Tractates B'rachoth and P'sachim*. Edited by M. Y. Blau.
    New York, 1964.

Meiri, R. Menahem. *Beth Habehirah*. *Berakhot*. Edited by Shmuel Deikman.
    2d ed. Jerusalem, 1965. *Pesahim*. Edited by Yosef Klein. 2d ed.
    Jerusalem, 1967. *Sukkah*. Edited by Abraham Liss. Jerusalem, 1966.

Meshulam of Beziers. *Sefer Hahashlamah* on Ber. in *Ginze Rishonim*. *Berakhot*.
    [Also edited by Blau. See Meir of Narbonne.]

*Methiboth*. Edited by B. M. Lewin. Jerusalem, 1933. Reprint. 1973.

Meyuhas b. Elijah, R. *Commentary on the Pentateuch*. *Genesis*. London, 1909.
    Reprint. Jerusalem, 1968.

*Midrash Samuel*. Edited by Salomon Buber. Vilna, 1925.

Moses of Quizi. *Sefer Miṣvot Gadol*. 2 vols. 1547. Reprint. Jerusalem,
    1961.

Naḥmanides. *Commentary on the Torah*. 2 vols. Edited by Ḥaim Dov Chavel.
    Jerusalem, 1962-63.

_____. *Complete Novellae*. Vols. 1-  . Edited by Moshe Hershler.
    Jerusalem, 1970-   .

_____. "Milḥamot HaShem." On Alfasi, *Hilkhot*. In standard editions of BT.

_____. *Novellae*. 3 vols. Jerusalem, 1928-29.

_____. *The Novellae Ḥullin*. Edited by Solomon Reichman. New York, 1955.

Nissim, b. Jacob b. Nissim, Gaon. *Libelli Quinque*. Edited by Shraga Abramson.
    Jerusalem, 1965.

Nissim b. Reuben Gerondi. Commentary on Alfasi. In standard editions of BT.

*Ozar HaGaonim*. Edited by B. M. Levin. 13 vols. Haifa and Jerusalem, 1928-43.
    To Tractate Sanhedrin. Edited by Ḥaim Ṣevi Tuyabas. Jerusalem, 1966.

Pardo, David. *Ḥasde David* on Tosefta. Vol. 1. Livorne, 1776. Reprint.
    Jerusalem, 1970.

Peres, Rabbenu. *Tosefot to Tractate Bava Meṣi^c a*. Edited by Ḥaim Hershler.
    Jerusalem, 1970.

_____. *Tosefot to Tractate Pesaḥim*. Edited by Shraga Vilman. New York,
    1970.

Qinon, Shimshon. *Sefer Keritut*. Edited by S. B. D. Sofer. Jerusalem, 1965.

Rabad of Posquires. *Novellae to Tractate Bava Qamma*. Edited by Shmuel Atlas.
    2d ed. New York, 1963.

Rabinowitz-Teomim, Elijah David. "Tov Yerushalayim." Commentary to PT. In
    Vilna edition.

Saadja Gaon, R. *Siddur*. Edited by Israel Davidson, Simḥa Assaf, and B. I.
    Joel. Jerusalem, 1941.

Sar Shalom Gaon, Rav. *Teshuvot*. Edited by R. J. Weinberg. Jerusalem, 1975.

Schiff, Meir ben Jacob HaKohen. "Ḥiddushe." In standard editions of BT.

*Sefer HaḤinukh*. Edited by H. D. Chavel. Jerusalem, 1956.

Sens, Samson b. Abraham. Commentary on Mishnah Zera^c im. In standard editions
    of BT and Ven., p. e.

Shapiro, Yehushua Isaac of Slonim. *Noam Yerushalmi*. 2 vols. Vilna, 1863-69.
    Reprint. Jerusalem, 1968.

*Sheiltot of R. Ahai Gaon*. Edited by Naphtali Berlin. 3 vols. Reprint.
    Jerusalem, 1961.

*Sheiltot of R. Ahai Gaon*. Edited by Shmuel Mirski. 5 vols. Jerusalem,
    1960-66, 1977.

*Sheiltot of R. Ahai Gaon*. Ven., p.e., 1546. Reprint. Jerusalem, 1971.

Shimeon HaDarshon. *Yalqut Shimoni*. Reprint in 2 vols. New York. 1944.
    1st. ed. Salonica, 1501, 1506-07. Reprint. Jerusalem, 1968, 1973. Based
    Upon Oxford MS, Cross-references, and Notes [= New critical ed.]. Edited
    by Aaron Hyman, Isaac Lerrer, and Isaac Shiloni. Vols. 1-  . Jerusalem,
    1973-   .

"Shiṭah Mequbeṣet."  See *Berakhah Meshuleshet*.

Shulsinger, Eliahu.  *Yad Eliahu*.  Vol. 1.  Jerusalem, 1971.

Simeon bar Ṣemaḥ.  *Perush HaRashbaṣ ᶜal Berakhot*.  Edited by David Ṣevi Hillman.
   Benei Brak, 1971.

Siponto, R. Isaac b. Malkiṣedeq.  *Perush HaRYBM"Ṣ* Commentary on Mishnah
   Zeraᶜim.  On side of page of M. Zeraᶜim.  In standard editions of BT.
   And in *Perush HaRYBM"Ṣ*.  Based upon London and Oxford MSS with notes,
   cross-references, and explanations.  Edited by Nissan Sacks.  Jerusalem,
   1975.

Sirillo, Solomon.  "Commentary" to Yerushalmi.  To Tractate Berakhot.  Edited
   with commentary "Meir Netiv" by Meir HaLevi Lehmann.  Mainz, 1875.  Reprint
   with text to Tractate Peᵓah in Vilna edition of PT.

_____.  To Tractates of Zeraᶜim and Sheqalim.  Edited with commentary
   "Emunat Yosef" by Ḥayyim Yosef Dinglas.  9 vols.  Jerusalem, 1934-1967.

_____.  Commentary to Yerushalmi.  British Museum MSS 403, 404, and 405 =
   Or. 2822, 2823, 2824.  Microfilm provided by British Museum.

_____.  Commentary to Yerushalmi.  Paris, Bibliothèque Nationale, Supplement
   Hebre MS 1389.  Microfilm provided ny Bibliothèque Nationale.

Sirkes, Joel.  "Bayit Ḥadash," commentary to Jacob b. Asher, *Arbaᵓah Turim*.

_____.  "Haggahot" to BT.  In standard editions of BT.

Solomon b. Isaac (Rashi).  Commentary on the Pentateuch.  In Rabbinic Bibles.
   Critical edition by Abraham Berliner.  *Raschi uber den Pentateuch*.
   Frankfurt, 1905.  Reprint.  Jerusalem, 1962.

_____.  Commentary to BT.  In standard editions of BT and Venice, first
   edition.

_____.  *Responsa Rashi*.  Edited by Israel Elfenbein.  New York, 1943.

Solomon b. Isaac (Rashi).  Pseudo-.  Commentary on Midrash Rabbah, in Vilna
   editions.

Strashun, Samuel b. Joseph.  "Annotations."  In standard editions of BT.

Tewel, Hirsch.  *Ṣion LaNefesh To Berakhot*.  New York, 1957.

Tosᵓafot.  In standard editions of BT and in Venice p.e.

Tosefot Anshe Shem.  In standard editions of Mishnah.

Tosefot Yeshenim.  In standard editions of BT.

Willowski, Jacob David Ben Zeᵓev of Slotz.  "Perush HaRidbaz" on PT.  In Vilna
   editions of PT.

Yellin, Aryeh Loeb.  "Yefeh Enayim."  In standard editions of BT.

Yellis, Jacob Tzvi.  Author of *Melo HaRoᶜim*.  "Novellae and Notes."  In back
   of reprint of Vilna BT.

Zundel, Hanoch.  "Eṣ Yosef."  Commentary in *En Yaaqov*.  Vilna, 1923.  Reprint.
   New York, 1955.

*iii. Other Ancient Authors and Works*

Cato, Marcus. *Cato the Censor on Farming*. Translated by Ernest Brehaut.
New York, 1933.

_____. *On Agriculture*. *Loeb Classical Library*. Translated by William D.
Hooper. Cambridge, 1934.

Charles, R. H., ed. *The Apocrypha and Pseudepigrapha of the Old Testament in
English*. Vol. 2: *Pseudepigrapha*. Oxford, 1913, 1969.

Columella, Lucius Junius Moderatus. *On Agriculture*. *Loeb Classical Library*.
Translated by E. F. Forster, Edward H. Heffner et al. 3 vols. Cambridge,
1941-55.

*Das Fragmententhargum: Thargum Jeruschalmi zum Pentateuch*. Edited by Moses
Ginzburger. Berlin, 1899. Reprint. Jerusalem, 1969.

*Josephus*. 9 vols. *Loeb Classical Library*. Edited by H. St. J. Thackerary,
Ralph Marcus, and H. Feldman. Cambridge, 1926-65.

*Philo*. 10 vols. and 2 supplementary vols. *Loeb Classical Library*. Edited
by F. H. Colson, G. H. Whitaker, and Ralph Marcus. Cambridge, 1929-62.

Pliny. *Natural History*. *Loeb Classical Library*. Translated by H. Rackham
et al. 10 vols. Cambridge, 1938-62.

Pseudo-Jonathan. *Targum Jonathan Ben Uziel* on the Pentateuch. Edited by
David Rieder. Jerusalem, 1974.

*Targum Des Chroniques*. Edited with commentary by R. Le Déaut and J. Robert.
2 vols. *Analecta Biblica*, 51. Rome, 1971.

*Targum Neofiti = The Palestinian Targum to the Pentateuch*. *Codex Vatican
(Neofiti)*. Makor ed. 2 vols. Jerusalem, 1970.

Varro, M. P. *On Agriculture*. *Loeb Classical Library*. Translated by William
D. Hooper. Cambridge, 1934.

For Dead Sea Scrolls, see Rabin and Yadin, below, in II.


II.  MODERN WORKS

Abramson, Shraga. *Inyanut BaSifrut HaGaonim*. Jerusalem, 1974.

Albeck, Chanoch. *Introduction to the Talmud, Babli and Yerushalmi*. Jerusalem,
1969.

_____. *Mavo LaMishnah*. Jerusalem, 1959, 1967.

_____. *Shisha Sidre Mishnah*. 6 vols. Jerusalem, 1954-59.

_____. "Studies in the (Babylonian) Talmud." *Tarbiz* 3 (1932):1-14.

_____. *Studies in the Baraita and Tosefta*. Jerusalem, 1944.

_____. "Variants in the Mishnah of Amoraim." In *Abhandlungen zur
Erinnerung an Hirsch Perez Chajes*. Hebrew Section, pp. 1-28. Vienna,
1933.

Alon, Gedalyahu. *History of the Jews in the Land of Israel in the Period of
the Mishnah and the Talmud*. 2 vols. Vol. 1, 4th printing. Tel Aviv,
1967; Vol. 2, 2nd ed. Tel Aviv, 1961.

_____. *Studies in Jewish History*. Vol. 1, 2nd printing, Tel Aviv, 1967.

Assaf, Simḥa. *Gaonica*. Jerusalem, 1933.

_____. *Tequfat HaGeonim Vesifrutha*. Jerusalem, 1955.

Atlas, Samuel. "On the History of the Sugya." *HUCA* 24 (1952-53):1-22, Hebrew
    section.

Attridge, Harold W. *The Interpretation of Biblical History in the Antiquitates
    Judaicae of Flavius Josephus*. Missoula, 1976.

Avi-Yonah, Michael. *The Jews of Palestine*. Oxford, 1976.

_____. *Trade, Industry, and Crafts in Ancient Palestine*. Library of
    Palestinology of the Palestine Exploration Society 9/10. Edited by
    S. Yeivin. Jerusalem, 1937.

Bacher, Wilhelm. *Agadot Amorei Eres Yisrael*. Hebrew edition 3 vols. in 6
    parts. Tel Aviv, 1925-36.

_____. *Die Agada der babylonischen Amoraer*. Frankfurt, 1913. Reprint.
    Hildesheim, 1967.

_____. *Die Exegetische Terminologie der Judischen Tradionasliterature*.
    2 vols. in 1. Leipzig, 1899 and 1905. Reprint. Darmstadt, 1965.

_____. *Erchē Midrash*. 2 vols. Tel Aviv, 1923. Reprint. Jerusalem, 1970.

_____. *Tradition und Tradenten in den Schulen Palästinas und Babyloniens*.
    Leipzig, 1914. Reprint. Berlin, 1966.

Bailey, H. W. *Zoroastrian Problems in the Ninth Century Books*. Oxford, 1943.

Baron, Salo. *A Social and Religious History of the Jews*. Vol. 6. New York,
    1958.

Barth, Lewis. *An Analysis of Vatican 30*. Cincinnati, 1973.

Beer Moshe. *The Babylonian Amoraim*. Ramat Gan, 1974.

Bendavid, Abba. *Biblical Hebrew and Mishnaic Hebrew Compared*. 1- . Tel Aviv,
    1967- .

Beuchler, Adolphe. "La Ketouba chez les Juifs des Gueonim et relations des
    communautes africaines avec la Babylonie et la Palestine." *REJ* 50 (1905):
    145-181.

Blidstein, Gerald. "Prostration and Mosaics in Talmudic Law." *Bulletin of the
    Institute of Jewish Studies* 2 (1971):19-39.

Bickerman, E. J. "Notes on the Greek Book of Esther." *PAAJR* 20 (1951):
    101-133.

_____. "The Septuagint as a Translation." *PAAJR* 28 (1959):1-39.

Bleinkinsoff, Joseph. "Prophecy and Priesthood in Josephus." *JJS* 25 (1974):
    239-262.

Bloch, Renee. "Midrash." In *Approaches to Ancient Judaism: Theory and
    Practice* [= *Brown Judaic Studies*. 1]. Missoula, 1978.

Bokser, Baruch M. "An Annotated Bibliographical Guide to the Study of the
    Palestinian Talmud." *ANRW*. II. 19, 2:139-256. Berlin, 1979.

_____. "Minor For *Zimmun* (Y. Ber. 7:2, 11c) and Recensions of Yerushalmi."
*AJS Review* 4 (1979):1-25.

_____. "Redaction Criticism of the Talmud: The Case of Hanina Ben Dosa."
Forthcoming.

_____. *Samuel's Commentary on the Mishnah. Its Nature, Forms, and Content.*
Part One. Leiden, 1975.

_____. "Talmudic Form Criticism." *JJS* 31 (1980):46-60.

_____. "Two Traditions of Samuel: Evaluating Alternative Versions."
*Christianity, Judaism, and Other Greco-Roman Cults. Studies for Morton
Smith at Sixty.* Edited by J. Neusner. Vol. 4, pp. 46-55. Leiden, 1975.

_____. *Passover Eve Celebration and Early Rabbinic Judaism.* Chico.
In press.

_____. *Philo's Description of Jewish Practices.* Center for Hermeneutical
Studies in the Hellenistic and Modern Culture. *Protocol of the Thirtieth
Colloquy.* Edited by Wilhelm Wuellner. Berkeley, 1977.

_____. "Proper Intent in Early Rabbinic Judaism. A Response to H. D.
Betz." In H. D. Betz, *Paul's Concept of Freedom in the Context of
Hellenistic Discussions About the Possibilities of Human Freedom.* Center
for Hermeneutical Studies in the Hellenistic and Modern Culture. *Protocol
of the Twenty-Sixth Colloquy:* January 9, 1977. Edited by Wilhelm Wuellner,
pp. 35-37. Berkeley, 1977.

_____. "Response to Catastrophe: From Continuity to Discontinuity."
Forthcoming.

Bokser, Ben Zion. *Pharisaic Judaism in Transition.* New York, 1935.

Bornstein, H. "Sidre Zemanim VeHitpathutam BiYisrael." *Hatkufah* 6 (1920):
247-313.

Bousset, Wilhelm. *Apophthegmata.* Tubingen, 1923. Reprint, 1969.

Boyce, Mary. *A History of Zoroastrianism.* Leiden, 1975.

_____. "Middle Persian Literature." In *Handbuch der Orientalistik. I.4
Iranisti 2. Literatur*, pp. 33-38. Leiden, 1968.

Boyce, Mary and Firoze Kotwal. "Zoroastrian *bāj* and drōn-II." *Bulletin of the
School of Oriental And African Studies* 34 (1971):298-313.

Brand, Yehoshua. *Ceramics in Talmudic Literature.* Jerusalem, 1953.

Brown, Francis, Driver, S. R. and Briggs, Charles A. *A Hebrew English Lexicon
of the OT Based Upon the Lexicon of William Gesenius.* Oxford, 1907, 1966.

Brown, Peter. *The Making of Late Antiquity.* Cambridge, 1978.

_____. "The Rise and Function of the Holy Man in Late Antiquity." *Journal
of Roman Studies* 61 (1972):80-101.

Bruce, F. F. *Biblical Exegesis in the Qumran Texts.* London, 1959, 1960.

Bultmann, Rudolf. *History of the Synoptic Tradition.* Revised ed. New York,
1963, 1976.

*Chicago Assyrian Dictionary.* 1- . Chicago, 1956-       .

Childs, Brevard S.  "Interpreting in Faith: The Theological Responsibility of
    an Old Testament Commentary."  *Interpretation* 18 (1964):43-49.

_____.  *The Book of Exodus* [= *The Old Testament Library*].  Philadelphia,
    1974.

Cohen, Boaz.  *Mishnah and Tosefta: A Comparative Study.*  New York, 1935.

Coronel, Nathan.  *Beth Nathan.  Lectiones Varias Tractatus Berachot.*  Vienna,
    1854.  Reprint.  Jerusalem, 1968.

Daube, David.  "Rabbinic Methods of Interpretation and Hellenistic Rhetoric."
    *HUCA* 22 (1949):239-264.

_____.  *Studies in Biblical Law.*  Cambridge, 1947.  Reprint.  New York,
    1969.

Driver, G. R.  "Glosses in the Hebrew Text of the Old Testament."  In *L'Ancien
    Testament et L'Orient* [= *Journees Bibliques de Louvain* 6], pp. 123-162.
    Louvain, 1957.

_____.  *Semitic Writing.*  Newly revised edition.  London, 1976.

DeVries, Benjamin.  *Studies in the Development of the Talmudic Halakhah.*  Tel
    Aviv, 1962.

_____.  *Studies in Talmudic Literature.*  Jerusalem, 1968.

Dimitrovsky, Haim Z.  *Exploring the Talmud.*  New York, 1976.

Dor, Zwi Moshe.  *The Teachings of Eretz Israel in Babylon.*  Tel Aviv, 1971.

Drower, E. S. and Macuch, R.  *A Mandaic Dictionary.*  Oxford, 1963.

Eissfeldt, Otto.  *The Old Testament.*  New York, 1965.

Elbogen, Ismar.  "Eingang und Ausgang des Sabbats."  *Festschrift zu Israel
    Levy's Siebzigsten Geburstag.*  Edited by M. Brann and J. Elbogen, pp.
    173-187.  Breslau, 1911.

_____.  *HaTefillah BeYisrael.*  A Hebrew Revised and Expanded Edition by
    Yehoshua Amir, J. Heinemann, H. Schirmann, et al.  Tel Aviv, 1972.

*Encyclopaedia Judaica* (1972).  2:454-455, s.v. "Ahavah Rabbah," by R. Posner;
    3:259-287, s.v. "Aramaic," by E. Y. Kutscher; 4:241-242, s.v. "Barley,"
    by J. Feliks; 4:484-488, s.v. "Benedictions," by Editor; 4:890-899, s.v.
    "Bible.  'Exegesis and Study: Medieval.  Allegorical,'" by Avraham
    Grossman and Alexander Altman; 6:1332-1333, s.v. "Five Species," by
    J. Feliks; 7:832, s.v. "Gourds," by J. Feliks; 7:838-841, s.v. "Grace After
    Meals," by Editor; 7:1489-1492, s.v. "Haver, Haverim," by [= from]
    *Encyclopaedia Hebraica*; 7:1492-1493, s.v. "Haver Ir or Hever Ir," by H.
    Freedman; 11:1507-1514, s.v. "Midrash," by M. D. Herr; 11:1521-1523, s.v.
    "Midreshei Halakhah," by M. D. Herr; 12:89-93, s.v. "Mishmarot and
    Ma$^c$amadot," by J. Licht and D. Sperber; 12:93-109, s.v. "Mishnah," by
    E. E. Urbach; 12:942-943, "Nehutei," by Moshe Beer; 13:1520-1523, s.v.
    "Rain," by J. Katsnelson; 14:155-156, "Rice," by J. Feliks; 14:1370-1374,
    s.v. "Shema$^c$," by Louis Jacobs; 15:79-81, s.v. "Soferim," by Y. D. Gilat;
    15:164-165, s.v. "Sorghum," by J. Feliks; 15:1025-1028, s.v. "Terumot and
    Ma$^c$aserot," by A. Oppenheimer; 15:1156-1172, s.v. "Tithe," by Moshe
    Weinfeld; 16:82-83, s.v. "Vegetables," by J. Feliks; 16:1590-1607, s.v.
    "Hebrew Language.  'Mishnaic Hebrew,'" by E. Y. Kutscher.

*Encyclopaedia Migrait* [= *Encyclopaedia Biblica*].  2:354-356, s.v. "BRKH," by
    M. Cassuto; 2:913, s.v. "ZYT," by J. Feliks; 3:103, s.v. "KYM⊃ WKSYL,"

by Editor; Supplement Volume (forthcoming), s.v. "Biblical Exegesis.
'Rabbinic,'" by Moshe Greenberg.

Epstein, J. N. *Der Gaonaeische Kommentar zur Mischnaordung Teharoth*. Berlin,
1924.

_____. *Grammar Babylonian Aramaic*. Jerusalem, 1960.

_____. *Introduction to Amoraitic Literature*. Jerusalem: 1962.

_____. *Introduction to Tannaitic Literature*. Jerusalem, 1957.

_____. *Introduction to the Text of the Mishnah*. 2nd ed. 2 vols.
Jerusalem, 1964.

_____. "LeLeqsiqon HaTalmudi." *Tarbiz* 1c (1930):131-136.

_____. "Mediqduqe Yerushalmi: I." *Tarbiz* 6 (1934):38-55.

_____. "The One Who Taught This Did Not Teach This." *Tarbiz* 7 (1936):
143-158.

_____. "Post-Talmudic Aramaic Lexicography II." *JQR* 12 (1921-22):299-390.

_____. "Sheiltot Fragments B." *Tarbiz* 7 (1938):1-30.

_____. "Some Variae Lectiones in Jerushalmi." *Tarbiz* 5 (1934):257-272.

_____. "ZYQYN und RWHWT." *MGWJ* 63 (1920):15-19.

Feldman, W. M. *Rabbinical Mathematics and Astronomy*. 2nd ed. New York, 1965.

Feldman, Uriah. *Samhe HaMishna*. Tel Aviv, n.d.

Feliks, Yehuda. *Agriculture in Palestine in the Period of the Mishna and
Talmud*. Jerusalem, 1963.

_____. "Go and Seed in the Seventh-Year Because of Arnona." *Sinai* 37
(1973):235-49.

_____. *HaHai BeMishnah*. Jerusalem, 1972.

_____. *Mixed Sowing, Breeding and Grafting*. Tel Aviv, 1967.

_____. "Pereq Zera$^C$im." In Mordechai Margalioth, *Hilkhot Eres Yisrael Min
HaGenizah*. Jerusalem, 1973.

_____. *Plant World of the Bible*. Tel Aviv, 1957.

_____. "The Prohibition of Plowing in the Summer Preceding the Seventh
Year." *BIA* 9 (1972) [= Memorial to H. M. Shapiro. Edited by H. Z.
Hirschberg. Ramat Gan, 1972]:149-220 and xvii-xxiii.

_____. "Rice in Rabbinic Literature." *BIA* 1 [= Pinkhos Churgin Memorial
Volume] (1963):177-89.

Fensham, F. C. "Aspects of Family Law in the Covenant Code in Light of Ancient
Near Eastern Parallels." *Dine Israel* 1 (1969):v-xix.

Finkelstein, Louis. "The Development of the Amidah." *JQR* 16 (1925-26).
Reprinted in Petuchowski, *Contributions to the Scientific Study of the
Jewish Liturgy*.

_____. *New Light from the Prophets*. New York, 1969.

_____. "The Prayer of David According to the Chronicler." *EI* 14 (1978): 126*-127*, 110-116.

Fischel, Henry A. *Essays in Greco-Roman and Related Talmudic Literature.* New York, 1977.

Fitzmyer, Joseph A. *The Dead Sea Scrolls: Major Publications and Tools for Study.* Missoula, 1975.

_____. "The Use of Explicit Old Testament Quotations in Qumran Literature and the New Testament." In *Essays on the Semitic Background of the New Testament.* Missoula, 1974.

Fleischer, Ezra. "Havdalah Shiv^c atot According to Palestinian Ritual." *Tarbiz* 36 (1967):342-365.

Florsheim, J. "On the History of Rav Hisda's Life." *Sinai* 71 (1972):121-31.

_____. "Rav Hisda as Exegetor of Tannaitic Sources." *Tarbiz* 40 (1971): 24-48.

Forbes, R. J. *Studies in Ancient Technology.* Vols. 1-3. Leiden, 1964-65.

Frankel, Zechariah. *Introduction to the Palestinian Talmud.* Breslau, 1870. Reprint. Jerusalem, 1971.

_____. *Talmud Yerushalmi, Seder Zera^c im. I, Berakhot, Pe^ɔah.* Reprint. Jerusalem, 1971.

Friedmann, M. *Tractate Makkoth.* Vienna, 1888. Reprint. Jerusalem, 1970.

Friedman, Shamma. "A Critical Study of Yevamot X with a Methodological Introduction." In *Mehqarim umeqorot.* Texts and Studies. *Analecta Judaica* of the Jewish Theological Seminary of America. Volume 1. Edited by H. Z. Dimitrovsky, pp. 275-441. New York, 1977.

Frye, R. N. *The Heritage of Persia.* New York, 1963, 1966.

Gafni, Isaiah. *Babylonian Jewry and Its Institutions in the Period of the Talmud.* Jerusalem, 1975.

_____. "Yeshiva and Metivta." *Zion* 43 (1978):I-II, 12-37.

Gereboff, Joel. *Rabbi Tarfon: The Tradition, the Man, and Early Rabbinic Judaism.* Missoula, 1979.

Gevirtz, Stanley. "A New Look At an Old Crux: Amos 5:26." *JBL* 87 (1968): 267-76.

Gilat, Isaac. "As to the Applicability of the Laws Plowing and Seeding on the Seventh Year." *Sinai* 70 (1970):200-210.

_____. "From Biblical Severity to Rabbinic Injunction." In *Benjamin DeVries Memorial Volume.* Edited by E. Z. Melamed, pp. 84-93. Jerusalem, 1968.

_____. *The Teachings of R. Eliezer Ben Hyrcanos.* Tel Aviv, 1968.

Ginzberg, Louis. *A Commentary on the Palestinian Talmud.* 4 vols. New York, 1941-61.

_____. *Genizah Studies.* 3 vols. New York, 1928. Reprint. New York, 1969.

_____. *Legends of the Jews.* 7 vols. Philadelphia, 1909-1938.

_____. *An Unknown Jewish Sect.* New York, 1976.

*Ginze Kedem* 5 (1934). Edited by B. M. Lewin.

Glatzer, Nahum N. "A Study of the Talmudic-Midrashic Interpretation of
Prophecy." *Review of Religion*, 1946. Reprinted in *Essays in Jewish
Thought*, pp. 16-35. University, Alabama, 1978.

_____. "The Attitude Towards Rome in Third-Century Judaism." In Alois
Dempf, et al., eds., *Politische Ordung und Menschliche Existenz*, pp.
243-257. Munich, 1962.

Goitein, S. D. *Sidre Ḥinukh Bime Hagge'onim.* Jerusalem, 1962.

Goldberg, Abraham. *Commentary to the Mishna. Shabbat.* Jerusalem, 1976.

_____. *Mavo LeMishnah UleTosefta.* Edited by Michael Asulin. Jerusalem,
1973.

_____. "On the Development of the Sugya in the Babylonian Talmud." In
*(C)hanoch Albeck Jubilee Volume*, pp. 101-113. Jerusalem, 1963.

_____. "Palestinian Law in Babylonian Tradition, as Revealed in a Study
of *Pereq ᶜArvei Pesaḥim.*" *Tarbiz* 33 (1963-64):I-II, 337-348.

_____. "Tosefta to Tractate Tamid." In *Benjamin DeVries Memorial Volume*,
pp. 18-42. Jerusalem, 1968.

_____. "R. Zeᶜira and the Babylonian Custom in Palestine." *Tarbiz* 36
(1967):319-41.

_____. "Review of Chanoch Albeck, *Introduction to the Talmud, Babli
and Yerushalmi.*" *KS* 47 (1972):9-19.

_____. "The Sources and Development of the Sugya in the Babylonian Talmud."
*Tarbiz* 32 (1962-63):143-52.

_____. "The Use of the Tosefta and the Baraita of the School of Samuel by
the Babylonian Amora Rava for the Interpretation of Mishna." *Tarbiz* 40
(1971):44-57.

Goldin, Judah. "On Change and Adaptation in Judaism." *History of Religions*
4 (1965):269-294.

Goldman, Felix. "Der Öblau in Palästina in der tannaitischen Zeit." *MGWJ* 50
(1906):563-580, 707-728; 51 (1907):17-40, 129-141.

Goldschmidt, Daniel. "Qiddush VeHavdalah." *Maḥanayim* 85-86 (1964):48-53.

Goldziher, Ignaz. *Muslim Studies.* Edited by S. M. Stern. 2 vols. Aldine,
1971.

Goodblatt, David. "Abraham Weiss: The Search for Literary Forms." In *The
Formation of the Babylonian Talmud*. Edited by Jacob Neusner, pp. 95-103.
Leiden, 1970.

_____. "The Babylonian Talmud." *ANRW.* II.19, 2:257-333. Berlin, 1979.

_____. *Rabbinic Instruction in Sasanian Babylonia.* Leiden, 1975.

Gordis, David. "On Rav's and Samuel's Exegesis of Mishnah and Baraita." Ph.D. dissertation, Jewish Theological Seminary of America, 1980.

Goren, Shelomoh. *HaYerushalmi HaMeforash*. Jerusalem, 1961.

Graetz, Heinrich. *History of the Jews*. Vol. 2. English ed. Reprint. Philadelphia, 1893. Hebrew ed. [= *Divre Yime Yisrael*] Edited and translated by S. P. Rabinowitz. Warsaw, 1907.

Green, William S. "Palestinian Holy Men: Charismatic Leadership and Rabbinic Tradition." *ANRW*. II.19, 2:619-647. Berlin, 1979.

_____. "Reading, Writing, and Rabbinism: Towards a Description of the Rabbinic Intellect." Lecture delivered at the American Academy of Religion Annual Meeting. New York, November 18, 1979.

_____. *Rabbi Joshua*. Leiden, 1980.

_____. "What's in a Name?--The Problematic of Rabbinic 'Biography.'" *Approaches to Ancient Judaism: Theory and Practice*. Edited by William S. Green, pp. 77-96. Missoula, 1978.

Greenberg, Moshe. "Biblical Exegesis: Rabbinic." *Encyclopedia Miqrait*. *Supplement Volume*. Forthcoming.

_____. "On the Refinement of the Conception of Prayer in Hebrew Scriptures." *AJS Review* 1 (1976):57-92.

Greenfield, Jonas. "Ratin Magusha." In *Exploring the Talmud. 1: Education*. Edited by Haim Z. Dimitrovsky, pp. 270-276. New York, 1976.

Gruber, Mayer Irwin. *Aspects of Nonverbal Communication in the Ancient Near East*. Ph.D. dissertation. Columbia, 1977. Published on demand Ann Arbor: University Microfilms, 1977.

Gulak, Asher. *History of Jewish Law*. Vol. 1: *Law of Obligation and Its Guaranties*. Jerusalem, 1939.

Gutmann, Joseph. *The Dura-Europos Synagogue: A Re-evaluation*. Missoula, 1973.

Guy, Jean-Claude. *Recherches Sur La Tradition Grecque des Apophtegmata Patrum*. Brussels, 1962.

Habermann, A. M. *Edah We-$^c$eduth*. Jerusalem, 1952.

_____. *Tefillot Me$^c$en Shemoneh Esreh*. Berlin, 1943.

Halevi, E. E. *Agadot HaAmora'im*. Tel Aviv, 1977.

Hadas, Moses. *Hellenistic Culture*. New York, 1959, 1972.

Halevy, Isaac. *Dorot HaRishonim* IIa. = Vol. 5. Frankfurt A. M. Reprint. Jerusalem, 1967.

Hatch, E. and Redpath, H. *Concordance to the Septuagint*. Reprint Greg-Austria, 1954.

Halperin, David Joel. "Merkabah and Ma$^c$aseh Merkabah According to Rabbinic Sources. Ph.D. dissertation at University of California, Berkeley, 1977. [Rev. ed., in press, *American Oriental Series*.]

Havizdorf, Eleazar. "Ḥaqirah BaInyan Seluta DeHavinenu." *Bet Talmud* 3 (1883): 279-281. [Repr. Jerusalem, 1969].

Hayes, John. *Old Testament Form Criticism*. San Antonio, 1974.

Heinemann, Isaac.  "Hitpathut HaMunahim HaMiqso<sup>C</sup>iyim Leferush Hamiqra."
     Leŝonenu 14 (1945-46):182-189, vol. 15 (1946-47):108-115, vol. 16
     (1947-48):20-28.

Heinemann, Joseph.  "The Formula 'Melekh Ha-<sup>C</sup>Olam.'" JJS 11 (1960):177-180.

_____.  "On the Meaning of Some Mishnayot." BIA 3 (1965):vii-viii; 9-24.

_____.  "Once Again 'Melekh Ha-<sup>C</sup>Olam.'" JJS 15 (1964):149-154.

_____.  Prayer in the Period of the Tannaim and Amoraim: Its Form and
     Structure.  Hebrew: 2d ed.  Jerusalem, 1966.  English revised edition:
     Berlin, 1976.

_____.  "Tefillat HaShabbat." Mahanayim 85-86 (1964):54-57.

_____.  Tefillat HaQeva VeHovah Shel Shabbat VeYom Tov.  Tel Aviv, 1976.

Hengel, Martin.  Judaism and Hellenism.  English, 2d rev. and enl. ed., 2 vols.
     Philadelphia, 1974.

Herr, Moshe David.  "Persecutions and Martyrdom in Hadrian's Days." Scripta
     Hierosolymitana 23 (1972):85-125.

Hershler, Moshe.  Talmud Bavli.  Masekhet Ketubot.  Diqduqe Sofrim HaShalem.
     2 vols.  Jerusalem, 1972-1977.

Higger, Michael.  Osar HaBaraitot.  10 vols.  New York, 1938-48.

Hoffman, Lawrence A.  The Canonization of The Synagogue Service.  Notre Dame,
     1979.

Hoffmann, David.  Mar Samuel.  Leipzig, 1873.

_____.  Sefer Devarim.  2 vols.  Tel Aviv, 1959-61.

_____.  Sefer Vayiqra.  2 vols.  Jerusalem, 1953-54.

Horgan, Maurya P.  Pesharim: Qumran Interpretations of Biblical Books.
     Catholic Biblical Quarterly Monograph Series 8.  Washington, D.C., 1979.

Horovitz, J.  "Nochmals HBR <sup>C</sup>YR." JJLG 17 (1926):264-266.

Hyman, Aaron.  Toldot Tannaim VeAmorim.  3 vols.  Reprint.  Jerusalem, 1964.

Interpreter's Dictionary of the Bible.  Supplementary Volume.  Pp. 3-5, s.v.
     "Abbreviations, Hebrew Texts," by Michael Fishbane; 296-303, s.v.
     "Exegesis," by L. E. Keck and G. M. Tucker; 336-337, s.v. "First Fruits,
     OT," by Jacob Milgrom; 391-392, s.v. "Heave Offering," by Jacob Milgrom;
     436-438, s.v. "Interpretation, History of," by Jacob Weingreen; 641-642,
     "Parable," by C. E. Carlson; 787-789, "Sayings of Jesus," by D. Lührmann.

Jacobs, Louis.  Studies in Talmudic Logic and Methodology.  London, 1961.

Jackson, Bernard S.  Theft in Early Jewish Law.  Oxford, 1972.

Japhet, Sara.  The Ideology of the Book of Chronicles and Its Place in Biblical
     Thought.  Jerusalem, 1977.

Jastrow, Marcus.  Dictionary of Talmud Babli.  2 vols.  New York, 1950.

Johnson, N. B.  Prayer in the Apocrypha and Pseudepigrapha.  JBL Monograph
     Series, 2.  Philadelphia, 1948.

Johnstone, Quintin and Hopson, Dan Jr. *Lawyers and Their Work*. Indianapolis, 1967.

Kadushin, Max. *Worship and Ethics*. New York, 1963.

Kahana, Isaac Ze⁾ev. "Rules for Decisions Found in the Babylonian Talmud." *Sinai* 6 (1939):336-43.

Kanovsky, Israel. *Rav Samuel* [= *Ma^c arkhot haTanna⁾im*, 2]. Jerusalem, 1974.

Kanter, Shammai. *The Legal Traditions of Gamaliel II*. Missoula, 1980.

Kasher, M. A. *Torah Shelemah*. 1-  . Jerusalem, 1929-   .

Kaufman, Stephen A. *The Akkadian Influences on Aramaic*. Chicago, 1974.

Kaufmann, Yehezkel. *History of the Religion of Israel*. Vol. 4. English Translation. C. W. Efroymson. New York, 1977.

Klein, Hyman. "*Gemara* and *Sebara*." *JQR* 38 (1947-48):67-91.

_____. "*Gemara* Quotations in *Sebara*." *JQR* 43 (1952-53):341-63.

_____. "The Significance of the Technical Expression ⁾L⁾ ⁾Y ⁾YTMR HKY ⁾YTMR in the Babylonian Talmud." *Tarbiz* 31 (1961):23-42.

_____. "Some Methods of *Sebara*." *JQR* 50 (1959-60):124-46.

Kohler, Kaufmann. "The Origin and Composition of the Eighteen Benedictions." *HUCA* 1 (1924). Reprint in Petuchowski, *Contributions to Scientific Study of the Jewish Liturgy*, pp. 52-90.

Kohut, Alexander. *Aruch Completum*. 2d ed. 8 vols. Vienna, 1926.

Kosovsky, Biniamin. *Otzar Leshon HaTanna⁾im: Concordantiae Verborum Mechilta D'Rabbi Ismael*. 4 vols. Jerusalem, 1965-66.

_____. *Otzar Leshon HaTanna⁾im: Thesauris Sifra*. 4 vols. Jerusalem, 1967-69.

_____. *Thesaurus Sifrei*. 5 vols. Jerusalem, 1971-74.

_____. "T⁾ ŠM^C." *Sinai* 50 (1962):470-74.

_____. *Thesaurus Nominus. Quae in Talmude Babylonico Reperiunter*. Vol. 1-  . Jerusalem, 1976-   .

Kosovsky, Chayim Yehoshua. *Thesaurus Mishnae*. 4 vols. Jerusalem, 1960.

_____. *Thesaurus Tosephthae*. 6 vols. Jerusalem, 1932-61.

Kosovsky, Chayim Yehoshua and Biniamin Kosovsky. *Thesaurus Talmudus*. Vols. 1-  . Jerusalem, 1954-   .

Kosowsky, Biniamin. See Kosovsky, Biniamin.

Krauss, Samuel. "HBR ^CYR, ein Kapital aus altjudischer Kommunalverfassung." *JJLG* 17 (1926):125-142.

_____. *Lehnwörter*. Vol. 2: Wörterbuch. Berlin, 1899.

_____. *Qadmoniot HaTalmud*. 4 vols. I,i. Berlin, n.d. I,ii. Berlin, 1923. II,i-ii. Tel Aviv, 1929 and 1945.

_____. *Talmudische Archäologie*. 3 vols. Leipzig, 1910-12.

Krauss, Samuel, et al. *Supplement Volume to Kohut. Aruch Completum*. Vienna, 1937. Reprint. New York, 1955.

Kutscher, Ezekiel, ed. *Archive of the New Dictionary of Rabbinical Literature*. Vol. 1. Ramat Gan, 1972.

_____. "Geniza (G) Fragments of the Mekilta of Rabbi Yišma^Cel." *Lešonenu* 32 (1967-68):103-116.

_____. "The Language of the Hebrew and Aramaic Letters of Bar-Koseva. A. The Aramaic Letters." *Lešonenu* 25 (1961):117-133.

_____. *Studies in Galilean Aramaic*. Translated and Annotated with Additional Notes from the Author's Handcopy by Michael Sokoloff. Bar Ilan Studies in Near Eastern Languages and Culture. Ramat Gan, 1976.

Le Deaut, Robert. "Apropos a Definition of Midrash." *Interpretation* 25 (1971):259-282.

Leichty, Erle. *The Omen Series Šumma Izbu*. New York, 1970.

Levine, Lee L. *Caesarea Under Roman Rule*. Leiden, 1975.

_____. "The Jewish Patriarch (Nasi) in Third Century Palestine." *ANRW*. II.19, 2:649-688. Berlin, 1979.

Levy, Israel. *Mavo UPerush LaTalmud Yerushalmi. BQ Chs. 1-6*. Reprint. Jerusalem, 1970.

Levy, Jacob. *Wörterbuch über die Talmudim und Midraschim*. 4 vols. Leipzig, 1876-89. Berlin, 1924.

Levine, Baruch. *In the Presence of the Lord*. Leiden, 1974.

Lewin, B. M. *Otzar Hilluf Minhagim*. Jerusalem, 1937.

Lidell, Henry George and Scott, Robert. *A Greek-English Lexicon*. Revised and Augmented Throughout by Henry Stuart Jones. With a Supplement by E. A. Barber. Oxford, 1968.

Lieberman, Saul. "Brief Commentary." In *The Tosefta*. Vols. 1- . New York, 1955- .

_____. "Eres Yisrael VeYahadut HaOlam BeTequfat HaMishnah VeHaTalmud." *Erev Iyun LeZeker Moshe Habib*, pp. 28-37. Tel Aviv, 1976.

_____. *Greek in Jewish Palestine*. New York, 1965.

_____. *Hellenism in Jewish Palestine*. New York, 1950.

_____, ed. *Hilkhot HaYerushalmi. The Laws of the Palestinian Talmud of Rabbi Moses Ben Maimon*. Text and Studies of the Jewish Theological Seminary of America. Vol. 13. New York, 1947.

_____. "Martyrs of Caesarea." *Annuaire de l'Institut de Philologie et d'Histoire Orietalis et Slaves* 7 (1939-44):395-445. New York, 1944.

_____. "Miscellanies: Emendations in the Yerushalmi (F)." *Tarbiz* 4 (1933): 377-379.

_____. *On the Yerushalmi*. Jerusalem, 1929.

_____. "Palestine in the Third and Fourth Centuries." *JQR* 37 (1946):31-54. Reprint in *Texts and Studies*, pp. 112-177. New York, 1974.

_____. *Siphre Zutta*. New York, 1968.

_____. *The Talmud of Caesarea*. Jerusalem, 1931.

_____. *Texts and Studies*. New York, 1974.

_____. *Tosefeth Rishonim*. 4 vols. 2-4. Jerusalem, 1937-39.

_____. *Tosefta Ki-Fshuṭah*. Vols. 1- . New York, 1955- .

_____. *HaYerushalmi Kiphsuto*. Jerusalem, 1934.

Liebrach, J. "The Benediction Immediately Preceeding and the One Following the Recital of the Shema[C]." *REJ* 125 (1966):151-164.

Loew, Immanuel. *Die Flora der Juden*. 4 vols. Vienna, 1924-34.

_____. "Lexikalische Miszellen." *Festschrift zum Siebigstem Geburstage David Hoffmann's*. Edited by S. Eppenstein, et al. Berlin, 1914. Reprint. Jerusalem, 1970.

Luncz, A. M. *Talmud Hierosolymitanum ad exemplar editionis principis*. 5 vols. Jerusalem, 1907-1919.

Lutz, H. F. *Viticulture and Brewing in the Ancient Orient*. Leipzig, 1922.

Luzzatto, Samuel D. *Ohev Ger*. Cracow, 1895.

_____. *Perush [C]al Ḥamishah Ḥumshe Torah*. Edited by P. Schlesinger. Tel Aviv, 1965.

MacMullen, Ramsay. *Enemies of the Roman Order*. Oxford, 1967.

Malter, Henry. *The Treatise Ta[C]anit of the Babylonian Talmud*. New York, 1930.

Mann, Jacob. *The Collected Articles of Jacob Mann*. 3 vols. Gedera, Israel, 1971.

Mandelkern, Solomon. *Concordanctiae Veteris Testamenti Hebraicae Atque Chaldaicae*. Reprint. Tel Aviv, 1964.

Margalioth, Mordechai. *Encyclopedia of Talmudic and Geonic Literature*. Tel Aviv, n.d.

See also Margulies and Margaliot.

Margalioth, Mordecai. *Hilkhot Hannagid*. *A Collection of Extant Halakhic Writings of R. Shmuel Hannagid*. Jerusalem, 1962.

_____. *Hilkhot Ereṣ Yisrael Min HaGinezah*. Jerusalem, 1973.

Margulies, Mordecai. *The Differences Between Babylonian and Palestinian Jews*. Jerusalem, 1937.

Meir, Ophra. "The Acting Characters in the Stories of the Talmud and the Midrash (A Sample)." Ph.D. dissertation, Hebrew University, 1977.

Melammed, E. Z. *An Introduction to Talmudic Literature*. Jerusalem, 1973.

Meyers, Jacob. *The Anchor Bible*. *I Chronicles*. Garden City, 1965.

Milgrom, Jacob. *Cult and Conscience*. Leiden, 1976.

Morris, William, ed. *The American Heritage Dictionary of the English Language*. Boston, 1969.

Motz, Lloyd. *This is Astronomy*. New York, 1958, 1963.

Naeh, Baruch, ed. *Gemara Shelemah. Masekhet Pesaḥim min Talmud Bavli*. Part One. Introduction by Menahem M. Kasher. Jerusalem, 1960.

Narkiss, M. "The Origin of the Spice Box Known as the Hadass." *EI* (1960-61): 189-198.

Neusner, Jacob. *Development of a Legend*. Leiden, 1970.

_____. *Eliezer Ben Hyrcanus*. 2 vols. Leiden, 1973.

_____. "From Scripture to Mishnah: The Origins of Mishnah's Fifth Division." *JBL* 98 (1979):269-283.

_____. *Formation of the Babylonian Talmud*. Leiden, 1970.

_____. "The Formation of Rabbinic Judaism." *ANRW*. II.19, 2:3-42. Berlin, 1979.

_____. *A History of the Jews of Babylonia*. 5 vols. 1966-70.

_____. *A History of the Mishnaic Law of Holy Things*. 1- . Leiden, 1978- .

_____. *History of the Mishnaic Law of Purities*. 22 vols. Leiden, 1974-77.

_____. *The Idea of Purity*. Leiden, 1973.

_____. *Invitation to the Talmud*. New York, 1973.

_____, ed. *The Modern Study of the Mishnah*. Leiden, 1973.

_____. "The Rabbinic Traditions About the Pharisees Before A.D. 70: The Problem of Oral Transmission." *JJS* 22 (1971):1-18.

_____. *The Rabbinic Traditions About the Pharisees Before 70*. 3 vols. Leiden, 1971.

_____. "Rabbis and Community in Third Century Babylonia." In *Religions in Antiquity, Essays in Memory of E. R. Goodenough*. Edited by Jacob Neusner, pp. 438-459. Leiden, 1968, 1970.

_____. *There We Sat Down*. Nashville, 1972.

_____. "The Written Tradition in the Pre-Rabbinic Period." *JSJ* 4 (1973): 56-65.

Nikiprowetzky, V. *Le Commentaire De L'Ecriture Chez Philon D'Alexandrie*. Leiden, 1977.

Obermeyer, Jacob. *Die Landschaft Babylonien*. Frankfurt am Main, 1929.

Oppenheim, A. Leo. *Ancient Mesopatamia*. Chicago, 1964, 1968.

Orlinsky, Harry M., ed. *Notes on the New Translation of the Torah*. Philadelphia, 1969.

Petuchowski, J. J. *Contributions to the Scientific Study of the Jewish Liturgy*. New York, 1970.

Pfeiffer, Robert H. *History of New Testament Times*. New York, 1949.

Pfeiffer, Rudolf. *History of Classical Scholarship*. Oxford, 1968.

Pinelis, Ṣevi. *Darkah shel Torah*. Vienna, 1861. Reprint. Jerusalem?, n.d.

Pope, M. *The Anchor Bible*. *Job*. Garden City, 1965.

Porton, Gary. "Midrash." *ANRW*. II.19, 2:103-138. Berlin, 1979.

_____. *The Traditions of R. Ishmael*. Part 1. Leiden, 1976.

Preuss, Julius. *Biblisch-talmudische Medizin*. Berlin, 1911. Reprint. Westmead, 1969.

Primus, Charles. *Aqiva's Contribution to the Law of Zera^Cim*. Leiden, 1977.

Rabin, Chaim, ed. *The Zadokite Documents*. Oxford, 1958.

Rabbinovicz, Raphaelo. *Diqduqe Sofrim*. 12 vols. Reprint. New York, 1960.

Rabbinowitz, Zevi Meir. *Halakhah and Aggada in the Liturgical Poetry of Yannai*. Tel Aviv, 1965.

Rabinovitz, Z. W. *Sha^Care Torath Babel*. Jerusalem, 1961.

_____. *Sha^Care Torath Eretz Israel*. Jerusalem, 1940.

Rappaport, Uri. "On the Meaning of Heber HaYehudim." *Studies in the History of the Jewish People and the Land of Israel*. Vol. 3. Edited by B. Oded, et al., pp. 59-67. Haifa, 1974.

Ratner, B. *Ahawath Zion We-Juruscholaim*. 10 vols. Reprint. Jerusalem, 1967.

Rivkin, Ellis. "Ben Sira--The Bridge Between the Aaronide and Pharisaic Revolutions." *EI* 12 (1975):95-104.

Rosenblatt, Samuel. *The Interpretation of the Bible in the Mishnah*. Baltimore, 1935.

Rosenthal, Eliezer Shimshon. "A Contribution to the Talmudic Lexicon-Elucidation of Words Based on Textual Variants." *Tarbiz* 40 (1971):178-200.

_____. "Leshonot Sofrim." *Yuval Shay. A Jubilee Volume Dedicated to S. Y. Agnon*. Edited by B. Kurzweil, pp. 293-324. Ramat Gan, 1958.

_____. "HaMoreh." *PAAJR* 31 (1963), Hebrew Section: 1-71.

Rousseau, Philip. *Ascetics, Authority, and the Church*. Oxford, 1978.

Rubinstein, S. M. *Leheqer Siddur Hatalmud*. Kovno, 1932. Reprint. Jerusalem, 1971.

Russel, D. S. *The Method and Message of Jewish Apocalyptic*. Philadelphia, 1964.

Sacks, Mordecai J. L. *Diqduqe Sofrim LeTalmud Yerushalmi 1*. Masekhet Berakhot. Jerusalem, 1943.

Safartti, G. "Addition to T^CH=ŠKH." *Lešonenu* 32 (1968):338.

Saldarini, Anthony J.  "Review [of E. P. Sanders, *Paul and Palestinian Judaism*
    (Philadelphia, 1977)]."  *JBL* 98 (1979):299-303.

Salonen, Armas.  *Agricultura Mesopatamica*.  Helsinki, 1968.

Sanders, J.  *The Dead Sea Psalm Scroll*.  Ithaca, 1967.

Sanders, E. P.  *Paul and Palestinian Judaism*.  Philadelphia, 1977.

Sarason, Richard S.  *A History of the Mishnaic Law of Agriculture*.  *Demai*.
    Part 1.  Leiden, 1979.

_____.  "Mishnah and Scripture: Preliminary Observations on the Law of
    Tithing in Seder Zera$^C$im."  Paper delivered at the Fourth Max Richter
    Conversation on the History of Judaism.  Brown University.  Providence,
    Rhode Island.  June 27, 1978.  [Forthcoming in: W. S. Green, *Approaches to
    Ancient Judaism*.  2.  Missoula, 1980.]

Sarna, Hahum.  "Hebrew and Bible Studies in Medieval Spain."  *The Sephardic
    Heritage*.  Edited by R. D. Barnett, pp. 323-366.  London, 1971.

Schiffer, Ira J.  "The Men of the Great Assembly."  In W. S. Green, ed.,
    *Persons and Institutions in Early Rabbinic Judaism*.  Brown Judaic Studies.
    Vol. 3, pp. 237-276.  Missoula, 1977.

Schiffman, Lawrence H.  *The Halakhah at Qumran*.  Leiden, 1973.

Scholem, Gersom G.  *On the Kabbalah and Its Symbolism*.  New York, 1965, 1969.

_____.  "Revelation and Tradition As Religious Categories in Judaism."
    [Originally published in 1962.]  In *The Messianic Idea in Judaism*, 282-303.
    pp. 282-303.  New York, 1971, 1972.

Shiloh, Shmuel.  "The Attitude of R. Yosef Migash to the Gaonim."  (Hebrew)
    *Sinai* 66 (1970):263-267.

Silberman, Lou H.  "Unriddling the Riddle.  A Study in the Structure and
    Language of the Habakkuk Pesher."  *Revue de Qumran* 3, part 11 (1961):
    323-364.

Simon, M.  Translation and Notes, *The Babylonian Talmud*.  *Berakoth*.  London,
    1948.

Smalley, Beryl.  *The Study of the Bible in the Middle Ages*.  New York, 1952.

Smith, Jonathan Z.  "Wisdom and Apocalyptic."  In *Religious Syncretism in
    Antiquity*.  Edited by Birger A. Pearson, pp. 131-156.  Missoula, 1975.

Smith, Morton.  "A Comparison of Early Christian and Early Rabbinic Tradition."
    *JBL* 82 (1963):169-176.

_____.  *Tannaitic Parallels to the Gospels*.  Philadelphia, 1951, 1968.

Smith, Payne.  *A Compendious Syriac Dictionary*.  Oxford, 1903, 1967.

Spanier, Arthur.  "Zur Formengeschichte des altjuischen Gebetes."  *MGWJ* 78
    (1934):438-447.

Speiser, E. A.  *The Anchor Bible*.  *Genesis*.  Garden City, 1964.

Sperber, Daniel.  *Roman Palestine: 200-400*.  *The Land*.  Ramat Gan, 1974.

Spiegel, Shalom. "Introduction (to *Legends of the Bible* by Louis Ginzberg.
    New York, 1956)." In *The Jewish Expression*. Edited by Judah Goldin,
    pp. 134-162. New York, 1970.

_____. *The Last Trial*. New York, 1967.

Sprengling, Martin. *Third-Century Iran*. Chicago, 1953.

Steinsaltz, Adin. "Links Between Babylonia and the Land of Israel." *Talpioth*
    9 (1964):294-306.

Sussmann, Jacob. "Babylonian Sugyot to the Orders Zera$^c$im and Tehorot."
    Ph.D. dissertation, Hebrew University, 1969. [In press: Israel Academy
    of Sciences and Humanities.]

Talmadge, Frank. *David Kimhi, The Man and the Commentary*. Cambridge, 1975.

Talmon, Shemaryahu. "The 'Manual of Benedictions' of the Sect of the Judean
    Desert." *Revue de Qumran* 2, part 8 (1960):475-500.

Tawil, Dalia. "The Purim Panel in Dura in the Light of Parthian and Sasanian
    Art." *Journal of Near Eastern Studies* 38 (1979):93-109.

Telegdi, S. "Essai sur La Phonetique Des Emprunts Iraniens En Arameen
    Talmudique." *Journal Asiatique* 226/227 (1935):177-256.

Towner, Wayne S. "'Blessed be YHWH' and 'Blessed art Thou YHWH': The
    Modulation of a Biblical Formula." *CBQ* 30 (1968):386-99.

Twersky, Isadore. *Rabad of Posquieres*. Cambridge, 1962.

_____. "The *Shulhan Aruk*: Enduring Code of Jewish Law." [Originally
    published in 1967.] In *The Jewish Expression*. Edited by Judah Goldin,
    pp. 322-343. New York, 1970.

Urbach, Ephraim E. "HaMasoret $^c$al Torat HaSod biTequfat HaTannaim." In
    *Studies in Mysticism and Religion. Festschrift Gershom Scholem*. Edited by
    E. E. Urbach, et al. Jerusalem, 1967.

_____. "Mavo LaMishnah [of H. Albeck] and One Hundred Years of Mishnaic
    Research." *Molad* 17 (1959):422-440.

_____. *The Sages*. Jerusalem, 1969.

_____. *The Tosafists*. Jerusalem, 1955.

Vermes, Geza. "Bible and Midrash: Early Old Testament Exegesis." In *The
    Cambridge History of the Bible*. Vol. 1. Edited by R. R. Ackroyd and
    C. F. Evans, pp. 199-231. Cambridge, 1970, 1975.

_____. "The Decalogue and the Minim." In *Memorium Paul Kahle*. Edited by
    Mathew Black, et al., pp. 232-240. Berlin, 1968.

_____. "The Qumran Interpretation of Scripture in its Historical Setting."
    [Originally published in 1969.] In Geza Vermes, *Post Biblical Studies*,
    pp. 37-49. Leiden, 1975.

_____. *Scripture and Tradition in Judaism*. Leiden, 1973.

Vermes, Geza and Millar, F. *Emil Schurer's History of the Jewish People.
    New English Edition*. Vol. 1. Edinburgh, 1973.

Wacholder, B. Z.  "On the Origins of Midrash."  Lecture delivered at the
    Seventh Annual Association for Jewish Studies Conference.  Boston,
    Massachusetts.  December 23, 1975.

Watters, W. R.  *Formula Criticism and the Poetry of the Old Testament.*  New
    York, 1976.

Weinberg, Jechiel J.  "The Talmudic Exegesis of the Mishnah."  In *Isaiah
    Wolfsberg Jubilee Volume.*  Edited by Yosef Tirosh,  pp. 86-105.  Tel Aviv,
    1955.

Weingreen, Jacob.  *From Bible to Mishna.*  Manchester, 1976.

Weiss, Abraham.  *The Babylonian Talmud as a Literary Unit.*  New York, 1943.

_____.  *Liqorot Hithavut HaBabli.*  Warsaw, 1929.  Reprint.  Jerusalem?, n.d.

_____.  *Notes to Talmudic Pericopae.*  Bar Ilan, n.d.

_____.  *On the Mishnah.*  Bar Ilan, n.d.

_____.  *Studies in the Law of the Talmud on Damages.*  Jerusalem, 1966.

_____.  *Studies in the Literature of the Amoraim.*  New York, 1962.

_____.  *The Talmud in its Development.*  New York, 1954.

_____.  *Studies in the Talmud.*  Jerusalem, 1975.

Weiss, I. H.  *Dor Dor VeDorshov.*  Vol. 3.  Reprint.  New York, 1924.

Weiss, P. R.  "The Controversies of Rab and Samuel and the Tosefta."  *Journal
    of Semitic Studies* 3 (1958):288-297.

Weiss Halivni, David.  "The Apodictic and Argumentational in the Talmud."
    Paper delivered at the Society of Biblical Literature Annual Meeting.
    New York.  November 15, 1979.

_____.  "Contemporary Methods of the Study of Talmud."  *JJS* 30 (1979):
    192-201.

_____.  "The Reception Accorded Rabbi Judah's Mishnah."  Paper delivered at
    the Conference on "Judaism and Christianity in the First Two Centuries:
    Problems of Self Definition."  McMaster University.  Hamilton, Ontario.
    June, 1979.

_____.  "Some People Bring Bikkurim."  *BIA* 7-8 (1970):73-79.

_____.  *Sources and Traditions.*  Vol. 1.  Tel Aviv, 1968.  Vol. 2.
    Jerusalem, 1975.

_____.  "Talmudic Criticism: A Historical Review."  Paper delivered at the
    Association for Jewish Studies, Fifth Annual Conference.  Harvard
    University, Cambridge, Massachusetts.  October 21, 1973.

_____.  "Whoever Studies Laws . . . "  *Proceedings of the Rabbinical
    Assembly* 41 (1979):298-303.

Weiss, J. G.  "On the Formula 'Melekh ha-$^{C}$Olam' as Anti-Gnostic Protest."
    *JJS* 10 (1959):169-70.

White, K. D.  *Roman Farming.*  Ithaca, 1970.

Widengren, Geo. "Holy Book and Holy Tradition in Iran: The Problem of the
     Sassanid Avesta." In *Holy Book and Holy Tradition*. Edited by F. F. Bruce
     and E. G. Rupp, pp. 36-53. Manchester, 1968.

Wieder, J. "The Old Palestinian Ritual-New Sources." *JJS* 4 (1953):30-37, 65-73.

Wiesenberg, E. J. "The Liturgical Term 'Melekh Ha-<sup>C</sup>Olam.'" *JJS* 15 (1964):
     1-56.

Winston, David. *The Anchor Bible. The Wisdom of Solomon*. Garden City, 1979.

Wiseman, D. J. "Books in the Ancient World." In *Cambridge History of the
     Bible*. Vol. 1. Edited by R. R. Ackroyd and C. F. Evans, pp. 30-48.
     Cambridge, 1975.

Wolfson, Harry Austryn. *Philo*. 2 vols. Cambridge, 1974, 1968.

Yalon, Henoch. *Introduction to the Vocalization of the Mishnah*. Jerusalem,
     1964.

_____. *Studies in the Hebrew Language*. Jerusalem, 1971.

Yadin, Yigael, ed. *The Scroll of the War of the Sons of Light Against the Sons
     of Darkness*. Oxford, 1962.

_____. *The Temple Scroll*. 3 vols. Jerusalem, 1977.

Yadin, Yigael. *Judean Desert Studies. The Finds from the Bar-Kokhba Period in
     the Cave of Letters*. Jerusalem, 1963.

Yaron, Reuven. *Gifts in Contemplation of Death in Jewish and Roman Law*.
     Oxford, 1960.

Zahavy, Tzvee. "A History of the Mishnaic Law of Blessings." Forthcoming.

_____. *The Traditions of Eleazar Ben Azariah*. Brown Judaic Studies.
     Vol. 2. Missoula, Montana, 1978.

Zeitlin, Solomon. "The Morning Benediction and the Reading in the Temple."
     *JQR* 44 (1953-54):330-336.

_____. "The Tefillah." *JQR* 54 (1964):208-249.

Zohary, Michael. *Flora Palestina*. Vols. 1-3. Jerusalem, 1966-72.

Zucker, Moshe. *Rav Saadya Gaon's Translation of the Torah*. New York, 1959.

Zuri, Jacob S. *Rav*. Jerusalem, 1925.

_____. *Toldot Darkhe HaLimmud Bishivot Darom, Galil, Sura, VeNeharde<sup>C</sup>a*.
     Jerusalem, 1914.

INDEXES*

The Index is made up of four parts: I, an "Index to Samuel's Traditions, by Number (1-143)," that is keyed to the number of the tradition as set out in chapters two and three; II, an "Index to Sources," to rabbinic and other ancient works; III, an "Index to Talmudic Terms, Formulae, and Patterns"; and IV, a "General Index." For the following categories, the Indexes include only commented upon instances of the entries: the numbered traditions in notes to chapters four through ten; the entries for Indexes II-III; the names of medieval commentaries for Index IV; and the items (e.g., names and concepts) only mentioned in Samuel's traditions when the traditions are cited in chapters four through ten. The items in the last category, however, may still be located by tracing the number of the tradition, through Index I.

I.   INDEX TO SAMUEL'S TRADITIONS, BY NUMBER (1-143)

*I thank Fred Astren, Edward Hanker, and Miriam Petruck for compiling the Indexes.

33   193, 382, 391

34   193-94, 382

35   194, 390

36   194, 237, 271-72, 382

37   194, 232, 237, 271, 272, 382,
     388, 390

38   195, 233, 237, 272, 382

39   10, 195, 233, 271, 272, 377, 391

40   10, 195-96, 382

41   10, 196, 272, 289, 382

42   10, 196, 233, 272, 281, 377,
     390

43   10, 196, 233, 264, 267, 272,
     287, 387, 388, 390

44   22, 196, 231, 233, 255, 298,
     299, 322, 327, 328, 331, 334,
     335, 354, 358, 407

45   22, 196-97, 231, 233, 255, 284,
     285, 298, 327, 328, 334, 335,
     356, 358, 364, 368, 369, 373,
     417

46   22, 197, 231, 233, 255, 284, 285,
     298, 327, 328, 334, 335, 356,
     358, 364, 368, 369, 373, 417

47   197, 231, 272, 382

48   197, 231, 234, 272, 382

49   197, 234, 235, 272, 382-84

50   197, 234, 235, 272, 382

51   24, 197-98, 272, 287, 302, 327,
     329, 331, 334, 343, 354, 355,
     445

52   198, 267, 347, 382, 385, 387,
     390, 398

53   198, 267, 347, 379, 382, 385,
     387, 390, 398

54   10, 26, 198-99, 255, 283, 284,
     304, 327, 329, 331, 334, 343,
     357, 364, 365, 463

55   10, 26, 42, 199, 287, 311, 312,
     319, 327, 329, 331, 334, 335,
     340, 357, 415, 428

56   10, 26, 117, 199, 255, 283, 284,
     293, 304, 310, 327, 329, 332,
     334, 335, 343, 357, 358, 364,
     365, 369, 373, 463

57   200, 232, 267, 272, 273, 345, 387,
     388, 390, 391

58   11, 32, 201, 255, 287, 309, 318,
     327, 329, 332, 334, 335, 366,
     463

59   11, 32, 201, 255, 287, 309, 318,
     327, 329, 332, 334, 335, 366,
     463

60   36, 201, 232, 279, 298, 300-1,
     327, 329, 332, 335, 364, 417

61   202, 236, 345, 379, 391

62   202, 345, 347, 379, 391

63   10, 202, 346, 377, 391, 428

64   203, 380

65   38, 203, 235, 255, 273, 288, 311,
     312, 319, 322, 327-29, 332,
     334-45, 350, 354, 357-58, 362-63,
     369, 373, 407

66   38, 203, 255, 280, 288, 311-12,
     319, 322, 336, 350

67   42, 203, 255, 257, 310, 322, 327,
     329, 332, 334, 350, 359-60,
     370, 415

68   42, 203, 255, 287, 304, 329, 332,
     334-45, 358, 370, 406, 415, 418,
     463

69   204, 377, 463

70   48, 205, 257, 286, 302-3, 318,
     327, 329, 332, 334-45, 340,
     342, 464

71   53, 205, 237-38, 255, 289, 305,
     336, 354, 370, 416

72   10, 53, 65, 205, 237, 238, 255,
     280, 289, 305-6, 311-12, 319,
     336, 344, 364-65, 370-71, 377,
     418, 428

73   53, 205, 237-38, 255, 289, 305-6,
     354, 370, 416

74   53, 205, 237-38, 255, 289, 305,
     336, 354, 361-63, 370-71, 416

75   53, 237-38, 289, 305, 336, 357-58,
     362-63, 369, 373, 416

II.   INDEX TO SOURCES:   RABBINIC AND OTHER ANCIENT WORKS

## III.   INDEX TO TALMUDIC TERMS, FORMULAE AND PATTERNS

IV.  GENERAL INDEX